Implementing Best Practices In Human Resources Management

Hugh Secord, B.A., M.B.A., CHRP

CCH CANADIAN LIMITED
90 Sheppard Avenue East, Suite 300
Toronto, ON M2N 6X1
Telephone: (416) 224-2248 Toll Free: 1-800-268-4522
Fax: (416) 224-2243 Toll Free: 1-800-461-4131
www.cch.ca

A WoltersKluwer Company

Published by CCH Canadian Limited

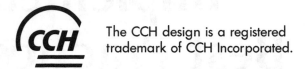

The CCH design is a registered trademark of CCH Incorporated.

National Library of Canada Cataloguing in Publication

Secord, Hugh, 1958 —
    Implementing best practices in human resources management/Hugh Secord.
Based on author's: Secord's A-Z guide for human resources practitioners.
Includes Index.
ISBN 1-55367-189-9

    1. 1. Personnel management.   I. Title.

HF5549.S43 2003   658.3   C2003-904730-X

ISBN 1-55367-189-9

Typeset by CCH Canadian Limited.
Printed in Canada.

Introduction

Implementing Best Practices in Human Resources Management is based on the CCH loose leaf publication, *Secord's A–Z Guide for Human Resources Practitioners*, and was undertaken as a project to rewrite a product from the United Kingdom, *Croner's A-to-Z Guide for HRM Professionals*, making it relevant in the Canadian context. In doing so, the focus was put on subject areas that were important not only to managing people within an organization but also, more importantly, to managing the organization's culture. Croner's takes an all-encompassing approach, whereas *Implementing Best Practices* examines only areas that have a strategic impact on an organization or that can strongly influence an organization's culture.

Implementing Best Practices in HR Management not only differs from the original *Croner's* guide in context and content but also departs from the original's academic approach. While an understanding of the fundamentals of organizational behaviour is an essential competency for the Human Resources practitioner, *Implementing Best Practices in HR Management* takes this as a given and approaches the subject areas from a more pragmatic angle. The practical application considers the fact that the only sustainable competitive advantage an organization can attain is through its people. Practitioners and their client managers generally understand this. They want to know how to achieve this competitive advantage.

An organization's culture is difficult to define. It is developed by many things, including the vision of the founders and leaders, the processes and means of communication within the organization, the values that are reinforced and accepted as norms, the visual artifacts (office decor, facilities, housekeeping, art) and the reward systems. The leaders define, through their actions and their words, the kind of organization they want. The success of developing the culture cannot be measured directly but is seen in the strength of the culture.

A strong culture is one in which all participants share the vision and values of the organization. Their activities are governed by these elements. This helps the organization to respond quickly to changes in its environment without the need to have formal communications. Employees within the organization can respond without specific directions because they are governed by the same set of cultural guidelines. At an extreme, this can be dangerous. Price-fixing is a behaviour most organizations would find taboo. However, in the absence of any direct prohibition on collusion, an employee might engage in this behaviour for the good of the organization.

Nevertheless, having a strong culture is preferable to having a weak one. In a strong culture, employees are retained because they do share the common values and goals of the organization. In weak cultures, employees often do not have a sense of direction or ownership in their work processes. Employees lack a true sense of belonging or that the work they do is important.

Weak cultures tend to breed counter-cultures that can run against the goals and objectives of the organization. Employees often organize under unions because they do not have a sense of having a voice in the organization or a sense of belonging. Unions can give them a sense of belonging and purpose. However, if the cultures between the organization and the counter-culture that develops within clash significantly, the relationship between management and employees can become dysfunctional.

Human Resources practitioners today struggle with a number of questions regarding their roles in an organization. The function still remains relatively new and, in many Canadian organizations, continues to be seen as an ancillary function rather than as an integral part of managing the organization. Practitioners would like to see their roles have a more strategic impact on the business. Many talk of being recognized as a business partner. They also seem to be searching for how they can truly add value to the organization. Correctly, many are realizing that in order to gain credibility with senior management, and in order to join the ranks of senior management, they need to have a solid understanding of the business. This means understanding what drives the business and makes it successful.

One of the most significant dilemmas facing Human Resources practitioners is their role *vis-à-vis* employees. One paradigm dictates that the practitioner should be an employee advocate. As a conduit to management, practitioners can position themselves as the voice of the employees. This is seen as bringing value to the organization by ensuring that employee concerns are addressed before they become problematic. With this style of practice, the practitioner runs the risk of being perceived as catering to the whims of individuals at the expense of business considerations.

On the other hand, the practitioner is viewed as a management representative responsible for ensuring that employees understand the organization's expectations and its policies and practices. At an extreme, the practitioner may be viewed by employees as the organization's policeman. Under this paradigm, the practitioner risks having line managers abdicate their roles for managing people and leaving it to the Human Resources Department.

Implementing Best Practices in HR Management has been written to help solve some of these issues for the practitioner. A number of subjects are specifically included because of their strategic importance and the significance of the role the practitioner can play in their implementation. This role is not the role of a business partner but rather is an integral and essential role in running the business.

Many of the roles the practitioner fills are that of an internal consultant. In order to be successful in fulfilling these roles, the practitioner needs to establish credibility with senior management. Credibility can be established in a number of ways. First, the practitioner needs to be a subject matter expert. In the Canadian context, this means understanding employment law, legislation, theories of organizational behaviour and Human Resources Management. *Implementing Best Practices in HR Management* provides practical advice on subjects related to Human Resources Management to help the practitioner gain credibility as a subject expert. The role is so varied that few practitioners, even seasoned generalists, can have the breadth of experience and understanding to be an expert in every area of Human Resources Management. Thus, *Implementing Best Practices in HR Management* can be used as a reference manual for the practitioner.

Secondly, in establishing credibility, the practitioner needs to understand strategy. *Implementing Best Practices in HR Management* addresses how each subject area impacts on the organization's culture, business objectives, or overall strategy. It also gives tips to the practitioner on how to develop Human Resources strategy. In particular, the "Employment Cycle" has been introduced to help practitioners develop a model for how they will manage Human Resources within their own organizations. The value practitioners bring must ultimately be measured in terms of their contribution to the key success indicators for the business. The Employment Cycle is intended as a construct for demonstrating how the practitioner influences culture through the management of employee performance. This is the key to adding value to the organization through Human Resources.

Implementing Best Practices in HR Management does not assume that either the employee advocate role or the organizational policeman role is the correct paradigm. Rather, the Guide assumes that the practitioner is a process manager who must design processes or systems that support, reinforce or even define the organization's culture. Ultimately, the role must be a proactive one that moves the organization forward by helping it create competitive advantage through its people. At a basic level, the practitioner can help an organization create a competitive advantage by helping it control labour costs. This could be attained by negotiating labour contracts to the organization's advantage or controlling the costs of providing employee benefits. These are important activities, and may even be strategic to a degree. However, they are activities that can be replicated by the competition.

In order to be truly strategic, the practitioner can add value to an organization by providing leadership in the development of its people. The strength of an organization's people, its "intellectual capital", provides it with a unique and sustainable advantage. Moreover, if the organization can become a learning organization, not only is the advantage sustained over time but also it can grow. The practitioner is in a unique position to provide the practical means of creating the organizational culture required to create and to maintain this advantage.

By taking a process approach to Human Resources Management, *Implementing Best Practices in HR Management* is intended to point the practitioner in the direction of solving organizational issues and providing added value rather than implementing "flavour-of-the-month" programs. Many Human Resources initiatives fail because they were introduced without line management's appreciation for the need to have such programs. *Implementing Best Practices in HR Management* points out the expected benefits of addressing issues and gives practical advice on the proper implementation of processes to gain those benefits.

When addressing different organizational needs, the practitioner should expect to encounter some problems. As the saying goes, "Everyone makes mistakes". As a practical tool, *Implementing Best Practices in HR Management* points out some of the common mistakes made and pitfalls encountered to help the practitioner learn from the experiences of others. However, one caveat should be heeded: even when we are informed of possible hazards beforehand, it is not a guarantee that we will avoid them. The practitioner should expect to encounter problems when implementing any new processes. *Implementing Best Practices in HR Management* will help the practitioner recognize these pitfalls and can provide advice on how to overcome them. While *Implementing Best Practices in HR Management* was written as a reference work for Human Resources practitioners, it is hoped that it will prove to be a useful tool for others in the organization. Chief Executive Officers (CEOs) and Presidents of smaller organizations that might lack in-house Human Resources expertise should find *Implementing Best Practices in HR Management* a useful starting point in understanding Human Resources issues. The practical advice provided should allow the executive to address issues systematically following good organizational theory and principles without having to engage expensive consultants or having to hire a practitioner.

Similarly, *Implementing Best Practices in HR Management* can be used as a training tool for educating line managers or aspiring practitioners. We would encourage training managers and practitioners to use *Implementing Best Practices in HR Management* as a starting point in developing programs to teach line managers about Human Resources Management issues.

We hope to receive input from the users of *Implementing Best Practices in HR Management* to create a dialogue with practitioners on how to develop it. Your suggestions, advice and criticisms are all invited.

About the Author

Hugh Secord is a graduate of the University of Toronto (Hon. B.A. in Sociology) and York University (M.B.A.). In 1997, he received the Certified Human Resources Professional (CHRP) designation. Hugh has been involved in Human Resources Management at a senior level for 21 years in a variety of industries, including manufacturing, mining and distribution.

Hugh has been a contributor to various CCH publications, and is a regular contributor to *Canadian Industrial Relations and Personnel Developments* in which he writes the monthly "Practitioner's Corner" and the "Feature Article". He has also taught courses in Organizational Behaviour and Employment Law for the Human Resources Professionals Association of Ontario (HRPAO) and for Mohawk College, Hamilton, Ontario.

Acknowledgements

Implementing Best Practices in Human Resources Management began as a rewrite of the *Croner's A-to-Z Guide for HRM Professionals*. The *Croner's* work served as the basis for *Secord's A–Z Guide for Human Resources Practitioners*. The guide in turn has been turned into this book to make it more accessible to a wider audience.

Best practices are, not too surprising, based on fundamental theories and principles of organizational behaviour and design that are applicable in any context of organizational life. The theme of *Implementing Best Practices in HR Management* is to provide practical guidance while at the same time asking the reader to take a strategic perspective. Before implementing a program or process, the practitioner should ask "Why are we doing this? What is it we hope to achieve? How will we measure the results and determine if we have been successful?".

Although with over 20 years of experience in a variety of organizations I have had opportunities to develop my own expertise, I have always found that teaching others was one of the best ways to learn more about a subject myself. From teaching, one gains a certain discipline for learning. While I have taught for a number of different institutions and conducted seminars for a variety of associations, I should acknowledge the Human Resources Professionals Association of Ontario (HRPAO), where I had the opportunity to teach organizational behaviour for several years. The Association continues to work towards developing professional standards for Human Resources practitioners and provides a forum for them to share experiences and learn.

It is my hope that ultimately *Implementing Best Practices in HR Management* will stir some debate or at least provide a forum for a continuous dialogue on Human Resource Management. I entered my career hoping to make a difference. Part of that desire was driven by ego — in hopes that I could be a big fish in the pond as they say. However, as I gain experience, I have realized that the best gains for human resources practitioners will come as we join our resources together as a community of subject matter experts. Collectively, we need to continue to work towards increasing our profiles and our credibility as vital contributors to the successes of the enterprises we serve.

All those who were involved with the publication of this book should be acknowledged for their expertise and their contribution, including especially Mary Elizabeth Bennett, David Iggulden, Janet Kim, and Martin Piertzak.

The most significant support mechanism an individual can have is an encouraging family. It is to Lesly that all my work is dedicated in thanks for her support, encouragement and occasional prodding. I would also like to thank my two sons, Tyler and Michael, who have been very supportive and were quiet when they needed to be.

Table of Contents

ALCOHOL AND DRUG ADDICTION

Definition/Background

Substance abuse is the term commonly used to describe both drug and alcohol misuse, including alcoholism and drug addiction. The Addiction Research Foundation estimates that 5% of the Canadian adult population are alcoholics and an additional 5% are problem drinkers. This is consistent with the findings of the General Social Survey (1993) reported in the *Canadian Profile* by the Canadian Centre on Substance Abuse that found that 9.2% of adults reported problems with their drinking, 5.1% reported that alcohol abuse affected their physical health and 4.7% said it had a definite impact on their financial position.

While there is an apparent act of volition involved in substance abuse, it is a recognized disease. The National Council on Alcoholism and Drug Dependence defines alcoholism as "a primary disease with genetic, psychosocial and environmental factors influencing its development and manifestations. The disease is often progressive and fatal. It is characterized by continuous or periodic impaired control over drinking, preoccupation with the drug alcohol, use of alcohol despite adverse consequences and distortions in thinking, mostly denial".

Statistics from the United States regarding the impact of alcohol and drug use in the workplace show the following:

— 6.6% of full-time workers report that they are heavy drinkers;

— 40% of industrial fatalities and 47% of industrial injuries are linked to the use of alcohol or to alcoholism;

— alcohol abuse costs the American economy $66.7 billion in productivity losses in 1992, while drug abuse contributed an additional $14.2 billion loss;

— absenteeism is 3.8 to 8.3 times higher among problem drinkers versus the average employee, and up to 16 times higher for employees with cross-addictions (addicted to more than one substance); and

— drug abusers will use three times the sick benefits of an average employee and are five times more likely to file a workers' compensation claim.

Quite obviously, substance abuse is a significant workplace issue. Employers can take a variety of approaches to deal with the problem.

Benefits/Expected Outcomes

Organizations can realize significant benefits from successful treatment of drug and alcohol abuse in the workplace, such as:

— reduced health care costs;

— improved productivity;

— reduced accident frequency and severity rates;

— reduced workers' compensation costs (and potential rebates);

— decreased absenteeism; and

— improved morale.

Companies invest a great deal of time and resources in training its employees. To protect their "human capital", employers should consider investing in proactive programs for the detection and treatment of substance abuse. Unfortunately, these programs will not reach all employees who are experiencing problems with their alcohol and drug use. Companies are also advised to establish internal policies to deal with alcohol and drug use.

Programming/Implementation

A. Identification

Problems with addictions and dependency come to light mainly through poor attendance and poor performance. Repeated short absence spells, pattern absenteeism (Fridays/Mondays), sloppy work habits, inattentive performance and unpredictable or erratic behaviours can be key indicators. In severe cases, use at work or reporting to work in an unfit condition will be detected.

If the problem becomes evident on the job, it is very likely that colleagues, including supervisors, will try to cover up for the problem employee, so management's attention is not drawn to him or her. While this action may protect the employee temporarily, it prevents proper treatment, care and, if necessary, decisive action from being taken. It also puts the company and fellow employees at risk.

It is not normally the day-to-day behaviour that will indicate a problem as this is specific and individual to the employee concerned. However, severe deviations from what is a normal behaviour pattern for that employee should alert a manager that something is awry. Sudden increases in absenteeism, deceased productivity or poor work performance may be indicators of an underlying substance abuse problem.

Even when alcohol or drug abuse is strongly suspected, managers are well advised to focus their attention on the performance or work related issues. Managers should not accuse or confront the employee with the suspicion of an addiction problem. A significant part of the cure is for the addict to overcome his or her denial and recognize the problem. Managers will also want to be wary of infringing on an individual's human rights. Substance abuse is only a workplace issue when it has a direct impact on the work being performed.

Use at work may also be difficult to detect. Fellow employees may collude in well intentioned, but misplaced, efforts to protect the individual. Beyond the obvious smell of alcohol on the breath (or smell of marijuana), other indicia of use include:

— bloodshot eyes or dilated pupils;

— slurred or impaired speech;

— restlessness;

— staggered walk; and

— erratic or violent behaviour.

B. Treatment

There are generally two approaches to dealing with substance abuse in the workplace. The proactive approach is to invest in an Employee Assistance Program that is designed for the detection and treatment of substance abuse (among other things). The reactive approach is to use disciplinary sanctions including dismissal as a deterrent to alcohol and drug use in the workplace. Both are necessary and should be implemented as complementary policies.

There are many different designs for employee assistance programs. With respect to substance abuse, the programs should provide an avenue for self-referrals such as confidential help lines and may include peer interventions or referrals. In organized workplaces, collaborative union–management efforts to persuade employees to use the resources of a third-party treatment provider can go a long way to reducing the stigma often associated with substance abuse. The key to an Employee Assistance Program is that it provides an opportunity for employees to seek help before their problems create employment issues for them.

Specific treatments include in-house treatment programs (commonly 28 days in residence), individual counselling and after-care programs such as Alcoholics Anonymous. In all instances, before embarking on a treatment program, the employee should seek the advice of his or her own physician. In some instances, drug interventions may be indicated.

C. Discipline

Progressive disciplinary sanctions (whether punitive or positive) should be used to deal with the manifestations of substance abuse and not with the addiction itself. There are a number of reasons for this. First, and perhaps foremost, managers run the risk of infringing on an individual's human rights when confronting the employee with an accusation regarding a suspected addiction. In some instances, the manager could simply have misread the signs. Even where addiction is the underlying cause, it would be discriminatory on a prohibited ground in many Canadian jurisdictions to sanction the employee for having a recognized disease. Notwithstanding, the disease does not excuse the employee from meeting his or her employment obligations.

The manager should simply address the work performance issues as he/she would in any other case. The manager can ask the employee if the employee knows of any reason or condition that might be contributing to the performance issues. The manager can also offer the services of the Employee Assistance Program. This does not presuppose an addiction. Rather, employee assistance programs offer a range of services to deal with personal issues that might impact on an employee's work performance.

This is not to suggest that discipline is never appropriate in cases of drug or alcohol abuse or misuse.

Where the employer has a clear policy prohibiting the use or possession of alcohol or drugs in the workplace, then a violation must be met with a disciplinary action, and often with dismissal depending on such factors as the nature and safety sensitivity of the work being performed. Employees who report to work intoxicated or unfit to perform their work because of the use of drugs or alcohol (and this includes being severely hung-over from the night before) should be disciplined. Discipline, in these instances, is usually severe and, for many employers, may involve immediate discharge. Severe discipline can often shock the addict into realizing he or she has a problem and should seek help.

Employers need to keep in mind that, at the point of discharge, a previously undetected addiction should be considered as a mitigating factor in substituting the dismissal for a treatment program and a "Last Chance Agreement".

D. Policies

Policies dealing with drug and alcohol abuse should recognize addiction as a known and treatable disease. The first emphasis should be on treatment. Employee assistance programs are put in place in order to provide employees with a means to seek help without employment consequences. Notwithstanding, employers are obliged to provide a safe and healthy workplace for all employees, and must deal harshly with employees who put the safety of others at risk through their misuse of controlled substances.

Workplace rules should stipulate that the use and possession of alcohol and non-prescription drugs at work is strictly prohibited. Employees who are using prescribed medications should inform their supervisors or, where applicable, a Health Nurse before commencing work. Employees who report to work intoxicated or in an unfit condition to work should be immediately suspended pending a disposition on their employment status.

Employers should also carefully consider the circumstances, if any, where alcohol use may be an acceptable part of an employee's workday. Some employers tolerate light consumption of alcohol at lunch breaks or when entertaining clients. This once common practice is declining as companies become more sensitive to the issues of abuse and more concerned with the possibility of a third-party liability suit.

Companies are also more sensitive to the use of alcohol off-duty at work related social gatherings. Many employers limit the number of "free" drinks that will be provided to employees by the company at such functions as Christmas or retirement parties. Others do not provide any. Some employers offer "no questions asked" cab rides to the employees home following a social function. Others are focusing social activities to family events where the use of alcohol is banned altogether.

E. Last Chance Agreements

Last Chance Agreements are contracts entered into between an employee and the employer to deal with substance abuse. They are usually made after the individual's employment has been terminated or has reached the point of discharge, and when the employee has come forth and admitted his or her addiction. The addiction is treated as a mitigating circumstance and the employee must undertake to seek the appropriate treatment to control the disease so that it does not affect his or her work. These agreements typically include the following provisions:

— agreement to seek in-patient detoxification and treatment;

— agreement to attend at any prescribed after-care treatment program;

— agreement to attend work regularly and certify that any absence is not related to substance abuse;

— agreement to undergo drug or alcohol screening as required; and

— agreement to abstain totally from the use of alcohol or non-prescription drugs.

These agreements can be of a fixed term but are increasingly becoming permanent in nature. The usual sanction for a breach of the Last Chance Agreement is immediate dismissal. Employers should be careful to include a clause stipulating that the agreement constitutes accommodation within the meaning of the applicable human rights statute. In unionized environments, the agreements should be written in consultation with the employees' union representatives.

F. Screening

Screening for alcohol or drug dependency, either as part of the recruitment procedure or intermittently during employment, is common in the United States but is not recommended in Canada. Employers cannot institute random testing as this would constitute an infringement on an individual's human rights. Testing is acceptable on an individual basis where the employee has undergone a treatment program and the testing is part of his or her after-care program or Last Chance Agreement. Testing can also be instituted in work environments where the employer can show the nature of the work is "safety sensitive" or where there are indications of widespread misuse/abuse. Employers should seek legal counsel before instituting a screening program.

G. Accommodation

Alcoholism and drug dependency are viewed as disabilities. As such, human rights legislation requires that employers must accommodate employees who have these disabilities. For some, this is a difficult concept to grasp because dependencies have an element of volition and therefore are often seen as culpable behaviours.

Despite these views, there is an onus on employers to accommodate employees who find themselves with these difficulties. One simple form of accommodation is to ensure employees have the opportunity to avail themselves of sick leave and/or short term disability insurance (when available) to seek rehabilitation treatment. Proactive employers will spell this type of accommodation out in the form of an employee assistance policy.

Even if the substance abuse comes to light in a disciplinary process, the employer will be viewed as having a duty to accommodate the disability. This is precisely because the substance abuse is a mitigating factor behind why the disciplinary response became necessary. Thus, the Last Chance Agreement can be viewed as a means of accommodating the employee's problem. Care must be taken when writing these agreements to ensure that conditions are not put into place that impose differential treatment on the employee, except for those conditions that are directly relevant to the treatment and eradication of the disease.

Take the example of the employee who is dismissed because of attendance problems and then is reinstated as a result of the need to accommodate substance abuse as the mitigating factor that caused the excessive absenteeism. The employer cannot impose a standard of attendance that is different than what is expected of other employees. The employer, however, can expect the employee to prove that absences were not the result of further substance abuse.

It is also important in ensuring the enforceability of Last Chance Agreements that the parties agree that such agreements represent accommodation in accordance with the requirements of the applicable human rights legislation.

The most controversial aspect of accommodation for substance abuse is determining how many times the employer needs to allow the employee to undergo rehabilitation treatment. There does not appear to be a consensus on this. If properly framed, Last Chance Agreements can limit this form of accommodation to one time only. Notwithstanding, compassionate employers will observe that even the most determined employee may have difficulty in not slipping up at some time in his or her recovery process. Whatever standard might be established, it should, of course, be consistently applied.

Role of the Human Resources Practitioner

Human Resources practitioners should be careful not to cast themselves in the role of counsellor. The treatment of substance abuse demands expertise that the practitioner is unlikely to possess. As well, the practitioner cannot have dual roles in counselling employees and advising managers on dealing with performance issues.

The practitioner should be involved in the following activities:

— developing policies regarding substance abuse and the use of alcohol;

— selecting an Employee Assistance Program provider;

— coaching supervisors and managers on dealing with problem employees;

— developing Last Chance Agreements; and

— developing screening programs, where applicable.

Barriers to Success/Common Pitfalls

Substance abuse is a difficult and sensitive issue with which to deal. The effort put into controlling it in the workplace pays obvious dividends, but the practitioner needs to be careful when proceeding. Substance abuse has an element of volition and carries with it a stigma that many people find difficult to overcome. Some managers may be resistant to recognizing it as a disease that must be treated.

A significant aspect of the disease is denial. This makes confidentiality a particularly important consideration. Employee assistance programs must be handled with great sensitivity and absolute confidentiality. Employees who self-refer must be assured that their employment status will not be affected and that their supervisors will not be informed. Even where the employee's problem has only come to light through the disciplinary process, the employee should be assured that his or her dignity will be respected and maintained.

In developing policies, particularly with respect to Last Chance Agreements, practitioners should familiarize themselves with the applicable human rights legislation and seek legal advice.

Cases

A sales executive had been demoted to a non-sales position. He subsequently met a client to say good-bye and to thank him for his loyalty and business. They had lunch together and consumed a great deal of alcohol. The client in an intoxicated state made an off-colour remark about the employee's wife and the two got into a physical altercation. The company fired the employee. He sued and was awarded damages by the court (*Ditchburn v. Landis and Gyr Powers Ltd.* (1995), 16 C.C.E.L. (2d) 1 (Ont. Ct. Gen. Div.); 97 CLLC ¶210-015).

The court's rationale was based on the employee's 27 years of exemplary service, his age (close to retirement) and the fact that this was an isolated incident. Generally, intoxication is grounds for dismissal, if

(a) the employee's ability to perform his or her duties is impaired;

(b) the workplace has been detrimentally affected, or harm has been brought to the business; or

(c) there has been a risk to the health and safety of the employee or others.

The concern over safety has been the central focus of two of the better known cases. Following the *Exxon Valdez* oil spill off the coast of Alaska, Esso made a decision to implement a policy regarding the use of alcohol and drugs that provided for random drug and breath testing for employees in positions deemed to be safety-sensitive. The policy also included provisions for mandatory medical examinations for employees in safety-sensitive positions, obligatory disclosure of substance dependency (past or present) and drug or alcohol testing for cause when employees were involved in a serious workplace accident.

The Communications, Energy and Paperworkers grieved the policy (*Esso Petroleum Canada and CEP, Local 614* (1994), 56 L.A.C. (4th) 440). The British Columbia Labour Relations Board ruled that, to enforce such a policy, the employer would have to demonstrate that there was evidence of a significant drug and/or alcohol problem in the workplace. Secondly, the employer should explore alternative means to deal with the problem in a less invasive way. In other words, the Board rejected much of Esso's policy. It accepted rules that dealt with possession of alcohol or drugs at work and intoxication while on duty. It also accepted random testing as part of a rehabilitation plan and mandatory testing for cause in the case of a workplace accident.

In a subsequent related case, the employee claimed that Imperial Oil had infringed on his right to equal treatment because of his handicap or perceived handicap (*Martin Entrop v. Imperial Oil Limited* (1995), 24 C.C.E.L. (2d) 87 (Ont. Bd. of Inquiry); 2000 CLLC ¶230-037). Mr. Entrop was employed in a safety-sensitive position and was thus required to disclose to the company that he had been addicted to alcohol. The company responded by reassigning him to a less desirable position that was not safety-sensitive. As a result of his complaint, the company changed its policy and allowed employees who had been abstinent for more than five years to maintain positions in safety-sensitive positions.

However, before Entrop could return to his former position, he had to provide medical evidence that he was alcohol-free for more than five years and to sign an agreement to allow the company to administer random tests twice each quarter. Mr. Entrop also had to agree to annual medical examinations and continued abstinence. After a period of a year, the conditions were again changed and Mr. Entrop was only required to continue his abstinence.

The Board of Inquiry found that the company had violated Mr. Entrop's rights when it required him to disclose his past alcohol dependence and when it removed him from his job. It further violated his rights when it imposed the ongoing conditions on him.

The importance of this case is that the Board laid out important guidelines for employers to follow when fashioning policies. These include:

⇨ recognition that alcohol and drug dependencies are handicaps within the meaning of the Ontario *Human Rights Code*;

⇨ pre-employment and random alcohol or drug testing is unlawful;

⇨ employers must use the least intrusive means available to accommodate employees with substance abuse problems; and

⇨ testing for cause is permissible.

Employers can dismiss employees for reporting to work in an unfit condition when the conduct presents a direct threat to the safety of the employee or others. However, in many contexts, organizations must be careful that their own actions have not led to the condonation of alcohol use. Sales representatives are often encouraged to entertain clients and this may involve the consumption of alcohol. Courts have found that employers cannot terminate sales representatives for becoming intoxicated when the organization has encouraged the practice of entertaining clients in situations involving the use of alcohol (*Hardie v. Trans-Canada Resources Ltd.* (1976), 2 A.R. 289 (C.A.)).

SAMPLE DRUG AND ALCOHOL POLICY STATEMENT

It is our company's desire to provide a drug-free, healthful and safe workplace. To promote this goal, employees are required to report to work in appropriate mental and physical condition to perform their jobs safely and efficiently in a satisfactory manner.

While on company premises or while conducting business-related activities on behalf of the company away from the premises, no employee may use, possess, distribute, sell, or be under the influence of alcohol or illegal drugs. The legal use of prescribed drugs is permitted on the job, provided such use does not impair an employee's ability to perform the essential functions of the job effectively and in a manner that does not endanger the individual or other individuals in the workplace.

Violations of this policy may lead to disciplinary action, up to and including immediate termination of employment, and/or required participation in a substance abuse rehabilitation or treatment program. Such violations may also have legal consequences.

Employees with questions or concerns about substance dependency or abuse are encouraged to discuss matters with their supervisor or a Human Resources Department representative to receive assistance or referrals to appropriate resources in the community.

Employees with drug or alcohol problems that have not resulted in, and are not the immediate subject of, disciplinary action may be able to participate in a rehabilitation program as part of the company sponsored Employee Assistance Plan. Please see a representative of Human Resources for more details.

The company does not engage in pre-employment or random drug and alcohol screening. However, drug and alcohol testing may be required under the following circumstances:

⇨ where, after the accident/incident, demonstrable losses have been incurred and there is suspicion that drug or alcohol use may have been a factor;

⇨ where there is evidence of drug or alcohol use contrary to this policy; or

⇨ where an employee's acknowledged substance abuse has led to a "Last Chance" agreement that includes post-rehabilitation monitoring.

Employees with questions on this policy or issues related to drug or alcohol use in the workplace should raise their concerns with their supervisor or the Human Resources Department without fear of reprisal.

———

SAMPLE LAST CHANCE AGREEMENT

Memorandum of Agreement

Between

A to Z Services Co. (the "Company")

and

Mr. I. M. Working (the "Employee")

and

Allied Workers International, Local 222 (the "Union")

Whereas I.M. Working reported to work on February 16, 2002 in an unfit condition to resume his duties;

Whereas contrary to Company policy the Employee was under the influence of alcohol;

Whereas the Company has suspended the Employee indefinitely without pay;

Whereas the Employee has admitted to a substance abuse problem requiring treatment;

Whereas the Union has filed a grievance on behalf of the Employee;

Whereas the parties hereto are desirous of a full and final settlement to all matters concerning Mr. Working's employment with the Company and the suspension thereof; and

Therefore, in this matter the parties agree on the following:

1. The parties agree that the Employee will enter an agreed to rehabilitation program on an in-patient basis and will be eligible for disability benefit coverage under the Company's benefit program while participating in such a program provided he abides by all the requirements of the benefits plan including abstinence from the use of alcohol or illegal drugs.

2. The period from February 16 until the Employee has successfully completed the stipulated rehabilitation program will be considered as a suspension without pay. This will not preclude the Employee from receiving disability benefits during this period if he otherwise qualifies under the terms and conditions of the benefit plans.

3. Upon successful completion of the prescribed rehabilitation program, the Employee will be reinstated to his former position without loss of seniority.

4. Once reinstated, the Employee agrees to abide by all Company policies and to maintain regular attendance at work.

5. The Company reserves the right to require medical proof that absences are not the result of alcohol use and to have the Employee tested for the use of alcohol periodically for a period of not less than one year.

6. The Employee agrees to abstain from the use of alcohol and illegal drugs at all times.

7. The Union and the Employee agree to withdraw all grievances and complaints related to the suspension of his employment and accept these terms and conditions as a full and final settlement of any and all claims he may have against the Company in that regard.

8. The Union and the Employee acknowledge that the breach of any terms or conditions contained herein may result in the termination of the Employee's employment for just and sufficient cause and that the subject of any grievance launched with respect to such termination will be limited to whether or not a breach in fact occurred and not the quantum of penalty imposed for the breach.

9. This agreement shall constitute accommodation under the *Human Rights Code*.

Signed this _____ day of March 2003

_____   _____
For the Company   I.M. Working

                                                        _____
                                                        For the Union

ALTERNATIVE DISPUTE RESOLUTION

Definition/Background

Alternative Dispute Resolution (ADR) refers to processes of resolving conflict in lieu of litigation. In common law employment relationships, as opposed to those governed by collective agreements under labour relations statutes, the parties have little recourse other than to sue each other when conflict escalates to the point that it threatens the continuation of the employment relationship, or has resulted in the termination of the relationship.

When parties choose to litigate a dispute, there is an underlying perception that one of the parties will win and, consequently, the other party will lose. In employment relationships, it can be argued that, in fact, both parties lose through litigation. The process is expensive. If an employee sues for wrongful dismissal, legal fees can easily eat up the gains made in severance pay. Moreover, the relationship between employee and former employer is forever strained. Employers who successfully defend an action by a former employee may gain a tainted reputation for being a difficult employer. The purpose of litigation is to make a determination as to who is right and who is wrong in a dispute. Under ADR, the purpose is to arrive at a mutually satisfactory resolution to the underlying dispute; the central premise is that by choosing an alternative route to resolving the conflict, the parties open up the possibility that they both can emerge as winners.

ADR processes assume that the parties will always have some common ground to settle any dispute amicably. They may have common interests, such as avoiding publicity, minimizing the cost of resolving the dispute and coming to a speedy conclusion to the conflict. In other instances, the interests may be divergent but compatible.

ADR processes include negotiated settlements, mediation and arbitration. For our purposes, we will also discuss below several internal dispute resolution mechanisms.

To be effective, all these methods should result in a written statement of resolution. This could be in the form of a written agreement between the parties, or a decision or award from a third-party arbitrator. Employment disputes can be relatively complex. The parties should be open to the possibility that some of the underlying issues may be resolved, while others remain in dispute. For the process to be completely effective, the parties must appreciate that settlements may only bring partial closure to the issues and that the unresolved issues may either remain unresolved or may have to be referred to arbitration or litigation for final disposition.

The written resolution is an enforceable contract. If either party fails to live up to the terms of the resolution, the other party can apply to a court for a summary judgment to enforce the terms of the agreement. The courts will not have to consider the underlying issues that led to the drafting of the agreement unless one of the parties raises concerns that there was no meeting of the minds when the agreement was struck, that the terms were not understood, or that the agreement was obtained through coercion, intimidation or undue influence.

Employers tend to have more power in a negotiating setting, even when the employment relationship has ceased and the ultimate sanction (termination of employment) is no longer available. Moreover, the organization usually has more resources available to it to resolve conflicts in its favour. In an ADR setting, the organization may assign responsibility to a Human Resources practitioner with a sophisticated understanding of employment law and litigation. This is perfectly understandable. However, that practitioner cannot take advantage of the relatively less sophisticated employee, and "bully" him or her into signing an agreement that is unconscionable or was reached without a full appreciation by the employee of the consequences of signing an agreement.

ADR is founded on the basis of "principled negotiations" or "interest-based bargaining". These concepts revolve around a process of engaging in a dialogue on the underlying issues and working together on a resolution, as opposed to staking out a position and using whatever means is at the party's disposal to have its position win over the other party's position.

A - B - C

In a labour relations context, the grievance-arbitration process has evolved into a very effective alternative system to resolving disputes. The process emerged as an alternative not only to litigation but also as an alternative to work actions such as slowdowns, work-to-rule campaigns and wildcat strikes. Moreover, a significant part of the process rests on the internal processes of hearing grievances through a variety of progressive steps before the matter is referred to a third-party arbitrator for a binding resolution.

These internal steps reinforce the "internal responsibilities" incumbent on the organization and the union to work cooperatively in resolving any disputes that arise out of the interpretation, administration or implementation of the collective agreement into which they have entered. When matters are referred to arbitration, the process is sufficiently relaxed to allow the arbitrator to mediate a possible solution before hearing the matter and rendering a decision as to which party is right and which party is wrong. It is widely accepted that the system is enhanced when the parties are able to reach a settlement rather than being dependent on a third party to resolve the matter for them.

In labour relations, the parties have the common interest of fostering positive relations, precisely because the relationship is ongoing. There is an assumed overarching objective of creating a productive working relationship between the parties that will supercede the immediate need to "win" each and every dispute. While the relationship between many employers and the unions that represent their employees have a long way to go to reach this point, most Human Resources practitioners recognize the importance of developing strong working relationships between themselves and the business agents who represent employees.

Unfortunately, in non-union employment relationships, most disputes arise at the point of termination. Employees under common law have little recourse during the term of their employment to take action against their employers when they believe they have been wronged. Employment statutes (including legislation on health and safety, human rights and employment standards) provide some protections and avenues for redress on specific issues. However, these tend to be very narrow in scope. Under occupational health and safety legislation, for example, employers are forbidden to take any form of reprisal against an employee who exercises a right under the law. Human rights legislation protects employees from differential treatment based on prohibited grounds such as race, gender, religion and handicap. Employment standards legislation requires employers to meet certain minimum conditions of employment.

Each of these avenues are limited in terms of scope and potential redress. Although they provide an accessible alternative to litigation, the processes are similar in as much as the ministerial branches processing complaints are predisposed to determining who is right and who is wrong. Some branches have introduced mediation services to address this deficiency.

Notwithstanding, for a great number of employees, either the issues they face go unresolved, or they are forced to leave their employment and seek recourse through litigation. Hence, some enlightened employers have established internal processes mirroring the grievance process that are accessible to non-union employees. Some have gone a step further and use the services of a third-party ombudsman as a final step in the process to bring closure to issues. Others have introduced arbitration as a final and binding step when the employment relationship has been terminated and the parties are in dispute as to the terms of the final settlement.

Benefits/Expected Outcomes

ADR processes have many significant advantages over litigating disputes. The advantages are as follows:

✓ The parties are open to the potential for a mutually satisfactory settlement.

✓ Speedier resolution — litigation can take years to bring closure to an issue, whereas ADR processes can usually be concluded in a few months.

✓ Lower costs — legal fees can add up and negate any potential gains for both parties.

✓ In employment relationships, there are many potential non-compensatory benefits for the employee that the employer can provide at little or no cost and that can resolve outstanding issues. Litigation cannot uncover these benefits.

✓ Some of the damages relate to emotional or "intangible" harm (hurt feelings, loss of face, damage to personal or professional reputation). These are brought to the surface through the open dialogue that is characteristic of ADR processes.

✓ Through an interest-based process, joint gains can be realized that are not possible when the parties are forced (as is the case in litigation) to take positions.

✓ Adverse publicity is avoided. Even when an employer wins a wrongful dismissal case, it can gain a reputation of being a difficult organization for which to work. Employers who embrace ADR may gain a reputation of being fair and progressive organizations. This ultimately can make them the employers of choice for many potential high-flyers.

Workplace conflicts that go unresolved create tension and undermine the organization's culture. Even if the matter at hand is resolved through litigation, the resulting settlement may not go beyond the surface issues to treat the root cause of the conflict. The employee who succeeds in a lawsuit for wrongful dismissal may get a sense of just rewards, but seldom overcomes the hurt feelings and loss of dignity that are often associated with the termination of an employment relationship. This can have an indirect effect on employee morale. Employees who believe that the former employee was treated poorly will foster mistrust and apprehension when dealing with management. Consequently, the organization will suffer in terms of reduced productivity, increased absenteeism and turnover, and diminished quality of work. Having an effective alternative may demonstrate to all employees that the organization is committed to the fair resolution of all employment disputes. The net result will be a close in the performance gap — that is, improved productivity and product/service quality and reduced turnover and absenteeism.

Even if the ADR process fails to bring closure in every instance, it can help reduce the costs of litigation and speed up the process. During the dialogue towards reaching a settlement, the parties can sign off on specific matters to which they agree (including statements of fact, procedural matters, admissions and any individual terms of settlement). This can reduce the amount of time spent on procedures before the court.

Employees can gain a lot from the ADR process that may not be possible through litigation. If the process is used before the employment relationship is irreparably dissolved, then re-employment may be possible. The organization may be influenced to consider other career possibilities within the organization or with an affiliate.

In some cases, the employee's ability to find other employment may be significantly enhanced through retraining or through the assistance of an outplacement counsellor. These alternatives may allow the employer to discount the amount of severance, thus saving money, while providing a benefit to the employee that has a greater perceived value. Moreover, employees often perceive that in a termination situation they carry a stigma which will hamper their ability to continue growing their careers. The employer can address these concerns in a number of different ways, not least of which is by providing a letter of reference that sheds a positive light on the employee's abilities and that explains the reason for departure in a way that removes the potential stigma.

Employees gain perhaps even more than organizations by having the disputes resolved as quickly as possible. Psychologically, the employee will want closure as quickly as possible. Moreover, the employee does not have the resources to engage in a protracted battle with the organization. An expedient and open means to discuss and resolve issues can, in itself, have tremendous value for the employee and in return may help "discount" settlement costs for the organization.

Addressing the psychological impact of termination can be one of the most significant gains for the employee. Work provides the individual not only with a means of financial support but also, as importantly, with a contributory role in society. A person's employment is an essential component of his or her sense of identity, self-worth and emotional well-being. Accordingly, when the individual is terminated from employment, he or she feels a grave loss in terms of dignity, self-worth and self-respect. Through an open dialogue, the organization can help restore these elements by listening with empathy and addressing the emotional components with some degree of sensitivity and concern. By merely expressing that the organization ultimately cares about the individual, the employer's representative can help the employee begin the healing process. This is not something that is possible in litigation.

Programming/Implementation

In the employment context, ADR processes must be negotiated. The parties need to establish, usually at the onset of employment, the processes they agree to follow in the event of a dispute. The parties to the agreement may include terms where:

❑ Agreement can be made as to the types of disputes that may be subject to the ADR process. This could be in the form of allowing the parties to opt in or out of the process. The party bringing a claim against the other may be given a choice to follow the ADR process or to litigate.

❑ Agreement can be made as to the specific ADR process to be followed in the event of a dispute and the procedures allowed within the process (particularly with respect to the arbitration of disputes).

❑ Agreement can be made as to the powers to be granted to a third-party arbitrator and as to whether that the decision will be considered binding and enforceable on both parties.

❑ Agreement can be made on internal dispute resolution processes and the subjects these processes are designed to address.

❑ Agreement can be made to have a third-party mediator assist with some parts of the processes.

❑ Agreement can be made that the ADR process will be considered a communication in pursuit of a settlement and any discussions that take place will not be entered as evidence in any subsequent legal proceedings.

While both parties may wish to have legal counsel in the event of a final and binding arbitration hearing, the parties may agree to exclude legal counsel from participating in earlier stages of the process. This is an important consideration. One of the advantages of the ADR process is that the parties themselves are direct participants. In litigation, lawyers for the parties can take over the dispute and the parties become separated from the process. In ADR, the parties are free to express themselves in their own terms. However, the employer's representative may have a perceived advantage in terms of power or leverage; Human Resources practitioners, who are familiar with employment law and ADR may be perceived by the employee as having an advantage. This may be one reason that employees are reluctant to embrace ADR. This is why the presence of a third party can be advantageous and is strongly recommended.

The third party serves as a mediator and can neutralize any feelings of disadvantage an employee may have. As well, the mediator can help define the way the matter will proceed to keep the dialogue on track and moving towards a positive resolution.

It is important to give the third-party mediator/arbitrator enough latitude to ensure the interests of both parties are well served. ADR is interest-based, not rights-based. The distinction is that the third party is not restricted to making a determination as to who is right or wrong. Rather, his or her mandate is to facilitate a process where both parties' interests find expression and a mutually agreeable settlement can be effected.

Mediation

Mediation is, in effect, a facilitated process of negotiating a settlement to a dispute. The process begins with an opening statement from the mediator in which he or she outlines the ground rules for the dialogue and establishes an agenda. In the opening statement, the mediator will explain that discussions held in pursuit of a settlement are to be considered confidential and therefore cannot be used as evidence in any subsequent legal proceeding (unless otherwise agreed to by the parties). In the same vein, the mediator cannot be compelled as a witness, regardless of the circumstances.

After the mediator has set the stage, the parties are allowed the opportunity to give brief opening statements. These may be given by legal counsel or by the parties themselves. This helps the mediator understand what issues are in dispute and what positions each party has adopted. The opening statements will also tell the mediator something about the stances the parties have taken in approaching mediation.

Despite agreeing to mediation as a method of resolving disputes, it is not automatic that the parties will arrive with a mindset to collaborate in finding a mutually satisfactory settlement. The agreement to use mediation-arbitration as a dispute resolution forum will usually be made when there are no issues in dispute. When a dispute arises, and in the employment context this invariably involves the loss of the employee's job, emotions will take over. The employee may be motivated to exact revenge, while the employer may be initially intransigent in defending its position.

The mediator will thus take time to gain a deeper understanding of the nature of the dispute. Usually the parties are met with separately. The mediator determines from discussions with each if a negotiated settlement is possible and with what issues he or she should specifically deal. The mediator's role is to assist the parties in creating solutions. Understanding the nature of the issues at dispute will help the mediator determine how to proceed. In some instances, it may be appropriate to deal with certain aspects separately, while in others it may be more appropriate to bundle issues. Skilled mediators are able to assist the parties to be creative in finding solutions.

Mediation is distinct from arbitration or litigation. The mediator must maintain neutrality. He or she may look at evidence to gain a clearer understanding of issues, but the mediator's role is not to determine the relative merits of each party's case. Having said that, mediators will take a measure of the evidence and suggest to the parties potential outcomes should the case proceed to arbitration or litigation. The mediator's mandate is to help the parties arrive at a negotiated settlement and avoid further proceedings.

In labour relations, it has become common for arbitrators to mediate potential settlements with the parties to a dispute prior to actually hearing any specific evidence in the case. There is a potential danger in doing this, in that the arbitrator may voice an opinion on the merits of the case and be perceived by one of the parties as carrying a bias into the hearing if the matter is not resolved. Skilled arbitrators avoid this and maintain an even-handed perspective. Moreover, the labour relations milieu has evolved over the past six decades and has become quite sophisticated. Experienced participants have no difficulty with this dual role.

Once the mediator has become familiar with the nature of the dispute, he or she will assist the parties in developing an exchange of information. In some instances, the initial exchanges may be through the mediator as an intermediary; however, ultimately, the mediator has to bring the parties together to gain a true meeting of the minds. During these exchanges, either party may provide information to the mediator that it wants to keep confidential from the other party. This may be intended to influence the mediator, but the real value comes in helping the mediator understand underlying issues that are typically hidden in other forums. The mediator will try to find ways to

bring this information forward if it seems relevant to the potential outcome.

During the process, the mediator will encourage the parties to engage in dialogue as much as possible. The mediator will act as a referee to keep the discussions close to the agenda and prevent the parties from getting heated in their discussions; however, the mediator needs to intervene sparingly to ensure the dialogue is productive. Some display of emotions is essential to the process and is psychologically healthy. Either party can also ask for a private conference to consult with counsel.

In the labour relations context, parties to mediation are usually experienced and sophisticated practitioners. They often do not involve legal counsel in the proceedings, primarily to save what they perceive is an unnecessary expense. In the employment law context, it is advisable for the parties to be allowed to have their lawyers present. Employers may feel comfortable not using lawyers at this stage, but employees are unlikely to have experience with the process and will benefit from having a skilled practitioner available to them to discuss strategy and to ensure their rights are protected.

Allowing the parties to have a private caucus with their counsel ensures that no party becomes uncomfortable with the proceedings. Information exchanged during mediation is usually considered confidential and cannot be relied on at subsequent proceedings. However, the parties can agree that the session will be used as a form of discovery and the mediator can allow evidence to be brought forward in a form of discovery.

If the matter is part of a process that can be finally determined through arbitration, then exchanging evidence at this stage will help reduce the amount of time required for an arbitration hearing. With the parties together, the mediator can facilitate an agreed statement of facts and help reduce the presentation of evidence at arbitration to matters in dispute. However, if failure to reach a settlement results in litigation, the mediator should refrain from managing evidence.

The skill of the mediator is very important. Each party will arrive at the session with its own agenda and with an anticipated approach. The mediator will need to encourage and influence the parties to adopt a collaborative approach to the dialogue for achieving the best possible negotiated settlement. Part of the benefit of

A - B - C

mediation, when it is successful, is to break down the confrontation and work towards the parties' mutual interests. It is not uncommon for one, or both, of the parties to arrive with a mindset of beating the other party. Mediation is not, in the end, successful if one party perceives it has won at the expense of the other. The ideal and desired outcome is for both parties to arrive at a satisfactory settlement with which they can live.

The mediator's primary role is to facilitate the process of dialogue. During discussions, he or she should refrain from intervening as much as possible. Thus, at the onset, it is important for the mediator to work with each party to get both sides to be open to settlement possibilities. The mediator will often spend sufficient time with each party to get them to "let down their guard" and be receptive to the other party's concerns.

Once the opening statements have been completed and the mediator has had an opportunity to meet with each side to gain an understanding of the nature of the dispute, the parties are brought together to discuss it in detail. This might be considered as a form of subjective discovery. The idea is not to restrict the exchange to mere facts, but to allow each party to express how it feels, what it believes and what it hopes to achieve. Each party can ask the other questions to clarify understanding. The mediator should be very clear on the ground rules in this phase. The parties should not be trying to win their case. They should be using this as an opportunity to gain a full understanding of and appreciation for the position of the other party.

The "subjective discovery" phase is an attempt to achieve the following:

⇨ create an atmosphere of trust, respect and mutual understanding;

⇨ reduce tension and eliminate confrontational approaches;

⇨ allow each party to give voice to its feelings and emotions, and to be heard by the other party;

⇨ allow each party to vent, while accepting that the other party holds certain beliefs and understandings;

⇨ create an understanding about the root causes of the dispute;

⇨ create an environment where defences are down and each party can openly admit its contribution to the cause of the conflict; and

⇨ break down the initial posturing by allowing each party to see the honestly held beliefs of the other and see it in a more human vein.

This phase is not about presenting arguments or winning points over the other side. The degree of success for the mediation process is largely dependent on each party abandoning certain paradigms and being willing to empathize with the other party. The idea is to assume that the best alternative is not to accept either party's version of events as being preferred over the other. Rather, the best alternative invariably lies somewhere in between.

One of the most important advantages of mediation is that it is a dialogue between the parties in a dispute. While perhaps idealistic, one of the most sought after outcomes is to have the parties each admit its complicity in the dispute. Apologies and expressions of empathy can go a long way to resolving an employment dispute.

When an employee has been terminated, he or she invariably loses a sense of personal identity. The employee will lose a feeling that he or she belongs and will gain a deep sense of alienation. This leads to hurt feelings. Having an employer express that the employee's service was valued and that he or she is missed can relieve some of those hurt feelings. Many terminations are the result of changing business conditions. In other instances, a shift in the required skills needed in the position has left the employee behind. Acknowledging the contributions the employee did make and sincerely expressing concern for the individual's future can help the employee regain some dignity and feelings of self-worth.

Certainly, in cases where cause is alleged, it will be difficult for employers to express sympathy. Practitioners who are involved in these kinds of cases need to separate the circumstances surrounding the cause and deal with the inherent value of the individual as a fellow human being. If there is no room for this kind of expression of empathy, then the mediation will not likely be successful. Fortunately, cases of dismissals without cause and cases of so-called "near-cause" are far more common than terminations for cause.

It is important for the mediator to emphasize that admissions and apologies are presented in confidence and are not to be used as evidence in subsequent hearings. Without such assurance, the parties will be extremely reluctant to open up; this removes the advantage of mediation to give voice to these underlying emotions. In many termination cases, the employee rationally understands the reason he or she has been let go. On an emotional level, the employee may have difficulty in accepting the loss. Often the only motivation in seeking redress is to vent anger and frustration. This is why mediation can be a very effective forum for resolving employment disputes. The future success of ADR processes is partially dependent on the extent to which organizations and practitioners realize this.

The final phase of mediation is the attempt to arrive at a negotiated settlement. Here the mediator's skill and experience can be helpful to the parties. The mediator can suggest creative solutions that might not have occurred to either party. One of the goals for both parties is to use the process to save money. Many solutions may be available that represent less cost to the employer and at the same time have a greater value for the employee.

For example, outplacement counselling can be made available. If the employee had to pay for these services personally, he or she would have to do so with after-tax dollars. The employer can pay directly and in exchange may expect a discount on the severance pay negotiated with the employee. In addition, by agreeing to the outplacement option, the employee can expect the employer to work with the outplacement counsellor to assist the employee. The employer has a vested interest (i.e., reduced costs) in having the outplacement process work quickly. The employer is in a position to work cooperatively with the outplacement counsellor in assessing the employee's strengths and weaknesses and in providing appropriate references for prospective employers.

It is not unheard of for an employer to use the organization's network to help the employee find "hidden" employment opportunities. Other possibilities may include enhancing pension benefits, extending health and welfare coverage, retraining, funding membership in professional associations, or including the employee in social events.

Given the confidential nature of mediation, either party is free to make a "without prejudice offer of settlement" to the other. If the final disposition of the case is through litigation, such an offer can be made in accordance with civil procedure (under the rules of civil procedure, offers of settlement can be produced to support arguments that the other party should bear the costs of litigation). The same rule could be accepted as part of the arbitration process, if the parties so desire. The idea is to encourage both parties to consider carefully any offer put forward rather than dismiss them out-of-hand and take a chance that a better result can be achieved through litigation.

Either party may also make a "with prejudice" offer of settlement. This is not common, but tactically could be employed should the matter proceed to a hearing, to demonstrate that the other party failed to take reasonable steps to mitigate damages.

Arbitration

In most negotiations, parties are reluctant to agree on single issues separately. They prefer working towards a full and final settlement of all issues. However, under ADR, the parties should be encouraged when they cannot reach a full settlement to narrow the scope of the dispute. This is in keeping with the objectives of using ADR processes to minimize costs and to arrive at an expedient resolution.

If a full settlement appears unlikely, then the parties may use the mediation phase to agree upon a number of "statements of fact" to speed up subsequent procedures. Even if there is not agreement on the facts, the parties should exchange all available evidence at this point. Neither party should lie in wait by holding back evidence. In some instances, the failure to disclose a certain piece of evidence may be the only thing hindering settlement.

Notwithstanding, some parties may be motivated to abuse the process in order to "win" in the final outcome. Procedurally, there should be an understanding that prior to proceeding beyond mediation, the parties are required to exchange all available evidence.

In a sophisticated ADR environment, the parties will choose arbitration over litigation. While arbitration proceedings are well developed in the labour relations context, they are still rare in Canadian employment law cases.

A - B - C

Conceptually, the arbitrator is a neutral third party, appointed by mutual agreement between the parties, to decide on the relative merits of each party's arguments and to render a final and binding decision to resolve the dispute. Arbitrators' decisions are binding and enforceable under law. The decision of an arbitrator can only be appealed if he or she makes an error in law or the decision is patently unreasonable (such as exceeding jurisdiction).

The arbitrator is appointed by mutual agreement. The individual may be the same person who attempted to mediate a settlement or may be an independent appointee. The advantages of having the mediator hear the case include the fact that the individual already has a high degree of familiarity with the facts of the case. In the labour relations environment, there should be little concern that the mediator will carry a bias over to the arbitration. Notwithstanding, given the general lack of experience with arbitration in the employment law context, the parties may be apprehensive about potential bias; if so, they can choose a different individual to arbitrate.

The arbitrator is bound by any relevant legislation (e.g., employment standards, human rights) and cannot change contractual arrangements between the parties. Arbitrators are not generally bound by legal precedents; however, most arbitrators will actively consider any relevant case law put before them in support of an argument.

Arbitration is not yet a common feature in resolving employment law disputes. No one can today compel another party to submit a dispute to binding arbitration. However, if the parties have contractually undertaken to have their disputes resolved through the arbitration process, then either party can compel the other to follow that course.

Agreements to submit employment issues to arbitration should describe exactly what types of issues may be submitted and the procedures to be followed. The provisions of the agreement should also clarify what rules or body of law will apply. For organizations that operate in several provincial jurisdictions, it is common to either stipulate that the laws of the employee's home province will apply in case of disputes, or that the laws of the province in which the organization's head office is located will apply.

The parties will also want to agree over which provisions of the provincial Act (e.g., Ontario's *Arbitration Act*) will apply. Parties to an arbitration agreement may agree to vary or exclude any provision of the Act with certain exceptions.

- Once the parties have agreed to submit an issue or issues to binding arbitration, they cannot then proceed with a lawsuit or other legal action on the issue(s).

- Parties to an arbitration may apply to a court for the following:

  ⇨ determining a question of law upon consent of the parties;

  ⇨ appointing an arbitrator when the parties cannot agree on a nominee;

  ⇨ enforcing an arbitrator's ruling;

  ⇨ appealing of an arbitrator's decision based on a question of law or fact, or if the decision is patently unreasonable; and

  ⇨ assessing of costs, including the arbitrator's costs.

- Parties are free to agree on any procedural matters, provided they are deemed to be fair and are equitably applied to both parties.

- The arbitrator must decide the dispute in accordance with existing law and may order any remedy or measure available to the courts.

- The arbitrator's ruling should be rendered in writing and is enforceable under law.

- Arbitrators may award costs of the proceeding to either party.

- The pre- and post-judgment interest provisions of the relevant legislation (e.g., Ontario's *Courts of Justice Act*) apply to arbitration awards.

In labour relations, it is common for the parties to agree to mutually share the cost of the arbitrator, regardless of the outcome. Given that employment law arbitration is relatively rare, it may behoove organizations to absorb the cost of arbitration at least in the initial launch. The savings to the organization in avoiding litigation should, in most instances, far outweigh the potential cost of arbitration. In the alternative, the organization may fix the amount of costs the employee will have to pay to make the option attractive to the employee. Having the employee pay a nominal, but not insignificant, amount to access arbitration will reduce any tendency to "roll the dice" in the hope of a favourable outcome. This should also provide some incentive for the employee to try earnestly to effect a settlement at the mediation stage.

Internal Dispute Resolution Mechanisms

ADR is clearly not for everyone. Organizations that are highly centralized and are characterized by command-and-control structures are not likely predisposed to becoming involved in a process that involves open dialogue and interest-based dispute resolution techniques. Decentralized organizations that emphasize empowerment and employee engagement are more likely to embrace both internal dispute resolution mechanisms and ADR. In these environments, employees are encouraged to give voice to their concerns and express their values and beliefs openly.

In empowered cultures, employees gain a certain level of confidence in themselves and are less prone to seek outside help (i.e., legal counsel) in resolving disputes with the employer. There is also a greater level of trust built between employees and management. Employees will be more willing to accept that the organization is motivated to use the ADR process to resolve issues fairly rather than to leverage it to an advantage.

Having effective internal dispute resolution mechanisms will create a positive environment, where ADR will be seen as a natural extension of those processes. Internal dispute resolution processes include:

- hierarchical;
- open door policy;
- peer tribunals;
- communication coordinators; and
- ombudsman.

Hierarchical Process

A common protocol in organizations dictates that an employee who has a complaint or dispute must first raise the complaint with his or her immediate superior. The boss should then be given sufficient time to attempt either to resolve the issue or answer the complaint. If the matter is not within the boss's authority to resolve, then it is taken up with the next level superior for resolution. The process continues until the matter is resolved to the employee's satisfaction, or it reaches the Chief Executive Officer, who is deemed the highest authority available to the employee.

This process often fails. At the first level, employees will not bring a concern to their boss if they fear potential reprisals, or if they believe they will not be listened to. Moreover, if the complaint is against the boss, the employee will be unlikely to bring the issue forward. In some organizations, managers at levels beyond the front-line are inaccessible to rank-and-file employees.

Typically, employees perceive that the process of complaining falls on deaf ears and will not pursue complaints. They believe that managers will close ranks and support each other.

Open Door Policy

Open door policies are formal complaint redress systems that address the deficiencies of the informal hierarchical processes by codifying the steps the employee should take. While these processes do not completely overcome the issues of employee reluctance or the fear of reprisals, they are a step in the right direction. Open door policies can be made more effective by specifying the kind of complaints the process is designed to address and training supervisors and managers on how to resolve disputes.

In organizations with an Human Resources department, the Human Resources practitioner can be assigned to provide assistance to the employee in formulating his or her complaint and presenting it to management. The practitioner can also conduct periodic audits or hold focus groups to check on the effectiveness of the process. The practitioner must assume a neutral role. In addition to assisting the employee in formulating the complaint, the practitioner should assist the supervisor in formulating a response. The practitioner acts, in effect, as a neutral third-party mediator to facilitate the process.

The number of complaints received in an open door process should never be used as a measure of process efficacy. A large number of complaints is not a sign that the system is not working, but rather the opposite. If employees feel the system is fair and equitable, they will be more willing to use it. However, too many complaints may signal more profound problems with management practices, or may be evidence of managers merely giving into employees.

Similar to the open door process, some organizations have formalized their internal complaints processes. Instead of following the chain of command, these processes specify that beyond the supervisor having the first opportunity to resolve an issue, unresolved disputes are to be heard by managers from other departments. This provides some level of independence at early stages and removes any perception of subjectivity.

In other organizations, a complaint process mirroring the grievance process found in collective agreements has been established. The first step, as with any internal process, is for the employee to submit the complaint to the front-line supervisor. If it is unresolved, then it is put in writing and presented to the next level of management. Finally, there is a concluding step where the complaint is submitted to a senior designated official, usually the senior Human Resources practitioner, for final resolution. Unlike union grievances, there is no recourse to a neutral third-party arbitrator.

Peer Tribunals

Peer tribunals are often introduced in organizations where team development is well advanced. These tribunals are commonly used to review employee misconduct and to determine the appropriate disciplinary sanctions. However, the tribunals can also be used to hear employee complaints regarding policies, including issues related to internal postings and promotions.

Peer tribunals have a significant influence over policies, but seldom are given full authority to decide on any matter. They are typically set up as advisory councils that have the mandate to make recommendations to management. There are a number of reasons for this. Management retains authority to serve as a system of checks and balances. As well, management cannot in effect delegate the responsibility to discipline an employee or, in the extreme, to terminate an employee's employment.

Peer tribunals can be set up as standing committees with a fixed membership, or can be set up on an *ad hoc* basis. In the latter case, the employee bringing forth the complaint or who is facing possible disciplinary action is permitted to name one member, a second member is arbitrarily selected from a list of volunteers and a third member is selected by manage-

ment. This third member is usually an Human Resources practitioner or another management representative who has been trained to facilitate the meeting and deliberations of the tribunal.

Communication Coordinators

This is a common strategy to use during times of rapid organizational change. To facilitate improved communications, employees from all levels of the organization are selected as communication coordinators. These representatives meet periodically with senior management to discuss the status of change initiatives. The emphasis is on discussion. These meetings are not mere briefings by management. Rather, the communication coordinators are expected to represent employee concerns. They are charged with the responsibility to bring forth questions on behalf of employees and to report on rumours and concerns.

The independence of these coordinators gives them a credibility that managers cannot achieve. More importantly, they are particularly effective when communication flows in both directions.

Ombudsman

A few large organizations (e.g., Bank of Nova Scotia, Magna) have established formal ombudsman offices to hear complaints, investigate their merit, report findings and make recommendations. These offices are functionally separate and usually are attached to the CEO. In order to be effective, they must be perceived as being relatively independent bodies with sufficient power to resolve serious conflicts.

The ombudsman's office may look into complaints of sexual/racial harassment, bullying, or other capricious supervisory behaviour such as nepotism or favouritism. The office gives employees an avenue to pursue outside the chain of command, and may be an appropriate channel for constructive "whistle blowing". Employees who witness unethical behaviour that breaks the bounds of the organization's espoused values, or of the law, need to know they have a place internally to which to turn for the just resolution of matters.

Ombudsmen are common in government contexts to provide citizens with a means to present grievances against public officials. Ombudsmen are not advocates. They are third-party neutrals who make recommendations to the organization based on the evidence they are able to gather. To be effective, the ombudsman needs to be speedy in his or her approach. Notwithstanding, the most important quality is thoroughness.

While they are often given a wide latitude in terms of the redress they can recommend, the nature of the complaints ombudsmen typically receive demands a specific decision be made to resolve the issues. For example, in a sexual harassment complaint, it would be very unusual to bring the parties together to discuss a mutual settlement. If the alleged harasser has abused his or her power in the working relationship, the resolution usually demands a disciplinary sanction be taken, up to and including the possibility of termination.

It should also be noted that the ombudsman typically has no official power, but does have a lot of influence on decision-makers. It only makes sense for organizations that go to the trouble and expense of establishing an office of ombudsman to listen closely to their recommendations.

Refer also to the chapter, Conflict Management at page 103 *et seq.*

Role of the Human Resources Practitioner

Setting the Table

Managing workplace conflict is a significant part of what Human Resources practitioners do. The practitioner plays many different roles in dealing with workplace conflict. These roles can be both proactive and reactive. One of the most difficult challenges faced by practitioners is to develop credibility as a neutral party whose chief role is to facilitate a dialogue and assist in the resolution of workplace disputes. Gaining the appropriate balance between working in the interests of the organization and acting as an employee advocate is a very difficult task for any practitioner.

In order to strike the appropriate balance, the Human Resources practitioner must develop a proactive strategy for addressing conflict and internal disputes. Implementing internal dispute resolution mechanisms is one important step in a proactive strategy. The ultimate goal is to create a positive employee relations environment where employees feel safe to give expression to their concerns and complaints. In

such an environment, employees learn to trust that there are avenues for recourse that are fair and equitable.

Creating a positive employee relations culture is an essential element for ADR to gain acceptance. If employees do not trust the organization to be fair in its treatment of employees, they will be reluctant to give up the power they perceive they have in litigation.

Establishing an ADR Policy

In the employment context, it is the Human Resources practitioner who will likely have to buy-into the ADR concept and sell it to the organization. The practitioner has to be convinced that the process adds to the overall culture the organization wants to create and provides certain benefits to the organization. If the practitioner is convinced that ADR is a viable alternative, he or she will likely have to sell senior management on the idea and this may involve putting together a business case.

This may be more compelling in large organizations where, given the litigious environment we find ourselves in today, lawsuits for wrongful dismissal are large enough in number to be meaningful. However, the more interesting argument in favour of internal dispute resolution mechanisms and ADR is the positive impact they each can have on the employee relations' environment.

Once the organization is sold on the concept, then the practitioner needs to establish organizational policies to support ADR and to write individual contracts that provide for the ADR alternative. This can be a potential show-stopper for senior management. There is a common fear that employees will see an ulterior motive behind the implementation of an ADR process and that it will raise apprehensions of a potential mass layoff or downsizing.

These concerns can only be alleviated in part through the selling power of the practitioner. In establishing new employment contracts, the practitioner can take a multifaceted approach. First, all new contracts could include a mandatory ADR clause that allows for mediation and arbitration in the case of any allegations of constructive or wrongful dismissal. Existing employees could either be presented with an option to sign on to the agreement voluntarily, or be given a contract (in conjunction with some consideration such as their annual salary increase) that allows them the option of ADR or litigation in the event of non-voluntary termination of employment.

Facilitator

The Human Resources practitioner's most neutral role is that of facilitator, particularly with respect to the internal dispute resolution mechanisms. In this role, the practitioner has to focus on maintaining the integrity of the processes and not presuppose the outcomes. The practitioner must not take sides, but rather offer advice to participants on how they should conduct themselves. Essentially, the practitioner takes an independent role as an internal consultant. The ultimate goal of a facilitator is to reach a mutually satisfactory agreement between the two parties involved in a dispute.

The role of facilitator is not an *ad hoc* one. Rather, it is imbedded in the policies and procedures of the organization. In some instances, the role may be seen as being reactive. However, the fact that processes have been put in place to deal with internal disputes makes it proactive. Some view the existence of internal dispute resolution as a means of breeding conflict. In their view, processes like open door policies give a voice to discontented employees who take the opportunity to be disruptive. These individuals view internal dispute resolution processes with suspicion and may be apt to undermine them.

In the alternative view, by giving a voice to employee grievances, the organization will learn how to cope with the stresses put on employees and how to transform dysfunctional conflict into productive and creative outcomes. In dealing with conflicts through institutionalized processes, the organization is introducing procedural fairness that will in turn breed open and honest communications.

In the open door process, the practitioner should be positioned as a third party. The practitioner can help the employee frame his or her complaint by reviewing the facts of the situation and relevant policies with the disgruntled employee. While the review of policy can itself resolve the issue, the practitioner should resist taking too narrow an approach to fixing the issue. Often, the real issue lies below the surface and, through opening up communications, the root cause of the grievance may be uncovered.

The practitioner also assists the supervisor or manager with an open door policy by coaching him or her on how to listen with empathy. The practitioner will also debrief with the supervisor or manager and assist him or her in writing the response. In this role, practitioners must guard themselves from owning the proposed resolution. If the employee rejects the proposed redress and wants to move further in the process, the practitioner must be able to keep an open mind and allow for alternative solutions that might emerge at different stages.

Practitioners should facilitate the convening of peer tribunals. These can demand a delicate hand to ensure openness and procedural fairness. As a facilitator, one of the primary roles for the practitioner is to educate the panel members on corporate policy, organizational precedents and, in some instances, employment law and statutory considerations. While the practitioner must maintain neutrality with respect to the issue at hand, he or she also has to serve as a guardian of the organization's interests. The practitioner may be able to maintain the balance between these aspects of the role by exercising finesse. However, at the onset, the practitioner should establish ground rules with the panel members. These ground rules will include asserting that the practitioner may veto any recommendation that contravenes law or is patently unreasonable.

Ombudsman

While the role of ombudsman is a neutral one, the incumbent will inevitably take a position on the matter brought before him or her. In essence, the very nature of the Human Resources practitioner's role is to serve as the organization's ombudsman. An ombudsman, by definition, is a person appointed to a role to receive and investigate complaints, report findings and make recommendations as to the fair and equitable disposition of the complaint. While some organizations have formalized the office of ombudsman, most expect the Human Resources Department to fulfil this function, particularly when it comes to complaints regarding capricious supervisory behaviour and abuses of power including, but not limited to, sexual/racial harassment and bullying.

In investigating matters, the practitioner must maintain objectivity. The types of complaints can be quite serious and may result in the termination of a supervisor or manager. The investigation has to be thorough, and to every extent possible rely on clear and cogent evidence of a wrongdoing before a decision is recommended. It must also be handled delicately to ensure an individual's rights are preserved at all times and reputations are not unnecessarily besmirched.

In addition to being objective, the practitioner must have a thorough understanding of employment law (including human rights and wrongful dismissal jurisprudence) to fulfil this role. Investigations are usually handled by senior practitioners who have had a wide experience in dealing with employee issues because of the sensitivity and importance of the subject matter.

In more advanced organizations, the role of ombudsman is strictly a third-party one that is formalized. In these contexts, the practitioner may be responsible for choosing the incumbent for the role and for providing such assistance and access as the ombudsman requires in the discharge of his or her duties.

Mediation/Arbitration

Depending on the perceived role of the Human Resources practitioner within the organization, he or she may represent the organization in mediation or be its advocate at arbitration. Alternatively, the practitioner may have a diminished role of helping to facilitate the process rather than having an active part in it.

Barriers to Success/Common Pitfalls

Some employers believe that when disputes are litigated, they have the opportunity to delay or obstruct the process. By forcing the process to be dragged out, they hope the employee plaintiff will run out of resources or willpower and abandon any claims. At times, representatives on both sides do not try to pursue interest-based solutions. They prefer confronting the other party and winning the dispute.

ADR processes are too new and untried. Employees generally have no familiarity with the concept. Employers also have little, if any, experience with alternative processes, and may lack the confidence that the processes will yield the desired results. Likewise, Human Resources practitioners are inexperienced with ADR, and have been reluctant to establish the process as an option under contracts of employment. This lack of experience often means they lack the necessary skills and competence to use ADR processes effectively.

Since the process is relatively untried in the employment context, there is a perception that the process will not work and the matters will be decided through litigation. Parties may be reluctant to spend the necessary resources on a process that is not proven or widely accepted. Moreover, they will not want to make an investment in terms of time and resources in the process when they believe they will end up in the courts, regardless of the ADR efforts.

Employees who are insecure or mistrust the employer, will be reluctant to opt for ADR. These employees will seek a sense of security by engaging a lawyer to act as their advocate. If the issue is particularly acrimonious, the resentment, and even hatred, will make litigation preferable. The hurt party will not be seeking a mutually satisfactory result. In fact, the preferred result may well be seeing the other party lose. Similarly, the organization's managers may fear the potential loss of face, although a skilled mediator will take whatever steps necessary to avoid this.

SAMPLE POLICY

Dispute Resolution Process

The company is committed to providing the best possible working conditions for its employees. Part of this commitment is encouraging an open and frank atmosphere in which any problem, complaint, suggestion, or question receives a timely response from supervisors and management.

The company strives to ensure fair and honest treatment of all employees. Supervisors, managers and employees are expected to treat each other with mutual respect. Employees are encouraged to offer positive and constructive criticism.

If employees disagree with established rules of conduct, policies, or practices, they can express their concern through the problem resolution procedure. No employee will be penalized, formally or informally, for voicing a complaint in a reasonable, business-like manner, or for using the problem resolution procedure.

If a situation occurs when employees believe that a condition of employment or a decision affecting them is unjust or inequitable, they are encouraged to make use of the following steps (the employee may discontinue the procedure at any step):

1. Employee presents problem to immediate supervisor as soon as possible after incident occurs. If supervisor is unavailable or employee believes it would be inappropriate to contact that person, employee may present problem to Human Resources Department or to any other member of management.

2. Supervisor responds to problem during discussion or within 10 calendar days, after consulting with appropriate management, when necessary. Supervisor documents discussion and provides a written response to the employee.

3. Employee presents problem to department manager within 10 calendar days, if problem is unresolved.

4. Manager responds to problem during discussion or within 10 calendar days, after consulting with appropriate management, when necessary. Manager documents discussion and provides a written response to the employee.

5. Human Resources Department counsels and advises employee, assists in putting problem in writing, visits with employee's manager(s), if necessary, and directs employee to the next step in the process.

6. Employee presents problem to the appropriate director in writing within 10 calendar days, if problem is unresolved.

7. Director responds to problem during discussion or within 10 calendar days, after consulting with appropriate management, when necessary. Director documents discussion and provides a written response to the employee.

8. If the problem remains unresolved, the employee may present the issue in writing to the President for final review and resolution. The President responds to problem during discussion or within 10 calendar days, after consulting with appropriate management, when necessary. Director documents discussion and provides a written response to the employee.

Not all problems can be resolved to everyone's complete satisfaction, but only through understanding and discussion of mutual problems can employees and management develop confidence in each other. This confidence is important to the operation of an efficient and harmonious work environment, and helps to ensure the job security of all.

Alternative Dispute Resolution Process

All new employees of the company will be required as part of their contract of employment to agree to a provision requiring them to submit any dispute arising in the course of their employment that is unresolved through the internal dispute resolution processes or any disputes related to the termination of their employment to final and binding arbitration as provided for herein.

Employees hired before the effective date of this policy may, at their sole discretion, opt to use the arbitration process for the resolution of disputes, or may seek any other legal recourse they choose. This election may be made in the form of an amendment to their employment contract, or may be made at the time the dispute arises. Notwithstanding, once an employee has elected to pursue arbitration of a dispute, he or she will be bound by the provisions of this policy, and shall be prohibited from seeking recourse through a lawsuit or any other legal proceeding.

Prior to proceeding to arbitration, the company and employees bound by this policy agree to have the matter referred to a mediator who will work with the parties to attempt to negotiate a settlement of the dispute. The mediator shall be appointed by mutual agreement from the list of mediators appended to this policy. The company reserves the right to amend the list of mediators at any time. However, in the event that none of the listed mediators is acceptable to the employee, the employee may suggest an alternative mediator, or may choose to have the courts appoint a mediator in accordance with the *Arbitration Act.*

Should the matter remain unresolved through the mediation process, either party may submit the issue to final and binding arbitration by providing written notice to the other party within 30 days of the conclusion of mediation. Unless otherwise expressly agreed to by the parties, the mediator shall also be appointed as the arbitrator in the matter. Once the mediation process has been initiated, either party may abandon the process and have the matter referred to arbitration.

Any evidence adduced during the mediation phase and any statements made will be considered confidential, and shall not be used as evidence in the arbitration process except in instances where the parties enter into written agreements to allow specific evidence or agreed statements of fact to be considered by the arbitrator. Offers of settlement shall not be entered as evidence as to the merits of either party's case, but may be submitted to determine the allocation of costs or to ascertain any mitigating factors that may affect the amount of an award. The mediator may establish any rules of procedure he or she deems appropriate under the circumstances.

Any matter referred to arbitration shall be subject to the following provisions:

❑ The decision of the arbitrator shall be final and binding on all parties to the dispute, and shall only be subject to appeal under the provisions of the *Arbitration Act.*

❑ The employee will be responsible for half of the cost of the arbitrator to a maximum of $500. The company shall be responsible for the remaining cost. The parties will bear the fees of their own legal counsel and any associated costs. Notwithstanding, should the arbitrator decide that the matter referred was frivolous or vexatious, at his or her own discretion, the arbitrator can assign all the costs to the responsible party.

❑ The arbitrator shall arrange for a hearing into the matter at a mutually acceptable date. The arbitrator shall make a final determination on all matters referred to him or her and shall render that decision in writing within 30 days of hearing the matter. The arbitrator shall have the authority to make any award consistent with the laws of (jurisdiction), and to order any remedies reasonable under the circumstances. The arbitrator, however, shall not have the authority to amend, add to or subtract from any existing employment contract between the parties except where such contract, or provision thereof, is not enforceable under law. Nor will the arbitrator have the authority to reinstate an employee to a position with the company in cases where the dispute has arisen from the termination of employment. The arbitrator does have the authority to award pre- and post-judgment interest on any monetary awards in accordance with the *Courts of Justice Act.*

❑ Arbitration awards are only binding on the parties to the arbitration. The award shall not be considered as precedent in any subsequent matters involving the company and another party.

❑ Any settlement agreed to by the parties at any stage during the process will be considered as confidential and shall only be divulged to legal counsel or, in the case of an employee, to his or her spouse/financial advisors.

ASSESSMENT CENTRES

Definition/Background

The term assessment centre or development centre, refers to an event at which a group of individuals take part in a series of activities to assess their business skills and competencies. These activities may be individual or group-based, and are designed to simulate situations that may test the individual's abilities and behavioural tendencies.

Assessment centre activities might include:

⇨ group problem-solving exercises;

⇨ business simulations, including case studies and "in-tray" exercises;

⇨ individual interviews designed to elicit participant's aspirations and goals as well as business acumen; and

⇨ psychometric measurement of behavioural tendencies, personality, natural abilities and aptitudes.

Assessment centres can be used as a selection tool or for development (including self-development) purposes. Candidates for a particular role can be assessed against the appropriate competencies identified for the job. The assessment centres are perceived to be equitable in that individuals are given an opportunity to demonstrate their strengths and skills in a variety of tasks and situations. The assessment centre, in particular, can be a powerful tool in reallocating internal resources during an organizational restructuring following a merger, acquisition or in times of rapid change. (See also Redundancy/Downsizing at page 391 *et seq.*)

Assessment centres can also be set up as a means to measure individual potential and identify development needs. During and following the assessment, the individual receives feedback on his or her strengths and weaknesses in order to initiate development planning. This method provides reliable data for career and succession planning. This can be an excellent way to identify "high flyers", individuals who will be fast-tracked in the organization. Alternatively, the organization may provide the feedback to the individuals who will then be held responsible for engaging in their own development. Many organizations today do not have the resources available to assist the individual and therefore expect high potential people to initiate actions for self-development.

A significant feature of assessment centres is the involvement of several assessors who observe the subject employees engaging in activities and provide objective feedback to the participants. This adds to the credibility and reliability of the centre as a tool for identifying individual strengths and skills. In addition, the managers used as assessors are gaining a useful skill through their participation. These managers can be relied upon not only to provide feedback regarding their observations but also can be asked to coach and mentor the participants throughout their development.

Assessment centres have traditionally been designed around the specific skills requirements of a particular job. This starts with an analysis of the skills and competencies that are to be assessed and an in-depth job analysis. However, this can be a very costly approach and may narrow the findings. Given the rapid changes most organizations face today, a broader approach is being adopted whereby a set of competencies related to the future demands likely to be placed on a group of individuals in similar positions are identified. Assessment methods can then be developed to measure these competencies in a variety of ways along several dimensions.

Benefits/Expected Outcomes

Well-designed and executed assessment centres will deliver accurate data related to business competencies on individuals or groups of individuals. The assessment centre method produces more valid findings than other single methods when considered alone. Accurate assessments of an individual's competencies helps to ensure:

✓ the best people-to-job matches in key organizational roles;

✓ useful feedback to individuals for planning their career development;

✓ appropriate design of development programs and activities;

✓ high potential individuals are identified early and developed accordingly; and

✓ the organization is able to communicate clearly its expectations regarding desired competencies in a particular role.

As mentioned earlier, managers who act as assessors receive training as observers and are able to improve their skill sets in managing individual performance, assessing the behaviours of individuals, providing (and receiving) feedback, understanding motivation and coaching.

Of course, the individual participants can be big winners. They gain self-insight, they learn about business issues through the activities, and they learn from the experiences of other participants. Participants are also able to embark on a course of focused development that can help them build on their strengths.

Organizations can take full advantage of the power of assessment centres by implementing them across groups of managers in key roles. For example, an organization may target its branch managers for assessment and development. These managers can be oriented towards the development of skills designed for the future needs of the business as represented by the identified competencies. Since these individuals are in strategic roles that can influence and affect the behaviours of others, the organization is, *de facto*, introducing change into the organization. Moreover, the nature of the assessment centre encourages individuals to become self-reflective and to take charge of their own development. This, in turn, can effect a cultural change wherein the self-development ethos becomes a cornerstone of the organization's value system.

If an assessment centre is set up as a one-off initiative, the organization will get limited value. However, if centres are used consistently to measure competencies in key roles, the organization should realize additional benefits such as reduced turnover in key positions, a higher promotion rate (improved bench strength), and improved performance.

Development centres can yield "soft" benefits that are difficult to measure but are nevertheless important to the organization. The emergence of a culture centred on self-development wherein individuals take responsibility for their own career planning is an important prerequisite to the creation of a learning organization.

Immediate bottom line benefits will not necessarily be evident but, as managers improve their skills at judging individual potential and hone their skills at observing behaviours, overall organizational performance will improve.

Individual satisfaction will also improve. This is indeed difficult to measure but over time should show up in improved employee morale as reflected in employee climate surveys. The reason for this is that individuals who participate in an assessment or development centre will have a clearer idea of what the organization's expectations are and a clearer notion of how to be successful.

Programming/Implementation

Historically, assessment centres were created to assess skills, behaviours and attitudes in situations that simulated those individuals would likely encounter in their future anticipated roles. It became well recognized that interviews, even those that are behaviourally based, are not reliable predictors of future performance. Therefore, senior managers wanted a better means to assess high potential individuals and to select candidates for key roles in the organization.

This gave rise to several tools that can be employed to gather data on the potential of individuals, including psychometric tests, group exercises, and in-tray exercises, in addition to the traditional interview. Assessment centres are merely an event whereby a group of individuals are brought together to undergo the same battery of exercises in order to assess their individual potential for a specific role within the organization.

The principal objective is to assess the future potential of the individual and to attempt to predict future performance in a particular role. The well regarded adage that forms the foundation of behaviourally based interviewing techniques states that "past behaviour is the best predictor of future performance". The assessment centre concept takes this a step further by testing the individual's behavioural responses in new and perhaps novel circumstances. The orientation of the assessment is on the future challenges the individual is likely to face in a given position.

It is because of this that assessment centres need to be carefully designed. Too narrow a focus on aptitudes will not result in good data to predict future performance in the face of the significant challenges that will be faced by an individual promoted to a senior position. Instead, the individual's ability to adapt to change and master different situational roles needs to be determined so that he or she can meet the demands of strategic and cultural shifts in the organization.

The first step in introducing an assessment centre into an organization is for the sponsoring executive, usually the human resources director, to "sell" the concept to the senior leadership team. It is imperative that the senior management group takes ownership of the process and supports it. Support has to be demonstrated in an overt way. Senior management can demonstrate their support by insisting on having candidates for senior level positions undergo the process and by following up on development activities.

Moreover, senior managers can lend their support by participating in the identification and analysis of the key behavioural dimensions to be measured. This involvement raises the credibility of the process and ensures it remains relevant and central to the needs of the business.

The design of an assessment centre begins with an analysis of the key behavioural dimensions of a specific role. A matrix of behavioural dimensions against individual methods of assessment ensures that each dimension is properly assessed.

In order to have a comprehensive assessment, a specific role may have as many as 15 key behaviours. However, it is recommended that the organization focus on just seven or eight dimensions. Too many behaviours to be assessed can be overwhelming to the observers. When an excessive number of dimensions are introduced, observers may have a tendency to rate related skill areas in a similar manner. That is to say that it becomes increasingly difficult for the observer to distinguish between discreet behaviours (e.g., interpersonal skills and relating to customers in a positive manner).

Once the specific dimensions have been defined and it is determined how they will be tested, the organization will need to select a group of key individuals to act as observers. This is an important feature of the assessment centre and thus the selection has to be made carefully. Observers are to be asked to make sound judgments regarding their observations of a range of tasks or exercises. These individuals will need to possess the appropriate skill set to make objective

findings and to avoid casual observations from clouding their judgments.

Even more importantly, observers need to be properly trained prior to the implementation of the assessment centre. This involves:

- introducing them to the dimensions and tasks — usually observers will be asked to perform the exercises themselves in order to become more familiar with what is being tested;

- focusing the observers on concrete data gathering techniques rather than subjective impressions;

- practising the use of rating scales to ensure consistency;

- familiarizing them with the practice of collating data from different observers during the centre conference; and

- fostering the art of coaching and development planning (for development centres).

Training is usually conducted by external consultants, typically industrial psychologists. Once the organization has incorporated the use of assessment centres into its culture and has developed a degree of internal expertise, it may rely less and less on these external consultants.

Assessment centres can be quite expensive to set up and implement. Development costs alone can reach into the hundreds of thousands. For this reason, organizations often want to maximize the number of participants and minimize the number of observers. However, if there are too many participants such that the quality of group exercises is greatly diminished, this context will lead to a breakdown in credibility. Too few observers will result in reduced opportunities for feedback and missed observations.

Ideally, the number of participants should be between six and 10, with a participant to observer ratio of 2:1. This means three to five observers need to be trained. The mix of observers should also be selected to represent line management, but should also include staff specialists who are trained to conduct specific psychometric tests.

The duration of the process will depend on its purpose. If the central purpose is selection, the centre can be conducted in a day. If the purpose is to identify development needs, the process may take up to three days inclusive of the tests and exercises. The centre conference is a gathering of the observers to share their observations and judgments and to arrive at consensus findings. This usually involves some degree of rigorous debate wherein the data is accumulated and interpreted. The net result is a final assessment of each participant on each competence. A final report is then published and shared with the participants at subsequent one-on-one meetings.

Practical Application

A large multinational distribution company has identified the long-term need to create a succession plan. The chief consideration for the plan is to ensure the organization has a consistent and continuous supply of candidates for General Managers. The company has 23 divisions, each with a General Manager. The senior leadership team has concluded that having key individuals with leadership skills in this position is vital to the realization of its strategic direction. The organization wants to identify whether or not the current incumbents in the role of General Manager have the skills necessary to move the organization forward. It wants to identify specific gaps and develop action plans to close those gaps. In addition, the company seeks to identify others in the organization who have the potential to develop into General Managers within the next five years.

The organization's senior vice-president of human resources proposed that an assessment centre be set up to evaluate the current General Managers and a selected group of high potential young managers who aspire to be General Managers in the foreseeable future. The first step was to engage the services of an industrial psychologist who specialized in performance management, selection and developing assessment centres. His expertise would assure success in establishing the assessment centre. His experience as well would help the organization integrate the results of the assessment centre exercise into other human resources management processes.

The next step was to form a taskforce of senior executives from a cross-section of the organization who could articulate what was expected from General Managers in terms of behaviours on-the-job. Their mandate was to establish a set of competencies to be measured through the assessment centre exercise. The key competencies they developed were as follows:

Leadership Model

Business/Technical Expertise

Definition: Understands the issues, trends and practices involved in successful business/technical operations relative to his/her respective profession and industry. Maintains the industry/technical knowledge needed to achieve business objectives. Willingly leverages business/technical knowledge by providing guidance to individuals and the organization. Understands and uses key financial/business indicators to track business performance. Develops and initiates contingency plans to deliver business results. Clearly communicates business/financial performance in oral/written form.

Champions Change

Definition: Adapts to and thrives in times of internal or external change. Supports others to adapt and remain effective. Successfully provides a visible anchor for others in times of change; for example, by re-affirming key goals or values. Helps others to understand the emotional impact of change. Leads others through the change process. Knows and understands how change processes work. Convinces others of the need for change due to critical organizational objectives. Learns and develops new skills or behaviours to adapt to constant, sometimes turbulent, change.

Decision-making

Definition: Makes timely and sound decisions. Takes ownership for decisions by standing by them and accepting resulting consequences. Seeks input from a variety of colleagues to make reasoned, educated decisions. Calculates and evaluates the long-term consequences of decisions. Makes timely decisions judged to be prudent for the business, even though they may be difficult, controversial, or in unclear circumstances. Takes time to gather information and input from a variety of sources before making a decision.

Develops People

Definition: Provides the structure, information, support and resources that encourage people continuously to develop their talents to benefit the organization. Provides appropriate resources to support the developmental needs of employees. Uses a variety of methods (feedback, personal example, coach, teach, etc.) to help individuals attain higher levels of performance. Helps others recognize their areas of strength and weakness in a beneficial and constructive manner. Actively promotes organizational learning (transfer of best practices, benchmarking, etc.). Develops and executes a personal development plan. Helps others view mistakes as learning opportunities. Actively engages in on-going development planning with direct reports.

Fosters Open Communication

Definition: Drives free flow of timely and accurate information and communication throughout the organization. Articulates viewpoints in a way that influences others in a positive way. Effectively communicates and relates to a broad range of people internally and externally. Seeks to understand others by noticing and responding to nonverbal behaviour. Utilizes active listening skills. Chooses appropriate communication vehicles for each message (voicemail, e-mail, direct communication, etc.). Presents opinions accurately and persuasively — both one-on-one and to a group. Channels his/her communication to all those who need to be informed.

Manages and Leads Teams

Definition: Collaborates with others to develop a stronger team and enhance team spirit. Sees teams as a vehicle to achieve business goals. Shares information, ideas and suggestions with team. Acts as one; puts team and organizational goals ahead of personal goals. When looking at team goals, is aware of team members' strengths and weaknesses, and assists members to improve team performance. Performs multiple roles such as leader, doer, or facilitator to support the work of the team. Fosters collaboration among team members by soliciting input and encouraging participation.

Results-oriented

Definition: Is willing and able to take calculated risks in growing the organization's profitability, while holding self and others accountable. Seeks to accomplish critical tasks with measurable results. Personally strives for excellence in performance by surpassing established standards. Shows a willingness to take calculated risks to accomplish project deliverables. Does not sacrifice long-term results for short-term gains. Commits significant resources and time to reach challenging goals that will improve company performance. Adapts/modifies current procedures or methodologies to effectively achieve a business result. Is persistent and maintains focus in the face of challenges. Devotes at least 80% of time to top 20% of

priority list. Advocates and enables a safe work environment. Does not sacrifice safety over results.

Strategic Thinking

Definition: Expresses a clear vision for future business opportunities and creates linkage between current and future activities. Communicates the future picture of the business and industry. Builds shared commitment for the organization's strategic and local plans. Continually sets and adjusts goals based on new information. Collaborates with the organization's leaders by providing new insights regarding future business opportunities. Understands and communicates the organization's strategic plan. Annually aligns local and business objectives with the strategic plan.

Walks the Talk

Definition: Evokes trust from others by keeping commitments. Sets a personal example by supporting the organization's shared goals, values and vision. Accepts responsibility and acknowledges problems or mistakes to others and commits to take necessary corrective action. Gains others' trust and loyalty by fulfilling the commitments he/she makes to them. Sets a clear example for others by following through on important commitments. Uses an honest, straightforward approach with colleagues. Takes actions that are consistent with stated personal and organizational values.

Demonstrates Courage

Definition: Confronts problems early on, drives hard on difficult issues and takes a firm stand in the face of controversy. Shows willingness to engage and act when personally at risk. Faces up to problem situations quickly, directly and without hesitation. Respectfully communicates own opinions for the benefit of the organization despite fear of rejection or repercussion. Takes unpopular actions in an appropriate manner when he/she feels they are necessary. Is willing to put self at risk to move forward an initiative in which he/she believes. Willingly admits mistakes and seeks to learn from these in the future. Demonstrates maturity and optimism despite personal or team setbacks.

These competencies were then used by the industrial psychologist to design the assessment centre (and are to be incorporated into the organization's performance management system and its selection process for external recruiting). A three-day development centre was then set up. Participants were selected from the current cohort of General Managers (those deemed to require development) and individuals identified in the company's succession plan as being likely to fill General Manager positions within the next five years. The centre involved the participants engaging in a variety of group exercises (both business- and process-oriented), interviews and psychometrics designed to measure the relevant behaviours and competencies identified by the taskforce.

In all, 12 managers were selected as participants. An additional six individuals were trained as assessors. These assessors were selected from the senior leadership team, human resources and among non-participating General Managers who were considered fully competent in the role. No one in a direct line relationship with a participant was selected to avoid potential bias in the observations.

Following the exercise, the assessors were brought together to compare notes and arrive at consensus ratings. This involved intense debate and dialogue, but resulted in an assessment report written by the industrial psychologist for each individual outlining the observed strengths and weaknesses and suggesting a development plan. The participant then had an opportunity to discuss the results with the psychologist. These discussions lead to an agreement on the content of the report that was then published to the individual, his or her line manager and a human resources practitioner in the business unit.

The next stage was the implementation of the development plan. For the most part, the intention was that the individual be held responsible for driving the development plan. However, through day-to-day coaching and the performance management process, the line manager was responsible for holding the individual accountable for taking actions. Assessors, having had some degree of specialized training, were available to any individual who wanted to seek specific coaching or feedback.

Different aspects of the experience began to creep into the organization's culture. For example, participants used what they had learned from an active listening exercise to correct one another in subsequent meetings on the use of open-ended versus closed-ended questions. More explicitly, many of the participants began to improve their observable performance and were seen as the high potential group. Others envied

them and began clamouring for another assessment centre to be conducted.

Role of the Human Resources Practitioner

The senior human resources practitioner is typically the initiator and sponsor of the assessment/development centre process. This individual must first "sell" the concept to the senior leadership team in the organization and gain their support. Once the senior management group is committed, the practitioner must market the process throughout the organization in order to establish its purpose and ensure it is received well by line management.

Line management must ultimately own the process to ensure it becomes incorporated into the organization's culture and to ensure the required follow-up is conducted. While the assessment centre is a singular event, it is intended to form a foundation for future development activities. The practitioner must solicit the involvement of line managers in the design and execution of the centre to lend credibility to the process.

The human resources practitioner will be consulted on the selection of line managers to participate in the design of the process, those who will participate as observers and internal candidates who will participate in the centres. In selecting line managers who will act as observers, the practitioner will need to select individuals who not only possess the requisite skills to act in an objective and detached manner but also will act as proponents of the process. It is important that these individuals are influence-makers who can assist in incorporating the process into the fabric of the organization's culture.

The practitioner is the key contact with the external consultants who will be commissioned to initiate the process. In contracting with the consultants, the practitioner will need clearly to articulate the organization's intended objectives and will subsequently need to measure the centre's effectiveness against these stated goals.

The practitioner is also responsible for planning the logistics: where and when the centre will be held, ensuring materials are available, ensuring lunches and refreshment breaks are provided, and so on. The human resources department is also the repository for test results. As such, they are in a position to monitor that follow-up actions take place. In this regard, it is imperative that confidentiality be maintained and that the information is only used for its intended purposes.

In this litigious society, keeping records of the results of assessment centres used for selection purposes is necessary to protect the organization from potential claims of bias or discrimination in its recruitment practices. Assessment centres, because of their reliance on multiple observations and testing that has been validated, are easily defensible. Moreover, because they create the sense of equitable treatment among participants, they reduce the likelihood that any participant would attack the integrity of the process.

Barriers to Success/Common Pitfalls

Although assessment and development centres can yield tremendous benefits for both the individual and the organization, internal participants can experience a high degree of anxiety about why the centre is being run and what impact the results might have on individual careers. People can be naturally suspicious about the "real" reason the centre has been established. This can be heightened if the centre is set up during times of rapid organizational change. Moreover, if senior line managers are skeptical about the value and purpose of the assessment/development centre, the success of the process can be much reduced.

To protect against these possibilities, the sponsoring executive should ensure the organization's commitment to the process by securing an overt commitment and support from the organization's senior leadership team. Moreover, senior level managers should be brought into the process and be involved in the delineation of the competencies to be measured.

The project sponsor should also take steps to market the concept of an assessment centre throughout the organization. Marketing activities will include informing potential participants of the following:

✓ where the assessment centre fits in relation to existing development activities;

✓ what the rationale is behind the implementation of the centre;

✓ what the implications are for the career potential of the individual;

✓ how the centre supports the organization's intended cultural change and underlying values; and

✓ what follow-up processes will take place and the commitment of the senior leadership team to make sure they do happen.

Common mistakes made in setting up assessment and development centres include:

● The identified competencies being measured lack credibility because they are insufficiently related to the business, or do not fit with the future strategic needs of the organization.

● Changing business needs make the underlying purpose of the particular assessment centre redundant or irrelevant.

● The competencies are developed without significant line input and therefore lack credibility with the participants.

● The exercise lacks the proper context and individual participants do not take it seriously or, conversely, take it too seriously. In the former instance, participants are too relaxed and do not stretch themselves to reveal full potential. In the latter instance, participants act defensively and may not behave in an authentic manner.

● Poor planning results in poor logistics.

● Observers are not sufficiently trained to provide reliable and meaningful feedback to participants.

● Observers focus on participants' weaknesses rather than strengths. A focus on strengths leads to better decisions regarding the appropriate deployment of individuals into positions where their skills are better matched to the requirements of the job.

● Follow-up becomes lax and processes do not exist to ensure line managers continue their involvement in the development of their charges.

● The emotional impact of the event leads to the individual becoming overly defensive and rejecting the feedback and coaching efforts.

● Early participants, either deliberately or inadvertently, undermine the effectiveness of the process by sharing their experiences with others in the organization. If the individuals found the exercise was not constructive or useful, the process will be damaged regardless of whether the deficiencies have been corrected. Even if the initial process was successful, future participants may be tipped off as to what to expect and may prepare for the exercise, which will skew the outputs.

A - B - C

ATTENDANCE MANAGEMENT

Definition/Background

In developing an approach to attendance management, the Human Resources practitioner should first recognize that absenteeism might be the result of many different things. In order to have an effective and defensible policy, an organization should make a distinction between culpable and non-culpable absenteeism. Each demands a different response.

Culpable absenteeism is blameworthy or controllable behaviour. If an organization has a requirement that employees must report an expected absence prior to the beginning of their work shift, failure to do so is considered culpable misconduct. The employee could have, except in extreme circumstances, telephoned the company to report the absence. As such, the appropriate response is disciplinary action. Subsequent repeat offences would be met with progressively more severe disciplinary sanctions according to the organization's disciplinary policy.

Most examples of blameworthy absenteeism are more serious than a failure to report an intended absence in a timely manner. Using sick leave for another purpose, such as going to a ball game, is a serious offence, and may be considered a form of fraud if the employee is claiming a benefit for his or her deceit. Thus, culpable absenteeism may warrant a significant disciplinary response, even for the first offence. In many instances, a final warning or termination of employment may be warranted.

Tardiness is usually considered a form of culpable absenteeism. An employee who never reports late but is tardy because of unexpected car trouble is likely innocent. Such an employee can be excused for the aberration. Similarly, when several employees are late because of a snowstorm, the employer can easily deduce from a quick look out the window that they are not blameworthy. However, the employee who is habitually late is probably not making the requisite effort to get to work on time.

Forms of culpable absenteeism include:

— misuse of sick leave;

— failure to report an expected absence;

— failure to provide a doctor's note when required;

— leaving company premises without permission or notification;

— falsifying a physician's statement;

— failure to return from an approved leave; and

— tardiness.

The bulk of absenteeism is not caused by culpable behaviour. Most employees absent themselves from work because of illness, injury or family emergency. These instances are examples of innocent behaviour. It seems to be common sense, therefore, that they should not be disciplined for their actions. They did not likely intentionally get sick.

Examples of innocent absenteeism include:

— sickness;

— accidental injury;

— workplace injuries;

— occupational illnesses; and

— family emergencies.

Employees may also not attend work because their attendance has been excused. Employees who are on vacation are enjoying an employee benefit; they are not absent. Nor are employees who are away on bereavement leave to be considered absent, from an attendance management point of view. Another exception is employees who have been excused from reporting by their supervisor. Employees should not be held accountable for absences that have been approved when it is fully in the supervisor's power and discretion to deny such leave.

Examples of approved leaves include:

— bereavement;

— approved leaves of absence;

— jury duty;

— vacation leave;

— statutory holidays; and

— leave for union business.

Absenteeism can be measured in a number of ways. It is commonly expressed as a percentage of hours absent versus the hours of available work. Some organizations also track the frequency of absences by counting the instances of absences of less than a week's duration and calculating them as a ratio per 100 employees.

In measuring absenteeism, an organization will need to track individual absenteeism, and absenteeism by shift, department, plant/location and enterprise-wide. Comparative statistics are important in identifying trends and possible root causes for absenteeism. The data should also be kept in a manner that allows for analysis of weekly, monthly and seasonal trends.

Benefits/Expected Outcomes

The management of attendance involves controlling absences and positively ensuring through proactive practices and policies the welfare and health of employees so that genuine causes for absence can be reduced. Any savings in the cost of absence can be set against the introduction of other benefits, such as wellness programs and employee assistance plans. Savings will also be obvious in improved productivity and from not having to pay for covering absent staff.

The "soft" benefits of managing attendance include improved morale and motivation, and hence increased productivity, adding value to the organization.

There are, however, significant real costs associated with absenteeism, including:

— weekly indemnity or sick pay;

— workers' compensation costs;

— increased overtime;

— lost productivity;

— relief staffing;

— increased administrative burdens (dealing with the absence, finding temporary staff, or arranging overtime, payroll administration of sick pay and overtime payments); and

— increased pressure on co-workers who cover for the absentee, with a potential increase in stress, lowering of morale and job satisfaction and, in the longer term, lower productivity generally.

Reduced absenteeism, therefore, can have a direct bottom line impact on the business.

Although the main reason for absence is usually given as sickness, other underlying factors can contribute to the problem of persistent short-term absences. This sort of absence may occur for the following reasons:

— substance abuse (drug and alcohol addiction);

— gambling addiction;

— marital problems;

— financial problems;

— non-work related stress;

— poor person-to-job match;

— role ambiguity; and

— poor work ethic.

Programming/Implementation

The first step is to define absenteeism and develop a policy covering culpable absenteeism and non-culpable absenteeism. A further breakdown of innocent absenteeism into casual, short-term and long-term absences will help delineate the appropriate steps to be taken to match the circumstances of the absence.

The policy needs to be reviewed with managers and, in particular, with front-line supervisors to ensure a comprehensive understanding of the policy and the underlying issues. Attendance management is a complex issue deserving of a planned and careful approach.

Employees also must be informed of the policy. It is important to keep the policy statement to employees simple. The company's main objective is to communicate its expectations of performance as it relates to attendance at work to the individual employee. The ultimate message should be: "We want you at work because we value your contribution". Of course, once the policy has been established, it should be reviewed with every new recruit.

One key to effective attendance management is to let the employee know that the organization truly and sincerely cares about his or her well-being. Regardless of what other steps an organization may take, it should insist that the supervisor talk directly to the employee who is absent and to keep regular contact with the employee during any extended absence.

Although this is a means of monitoring the employee, its primary goal is simply to demonstrate that the supervisor, and hence the organization, cares.

In order to manage absenteeism, we need to measure it. A thorough analysis of attendance statistics will help the organization define what expected regular attendance is for its workplace. Usually, absenteeism rates distinguish between short-term absences (absences of a week or less in duration) and long-term absences. This is done to prevent long-term absences from skewing the rate upwards. It also considers that long-term absences are not controllable and, therefore, need to be dealt with in a different manner.

The benefits of calculating an average absenteeism rate is that, as improvements are made in the worst cases, the average will improve, thus moving the standard. It also gives the supervisor an objective standard of comparison to help the employee understand the severity of the problem.

Measuring absenteeism allows for an analysis of trends and patterns. On an individual level, the supervisor may detect a trend on a weekly basis (absent most frequently on Mondays and Fridays), or seasonal basis (absenteeism increases in the summer months). When counselling the individual employee, the supervisor can identify these trends to assist the employee in determining the root causes that create the attendance problem.

On an organizational level, trends may be detected based also on time of week or month or year. The organization can also compare absenteeism rates between shifts, departments, or locations to see if any contributing factors can be identified.

The organization may be contributing to the absenteeism rate and needs a means of identifying possible causes. The organization can contribute to poor attendance as a result of the following:

— absenteeism may be seen to be tolerated, and the policy and procedures to deal with absence may be unclear;

— employees may experience problems with management (management style, personality traits) or co-workers;

— there may be a performance issue that creates stress for the individual;

— there may be frustration with the job content or role definition;

— the employee may be poorly matched to the job requirements, creating a problem with his or her motivation to perform;

— the culture of the organization may influence attendance by not valuing or treating employees as individuals;

— the work may be inefficiently organized, leading to frequent changes and confusion; and

— the working environment may contribute to increasing the rate of absenteeism (for example, excessive heat, cold, noise, type of equipment available to do the job, peaks and troughs in the work).

Over time, the organization needs to identify any of these that may apply to it and take the appropriate steps to rectify them. Developing an attendance management policy will address the first issue.

It is important to develop the approach to non-culpable absenteeism as a problem-solving approach. Management needs to have a sincere interest in improving the health and welfare of employees and not simply in taking a cost-saving measure. When employees become aware that the company is monitoring attendance and will be taking a proactive and consistent approach to managing it, a certain amount of self-monitoring takes place. Interestingly, by measuring the problem, some organizations realize an immediate improvement in attendance. This simply reflects the fact that employees will react in a positive manner to management's effort to take a clear approach to tackling the problem.

Once the measures have been initiated, then the supervisor needs to meet with those individual employees who have attendance issues. The usual first step in introducing an attendance program is to meet with employees who have high rates of casual absenteeism. Casual absenteeism is defined as frequent absences of one day. Other short-term absenteeism users can be dealt with in the same way. Discussions should always begin with the highest users. Objectively, the supervisor is not singling out any individual on any basis other than his or her high absenteeism.

Attendance discussions are fairly simple. The supervisor will want to show the employee his or her attendance record and discuss what the root causes might be. The supervisor should probe with the employee possible causes, but at no time should the supervisor speculate as to the nature of the underlying cause of the absenteeism. The employee must always bear the onus of discovering the cause and taking ownership for fixing any contributory behaviour.

In addition to the organizational issues that may contribute to high absenteeism, there are a number of external factors that will affect the individual. These are the short-term issues that can be addressed through counselling the employee. They include:

— chronic poor health due to a lack of physical fitness;

— poor attitude towards work or the organization;

— substance abuse;

— family issues;

— financial issues; and

— recurring illness (e.g., multiple sclerosis, persistent back problems, HIV-related illness, the aftermath of an accident).

Supervisors are not usually trained to counsel employees on how to deal with these often complex issues, nor should they be. The level of counselling a supervisor should provide is to help the employee recognize his or her absenteeism as a problem and to try to identify possible causes. If a specific cause is identified, the supervisor can then suggest avenues for the employee to seek proper professional assistance (family physicians, employee assistance programs). The supervisor may also be able to explore if any job related changes could be made to accommodate the employee.

The purposes of the meeting with the employee are:

— to identify the absenteeism as a problem that must be addressed;

— to have the employee accept responsibility for fixing the problem;

— to identify possible root causes;

— to define goals for improvement;

— to demonstrate the organization's concerns for the employee; and

— to schedule a follow-up to monitor improvements.

As any Human Resources practitioner knows, all discussions with employees related to performance must be documented. This includes not only every meeting to discuss the employee's poor attendance but also any meeting held to discuss the employee's improved attendance.

At a follow-up meeting, the supervisor should first acknowledge any improvements. If there have not been any, the supervisor should once again go through the employee's attendance record and stress the importance of making an effort to improve. Each organization will have to decide how many meetings are sufficient before alternative steps are to be taken. Ultimately, attendance at work is a *bona fide* job requirement. Employees who are unable to fulfil that requirement may have frustrated their contract of employment. At this point, the supervisor or manager should consult with his or her Human Resources practitioner to review what steps should be taken with respect to accommodating any known disability the employee may have or terminating employment. Such a termination is "not for cause" but rather is the result of the employee's inability to attend work and fulfil his or her side of the employment bargain.

Several meetings should precede termination, the number of which will depend on the organization's policy and should take into consideration the employee's level of service. Many organizations introduce an element of progression by having the employee interviewed by successively higher levels of management after the second or third interview. Prior to termination, the employee must be given an explicit warning that such a possibility is imminent.

If any mitigating circumstances have been identified that require accommodation, the supervisor should be referred to the Human Resources practitioner or the organization's legal counsel. These cases require a program for accommodation to be established. A common example is to establish a "Last Chance Agreement" for employees with chemical dependencies.

Other aspects of a comprehensive attendance management policy include the following:

— Require chronic users of sick leave to provide physicians' notes to substantiate any absence. This assures the organization that the employee is getting treatment and that his or her family physician may be aware of any recurring problems.

— Introduce an aggressive return-to-work program to rehabilitate injured employees. This should cover both work related and non-work related injuries. Some employers fear the latter because they do not want to run the risk of re-injuring the employee and having an accident counted against the organization. Experience suggests this risk is minimal and workers' compensation boards usually indemnify the organization in these instances.

— As part of the early return-to-work program, organizations should consider graduated return-to-work programs where employees can start back with reduced hours and work their way back to a regular schedule.

Long-term absence through prolonged ill health requires a different response to that appropriate for persistent short-term spells of absence. In the former, it is good practice to maintain contact with the employee, either by telephone or in person. Initially, after a long period away from work, it is becoming increasingly acceptable to rehabilitate employees back into the workplace slowly as, for example, through working flexibly, part-time working and combining home/office working. Redeployment is an option if some disability is permanent as a result of the illness or injury.

If the absence is of indefinable length and a return-to-work seems improbable, medical severance or ill health retirement may be appropriate. Organizations should work closely with medical and legal advisors in such cases (either the employee's family doctor, or its own occupational health advisors).

Role of the Human Resources Practitioner

The Human Resources practitioner should be the initiator of the attendance management policy. The practitioner needs to define the acceptable norms for attendance. The practitioner will serve an important role in the implementation of the policy.

The practitioner's responsibilities include:

— designing the policy and defining the appropriate measures (and how they are to be gathered and reported);

— communicating the policy to managers, supervisors, employees, union representatives and new recruits;

— training supervisors on conducting attendance interviews;

— developing support mechanisms such as employee assistance programs;

— drafting accommodation plans and Last Chance Agreements, when appropriate;

— coaching supervisors on problematic cases;

— monitoring overall success of the attendance management policy;

— designing complementary policies such as early return-to-work programs and attendance recognition programs; and

— managing long-term cases.

Barriers to Success/Common Pitfalls

Attendance management is complex and requires a great deal of patience. Many supervisors find the nuances of the policy difficult to put into action. As a result, many fall back to applying traditional progressive discipline. When these efforts fail, they resort to doing nothing at all.

There is nothing easy about managing attendance. Senior management needs to empathize with the supervisor's task. It is of tantamount importance that supervisors receive adequate training on how to interview employees with attendance problems and are made fully aware of the support mechanisms that are in place to support their efforts.

While the issue is complex, the policy should be communicated to supervisors and employees in clear, concise and succinct terms. Keep it simple.

The process is an ongoing management practice. Many organizations have experienced substantial initial success in controlling absences, only to find after a couple of years that their experience has deteriorated. Managing attendance should not be a temporary measure.

Unfortunately, many health professionals and union representatives are unaware of the proactive steps enlightened organizations are taking to improve

A - B - C

attendance by addressing the underlying causes of absenteeism. They are distrustful of these efforts and sometimes block well-intentioned initiatives. Whenever possible, these people should be debriefed on the policy and kept abreast of the company's efforts in individual cases.

In this regard, supervisors are often unaware of their and the organization's rights to manage employee attendance. The Human Resources practitioner needs to be somewhat aggressive and assert these rights at the implementation phase of the process to overcome the resistance of employees, their physicians, union representatives, and supervisors alike.

Managing attendance requires empathy and caring. It can be a true test of a supervisor's suitability to the role of managing people. If the organization does not strongly support the initiative, it will send a signal to supervisors that this aspect of their job is not important. However, there is no more important part of the supervisor's role than to manage the organization's most important asset.

Sample Attendance Management Program

Introduction

The aim of this attendance management program is to provide a consistent approach to dealing with absenteeism. It is recognized that many absences are unavoidable, but it is also recognized that proactive, positive and ongoing intervention with employees can assist greatly in improving attendance. Therefore, this program is focused on improving attendance through awareness and managing individual cases in a consistent and supportive manner.

An important part of the attendance management program is the ability to measure and track absences. It is also essential that defined thresholds exist to review employees' attendance records as part of an effective program. Defining these thresholds ensures that the same criteria are used in deciding when employees' absences become a problem and require action. Conversely, it is just as vital that employees with excellent attendance records be recognized formally with a letter on file.

To aid in reaching the overall goal of attendance improvement, the attendance management program focuses on several objectives that combine to create a proactive approach. The objectives of this program are:

- to treat absences as non-disciplinary until there is evidence to the contrary — the approach should be supportive, providing the employee the opportunity to explain the reasons for his or her absences, and offering company support and assistance that will help in dealing with the causes of absenteeism;

- to ensure that each employee understands that attendance at work is valued and that his or her presence contributes to the success of his or her team and to the company's success as an organization;

- to monitor attendance levels and the reasons for the absence;

- to decrease the incidence of sick leave without legitimate reason;

- to communicate attendance expectations to employees and to provide sufficient opportunity to improve their attendance;

- to deal with continuing absenteeism issues in a progressively more formalized manner, including the use of letters, which will become part of an employee's work file;

- to communicate the need for employees to provide medical documentation for absences that are longer than three consecutive days, absences that go above the department threshold, or where there is a question about the legitimacy of the sick time;

- to build flexibility into the program so that each individual case is considered on its own merits; and

- to assist the employee in returning to work quickly.

Step 1 — Counselling Discussion

The employee attendance record provides the information needed to decide if a first meeting should take place. When the employee has exceeded the acceptable attendance level, a meeting should be scheduled. Prior to the meeting, the attendance record of the employee should be reviewed and the concern identified. The primary objective of this discussion is to motivate an employee to attend work regularly and, as a result, avoid what may become a major attendance issue.

The meeting provides an opportunity to notify the employee that his or her current absenteeism level is above the department and/or company average. The employee should have the ability to view the record and the manager/supervisor should use the record to help in a discussion about how the employee is dealing with the absences.

This meeting may be perceived by the employee as disciplinary in nature. It should be explained to the employee that the discussion is not to initiate disciplinary action, but to discuss concerns regarding his or her individual absences as they compare to the department and/or company average. The absenteeism needs to be approached as "blameless".

Guidelines that can shift this perception away from a disciplinary nature:

❏ Demonstrate a concern for the employee's well-being.

❏ Demonstrate a concern for the employee's work team since generally the team has to share in the extra work the absence has created.

❏ Encourage the employee to ask questions, which may ease his or her anxiety about the process.

Guidelines for the discussion should:

❏ Explain how the employee's absences affect the delivery of service and the work unit.

❏ Review the employee's record and advise where he or she stands compared to the department/company average.

❏ Ask if there are medical or other reasons that may hinder his or her ability to attend work on a regular basis. Explain to the individual that he or she is not required to divulge any personal or medical information.

❏ Offer assistance that may be helpful in dealing with the source of the absences. Assist in finding appropriate resources. The company should not be involved in providing a diagnosis as it is not acting in the capacity of a physician.

❏ Summarize the interview, and set an attendance goal and a date for a follow-up meeting within two months.

❏ Document the meeting and follow up with a letter for the employee within a week. Place a copy of the letter in the employee's file.

❏ The manager/supervisor should complete the attendance management checklist (refer below) as a way of ensuring consistency in dealing with employees.

Note: The attendance management checklist can also be used as a quick reference to answer questions about a particular employee.

Following this first meeting, the employee's attendance should be closely monitored. After the follow-up period, if the employee has demonstrated a noticeable improvement, the manager/supervisor should still have a meeting to acknowledge the improvement and support the employee to continue with this improvement. A letter should document this, and be put in his or her file. As well, a copy should be given to the employee.

Step 2 — Counselling Discussion

After the follow-up period, a second meeting will be held as previously scheduled. If the employee's attendance fails to show an improvement, the record should be reviewed and the concern identified. The employee should have the opportunity to view his or her attendance record, and the manager/supervisor should use the record as an aid in discussing the reasons for the continued absences.

The *primary objectives* of this discussion include:

● communicating the continued absenteeism issue and the effect on the work unit;

● motivating the employee to attend work regularly; and

● communicating expectations for improvement.

Guidelines for the discussion should:

❏ Explain how the continued absenteeism is affecting the work unit.

❏ Summarize the first interview and spend time gathering information as to why the employee has not made substantial improvements.

❏ Ask if there are medical or other reasons that may hinder his or her ability to attend work on a regular basis. Explain to the individual that he or she is not required to divulge any personal or medical information.

❏ Offer assistance that may be helpful in dealing with the source of the absences. Assist in finding appropriate resources. The company should not be involved in providing a diagnosis as it is not acting in the capacity of a physician.

❏ Summarize the interview, and set an attendance goal and a date for a follow-up meeting within two months.

❏ Document the meeting and follow up with a letter for the employee within a week. Place a copy of the letter in the employee's file.

❏ Indicate to the employee that his or her attendance will be closely monitored.

❏ The manager/supervisor should complete the attendance management checklist (refer below) as a way of ensuring consistency in dealing with employees.

After the follow-up period, if the employee has demonstrated a noticeable improvement, the manager/supervisor should still have a meeting to acknowledge the improvement and support the employee to continue with this improvement. A letter should document this, and be put in his or her file. As well, a copy should be given to the employee.

Step 3 — Counselling Discussion

After the follow-up period, if the employee's attendance still fails to show improvement, the process will begin to take a more serious tone in nature. A meeting should then be scheduled once again.

The *primary objectives* of this discussion include:

- communicating to the employee that the continued absenteeism is becoming a greater concern for effective and efficient service delivery and for the work team; and

- motivating the employee to attend work on a regular basis.

Guidelines for the discussion will remain the same as previous discussions, but:

❏ Summarize the past interviews, spend time gathering information as to why the employee has not made substantial improvements, and emphasize the importance of regular attendance.

❏ Advise the employee that the matter is of concern and that his or her attendance is under scrutiny.

After the follow-up period, if the employee has demonstrated a noticeable improvement, the manager/supervisor should still have a meeting to acknowledge the improvement and support the employee to continue with this improvement. A letter should document this, and be put in his or her file. As well, a copy should be given to the employee. It should also be made clear to the employee that his or her attendance will continue to be closely monitored to ensure continued success.

Step 4 — Counselling Discussion

If there still is no improvement, it will be necessary to meet again. Discussions need to be held with the Manager of Human Resources, the Department Manager and the employee regarding the situation to develop a plan of action. At this stage, it may become evident that, while it can be non-culpable absenteeism, such absences can reach a stage where the employee can no longer fulfil his or her part of the employment contract. In such cases, the company may eventually terminate the employment of that employee. However, in order to justify terminating an employee for non-culpable absenteeism, the company must demonstrate that the employee in all likelihood is incapable of regular attendance in the future. Under circumstances like these, employees should be directed to undergo a medical assessment to determine the prognosis for sustained, consistent attendance at work.

The *primary objectives* of this discussion will be the same as Step 3 with the addition of having the employee obtain a medical prognosis on capability of regular attendance in the future.

The *guidelines* for discussion also remain the same, but should include the following:

❏ Summarize the past three meetings.

❏ Request the employee obtain a medical prognosis from a physician. Explain that this is needed to ascertain whether or not there is an underlying medical condition that causes excessive absenteeism. Make it clear that the company is not looking for the diagnosis of a potential medical problem, but rather a prognosis for sustained, consistent attendance at work. A letter will be provided for the employee's doctor.

❑ Indicate that attendance will be closely monitored over this period and, if there is no improvement, his or her continued employment may be in jeopardy.

Step 5 — Counselling Discussion

If there is still no improvement in attendance and the employee has either refused to provide a medical prognosis or the medical prognosis states the employee is fit, then the employee's employment may be in jeopardy. The manager/supervisor will meet with the Manager of Human Resources to outline the particular situation and obtain guidance regarding the approach to take with the employee on his or her return to work.

The *primary objectives* of this discussion include:

● communicating to the employee that the continued absenteeism is a serious concern for effective and efficient service delivery and for the work unit; and

● motivating the employee to attend work on a regular basis.

The *guidelines* for the discussion remain the same as previous discussions, but include:

❑ Summarize all past meetings and review the medical prognosis, if one is obtained.

❑ Indicate that attendance will be closely monitored over this time period and, if there is no improvement, his or her employment may be terminated.

Step 6 — Termination

After the follow-up period, if there is no substantial improvement in attendance, the reporting manager should contact the Manager of Human Resources for advice prior to the employee returning to work. The Manager of Human Resources will work with the manager to determine the best course of action. If it is decided that employment will be terminated, the manager/supervisor will be required to have union representation present at the final meeting.

Request for Medical Certification

The company has the right to request substantiation of an illness by a doctor's note; therefore, the man-

ager/supervisor can require an employee produce a doctor's note upon his or her return to work.

As a general rule, a medical certificate from the employee's doctor should be requested from an employee for:

⇨ absence of more than three consecutive days (usually this will be provided in the copy of the health and welfare form for short-term disability);

⇨ absences that exceed the department threshold; and

⇨ absences that are believed to be malingering (fraudulent claims of illness) in nature.

A medical certificate from a qualified medical practitioner should be obtained on the *date of request* and must have an *objective medical statement* confirming illness or injury during a specified time period. An example of an *unacceptable* note would be, "*Patient states* he was sick, which prevented him from working"; there is no objective information to confirm illness in this statement. An acceptable note would read, "I examined the patient today and due to illness have recommended he not work for the period of X to X".

A standard form can be used to have employees submit to their physicians. The form (a sample of which appears below at the end of this chapter) should be sent to the employee's doctor by fax, either prior to or after a visit to the doctor. The form is to be completed by the attending physician to confirm that the employee's illness was serious enough that it prevented him or her from being able to work. It also serves the purpose of having the doctor objectively validate the reason an employee was away from work. After it has been completed, the form should be returned by fax to the manager/supervisor.

Requesting a doctor's note requires discretion. If you know that a person is having surgery, you should not be requesting a medical certificate. It is the long occurrences, frequent and sporadic situations, and those suspected of malingering that most often require a doctor's note.

Attendance Management Checklist

Complete this checklist each time an attendance management counselling discussion takes place:

A - B - C

✓ review attendance record — you may need to go back a year or two;

✓ review any previous discussions that took place on the issue of attendance;

✓ explain how the employee's absenteeism affects the level of work being done and the delivery reliability of service;

✓ reinforce the responsibility of the employee to maintain regular attendance;

✓ ask if there are any reasons that may hinder the employee's ability to attend work on a regular basis;

✓ remind the employee that the company is committed to assist him or her in improving the level of attendance;

✓ discuss what the employee plans to do to improve his or her level of attendance;

✓ summarize the meeting and set an attendance goal and date for a follow-up meeting;

✓ indicate that the employee's attendance will be monitored;

✓ document the meeting in both note form and formal letter; and

✓ obtain medical documentation, if required.

MEDICAL CERTIFICATE — CONFIDENTIAL

PHYSICIAN'S STATEMENT

Following examination, I hereby certify that _____

                                                        Employee's Name

was unable to attend work on _____   due to _____

                                 dates

_____

                          describe the general nature of the problem

This illness prevented him/her from working   Yes _____   No _____

He/she was seen by me regarding this illness/injury on _____

I estimate that he/she will return to work on _____

Please provide general information about how the illness prevents the employee from working

_____

_____

_____

_____

Physician: _____ Phone: _____

Date: _____

Please return this form to Human Resources by fax at xxx-xxx-xxxx

Questions about the use of this form can be directed to Human Resources at xxx-xxx-xxxx

AUDITING THE HR FUNCTION

Definition/Background

An audit is a comprehensive and open assessment of management processes designed to assist management in finding ways to improve those processes. In part, audits are conducted to ensure managers and employees throughout the organization are complying with established policies, procedures and guidelines. Auditing for compliance is not specifically intended as an enforcement activity, but rather is done to study the efficacy of processes and to make recommendations on how the organization can ensure compliance in the future.

Auditing looks both at the effectiveness of existing practices and examines the interrelations of activities within the organization to determine if desired outcomes are being achieved. The idea is not simply to look for what might be going wrong or right with current processes but also to assess whether the organization is engaged in all the activities it needs to be to achieve success.

Audits are not intended to form part of the individual performance appraisal process and should not be used as a means of directly evaluating an individual. Indirectly, an individual can be held accountable for developing action plans to correct deficiencies uncovered by the audit or for ensuring compliance to policies and procedures. It may seem to be a moot point; however, managers should welcome the audit as a tool for helping them manage their functional responsibilities better. If the audit score is used directly as a performance measure, managers may fear the process or attempt to manipulate audit results in a number of different ways.

Few organizations audit their Human Resources Management activities. Audits can be time-consuming and costly to conduct. Moreover, there is a tendency for managers to spend time and resources preparing for an audit so they can get a good score. This is an additional tax to the organization's resources.

Arguably, managers should not prepare for an audit. One presumes first that the managers will be following established practices. If not, the manager should not attempt to correct deficiencies simply in preparation of an audit. In some ways, maintaining the *status quo* not only provides a more honest and accurate portrait of organizational practices but also allows the auditors an opportunity to delve into the question as to why those practices are not followed.

The audit should evaluate how well the organization is doing with respect to its own established policies and procedures as well as provide recommendations on how to correct any discovered deficiencies. A skilled auditor will be able to identify deviations from the established practices and be able to make a determination as to what caused the deviation. The auditor further requires the knowledge and experience to make informed recommendations as to the proper corrective actions.

Audits can take several forms. An audit can take a comprehensive approach and examine every aspect of the Human Resources function, the delivery and efficacy of services, the quality of managing the function and its related processes, the experience and effect of Human Resources practitioners throughout the organization, major initiatives and the metrics that determine if the function is achieving its stated organizational goals and objectives. Comprehensive audits can take a considerable toll on time and resources. An alternative approach is to conduct focused audits on selected programs or practices.

A focused audit may look at the effectiveness of the performance management system or the compensation and rewards practices. A specific plan to use focused audits over time to examine the entire function is a means of efficiently using scarce organizational resources and still developing a comprehensive overview of the Human Resources Management function. Alternatively, the focused approach may be employed to examine a specific functional area because of an emerging issue. Given the shifting labour market, an organization with concerns over employee retention may want to examine, in particular, its recruitment practices and retention strategies.

Scope of the Human Resources Management Audit

A comprehensive Human Resources audit may look at the following aspects of the organization's people practices:

⇨ mission and strategic objectives;

⇨ culture;

⇨ goals and objectives;

⇨ corporate policies;

⇨ management practices (e.g., recruiting, orientation, performance management, discipline, attendance management, personnel development, mentoring, compensation/rewards);

⇨ structure;

⇨ staffing;

⇨ employee relations;

⇨ employee services; and

⇨ facilities and equipment.

Benefits/Expected Outcomes

The purpose of a Human Resources Management audit is to measure whether or not policies, procedures and processes established for the management of people within the organization are being followed. In addition, the audit will review whether or not the desired outcomes are being achieved by those activities. In order to properly conduct an audit, the Human Resources function should first be tracking a relevant set of metrics against established standards and objectives. In the absence of these, the auditor will have to select specific metrics for examination. This will add considerably to the cost and amount of time necessary for the audit.

Auditing is a means of establishing management accountability and control. However, used effectively, the auditing of the Human Resources function can lend credibility and develop faith in the Human Resources Department. Taking the initiative to measure the effectiveness of the department's delivery of service demonstrates to the organization that the Human Resources practitioner has integrity. Initiating a continuous audit process tells the organization that the practitioner is willing to be held accountable for organizational outcomes. It further signals a readiness to take the necessary corrective action to add value to the organization.

In the current business environment, organizations have a growing concern in their codes of business conduct (whether they be explicit or implicit). A Human Resources audit can be a *de facto* "deep dive", to check on potential management abuses in areas such as conflicts of interest, favouritism/nepotism, ethical hiring practices and general compliance with organizational rules. Weeding out these abuses ultimately serves to strengthen the organization's core values and the integrity of its culture.

In summary, an audit serves to:

✓ review the appropriateness of existing policies, procedures, practices and plans against the needs of the organization, its strategic plans and its readiness to adopt Human Resources Management processes;

✓ determine the level of compliance with existing policies and procedures;

✓ identify the organization's key Human Resources Management issues, those areas most in need of improvement;

✓ develop an understanding of organizational issues and identify from them opportunities for Human Resources Management solutions;

✓ identify deficiencies in current practices and determine the appropriate corrective steps;

✓ review the efficacy of processes and the need for management controls;

✓ determine the quality and performance of the management group with respect to the implementation of Human Resources Management programming;

✓ provide a basis for strategic Human Resources planning;

✓ identify opportunities for improving the cost-effective delivery of Human Resources Management products and services; and

✓ develop a positive employee relations climate through improved policies, procedures, practices and programming.

Programming/Implementation

The senior practitioner may decide on a number of different types of audits to be conducted. Some of these may simply involve the Human Resources Department in an established organizational audit. Two such areas that might impact the management of the Human Resources function are *financial audits* and *quality audits*.

A financial audit examines the organization's financial statements for accuracy, completeness, fairness and compliance with generally accepted accounting principles. Most financial audits are conducted by outside firms that attest to the appropriateness of the organization's financial reporting. Larger organizations may periodically employ internal auditors to check accounting and reporting procedures to ensure internal controls are being maintained.

Human Resources practitioners may be asked to participate in financial audits in a number of ways, including ensuring the necessary controls are in place with respect to payroll administration (authorization of new hires, processing of wage and salary increases, payment of settlements with respect to grievances or employee terminations), accounting for employee expenses within the department, or following established purchasing procedures for goods and services.

Quality audits take many forms. They are designed primarily to examine the adequacy of production process controls. They specifically compare documented processes and procedures against actual production practices. To be complete, a quality audit will also look at finished goods to ensure products being made or services provided meet the standards established by the organization.

Human Resources practitioners are usually specifically involved in ensuring training programs are in place to teach employees the skills necessary to comply with the detailed processes established for each job. This means having ready documentation on the specific procedures the employee is to follow in performing his or her job. It also means having an established methodology for testing employee skill proficiency and a process of documenting when training was conducted and what the outcomes were of that training.

The senior Human Resources practitioner who heads up a well established and mature Human Resources function may choose to implement an audit specific to the function itself. Such an audit may be comprehensive to examine the entire breadth of Human Resources Management activities, or may be focused on one or more key Human Resources processes.

When planning a Human Resources Management practices audit, the practitioner should follow these principles:

❑ Audits must be planned so that the necessary time and resources are allocated to the activity.

❑ Audits are not *ad hoc* investigations. They must be consciously designed and implemented. A docu-

mented audit process, which can be sent to individuals involved in the process to allow them to prepare, demonstrates that the process is a meaningful and important exercise.

❑ Audits need to be relevant to the organization's strategic mission and its objectives. Human Resources practitioners need to be wary of auditing against practice standards that are beyond the level of sophistication of their respective organization.

❑ Audit findings and assessments must be objective and based on documented evidence or observations, not on opinion, conjecture or speculation.

❑ Audit results must be reliable. Having a documented audit protocol that will allow an independent auditor to replicate the findings and conclusions ensures the process is free of individual bias.

❑ Auditing the Human Resources function must involve the department's key internal customers. Successful Human Resources audits are conducted in collaboration with, and with the full cooperation of, the other departments within the organization (e.g., Operations, Finance, Marketing, Sales).

❑ Audits are not one-time efforts. When introducing an audit process, the practitioner must consider the need to establish a continuous process that will become an enduring feature of Human Resources Management.

❑ Audits should be supported to every extent possible by established Human Resources metrics. In areas that are not readily measurable, the auditor should rely on documented evidence or specific observations. To maintain credibility, an auditor must avoid generalizations and unsupported innuendo.

❑ Audits should be manageable. Human Resources audits are not commonplace today. If they are to become part of the organizational landscape, they must be conducted in a cost-effective manner with minimal disruption to the organization's principal activities. This again relates to the concept of being planned in an appropriate manner and well designed to address the specific needs of the organization.

In order to be successful, the practitioner should gain full senior management support for the auditing process at the outset. Involving senior management and key influence-makers among the internal client

A - B - C

groups in the design of the audit process is an effective way of getting support for the process.

Training the auditors and the rest of the Human Resources staff is also a must. Auditors need to be skilled in terms of following the auditing protocols, gathering the appropriate data, making valid observations and interpreting the results of their findings. The staff need to be taught how to prepare for an audit, what to expect and how to manage the results.

Audit Steps

The following is an outline of the steps taken once the senior practitioner has decided to conduct an audit of Human Resources Management practices. These steps should be taken regardless of whether the audit is comprehensive or is focused on a single aspect of Human Resources Management. They include:

- **Establish audit scope and objectives:** This is done in collaboration with the senior leadership team, divisional and department heads and any other key internal clients. The scope of the audit should define the desired end results, the functional areas to be investigated (e.g., management development, personnel assessment, succession planning), the physical locations to be visited, the key contacts to be interviewed, the documents and information to be reviewed and the time lines expected for completion.

- **Appoint, orient and train the audit team:** A team captain should be appointed and the senior Human Resources practitioner should provide that individual with a written mandate. If the senior practitioner chooses to develop an internal audit team, the team members will have to be trained on data gathering methodologies, making observations, analyzing and interpreting data, drawing conclusions and making recommendations. For external teams (consultants), the practitioner should develop an orientation program to familiarize the team with the organization and the scope of the project.

- **Orient the Human Resources Department staff:** Those members of the Human Resources Department who are not directly involved in the audit process should be briefed on what to expect in terms of the process and outcomes. These individuals need to buy-in to the process and become collaborative participants. During their orientation, the senior practitioner should address any fears or

skepticism the staff may have regarding the audit process.

- **Prepare a plan:** The audit team needs to prepare a detailed plan of action, including a schedule of events, standards to be applied, documents to be reviewed, locations to be visited, individuals to be interviewed and data to be collected. A comprehensive plan will involve such tools as checklists and interview scripts for the auditors' use to ensure nothing is forgotten or omitted as an oversight. Before implementation, the senior practitioner may want to review the plan with the senior leadership team and the Human Resources Department staff to ensure buy-in.

- **Gather data and make observations:** This involves reviewing documents, conducting interviews and making observations. Documents to be reviewed might include policy manuals, minutes of Committee meetings, personnel files, budgets, operational reports (safety statistics), Human Resources reports (key metrics), procedural manuals, training reports and previous audit results.

- **Analyze organizational performance:** Key Human Resources metrics such as turnover, retention rates and absenteeism should be compared to stated objectives, compared across divisions and benchmarked against industry or regional norms (as applicable). In addition, key organizational performance measures such as productivity, costs of goods and return on capital employed should be examined to see if any correlations exist with Human Resources Management activities.

- **Interpret data and develop conclusions:** This requires a seasoned Human Resources practitioner who has a firm understanding of the organization. The key is to identify the strengths and weaknesses inherent in the current Human Resources Management practices within the organization and to identify key opportunities for improvement. Where strengths are identified, the practitioner will want to figure out ways to exploit them. For example, in reviewing the data, the practitioner may see an emerging core competency that the organization can use to strategic advantage.

- **Develop recommendations and suggested action plans:** The focus here should be on developing reasonable and practical action plans. The idea is not to attempt to reach perfection in a short period of time, but rather to address the most telling deficiencies and strengthen those areas that bring the most value to the organization. The practitioner must remember to tailor any recommendations to the level of sophistication of the organization, its available resources and the state of readiness in accepting organizational changes.

- **Validate the results:** A preliminary report is issued to key managers and Human Resources staff for review. If any areas seem unclear or require further investigation, this can be done before official results are published and action plans acted upon. Often this involves nothing more than a "smell test". Key individuals are simply asked how they feel about the report and if they have any concerns with the findings.

- **Report the findings and recommendations:** The final audit report is presented to the senior leadership team who are asked to accept the report and to determine which of the recommendations will be acted upon. Their decision then filters down to the key managers in the organization who must incorporate the recommendations as part of their organizational objectives.

- **Implement action plans:** Depending on the nature of the recommendation, the practitioner will determine how to correct any deficiency or exploit an organizational strength. In some instances, the responsibility for addressing the issue will rest with line management with the support of the practitioner; in others, the Human Resources Department will be accountable. Action plans might include developing a policy, engaging in training and development activities, forming a task force or putting together a project team.

- **Follow up:** Each action plan should identify milestones to be met and objectives to be achieved. The plan should also identify when and how progress is to be measured.

Role of the Human Resources Practitioner

The senior Human Resources practitioner ultimately owns the responsibility for continuously ensuring the organization's management of its people is done in accordance with the organization's stated values. The practitioner is accountable for ensuring that the resources spent on recruitment, hiring, orientation, training, management development, performance management and using human capital result in a fair return to the organization.

The motivated Human Resources practitioner will not want to leave the audit function up to a professional auditor alone. The senior practitioner has a vested interest in using the audit as a tool for improving the delivery of Human Resources Management services and programs and as a vehicle for enhancing the credibility of the function. Moreover, the practitioner can use the tool to ensure planned Human Resources Management activities are aligned with the organization's strategic goals and match the organization's culture.

Many practitioners lose sight of the culture of the organization and are prone to introducing programs or processes that the organization does not need, does not want or cannot absorb. Even when an organizational need is identified, the practitioner must ensure the organization perceives the need and is able to assimilate the program or process into its culture. The audit is one tool for the practitioner to use to align his or her action plans with the organization's priorities. Moreover, after a few iterations of the planning for an auditing cycle, the practitioner will be in a much better position to influence organizational outcomes and priorities.

Barriers to Success/Common Pitfalls

The term "audit" seems to strike fear in many managers. Audits are perceived as a threat to managers. Managers may believe they are being audited in order to uncover some wrongdoing and punish the perpetrator for the abuse. This, in fact, may be the case in some organizations. Some unscrupulous senior managers may use the audit as a tool to enforce compliance. This will run in a counter-productive way to the desired outcome of making the audit a central feature of managing processes and outcomes.

To overcome this fear, the first step is to emphasize that audit scores will not be used to directly assess the performance of any individual manager. Instead, managers will be assessed on their implementation of corrective action plans to overcome deficiencies identified in the audit. Punishment should never be meted out in any manner as the result of an audit. The only exceptions would be the uncovering of some egregious misconduct of a criminal or unethical nature.

Human Resources programs and initiatives often do not lend themselves to precise measures. Nor is it always possible to draw meaningful comparisons between departments or divisions with respect to the quality of implementation of Human Resources programs. In some instances, the audit should simply measure whether or not there is objective findings of compliance.

For example, measuring the effectiveness of the performance management process is difficult except by proxy. If there are distinct measurable improvements in performance following the implementation of a performance management system, then it can be concluded that the system was effective. Another means of measuring the effectiveness is to draw correlations between productivity and levels of compliance. If one division has completed all of its performance appraisals and posts better productivity numbers than a division that has only completed half of its appraisals, then it might be concluded that the system is effective when used. However, such measures may not be readily available and analyzing the results to account for other variables may be very complex. Instead, the audit may simply look to measure compliance. The quality of the process might be better measured by surveying employee opinion.

Unfortunately, one of the most common problems faced today by Human Resources departments is the lack of any established metrics or other standards of performance to measure program effectiveness. As a matter of process, a senior practitioner may be well advised to forgo implementing an auditing process until the department has established meaningful metrics and standards of performance. Notwithstanding, designing the potential audit protocols may create a foundation for establishing those measures and standards. (See also Human Resources Metrics at page 185 *et seq.*)

The first key principle to developing a successful auditing experience is proper planning. Not surprisingly, therefore, one of the expected common pitfalls is the lack of proper planning. Without defining the procedures that are to be followed, the auditor faces being understaffed and under-resourced. Many practitioners today conduct *ad hoc* focused audits (or reviews) of specific processes. However, without a comprehensive plan, these reviews are seen as one-off activities, and lack the necessary credibility to add much value to the function or to add to its acceptance as an integral part of the organization.

Any audit will suffer if the people conducting the evaluation lack objectivity or the skills necessary to interpret the data collected properly. Unfortunately, there are few experienced external auditors who specialize in the area of Human Resources Management audits (and even fewer who have well documented and established protocols to follow). Audits of the Human Resources function are largely conducted by practitioners themselves. In doing so, the senior practitioner should be aware of some common interpretation errors. These same errors can occur when interpreting the results of employee opinion polls. They include:

⇨ basing reports on single observations;

⇨ assuming consensus based on the opinions expressed by a small group;

⇨ dismissing single observations without further investigation;

⇨ interpreting reports at face value without probing for meaning; and

⇨ reaching conclusions based on a majority of observations or "opinions" without regard to the minority perspective (for example, if 51% use the performance appraisal form, it is true that the majority use it — it is also true that almost half do not).

Communication is an essential ingredient throughout the audit process. However, the senior practitioner must take care not to over-promise and under-deliver. Realistic target dates for completing data gathering, analyzing results and reporting the findings must be set. More importantly, they must be met. If there are delays, these should be communicated to the client group as soon as possible.

BENCHMARKING

Definition/Background

Benchmarking is defined as the process of continuously and systematically comparing products, processes and practices with the best practices in other organizations, or other parts of your own organization, with the aim of adapting and implementing them in order to improve the organization's performance. Best practice benchmarking involves identifying the top levels of performance being achieved by other organizations for each activity in the business, and finding out how they achieve these performance levels. These practices are then adapted, rather than copied, to meet one's own business needs and implemented in order to improve one's own business performance levels.

There are two elements to benchmarking. First, there is goal setting, based on the best measures of performance identified in other comparable organizations. These measures are called metrics. Second, there is process improvement, identifying the practices that other organizations use to achieve high levels of performance and implementing these practices in one's own organization by adapting them to the unique culture and circumstances of one's organization.

The objective of benchmarking is to improve business performance by learning from others. By looking at best practices in other organizations, target performance levels can be set which are based on what is being achieved elsewhere. Analysis of how these performance levels are being achieved can enable the development of new methods and procedures that can be adopted by the benchmarking organization.

Best practice benchmarking analysis involves four different types of benchmarking.

1. **Internal Benchmarking.** Comparisons are made between different divisions, subsidiaries, plants or departments within the same organization. This has the advantage of virtually free access to all information with few problems of commercial confidentiality. It should be a part of any benchmarking exercise as it would ensure that existing internal processes are fully understood before looking at processes in other organizations. However, it is not sufficient on its own. It can lead to complacency and it provides no opportunity to learn from other organizations.

2. **Competitive Benchmarking.** Comparison with the performance of direct product competitors is important in order to identify areas where improvement would have the greatest competitive impact. It is unlikely that direct competitors will allow direct access to their plants, but a lot of information is available in the public domain in the form of annual reports and press articles. Also, competitors will sometimes share information through an independent third party provided that anonymity is maintained. This often means that information is restricted to the average range of industry performance levels.

   It is also possible in some industries to benchmark with organizations who produce like or similar products but who do not compete in the same geographic market. Overseas organizations who do not compete in your market because of the high cost of transporting goods may be willing to share information and processes.

   Suppliers, who commonly provide goods and services to competing firms, can sometimes be excellent sources of information regarding different processes and performance levels among competitors. The amount of information available from these sources may be restricted by confidentiality covenants.

3. **Functional Benchmarking.** This involves taking a specific function, such as distribution, and benchmarking against best practice organizations for that function. It is important to choose organizations which are similar to your own in terms of size and customer requirements, but they do not need to be manufacturing similar products or even be in the same industry. This has the advantage that they are likely to be more willing to share information than would be the case with a direct competitor.

   This is an area where creative thinking can be a tremendous competitive advantage. Organizations who can see similarities in the way a function is managed in decidedly different industries may be able to capitalize on "best practices" in ways that are unimaginable to their competitors. Manufacturers who look at distribution companies to learn how to optimize their logistics may gain a lot more insight into the function than those who narrow their scope on "like" industries. The company that makes widgets can learn about distribution networks from a food service distributor or a transportation company.

This type of benchmarking involves comparing in detail the methods that different organizations use to achieve high levels of performance. It is not enough to know that a company achieves 99.8% on-time delivery. You need to define what "on-time delivery" means and find out how the organization achieves it.

4. **Generic Benchmarking.** Some processes and activities are similar for almost all organizations. For example, billing of customers is likely to be similar regardless of the product or service that has been purchased. Consequently, when benchmarking such generic processes, the search for best practices can be much more wide-ranging. It is generic benchmarking that is most likely to produce really innovative and potentially valuable ideas. Taiichi Ohno of Toyota is said to have come up with some of the ideas that form the basis of just-in-time production while watching shelf replenishment in an American supermarket. However, generic benchmarking does require the imagination to visualize how a practice seen in one context might be adapted to meet the needs of a quite different type of business.

Benefits/Expected Outcomes

The following benefits can be expected from the successful application of benchmarking:

⇨ A better understanding of the needs of customers and the extent to which the organization is meeting these requirements. Companies need to match the needs of customers to their organization's capabilities. Often an organization will spend a great deal of effort and resources attempting to meet a perceived customer requirement that does not really exist.

⇨ Reduced costs as a result of higher levels of productivity and lower levels of waste. The disciplined approach of benchmarking requires a full understanding of existing processes. Thus, the organization can compare existing processes against best practices and identify areas where losses of productivity and other wastes occur.

⇨ A better understanding of existing processes and how well they are being performed. Without a benchmark to compare to, it is difficult to assess the organization's level of performance.

⇨ Increased market share as a result of more competitive performance levels and greater customer satisfaction. Organizations that benchmark tend to have a much better understanding of their markets and how to compete at a world class level.

⇨ More effective management as a result of better understanding of business processes.

⇨ The ability to set targets which are challenging but credible. This, of course, is a vital element to any effective performance management process. By using an outside benchmark the organization will increase motivation by giving employees a credible and identifiable mark to shoot for. It is the old AVIS slogan, "We're number two so we try harder".

⇨ Identification of the areas with the greatest potential for improvement. Following the "Pareto principle", organizations have a limited number of resources and, therefore, should focus those resources on the 20% of processes that will yield 80% of potential gains.

⇨ Reduced resistance to change as the success of the methods being proposed can be demonstrated in other organizations.

⇨ More rapid awareness of successful business innovations. Benchmarking can become habit forming. It is an essential process for the "learning" organization.

⇨ Avoidance of the long learning curve often associated with the implementation of new techniques.

If benchmarking is to have the desired effect in changing and improving methods and procedures within the organization, then everyone will be affected to some extent. Senior management will play a key role in ensuring that benchmarking is adequately resourced, determining the processes to be benchmarked and co-ordinating the implementation of the project findings. Participants in the benchmarking projects will need training in a new set of data collection and analysis skills to ensure that they can identify and modify processes found in other organizations in order to make them suitable for use in their own.

Staff in the departments affected by the changes in processes will need to have the reasons for the changes and the revised performance objectives explained to them. They will also need training in the new methods. If possible, the staff most directly affected should visit the organizations that have been benchmarked so that they can see for themselves how other organizations handle tasks similar to their own and the results that are possible.

As benchmarking becomes a routine part of work within an organization, there will be a number of organizational effects. While initially a specialized benchmarking group may need to be established, over time the activities of this group will be progressively absorbed into the individual departments. Since benchmarking is project-based and usually involves multi-functional teams, organizations with a fairly rigid hierarchical structure may need to move to a more flexible structure. It is also quite likely that one of the outcomes of benchmarking will be the identification of the need to make major changes in organizational structure in order to achieve the targeted improvements in performance. (See also Change Management at page 67 *et seq.*)

While many of the benefits of benchmarking will be gained relatively quickly and should be easy to quantify, the real pay-off is in the longer term. Benchmarking is part of the process of evolution into a learning organization where continuous change and improvement is the norm. This is very difficult to express in financial terms, but without it organizations will find their performance falling further and further behind that of the competition and, in the long term, their very survival may become in jeopardy.

Programming/Implementation

Benchmarking is a continuous iterative process that has become a way of life in many organizations. However, when first starting, it is important not to try to cover too much initially. If you try to benchmark everything simultaneously, the results tend to be rather superficial, and by the time they are ready, they are likely to be out of date. It is far better to choose a single process for the first benchmarking project and extend benchmarking to other processes as experience is gained. Even then, the first project can be expected to take about a year in total, of which the first two months will be needed for initial set-up, identification of suitable benchmarking partners and project design. The remaining 10 months are used for data collection and analysis.

Benchmarking will typically involve the following steps:

☐ **Select the process to be benchmarked.** The process selected should be one for which an improvement in performance will have a significant impact on the organization, either by reducing costs or increasing market share. Many organizations start with a questionnaire survey of customers in order to identify critical success factors. These are the aspects of performance that are most important to customers in selecting a supplier. If customers are asked at the same time to rate the benchmarking company's performance on each critical success factor relative to competitors, this should help identify those processes that, as well as being important, have considerable scope for improvement.

☐ **Select a benchmarking team.** The team should be multi-disciplinary so that the process under investigation will be viewed from more than one perspective. The team should also consist of the people who are responsible for the process and for the implementation of any changes rather than staff specialists.

☐ **Map the internal process.** It is important that before any external data collection takes place, the team fully understands the process within its own organization. The best way to achieve this is to prepare a detailed map of the existing process. This will provide an understanding of existing methods and procedures, performance measures being used and current levels of performance. This analysis will usually reveal deficiencies and anomalies that can be rectified immediately before the benchmarking exercise proper takes place. At this stage, you will also need to decide which metrics are to be benchmarked and how they are to be calculated.

☐ **Identify suitable benchmarking partners.** Benchmarking partners will fall into three groups. These are internal, external, and best practice organizations.

Most organizations will use all three at different stages in the benchmarking process. The first stage will be an internal benchmarking exercise that compares different parts of the benchmarking organization. This can be a valuable way of developing benchmarking experience before approaching outside organizations. Also, it is frequently the case that levels of performance and operating methods are very different in different parts of the same organization. Adoption of the best of these practices across the whole organization can lead to immediate improvements in overall performance even before the external benchmarking process has started.

The next stage will be an external benchmarking exercise comparing the benchmarking organization with the best performers in its own industry. This will be a desk exercise involving a survey of published information, but a surprising amount can be learned in this way. Studies of annual reports, newspaper articles, trade journals, trade association reports and conference proceedings can reveal a great deal. This process is now greatly simplified by the availability of electronic databases that can be rapidly searched for all references to the organization being investigated. There are also consulting services that specialize in preparing comparative analyses of organizations within an industry on behalf of clients.

It is the selection of organizations to be included in the third stage that is most difficult, as the range of potential organizations to be considered is so large. The first step should be to draw up a list of organizations generally considered to be excellent at the process of being benchmarked. This can be based on a literature search and discussions with experts in the field at universities and in trade associations. The next step is to reduce this to a shortlist of organizations that face similar problems to those that the benchmarking organization faces but which are not direct competitors. The final step is to approach the shortlist of organizations

and see which ones would be willing to share data for benchmarking purposes.

☐ **Decide on the data collection method and collect the data.** First, the data to be collected must be identified. Then, the method of collection must be decided. In some cases, a third-party organization is asked to carry out the research and prepare a report. In other cases, groups of organizations from similar but non-competing organizations will combine forces and share information.

The following methods of data collection are used, usually in combination:

- *Surveys* — This will usually involve each participant completing a questionnaire or being interviewed on performance levels and procedures within his or her own organization.

- *Meetings* — The participating organizations meet at regular intervals to exchange data on performance measures and procedures. At the meetings, each of the participants presents the information gathered since the previous meeting and together they decide what should be collected for the next meeting.

- *Site visits* — Many experts believe that these are only of value if they are highly focused and the purpose of the visit is precisely defined. It is further believed they should only take place after as much information as possible has been collected using the first two methods. However, often investigating how others perform a given function, or simply visiting an admired organization to see how they do a variety of things, provides the impetus for creative thought. It is sometimes the accidental discovery of a different process or a different paradigm that causes us to question our own way of doing things. As much as benchmarking is intended to be a disciplined approach to adopting best practices, it should not be viewed so rigidly as to prevent creative learning. In other words, it is sometimes worthwhile to take a site visit just to see something different.

☐ **Communicate the benchmarking results.** Once the benchmarking survey has been completed, the results must be reported back to senior management and to those who will be involved in, or affected by, implementation of the findings. To every extent possible, the findings should be documented and quantified. The results should be disseminated through face-to-face presentations. Newsletters and written reports can be used to let the wider organization, those not directly impacted by any changes brought about by the benchmarking results, know about the successes and failures of the specific project. This helps legitimize the process of benchmarking itself and may stir others to participate or develop project ideas of their own.

- [ ] **Determine the performance gap.** Once the data have been collected, a comparative analysis of the benchmarking organization's performance against the performance measures at each of the benchmarked organizations should be carried out. For each performance measure, reasons for the gap between organization performance and best performance should be identified.

- [ ] **Develop an improvement plan.** For each performance gap identified in the previous stage, an action plan needs to be drawn up that details how the gap is to be closed. This will cover the detailed changes of method to be introduced, a schedule for their implementation, the resources required and the expected results.

- [ ] **Implement and monitor progress.** Benchmarking is only successful if the ideas that it generates are implemented, leading to improvements in performance. In order to ensure this, there should be a clear allocation of responsibility for each aspect of the implementation. A formal monitoring system should be set up so that senior management receives a regular summary of actual performance on key metrics in comparison with target performance.

- [ ] **Start again.** It is important to remember that benchmarking is a continuous, iterative process. Other organizations are constantly improving and introducing new practices. Once the findings of the first benchmarking project have been implemented, the process should be repeated to determine whether any new best practices have emerged.

Role of the Human Resources Practitioner

As benchmarking requires the development of new attitudes and the learning of new skills, Human Resources practitioners will need to play a major training role. During the establishment of benchmarking within an organization, workshops will be needed to convince staff of the value of the technique, and the staff involved in carrying out the benchmarking exercises will need training in the techniques and discipline of benchmarking.

In some instances, benchmarking may result in recommendations that require significant changes in organizational structure. In others, the improved processes may result in the displacement of staff. In yet others, the result may dictate a major transformation in the organization's culture. The Human Resources practitioner thus may be required to develop new position descriptions and evaluations; create severance packages and "survivor" strategies; and assist in the change management process.

In sophisticated organizational contexts, the Human Resources practitioner may be a champion of the benchmarking process itself. The practitioner will require a solid understanding of process mapping and performance measurement. Ideally, they will borrow from the discipline of approaches like Total Quality Management and/or capital budgeting for decision making tools like Pareto analysis or cash flow analysis. The practitioner can serve as a facilitator for the process to ensure the steps are followed and, in particular, that there is follow-up by senior management to ensure the effectiveness of the benchmarking process itself.

Finally, the seasoned practitioner who has significant business experience will be able to deliver the skills necessary for effective benchmarking on a just-in-time basis. One mistake often made is to over-train line staff on the tools needed for benchmarking. Rather than going through all the details of how to build a house, the effective trainer knows to start by teaching the apprentice how to saw a single board. As the trainee develops, the trainer adds to the skill set as needed. This prevents overload and assists in securing a buy-in to the process from the line participants.

In order to have credibility as a champion of the process, or even as a facilitator, it is important for the practitioner to apply benchmarking to the Human Resources function itself. This has its own unique challenges.

Benchmarking the Human Resources Function

Of course, the Human Resources function will need to benchmark its own activities against those in other organizations in order to identify ways in which its own performance can be improved. Benchmarking can be applied directly to Human Resources Management. As such, it is one example of functional benchmarking. The main questions to consider are, "How well is the Human Resources function performing now, and can we assess its performance in relation to other Human Resources functions both now and in the future?"

However, as a function that is not directly responsible for the organization's output, Human Resources does not have such obvious measures to use for benchmarking purposes and therefore presents a much more problematic challenge for benchmarking than areas such as production or inventory control. Consequently, the Human Resources practitioner has to approach the subject of benchmarking by creating his or her own benchmarking framework, which should be able to cope with internal as well as external benchmarking activities.

Internal — Efficiency

Before trying to compare notes with similar Human Resources groups in other organizations, a view should be taken on the role that the Human Resources function plays within the organization. Benchmarking in this area is very much focused on the measurement of specific activities. Examples include absenteeism, staff turnover, the time it takes to fill a vacancy and so on. Baseline measures can be produced for all of these activities and used to set improvement targets.

Equally, Human Resources functions from different divisions within the same organization should have some means of comparing their efficiency at performing a range of minimum, but critical, tasks (e.g., payroll). Referring to such tasks as "minimum" tends to underestimate their importance. Much of the focus in benchmarking is on improvement and there is a tendency for Human Resources practitioners to want to have a role that contributes at a more strategic level.

While this may be laudable, if it is at the expense of ensuring that the minimum/critical role is fulfilled properly, then it can have serious consequences.

Perhaps the best example that illustrates this point is when two organizations merge. Shortly after a merger, discussions take place at the strategic level concerning Human Resources issues such as trying to bring together the cultures of the two companies. While these discussions take place, however, the staff are not likely to be very interested in such larger issues if their pay contains errors. Hence, the more appropriate term "critical". Efficient payroll systems may not differ much from one company to another, but any problems caused will have serious Human Resources implications.

Role Definition

After ensuring that the minimum administrative role is fulfilled effectively and efficiently, the next question to consider is what other aspects of Human Resources Management can be benchmarked. This moves the discussion onto a broader consideration of the role of the Human Resources practitioner.

Every organization will have its own view on the contribution the Human Resources practitioner can or should make to the business. For many practitioners, providing the level of service that fits the level of sophistication and maturity of their organizations is a sufficient challenge. For others, the challenge is to advance the function of Human Resources Management so that it is less focused on administrative responsibilities and more on adding value through the strategic alignment of the organization's capabilities and the business plan.

This could, perhaps, be put on a continuum. In recruitment, for example, at the base level, the Human Resources function provides a service that organizes internal and external advertising and preparation of job descriptions and job specifications, sifts application forms and arranges interviews.

As the function and its host organization mature, the Human Resources practitioner should be involved in the interview and selection process with the line manager. With a shift in mindset by both the Human Resources practitioner and line management comes involvement at an earlier stage. The practitioner is able to ask questions, such as "Do we need to fill this vacancy with a similar person or should we actually be looking at a new role?" This is a move towards internal consulting.

The business partner stage would be another developmental shift as the questions from the practitioner become more focused on real business objectives. For example, does this manager have the right type of people doing the right jobs for the way the business needs to operate? Finally, at the most advanced level, the practitioner has to become the expert at designing departmental structure and the organization as a whole. Now the practitioner's activities move into organizational structure and process analysis. Both of these are activities that can have a significant impact on an organization's performance, and thus can be regarded as, potentially, the highest added value service that a Human Resources practitioner can offer.

The role evolves over time. The challenge for the practitioner is to define where his or her function fits on the continuum. The focus of benchmarking then is to determine how to optimally deliver the level of service that best fits the organization at the time. Furthermore, the practitioner will want to find out how best to advance the function within the organization to the next level of sophistication.

External

One simple area that helps to highlight the fact that different organizations have Human Resources functions that have developed to different degrees of sophistication, advancement and strategic contribution is the use of appraisal systems. These can vary greatly from the typical, traditional, one-on-one, subordinate/superior, paper-based process, to the latest 360-feedback system using computers for data gathering and collation.

How can one appraisal system be compared with another? To answer this requires consideration of the context in which the system is operating. Is the process being used well, and do managers understand exactly how to use the process and what is its purpose?

Measurement is still the key to benchmarking so the basic activity could be measured (e.g., the number of appraisals that are completed on time), the quality of the appraisal could be measured (e.g., the percentage of SMART (**S**pecific, **M**easurable, **A**ttainable, **R**eliable and **T**ime bound) objectives set) or, most importantly, the added value of the activity could be gauged (e.g.,

whether appraisal helps the department to reduce its operating costs or achieve any other specified objectives).

While performance measurement is a key element of benchmarking, it can also be viewed as a subject in its own right. If we define performance as "the achievement of business plans", then all organizations have to perform to survive. This could be called absolute performance. Another view is the longer term, relative nature of performance. In other words, if the organization were not performing at least as well as its competitors, then it would be very difficult to regard the achievement of its plans as "performance" in any true sense because, over a period of time, it would lose out to the competition.

It is important to understand the difference between absolute and relative performance for Human Resources because it is necessary to distinguish between efficiency, effectiveness today and added value for the future. For example, a Human Resources practitioner may manage labour relations very efficiently (i.e., few resources are needed) and effectively (there are few arbitrations or little work disruption), but this cannot be regarded as adding value if an organization's competitors do not have a union to contend with. It is helpful, therefore, to subdivide Human Resources Management performance measures into efficiency, effectiveness and added value measures.

Activities and Processes

It is important to distinguish between activities and processes. The recruitment process, for example, starts when a vacancy occurs and finishes when that vacancy is filled.

Within this process, there are many activities which all contribute to the final outcome. Advertising, screening and interviewing are just some of the activities which contribute something to the overall process.

If an activity is not contributing to the process, then it is a "pure" activity that does not add value. So, for example, is the activity of sending out information packs to each and every candidate an integral part of the overall process, or does this activity add nothing? In other words, when trying to measure the performance of the Human Resources function, it is necessary to concentrate on meaningful measures, that is, those that relate to the process.

Assuming that the activities are worth measuring, we can then start to assess how well they are performed.

Efficiency Measures

Efficiency measures can be applied to any Human Resources activity and are probably the easiest measures to produce. They tend to refer either to cost or to speed. The most obvious areas to consider cost efficiency are probably recruitment and training, where the average cost per recruit or trainee should be readily available. Perhaps less obvious are the costs of general Human Resources administration that can be expressed as a total cost or as a percentage of total business costs.

Cost, however, is only a limited aspect of the Human Resources practitioner's performance. Speed is another important consideration. Issues to consider in this respect will include how long it takes to fill a vacancy or to process employees' benefit claims.

Effectiveness Measures

While efficiency will always be a concern for Human Resources, effectiveness may be more significant. Measures of effectiveness are slightly more difficult to obtain than simple efficiency measures. Even in recruitment, it is not straightforward. For example, effectiveness could be viewed from several angles. Were there a sufficient number of applicants and were they of the right caliber? Alternatively, whether the vacancy was filled internally may be a better measure of the practitioner's performance in retaining, developing and rewarding staff.

Probably the best — and some would argue the only — measure of effectiveness of Human Resources is the performance of employees themselves. There is little point in measuring the speed of the recruitment process and then trying to improve the speed of that process, if the quality, or performance, of the employees that are recruited suffers.

Methods of measuring and managing employee performance have become more and more important as competition and cost pressures increase. Consequently, if the practitioner can show an improvement in employee performance measures over a period of time, then these could be a good indicator of his or her own performance.

At their most basic level, performance measures are provided during the appraisal process, usually using a simple rating scale. Even though these may be rather subjective, collecting and aggregating this data as a baseline measure and then checking the changes over a year will give a simple indication of a shift in performance.

One of the immediate obstacles to this approach is the question, "How do we know that it is the Human Resources function which is improving performance?" This can seem to present an insurmountable obstacle in measuring the function's effectiveness. An added complication is that Human Resources is often perceived as working in an area which is inherently intangible. Motivation, morale, attitudinal and behavioural change are all seen as targets for improvement through Human Resources initiatives, but they are usually seen as "soft" rather than "hard" factors and are, therefore, less easily measured.

One way to address this issue is to at least measure some of the soft factors in subjective terms (e.g., through the use of attitude surveys) and to chart any trend changes. However, it could be argued that regarding such matters as soft is a fallacy. If better motivation means anything, it means that employees will perform better as a consequence of being motivated.

Moreover, organizational performance is always, ultimately, measured in terms of hard costs, outputs or profit. So, when measuring the performance of Human Resources, we need to focus activities, processes and initiatives that are directly focused on improving an existing performance measure. This approach requires a fundamental shift in thinking for those who still regard Human Resources as dealing with intangible issues. In broad terms, whatever measures are chosen for Human Resources, they should be as meaningful as possible. They should be meaningful not only to the practitioner but also to the wider group of business stakeholders.

Highly subjective and soft measures will continue to be used to demonstrate Human Resources Management's performance, but the more objective and more business focused measures will always be more meaningful, particularly to line management and the board.

Barriers to Success/Common Pitfalls

There are a number of common reactions when benchmarking is first proposed within an organization. First, there is the belief that the organization is unique. No other organization has quite the same product range, business strategy and market conditions, and so benchmarks based on other organizations would be irrelevant. While this may be true for the organization as a whole, it is still possible to identify organizations that are sufficiently similar with regard to specific processes for their performance to be relevant.

It is important to draw attention to the benefits that other organizations have gained from benchmarking and to emphasize the fact that the intention is not blindly to copy methods used by others. Instead, ideas from other organizations will be used as a catalyst for the development of procedures specifically suited to the special requirements of the benchmarking organization.

There is also a frequent belief that copying the methods of other organizations can never be so effective as original ideas. Copying someone else can only result in being second best. Such a reaction is really missing the point. Benchmarking is not instead of, but in addition to, the development of new methods within the organization. What we want to avoid is re-inventing the wheel. What we should be doing is building on and improving the ideas and procedures that have been successfully implemented elsewhere. If we are second best, it will be to a different organization, often not a competitor, for each function. Being number two in the world on every single performance measure would lead to an overall level of performance that is unbeatable.

There is also the "not invented here" syndrome. Managers and employees may resent the notion that someone else can show them how to do their jobs better. They can feel threatened by the idea that their function needs improvement. This is a significant cultural issue. The challenge is to create an environment where everyone accepts that learning and continuous improvement is a higher superordinate goal.

Finally, there is usually a concern that benchmarking is just another word for industrial espionage and that any co-operative benchmarking activity will lead to our competitors gaining commercially sensitive information about us. This is a very real fear and to combat it organizations using benchmarking on a regular basis have drawn up a code of ethical conduct. This is designed to ensure that the organization never asks for information that it would not be willing to provide about itself and that no benchmarking group ever indulges in activities which would be illegal under anti-combines legislation.

Common mistakes leading to lack of success in benchmarking include the following:

⇨ Lack of support from senior management so that insufficient resources are devoted to benchmarking and no action is taken to implement the changes recommended as a result of the exercise.

⇨ Trying to benchmark every single aspect of the business at the same time so that the exercise becomes very superficial. The concept should be piloted first using a single, albeit significant, process.

⇨ Putting too much emphasis on comparing performance levels rather than comparing the methods by which improved performance is achieved.

⇨ Choosing inappropriate benchmarking partners whose methods and procedures are not relevant or readily adaptable to the benchmarking organization.

⇨ Choosing benchmarking partners who are unable or unwilling to provide data at the level of detail required. Benchmarking requires a fair level of commitment from both organizations. If your organization is asked to assist another in its benchmarking activities, you will need to be prepared to set aside a significant amount of time and resources to be of any help.

⇨ Attempting to transplant procedures seen in other organizations without sufficient consideration of how they will need modifying to meet the special needs of the benchmarking organization. Copying the processes of others is rarely, if ever, successful. You must adapt what you have learned from the other organization to your particular fact situation.

⇨ Failing to define one's own processes fully before looking at those of others. As with any process or project, there is no substitute for preparation.

A - **B** - c

CAREER MANAGEMENT

Definition/Background

Career management processes in organizations arise normally from defined needs. From the organization's perspective and, at a practical level, these could be plans about the succession of senior managers known to be retiring in the future. More strategically, the need is often the creation of competitive advantage through the talents of an organization's employees. From the individual's perspective, the need may be to sustain interest in work through the prospect of promotion or job change.

"Our principal asset is our people" is a platitude that peppers many company annual reports. However, there are organizations whose strengths depend primarily on employee know-how and knowledge rather than capital assets such as cash or buildings, and it is these which are likely to take career management processes most seriously. These so-called "talent-intensive" organizations include those from the sectors of electronics, telecommunications, e-commerce, pharmaceuticals and financial services.

The career management of technical and professional groups presents a particular challenge in talent-intensive organizations. Technically-driven people may lack managerial aspirations and may be unwilling to relinquish technical components of their work. One way of solving this problem is to establish a dual career path, allowing advancement up a technical or managerial ladder.

Dual-career marriages, where both spouses work, present another challenge. The pattern is changing to one where the careers of both partners are seen as of equal priority and, because of two pay cheques, some couples cannot afford to relocate. Organizations are responding by using temporary transfers or helping to find work for the partner, sometimes in the same organization.

In general, career management processes aim to ensure that, in the longer term, talent-intensive organizations have the necessary "intellectual capital" and managerial talent to achieve their goals. To achieve this, organizations need to define the kind of managerial abilities that will be required in the future. Knowledge of core business processes is likely to be impor-

tant, but some of the key generic competencies include:

⇨ the ability to adapt and capitalize upon change in the business environment;

⇨ the ability to work across business boundaries (increasingly important as non-core activities are spun off and contracted out); and

⇨ the ability to self-manage careers as flattening organizations reduce opportunities for promotion. A recent trend, reinforced by organizations wishing to motivate their people and sensing, perhaps, an obligation towards their employees, is to encourage "self-managed development".

The skills required of managers will vary in relation to the development of an organization. A company in a "turnaround" situation will require different skills from a company in "start-up". Large organizations will need a variety of skills to enable them to seize on the opportunities created by changes to the business environment. Career management processes should aim to nurture a degree of diversity of talent and avoid corporate cloning. They should be as much about building on strengths and the unique qualities of managers as about addressing limitations.

The dictionary definition of career is "a person's course of progress through life". Assuming a society in which individuals tend to work together in some form of productive endeavour, there are two relevant perspectives — that of the individual and that of the group, normally an employing organization.

The Individual

From the point of view of the individual, career management is best thought of as the planned means of creating work-related opportunities that allow personal goals to be achieved. On this definition, few engage in career management, since many observe that their own careers are essentially unplanned, arising from a series of opportunities coinciding with particular needs which vary in relation to life circumstances.

A conventional means of describing career pathways distinguishes four stages:

1. exploration, during which different options are investigated or a career embarked upon;

2. establishment, when an individual reinforces skills and interests;

3. maintenance, when a certain status has been achieved; and

4. decline.

However, this model is too simple to accommodate the variegated and complex careers seen in contemporary society. With maturity and financial independence, successful individuals may take on an unrelated career in later life. Men and women commonly place different emphasis on their career, as their families assume greater or lesser importance.

Career flexibility is likely to become increasingly important in the future. This reflects not only differing patterns of employee motivation but also the increasing rate of change in organizational life leading to less certain career pathways. Flatter organizations imply fewer career development opportunities by means of promotions. Organizations focusing on core activities are seeking to draw on non-central skills through fixed-term contracts and the use of consultants, again reducing further the chances for broadening career opportunities. As a result of these factors, managers are taking increasing responsibility for their own careers and are recognizing that changing organizations can be a powerful learning experience — as well as at times a necessity.

Successful career management, from the personal perspective, therefore requires individuals to recognize and balance their life and career goals, and create the opportunities to achieve them. This is often more to do with keeping open options than making clear choices that may rule out future opportunities.

The Organization

From the point of view of the organization, career management refers to those processes that create the level of skills necessary to achieve present and future business strategies. These include succession planning, internal recruitment, performance appraisal, and training and development. This often requires a high degree of central planning and administration.

In the changing climate of the world of work, emphasis will continue to shift from long-term employment to contract work, and employees who move across organizations as well as from project to project. The change includes a move away from specific jobs towards sets of skills and competencies — and employees who will come to see themselves as independent suppliers of these skills. An organization that recognizes these shifts will be interested in developing a pool of people who can supply it with the necessary competencies. It will be through the availability of such skill-based workers that an organization can have the flexibility needed for being at the competitive edge.

Organizations also need to recognize that instead of offering potential recruits stability and job security, the organization needs to provide individuals with opportunities to build their careers and enhance their employability.

Key needs that organizations attempt to address through their career management processes include:

⇒ the ability to ensure an adequate supply of managerial talent in the future to help achieve the organization's strategic objectives;

⇒ the ability, more specifically, to fill senior key roles, when they become vacant, with talented managers developed within the organization;

⇒ the ability to develop managers through planned job placement, in recognition that most managerial learning takes place "on the job";

⇒ the ability to retain and motivate the most able managers by the prospect of promotion or lateral moves which develop skills and hence employability; and

⇒ the creation of a mobile population of managers in the workforce, creating opportunities for the most able to shine and allowing those without the highest levels of ability to find productive niches or leave the organization.

At times, these organizational needs conflict with the needs of individual managers. This conflict is often most apparent in mid-life, when an individual's aspirations may exceed the organization's perceptions of potential, or when an individual may have difficulties in resolving career, family and personal goals.

Benefits/Expected Outcomes

A balance needs to be struck between the individual's increasing need to manage his or her own career and organizational requirements. Precisely where this balance is struck depends on the needs of the business and the benefits that will ensue. These benefits include:

⇨ the creation of a managerial pool with the depth and breadth of understanding to achieve business strategies;

⇨ cultures which emphasize co-operation, the growth and sharing of skills and the creation of synergies between business units (these benefits are most likely to arise when managerial experience embraces a number of operating companies);

⇨ the ability to reinforce and shape strategically important skills and behaviours (management competencies — key skills seen as having strategic value — can serve to bind together appraisal, assessment and development policies and present a coherent view to managers about the skills expected of them); and

⇨ ensuring that managers are motivated by the prospect of job variety and the acquisition of new skills, which is increasingly important as the allure of successive promotions is reducing with flatter organizational structures.

Although there are large variations in how organizations respond to the need to manage the careers of their managers, some clear trends are evident. Organizations that benefit most from formal career planning processes include:

✓ knowledge-intensive companies (e.g., consulting firms and pharmaceuticals);

✓ integrated companies requiring considerable co-operation between parts of the business and company knowledge (e.g., oil, banking and primary manufacturing);

✓ multinational companies with a need to create cohorts of managers with experience of managing across boundaries; and

✓ those wishing to foster distinctive and elitist cultures (e.g., advertising and marketing-led companies).

Organizations which ascribe less importance to career management processes include smaller, cost-driven companies (e.g., contract security and catering) with their emphasis on general management skills and decentralized conglomerates.

Programming/Implementation

Today, development of managers is seen as the joint responsibility of managers themselves and their superiors, although the extent to which this attitude prevails varies from one organization to another. Nonetheless, most organizations will nominate one individual to oversee its career management processes — typically, a management development manager or other Human Resources practitioner.

Successful implementation of career management processes depends on:

⇨ the support of key senior executives who act as role models and signal appropriate behaviours to those around them;

⇨ a developmentally-attuned culture;

⇨ career management serving business as well as personal goals (management development processes need to be clearly in-step with the business; those working in management development need to be credible and close to strategic developments); and

⇨ sufficient opportunities in the business to enable the creation of roles to which managers will aspire.

Where career management adopts a role in a business depends upon how a business is naturally grouped into its related constituents and the benefits that follow. The need for career management processes to serve the goals of the business means that much of the relevant work will be carried out firmly within operating companies, perhaps with the support of the Human Resources practitioner. For example, in a divisionalized company with quite separate activities, there may be little benefit in managing careers across those divisions. Rather, most of the job moves will be within a division. Those responsible for career management are therefore best located within those divisions.

In large, complex or multinational organizations, central involvement may extend to:

⇨ the overseeing of career management policies and processes;

A - B - **C**

⇨ the career management of selected, high-potential managers; and

⇨ the career planning and management of the most senior managers (often the responsibility of the Human Resources practitioner in conjunction with a chief executive).

The general requirement that follows from the needs outlined above is for processes that identify individual potential and aspirations that are matched with the goals of the business.

Identifying Potential and Aspirations

It is now widely recognized that a principal responsibility of managers is to consider the development of their subordinates. This includes considerations of the subordinates' strengths, development needs and career thinking, and is normally carried out, more formally, as part of the performance review. Such reviews will usually involve an indication of the perceived level of potential of the individual and some possible career steps that will build up strengths or broaden experience.

The performance management system needs to be designed so that the organization can identify individual development needs and, in particular, to identify "high fliers". Managers have to be well coached in conducting performance review interviews, as some may have difficulty in extrapolating their own observations to future, hypothetical situations. In addition to identifying the high fliers, whose careers may be centrally managed and who may subsequently be given access to the most challenging and beneficial roles, a system needs to be in place to identify late developers. The possibly demotivating effect of being identified as a non-high flier needs addressing, normally through the prospect of later reconsideration of the assessment, or through a healthy emphasis on internal jobs being open and candidates believing that they will be judged on the basis of merit.

Career Counselling Programs

Some organizations have established career counselling programs, primarily for individual benefit, which help to promote the idea that individuals are responsible for their own career management. These take a variety of formats. Group sessions can provide the stimulation of numbers and the sharing of experiences, while being cost-effective. Personal, one-to-one

interviews will be a necessity. For initial assessments and ongoing consultations, an outside consultant can be most effective at gaining credibility and ensuring trust. Confidentiality of personal discussions is key. When action plans are formulated, senior managers in the organization can be involved as appropriate, perhaps as coaches or mentors.

These change the employee–organization relationship from one of catering to a culture of dependence, to one in which employee and organization share joint responsibility. Flattening career structures and the reduced prospects of promotion, along with an increasing tendency to broaden careers by moving from organization to organization, have changed the focus of career management to be directed more towards the individual than the organization. The so-called new employment contract demands organizations provide the employee with an opportunity to increase his or her employability.

People make career decisions within the context of their whole life experience. Many theorists separate stages of career development tasks into life ages. Although age parameters may vary, there is large agreement on typical stages.

Teenage years are a period of exploration, self-examination, and occupational and role exploration. The twenties, with perhaps early trial-and-error and job changes, lead to establishment in the world of work. In the next 10 to 15 years, there is consolidation of work commitment and, while there might be some questioning of goals, a settling into a serious career. At mid-life, questions arise about work and other values, with a feeling of time passing and dreams running out. Some not only question their career choice but also make major life changes. From the late forties into the fifties, the emphasis is on consolidating one's position and maintaining or building on earlier work initiatives. The final period of career development tends to be marked by deeper evaluation of life successes and failures, often with increased mentoring of younger workers.

Stages of life/work patterns may differ for women. In their early twenties, some choose care giving, marrying and having children, and at that point do not think about other roles than the domestic one. Others choose "either-or" — an initial commitment to work with deferral for nurturing, or initial marriage and children with deferral of non-domestic achievement.

Other women attempt to combine marriage, career and children.

In addition to taking into account different life stages, theories of career development attempt to incorporate the following factors:

— personality traits;

— values;

— interests;

— self-concept;

— family background; and

— sociological factors.

Given all these variables, it becomes clear why there is no one, all-encompassing theory. However, while emphasis on these many factors may vary according to the particular theorist, all career development involves the individual making decisions about his or her work based on personal experience.

Whatever the overall model, formal career development has common elements in the process. An initial assessment aims at gathering as much information as possible about the individual. This is usually achieved through an in-depth interview that may be supplemented by results from a variety of psychometric tests. The information provides the person with a full picture of his or her strengths, weaknesses, interests, values, life patterns, skills and experiences. For many, this may be the first opportunity to gain such an organized, coherent self-awareness. It provides a strong base from which to move forward to effective change. Knowledge of key strengths allows the individual to consider those situations where his or her strengths are best harnessed.

Once the data have been synthesized, alternatives can be generated. Then is the time to obtain occupational information and to learn more about practical realities and constraints. A key objective is often to create future work opportunities. Then choices can be selected, plans made and implementation of those plans begun.

If an organization provides career counselling, it puts in place a system whereby employees assume more control over their own careers. In this way, it helps to remove the assumption that the organization knows what is best for employees and should take care of them. It changes the relationship from caretaking of dependants to one in which employee and organization share a joint responsibility. The organization gains by having employees who are clearer about their fit within, and their potential contribution to, the organization, and who then act upon that knowledge. Employees gain an understanding of their needs, interests, and skills, and greater responsibility for their personal and career development.

In general, most career counselling occurs between friends, family members and colleagues. Each will have a particular view of the individual and perhaps will have his or her own motives, and therefore may never be seen as entirely independent counsellors. Hence, the role of the independent professional. However, within organizations, it is the Human Resources practitioner who often gets the first call when a need for career counselling is identified. The practitioner is generally in a good position to advise on possible job opportunities. However, he or she is probably not in the best position to embark upon intensive, counselling-oriented discussions. Again, the independent professional will help to ensure trust and confidentiality.

This said, there is no professional body of career counsellors. Management consultants and professional psychologists may feel equally well qualified to do the work to high standards. Where psychometric tests are used as part of an assessment, care should be taken to make sure that an appropriately qualified individual makes the interpretation of the test.

Matching Individual Talents and Aspirations with Business Needs

Assuming the accurate identification of individual talent, the challenge is to harness this information in a way that satisfies the needs of the individual and the organization. Two principal means by which individuals are funneled into particular roles are through succession planning and internal job postings.

Succession Planning

At its simplest, succession planning normally involves a manager considering his or her own replacement and what his or her subordinates might need to achieve in order to be regarded as a likely successor. This process, in itself, has a number of benefits. Subordinates can plan their career thinking around their manager's future plans and make lateral moves if they see future progress barred or unlikely.

A - B - **C**

Development themes that arise from these discussions have a dynamic, future-oriented quality. Furthermore, when collectively reviewed, succession plans can reveal gaps in managerial resources as the organization projects itself forward.

Some organizations have attempted to consider succession planning three or four jobs removed. Such an overly deterministic approach is likely to be negated by rapid organizational change and delayering. Modern succession planning involves thinking ahead and considering various future scenarios in a way that accommodates such change. A key requirement in any organization is the creation of opportunities for individuals to gain work experience in as diverse a variety of roles as possible. Equally important, however, are individuals' needs to feel that, if suitable internal job opportunities arise, they will be able to make an application.

Internal Job Postings

This method of filling jobs is the best known, although it is not always well executed, even in those organizations with an explicit policy to advertise jobs internally. Announcements sent to managers at the appropriate level are another method. This has the benefit of encouraging managers to speak with their subordinates about job opportunities, although this can be logistically troublesome and places a great reliance on the commitment of managers who might not be motivated to encourage one of their star-performers to move.

The possible conflict, between a manager pursuing his or her own goals by protecting subordinates from the allure of jobs elsewhere and the needs of the business as a whole to develop its managers, can be partially resolved by collective discussions about management succession issues. Most large organizations that recognize the benefits of career planning have a suitable forum in which these discussions can take place (e.g., a staff planning committee or management development committee). Managers need to sense that it is a good thing to develop their most able subordinates and seek to place them in roles that are developmentally helpful to them. Some organizations rely entirely on these processes to broker people into management roles, although to work well the following are necessary conditions. There should be:

✓ free and open discussions between subordinates and their managers about possible future job moves;

✓ a well-developed central Human Resources management function which can act as a conduit between opportunities in the form of future vacant roles and people who are seeking a job move (some kind of database can help if numbers of managers are large); and

✓ an honest and trustworthy environment where, for example, the decision to recruit externally is not made without a sound and sensitive exposition of the reasons.

Portfolio Careers

For some individuals, in fact, a growing number, working one job is simply not enough to keep them satisfied. British management expert Charles Handy coined the phrase "portfolio career" in his 1989 book *The Age of Unreason* to describe how he balanced his core work as a consultant with other work done for personal fulfilment and enjoyment.

Many professionals today find that their primary income-producing job is not enough to give them a sense of personal fulfilment and satisfaction. In order to get a feeling of completeness, they must seek other work opportunities to give expression to their skills and abilities. These individuals may have reached a plateau in their on-the-job careers and are seeking new ways to develop their personal growth other than seeking new employment or advancement with other organizations.

Many individuals who develop a portfolio career do so unconsciously. They are restless individuals who need a variety of outlets to express their creativity and to expend their energy. Some individuals find avenues for this expression through charitable works or community service. Others need to have a sense of being productive through channels that will augment their income. This is not the same as "moonlighting". The added income is more a measure of the value of their skills than it is a necessity.

Quite often, the added work is related to the core activity. For example, a Human Resources practitioner may also write newsletter articles or even a book on Human Resources related subjects, or the practitioner may choose to teach Human Resources related subjects at a local community college or university. By doing so, the practitioner is not only giving back to the community but also is growing a different personal skill set.

Other portfolio careerists seek variety in their choices. An operations manager may produce and sell pieces of artwork (paintings, pottery, jewellery), or follow a calling such as doing missionary work. For many, developing a side interest is just the beginning of a transition out of the mainstream and into a field they truly enjoy. Some begin this new path in life by returning to school on a part-time basis.

A true portfolio career is different than just having a second source of income. It is characterized by the diversity of activities. For example, many professionals choose to leave full-time, permanent employment and work as contract or interim executives. This type of arrangement allows them to take time away from the job to invest concentrated time in other activities. They may sign onto a nine-month assignment each year and spend the other three months writing the next great Canadian novel. Others may reduce their core activity to part-time hours as their income and savings permit, and increase the hours spent on the second career.

Some portfolio careerists fall into piecing together a career accidentally. Executives who have been "downsized" after a long and successful career but are not yet ready to accept retirement may find a contract assignment and at the same time take on a teaching engagement to augment the reduced income. After some time, these executives find the improved quality of life and the control over their destiny too good to give up. Others merely use this as a transition strategy while they seek a new opportunity in a full-time position. (See also Interim Executives at page 221 *et seq.*)

On the other end of the scale, recent graduates who have difficulty finding the right opportunity may put together a variety of work assignments to round out their résumés. A graduate may find a full-time position in a low-skilled field (bartending, construction labourer) to pay the bills, and augment this with a non-paying engagement in the volunteer sector to develop his or her core skills. These types of activities augment a résumé and help graduates find the full-time assignment they really want. A true portfolio careerist sets his or her sights on continuous variety.

Having a portfolio career is generally quite difficult. While a few can make it lucrative, most portfolio careerists find that they earn less than they had in full-time positions. In order to develop a portfolio, careerists must have the skills to sell their talents. They must invest a significant part of their time in securing paid assignments and have the resilience to accept rejection.

For organizations, the growth of this segment of the working population may present interesting and beneficial opportunities. However, the concept of portfolio careers challenges the organizational paradigms. Canadian organizations still demonstrate a preference to hire full-time, permanent staff to fill their needs. Even when they see an assignment may be transitional or project-based, they are more apt to turn to expensive consulting firms than they are to engage interim professionals.

For the Human Resources practitioner, the concept of the portfolio career presents both challenges and opportunities. For example, practitioners should consider providing sabbaticals for staff members who may want to develop a portfolio of activities to round out their lifestyles. As well, practitioners may find enormous benefit in considering the use of contract executives to help manage parts of the business that are undergoing transition. The skills needed to transform part of the organization in a change management initiative are quite different than the skills required to maintain the business on a transactional basis. Organizations that hire a transformational leader in the wrong context find that the individual becomes bored once he or she has effected the requisite changes and then leaves the organization. Since this is in many cases an inevitability, organizations are well advised to plan for it.

In one example of an individual building a portfolio career, a safety director had a desire to seek variety through consulting work. However, the individual liked the security he had from full-time work with one employer. Fortuitously, the director was asked to sit on a multi-function task force that was given the mandate to find ways to "rationalize" the organization. The director, thinking somewhat "out-of-the-box", proposed that his job be changed to a contract for services. He would provide the same level of service on a fixed fee to be renegotiated each year. He would charge for a set number of hours each week; however, both parties would work towards reducing those

A - B - **C**

hours over time to save the organization money. Through this arrangement, he would be free to pursue contracts with other organizations. He now spends about 60% of his time working as the primary organization's safety director, and spends the remainder of the time with other clients, providing community service to employees who experience problems with their Workers' Compensation claims and helping out local safety associations.

The rewards in having this portfolio are a greater sense of achievement and fulfilment, task variety and freedom of choice. Being able to manage one's own time is a luxury few full-time executives have but for which most would sacrifice something to attain.

Role of the Human Resources Practitioner

Career management processes critically affect the Human Resources practitioner. Not only is it an area where the practitioner can add significant value to a business but also it requires a good deal of administrative capability. It is an area that allows the practitioner to get closely involved in the strategic aspects of a business. Indeed, this involvement is essential if career development is to anticipate emerging business requirements.

Career management processes lend practitioners a power and a certain mystique that require sensitive consideration if they are to be seen as helpful and trusted. To maximize trust, practitioners need to ensure that they are open in their policies, even-handed in their approach and seen to be serving the needs of the organization through the sensitive career management of its employees.

Barriers to Success/Common Pitfalls

Common mistakes include the following:

⇨ Bureaucratic involvement of a corporate centre, which runs the risk of becoming divorced from business goals, and being insufficiently flexible to deal with changing business needs. This can result in career development becoming "paper-led" and the disempowerment of managers taking responsibility for their own (and their subordinates') development.

⇨ An excess of data that are gathered over and above what can be readily put into use.

⇨ Excessive external management recruitment to fill vacancies. It is important to recognize that most management learning occurs through new job experiences. Therefore, internal recruitment is key in an organization's career management. Organizations therefore need means to match talent against job opportunities and to guard against vacancies being filled by informal, "behind-closed-door" processes that can be deeply demotivating. Some organizations have an explicit policy stating a guideline for the proportion of external hires, to balance the benefits of external recruitment (the importing of new skills and approaches) against the benefits of recruiting internally (the motivation and development of existing managers).

CHANGE MANAGEMENT

Definition/Background

All organizations are subject to changes of various degrees of complexity and significance. Changes occur in the organization's environment through technological innovations, legislative amendments, new competitive challenges, shifting demographics, and globalization. The management of change is the process by which the organization adapts to these changing conditions. It represents a significant challenge to the Human Resources practitioner who needs to assess the organization's readiness to adapt and to champion the process. Simple, incremental changes occur almost imperceptibly as the organization grows. However, as shifts in the environment occur more frequently and are more powerful, the need for fundamental or transformational change has become necessary for the very survival of many organizations. Thus, the management of change most often refers to the dramatic transference of an organization from its present state to an entirely new state. It requires careful attention and planning in order to be successful.

The requirement to change most often is imposed from outside forces. In exceptional cases, senior management may recognize the need to do things differently in order for the organization to remain competitive and to ensure its very survival. As profits erode, market share declines and the organization faces the prospect of downsizing its operations, new management thinking is required so the organization can reinvent itself to meet the challenges of its new environment.

Organizational change embraces corporate-wide changes which may embrace new processes, changes to the organizational structure, downsizing, cultural change, outsourcing, mergers and acquisitions, forming alliances or partnerships, and many similar complex moves. For the Human Resources practitioner, the challenges of major staff reductions, restaffing and changes to the organizational competencies have thrust them into a position of far more strategic importance than was, perhaps, previously perceived. The Human Resources practitioner must develop processes to create an acceptance of change and to develop a learning organization that is more adept at adjusting to an environment of continuous changes. This means assisting employees to cope with the changes and in forming new attitudes towards their work and their organizations.

Unfortunately, the challenge is so significant that most efforts to transform organizations simply fail. Studies put the failure rate at a staggering 70% to 80%. This includes the success rate of the ever-popular mergers and acquisitions. In the majority of cases, mergers and acquisitions have failed in realizing any significant increase in the combined value of the merged organizations. The goal of achieving perceived synergies is extremely elusive.

Significant change management approaches have routinely become viewed as flavour-of-the-month management initiatives. As such, they fail to capture the imaginations of employees and, in turn, fail to become ingrained as part of the organizational culture. Re-engineering, Total Quality Management, Quality Circles and many other interesting approaches have become fads of the past. In many instances, these processes have been soundly designed and ought to be effective. Nevertheless, they have been relegated to the trash heap because of poor implementation. Organizations usually fail to understand the level of commitment required to make these approaches successful. Regardless of the approach chosen for transforming an organization, the significance of the required transformation dictates that the senior management group adopts a fundamentally different paradigm in order for it to be a success. Otherwise, they will not carry the much-needed commitment and desire to make the change happen.

On the assumption that the strategy behind a change is well founded, the major factor for success is how the change is managed. The purpose of change management thus is to ensure that the organization can effectively implement the change, and is able to operate effectively after the change. The second part of this statement is as important as the first. It means that the change management process goes beyond the first phase of a change, such as making employees redundant, or successfully gaining control of another company. The purpose includes dealing with the next stage: successfully running the business in the way intended after those dismissed have left, or making

A - B - **C**

the acquired company integrate to the degree required to achieve the strategic intention behind its purchase.

Boiled Frogs and Dry Monkeys

Throughout the rapid changes of many organizations in the 1990s, two popular analogies were often repeated. These illustrate the need for organizations to change ("boiled frogs") and an understanding of the complexities of organizations as learning organizations ("dry monkeys").

If you place a frog in a pan of water and bring it slowly to a boil, the frog will remain in the water and will boil to death. (*Author's note:* I am led to believe this by the fable. I have never tried this, nor intend to.) However, if you try to place a frog in boiling water, it will instantly try to escape. (Again, so I am told.)

In the first instance, the frog is oblivious to the subtle and gradual changes in its environment. It will not realize its existence is imperilled until it is too late. Unfortunately, most organizations suffer the same fate. They fail to recognize the environment around them changing until the need for radical transformation becomes necessary for their survival. When the threat is sudden and dramatic, organizations are often able to respond.

Witness organizations that manufactured buggies before the advent of the automobile. Those who focused on improving their operations and improving the quality of their products were able to become the last to go out of business. Nevertheless, despite being the best producers of buggies, they failed to survive. Those that adopted their technologies to the production of automobiles not only survived the threat but also were able to become more successful than they were previously.

Organizations, however, have difficulty in learning new ways. It has been said that an experiment was once conducted where 12 monkeys were placed in a large cage. High above the floor, the experimenters placed a bunch of bananas with a rope for the monkeys to climb up to them. However, when the first monkey attempted to climb the rope, it activated a shower of water that drenched all the monkeys. After a few repetitions, the monkeys learned not to climb the rope.

The experimenters then disconnected the shower so that climbing the rope was perfectly safe. They then replaced one of the "wet" monkeys with a "dry" monkey. The new monkey quite quickly attempted to climb the rope and was stopped by the 11 wet monkeys. The experimenters continued to replace wet monkeys with dry ones until all 12 monkeys were now dry. None of these monkeys had ever experienced being drenched by the shower. Yet, no monkey was allowed by the others to climb the rope.

The iterations were continued for several "generations" of dry monkeys before finally a monkey was successful in climbing the rope and getting a banana. Organizations often suffer from the same kind of inertia. New things are not tried simply because that is not the way things are done around here. Unlike the monkeys, however, we are able to rationalize why things are done the way they are, and are able to experiment with different methods and predict the possible outcomes from doing things differently.

The simple lesson to be learned from these fables is that organizations need to be in tune with their environments so that they can proactively adapt to change. Second, organizations need to create learning cultures to prevent inertia from keeping them from reaping the benefits of trying new things.

Benefits/Expected Outcomes

The benefits of effective change management are, perhaps, obvious. Organizations embark on the process of transformation in order to survive and grow in changing environments. By deliberately and consciously managing change, organizations hope to achieve the following benefits:

— the change strategy reaps the desired results;

— the disruptive and negative impact of changes on employees and other stakeholders are minimized;

— the employees and other stakeholders understand and support the need for transformation;

— losses that might result if change does not occur are avoided (loss of revenue, loss of market share, loss of profits, decreased capitalization); and

— the organization learns to deal with change and is better positioned in adapting to future changes in their environment.

Programming/Implementation

The following elements need to be considered when planning and designing a strategy for transforming the organization to a new state:

— assessing the environment and the organization's readiness for change;

— assessing the impact of change/resistance to change;

— contingency approach to change management;

— transformational leadership; and

— downsizing and survivor management.

A. Assessing the Impact of the Change

The first step in any change process is to assess the implications of the change. This is somewhat different from the task of envisioning the change. Envisioning is about foreseeing what the organization will be like as a result of the change, and the benefits that this will bring. The assessment stage may contribute to the definition of a more accurate vision of the future state, but is much more basic. It is about the detailed way in which a change will impact on the various components of the organization. It is necessary to ensure that all aspects of the change are properly understood, so that action can be set in place to deal with the things that may make the change harder to implement, or even render it ineffective.

Part of the assessment deals with the obvious. If a factory is to be closed in one country, and production transferred to another, the initial impact is not difficult to see. If a downsizing decision will lead to the redundancy of 10% of employees, it is an immediate conclusion that action has to be taken to set a fair redundancy program that meets the requirements of employment law and any relevant collective agreements.

The less obvious requires more intense examination. For example, if 10% of employees leave the organization, how will this affect the jobs of the remaining 90%? If layers of middle managers are removed, can we assume that those at the top and bottom of the organization can continue to manage and be managed in exactly the manner of the past?

The following elements should be assessed in determining the impact of change on the organization.

1. Strategy

The change strategy should be interpreted broadly as the position the organization is trying to reach, and the means by which it intends to get there. With this broad definition, there is no need to be concerned about whether it is corporate, business unit, or departmental strategy — it covers them all. It may also be interpreted as the change the organization is making.

2. Tasks

These are the things that the organization has to do in order to make the change and operate under the new conditions. It includes the non-repetitive tasks to handle the change itself, and, as importantly, the new tasks that have to be undertaken continuously under the changed conditions.

3. People

We know what has to be done, but do we have the right people in the right numbers to do it? This looks closely at the way the change will affect the skills, attitudes and competencies of people within the organization, and should identify very carefully the actions to meet the new requirements.

4. Structure

This is the way tasks are grouped into jobs, and jobs into reporting relationships. The need is not just to look at the change itself, but also the impact on the motivation of those affected.

5. Reward Systems

It should not be assumed that existing reward systems will meet the new situation. A change to a stronger customer orientation might well mean that the current reward system for salespeople drives them in a different direction from that now intended. The reward system and the objective must be aligned.

6. Control Systems

The way in which the organization exercises control may also be inappropriate for the new situation. For example, if the aim of a change is to have a team-based approach to achieve particular results, it is pointless to continue with a control system that only assesses individual contributions.

7. Decision Processes

This heading covers both the process by which decisions are made, and who is empowered to take them.

A - B - **C**

The way in which decisions are reached often has to respond to the new shape and direction of the organization. A de-layered organization cannot function effectively unless there is clarity about empowerment (and this takes us back to how the tasks will change, and then to whether the people possess the competencies to enable empowerment to work).

8. Culture

Does the culture of the organization support or retard the intended change?

9. Information Systems

Information is part of the blood stream that makes the body corporate function. Any change can bring a need to review the information system, in terms of what is collected, how it is aggregated, and to whom it is disseminated.

To implement the integrated approach outlined above, knowledge of the present situation and of the change is required, and a measure of insight that enables an assessment to be made of the implications. Sometimes it is worth beginning with a basic review, looking at which of the numerous items under each of the headings hinders the change, which facilitates it, and which is neutral. The aim, of course, is to take action.

There are many ways of implementing such an approach, and factors that affect the choice would include the degree of secrecy about the planned change, the availability of people to undertake the assessment, and the degree of urgency. It may be desirable to use outside consultants in certain circumstances. Undoubtedly, one of the most effective ways of implementing the approach is to use task forces made up of staff specialists and line managers.

Although it is desirable to make as full an assessment as possible before the change is implemented, there may be circumstances when part of this work can only be done during the change process itself. This may still be valuable. A workshop of Human Resources specialists and line managers may be a very good way of identifying actions that need to be taken to make the change effective.

B. Resistance to Change

It would be wrong to suggest that change is always resisted, or that resistance is always bad. Most people welcome a modicum of change, and even drastic change may be accepted without question if it offers a better future than would a continuance of the present state. In other situations, there may be no resistance because of total faith in the leader. There would have been little human progress without some willingness to change. Resistance to an announced change may also be helpful in some situations, where, for example, the change had not been thoroughly thought out, and the deficiencies are brought to the fore by the objections.

However, in most situations of fundamental change, and some of incremental change, resistance may be encountered and, if not dealt with, may frustrate the change process. Although people may appear to be closed-minded and irrational, they may have good reasons to resist, and understanding those reasons can lead to strategies to overcome them.

Resistance may be overt or covert. The latter sometimes is the hardest to come to grips with because, on the surface, there appears to be agreement with the change. Covert resistance may take many forms, varying from lack of motivation, passive resistance, the spreading of rumours to frustrate the change, and sabotage. Overt resistance may be difficult to deal with, but the source is at least visible.

There may be many reasons for resistance, most of which are understandable if looked at from the employee's viewpoint. These are set out below.

— **Perceived threat of loss of job, job security or status:** often this fear is totally justified, as the change means that there will be such an impact on some of the employees.

— **A breach of the psychological contract:** something about the change may alter how a person operates in a certain job, and this may be something that is particularly valued. Although a change may not threaten title or salary, it may still be disturbing if it breaches the psychological contract. This cause is worth stressing because it is sometimes overlooked by those leading a change.

— **Resentment because a change is imposed:** this may be a particular concern when the vision is not shared, and the reasons for the change are not clear. There may be a feeling of insult if, for example, someone arrives at work one morning to find that his or her desk or workbench has been moved somewhere else without warning because management has not considered it important to tell that person about the planned change.

— **Distrust of those leading the change:** if the leader is not trusted, there may be a fear that the change is merely done for the sake of change, for his or her personal prestige, or to show that something is happening. This may lead to fear that the leader does not possess the capability to see the change through, or a feeling of being a pawn in someone else's power game.

— **A genuine belief that something important has been overlooked:** the change is opposed on the grounds of technical or specialist knowledge, and may be justified. However, this can also be a rationalization that gives respectability for resistance that has really been triggered by other causes.

— **Fear of the unknown:** venturing into a completely new situation can appear frightening when compared with the apparent safety of the old. Some people will resist the new for no other reason than that it is new.

The degree of resistance expected in relation to the urgency of the change will affect the choice of style used in the change management process. The suggestions given below for reducing resistance should be considered in relation to the situational factors, and the points made are indicative only.

— **Identify possible causes of resistance.** As part of the planning for the change, an attempt should be made to identify which of the causes are most likely to trigger resistance in different areas and levels in the organization. It should not be assumed that the cause would be the same everywhere. Although it is rarely possible to think through the triggers from the viewpoint of every individual, it may be worth doing this with one or two people who will be key to the success of the change, so that they can be given early and personal consideration.

— **Choose approaches which avoid resistance.** Forethought can sometimes mean that the same ends can be reached by means that reduce the resistance. This should not be read as a suggestion that essential changes should be abandoned because of possible problems.

— **Solicit participation and involvement.** A collaborative or consultative approach can sometimes reduce resistance, unless it is too heavily entrenched for those invited to participate to make a genuine effort to take part. Where it is not appropriate to have widespread involvement at the outset, much can often be gained by inviting involvement in the processes during the implementation of the change.

— **Communicate, communicate, communicate.** Whatever the style of the change management approach, clear and regular communication is essential to manage expectations, and to ensure that the reasons for the change are clear and everyone knows what is happening. It is not enough to paste a memo on notice boards. A complete communication strategy is needed, using a multiplicity of methods. Failure to communicate can cause resistance, where none might otherwise have existed.

C. Contingency Approach to Change Management

The right approach to change management is contingent upon the situation in the organization. The variation is not so much in the types of things that should be considered, but in the style of the change management process, and the amount of effort put into the various elements. Style in this context is related to the degree of participation in the change by those affected. The style can be collaborative wherein the manager seeks the active input of those affected by the potential change and decisions are reached through agreement or consensus. Another approach may be consultative. Here the manager seeks inputs and gives careful consideration to the opinions of others, but in the end makes the decision. In some instances, the approach may be directive. The manager decides on the course of action and leads employees through it. Finally, particularly if there is significant resistance, the approach may be coercive. Do this or else!

The issue is to determine which style is right for the particular situation. It is not hard to see how the choice of style will affect how the process is managed. There are penalties for getting the style wrong. Some may be immediate, such as a failure of the initiative. Others may be longer term, in that the change appears to have been effective, but at the cost of low morale, passive resistance, unwanted turnover of staff,

A - B - **C**

and occasionally sabotage that continues long after the change has happened.

Implementation of this concept requires a determination and consideration of those facts that are germane to the situation. Initially, eight situations will be indicated, all of which require a specific response. Later, an examination will be made of further factors that may modify those suggestions. In all situations, change has to be led. The first four situations relate to incremental change, the second four to transformational, or fundamental, change. In all cases, it is assumed that the change has significance for the organization, and we are not discussing trivial changes. Two main types of change are examined in relation to the strength of expected resistance and the degree of urgency.

1. Incremental Change (More of the Same)

Low urgency, low resistance

This situation is ideal for a collaborative approach. There is time to involve those affected by the change, which may lead to better ways of implementing it, and to higher motivation. At the same time, the widespread support for the change means that such participation should be effective.

High urgency, low resistance

In this situation, time is not on our side, unless the number of people who are affected is small. This may force a mix of collaboration and consultation, where the former is focused on fewer key people, and the majority have an opportunity to give feedback but are less involved in determining how to make the change work.

Low urgency, high resistance

Time is available, so it may be possible to use a collaborative style, but the degree of resistance means that this must also be persuasive, to try to increase the degree of support. In an incremental change situation, where people's jobs may not be threatened, it may be possible to demonstrate that the change benefits the individual as well as the organization. This is not possible on a widespread basis when redundancies are involved.

High urgency, high resistance

In this situation, there may be a need to balance the benefits of persuasive consultation against the need for a more directive approach, with persuasive under-

tones. In cases of extreme urgency and extreme resistance, the only solution is to be coercive, but this style should be used only as a last resort.

2. Transformational (or Fundamental) Change

The degree of urgency cannot be low, as there is little point in fundamental change that does not appear to be needed. The extremes are therefore high and crisis. In all fundamental change situations, the style requires a strong visionary element on top of the involvement dimension.

Low resistance, high urgency

Involvement is still appropriate, although it may vary between collaboration with key people, to consultation and informing others. The visionary element is important, and a charismatic leadership style will often work well here. Because resistance is low, people are willing to follow the lead of someone they trust who inspires them.

Low resistance, crisis situation

This situation is more difficult than low resistance, high urgency. The visionary element is important in helping the people to see how the organization can come out of the crisis, but collaboration will be restricted to a few key people. Widespread communication is important (i.e., telling it how it is, but also persuading people that the changes will solve the crisis). There may be a need to lean towards a directive approach.

High resistance, high urgency

The judgment is whether persuasive or consultative approaches can reduce the level of resistance fast enough to allow the changes to be implemented. The visionary element remains important, but the style for all except the top team may be directive, and sometimes even coercive. The change has to take place quickly. Communication and explanation remain very important, as there may be less opportunity for people to discuss the changes with senior management.

High resistance, crisis situation

A visionary dictator may offer the only solution to make the changes in time! However, in this case, even more attention needs to be put on management after the change, when people may need a much more supportive style.

Selecting the best style is not a dogmatic exercise, and there are many factors that may affect what is possible. It may be desirable to increase involvement when employees have all the skills needed for the change, but to reduce it when the contribution they can make is too limited. In situations of low morale and motivation, a judgment has to be made about whether involvement will improve morale, or reinforce the negative feelings.

Similarly, the culture of the organization may force a move to a lower level of involvement, simply because to behave differently would be viewed with suspicion. Involvement may have to be reduced when the issue is highly confidential. In all situations, it is important to consider the effect which the chosen style will have on the long-term, post-change situation, so that appropriate strategies can be put in place once the change is implemented.

D. Transformational Leadership

The management of fundamental change requires more than charismatic leadership. Many authorities have researched what is involved in the successful management of fundamental change, and ideas drawn from a number of sources have contributed to the model shown below. It is valid for all types of change situations, although for incremental change, it may not be necessary to follow every stage in the model in depth. For fundamental change, where the issues are more complex, and the future is not always a smooth transition from the past, it is vital that none is omitted. However, the style that determines how the stages are applied may vary.

Stages 1 to 3 of the model are essentially behavioural. These may get everyone excited about a change, but will not normally bring it about unless linked to stages 4 to 6, which are essentially concerned with analysis and systems, although each of these stages has behavioural implications. All the stages are connected; at any one time, they could be happening simultaneously, and the results of actions taken in any stage could affect future actions taken in any other stage. The fact that they are labelled sequentially does not mean that everything happens once, and in this order.

The initial letters of the labels provide the mnemonic EASIER, which is a memory aid and not a suggestion that this method simplifies complex change.

1. Envisioning

This is the process by which the leader of the change sets out his or her intentions as a word picture of what the future will look like after the change. It can best be compared to the famous "I have a dream" speech of Martin Luther King, and provides a coherent view of where the change will take the organization. It also acts as a beacon, a reassurance, and a driving motivation for the change.

Effect visions of the future of the organization must be believable. The employees must see that the future the organization is striving for is possible. It also must be challenging. It is difficult for employees to get excited about mundane goals. The vision must make the change effort worthwhile. It must also be coherent and consistent. If the vision seems to be fragmented and inconsistent, employees will not be able to buy in to it.

The vision needs to be clear. Employees must fully understand the direction the organization is going in and how they can contribute to it. If they do not know what is expected of them, their behaviour and conduct will not change and the objectives may not be reached. The vision should relate to the past, present and future. The future may represent discontinuity from the past, but avoid all temptation to denigrate the achievements of the past, or to criticize previous managers.

Certainly, the person formulating the vision must believe in it. The more passion he or she has for the vision, the more likely others will be compelled to follow that lead. The leader will demonstrate belief in the vision through his or her day-to-day activities. This will give employees a model to follow and help them translate through day-to-day actions.

2. Activating

This is the motivation of the organization to follow that vision. It is the process of creating commitment to it. This first means ensuring that others in the organization understand the vision and the reasons for the change, and that the vision is shared, firstly with the key players in the change, and eventually across the whole organization.

The leader must demonstrate a personal belief in the vision and in a culture change, and should be the best example of the new culture. Personal communication of the vision and its implications should stretch as far

A - B - **C**

as possible through the organization, and with frequency. The transformational leader must communicate the vision at every opportunity.

Organizations implementing change strategies should consider using workshops as a way of building commitment, and ensuring that all the implications have been understood. This is one of many ways to create opportunities for two-way communication. Another is to use all routine management meetings as a vehicle for emphasizing the message.

Personal communication is vital, but supplement this with all available tools, such as company newsletters, video, personal letters, e-mail and, where appropriate, obtain press or television coverage. Use examples of success from inside the organization to reinforce the value of the change. Deal honestly with the difficult questions, such as reductions in the number of employees; be empathetic to those losing their jobs, and ensure that they receive fair treatment and help in relocating.

Use internal training to build understanding of the change, to remove fear of failure, and to develop new competencies and skills. Pick with care the key members of the team who will help implement the change and ensure they are adequately equipped with the skills necessary to act as influence makers. Similarly, deal quickly with key managers who are frustrating the change. If they cannot be convinced to join the movement, they will need to be replaced. While this is often a difficult decision to make, particularly if the manager is a long-service employee who functioned well under the organization's previous culture, failure to act may sabotage the change process.

Empower others in the organization to play a part in the change process, and ensure that they have the necessary change management skills. Realize that leading change takes skills that may not have been needed in the past, and either acquire these or choose someone to work closely with on the change process who has those skills. Do not ignore difficult situations that require tough decisions — they will not get any better unless they are addressed.

3. Supporting

This refers to the encouragement, coaching, and other help given to those involved in the change, to help them fulfil their parts in the change process. The trans-

formational leader needs to demonstrate confidence in the other members of the team who are helping to implement the change. He or she will give coaching where needed, and use this as a means of boosting confidence. The leader will ensure that all involved are properly empowered, and that there is clarity in the role they have to fulfil.

Although the pursuit of the vision must be unwavering, the transformational leader must make provisions to listen to people's concerns. The leader's behaviour must be consistent; it is not credible to behave differently on change matters than on day-to-day management. In fact, his or her day-to-day management of the organization has to be designed in a way that fully supports the contemplated change. The leader must live the vision. He or she must give a high priority to providing support, and not allow other pressures of time to push this activity into the background.

4. Installing

This term covers the essential planning steps that ensure that the change can take place. It may be a timetable for change, a budget, a critical path analysis, or one or many of a number of similar tools and systematic approaches. It provides a clear analysis of all the actions that can be foreseen, which must take place to make the change work, and provides the resources that make this possible.

5. Ensuring

This is the monitoring and controlling process, which enables the progress of the change to be monitored, and further action taken, if things are not working to plan. There may be very strong behavioural implications within a control process, since the intention is to make things happen and hold people accountable, as well as to track overall progress.

6. Recognizing

This is the way the role played in the change by key people in the change is acknowledged. It may be through salary increases, special bonuses, promotion, or less tangible marks such as acknowledgement as a source of expertise and advice, or even publicly expressed thanks. Measures such as an annual chairman's award to a person or team can also have a role here.

In addition, the leader should:

— set adequate budgets to provide for the costs of the change;

— ensure that the plans and other mechanisms are specific to the changes, so that it becomes possible to monitor progress;

— set realistic timetables for the implementation of the numerous actions that must be undertaken to implement the change; and

— make sure that the accounting and other information systems can provide feedback of progress at regular intervals — a plan that cannot be monitored may have little value in the change process.

E. Downsizing and Survivor Management

Change management does not always involve significant reductions in the workforce. In fact, it has become an unfortunate, popular perception that change management strategies (like re-engineering) are synonymous with the major loss of jobs. Even when the changes result in making certain positions redundant, it is possible to retrain people and use them to help grow the new revitalized organization.

However, most change strategies are arrived at through necessity. Organizations faced with the question of their very survival are usually the ones who choose to reinvent themselves. Few organizations who are thriving in their existing environments decide to embark on major change initiatives to meet the challenges of a possible future threat. Therefore, those organizations that do undergo major change can often ill afford to carry extra employees as a buffer for growth. So, while sound in theory, the reality is that most change management strategies are going to have to deal with a major displacement of people.

A change where people lose their jobs has an obvious impact on those who have to leave. Somewhat less obvious, but to be expected, is the impact on the survivors (those that remain), and the effect this can have on the ability of the organization to perform effectively after the change. The pressure of the moment may direct attention to the task of dealing with those who have to go, and it is easy to overlook the fact that part of the survivors' reactions and feelings are shaped at this time. Early attention can reduce the problems that may otherwise arise.

The reactions of survivors to the forced departure of colleagues may include disbelief, fear, anger, a sense of betrayal, and a loss of trust in management (which can add to the other negative feelings, if previous levels of trust have been high). Relief at not being forced to leave may be tempered by feelings of guilt, especially if those who survive realize that their own survival has more to do with luck than merit.

A number of research findings about the factors that influence the feelings experienced by survivors are set out below.

⇨ Whether the loss of jobs was expected (as in a failing organization), or seen as a bolt from the blue (as in a successful firm where the need to change is not obvious).

⇨ The perception of the fairness in the treatment of those who are told to leave (financial treatment, help given, the basis of selection and the way they were told). Adverse feelings may be mitigated if the perception is that those who leave will find new jobs easily.

⇨ The degree to which the jobs of the survivors are interdependent with those of the leavers. Insecurity may be heightened if the survivors can no longer see how they themselves will function after the change.

⇨ The feeling of identification by the survivors with those leaving. There may be little empathy among the organization's employees in Vancouver to the plight of those affected by actions taken in the Quebec factory, because of lack of contact, or little perception of any commonality of values.

⇨ The individual feelings of insecurity of those who survive, which will be affected by personal experiences they have had of previous redundancy situations. Not all survivors will have the same reactions. Apart from differences because individuals are not clones, level in the organization and function will alter the perceptions and, hence, the feelings of survivors.

The model of transformational leadership above can be used as a background to the specific matters listed here. Survivor reactions may be more beneficial to the organization if attention is given to shaping expectations at the outset, and taking actions to reduce or mitigate the negative feelings.

A - B - **C**

⇨ *Manage expectations up front.* This can be assisted by ensuring that clear explanations are given to both survivors and leavers of the need for the change, that the plan for the change (including the timetable) is clear, and that the survivors can see a future beyond the upheavals of the redundancies. If the vision for the future is understood, and commitment to it is built, the negative feelings of survivors will be reduced.

⇨ *Provide opportunities for consultation and two-way communication.* It is rarely possible to have widespread collaboration down the organization when the decision will result in the widespread loss of jobs, and the uncertainty before decisions are made creates more problems. However, once the decision is announced, it is possible to consult with people in relation to their specific jobs, concerning how to make a success of the new situation. As a minimum, opportunities should be created for two-way communication to enable issues and concerns to be raised, and properly dealt with. It is essential that this is dealt with adequately, and that people are not left with a feeling that they have been fobbed off or that management does not know what will happen next. Both approaches can reduce anxiety and the consultation approach may remove some of the feelings of powerlessness. Apart from giving further opportunities for making the reasons for the change understood, such moves can help remove individual uncertainties about the roles people are expected to play after the change.

⇨ *Behaviour towards those who are leaving.* There are many true stories of appallingly handled redundancy situations where, for example, a person is not told of the situation by a member of staff, but is simply handed a note on leaving the place of work, which says little more than "don't come back on Monday". Survivors need to feel that the organization accorded those who had to leave the dignity due to human beings, that they were given time to say goodbye to colleagues who were staying, that the financial terms given to them were fair, and that the organization did all that it could to help them seek replacement jobs. Survivors need to feel that the choice of people to leave was fair, and that it was not a question of old scores being settled. Communication by the organization can make some of this clear, but the main

impact will come from what those who leave say to those who stay. Forbidding people to return to their desks and having them escorted from the premises by a security person does not prevent them from being in touch with former colleagues. One example of bad treatment will spread far faster than 100 examples of good treatment, and the only way to prevent an unnecessary impact on survivors is to ensure that there are no bad examples.

⇨ *Training for the new roles.* One way to demonstrate that future roles have been properly considered is to provide training for people who will need different competencies in the new situation. This not only demonstrates that management knows what it is about, but also implies that the survivors are considered to be important to the organization.

Role of the Human Resources Practitioner

The Human Resources practitioner should be involved in all major changes, in both the planning and implementation stages, as there are few complex changes that do not have "people" implications.

The Human Resources practitioner is rarely the leader of a change management process, but should play a major part in it. The role, and the information needed, will vary with the nature of the change. In a downsizing and de-layering initiative, for example, the Human Resources practitioner requires information to determine a fair redundancy program, to set the terms for this and for any early retirements, and to determine whether employees need help in finding other jobs. There needs to be knowledge of the way jobs will change as a result of the initiative, and the extent to which retraining should be provided to help the change. Information on morale is important, so that actions can be taken to improve the situation where possible.

Consideration needs to be given to the longer-term implications of the change, such as career management. The Human Resources practitioner must be able to give advice on the industrial relations climate, and the steps needed to negotiate changes with employees and unions, when this is necessary. Perhaps the most important information needed, and the most difficult for Human Resources Managers to think about, is an assessment of the implications of such a change on the whole organization, so that attention is given to managing the survivors, and to ensuring that Human Resources' involvement does not stop with the redundancy exercise.

Potentially everyone in the organization can be affected by the way change is managed. The responsibility for ensuring the success of the change management process falls on different managers, at various levels, depending on the nature of the change. So any manager could find himself or herself in a position where change has to be initiated and managed. The prime responsibility is with line managers, although the support of the Human Resources function and other specialists may be important for success.

When the change is fundamental and corporate-wide, the responsibility is clearly with the chief executive, the supreme line manager of the organization, and ideally supported by other key executives. In some situations, the chief executive may be the only visionary who initially sees the need for the change, and part of the task is to create a shared vision across the organization.

The planning and organizational development managers, if the organization has them, may play a key role. Sometimes a chief executive may appoint a number of advisors to help with the change process, who may be drawn from anywhere in the organization. External consultants may also be engaged.

Barriers to Success/Common Pitfalls

⇨ Failure to think through all the implications of a change, so that avoidable problems are not prevented from arising.

⇨ Inadequate attention is given to systems and processes for monitoring the change.

⇨ Failure is made to consider the behavioural implications of the change.

⇨ Inability to think of how people in the organization will perceive the change.

⇨ Inadequate change leadership is put in place.

⇨ Responsibility for the change process is abdicated to consultants and staff.

⇨ Senior management fails to demonstrate their belief in the change through their actions.

⇨ Failure to identify and deal with obstacles to change.

⇨ There is a belief that the benefits of the change are so self-evident that everyone will welcome them.

⇨ Consideration of the implications of a change is cut off at too early a stage (e.g., the de-layered organization has to be working effectively for the change to be completed). The main task begins after the redundancies of those who have to leave, although some organizations treat this as the conclusion of the change process.

People in the organization sometimes welcome change, but this is not always the case, particularly when people are in fear of losing their jobs, or when they are forced to make changes with which they do not agree. Sometimes resistance is almost subconscious, in that a manager may agree with the logic, but still be a passive resistor because of changes to his or her psychological contract. Unfortunately, there is no single solution to overcoming these problems, as the best approach is situational. The right solution depends on the degree of urgency of the change (how much time is available to overcome resistance), the depth and ferocity of resistance (which affects both the time needed to overcome it, and the actions that may be successful), the capabilities of the management team, and the importance of the change to the organization. Communication and the development of strategies to deal with the problems that concern people are always important.

Consultation and involvement, often given as the one route to success, are only possible in some situations. No amount of involvement would have removed resistance to the changes that have taken place in newspaper production, and the dictatorial approach taken by management was probably the only way forward.

A critical barrier to success in change management is ignorance. Although the dictatorial approach is appropriate in certain circumstances, it is sometimes applied through lack of understanding of how to manage change. Ignorance can be removed by management training, the hiring of people with expertise in this area, and/or the use of external consultants. However, it remains one of the areas on which the Human Resources practitioner should concentrate efforts, as enormous and avoidable damage can be done to the organization by managers who attempt to implement change without understanding how to manage it.

A - B - **C**

COACHING

Definition/Background

Coaching is a powerful tool which managers can use to improve the performance of individuals and of teams. Managerial coaching can be defined as "helping people to develop and perform to their full potential". This means that the manager is focusing on the needs and style of the learner, as contrasted with a more traditional telling or instructing approach. The outcome is that people are helped to act independently and to solve their own problems.

The emphasis in a managerial coaching activity is on the employee who is encouraged to take ownership and responsibility for his or her own development and performance. The staff member is engaged in a learning process, a key element which distinguishes coaching from traditional delegation. The intended output from coaching is the improved performance of individuals (i.e., performance in relation to the overall goals and objectives of the organization). The aim is to narrow the gap between the individual's actual and potential performance, either in his or her current job or in relation to a possible future career.

The purpose of managerial coaching can be condensed into the phrase "making the best use of your best asset". A manager who is entrusted with the stewardship of any major resource of an organization would be expected not just to maintain but also to develop that resource. Managers should similarly be expected to develop their human resources and this should be one of the key measures of their performance as managers.

Thus, the goal of the manager as coach is to enable the individual being coached (the learner) to learn, grow and develop. And the purpose of this learning is clearly understood by all parties to be to improve the performance of the individual staff member. In this way, of course, the performance of the employee's manager is also enhanced, as is that of the whole organization.

Most people would probably argue that learning is a desirable goal in its own right. But we do not need to rely on that general argument in order to convince managers that coaching is a worthwhile activity in the

organization and a very important part of their managerial role.

Coaching does not need to start with a learner's performance problem (remedial coaching). A manager can equally well coach an excellent performer to even better results (developmental coaching). This point should be stressed because much of the available coaching literature (especially American) appears to assume that coaching is always remedial.

Although this section focuses on the need for managers to coach the staff who report to them directly, the insights and skills needed to be an effective coach are in fact needed by almost every individual in today's organizations.

A coaching approach does not, by itself, change the structure of an organization. However, coaching and structure are closely linked in at least two ways:

1. An organization where coaching is accepted and widespread is more likely to be able to introduce and operate some of the newer structures and ways of working that are becoming increasingly important, such as:

   — cross-functional teams;

   — project teams;

   — self-directed work teams;

   — wider spans of control; and

   — fewer layers of management and supervision.

2. Conversely, an organization that has introduced these structures is probably in a position to promote coaching as its preferred management style; indeed, they may be unable to operate effectively in these structures without adopting coaching.

Benefits/Expected Outcomes

There are many individual managers who are enthusiastic about acting as coaches; they have acquired the necessary insights and skills through formal courses, by being coached by their own managers, by reading and study or, more intuitively, by just trying it and finding an approach that works.

A - B - C

There are also many organizations that are adopting a coaching approach, usually as part of a broader culture change program towards a more empowering and less directive management style. They are equipping their managers to act as coaches and are also preparing staff members to be coached. They are convinced that:

— coaching is the most cost-effective way to develop people because real work is being carried out as the learning vehicle and there are no external course fees or expenses to be paid;

— the hands-off approach of real coaching engenders commitment, independence and innovation in staff at all levels; and

— coaching is, in many cases, the only way for managers to operate in today's business and organizational climate.

To be more specific, coaching can contribute to enhancing the organization's level of performance, by encouraging people to value learning and to be more open to change and providing instant feedback about performance, and thereby accelerating the learning and performance improvement processes.

Managing people in new types of structure as, for example, cross-functional teams (perhaps in re-engineered business processes), project teams, self-directed work teams, or where managers have wider spans of control as the result of a delayering exercise, requires a different managerial approach over the traditional delegating and instructing.

Developing individuals is gaining more recognition as a key managerial competency. In particular, it can reap the following benefits:

— it is seen as a means of helping people to develop other competencies;

— many larger organizations have embraced mentoring (which is a form of coaching by somebody who is not the direct line manager of the learner);

— organizations get more value for money from formal training;

— coaching/mentoring are means to meet the expectations and wishes of many of today's younger staff;

— it is an increasingly necessary means of grooming a successor, particularly in smaller organizations; and

— enlightened organizations use it as a way of developing plateaued staff in new areas.

Other benefits gained from training managers in coaching skills include:

— managers taking on their first people-management role can make coaching part of their natural way of working;

— managers with many years' experience of managing people would benefit from reflecting on their style and acquiring any necessary extra coaching skills;

— individuals who act as mentors to staff outside their direct control will find that a coaching approach is the most effective way to help the other person to learn;

— managers of cross-functional or project teams may not always be responsible for the formal appraisal and development of their team members, but a coaching approach may be highly relevant to their day-to-day role (especially when their team members have specialist skills and knowledge with which the manager is less familiar, and who cannot therefore be developed by the manager instructing them);

— managers and specialists in supporting functions (e.g., Human Resources Management, finance, information systems) often need to help their colleagues from other areas understand key concepts and frameworks. Coaching skills will help them to carry out this role more effectively; and

— even trainers who conduct classic classroom programs will find it useful to develop the non-directive coaching skills needed to balance their formal instructional skills.

Programming/Implementation

If an organization develops (or selects) a coaching skills training program, this should include such learning objectives as:

— to appreciate how coaching differs from traditional management;

— to understand the benefits which coaching brings to individuals, to managers and to the whole organization;

— to be able to create a climate in which people feel able to take limited risks and to make (and learn from) mistakes;

— to develop the face-to-face skills of coaching individuals and groups;

— to be able to identify opportunities for implementing coaching which meet both the needs of the organization and the personal interests and aspirations of individuals;

— to identify and work constructively with organizational factors which support or hinder coaching; and

— to enhance their own receptiveness to being developed through coaching methods.

Coaching Techniques

The core coaching skills are as follows:

Observation and analysis: the ability to watch a learner in action, to conclude what is needed for him or her to raise the level of performance still higher, and to identify the best way to help that individual.

Structuring the coaching process: this involves selecting the right approach for each individual learner, preparing carefully, deciding when and how to intervene, agreeing upon realistic but challenging goals and plans.

Questioning: this is the absolute number-one skill. It is sometimes referred to as the Socratic method of teaching, after the famous philosopher who is credited with its introduction. The "GROW" model (see page 82) is a useful and practical framework. The coach does not use questions to get information (which is, of course, why we ask questions in normal conversations), but to develop the learner's awareness, sharpen focus, stimulate responsibility, help find his or her own answers and to ensure that he or she takes ownership of the coaching process.

Listening: there is obviously no point in asking questions without the skill of listening to the answers. This also includes tuning in to the unspoken messages from the learner (i.e., being sensitive to his or her tone of voice, body language, personal wishes, expectations and emotions).

Giving and receiving feedback: managers often feel uncomfortable about giving direct feedback to their staff, whether positive or negative (and are even

less comfortable about receiving it). Yet, people often complain that they have been starved of feedback and would have appreciated more of it, even if it is negative.

Communicating: even if the manager prefers to use a questioning approach to coaching, there will be times when he or she must pass on information, ideas and instructions in a more direct way.

Motivating: the coach can motivate the learner by showing his or her own enthusiasm for coaching, respect for the learner, his or her wish and expectation that the learner will succeed, and an appreciation for success.

Delivering the Training

The hands-on skills of coaching cannot be developed simply by reading books or watching videos. Two possible approaches are as follows:

1. An experienced coach can actually coach another manager to develop coaching skills (whether or not they work together in their day-to-day roles). This provides a valuable synergy, because the process of the coaching is then, at the same time, its content.

2. There are business schools and consultants who can conduct coaching skills training programs. These can be a cost-effective way of developing the skills of a number of managers at the same time and can ensure a common language and approach throughout an organization.

Skills Audit

A particularly useful tool in assessing a coaching program is a skills audit at the individual level. This requires a feedback instrument, such as a "Coaching Behaviours Questionnaire", which managers can give to their staff (and to their own manager). This identifies a number of coaching behaviours, and the staff concerned respond by indicating how often they see their manager acting in each of these ways.

This is done anonymously and the results are presented by a tutor to the manager concerned in such a way that individual feedback cannot be directly linked to the respondent (although both parties are encouraged to discuss this in person later if they wish to do so). Managers complete a self-perception form of the same instrument and then compare their own view of their coaching style with the views of their learners. In this way, they identify specific areas where they can develop their skills further.

Such a questionnaire could be used again after, say, six months as an evaluation instrument. It will indicate whether managers are perceived to have changed their coaching behaviours and whether these changes are appropriate.

If a manager tries to implement newly-polished coaching skills, it is important that the employee's own manager supports him or her in this — in fact, acting as his or her coach. For this reason (among others), a top-down approach is highly desirable if an organization-wide move towards a coaching culture is being introduced.

However, a manager should not be discouraged from trying to act as a coach if his or her own manager seems unaware or unsupportive of coaching. There are many examples of managers who have become enthusiastic about coaching and who have practised it surreptitiously like a virus, infecting that part of the organization's body which immediately surrounds them, but taking care to be discreet enough not to trigger off a rejection by the corporate immune system!

Since questioning is the most important coaching skill (and usually the most underdeveloped), the example below is based on a particular model of questioning presented by Sir John Whitmore in *Coaching for Performance* (Nicholas Brealy Publishing, London, 1992). It is called "GROW" (**G**oals, **R**eality, **O**ptions, **W**ill), which reminds the coach to ask the following questions:

Goals

- What is it that the learner wishes specifically to learn?

- How will the learner know if he or she has reached the goal?

- When will the learner wish to achieve the goal?

- Is the learner challenged?

Reality

- How would the learner rate his or her present skill level in this area?

- What has the learner done already to try to reach his or her goal?

- Whose help or support does the learner need in order to reach his or her goal?

- Who else does the learner know who has been successful in what he or she is trying to do? What can he or she learn from them?

- Are there any internal or external obstacles or constraints holding the learner back?

Options

- What else could the learner do?

- If money was no problem, if the learner was in complete control, if the learner had a clean sheet (no politics, no history), what could he or she do?

Will

- What is the learner's own level of commitment to achieving this goal?

- How would the learner score his or her own commitment (on a 0–10 scale)?

- Are there other priorities which will take the learner's energy and motivation?

Managers may well be intellectually convinced of the value of coaching, but unsure where to start in practice. Your starting point could be yourself, it could be your learner, it could be your organization.

Starting with You, the Coach

Whenever you perform a task that somebody else could do, you prevent yourself from doing a task which only you can do. Which of the tasks that you currently perform could, in fact, be delegated as coaching assignments for one of your staff?

- *Decisions which you make most frequently.* Delegating some of these would give you the biggest payoff in terms of saving your own time.

- *Tasks which you enjoy the most.* Have you perhaps kept these for yourself when they should have been delegated or shared a long time ago?

- *Tasks which you do not enjoy.* It is possible that somebody else might actually enjoy doing something that you find boring or which no longer challenges you.

- *Tasks in which you are particularly competent.* Is it not time to coach other people to acquire some of these competencies? How can you be released for promotion if your personal skills and knowledge are irreplaceable?

- *Tasks in which you are less competent.* There are likely some tasks which your staff could do better than you. Coach them to do so.

Starting with the Learner

- *Looking at his or her present job.* How could your learner be coached to perform even better in his or her current job? This might mean remedial coaching (where you have identified that there is some sort of performance problem), or developmental coaching (where a learner who is already a good performer is coached to broaden his or her job, to extend his or her repertoire of skills or to take on more responsibility).

- *Looking to his or her future.* What new skills or knowledge does the learner need for his or her next job?

- *Offering resources to the learner.* For example, some organizations give employees a sum of money to spend on a learning project of their own choice, with no preconditions about it being related to their current or future jobs. Such organizations believe that it is in their own interests if staff at all levels are excited about learning and have developed some learning skills.

Starting with the Organization

Instead of starting by considering the individuals concerned (you and the learner), you could start by looking at the current and future needs of your organization. For example, you might be planning to introduce a new computerized information system, to expand your range of products or services, to set up a quality improvement team, or introduce some sort of process re-engineering. Could any of these tasks be assigned to somebody as a learning project?

If so, it will be important to remember to identify two different types of objectives — task objectives and learning objectives. Without the former, you may miss some real practical benefits to your organization; without the latter, you may waste the opportunity for some real learning and development for the individuals concerned.

The Diary Challenge

Step One

Look back in your diary over the last three months. Can you find anything that you did yourself but that (in hindsight) could have been used as a learning opportunity for one of your staff? Was it essential that you made a presentation, met a customer, handled a problem, attended a meeting, received some visitors, concluded a negotiation?

Step Two

Now look ahead in your diary for the next few months. What have you written there as a task for yourself, but which you could coach one of your staff to do instead?

Delegation

Do you have plans to attend a training course, go to a conference, make an overseas trip or take a holiday? If so, you will no doubt delegate some key tasks to your staff to handle in your absence. Some of these will be fairly routine and are unlikely to inspire anybody to heights of creativity or learning, so coaching would not be the right word to use. However, with some forethought and preparation, your impending absence gives you an opportunity to delegate more important work to somebody — provided that you are prepared to take the time to coach him or her. You could even plan to be absent at a critical time, in order to persuade a hesitant learner to take on a new task.

As this section is aimed at individual managers who want to get started with coaching, below is a sample of what some real-life managers have said about their daily role as coach. One of the key messages is that coaching can be a mixture of formal and informal, structured and spontaneous activities. It is by no means limited to large, formal coaching projects.

> Coaching is very important, but it does take time: telling people the answer is usually the quickest solution, but this is not so effective in the longer term.

> Coaching often takes place informally, when people just drop in to bounce ideas around with me. In fact, these discussions are often the most effective for solving current problems: people are less guarded, more open, and they find it easier to recognize and discuss their own feelings. But you do need a lot of mutual trust for this to work.

A - B - **C**

I try to get my people to coach each other. Mary is working on this too — why don't the two of you get together and share ideas?

When we reach an agreement about a coaching assignment, I often apply what I call the sleep test: we double-check the next day that we are both still committed to what we agreed. There is always a risk that we jump to conclusions too quickly at a busy meeting, or that we have different perceptions of exactly what was agreed. The sleep test also helps me to resolve my own doubts if I am not quite sure that they can handle the assignment; I have often convinced myself by the next day, whereas I would damage their self-confidence if I reacted too quickly at the earlier discussions.

Coaching for the future is more important than remedial coaching: but it is also more difficult, because of the time pressures. One of the best opportunities to do this is at a formal performance review meeting, where future development should always be an agenda item. This works well here, because we have these meetings every quarter.

Right now, I am working with one of my people to groom him to become a senior product manager. We have agreed exactly which competencies he will need to demonstrate to show he is ready for this promotion; we have agreed success criteria for these; and we have agreed a number of extra tasks which will enable him to acquire these competencies.

Sometimes I think you should allow people to do things simply because they want to, even if there is no immediately visible bottom line benefit. For example, I agreed recently to one of my people spending some time on a project to help handicapped children.

My advice to managers who are considering coaching? Just try it! You will have to work at it, but it will give you great satisfaction as well.

The following framework can be used as a checklist of the most important coaching roles. Managers may decide that they themselves are not the best individuals to fill every single role. However, they should be aware that these roles do need to be filled and should ensure that the learner has access to other people who can do so.

✓ *Motivation:* stimulating the learner's enthusiasm for the learning activity.

✓ *Role model:* showing what is possible, what success looks like, and the benefits of this.

✓ *Feedback provider:* helping the learner to identify areas where he or she can develop further (not necessarily areas of weakness).

✓ *"Accountant":* somebody to whom the learner has made a commitment for which he or she feels accountable.

✓ *Opportunity:* creating and supporting opportunities for learning.

✓ *Expert:* a process expert (in learning strategies, organizational processes, coaching skills), or (perhaps less importantly) a content expert or specialist.

✓ *Dialogue partner:* stimulating the learner's reflective thinking (e.g., by questioning techniques).

✓ *Practice partner:* helping the learner to test and sharpen specific skills.

✓ *Assignment broker:* identifying and assigning specific projects or tasks which can act as learning opportunities.

✓ *Feedback provider:* helping the learner to review and evaluate his or her own progress.

✓ *Support:* building confidence and self-esteem, reinforcing successes.

✓ *Counsellor:* helping the learner to deal with the emotional side of learning.

✓ *Friend:* showing the learner that he or she has an ally and supporter.

✓ *Cheerleader:* encouraging from the sidelines, while the learner performs; expressing and giving confidence.

✓ *Reinforcer:* acknowledging and rewarding progress and success.

In order to implement a coaching approach, managers need to reflect on the following aspects of their personal values and way of working.

Personal Values

The coach's values will shine through his or her actions. A coach who believes strongly in the importance of helping people to learn and to grow will communicate this in all sorts of subtle and unintended ways. By contrast, a manager who is only acting the role of a coach, not convinced of its value, will find it almost impossible to hide this insincerity from the learner.

The Coach's Motivation

It is important for coaches to reflect on their own motivation before they embark on a coaching project. They can rate their readiness and enthusiasm to coach by asking themselves the following questions:

1. Will there be a clear business benefit if I coach this person?

2. Will my own manager recognize my efforts in coaching this person?

3. Will I get personal satisfaction from coaching?

4. Can I organize my own time to coach?

5. Will this person welcome being coached?

6. Am I confident of my own competence in coaching?

7. Will my colleagues accept that my time is well spent in coaching?

Self-awareness

Before managers start to coach, they should reflect on how they themselves operate and why they are successful. The reasons for their success may not be immediately obvious, especially in areas of human skills such as handling people or dealing with customers.

Flexibility: A Range of Options

The effective coach can accept that a range of options exists and that there is not just one solution or answer. Flexibility means having the humility to acknowledge that you may not always be right and that there may be other ways to do things which you are not aware of.

Also, because no two learners are the same, and no two learning situations are identical, the coach must be flexible enough to choose an appropriate coaching approach or style. There is, in fact, an unexpected reward for the really flexible coach: his or her learner will find solutions and answers which the coach never dreamed of.

Coaching Style

Effective coaches are aware of their own preferred way of working (personal style), and are also aware of the impact that this might have on the learner. They are able to adopt a style that is not their usual preferred choice if they judge that this is necessary. There are

many models of management style and personal style, and there are many valuable instruments that can help coaches to look more objectively at their own preferences and behaviours.

Directive

In this approach, the coach takes the leading role on behalf of his or her learner. It takes into account the first three interventions:

1. *Prescribing:* the coach gives directions, advice and recommendations to the learner.

2. *Informing:* the coach gives information and knowledge to the learner.

3. *Confronting:* the coach challenges the learner's assumptions and stimulates that individual's awareness of his or her own behaviour, attitudes or beliefs.

Facilitative

In this approach, the coach helps the learners to become autonomous and to take responsibility for themselves and for their own learning. It takes into account the last three interventions:

1. *Cathartic:* the coach helps the learner to a process of tension release and to get rid of, or come to terms with, emotions which are blocking his or her progress.

2. *Catalytic:* the coach helps the learner to a process of self-discovery, to self-directed learning and to owning and solving his or her own problems without involving the coach directly in the change.

3. *Supporting:* the coach builds up the learner's self-esteem, self-confidence and self-respect.

Each of these interventions may be needed at different times during a coaching project. What is needed from the coach is to select the right approach and to use it with sensitivity and skill.

Each individual coach will find some of these interventions easier and more comfortable than others. For example, a hard-driving, results-oriented manager may well find it difficult to adopt the cathartic or catalytic approaches, since these require him or her to coach in an indirect and hands-off manner. A more people-oriented manager, on the other hand, might find it difficult to give people challenging feedback and to confront their mistakes and assumptions when necessary. Thus, the core message of Heron's model (as with most models of personal style) is that the most effective coach is the one with the widest range of options from which he or she can select.

Role of the Human Resources Practitioner

In situations where it is individual managers in an organization who decide that they want to act as coaches, there is little direct impact on the Human Resources practitioner (apart from those practitioners who want to act as coaches themselves).

The most likely impact in this case is that managers will approach Human Resources practitioners to ask how they can acquire the necessary skills and tools to be effective coaches. Therefore, the practitioner will find it useful to keep abreast of ideas in this field (through books, videos, articles, conferences) and will need to be able to recommend training programs to equip managers with these skills.

If, however, there is an organization-wide move towards coaching (probably as part of a broader and fundamental culture change), the practitioner will need to be much more closely involved. He or she has a role to support the initiative by:

— diagnosing the current climate and practice in the organization (e.g., by means of employee or opinion surveys) — inputs to the change;

— working with management to define the desired new approach — outputs from the change; and

— consulting with management about how to introduce the change — the process of change.

Managerial coaching is much more than the application of some particular face-to-face skills when managing individuals or teams. It can only be effective if a number of organizational conditions are met. Therefore, the Human Resources practitioner will be concerned about such issues as:

- Does a climate exist in which people are willing to take the risk of learning and applying new skills and, if not, how can this be developed?

- Is it a required performance indicator for all managers that they invest time in developing and coaching their staff, and how can they be formally appraised for this?

- What sort of balance do managers strike between short-term financial results and long-term people development?

- Are top managers setting visible examples in coaching their own staff?

Barriers to Success/Common Pitfalls

The effective coach will be sensitive to potential organizational barriers to coaching, and will find ways of operating within these constraints, choosing when to work with the grain of the organization and when to take a stand on his or her beliefs. The barriers might include:

⇨ **hard factors**, such as procedures and systems (e.g., performance appraisal and reward systems, availability of resources for learning);

⇨ **soft factors**, such as styles and ways of working, attitudes to risks, tolerance of mistakes, willingness to give and receive open and honest feedback, openness to new ideas.

At a personal level, managers give a number of reasons why they do not do more coaching.

"I don't have the necessary technical knowledge to coach my staff." It is generally accepted in the world of sport that the best coaches are not necessarily the best performers. However, managers are often reluctant to accept that this principle applies to them too: "I couldn't coach John to do his job better, because he does it better than I could already!" This shows a fundamental misunderstanding of what coaching can achieve. Perhaps this is because such managers focus on telling and teaching rather than on helping to learn. It may be that their staff also have an expectation that "the boss knows best".

"I don't have the time to coach." The classic vicious circle of: "I'm overworked — so I don't have time to coach — so I do it all myself — so I'm overworked".

"I won't get the visibility or the credit if I coach my people to do things in my place." "I feel I'll lose control if I coach instead of teach."

"I've never acquired any coaching skills."

"If I get too close to the learner, I won't feel able to take any tough decisions which might be needed."

"I enjoy my work too much to want to share it."

"Coaching isn't recognized or rewarded in this organization."

"If I coach my people too well, they will be a threat to me."

"If I coach my people too well, they will leave me."

"I prefer my people to remain dependent on me, so I don't want to coach them."

Many of the possible traps have already been alluded to above. They include the following:

At the Level of the Organization

⇨ Expecting managers to seize on coaching with enthusiasm when they do not perceive their own managers acting as coaches.

⇨ Expecting managers to coach when they do not believe that the time and energy that they invest will be recognized or rewarded.

⇨ Prescribing desirable changes in behaviour (e.g., coaching), without ensuring that the organization's systems, procedures and practices are in line with (and actually encourage and reward) the new behaviours.

⇨ Not providing training (or coaching) support for managers to equip them with the skills and confidence to act as coaches.

At the Level of the Individual Coaching Manager

⇨ Offering (or imposing) solutions before the learner has time to find his or her own solution.

⇨ Imposing coaching when it is not wanted.

⇨ Assuming that everybody learns in the same way as the coach.

⇨ Adopting a style of coaching that is actually disguised directing or pseudo-coaching.

⇨ Starting a coaching project but not completing it with an in-depth learning review.

⇨ Starting a coaching project but taking over or interfering so that the learner feels no ownership of his or her own learning.

⇨ Pushing a learner to undertake an activity without adequate resources or preparations.

⇨ Not listening to the learner's ideas. (Why should the coach imagine that he or she has a monopoly on creativity and wisdom?)

⇨ Not obtaining the learners' commitment and enthusiasm. (Why should they want to be coached?)

⇨ Handling the learner's mistakes in such a way that he or she feels punished or humiliated.

The list is extensive and could be much longer.

COMPETENCY

Definition/Background

Managerial competencies can be described in a number of ways, and despite the widespread use of the term in Human Resources development contexts, there is not at present a clear and shared understanding of what it means. One reason for this is that different practitioners have different areas of interest (e.g., recruitment, assessment, job design, or training and development) and these interests will colour the notion of competencies with which they work. For example, there is a sharp contrast between the way that competency is defined under various provincial statutes and the way it is defined in competency-based management development systems used by organizations.

An organizational approach to defining competence is based on the underlying characteristics of a person. These characteristics can be predictors of the effective and/or superior performance of that person in a particular job.

An underlying characteristic, for example, can be:

— a motive;

— a trait;

— a skill;

— an aspect of one's self-image or social role;

— a body of knowledge.

These competencies can be identified through such techniques as critical incident review, behaviourally-based interviews and performance management tools (e.g., 360-degree feedback). *The objective is to identify dimensions of behaviour or personal qualities that differentiate effective or superior performance.* A set of competencies that are identified and validated in this way can then serve as criteria for assessment and development, performance management and recruitment processes.

The concept of competency implies standards of performance; distinctions are often made between basic or "threshold" competencies and high-performance competencies, and between differing levels of performance (ineffective, effective, superior) of any given competency.

It is important to note that the whole notion of competency, as it is generally used, is based on the assumption that management activity can be broken down into a set of individual competencies which, if performed well, will ensure effectiveness. Critics of the approach emphasize the danger of oversimplifying or mechanizing what is a complex, social activity. It is easy to recognize that managers may be assessed as possessing a competency but that they may not be able to use that competency effectively across a wide range of situations, or that they may choose when and how to use it in inappropriate ways. These limitations are worth bearing in mind when considering the use of a competency approach.

In today's increasingly complex and competitive environment, an organization's sustainable advantage depends on the quality and adaptability of its management. The key purpose of a competency approach is to improve the overall effectiveness of the organization by improving the individual effectiveness of managers, as well as by providing a common language and focus to performance management in general. The identification of key competencies can provide a benchmark that aligns the recruitment, assessment and development of managers to the strategic business goals of the organization.

A competency approach can be a support to ongoing strategic change because it focuses management attention on required behavioural changes and it provides a framework for relevant feedback to managers. It can help to develop a culture in which a vision of effective performance is shared and understood in terms that are immediately relevant to managers and is reinforced by the organization's appraisal and reward systems.

Competency can also serve as an important tool for individual self-development. Managers are increasingly taking, or being asked to take, responsibility for their own development. In order to do this, they need to have a way of building an accurate picture of their own effectiveness and identifying gaps to be addressed. This picture clearly needs to be linked to the organization's strategy and long-term competitive success. A defined set of competencies, if timely, relevant and accurately described, can assist a manager in gaining feedback and help in auditing his or her present position and planning appropriate development activities.

The development of a management competency clearly involves learning in some fashion but it may also be part of a broader development experience for individuals. In order to explain this further, it is worth taking a closer look at the concept of "development".

For some people, development and learning are almost synonymous and interchangeable terms. Development describes a process by which we learn new things and improve our performance as it may be related to career development. For others, development encompasses the idea of learning but also implies movement or growth towards an ideal, such as realization of personal potential or self-fulfilment. It can involve "unlearning" old habits or ways of looking at things.

Building on the idea of growth, some practitioners view development in a more specific way based on the idea that adults continue to develop their capacities and perspectives in particular ways throughout their lives. They believe that there are general patterns of development that are widely applicable to adults.

There are a wide range of "stage models" of adult development. These models all have in common a number of core ideas:

— development progresses in one direction along a line that is characterized by a sequence of milestones or stages;

— each stage represents a transformation that builds on previous stages;

— movement between stages occurs when, either internally or externally, something is required of us that is not possible at our current stage of development.

This idea has been applied to managers by describing stages of managerial development.

As managers go through these stages in their development, they move from a dependence on external factors (such as rules, norms and conventions) to a dependence on internal factors (e.g., reliance on their own judgment in situations of uncertainty, greater confidence) through to a higher awareness of self, others and the situation, and a greater sense of purpose. Development in this model is associated with individuals becoming more confident and creative, more able to deal with responsibility, change and ambiguity, and having a wider repertoire of managerial styles from which to choose.

Moving from one stage to another involves a type of change that is of a different quality than that typically associated with learning. Although learning is certainly part of the process, developmental change often implies a more fundamental level of change, that can involve more emotional ups and downs, periods of confusion, depression or resentment, and which generally takes place over a longer time frame. At the end of the process, individuals generally feel differently about themselves in a significant way. They feel they have "grown"; they see themselves in a new way, and are more confident and capable. Developmental change can result from a wide range of experiences: changing jobs/roles, taking on new responsibilities; living and working abroad; working with new and different types of people; parenthood; dealing with aging, and so on.

The key to understanding the competency approach is to understand that they are manifest in behaviour. An individual may cognitively understand what needs to be done but is not capable of executing the required behaviour. For example, many interviewers fall into the trap of asking hypothetical "What would you do in this situation?" type of questions. The responses tell you what the interviewee knows and not necessarily how he or she will in fact behave. It is better to ask what the individual has done in like situations. Past behaviour is an excellent predictor of future behaviour.

Any approach to business strategy must be underpinned by a thorough understanding of the human capability needed to implement a given strategy. The systems and processes of the organization (both formal and informal) then need to reflect this understanding in the way that they recognize and reinforce key behaviours.

A competency approach can provide a framework in which managers at a variety of levels can develop a shared understanding of what constitutes effective behaviour in their organizational context. It is used as a more formal system to spread that understanding of the required behaviours throughout the organization, and serves as a benchmark in recruitment, performance management and reward systems. This ensures that the focus of the organization is centred on those behaviours that support rather than detract from the overall strategic direction of the organization.

Benefits/Expected Outcomes

As with most systems or methods, the benefits of a competency approach depend not only on the system itself but also on the way it is used. It is no more than a vehicle that provides a clear focus and understanding on the behavioural expectations placed on the employee. It can act as a catalyst to meaningful communication between managers on how specifically to improve the organization's performance.

As such, a competency approach can provide the following specific benefits. It

— integrates core Human Resources Management activities with business goals, corporate strategy, and the management of strategic change;

— involves senior management in key Human Resources activities;

— improves the behavioural literacy of managers by providing a common language and focus for the effective management of performance and development;

— gives a sense of ownership of the performance management and development process to managers and staff by providing them with an important tool for self-development;

— improves the variety and quality of performance feedback to managers and staff by providing a clear focus on real job-related behavioural issues for appraisal and development and for disciplinary or remedial action;

— provides a vehicle for describing, valuing and recognizing managerial (as opposed to functional) capability within the organization.

Assessing the Benefits

It is difficult to assess separately the benefits of a competency approach from an evaluation of management development or management performance as a whole. Evaluating these areas is not always a straightforward task. However, assessing the approach itself also depends on the reasons for using it (e.g., performance management, strategic change, self-development, etc.). Generally, some type of comparison would need to be made to see if any improvements can be detected. Sources of information could include:

— existing indicators of management performance (e.g., appraisal data, performance-related bonus schemes, salary increases based on merit, sales performance);

— key areas of management performance related to particular competencies (e.g., quality of customer relationships, performance of project teams, number of new product ideas);

— the level of development activity generated by the initiative (e.g., training course attendance, partnering or mentoring relationships established, individuals seeking feedback on an ongoing basis); and

— the degree to which incoming recruits demonstrate capability in their new jobs (i.e., performance data as well as turnover rates coupled with reasons for leaving).

In addition, a simple means of assessing the perceived effect of a competency approach is to survey the managers involved. Such data would indicate the overall value of the system to managers who use it and provide an ongoing source of feedback to improve its use.

Programming/Implementation

Competency approaches to Human Resources Management contain common elements.

A Competency Model

This consists of a description of key competencies or clusters of competencies appropriate to managers in the organization. It may be broken down in terms of level or differing roles in the organization. The descriptions of competencies are detailed enough accurately to outline effective and ineffective behaviours, and often give indications of appropriate attitudes and self-image aligned with particular competencies. (For an example, see Sample Competency Model, page 97.)

A - B - **C**

A Self-assessment Process

This is often in the shape of a manual that explains the competency model and helps managers to determine which competencies are most relevant to them. It then provides a questionnaire or rating scale that allows managers to assess themselves against those competencies. However, this is not an end in itself but preparation for a focused discussion about current and future performance. It provides a basis for an individual's manager to give him or her supporting or contradictory feedback in relation to the self-assessment; together the pair can then identify development goals.

A Developmental Planning Process

Through structured forms or checklists, this helps an individual and his or her manager explore relevant options for developing the identified competencies. Often, information is provided about opportunities for development such as external programs, internal events, career development groups or learning groups, and expected experience requirements.

An Explanation

This can be an explanation of how the competency approach links to performance measures, reward systems, recruitment and induction, and succession planning, as appropriate.

A competency approach is similar to other approaches such as developing a customer focus, or ensuring total quality, in that it requires a paradigm shift. It is not enough simply to introduce a formal system or procedure. Its success depends on it becoming a shared attitude towards effective performance management as an integral part of the organizational culture. As such, it affects everyone in the organization.

Identifying Key Role Models

In order for this to happen, it is important to identify key role models in the organization who have a good understanding of how the competency system should work and who behave in a way which demonstrates the desired competencies and use of the system. Most obviously, senior management's role in, and use of, any competency system will have a major impact on how others view and use it themselves. Senior management should be involved in generating and validating a competency model for the organization and should be seen to be actively involved in required assessment and training activities that support the competency model. In addition, they have a key role in communicating the purpose and use of the competency system throughout the organization.

Other key role models are the functional line managers who are seen to be opinion-formers in the organization. It is particularly at the middle management level that change initiatives, which are a departure from the current organizational culture, can often be blocked. It is important that managers at this level buy into the whole competency concept, and particularly the content of the competencies themselves. They need to see a competency framework as a real, relevant tool that they can use to manage and develop their staff. Rather than trying to get all line managers to adapt to the new approach, an effective change strategy is to reach the influence peddlers among them, the line managers who willingly adapt to new processes and serve as models for the others to follow.

Involving all line managers at an early stage in the process (e.g., in generating a competency list) will provide important information to validate competencies and help to gain their commitment. Developing a sense of ownership of the competency approach on the part of line managers at all levels will enable them to use it effectively, as opposed to seeing it as a system developed and imposed by the Human Resources practitioner, to which they will only pay lip service.

The key area of impact of a competency approach will be in management practice (formal and informal systems and procedures) rather than organizational structure. In many cases, a competency approach may in fact be initiated by a restructuring. The current move to flatter, more flexible organizational structures and the premium this places on effective management has been a driving force in promoting the use of competency approaches in organizations. In particular, the focus on core personal effectiveness competencies rather than strictly defined job roles is a response to a more fluid and dynamic environment.

The structure of an organization, especially in the extent to which it reflects industry conditions, will have some effect on determining the types of competencies needed, the level of detail and functionality that is appropriate, and the "shelf life" of given competencies. A more bureaucratic, multi-layered organization in a relatively stable industry would focus on competencies that are more functional and procedural in nature, whereas a flatter, more fluid organization in a fast-changing industry would focus on core personal qualities that transfer across a multiplicity of roles and/or functions. Competencies may need to be revisited and validated more frequently as industry conditions change.

As with other management development activities, structure can potentially interact with the effective use of competencies in a number of ways. Expectations of career development may be hard to satisfy in traditional ways where there is an emphasis on moving up the structure, when the structure is at the same time becoming flatter. However, competencies can also be used to counteract this by providing a development framework that allows people to prepare specifically for other more responsible roles across the organization at a similar level. The focus becomes one of developing additional skills rather than moving up the hierarchy.

Structure can also become an issue if it results in those managers responsible for appraisal and development having little opportunity to see or work with their staff (e.g., through geographic distance). Sources of feedback and responsibility for development need to be carefully thought through in these cases. This is where more sophisticated assessment tools, like a 360-degree feedback mechanism can be of particular value.

An understanding of adult development is particularly relevant to the development of managerial competencies. By their very nature, many of these competencies require the degree of self-knowledge and self-management that is the result of a developmental process. It is therefore important that in managing a competency development process, a good understanding of both developmental change and learning is applied. This particularly requires the following mechanisms.

Clear Goals

A competency model can provide a basis for external and self-assessment. It is most helpful when competencies are described in detail so that a clear picture of effective and ineffective behaviours emerges. However, any competency model must be related to on-the-job behaviours and performance. It serves best as the basis for a discussion about current and future performance and areas for improvement.

Exploration of Opportunities for Development

These can be both on-the-job and off-the-job. In many cases, an external development event or course can be an important catalyst and source of information. They are particularly useful in providing new perspectives, guiding and structuring learning, and providing both challenge and emotional support in enabling individuals to take large developmental steps. On-the-job opportunities can be found within one's current role, as well as through an expanding role, new projects, secondments, receiving coaching, and observing others. It is important that the goals are clear in each situation and that appropriate ways of achieving feedback, reflecting on observations and generally reviewing the experience are identified.

Providing Support

As described above, a development process can be difficult and demoralizing if not implemented carefully. In addition, it requires outside information (i.e., feedback) at various key points. However independent one may be, no one can do it completely on his or her own. As part of a development plan, care should be taken to address the issue of support. This can be formal, such as the appointment of a mentor or a commitment to provide resources. Specific review points should be scheduled. Political support and/or protection might be necessary.

Informal support, which is part of an ongoing relationship, is invaluable. A manager who is perceptive, who sees the often hidden signs of emotional ups and downs, who is skillful at listening, counselling and coaching is a great asset in the development of his or her staff. No amount of checklists, action points, or appraisal meetings can substitute for this kind of support.

The key message here is that any competency framework or system can help in focusing and structuring an approach to development, but it cannot in itself provide a development process. That development process is personal, complex and must involve integrating external experiences with on-the-job experience over a longer time frame. The role that an individual's own manager, mentor and/or colleagues play in that process is obviously critical to the successful improvement of competence.

A - B - **C**

Relationship to the Performance Management System

Studies have shown that results-oriented managers tend to get better measurable performance out of their business units than do managers who are rated highly in people or relationship orientation. This is likely linked to the fact that a fundamental motivator is goal setting. When employees clearly understand what is expected from them in terms of output, they are able to achieve the desired results.

The cost of having a high results orientation is increased dissatisfaction that is ultimately manifested in behaviours such as absenteeism and higher turn-over. Managers may be willing to consciously adopt a results orientation if the increase in productivity and the resulting increase in profitability are greater than the losses experienced through higher turnover and absenteeism. Moreover, the true costs of absenteeism and turnover are not often measured and therefore cannot be directly measured as part of the overall performance of the business unit.

Typically identified competencies used to assess the development needs of a manager centre around people skills. Managers commonly have the technical skills and qualifications for their jobs. These are considered threshold requirements and managers lacking the basic understanding of the business or the functional specialty they head up are quickly weeded out. The performance management system is then focused on identifying the desired results in terms of goals and objectives. This combination makes it highly probable that managers will tend towards a high results orientation.

The best managers have both a high results orientation and a high people orientation. They strike a balance between driving for performance improvements and establishing strong working relationships with their staff. These managers, who are the exception, tend to have better performance coupled with high job satisfaction in their business units. Thus, they will have high productivity, lower production costs, better employee retention and lower absenteeism. The idea of evaluating and developing people management skills through the competency based assessment process is intended to add a dimension to the performance management system that will drive improvements in overall performance.

In addition, many organizations have examined their cultures and the inherent values that define their organizations, and have come to the conclusion that single-mindedness with respect to profitability and financial goals is not consistent with the reputation they want to build. Many organizations have recognized that there are more stakeholders to consider in managing an enterprise than just the owners (shareholders). Other stakeholders include the customers, suppliers and employees. These groups demand much more than just strong financial performance from the organization. In fact, the most important element these groups look for is strong relationships.

Managers who build a positive employee relations environment reap the benefits of having a staff that will tend to, in turn, build strong relations with suppliers and customers. This then has the reciprocal effect of building better supplier contracts and increasing sales. Many of the competencies identified in a typical model will include skills related to building relations with these three key groups of stakeholders.

The performance management system is established to set performance objectives in terms of desired outputs and results. A typical performance system revolves around Management-By-Objectives (MBO), where organizational goals are cascaded down from level to level within the organization. Individuals at each level are asked to determine their objectives in a way that supports the overall organizational goals. These objectives are sometimes referred to as SMART goals, because they are **S**pecific, **M**easurable, **A**ttainable, **R**eliable and **T**ime bound. The metrics established under an MBO-type system are usually quite clear to the individual. The competency model essentially introduces the concept that how the goals are achieved is equally as important to what is achieved.

The competencies therefore must also relate to what is important to achieving the specific goals of the position. By developing and improving these competencies, the individual can expect to be able to deliver superior performance outputs over time. Measuring individuals on how they perform their duties also ensures that management behaviours are consistent with the core values of the organization.

Managing change in an organization can be hindered if the stated goals and objectives given to the manager are incompatible with the desired culture. Rating a manager solely on his or her contribution to results may be counterproductive in an environment where the organization wants to foster a culture of teamwork and employee empowerment. Adding the dimension of assessing competencies allows organizations to retain their key performance indicators as metrics to manage individual performance, and adds a dimension that communicates to the individual the importance of achieving those results in a particular way consistent with the mission and values of the organization.

Human Resources practitioners need also to keep in mind the changing nature of employee expectations when creating a set of relevant competencies. Under the "new employment contract", employees expect more than just a "fair day's pay for a fair day's work". Employees want to achieve personal growth and satisfaction from their work. This does not necessarily mean every employee is looking to advance up the corporate ladder. Rather, many employees today are demanding that they learn something from their work or are able to gain a sense of personal satisfaction from being involved in a worthwhile endeavour.

Part of the process of establishing personal development objectives around the identified competencies is to negotiate with the employee as to what activities have the greatest payoff for both the organization and for the individual. The development activity itself may then become a form of reward to the individual who gains in terms of self-fulfillment or self-actualization.

Competencies include behavioural traits such as:

⇨ adaptability;

⇨ initiative;

⇨ effective communication skills;

⇨ being a team player;

⇨ customer focus;

⇨ champion of change;

⇨ develops people;

⇨ decision-making;

⇨ strategic thinking;

⇨ subject matter expertise;

⇨ talks the talk and walks the walk; and

⇨ takes risks.

Each needs to be defined in a manner that allows the manager and the manager's assessor to evaluate the demonstrated proficiency objectively. The first step for any organization is to identify the competencies relevant to the organization and to the particular position. The competencies should correlate with the organization's espoused values and mission. They should also be linked to the stated objectives of the job. However, smaller organizations may develop a single model that encompasses all management positions.

Identifying competencies should begin by reviewing the organization's strategic plan and considering which core competencies define the organization's culture and its competitive advantage. If the organization has also defined a set of core values, it should consider what behaviours would drive those values and make them an implicit part of the organization's culture. A good method for developing an initial set of competencies is to establish a cross-functional task force to review and debate what may be relevant attributes that will drive the organization towards its stated objectives. Such a task force should be managed by an experienced facilitator with expertise in the performance management field.

Each competency must be well defined in a way that allows assessors to reliably rate the individual based on observed behaviours. For example, a "Champion of Change" may be defined as someone who:

⇨ facilitates change company-wide, or for a division or function;

⇨ strives continually for a depth of knowledge to be on the leading edge of global and industry practices, and institutes appropriate change to meet customer needs based on these trends;

⇨ influences senior leaders and broad employee groups on the need for change and justification for corporate resources;

⇨ articulates the organization's mission and strategic direction consistently and continuously;

⇨ builds a support network of influential people to take accountability for achieving change objectives;

⇨ mobilizes and establishes accountability among resources across the organization to support change; and

⇨ develops and drives the change process for division/business unit.

For each of these competency dimensions, the assessor will need to know what behaviours result in the demonstration of the competency. To facilitate change, the individual needs to have the skills of a facilitator. Sending out a memo that changes are needed does not constitute facilitating change. However, arranging a retreat for senior managers to discuss new business processes and create a set of deliverables that will drive a dramatic shift in how the division conducts its business, does.

Measuring proficiency on each competency is not easy. First, the organization must establish a scale. A simple nominal description can be used such as:

- has not demonstrated competency;

- somewhat effective;

- effective; and

- highly effective.

The assessor is then asked to give anecdotal evidence to support the rating. In reply, the managers being assessed can also give examples of where they believe they have demonstrated the competency.

More sophisticated definitions can be developed to describe what each competency looks like at different rating levels. However, this can be an onerous task. If 10 competencies are identified with a four-point rating scale, then 40 definitions will have to be written. If the organization opts to define each competency for every position, then the task can become very expensive and cumbersome. The degree of sophistication required will depend on the level of sophistication in the organization, its size and the complexity of its operations.

Tying all of this to the performance management system is difficult. Human Resources practitioners know that managers already complain about not having sufficient time and resources to evaluate each individual on the achievement of measurable objectives under an MBO-type system. Convincing them to add an assessment on individual competencies will not be an easy task. Moreover, in some ways, the "development aspect" of managing an individual's performance should be separated from the achievement of results. While arguable that the two dimensions are strongly correlated and therefore inextricably linked, separating them removes the possibility of an individual perceiving that negative consequences are attached to not reaching his or her development goals.

Managers are responsible for giving individuals feedback on how they achieve the results they get out of performance. However, it is the individual's awareness, acceptance and commitment to change that will drive the changes in developing his or her competencies. The individual must buy into the need to develop in order for him or her to invest the time and energy needed to change. The degree to which the individual must develop will also depend on the individual's aspirations.

It is suggested that the discussion around individual competency be a separate, yet integrated part, of the performance management system. One suggestion is to conduct performance appraisals at the end of each fiscal year with emphasis on performance against measurable results and a simple update on development activities. Then, at mid-year, the emphasis shifts to assessing individual competencies and developing action plans around learning, combined with a brief update on measurable results.

When reviewing an individual's competencies, managers are not always in the best position to assess an individual's demonstrated behaviours. Performance objectives are measurable and a manager can rely on simple metrics and supporting reports to assess how well an individual did against defined objectives. However, competencies are demonstrated through what the individual does on a day-to-day basis. The individual's supervisor is often not there to see him or her in action. This makes assessing competencies particularly difficult.

One way to periodically assess individuals is to establish a management assessment centre (see Assessment Centres at page 25 *et seq.*) However, this can be expensive and does not provide for an on-going check of the individual's progress. Instead, the organization will need to establish a well-defined process that will include regularly gathering and soliciting feedback from others (peers and external/internal clients), documenting individual accomplishments and periodically observing on-the-job performance.

A manager assessing the competency of a sales representative may want to shadow the representative on a sales call, audit a sales presentation given by the individual, ask customers what they observed from the individual and ask the representative's peers to complete an assessment rating. All of this data is then reviewed to give a complete picture of how the individual performs his or her duties.

This example also demonstrates how a Human Resources practitioner may validate the relevance of a set of competencies and the reliability of the rating methodologies. If the competencies are properly defined and the assessment tool is reliable, then in theory the top performer should have the strongest set of competencies. The trick is to ensure all aspects of performance are being considered. Results are not the sole determinant.

It should be emphasized that direct observation of the individual performing is essential for the credibility of the assessor. Moreover, feedback that can be given immediately following an observation will have the strongest influence in getting the individual to make adjustments. Individuals tend to perform better when their supervisors have direct knowledge regarding their work performance and are able to give them immediate feedback. Competencies are not merely developed through a formal assessment process, but are enhanced when the supervisor or manager is able to create a learning environment for the individual.

Relationship to Other Human Resources Management Processes

In sophisticated Human Resources Management environments, defined competencies for each position are used to determine the candidate specifications when recruiting to fill a vacancy. Having identified the competencies, the practitioner can develop interview guidelines for the line managers to use that will elicit responses to demonstrate proficiency in a given competency. In addition, some psychometric tests can be utilized to check for behavioural tendencies that support the requisite competencies.

Hiring decisions can be made based on the candidate's accomplishments and his or her personal style. Even if a candidate is deficient in a particular competency, the hiring manager may proceed knowing what development has to take place. During induction and orientation, the manager can review the perceived area for improvement with the new hire and begin the development and coaching activities immediately.

Having well-defined competencies allows the Human Resources practitioner to engage in more meaningful dialogues with managers when consulting with them on performance issues. By having a shared set of understandings on how a job is to be performed, the manager and the practitioner can "speak the same language" when creating a corrective action plan for the employee.

Identifying competencies can lead to inventive ways for individuals to develop and grow with the assistance of the organization. The practitioner might direct an individual who wants to work on team building skills to participate in company sponsored activities such as task forces or project teams, or the practitioner might suggest that the individual gets involved with the Employee Social Committee. Individuals who want to work on facilitation skills might get involved in a charity drive.

Practical Application

Sample Competency Model

The following defines a set of competencies that may be applied generically to management positions. Each competency is titled and given a brief definition, followed by a series of descriptive statements. The descriptors are not intended to be inclusive, but rather are meant as illustrations of the type of behaviours that might be observed. This model defines the ideal state. In other models, each competency might be followed by descriptors for each rating (i.e., highly effective, effective, somewhat effective, not demonstrated).

For each position or level in the organization, there should be between five and 10 identified competencies. Too few will result in ineffective development plans; too many will make assessment and follow-up too onerous.

Competency: Strategic Thinker

Defines organizational capacity and core competencies, assesses key opportunities and threats, develops action plans to capitalize on opportunities, evaluates current and needed resources and sets clear priorities.

Demonstrated by:

- establishing business unit strategies and priorities considering the long-term operating environment and the organization's stated mission;

A - B - **C**

- developing the organizational structure and resources needed to deliver on the business strategy;

- using his or her knowledge of the total enterprise to create solutions and ideas that drive business results and the achievement of competitive advantage;

- leading and influencing business initiatives and aligning resources to meet business demands;

- ensuring that processes and initiatives support the key business objectives, strategies and goals of the organization and business units;

- anticipating opportunities based on identified trends and industry best practices;

- reviewing continuously the operating processes to ensure they achieve added value for the organization or are re-engineered;

- partnering with senior business managers in strategy planning and execution based on shareholder and other stakeholder value goals; and

- understanding strengths and development areas within the business unit and developing action plans to exploit opportunities for improvement and the creation of competitive advantage.

Competency: Champion of Change

Proactively challenges the organization. Builds the organization's capacity to embrace and capitalize on change. Provides the organization with a model for change and educates and supports the organization in change efforts.

Demonstrated by:

- facilitating change company-wide, or for a business unit or function;

- striving continually to be on the leading edge of global and industry practices, and institutes appropriate change to meet organizational and customer needs based on these trends;

- influencing senior leaders and employees of the need for change;

- assessing the need for corporate resources to optimize change management efforts;

- articulating position and builds a support network of influential people to take accountability for achieving change objectives;

- mobilizing and establishing accountability among resources across the organization to support change; and

- developing and driving the change process for division/business unit.

Competency: Decision Making

Makes timely and sound decisions. Takes ownership for decisions by standing by them and accepting resulting consequences.

Demonstrated by:

- seeking input from internal and external colleagues to make reasoned and educated decisions;

- evaluating the future consequences of decisions;

- making timely decisions judged to be right for the business, even though they may be difficult, controversial, or circumstances may be unclear;

- taking time to gather information and input from a variety of internal and external sources before making a decision; and

- sharing the rationale underlying the decisions made.

Competency: Develops People

Provides the structure, information, support, coaching and resources that encourage people to continuously develop their talents.

Demonstrated by:

- providing appropriate resources to support the developmental needs of employees;

- using a variety of methods (e.g., feedback, personal examples, coaching, teaching) to help individuals attain higher levels of performance;

- helping others recognize their areas of strength and weakness in a beneficial and constructive manner using the established performance management tools;

- promoting actively organizational learning (e.g., transfer of best practices, benchmarking);

- developing and executing a personal development plan;

- helping others view mistakes as learning opportunities; and

- engaging actively in on-going development planning with direct reports.

Competency: Fosters Open Communication

Drives the free flow of timely and accurate information and communication throughout the organization.

Demonstrated by:

- articulating viewpoints in a way that positively influences others;

- communicating and relating effectively to a broad range of people internally and externally;

- seeking to understand others by noticing and responding to non-verbal behaviour;

- utilizing active listening skills;

- encouraging employee interaction and dialogue;

- choosing appropriate communication vehicles for each message (e.g., voicemail, e-mail, direct communication, meetings, presentations);

- presenting opinions accurately and persuasively (one-on-one and in groups);

- sharing information with all those who need to be informed; and

- being receptive to the opinions of others and demonstrating a willingness to consider the input of others.

Competency: Manages and Leads Teams

Collaborates with others to develop a stronger team and enhance team spirit. Sees teams as a vehicle to achieve business goals.

Demonstrated by:

- sharing information, ideas and suggestions with team;

- putting team and organizational goals ahead of personal goals;

- aligning team goals with organizational and business goals;

- being aware of team members' strengths and weaknesses, and constructively utilizing and combining employee strengths to improve overall team performance;

- performing multiple roles such as leader, doer, or facilitator to support the work of the team;

- fostering collaboration among team members by soliciting input, resolving ambiguity and encouraging participation; and

- seeking diversity of people and perspectives in a team, and demonstrating commitment to developing diverse teams.

Competency: Serves as a Role Model

Evokes trust from others by keeping commitments. Sets a personal example by supporting the organization's shared goals, values and vision.

Demonstrated by:

- accepting responsibility and acknowledging problems or mistakes to others, and committing to take necessary corrective action;

- gaining others' trust and loyalty by fulfilling the commitments he/she makes to them;

- setting a clear example for others by following through on important commitments;

- using an honest, open and straightforward approach with colleagues;

- taking actions that are consistent with stated personal and organizational values; and

- refusing to engage in hidden agendas.

Competency: Demonstrates Courage

Confronts problems early on, drives hard on difficult issues and takes a firm stand in the face of controversy. Shows willingness to engage and act when personally at risk.

Demonstrated by:

- facing up to problem situations quickly, directly, and without hesitation;

- communicating respectfully one's own opinions for the benefit of the organization, despite fear of rejection or repercussion;

- taking unpopular actions in an appropriate manner when he/she feels they are necessary;

A - B - C

- willing to put self at risk to move forward an initiative in which he/she believes;

- admitting mistakes willingly and seeking to learn from these in the future;

- demonstrating maturity and optimism, despite personal or team setbacks; and

- refusing to compromise ethics in questionable situations.

Role of the Human Resources Practitioner

The role of the Human Resources practitioner is one of providing expertise, or gaining expertise from outside of the organization (i.e., bringing in consultants as appropriate) and facilitating the process of developing and implementing a competency system. Although the initiative may be started by the practitioner, it is important that it is not seen to be entirely driven and owned by Human Resources.

There is an important range of expertise to be provided by the practitioner in:

— defining and validating competencies;

— running assessment/development centres;

— training managers in observation, assessment and feedback skills;

— developing documentation that describes the competencies and their use, and may provide rating scales or other means of self-assessment.

The Human Resources practitioner has a key role to play in developing and implementing a competency approach. This forms part of his or her broader management development role. The development of a competency approach will be based, in part, on the output of a management development audit.

Key questions that need to be asked in considering and using competencies are as follows:

1. What is our understanding of the business strategy and how does this need to translate into managerial behaviour and practice?

2. What are we looking to gain by using a competency approach?

3. What types of competencies are we aiming to define? Competencies can be:

— generic or specific to certain roles;

— taken from outside and adapted to the organization, or generated solely from within;

— focused on personal characteristics or job outputs.

4. Where and how will the competencies be used (e.g., in recruitment and selection, in assessment and appraisal, in training and development)? It is important that these areas are integrated by asking:

— Will we start in one area and then roll out, or tackle everything at once?

— Will assessment or development centres be used?

— How will competency development be addressed?

— How will we gain commitment? Who needs to be involved and at what points?

5. How will we generate and validate our competencies? Options include:

   (a) adapting an external model or list;

   (b) job analysis;

   (c) brainstorming;

   (d) critical incident;

   (e) behaviourally-based interviews.

6. Will we use an outside consultant at any point in the process? If so, for what purpose, and at what points? How will it be managed?

7. How will the approach be communicated and documented? This should include pre-launch information (possibly counselling), briefing, work shops/training, documentation and getting feedback on how the approach is being used. The use of informal as well as formal processes is important here, as well as the identification of key role models.

8. How will the competency approach integrate with other systems (e.g., recruitment, appraisal, reward, career planning)?

Human Resources practitioners will need to assess their own skills and capabilities in the areas of competency, assessment, facilitation, counselling and feedback to determine their training needs and the appropriateness of using outside expertise or skills in some areas.

Barriers to Success/Common Pitfalls

The critical areas in which the introduction of a competency approach can falter are:

— organizational culture;

— the relationship between the Human Resources practitioner and line managers;

— the link between competency, performance management and development; and

— the perceptions and associations that people have of the competency approach itself.

Organizational Culture

Organizational culture is a broad term but it encompasses the idea of current attitudes, practice, language and values. In some cases, a competency approach may run counter to existing attitudes and practice. For example, in a culture which values functional expertise over managerial capability, in which managerial performance is not recognized or valued, and where such things as appraisals are only carried out in a cursory manner, the introduction of a competency approach will be completely alien. Similarly, if managers are being expected to demonstrate a high degree of sophistication in observing and describing managerial behaviour and yet no such language exists in the culture, they will struggle to use a competency system effectively. Finally, if the style of the competency system differs greatly from other practice (i.e., highly bureaucratic, lengthy, or "mechanical", or conversely too loose, open-ended, or vague), it may not be used effectively.

The extent to which a competency approach matches existing cultural norms is important in making the decision to implement. If the competency approach represents a major cultural change, then it needs to be regarded as such and planned for on an appropriate scale. This requires such things as the involvement of key people, winning over opinion-formers, starting with a successful pilot, and aligning other relevant systems and procedures.

The Relationship Between the Human Resources Practitioner and Line Management

The relationship between the practitioner and line managers is a critical factor. This will determine:

— how line managers receive initiatives;

— how welcome the involvement of line managers is in the process at an early point;

— how open the dialogue can be between the two during and after introduction of the scheme; and

— how issues of ownership will be managed.

Without doubt, the best foundation is the development of an open, trusting relationship between the two, in which line managers view the practitioner as working with them to achieve relevant business goals. In this light, it is important that line managers see a competency initiative as addressing a business need which is important to them as, for example, the management of performance, or focusing limited resources in the most effective way, rather than as an intrusion. A strategy to communicate with and involve line management is crucial here.

The Link Between Competency and Development

The link between competency and development is one of the problematic areas in current practice. To date, a good deal of effort has been spent in defining competencies and assessing managers against them. The question of how an individual develops a particular competency is a complex one. It may not only require the learning of knowledge or skills but also the development of self-insight and the ability to question and adapt attitudes and motivations appropriately. A development approach needs to include both a phase in which the problem can be identified and a motivation to change is mobilized, and a phase in which testing and support can take place that are related to real work behaviour.

Most competency approaches include the use of some type of personal development plans. As part of this planning process, careful thought needs to be given to the means of development (e.g., counselling, on-the-job coaching, mentoring, or external development programs). The use of external programs can be particularly beneficial in many cases but these need to be

A - B - **C**

chosen carefully. External providers should demonstrate a good understanding of the development process underpinning the required competency.

The Importance of Communication

The attitudes that individuals have to a competency approach will have a great impact on their commitment to using it effectively. These attitudes will be based on perceptions and associations. For example:

— if associated with a wave of redundancies, a competency approach may be cynically regarded as a way to rid the organization of undesirables;

— if associated with career and promotion, the approach may be seen as a way to select high fliers;

— if associated with "meaningless" competencies, the approach will be regarded as symptomatic of Human Resources or senior management distance from the "reality" of the field.

A high-quality and ongoing communication process is key here in order to determine what associations are operating and influencing individuals in a positive manner.

Common Mistakes

The following problems may need to be addressed:

1. Competencies themselves are not aligned to business strategy, or are not seen as relevant by practicing managers.

2. Competencies are not described well or understood by managers who need to use them. It is important that a competency (e.g., "initiative") can be translated into behaviour relevant in the organizational context.

3. There is a lack of effective communication throughout the implementation process. It is particularly important that people understand why and how a competency approach is being used and see some benefit to them.

4. There is a lack of senior management commitment and modelling/involvement.

5. A competency approach which is taken as a prepared package from an external source and which is not well understood or owned by the organization (and, in particular, line management).

6. There is an over-emphasis on systematizing and documenting the approach, without a dialogue with line management or training for line management. This results in competencies simply being used as a meaningless checklist rather than a vehicle for quality performance discussions with staff.

7. A competency approach is introduced that relies on psychometric and simulated data (e.g., an assessment centre) more than on-the-job performance in its assessment of competencies. While external sources can be useful, they can also be subject to bias. They should only be used to complement other forms of assessment. Observations of on-the-job behaviour should be the primary benchmark.

8. The process by which individuals develop competence is not always well understood.

There is a lack of consistent follow-up to ensure the approach becomes enshrined in the organization's culture. Like many Human Resources initiatives, the competency approach as part of a performance management process runs the risk of being viewed as a flavour-of-the-month if there is not a consistent follow-up. Any commitment to the process has to be perceived by employees as a long-term commitment to impact on the organization's culture.

CONFLICT MANAGEMENT

Definition/Background

Conflict in the workplace is common. Even in healthy organizations, it is inevitable. Human resources practitioners find that a substantial amount of their time, both planned and unplanned, is taken up in dealing with conflict. Effectively dealing with conflict will lead to a more dynamic, creative and healthy environment. Ineffective handling of conflict will lead to organizational dysfunction.

When managers and supervisors are asked what training they would like to receive, one of the most common responses is to be taught how to deal with conflict. In most instances, what they are really asking for is to be taught the skills to be able to confront employees on issues in an effective manner. No one wants to deal with confrontations that lead to arguments and open disputes.

Conflict arises from many sources. We are in conflict with anyone who we believe has taken steps to block us from doing what we want to do. We are in conflict with people who we believe pose a threat to us because they are different or hold different views.

The secret to managing conflict effectively is not to attempt to eliminate it or suppress it, but to channel its expression into positive outcomes. Avoiding conflict can cause other problems in the organization. In very cohesive work groups, for example, team members are so motivated to maintain harmony that they are willing to compromise their beliefs and opinions in order to conform to the majority. This withholding of opinions can lead to "groupthink".

Groupthink leads to many undesirable outcomes. The team or work group can underestimate the risks inherent in their decisions because individuals are reluctant to point out potential weaknesses. In extreme cases, groups can engage in questionable or even unethical decisions precisely because the group has developed an unquestioning belief in its own ability to reach the right conclusions. Information that is inconsistent with the group's thought pattern is dismissed or rationalized away, leading to faulty logic and unexamined assumptions.

Groupthink is a regularly occurring phenomenon among homogeneous teams that have had some degree of past success, are held together by a dominant and forceful leader who the team members can easily defer to, and is relatively isolated from outside influences or pressures. The point is that complete peace and harmony is not a desired state because it can lead to complacency and inertness. The ideal solution is to create an environment where conflict is channeled into creative behaviours.

In the heterogeneous work environments of today, it is unlikely that people will adapt naturally to working together in harmonious balance. Rather, the diversity of the work environment demands specific leadership skills to direct inherent tensions into positive organizational outcomes.

The first step to managing conflict is to understand its sources. Conflict originates with an individual's interpretation of an event or another person's behaviour. How the individual chooses to respond to the event or behaviour will be dictated by their perceptions, which will be further coloured by their beliefs, values and experiences. The initial response to conflict is emotional. The individual may like or dislike what he or she believes has just happened. This leads to an overt behaviour to show approval or disapproval of the event or behaviour. The overt behaviour will be tempered to some degree by the context in which the behaviour takes place.

Sources of conflict

Specific sources of conflict include:

⇨ **Goal Incompatibility:** Goal incompatibility can exist between individuals, between the individual and the organization, or between a work group and the organization. Everyone has a set of personal goals and objectives that are separate from the goals and objectives of the work team and the organization. One individual may be seeking higher pay or a promotion, while another may hope for a more challenging assignment to test his or her skills, and a third may hope for more time off to travel.

Differences in individual goals and objectives do not inevitably lead to conflict unless they are incompatible. For example, when two people aspire to the same job, their goals are mutually exclusive. Only one can be appointed to the position. The competition for the job creates a tension between the two because each perceives the other's ambitions as a potential barrier to achieving their own personal objectives.

Personal ambitions are not necessarily incompatible with organizational goals. Organizations grow and prosper precisely because they provide opportunities for personal growth to individuals. In some instances, however, individual ambitions may clash with organizational goals. In rare cases, one individual's blind ambition may lead him or her to behave in ways that are contrary to the values and interests of the organization. In more subtle ways, a person's on-the-job behaviour may simply not fit with the style of the organization. The individual who values individual achievement and recognition, for example, will be a poor fit in an organization where teamwork is highly valued.

⇨ **Differentiation:** Differentiation exists in large complex organizations. For example, when one organization merges with another, each brings a different set of organizational norms and values. If these norms and values are not compatible, conflict is inevitable.

As a result of the recent acquisition of Canadian Airlines by Air Canada, two large groups of employees from different organizational cultures were brought together. A dispute emerged early on as to how seniority was going to be handled. The end result was that the seniority of Canadian employees was end-tailed onto the seniority of Air Canada employees. This meant that a senior Canadian employee could end up being treated as junior to an Air Canada employee who might have less service with the company.

The perpetuation of this type of differentiation can block any attempt to create a common culture and leads to continuous clashes between groups of employees. Continuing with the Air Canada example, the airline's attempt to create a new discount carrier called ZIP is being marred by a clash between those employees represented by the CAW and those represented by CUPE over which

union should represent flight attendants. The continuous conflict that emerges from differentiation ultimately manifests itself in the quality of customer service and care.

⇨ **Cultural Diversity:** In addition to organizational differentiation, organizations today are influenced by the diversity of cultures their employees represent. In Canada's cultural mosaic, people from different lands are encouraged to hold onto their heritage.

In the workplace, having employees with diverse cultural backgrounds and experiences is desirable, but not without inherent difficulties. The different values and norms represented in today's workplace can lead to serious conflicts and such undesirable behaviours as racial harassment, prejudice and unlawful discrimination.

Heterogeneous work groups benefit from a wealth of different experiences and cultural norms. Members of such groups can learn from each other and gain new insights into the world. However, because of their diverse backgrounds, members are also likely to have different perceptions and interpretations of events and behaviours that can lead to significantly different responses.

People from different cultural backgrounds will, for instance, respond differently to different leadership styles. People from cultures where it is natural to defer to authority will respond more positively to an authoritarian style than will people where individuality is highly regarded.

⇨ **Task Interdependence:** Work in organizations is organized as a series of intertwined processes. The way in which work tasks or processes are integrated can lead to different types of conflicts.

The weakest form of interdependence is where two work units share a common resource. Two departments may share a fax machine, for example. If one department uses the machine to such a large extent that they interfere with the work of the other department, conflict will result. Within any organization, financial resources are shared and therefore there will be some degree of competition for the pooled resource.

In work processes organized sequentially, the work output of one department is the work input of another. The receiving department depends on its internal supplier to produce inputs in sufficient quantity and quality on a timely basis to allow it to meet its production goals. If the internal supplier makes errors or has production difficulties, these problems will be transferred on through the process. Similarly, the receiving department can cause problems for the supplier if it is unable to keep pace with the supply of inputs.

In other process arrangements, the work output is exchanged among work units. An example of this is the relationship between production departments and maintenance. Both share the common goal of keeping the production machinery operating at an optimal level. When breakdowns occur, the production department depends on maintenance to repair the equipment quickly and to manage preventative maintenance programs effectively to minimize the amount of downtime experienced. The maintenance department depends on production employees to operate the equipment within acceptable operating parameters and to take proper routine care of it.

An unfortunate incident happened a number of years ago in the employee parking lot at Domtar's Caledonia gypsum mines. One evening after the day shift was over, an equipment operator sought out and assaulted a mechanic. The resulting fistfight left both employees injured and their continuing employment in serious jeopardy. At the root of the altercation was each employee's perception that the other's efforts with respect to the care of a certain piece of equipment were negligent.

The operator ran a piece of equipment called a scoop-tram, which is a front-end loader used in mining operations. The scoop-tram had been experiencing hydraulic problems and was constantly in the shop because of low fluid levels. The mechanic was frustrated because of the amount of time he was spending on refilling the hydraulic fluid on this particular machine. He felt the operator must have abused the machine for it to need such attention. The operator did not believe the mechanic was properly servicing the machine and blamed him for the constant breakdowns.

The actual cause of the problem was an improperly specified fitting that had escaped the mechanic's attention. However, because each

depended so much on the other to keep the equipment in proper running order, it was easy for them to blame each other. The result was that the operator was terminated and the mechanic missed several weeks of work recuperating from his injuries. The lesson to be learned was that better communication and a common problem-solving approach could have helped the organization avoid this conflict all together.

⇨ **Scarce Resources:** All resources are ultimately finite and therefore potentially scarce. The organization has a finite amount of capital, equipment and time available to achieve its goals. It is natural for individuals to compete for these resources.

Capital budgeting protocols are established to provide objective standards in decision-making processes. Divisions, business units and departments in complex organizations have to compete for funds to finance their projects. As a result, projects in other divisions or departments may be seen as potential blocks in the way of an individual's "pet" project. One of the results of the scarcity of critical resources such as capital is political behaviour. Political behaviour in this context is any behaviour that is motivated by personal interests over organizational interests. If this behaviour continues unabated, it can lead to organizational dysfunction.

The boss's time is another example of a scarce resource. If one employee is seen to be monopolizing the time of a manager, co-workers may perceive this as a threat to their own development and ambitions. The other employees will resent the employee who is seen to be spending so much time with the boss and this resentment may spill over into a lack of respect for the boss, who will be seen as not making his or her time available on an equitable basis.

Petty conflicts can emerge out of something as simple as photocopier time. One department may be seen as monopolizing the use of the photocopier simply because there is not enough photocopier capacity (enough copying machines) to satisfy the demands at peak times.

⇨ **Ambiguity:** Ambiguous goals or directions are those that leave a lot of room for interpretation. Individuals' different experiences and belief systems will inevitably lead to different perceptions of

A - B - **C**

what the goals and directions are meant to achieve. In these situations, individuals may begin to work at cross-purposes.

In strong organizational cultures, ambiguous directions can be given with minimal conflict precisely because individuals have an overall sense of shared expectations and desired outcomes. In these environments, individuals are also more likely to openly discuss their interpretations and work towards developing a consensus as to the directions to take. Ambiguity is therefore particularly problematic in organizations with weak or undeveloped cultures.

⇨ **Poor Communications:** The potential for dysfunctional conflict can be further exacerbated by poor communications. The more work groups and individuals who depend on one another to complete their work processes, the more important good communication will be. The efficient coordination of work efforts requires a constant flow of information between dependent work groups.

Differentiation and diversification (see above) further complicate communications efforts. People from different backgrounds and with different experiences are likely to interpret the same information in different ways. A corporate directive to improve cost effectiveness might be interpreted as a directive to cut all discretionary spending by some and as a directive to invest in more efficient work methods by others. Seeking clarity means more than just eliminating any specific ambiguity in the delivery of the message. It also means getting feedback so that the sender of the message is able to validate that the receiver understood precisely what was intended.

⇨ **Ineffective Problem Solving:** Diversity and differentiation can also lead to different problem-solving paradigms that can ultimately create conflicts. Individuals with different experiences can define a problem in different ways and suggest different solutions. Moreover, individuals tend to take ownership of their proposed solutions and defend them rigorously against alternatives.

Organizations that lack a disciplined problem-solving process can run into a number of conflicts over process issues because of the failure to identify root causes.

Dysfunctional conflict in the workplace can result in losses to the organization in the form of:

● increased absenteeism;
● increased employee turnover;
● fighting (physical and verbal abuse);
● job actions (strikes, lockouts, wildcats, slowdowns, sick-outs;
● sabotage;
● political behaviour;
● amplified personal animosity;
● reduced productivity;
● poor employee morale;
● poor customer service;
● poor product quality;
● harassment; and
● litigation.

On the other hand, conflict is not in itself inherently bad. The organization suffers when individuals react to conflicts in inappropriate ways. When conflict becomes dysfunctional, it causes the organization to divert energy and resources away from productive activities in order to deal with inappropriate behaviours and other outcomes of conflict. Unbridled conflict can lead to increased stress in all of its manifestations. Organizations unable to deal with conflict may find that individuals' perceptions and understandings of the organization's goals and objectives have become distorted. Conflict can even result in the emergence of organizational subcultures that further undermine the efforts of the organization to create a set of shared expectations among its stakeholders.

Benefits/Expected Outcomes

Managing conflict is not about eliminating all sources of conflict. Even if such a thing were possible, the result would be a homogeneous population that valued harmonious relationships above all other considerations. As discussed above, these groups are susceptible to groupthink. They are unable to be creative and are likely to be either complacent or take ill-advised risks.

Managing conflict is about balancing the diverse interests and abilities of individuals with the goals and objectives of the organization. The most productive way to manage conflict is to channel it into positive behaviours, to find the root causes of issues and to allow people to pursue common goals while also accepting the differences that exist among them.

Managing conflict also involves creating a forum to resolve issues. One of the benefits of diversity and conflict is that they enable organizations to better identify problems and issues. Contrast this with the homogeneous group that is apt to suppress differences of opinion, even to the point of covering up logical flaws in group decision-making.

Dysfunctional conflict manifests itself when there are no avenues available for the voicing of different opinions or the expression of alternative points of view. Healthy organizations create such avenues so that misperceptions can be corrected and differing opinions can be heard and utilized. Finding healthy outlets for conflict enhances the organization's ability to deal with change and is an integral part of any Learning Organization.

Some organizations may find that their growth and creativity has stagnated because they have fostered a homogeneous culture that dominates to such an extent that differentiation has been obliterated. While these cultures may be remarkable for their harmony, such organizations are in as much danger of perishing as are organizations marked by overt dysfunctional conflicts.

Introducing conflict into workgroups suffering from groupthink or stagnation is a way to stimulate creativity and learning. However, organizations should be careful to maintain a healthy balance by ensuring that team members know how to deal with conflict in appropriate ways before introducing it.

The benefits of introducing conflict into a team environment include:

- improved decision-making;
- improved team dynamics and cohesiveness;
- improved creativity and learning;
- increased awareness of the importance and salience of team goals;
- strengthened task orientation;

- identification of underlying issues; and
- elimination of groupthink through constructive controversy.

Organizations that learn to manage conflict effectively can expect to have higher employee morale, improved attendance and fewer turnovers. Effective conflict management also pays dividends in terms of improved productivity and a reduced incidence of aberrant behaviours such as theft and sabotage. Moreover, the proactive application of tools to channel energy that would otherwise be used up dealing with dysfunctional conflict creates an environment of employee empowerment and involvement.

Every organization should have mechanisms in place to deal with unresolved issues and internal disputes. Medium-to-large-sized organizations rely at a minimum on their Human Resources practitioners to act as informal ombudsmen.

Programming/Implementation

Managing conflict involves several different approaches. These include:

- coaching in individual strategies;
- eliminating organizational politics;
- reducing conflict within work groups;
- reducing conflicts between work groups; and
- stimulating team dynamics through conflict.

Organizations may also have to deal with workplace harassment or bullying. This will be dealt with in a separate chapter.

Individual Strategies

Managers and supervisors at every level of an organization should receive some training in individual strategies for managing conflict. This will give them the necessary skills to channel conflict into productive and proactive activities. It is also an excellent way to teach these managers how to deal with the stress of their jobs. Managing conflict is an essential managerial competency, but this does not mean that it comes naturally. In fact, it is a difficult skill to master.

There are five basic ways to approach conflict:

⇨ **Avoiding:** For many people the easiest strategy seems to be to simply avoid conflict situations alto-

A - B - **C**

gether. They believe they cannot cope with conflict and that facing it will only cause them distress. Avoiding the situation or smoothing over the conflict allows them to escape confrontation.

As a strategy, avoiding may go so far as to influence a person's choice of career path in a direction where there is unlikely to be much conflict. It is not a strategy that should be chosen by those who aspire to managerial or supervisory positions, because conflict is all but inevitable in those roles. Avoiding is an advisable strategy when the underlying issue is trivial and is likely to be resolved in the future without confrontation.

⇨ **Competing:** Assertive individuals naturally choose to compete when faced with conflict. They have a strong tendency to want to win. However, being overly assertive or being assertive in the wrong context may create the impression of closed-mindedness. People who compete all the time are not seen as team players. They have to win every time, and in order to win, someone else has to lose.

Competing is an appropriate strategy when the issue at hand is important to the individual and he or she is very certain that his or her assumptions are correct. Competing is particularly important when a matter of principle is at stake or when there are time constraints on arriving at a decision. As a strategy, competing also requires that the individual have sufficient power or influence to win.

⇨ **Accommodating:** This basically means giving in to others, but can also be used to extract concessions from the other party on issues that are important to the individual. This "horse trading" is a common tactic in complex negotiations.

Accommodating is a good strategy when the issue at hand is not important to the individual and when allowing the other party to win will allow him or her to save face. Individuals should be accommodating when their position is flawed or when the other party has significantly more power.

⇨ **Compromising:** Some individuals confuse compromise with negotiation. Whereas negotiation is a complex interchange that will involve all five strategies at one point or another, compromising merely seeks the middle ground. In a way, it is similar to reaching a consensus. The parties reach a

solution somewhere between their respective positions that they can both live with.

In some contexts, compromising can be extremely ill advised because it can potentially lead to a lose–lose resolution. Take for instance an individual who wants to sell his or her home. The minimum he or she is willing to accept is $250,000. A buyer comes along who is willing to offer a maximum of only $200,000. A compromise might yield an agreed upon price of $225,000. At this price, both parties have lost and will be unhappy with the result.

Compromises may be effective where the issue is relatively unimportant to both parties and a speedy resolution is required.

⇨ **Collaborating:** In order to collaborate, both parties in a conflict must recognize their mutual interest in finding a common solution. Typically, when facing a problem or issue, we decide which solution we prefer and take position accordingly. When another party has an alternative solution, we may ignore the shared interest in the underlying issue and merely focus on the fact of the opposing positions. The result is that the parties choose to compete to see whose position will be adopted or, worse, they compromise.

Collaboration means dropping the taking of sides and focusing on the underlying issues. The parties can then operate in an environment of openness and trust to arrive at a single mutually acceptable solution. The resulting solution may be quite different than the original solutions arrived at by the individuals. It will inevitably result in better decision-making.

Collaborating results in buy-in by all parties. It also ensures that every point of view is taken into consideration before a decision is made.

The style an individual adopts will depend on the situation. Everyone has a natural style they fall into. Some will naturally avoid conflict. Others will focus on the importance of relationships and are quite willing to be accommodating. Others are naturally assertive and choose to compete. Collaborating, while it is an ideal way to resolve conflict, is not natural and individuals need to practice it. Learning good problem-solving skills and understanding work processes will help an individual abandon the tendency to jump to conclusions and to be willing to consider alternatives openly.

Eliminating Organizational Politics

People often engage in political behaviours at work in order to promote their self-interests and achieve personal objectives. These behaviours are discretionary behaviours. They are neither supported by the organization nor are they discouraged. While political behaviour may be engaged in for personal gain, it does not necessarily follow that political actions are inherently bad. If the organization's interests and the interests of the individual coincide, then political behaviour may be seen as furthering the interests of the organization as well as the individual.

Leaders are often natural politicians. Positioning themselves to gain organizational power can only benefit the organization. However, the tactics used when engaging in organizational politics can have negative consequences and may create dysfunctional conflicts. Political tactics include the following:

- blaming or attacking others;
- naming scapegoats;
- withholding or filtering information;
- distributing information selectively;
- covering up mistakes;
- controlling channels of information;
- forming coalitions;
- cultivating networks;
- creating obligations; and
- managing public images.

Some of these behaviours are so aggressive that they cannot but create conflicts. Blaming others for mistakes in order to shift attention from oneself is bound to create a conflict. The office politician who engages in this kind of behaviour must be sure he or she has the power and clout to pull it off.

Other political behaviours may appear neutral on their face. Filtering information, for example, is a necessary task in today's information age. Managers would be overwhelmed by the amount of information they received if they did not rely on others to act as filters. Politicians, however, will filter information so that nothing gets through that reveals a weakness on their own part. They may also take steps to ensure that information damaging to an organizational rival will always get through to the decision makers.

Other behaviours are usually considered to be positive and are, in fact, encouraged. Forming coalitions implies collaboration. This demonstrates willingness on the part of the individual to work in a team and to find mutually beneficial solutions to complex problems. However, whether forming a coalition is ultimately considered good or bad depends largely on the underlying motive. Political players often form coalitions in order to create obligations from others. They may be willing to support a relatively benign project in order to get support for a pet project they know may prove to be unpopular.

Eradicating political behaviour in organizations is likely not possible. Steps can be taken, however, to minimize the adverse impact of overt politicking. One of the most obvious ways to curtail political activities is to make policy statements to discourage such behaviours. Many organizations today are making deliberate attempts to engage employees in a dialogue on organizational values. These forums create excellent opportunities for discussing political behaviours in the context of what is and is not acceptable behaviour reflective of organizational values.

Political behaviours emerge in organizations where people have to compete for scarce resources. In this context, political behaviour is a manifestation of the conflict created when two or more people compete for the same limited resources. Principal among the resources people compete for in organizations is capital. The size and growth of a department's budget may be greatly influenced by the organizational power of the department head. In some organizations, like Pet Valu, there are no departmental budgets. Instead, money is allocated to specific purposes in accordance with an established set of criteria. The department with the largest allocation this year could well have the smallest allocation next year, depending on the relative value of the projects it is involved in. More to the point, money is allocated to projects and specific purposes. Projects are seen as belonging to the organization as a whole, rather than as belonging to a specific department.

The existence of a strong set of rules to govern the allocation of resources can deter political behaviour. In capital budgeting, cash flow analysis and the use of

A - B - **C**

decision-making criteria such as Net Present Value and Internal Rates of Return are designed to take discretion out of decisions regarding resource allocation. The more objectively based decisions are, the less likely it is that political actions will be encouraged.

Another strategy for eliminating political behaviour is to avoid hiring individuals who might have a tendency to engage in such behaviour. However, this strategy is neither practical nor desirable. People with a strong need for personal power and an internal locus of control may have a propensity to engage in political behaviour. They are also likely to be good leaders. Organizations are not likely to want to screen these people out and leave themselves with little bench strength in their succession plans.

The most effective means to combat negative political behaviours is to create forums for open dialogue and to ensure that all communication flows freely. Many senior managers will step out of the hierarchy to engage employees at all levels in discussions. This ensures that the senior managers are getting the full story about what is happening in the workplace. Creating effective vehicles for upward communications such as focus groups, employee "climate" surveys and suggestion programs will help to discourage political behaviour.

Strong performance management processes based on objective criteria will also prevent the politicians from taking credit for the work of others or laying blame on their doorsteps (see Performance Management Process at page 303 *et seq.*).

Finally, senior managers need to recognize the damaging political behaviours of their subordinates and take steps to coach these individuals to direct their energies in a more productive way. One of the most despised political animals found in organizations is the "management toady", otherwise known as the "yes man". As we have noted throughout this section, conflict has positive consequences when it challenges the *status quo* and questions underlying assumptions. "Only a fool wants to hear the echo of his own voice" is an adage that translates into strong managers surrounding themselves with people who have different experiences and backgrounds and who will help them arrive at better decisions.

Reducing Conflict Within Work Groups

Leading edge dispute resolution mechanisms include:

- **Hierarchal Process:** Most organizations rely on an unspoken policy whereby employees are expected to bring conflicts and internal disputes to the attention of their supervisor first. If the supervisor is unable to resolve the issue, the employee can then take the issue to the department manager, and so on up the chain of command.

In theory, such informal processes should bring resolution to a wide variety of issues. However, many supervisors and managers are ill equipped to deal with workplace disputes. Moreover, many employees are reluctant to complain to their bosses. They believe that the complaint will either be summarily dismissed as inconsequential or that there will be reprisals.

- **Open Door Policy:** Open door policies are formal complaint redress systems that address the deficiencies of the informal hierarchal processes by codifying the steps an employee should take. While these processes do not completely overcome employee reluctance or fear of reprisals, they are a step in the right direction.

Open door policies can be made more effective by specifying the kind of complaints the process is designed to address and by training supervisors and managers how to resolve disputes. In organizations with a Human Resources Department, the Human Resources practitioner can be assigned to provide assistance to the employee in formulating their complaint and presenting it to management. The practitioner can also conduct periodic audits or hold focus groups to check on the effectiveness of the process.

The number of complaints received in an open door process should never be used as a measure of process efficacy. A large number of complaints is not necessarily a sign that the system is not working, but rather the opposite. If employees feel the system is fair and equitable, they will be more willing to use it. However, too many complaints may signal more profound problems with management practices, or may be evidence that managers are merely giving in to employees.

- **Internal Dispute Resolution Processes:** Some organizations have formalized their internal complaints processes, but instead of following the chain of command (as with an Open Door Policy), these processes specify that after the supervisor has had the first opportunity to resolve an issue, unresolved disputes are to be heard by managers from other departments. This provides some level of independence at early stages and removes any perception of subjectivity.

- **Third Party Mediation:** Organizational disputes arising between employees and their organization are rarely handled by third party mediators. Under Ontario civil law, selected cases (including wrongful dismissal suits) can be referred to mediation. The actual process involves a private mediator who attempts to bring the parties to a settlement and avoid litigation.

- **Third Party Arbitration:** Arbitration is a well-developed method of resolving employment disputes that arise from the interpretation, application or administration of a collective agreement. In Canada, the system of arbitration has evolved over some 40 years and is an exemplary model of the value of third party arbitration, particularly in cases involving a specific branch of law such as labour relations.

  Arbitration offers a relatively inexpensive alternative to seeking redress through the court system. In labour relations, the arbitrators have a particular expertise that can be of significant assistance to the disputing parties. Moreover, because the system has a significant history, there is now a well-developed body of law that is easily accessible to interested parties. This adds to the procedural fairness and equity of the system.

  Under the labour relations model, the key advantage to the employees is that they can enter into a dispute with their employer without fear of reprisal. More to the point, the employees do not have to give up their employment in order to seek redress from the employer.

  Despite the well-documented advantages of arbitration, it has not yet been introduced as a viable alternative in the rest of employment law.

- **Peer Tribunals:** Peer tribunals are often introduced in organizations where team development is well advanced. These tribunals are often used to review employee misconduct and to determine the appropriate disciplinary sanctions. However, tribunals can also be used to hear employee complaints regarding specific policies, including those related to internal postings and promotions.

  Peer tribunals have a significant influence over policies but are seldom given full authority to decide any particular matter. They are typically set up as advisory councils that have a mandate to make recommendations to management. There are a number of reasons for this. Management retains its authority so that there is a system of checks and balances. In addition, management cannot delegate its responsibility to discipline an employee — or, in the extreme, to terminate an employee.

  Peer tribunals can be set up as either standing committees with a fixed membership or on an *ad hoc* basis. In the latter case, the employee who is bringing the complaint forward or who faces possible disciplinary actions, is permitted to name one member of the *ad hoc* committee. A second member is selected arbitrarily from a list of volunteers and a third member is selected by management. This third member is usually a Human Resources practitioner or another management representative who has been trained to facilitate the meetings and deliberations of the tribunal.

- **Communication Coordinators:** This is a common strategy to use during times of rapid organizational change. To facilitate improved communications, employees from all levels of the organization are selected as communication coordinators. These representatives meet periodically with senior management to discuss the status of change initiatives. The emphasis is on discussion. These meetings are not intended to merely be briefings by management. The communication coordinators are, rather, expected to represent employee concerns. They are charged with the responsibility of bringing forward questions on behalf of employees and to report on rumours and concerns.

  The independence of these coordinators gives them a credibility that managers cannot achieve. More importantly they are particularly effective when communication flows in both directions.

- **Ombudsmen:** A few large organizations (e.g., Bank of Nova Scotia, Magna) have established formal

Ombudsman Offices to hear complaints, investigate their merit, report findings and make recommendations. These offices are functionally separate and usually attached to the CEO. In order to be effective, they must be perceived as being relatively independent bodies with sufficient power to resolve serious conflicts.

The Ombudsman's office may look into complaints of sexual/racial harassment, bullying or other capricious supervisory behaviour such as nepotism or favouritism. The office gives employees an avenue of redress outside the chain of command and may be an appropriate channel for constructive "whistleblowing". Employees who witness unethical behaviour that breaks with the organization's espoused values or the law need to know they have a place to turn to internally to have the matter properly dealt with.

Ombudsmen are common in government contexts where they provide citizens with a means to present grievances against public officials. Ombudsmen are not advocates. They are neutral third parties who make recommendations to the organization based on the evidence they gather. To be effective, ombudsmen need to be speedy in their approach. Notwithstanding this, the most important aspect of the ombudsman's role is thoroughness.

While ombudsmen are often given a wide latitude in terms of the redress they can recommend, the nature of the complaints they typically receive demands a specific decision be made to resolve the issues. For example, in a sexual harassment complaint, it would be very unusual to bring the parties together to discuss a mutual settlement. If the alleged harasser has abused his or her power in the working relationship, the resolution usually demands a disciplinary action be taken, up to and including the possibility of dismissal.

It should also be noted that while an Ombudsman typically has no official power, he or she often has a lot of influence on decision makers. It only makes sense that organizations that go to the trouble and expense of establishing an Office of Ombudsman are going to listen closely to its recommendations.

Reducing Conflict Between Work Groups

- **Emphasizing Superordinate Goals:** In multiproduct manufacturing environments, the production department usually prefers to have long production runs to reduce the amount of time taken to change equipment over from one product run to another. The warehouse group, on the other hand, wants to keep inventories to a minimum so they can optimize the use of their space and keep the cost of inventory low. Nevertheless, the warehouse will recognize the need to carry a minimum amount of safety stock on hand to accommodate rush orders. But they usually prefer to have production build to order.

Even though each department should be working towards the overall objectives of the organization, the competing priorities of the two departments is very likely to lead to conflict. Short production runs usually command higher margins, but if there are too many changeovers the margins can be eroded by losses in efficiency. Production and warehousing need to coordinate their efforts to ensure that they are able to fulfill customer orders and maximize company profits. While compromises are seldom advisable, in instances like this, a compromise should result in a win for the organization, even though each department has to sacrifice its own wishes.

- **Reduce Differentiation:** In large organizations, the division of labour has led to the specialization of tasks. Specialization creates an artificial differentiation that can exacerbate organizational conflict. Specialists may have a tendency to be protective of their roles and to be dogmatic in their approach to problem solving. The very nature of being a specialist means that the individual is an expert who can rely on his or her expertise to create personal advantages.

Specialists sometimes lose focus of the overall goals of the organization and focus instead on their own narrow departmental or personal agendas. Information technology specialists, for example, are often in conflict with others because they are perceived to be out of touch with the "business" of the organization and its central purpose. They often cloud their expertise in a haze of jargon and secrecy to accentuate how special they are. Some information technologists refuse to document software codes in order to make themselves more valuable. These behaviours obviously accentuate the differences between these specialists and the user groups who depend on them.

In manufacturing, maintenance departments often act in a similar way. The organization depends on these individuals to keep the equipment running. However, maintenance mechanics are often reluctant to communicate what they do to repair machines and often resist attempts to document repair procedures. They can be very protective of their specialty and will oppose any attempts to have part of it handled by production personnel. Mechanics, for example, will argue that production people are not qualified to conduct routine lubrication on machinery.

These forms of political behaviour can damage the optimum efficiency of the organization. One way to combat it is to reduce differentiation by cutting the number of specialists and cultivating individuals who have more general experience. Employees from the IT department can be assigned to cross-functional teams to broaden their organizational perspectives. They may even be given assignments in other departments so that they can gain an appreciation for specific work processes.

In team manufacturing environments, such as Crown Cork & Seal's Mississauga, Ontario plant, maintenance mechanics are required to spend a year in production on a rotational basis. Production personnel are also required to spend time in maintenance performing basic functions such as greasing and oiling the equipment. This experience helps the team members maintain a common set of goals and to appreciate each other's efforts.

Organizations also need to be more insistent and disciplined when it comes to documenting processes that increase differentiation. By documenting software coding or maintenance procedures, the organization prevents individuals from becoming too specialized. Many organizations have faced the dilemma of a single individual who commands a significant amount of organizational power simply because he or she is the only one who knows how a particular program works or how to fix a particular machine that has been modi-

fied over time. Good documentation ensures that any qualified individual can perform the work.

This will reduce conflicts that can arise if one individual dominates the call for overtime. User groups and production people are also quick to blame the specialist for making a process so complicated that few can fix it. If the software constantly crashes or the equipment is susceptible to continuous breakdowns, they will blame the specialist for introducing unnecessary complexity. Documentation also allows people with general knowledge to gain some understanding of how a system works. This increases the opportunities for discussions between the specialist and the client group, and helps break down communications barriers.

- **Reduce Task Interdependence:** Issues that arise between groups will be accentuated by the degree of dependence each has on the other. There are several ways to reduce the level of dependence and thus reduce the magnitude of intergroup conflicts. In manufacturing, where separate processes are organized sequentially, the potential for conflict arises when one work group cannot keep pace with the other. In complex operations, this can be quite common because the designed capacities of the different processes cannot always be kept in alignment. One costly way to combat this is to build inventory buffers between the groups. Then a production problem in one area does not have an immediate impact on its internal customer. The cost of this has to be weighed against the cost of potential disputes between the work groups.

- **Clarify Rules, Policies and Procedures:** Rules help to codify behaviour and delineate what is and is not acceptable. They also ensure consistent treatment of all employees. Rules are set up so that employees know what is expected of them and what to expect when they break the rules.

Ambiguous rules or uncertain consequences can lead to inconsistent interpretation and application and thus create conflict. To be effective, rules have to be communicated well so that every employee is aware of them. The rules should not be arbitrary but should rather address an organizational need. Rules should be reasonable, meaning that they are demonstrably necessary to protect the interests of the business. Finally, the consequences for an infraction of the rules should be consistently applied and

A - B - **C**

should be appropriate to the seriousness of the misconduct.

Policies also help to reduce ambiguity. Policies are designed to ensure consistent application and equitable treatment of employees. When writing policies, human resource practitioners emphasize that the intent is to lay the groundwork for the equitable treatment of employees and not necessarily equal treatment. In organizations that have developed a culture of entitlement, conflicts can arise because employees have been led to believe there should be equal treatment.

For example, a conflict might arise when employees who do not have children feel discriminated against if employees with children are given a fixed number of days off to attend to a sick child. Some employees feel that equal treatment means that everyone should be given the same number of days off regardless of their needs. The simple fact is that the organization in this case does actually intend to be discriminating: by providing a benefit to employees with children, the organization is accommodating their specific needs. The organization needs to emphasize that they are accommodating a specific need rather then providing a special benefit. One way to do this is to avoid specifying a fixed number of days, so that it is well understood by everyone what the purpose of the policy is.

Procedures are another possible source of ambiguity. Organizations often find there is a certain degree of drift away from proper procedures over time. Employees who have not received adequate training will find their own way of doing things and adopt procedures according to their comfort level. However, depending on the degree of task interdependence, their way might conflict with another employee's way.

Written procedures reduce ambiguity by specifying an approved way of performing a particular task. Organizations that have undergone certification under the International Standards Organization (ISO) have found that documenting procedures and training employees how to follow them consistently not only reduces conflict, but can also dramatically improve productivity and product quality.

- **Negotiation:** The art of negotiation is probably one of the most coveted business skills. Negotiation is a deliberate attempt to resolve issues jointly with another party and to lay out a definition for the ongoing relationship. Some negotiations are relatively simple. Purchasing agents, for example, are required to negotiate the purchase of a wide range of products on a daily basis. More complex negotiations take place between parties who have relationships that endure over long periods of time. Buying a piece of office equipment can be relatively simple when the purchaser is not bound to any particular supplier. Collective bargaining for a new labour contract, on the other hand, can be a very complex process and will demand the talents of a skilled negotiator.

In the employment context, negotiating is more common than one might assume. Employees often negotiate with their supervisors to exchange extra efforts for extra time off. Senior managers become involved in complex negotiations over their compensation packages and bonuses before they agree to terms with their new employer. Employees with a penchant for office politics will frequently negotiate with others to extract some personal advantage.

Negotiation is a good strategy because it involves the feuding parties in the process, meaning that they can own the outcome. If the relative bargaining power of the parties is not equal, however, the weaker party may not find negotiating a settlement to be a fair means to resolve differences.

- **Relationships by Objectives:** This joint problem-solving process (also known as Inter-group Mirroring) involves having the two conflicting groups share their perceptions of each other and then coming up with a plan to change the other's perspective and address the issues put before them.

The Relationships by Objectives process requires a skilled facilitator who first meets with the two groups separately, in order to ascertain whether or not they are both ready to resolve their differences. The clear desire to settle matters has to exist on both sides for the process to work. It also requires the participant to approach the issues with a great deal of emotional maturity. This requires them to "park their paradigms" by suspending judgment and keeping open minds, and to be willing to accept the perceptions of the other group as fair representations of reality.

If the facilitator is convinced that the two parties are earnest in their desire to resolve their differences, and are prepared to approach the process with open minds, he or she will arrange for an offsite working session. Depending on the size of the group, this session can take from one to three days. It is important to hold the session offsite whenever possible. Not only does this ensure some freedom from the distractions of the office, but it also provides neutral territory.

Once offsite, the facilitator meets with each group separately and helps them prepare a list of grievances against the other party, along with their perceptions of the relationship. It is important that these grievances and perceptions are presented in an objective fashion. Issues concerning individuals should focus on behaviour and personal commentaries should be avoided.

Once both lists are completed, the groups are brought together to share their grievances. A representative from each group may be called upon to read the list to the other group. The receiving group is not permitted to comment on the list or to attempt to defend its actions. Members of the receiving group are, however, permitted to ask questions to clarify meaning and may ask the other group to cite examples. The facilitator acts as a referee to ensure the rules of engagement are respected at all times.

Next, the groups are separated again. This time each is responsible for responding to the other's list. Given that the list has to be accepted as it is, suitable responses must address the issues it raises, offer solutions and take ownership of those solutions. Neither group can offer solutions that require the other group to make changes. Sometimes it is acceptable to explain why a situation exists that cannot be changed, but groups should be encouraged to keep these to a minimum.

The groups are then united again to share their action plans. Each is permitted to seek clarification of any of the solutions being proposed. Together they negotiate a final action plan that is documented and signed off on. It is important to create this document as a binding settlement. Each group is promising to take certain actions to settle their differences.

Finally, the session is adjourned and the parties go back to work and begin the implementation of the action plan. Like any good action plan, it should contain a time line and define responsibilities clearly. The groups or their representatives should meet periodically to review progress. In some cases, this can evolve into a continuous process; in others, once the action plan is concluded, the process is simply adjourned.

The process will take months of committed time and may even result in changes that take place over a number of years. The success rate of Relationships by Objectives is incredibly high. Some facilitators can legitimately lay claim to a success rate of one hundred percent. The most important factor in creating such a high success rate is the willingness of the parties to resolve the disputes and look for mutual gains.

As illustrated by the following example of two credit clerks who could not get along, Relationships by Objectives can be used as a tool in fixing relationships between two groups of virtually any size. Despite the fact that these two clerks held the same job and worked at adjoining desks, they seldom spoke to each other during the course of their workday. When they did have words, they were typically heated. They refused to share information and insisted on working independently. When speaking to others in the office they constantly complained about each other to the point where their actions were negatively affecting overall morale.

The situation eventually got the attention of management. Productivity in the department was declining to the point where credit claims were backlogged and credit applications were taking an inordinate amount of time. The department manager was frustrated to the point that he wanted one or both of the clerks replaced. He approached the Human Resources Department, which suggested that the dispute be investigated and an attempt be made to resolve the differences between the two.

Now it may appear obvious in this example that both clerks were motivated to attempt to resolve their differences because of the potential threat to their continuous employment. This is true, but it is also common. Parties in a dispute often do not come to realize that they need to fix the relation-

A - B - **C**

ship until the relationship faces the threat of extinction. In the work context, the existence of relationships between workgroups is longstanding. If a union and management cannot find peace in the long run, the organization will not be able to compete.

In the example of our two clerks, each appeared to be mature and willing enough to take steps to resolve the underlying issues. The senior of the two clerks handled claims and applications for Eastern Canada. She believed the other clerk was not carrying her share of the workload. The senior clerk felt her junior counterpart took excessively long breaks and was unwilling to work overtime. As the more skilled of the two, she felt there was increasing pressure on her to perform while the junior clerk seemed to be given some slack because of her relative lack of experience.

The junior clerk was responsible for claims and applications for Western Canada. She believed the senior clerk hogged the work and was unwilling to share more interesting claims. She also believed the senior clerk made little effort to train her or provide assistance and that the senior clerk worked longer hours and refused to take breaks as a way of ingratiating herself with management. Furthermore, she believed this was a deliberate attempt on the part of the senior clerk to make her look bad.

This is a simple example and the underlying problem became quite obvious to the two clerks once they shared their grievances. They resolved to reorganize the work equitably by assigning a specific number of clients to each other rather than organizing the work along geographic lines. They also agreed to adjust the workload between themselves when it fluctuated. By doing this, the junior clerk reduced the time she spent on breaks and became more interested in her work. The senior clerk had more time available and was able to show her coworker how to handle difficult claims. The senior clerk no longer had to put in long hours and was now able to join her newfound friend on breaks.

The point of the example is to demonstrate that Relationship By Objectives is a relatively simple process of involving feuding groups in a joint problem-solving dialogue. Opening up communications can go a long way toward fixing broken relationships.

Introducing Conflict into Team Dynamics

There are different stages in the development of teams. How a team handles these various stages — and the individual team members' abilities to cope with the dynamics inherent in each stage — will have a profound impact on the effectiveness of the team to perform its mandate. In a 1977 study *Stages of Small-Group Development Revisted*, B.W. Tuckman created a five-stage model to describe how teams form. This model includes:

⇨ **Forming:** The members join the team and learn about each other and the benefits of membership in the team. Members are "socialized" as to what is expected of them and what they can expect from the others in the group.

⇨ **Storming:** Members become more proactive, roles are defined and tasks assigned. *This stage is marked by interpersonal conflict as members compete for leadership and other positions on the team.* It is at this stage that the group's ability to manage conflict is tested. If it has appropriate coping mechanisms, the conflict will be channeled into productive activities rather than being suppressed.

⇨ **Norming:** The group begins to be more cohesive and establishes rules and boundaries to govern behaviour. Conflict is channeled through open feedback between members and self-disclosure. Team members accept each other as individuals and appreciate the value that differences in background and experience offers to the team.

⇨ **Performing:** The team fulfills its mandate in a coordinated and efficient manner.

⇨ **Adjourning:** The team breaks up or is renewed through the introduction of new members.

Some teams are brought together to accomplish a single task and are then broken up. Others are more permanent bodies that are brought together to perform an ongoing role, such as a functioning department. In the latter case, the group can become complacent and ineffective if it achieves too high a degree of cohesiveness. Team cohesiveness can be achieved by recruiting people with common backgrounds and experiences and who share common values. Entire organizations can become too cohesive and suffer from a culture of complacency and groupthink.

Introducing conflict to a longstanding cohesive team in effect amounts to taking them back to the storming stage of development. In the vernacular, the idea is to "shake things up" in order to stimulate growth and creativity. To accomplish this, the team has to be reshaped by transferring some members out and bringing new members in, preferably individuals who have different backgrounds and a different set of experiences.

In addition to adding new members to the team, there are other ways to stimulate conflict. These include:

- **Increase Resource Scarcity:** Reducing conflicts that arise when two individuals or groups are competing for the same scarce resource by simply adding resources allows them to avoid the conflict and, in a sense, it deprives them of the opportunity to develop alternative solutions.

  If, for example, two groups have a conflict over the use of a photocopier, eliminating the conflict may simply involve purchasing a second photocopier. Instead of buying another photocopier, however, the organization might insist that the two groups get together to discuss the dispute. In this way, they might learn something about each other's work processes and may be able to reorganize their work to accommodate each other in a mutually productive way. Not only would the organization save the cost of a photocopier, but it might also create an ongoing dialogue between the two work groups that encourages them to find other process improvements.

  If an organization puts new restrictions on capital spending, it will force competing groups to discuss projects and arrive at decision-making criteria that might otherwise be overlooked. Competing project teams might discover synergies that will allow them to work together and save the organization money that would be spent on redundant resources. Encouraging such a dialogue may allow the organization to move forward on two projects, whereas before it had to choose between competing interests.

  Putting constraints on decision-making forces the decision makers to be more creative and ideally to

collaborate with others in order to get projects done. The legendary "skunkworks" that led to the creation of such innovative products as the Ford Mustang and Jaguar's XJ-220 "super car" emerged precisely because the organizations did not allocate the necessary resources to get the projects off the ground. Innovators within these organizations looked for creative ways to get around the restraints, rather than simply accepting the lack of resources as a "deal breaker".

- **Increase Task Interdependence:** The introduction of just-in-time inventory management systems forces departments in a sequential production flow to work very closely together to ensure inventory levels are kept to a minimum, while also ensuring that work flows are continuous and free of disruptions. Just-in-time systems require departments to coordinate work schedules with their internal suppliers and internal customers alike.

  This strategy is the antithesis of introducing production buffers, such as inventory buffers and accumulators designed (in part) to eliminate conflicts that might arise because of the different pace of production among work groups in a production sequence. Removing these buffers forces the groups to coordinate their efforts. The organization gains from the obvious reduction in the costs of carrying extra inventory. In a more subtle way, the organization will realize significant gains in overall productivity if the groups are able to work together to discover where the bottlenecks in production are occurring and resolve them.

- **Increase Ambiguity:** This is a trick often employed by astute managers when bringing heterogeneous work groups together to resolve complex problems. Minimizing the parameters contained in a project team's mandate allows the team creative freedom. Introducing ambiguity into an existing work group should force the group into a dialogue from which it will eventually arrive at a consensus as to the approach they will take and what constraints they will place on themselves in completing the project.

  At a minimum, introducing ambiguity should result in improved communication, because the work group will inevitably seek clarification. In order to resolve the ambiguity, the work group must ask questions.

A - B - **C**

- **Introduce Devil's Advocacy:** The devil's advocate is not merely a naysayer. Devil's advocacy requires an individual to be something of a sophist — someone who takes an alternative viewpoint and deliberately tests the assumptions made by the majority. The point is not to disagree for the sake of disagreeing. The focus is on ensuring every consideration is aired before a decision is struck.

- **Emphasize and Reward Departmental Goals:** A common application of this approach is to have "shift-of-the-month" awards. In manufacturing environments, some organizations have introduced a friendly competition among shifts to encourage each work team to optimize its safety, quality and production efforts. This type of conflict can lead to improved group cohesiveness within the shift as employees cooperate to overcome a common adversary — the other shifts.

Introducing conflict to stimulate creativity and create a more dynamic decision-making environment might be viewed as a model for organizational change. In the early stages of their formation, organizations have a tendency to recruit people with backgrounds and experiences similar to the founders. In these early stages, the harmony created by having homogeneous work groups allows employees to focus their energies on productive activities. Having employees who share common values and beliefs makes communications effortless and allows the organization to respond quickly to its environment. However, as the organization grows, not only does it become more difficult to find people with a common background but it also becomes undesirable.

Role of the Human Resources Practitioner

Managing workplace conflict is a significant part of what Human Resources practitioners do. Practitioners play many different roles in dealing with workplace conflict. These roles can be both proactive and reactive. Unfortunately, one of the roles the practitioner is often thrust into is that of organizational policemen.

In this policing role, the Human Resources practitioner is asked to monitor employee behaviours like absenteeism. When an employee exceeds the norm for absenteeism, the practitioner is asked to intervene and take the appropriate actions to get the employee to correct the underlying problem. In large industrial organizations, the role of disciplinarian may be given to the Human Resources practitioner. This is a form of specialization that allows supervisors more time to attend to administrative duties and allows them to maintain a positive relationship with their subordinates.

In the long run, however, assigning policing duties to the Human Resources Department is counterproductive. With a specialist on hand to do the "dirty work", supervisors are able to abdicate their responsibilities. Most supervisors welcome this because it means they can avoid potential conflicts with employees. Creating this "good cop, bad cop" scenario impairs the development of supervisory skills. Potential conflicts in the workplace increase as an individual moves up the organizational ladder. It is therefore important for the development of future managers that supervisors learn how to confront difficult issues early in their careers.

The most troubling aspect of the policing role is that it prevents the Human Resources practitioner from being viewed as a neutral party. If the Human Resources practitioners are primarily responsible for doling out discipline, employees will not trust them with issues or feel comfortable relying on them to resolve employee grievances. Gaining the appropriate balance between working in the organization's interests and acting as an employee advocate is one of the biggest challenges for any Human Resources practitioner.

If the practitioner is the chief disciplinarian then employees who are being harassed by their supervisors will believe they have no where to go internally for redress. As a result, they will either repress their grievances or will seek third party assistance to resolve the issue. If the supervisor can go to the practitioner to have an employee disciplined or suspended, employees will view the Human Resources Department as having an inherent bias. Even when the supervisor is merely seeking advice about how to proceed in a disciplinary matter, this perception will remain.

The best method for striking a balance is to move the Human Resources Department away from a reactive role towards a proactive one. A strategy used by some organizations has been to separate certain aspects of Human Resources Management from others. Functions that necessitate a slant towards the organization and involve potential confrontations with employees

— such as labour relations — are separated from the others and will have a different reporting line. This allows the rest of the Human Resources Department to be employee advocates, or at least neutral parties in the internal dispute resolution process.

One danger of this separation is that the labour relations function can be at odds with the direction of the Human Resources Department and inadvertently undermine efforts to build a strong organizational culture. Labour relations specialists can have a propensity to be more reactive then proactive. They can also be more conservative in their approach and rely on practices that were suitable in the past but do not meet present organizational needs. The potential result is that collective agreements can restrict what the organization wants to accomplish in the way of organizational changes.

As discussed above, increased specialization can breed conflict. Separating the labour relations function from the rest of Human Resources Department can lead to conflicts between the two departments. If there are two separate reporting lines, there is further potential for a breakdown in communications that can accentuate the differences in their respective approaches. It is almost inevitable that conflicts between Human Resources specialists and labour relations specialists will develop over time. The best way to combat this conflict is to develop Human Resources generalists who have a thorough knowledge of labour relations issues and human resource management practices.

In lieu of specialization, the balance between the practitioners' duties to the organization and his or her duties to the employees will be achieved according to the way the practitioner exercises the craft. Finding a balance is further complicated by the fact that a certain type of person is often attracted to the field of Human Resources Management. People with strong relationship orientations are initially attracted to Human Resources because they want to "work with people". They put a high value on relationships and have a strong desire to be liked and recognized as someone who is helpful. In organizations where the Human Resources role is defined as an advocacy role, these people can do quite well. They will struggle, however, in achieving a balance and are therefore not well suited to the more typical role of the Human Resources practitioner.

The primary reason why these people struggle is that they will consistently seek ways to improve personal relationships when dealing with conflicts. In the interest of maintaining the relationship, they will tend to avoid confrontation and will have a propensity for compromising on issues. Thus, in dealing with conflict, they are apt to dismiss the underlying issues as being of secondary importance. A "country club" atmosphere can be bred in organizations where the entire Human Resources function adopts this paradigm and this will have a significant influence on the organization's culture.

People in Human Resources roles who have strong relationship orientations are also prone to "burnout". Their primary focus is on being employee advocates. They want to help people. However, when dealing with conflicts, they inevitably find that they have to deal with many parties who all have different viewpoints and different interests. As well, they are likely to find that the breadth of "people issues" can be enormous.

By way of illustration, consider a Human Resources practitioner who has been assigned the unfortunate duty of closing an operation and permanently laying off hundreds of individuals. The practitioner with a high relationship orientation is going to strongly empathize with the employees who are losing their jobs. This may well prove to be overwhelming for such a person.

The first rule of achieving a balance in the Human Resources function therefore is to hire individuals who have the behavioural traits that match the demands of the job. Most people hold the view that Human Resources practitioners should be, above all else, "people people". Oddly perhaps, the opposite is true. Successful practitioners need to be somewhat assertive. They are thrust into situations involving conflicts daily and must be willing to assert themselves into those situations. In order to be balanced in their approach, practitioners need to be very objective in their assessments. This is their most important trait. Objectivity allows practitioners to distance themselves from the emotionally charged aspects of conflicts and get to the root cause.

The practitioner has to be able to handle multiple tasks and establish priorities in an ever-changing environment. Practitioners are the guardians of organizational policies and practices and must have an appreci-

A - B - **C**

ation for the importance of maintaining consistency in the application, administration and interpretation of those policies and procedures. However, the practitioner also needs to be creative and willing to think outside of the box when resolving issues.

In the multi-tasking organization of today, the practitioner achieves a balance by being many different things to different people within the organization. These roles include:

- **Coach:** Managers and supervisors must deal with conflict and potential conflict on a regular basis. In the course of their duties they also often have to confront employees regarding difficult issues related to work performance and other problems. The Human Resources practitioner can help managers and supervisors deal with these situations through coaching.

  This can involve discussions regarding individual strategies for dealing with conflict (avoiding, accommodating, compromising, competing and collaborating) and management style. Role playing is another effective way of coaching because it allows the supervisor an opportunity to test his or her skills in a non-threatening context. Feedback can help the supervisor make adjustments and get comfortable with his or her individual style. It also helps the supervisor anticipate a number of different scenarios that he or she may face.

  The practitioner's role as a coach is continuous. Advice is best delivered on a just-in-time basis. Supervisors should rely on the Human Resources practitioner as a sounding board to go over how they are going to approach a disciplinary meeting or performance review. This can help them practice their approach and get helpful tips. In some cases, the supervisor may want the practitioner to attend the meeting as an observer to provide feedback afterwards as to how well the meeting went.

- **Facilitator:** The Human Resources practitioner's most neutral role is that of facilitator. In this role, the practitioner must focus on maintaining the integrity of the processes and not presuppose the outcomes. He or she does not take sides but rather offers advice to participants about how they should conduct themselves. Essentially, the practitioner takes an independent role as an internal consultant. The ultimate goal of the facilitator is to reach a

mutually satisfactory agreement between the two parties involved in a dispute.

The role of facilitator is not an *ad hoc* one. It is rather imbedded in the policies and procedures of the organization. In some instances, this role may be seen as reactive. However, the very fact that processes have been put in place to deal with internal disputes makes it proactive. Some view the existence of internal dispute resolution as a means of breeding conflict. In their view, processes like open door policies give a voice to discontented employees who take the opportunity to be disruptive. These individuals view internal dispute resolution processes with suspicion and may be apt to undermine them.

An alternative view is to see that by giving a voice to employee grievances, the organization will learn how to cope with the stresses put on employees and how to transform dysfunctional conflict into productive and creative outcomes. In dealing with conflicts through institutionalized processes, the organization is introducing procedural fairness that will in turn breed open and honest communications.

In the Open Door process, the practitioner should be positioned as a third party. The practitioner can help the employee frame his or her complaint by reviewing the facts of the situation and going over relevant policies. While the review of policy can itself resolve the issue, the practitioner should resist taking a too narrow approach to fixing the issue. Often the real issue lies below the surface and it is only through opening up communications that the root cause of the grievance may be uncovered.

The practitioner also assists the supervisor or manager in the Open Door by coaching him or her on how to listen with empathy. The practitioner will also debrief the supervisor or manager and assist in writing a response. In this role, practitioners must guard themselves from owning the proposed resolution. If the employee rejects the proposed redress and wants to move further in the process, the practitioner must be able to keep an open mind and allow for alternative solutions that might emerge at different stages.

Practitioners should also facilitate the convening of Peer Tribunals. These require a delicate hand to ensure openness and procedural fairness. As a facilitator, one of the primary roles for the practitioner is to educate the panel members on corporate policy, organizational precedents and, in some instances, employment law and statutory considerations. While the practitioner must maintain neutrality with respect to the issue at hand, he or she must also serve as a guardian of the organization's interests — a role that requires considerable finesse. At the outset, however, the practitioner should establish ground rules with the panel members. These ground rules will include asserting that the practitioner may veto any recommendation that contravenes the law or is patently unreasonable.

Depending on the nature and complexity of the underlying conflicts, the skilled practitioner may facilitate a Relationships by Objectives exercise. In large organizations, it may be possible to use Human Resources practitioners from a corporate office or from another division to accentuate their neutral role in the process. In any case, it takes a great deal of experience and skill to facilitate an intergroup process like Relationships by Objectives and it may be best left to external consultants to act as intermediaries.

The practitioner can also play a very rewarding and interesting role in the facilitation of any team of people brought together to perform a task. The practitioner should be involved at every stage of the team's development. When establishing a team, the practitioner should be consulted so that good Human Resources practices are employed in selecting team members. The dynamics of group formation, particularly through the "storming" and "norming" stages (as discussed above) must be channeled to ensure positive outcomes. The practitioner can play an important role in teaching team members how to deal with confrontation and conflict in an appropriate manner and in teaching the group in how to develop mechanisms to handle disputes.

- **Ombudsman:** While the role of ombudsman is a neutral one, the incumbent will very likely take a position on the matter brought before them. In essence, the very nature of the human resource practitioner's role is to serve as the organization's ombudsman. An ombudsman by definition is a person appointed to a role to receive and investigate complaints, report findings and make recommendations as to the fair and equitable disposition of the complaint. While some organizations have formalized the office of ombudsman, most expect the Human Resources Department to fulfill this function — particularly when it comes to complaints regarding capricious supervisory behaviour and abuses of power including, but not limited to, sexual/racial harassment and bullying.

When investigating these matters, the practitioner must maintain objectivity. Some complaints can be quite serious and may result in the termination of a supervisor or manager. The investigation has to be thorough and to every extent possible must rely on clear and cogent evidence of a wrongdoing before a decision is recommended. Investigation must also be handled delicately to ensure that an individual's rights are preserved at all times and reputations are not unnecessarily besmirched.

In addition to being objective, the practitioner must have a thorough understanding of employment law (including human rights and wrongful dismissal jurisprudence) to adequately fulfil this role. Investigations are usually handled by senior practitioners who have had a wide experience in dealing with employee issues because of the sensitivity and importance of the subject matter.

- **Mediator/Arbitrator:** When some conflicts are brought to the attention of the practitioner, it is not clear that there is a sole instigator or a clear-cut villain in the matter. Disputes between peers may emerge, for example, when there is a breakdown in communications between two people. In some instances, a structural approach — like Relationships by Objectives — may be indicated. However, a more common approach is for the practitioner to act as a mediator. This essentially involves facilitating a dialogue between the two parties to help them resolve the dispute.

The practitioner may also serve as an arbitrator in the event that the parties are unable to resolve the matter between themselves. This is an informal process and is not binding on the parties in the way that mediation/arbitration processes are in a labour relations context. The practitioner's ability to get disputing parties to talk matters through in an appropriate manner can go a long way toward resolving conflicts.

Barriers to Success/Common Pitfalls

Creating channels to divert conflict into productive avenues can reduce workplace stress and eliminate the negative effects of organizational dysfunction. However, in order to deal properly with conflict, the organization must set up processes that confront the issues. The natural tendency for a lot of people is to avoid conflict. They are willing to accommodate others or compromise their own interests in order to avoid confrontation. Unfortunately, this means suppressing their opinions and ideas.

There are a few organizations where there is little conflict. The most common mistake made in managing conflict is failing to recognize that conflict is a necessary element in the health of an organization. As a result, the organization adopts inappropriate and ineffective mechanisms for dealing with it. The result is usually a stagnant organization that is unable to grow. These organizations may have an unrealistically heightened sense of organizational performance and may take inadvisable risks. In order to grow and maintain a competitive edge, these organizations need to introduce conflict and learn how to channel it appropriately.

One way many supervisors and managers cope with conflict is to trivialize it. They may acknowledge that a conflict between two employees exists, but they will assert that the issue is merely a "personality conflict". As we have seen above, personality may be an influencing factor in a conflict, but it is never the root cause. Supervisors and managers who do not recognize this fact are unlikely to investigate conflicts to find their root causes and arrive at solutions that will ultimately better the organization.

Conflicts labelled as personality clashes are rarely addressed in the early stages of the confrontation. The conflict is instead left to fester and grow until the point when a decisive action must be taken. In extreme cases, the conflict can lead to altercations between the employees (including physical assaults) and the organization will be forced to take drastic measures, including the possibility of terminating the employee.

Too often there are no suitable or effective venues for conflict to be brought out in the open. As a result, organizations may face the prospect of nurturing political behaviour. Some organizations fail to recognize the potential damage that unchecked political behaviour can have on organizational culture. In general, organizations also fail to recognize the importance of dealing with conflict in a structural way. The Human Resources practitioner needs to be very persuasive in ensuring processes like open door policies or other complaint resolution mechanisms are implemented.

A multifaceted approach is required. Good Human Resources Management practices like objective performance management systems will go a long way toward reducing the potential for confrontations (see Performance Management Process at page 303 *et seq.*). As well, organizations that provide avenues for employees to voice their objections and grievances will see a reduction in the ill will that can be bred by miscommunication.

When implementing any conflict management initiative, the secret ingredient is to ensure that everyone involved in the process is capable of accepting responsibility for the resolution of conflict. To make the process work, the individuals involved have to experience a paradigm shift. Training alone will not achieve this. It is a common complaint among supervisors and managers that they are not well trained in dealing with conflict. What this usually means is that they have difficulty in handling confrontation. A common mistake, though, is to assume that a training course in conflict resolution will act as a panacea.

In the worse-case scenario, there may be a tendency to lay blame on the employee who raised a complaint or voiced an alternative opinion. Unfortunately, some victims of sexual harassment have found themselves in this predicament. Investigations may be cursory and may focus on the actions of the victim. In a rather unfortunate example, a new female employee on probation was subjected to verbal abuse, leering and some physical contact by her male supervisor. As a result, she suffered considerable distress causing her to be distracted from her work. Her performance was understandably sub-par. The investigation into the matter focused on her poor work performance. Some evidence of wrongdoing on the part of the supervisor was found, but the end result was that he was given a written reprimand while she lost her job. The company settled the matter with the employee rather than face a human rights investigation.

The organization must develop a culture wherein open and honest communication is encouraged. In such a culture, everyone must be willing to empathize with others and make earnest attempts to see the point of view of others. This does not mean capitulating. In one organization with an open door policy, a certain division had far more open door issues raised by employees than all the other divisions combined. This is usually a sign that employees feel comfortable with the process and that issues were being resolved. However, every issue raised was resolved in favour of the employee at the plant manager level. The plant manager was abusing the system in a rather unique way. He did not want any issue moving on to the next step in the process, regardless of its merits or lack thereof. So he gave in to every employee issue. It became well known among employees that raising complaints could result in windfall gains for the employee. By accommodating employees the manager had exposed the process to flagrant abuses. Moreover, he undermined the authority of his supervisory staff who had made honest attempts to listen to employee issues but had found the complaints wanting.

In another division at the same organization, the opposite was happening. The division produced no open door grievances at all. The head of the division asserted that the process worked very well and that all employee issues were being addressed. However, an audit uncovered the fact that not a single complaint had been raised in over four years and that a clear majority of the employees in the division were completely unaware that the open door policy existed. Those few who were aware of the process cited that they were afraid of reprisals if they were to use it.

Employee complaints and other sources of conflict present an opportunity for improvement. Instead of viewing them as challenges to a manager's authority, they need to be seen as an opportunity to correct skill deficiencies or to correct process problems. Even the complaints that have no substantive merit must be seen as valuable. They provide an insight into how well the organization communicates its policies and values.

Let's say, for example, an employee feels that he or she was denied the use of personal days. The organization may have a policy to provide days off to employees who need to deal with family emergencies. The employee in question had no family emergencies, but still believes he or she was entitled to the days off regardless. The fact that the employee holds a particular belief about a company policy in error signals to the organization that it has not done a good enough job in communicating its policies. So even if there is no specific redress for the employee who raised the complaint, there are steps the organization should take to correct the underlying problem.

In most organizations, individuals who are competitive and ambitious tend to be the people who receive recognition and get promoted. They are the home run hitters. Their wins however come at the expense of others. The problem is that organizations tend to reward these individuals, the "winners". As these competitors become more successful, they gain power through promotions. The people who lose become disheartened and learn not to speak out in opposition to the *status quo*. The alternative is to encourage an integrative orientation wherein employees believe that by working together the pie will grow and each individual's share will grow commensurately.

Leaders in an organization that espouses an integrative orientation as a core value tend to be rewarded for behaviours that help others achieve their goals. These leaders listen to ideas with an open mind and empower employees to try new ideas. Empowerment means allowing the employee to own an idea and to receive recognition for its successful implementation. The true leader stands out because he or she is able to contribute to the development of others.

The most significant barrier is therefore the organizational culture. Instituting an open door policy alone will not do much in the way of managing conflict. To truly get a handle on conflict an organization must take a broad approach. A starting point may be, for example, to review the current role and perceptions of the Human Resources Department. It plays the central role in conflict management so it is vital that this role be well defined. Once the appropriate mandate is established, the senior practitioner should review the current skills inventory within the department and honestly assess whether or not the current practitioners can fulfill the general requirements discussed above. They should then be trained and coached in areas where they are lacking.

Related to this are the misperceptions among senior managers regarding conflict. They may believe that the absence of overt conflict is a sign of organizational health and harmony. On the other hand, some may believe that employee complaints and grievances are a sign of organizational dysfunction. Healthy organizations achieve a symbiosis wherein conflict is well balanced. The point is that, in conjunction with implementing structural approaches to managing conflict, the organization should take regular stock of its health through the use of tools like employee surveys, focus groups and Human Resources audits to ensure it is maintaining a balanced approach.

CONTRACTS, EMPLOYMENT

Definition/Background

All employee-to-organization relationships are contractual. There is an implied exchange of services (labour) for remuneration. Employment contracts can be simply oral agreements with implicit understandings, or they can be well-documented written contracts (or something in between).

All employment contracts carry certain implicit understandings. Unless specified as a "fixed-term contract", employment contracts are continuous. There is the implied duty that the employee will perform the agreed upon work faithfully and will be loyal to the organization. This means that the employee will not work for a competitor or otherwise divulge confidential information that would bring harm to the organization.

Since the employment contract is considered to be a permanent arrangement, the parties implicitly agree not to terminate the contract without cause or without reasonable notice. The whole basis of "wrongful dismissal" jurisprudence (in addition to determining what is or is not "cause") is to determine what reasonable notice is.

At their simplest, contracts contain three elements:

(a) an offer;

(b) acceptance of the offer; and

(c) consideration.

Today, most employers make an offer of employment in writing to the prospective employee, and ask the individual to sign a copy back to acknowledge his or her acceptance. Once the employee begins work, he or she receives a pay cheque which is the consideration that consummates the contractual arrangement. Thus, the simple "Letter of Offer" is, in fact, an employment contract. While it is not all-inclusive, it sets the basic terms of the relationship. Usually, letters of offer include the starting date, the agreed upon salary, benefits entitlement, vacation entitlement, reporting relationships and job duties. Other more specific terms may be deemed to be included implicitly.

In legal terms, there is no finite or exact definition of what distinguishes an employee from another provider of services. Organizations should clearly consider what the terms of employment will be before drafting a contract. Some employers mistakenly believe they are hiring an independent contractor when they are, in fact, taking on a new employee.

Common clauses included in employment contracts are the following:

- **Remuneration** — How much the employee will be paid, when he or she is paid, applicable bonuses and the employee's eligibility for bonus payments.

- **Term** — Most employment contracts are implicitly permanent; however, organizations may opt to hire an employee for a fixed term. The beginning and end of the contract should therefore be stated.

- **Job Description** — This may involve a brief description of job duties or the description itself can be included by reference.

- **Probationary Period** — This is a contracted period of time during which the organization can assess the employee's fit to the position and the organization's culture. If the employee is found not to be a fit, the standard of proof for determining cause is less than with regular employees and, therefore, notice of termination is restricted to the statutory requirement.

- **Relocation** — Specifies that the employee may be relocated to another geographic location. By specifying this, the organization negates potential claims that an offer to relocate is tantamount to constructive dismissal.

- **Entire Agreement Clause** — This important clause specifies that the agreement represents the entire offer made to the employee. If, during the hiring process, an interviewer implied a different understanding, it is negated by this clause.

- **Non-competition, Non-solicitation Clauses** — These protect the organization from having employees leave their employment and use their knowledge of the industry to solicit clients or customers away from the organization, and protect the organization from former employees poaching its staff.

- **Confidentiality** — While there is an implicit duty to act in good faith and protect the interests of the organization, many organizations include a confidentiality agreement in their offers of employment. These are agreements that any information gained on the job which could be used to the organization's detriment will be kept confidential.

- **Mandatory Retirement** — Many terms of employment can be included in the contract by reference to the organization's Human Resources policies. Some organizations specify the mandatory retirement age in their letters of offer to ensure it is clearly understood.

- **Choice of Law** — Organizations that operate in more than one jurisdiction may want to specify which jurisdictions laws will apply to the interpretation of the contract in the case of a dispute. There must be a clear rationale for the choice rather than picking a jurisdiction to the organization's advantage. Usually, it is the jurisdiction where the organization's corporate offices are located, or the jurisdiction in which the employee works.

- **Severability** — Employment contracts can be complex and are subject to changes in relevant employment legislation. Changes in legislation could potentially render an employment contract void. A severability clause essentially states that, if one clause is voided under law, the rest of the contract will remain intact and enforceable.

- **Wage Deductions** — Some Employment Standards Acts specifically prohibit any offset from wages without the employee's expressed consent. The employment contract can be used to gain this consent.

- **Severance** — Specifies the amount of notice and severance that will be provided to the employee if it becomes necessary to terminate the contract for other than "cause". In the case of executive employees, an added feature may be to specify certain conditions (such as a change of ownership or control of the organization) under which the employee can trigger the severance clause unilaterally. These clauses are known as "golden parachutes".

- **Arbitration** — These clauses are not common in Canada but may be found in certain sectors such as financial services. They stipulate that, rather than refer disputes to the courts, the parties will submit any contractual disagreements to an independent arbitrator for adjudication.

Benefits/Expected Outcomes

Having explicit written contracts can provide advantages both to the individual employee and the organization. A written contract should be the outcome of informed discussions between the parties. Organizations should not simply impose contractual terms but should spend the required time to go through the contract terms with the employee before signing. This will take some of the edge out of the contract language. Employees or potential employees can become unsettled with the legalese that typifies written contracts.

Organizations can benefit from a written contract in the following ways:

1. The organization can limit its liability at common law in the case of a termination for other than cause, by stipulating the severance and notice requirements when the employee first enters employment with the organization. Of course, a contract cannot allow the organization to escape its statutory obligations under the various Employment Standards Acts.

2. The organization can outline certain expectations up front with respect to future changes in the terms and conditions of employment. For example, the organization can specify that the employee can be relocated, assigned other responsibilities, or required to undertake extensive travel.

3. The organization can protect itself from future harm if the employee leaves the organization, by including restrictive covenants with respect to the use of confidential information, the solicitation of the organization's clients/customers, or any attempt to entice its employees away.

4. The terms and conditions of employment will be clearly understood by both parties and there can be a true meeting of the minds.

5. Standards of performance can be established in a contract to help the organization determine cause for dismissal if the employee fails to live up to his or her part of the bargain.

The benefits for the individual can vary depending on the level of responsibility and position in the organization's hierarchy. The general rule is the more senior the position, the more the need for a written contract. Employees can benefit from a contract in the following ways:

1. Senior managers can protect themselves from the downside impact of a change in ownership or control by negotiating a "golden parachute" clause.

2. All employees can benefit from a clause stipulating what their compensation would be if their employment was terminated for other than cause.

3. Employees can benefit from provisions that give recognition to their past experiences and service.

4. Implicit considerations are not left ambiguous when they are made explicit in a written contract.

5. Employees can protect themselves against sudden and unilateral changes to their positions or terms and conditions of employment.

Programming/Implementation

Implementing the use of written employment contracts is relatively simple. The organization should establish certain templates to be used for various types of contractual arrangements (executive, regular employee, fixed-term contract, part-time employees).

The largest issue is how to apply contractual arrangements to existing employees. For example, if the organization wanted to impose a mandatory retirement age when none previously existed, it may choose to notify all employees that they would be covered by a new employment contract with this term added. The organization needs to do two things to make such a contractual arrangement binding: it should provide reasonable notice of the change, and it should provide consideration. Notice will vary from individual to individual, depending on years of service, age and possibly other factors. Consideration could be in the form of additional remuneration (i.e., a raise in pay) or continued employment.

The organization may want to have all employees bound by written contracts at some point in time. The best way to implement this type of program is to introduce the written contract when there is a significant job change (transfers or promotions), a significant change in the terms and conditions of employment that affect all employees (a new benefits package), or during a regular, annual salary review.

Contracts are legal documents. Their style (legalese) can be intimidating to some employees. If the employee is too intimidated, the contract may be later found unenforceable because the employee did not understand the terms or felt coerced into accepting the terms. To be enforceable, there must be a clear meeting of minds between the parties.

To a certain extent, the use of employment contracts can set the tone for the organization's culture. They can imply to the prospective employee that the organization is rigid and rule-bound. They can also imply that the organization has faced problematic issues with former employees. These implications can have a negative effect on the culture.

To circumvent these effects, the organization should take time to go over the contractual terms in detail with the prospective employee (or existing employees as the case may be). The employee should be given latitude to negotiate and question the terms of the agreement. As well, employees should be given a sufficient amount of time to consider the contract terms and seek legal advice before they sign anything. The organization does not have to verify that legal counsel was sought but only needs to provide the employee with sufficient time to do so. A week is usually sufficient.

The whole secret is to take the mystery out of the contract. Organizations should ensure not only that employees understand the terms of the contract but also understand why the contractual arrangement is important to the organization.

Role of the Human Resources Practitioner

The practitioner should be responsible for drafting contracts or the templates to be used. He or she should write contracts to cover the relevant aspects of law, but may want to consider drafting them in plain language to every extent possible, to make them more accessible and understandable to the average employee (and manager). In some cases, the organization may require legal advice, and the practitioner is the natural contact between the lawyer and the organization.

The practitioner may be the person responsible for going over the terms of the contract with employees and prospective employees, or should train line managers on how to do it. It is important that those involved in reaching a contractual agreement between the organization and an individual understand the terms and why they exist. It is not acceptable to tell a prospective employee that the contract is simply the way the organization "does things".

Any issues regarding the interpretation, application or administration of employment contracts should be referred to the Human Resources practitioner. In Canada, understanding employment law is an essential competency for the Human Resources practitioner. If disputes arise, they are usually in the form of a claim for either "constructive dismissal" or "wrongful dismissal". The practitioner should be sufficiently versed in employment law to address any initial claims tactfully and expertly.

Barriers to Success/Common Pitfalls

The most significant barrier to the use of written employment contracts is the nature of the contracts themselves. They are legal documents that can put off employees. The language of contracts can be confusing and intimidating. They can suggest to a prospective employee that the organization is overly restrictive and bound by regulation.

Common mistakes in the use of employment contracts include the following:

— inconsistent application (some employees have signed confidentiality agreements, others have not);

— omission of important clauses (entire agreement clauses are essential);

— poorly drafted language;

— contractual terms are offered to the employee after he or she has started employment and, therefore,

are not provided with consideration or with the alternative not to accept;

— contract has expired and not been renewed explicitly;

— contract voided because a clause violates a provision of Employment Standards legislation; and

— contract voided because the employee was not given time to seek advice (the employee was not sufficiently sophisticated to understand the terms he or she was agreeing to, or the employee felt coerced into signing the agreement).

Confidentiality and Non-Competition Agreement

Employees are generally bound to protect the interests of their employers. This means, among other things, that employees will not disclose any information about the organization which might be considered confidential or proprietary, particularly when disclosure could bring harm to the organization. Further, employees are obligated not to engage in activities that could create a real or perceived conflict of interest such as working for a competitor.

These concurrent duties of loyalty and good faith have a life beyond the employment contract. Employees are not relieved of the responsibility to refrain from using any information or advantage they have gained in employment in a way that might bring damage to the employer. Notwithstanding, the employee has to be permitted to "sell" his or her skills to other employers once that person has left the organization. Employees may leave an organization and join a competitor provided they do not use any confidential information they have received (such as customer lists, marketing plans, pricing strategies or business plans) to assist the new organization to gain advantage. Moreover, the employee is restricted from soliciting business from a former employer or to "poach" former colleagues.

While these principles are grounded in civil law precedents, they are not "black and white" concepts. A former employee does not have to refuse to deal with a customer of the organization who has approached the new organization. Similarly, the employee can accept inquiries from former colleagues about employment prospects at the new organization. Certainly, there is no continuing claim by the former employer on the skills acquired by the individual while in its employ.

It is precisely because these concepts are somewhat "grey" that employers ask new employees as a condition of employment to sign confidentiality and non-competition/non-solicitation agreements. In the alternative, employers who are dismissing employees may seek to gain agreement from the employee to sign such an agreement in exchange for the considerations contained in a severance package. To consummate a contractual obligation from the employee, some "consideration" should be given to the employee. For new hires, the consideration is the offer of employment itself; for departing employees, it is payment of a severance package beyond the minimums required by statute.

Confidentiality agreements are, for the most part, redundant. It is clear that, with the exception of disclosing illegal activities, employees are bound to protect the employer's interests at all times, including after they have left the organization. Nevertheless, many organizations ask employees to sign off on a confidentiality agreement as a means of documenting the understanding of what constitutes confidential information. It also lets the employee know that the organization takes the obligation of loyalty seriously.

Non-competition and non-solicitation agreements are somewhat more problematic. Employers do not have a claim if the former employee engages in a competitive activity but does not use any confidential information gained in his or her former employment to create an unfair advantage. This aspect of the duty of loyalty to an organization is not so clear-cut as the duty to maintain confidentiality. Therefore, many organizations also ask employees to sign non-competition/non-solicitation agreements. These agreements are not always enforceable in law and must be limited in scope, both geographically and temporally, to pass the scrutiny of the courts.

Refer to the following page for a **Sample Confidentiality and Non-Competition Agreement**.

SAMPLE CONFIDENTIALITY AND NON-COMPETITION AGREEMENT

I hereby acknowledge that, in the course of my employment with XYZ Incorporated (the "Company"), I may have access to and receive confidential and proprietary information belonging to the Company as well as confidential information belonging to or regarding its customers. Collectively, this "Confidential Information" may include, but is not limited to, information such as:

— labour contracts;

— sales and marketing information;

— product pricing;

— strategic business plans;

— financial summaries;

— new product information; and

— medical records.

In consideration of my employment with the Company, I hereby acknowledge, covenant and agree that I will fulfil my obligations to hold confidential that information I have received during my employment with the Company. I recognize that, in my employment, I may acquire information about certain matters which are confidential to the Company and which information is the sole and exclusive property of the Company and/or its customers that cannot be used in any manner without the express written permission of the Company. I therefore agree that in accordance with my obligation of confidentiality, I will not use in any manner or disclose any other confidential information I have obtained from the Company to anyone other than for purposes for which I have been expressly authorized to use that information in the course of my employment.

I understand that Confidential Information may only be used for such purposes as required in order to carry out my work with the Company and that I will not use Confidential Information for any purpose whatsoever at any later time should my employment with the Company be terminated with or without cause or for any reason whatsoever. It is understood that no copy or reproduction of any Confidential Information will be made without the prior written consent of the Company's President or except as required to carry out my employment requirements with the Company.

And further, for said consideration, I hereby acknowledge, covenant and agree that should my employment with the Company be terminated with or without cause or for any reason whatsoever I will not seek employment with, provide services to, or engage in any business activities with any known competitors of the Company in the province of _____ for a period of not less than one year from the date of this general release. I further agree that should my employment with the Company be terminated with or without cause or for any reason whatsoever I will not solicit or otherwise seek the services of any of the Company's employees for a period of not less than one year from the date of this general release.

Following the completion of my employment, I will immediately return to the Company all Confidential Information, including all copies thereof, which are in my possession, charge, control or custody.

I understand that any willful breach of any of the terms and conditions of this Agreement will result in the termination of employment and may result in such other action as deemed appropriate under the circumstances.

I have read, understand and voluntarily agree to the terms of this Agreement.

This Agreement continues indefinitely.

DRUG AND ALCOHOL TESTING

Definition/Background

Drug and alcohol abuse is a significant social issue that ultimately affects all employers. Many human resource practitioners are uncertain about employers' legal rights to screen both potential and current employees for drug and alcohol use.

In Canada, there is little data on the potential costs of substance abuse to employers. Generally, it is accepted that at least 10% of the population has a problem with addiction or chronic abuse. People with addictions pose heightened risks to the employer. They may be prone to higher absenteeism rates, a higher frequency and severity of accidental injury, reduced productivity and increased error rates. Figures from the U.S. suggest that drug or alcohol use is a factor in as many as 40% of industrial accidents. Unfortunately, similar statistics are not available for Canada.

Employers in the transportation sector are particularly sensitive to the potential for catastrophic losses when the use or abuse of drugs or alcohol impairs an operator's abilities. The role played by alcohol in the *Exxon Valdez* accident, for example, highlighted these concerns for many employers. Some employers in security sensitive industries have also expressed concern about the potential risk that employees with addiction problems might steal from them or otherwise engage in illegal activities. Drug habits can become very expensive to support. There are many incidents where such a habit has grown beyond the employee's ability to pay for it and the temptation to take from the employer has proven to be too great. In addition, many organizations have to concern themselves with the public's perception of them. Banks, for example, can ill afford a negative image that portrays them as employing a criminal element.

In the U.S., employers in every sector have instituted mandatory pre-employment drug testing and mandatory random testing during employment. Most of these policies carry significant penalties. Testing positive during pre-employment screening, for example, will result in the candidate not being hired. Being caught in a random check will often result in the termination of employment.

The theory supporting these policies is simple: the use of drugs impairs an individual's judgment and response times, leading to a higher potential for accidental losses and reduced productivity. The use of controlled substances is an illegal activity and the individual cannot assert a right to engage in an illegal activity. It is in society's interest to ensure everyone's safety is protected and this takes precedence over the rights of the individual. Employers, however, have no right to question or act on the off-duty behaviour of their employees unless that behaviour has a direct adverse impact on the employer.

In Canada, employers face a different situation. Canadian human rights legislation has been interpreted to include drug and alcohol addictions as handicaps and thereby affords some protection to the individual against discrimination. For some practitioners, this has led to a belief that employers are virtually powerless to deal with the problem. At the very least, employers are perceived to be highly restricted in what they can and cannot do.

An understanding of the legal implications of drug testing in Canada can, however, provide the practitioner with insight into setting up testing programs to reduce the losses his or her employer may be experiencing because of substance abuse.

Benefits/Expected Outcomes

Employers who implement drug testing as part of the recruiting process set a high standard that sends a powerful message about the organization's culture. Potential employees understand that the issues of drug use and workplace safety are significant considerations. In some cases, potential candidates who are unwilling to subject themselves to drug testing might take themselves out of the running for a position.

Drug testing may also be used to detect drug use among existing employees. While the benefits are the same as with pre-employment screening, the emphasis has to be on identifying a real need for engaging in drug testing. General attitudes regarding widespread drug use do not constitute sufficient or compelling reason for engaging in drug testing. The organization cannot simply select employees at random for testing.

D - E - F

It must demonstrate that drug use is prevalent in the workplace and that such use poses a significant risk of losses (such as increased accident exposure, significant absenteeism, decreased productivity or loss of reputation) to the employer. To compel an individual employee to submit to a drug test, the employer must have some indication of drug use on the part of that individual.

Drug and alcohol testing is most commonly used in Canada as part of a "Last Chance" agreement struck with employees. "Last Chance" agreements are typically arrived at after an incident occurs in which the employee's addiction problem is brought to light. For example, the employee could report to work obviously under the influence of a controlled substance. Or there might be an accident where through investigation the employee is discovered to have been under the influence. In the agreement, the parties will need to agree on when testing will occur and how it will be conducted. The benefit of including testing in the agreement is that it provides an incentive for the employee to abstain from the use of the substance they are addicted to.

Drug testing does not eliminate drug addiction. It does identify people who potentially have a problem and thereby provides the employer and the employee an opportunity to deal with it. Once a problem is identified, the employer must treat the issue as a disability, meaning he or she has a duty to accommodate the employee.

Programming/Implementation

A. Discrimination

Until quite recently, a distinction was drawn between "direct" and "adverse effect" discrimination. Direct discrimination occurs when a workplace policy or rule is discriminatory on its face. If, for example, a company had a rule that said "no women" could apply for a certain position, it would be directly discriminating against women. However, it is unlikely that any employer would have a policy that so blatantly discriminated against a given group.

Adverse effect discrimination (sometimes referred to as "indirect" or "constructive" discrimination) occurs when the workplace policy or rule is on its face neutral but has the effect of inadvertently discriminating against individuals in a given group. An example might be a height restriction that requires employees to be of a minimum height. While neutral on its face, this rule could restrict many individuals of certain ethnic backgrounds that are on average shorter than the required height.

Direct discrimination is simply unlawful. In adverse effect cases, however, employers have a defense if they can show that the workplace policy or rule is a "*bona fide* occupational requirement". In addition, unless the policy or rule accounts for individual differences and accommodates them to the point of undue hardship to the employer, it remains discriminatory.

In two recent decisions, the Supreme Court of Canada erased the distinction between direct and adverse effect discrimination [see: *British Columbia (Public Service Employee Relations Commission) v. B.C.G.S.E.U. (Meiorin)*, [1999] 3 S.C.R. 3, 176 D.L.R. (4th) 1, and *British Columbia (Superintendent of Motor Vehicles) v. British Columbia (Council of Human Rights) (Grismer)*, [1999] 3 S.C.R. 868, 181 D.L.R. (4th) 385]. The Court decided that the distinction between the two kinds of discrimination was artificial and, ultimately, not meaningful. Moreover, the remedies in a given case could depend on how the discrimination was classified and such differences in remedies are difficult to justify in a human rights regime. Why? Because an employer could intentionally discriminate against a group with a policy that is neutral on its face. In such a scenario, the distinction previously drawn could lead to legitimizing systemic discrimination. The Court therefore sought to find a uniform way to deal with discrimination.

McLachlin J. made the following observation in *Grismer*:

> Meiorin announced a unified approach to adjudicating claims under human rights legislation. The distinction between direct and adverse effect discrimination has been erased. Employers and others governed by human rights legislation are now required in all cases to accommodate the characteristics of affected groups within standards, rather than maintaining discriminatory standards supplemented by accommodation for those who cannot meet them. Incorporating accommodation into the standard itself ensures that each person is assessed according to her or his own personal abilities instead of being judged against presumed group characteristics.

B. Threefold Test

Meiorin established a threefold test for employers. They must meet all three requirements in order to justify a *prima facie* case of discrimination.

1. The employer must establish that the workplace rule, policy or standard was adopted for a purpose rationally connected to the performance of the job.

2. The employer must establish that the workplace rule, policy or standard was adopted in an honest and good faith belief that it is necessary to the fulfillment of the work-related purpose.

3. The workplace rule, policy or standard must be reasonably necessary to the accomplishment of the legitimate work-related purpose. That is, there are no reasonable alternatives available to accommodate the employee without undue hardship to the employer.

By applying this threefold test and taking into consideration how it has been applied in the jurisprudence on drug testing, employers can develop drug testing policies that help them protect their interest while respecting the privacy of the individual.

The first test is simple. Employers have an interest in and, in fact, are obliged to protect the health and safety of their employees, the public and the environment. In order to fulfill this obligation, employers can reasonably expect employees to do their jobs free of the impairment caused by drugs or alcohol. It is well established that impairment from drugs or alcohol increases the risk of accidents. A simple rule that all employees must report to work and perform their work free from impairment is clearly consistent with the performance of the job and is in the legitimate interest of the employer. If an accident occurs, the employer can reasonably insist that the employee involved demonstrate that he or she was not under the influence of drugs or alcohol at the time.

The second test involves more than simply asserting a belief. Despite the commonality of substance abuse, it is not an automatic given that every employer needs the same level of protection from employee substance abuse. In the manufacturing and transportation industries, the issue of safety both for employees and the public is acute. The retail industry, on the other hand, does not face the same type of issues. Operating heavy equipment and motor vehicles is dramatically more risky then selling merchandise.

The fact that drug and alcohol abuse is widespread in society does not automatically justify the presumption that it therefore must be present and having an effect in the workplace. Some employers experience very evident problems with drug and alcohol use in the workplace. This is particularly true in environments where employees are left unsupervised for most of their time at work. Evidence of specific abuses in the workplace, coupled with demonstrations of the safety-sensitive nature of the work, will support an assertion that the rule was adopted in good faith.

The third test is the most problematic. There are many alternatives to drug testing that can reduce the risk of losses in the workplace due to substance abuse. Three such alternatives are: employee assistance programs, drug and alcohol abuse education programs, and training programs for supervisors in detection and intervention.

C. Accommodation

When formulating a policy, employers must consider how they plan to accommodate an addicted employee. Once it is established or perceived that the employee has a substance abuse problem, the employer must recognize it as a handicap and take appropriate steps to accommodate the employee in dealing with the issue. Common forms of accommodation include providing sick benefits that cover rehabilitation programs, assisting the employee in receiving treatment from a recognized treatment facility and, in some instances, drafting a "Last Chance" agreement that includes clauses on abstinence and after-care programs.

Automatic sanctions for testing positive, particularly severe ones like automatic dismissals, do not take into account individual circumstances and, therefore, cannot be viewed as accommodation.

D. Drug Addiction Versus Recreational Use

When an employee tests positive for drug use or is discovered using drugs in the workplace, it is commonly assumed that a substance abuse problem exists. This is a leap in logic. Furthermore, common forms of drug testing, like urinalysis, can be problematic because they do not measure addiction.

Use of alcohol or illegal drugs does not equal either abuse or addiction. Some people merely experiment with illegal drugs and some are what is termed "recreational users". These people use drugs or alcohol in social settings occasionally, but not as a routine part of their normal lives. Chronic users, on the other hand, use drugs or alcohol so frequently that it defines part of their lives. Excessive chronic use is another way of saying "addiction".

Bingeing is another form of abuse. While an individual might not use drugs or alcohol routinely, he or she might "binge" fairly regularly. Often, this evolves into a pattern of more frequent and chronic use.

Most pre-employment drug testing in the U.S. relies on urinalysis. Urinalysis, however, is somewhat limited in its findings. The results do not demonstrate the degree of impairment nor do they provide any measure of addiction. It merely measures whether or not the subject has used a controlled substance in the recent past. Because of this, urinalysis would be of limited use in the Canadian context. Blood tests can provide a more accurate measurement but they are more intrusive and costly.

In the case of alcohol, Breathalyzer tests can measure the degree of impairment. When an accident occurs, a Breathalyzer test can be used to determine if an employee is intoxicated or to confirm supervisors' suspicions that an employee is under the influence.

E. Policy Elements

Pre-Employment Drug Testing

Human rights legislation in Canada prohibits employers from denying employment opportunities to individuals with real or perceived handicaps. Drug screening can thus only be done after an offer of employment has been made.

Once the offer has been made, the employer can insist that the potential new employee undergo drug screening as a condition of employment. If the candidate refuses the test, his or her refusal can be used as grounds to withdraw the offer. If, on the other hand, the candidate agrees to the screening process and subsequently tests positive, the employer is obligated to follow through with the offer and find a means to accommodate the individual's drug use.

Accommodation of a positive test in a pre-employment context should involve informing the individual of the results, providing counseling to determine if a chronic problem exists, rehabilitation (if indicated), follow-up monitoring and testing, and enforcement of rules related to possession and use in the workplace.

Bear in mind that the testing itself must serve a legitimate business purpose. If safety is an issue, as with truck drivers or equipment operators, the testing can be defended as a necessary means of ensuring that the employee is free from impairment while at work. The Toronto-Dominion Bank's drug testing policy, however, was ruled to be discriminatory largely because the Bank was not able to demonstrate that the policy was reasonably necessary to the running of its business. [See *Canadian Human Rights Commission v. Toronto-Dominion Bank*, [1998] F.C.J. No. 1036, (July 23, 1998)]. The distinction between direct and adverse effect discrimination may also have played a role in the court's decision. Today, under the threefold test, the Bank might be able to demonstrate that its program provided accommodation based on individual circumstances and that the testing was a *bona fide* occupational requirement. At the time, though, its policy was seen as direct discrimination and this defense was not available to it.

Employers should only engage in pre-employment drug screening in the following circumstances:

- prevalent drug use is evident in their workplace;

- the company employs people in safety sensitive roles where significant loss or harm could come to the individual, fellow workers, customers, the public or the environment if an employee is under the influence; and

- the nature of the job makes it difficult for the employer to monitor an employee's work performance on a regular basis.

Drug and Alcohol Testing for Existing Employees

Random drug and alcohol testing is generally considered to be a discriminatory practice. It is also seen as somewhat intrusive and a potential invasion of privacy. Since drug testing only reveals recent use and is not necessarily indicative of impairment, any sanctions taken against employees for testing positive may be seen as discrimination.

Instead of random tests, the employer may want to require mandatory testing in certain circumstances. For example:

- when an accident happens after which recordable losses occur;

- where there is evidence of drug or alcohol use; or

- where an employee's acknowledged substance abuse has led to a "Last Chance" agreement which includes post-rehabilitation monitoring.

In a post-accident scenario, the employee(s) involved should be tested for the presence of alcohol or drugs in order to rule them out as possible causal factors and to protect the innocent from suspicion and innuendo. Using this policy, the employer does not seek to discover whether the employee has an addiction (and, hence, a handicap). The employer is, rather, simply trying to determine if the employee was impaired at the time of the accident. If the employee was impaired, the employer can take action based on the reasonable workplace rule that employees must be free from impairment while at work.

Similarly, when a supervisor detects signs of impairment and confirms these suspicions by testing, he or she is acting on the specific behaviour and breach of company policy. In either case, the employee is free to raise the issue of addiction as a mitigating factor in determining the level of sanctions appropriate to the circumstance.

Looking at the issue in a different way is sometimes helpful in making the distinction. As stated above, not all drug users are addicts. Let's say an employee who is a recreational user makes an error in judgment and smokes marijuana while at work. The employee is then involved in an accident which results in significant property damage and an injury to another employee. During the accident investigation, the supervisor detects the odour of marijuana on the employee and notes that the individual appears to be "stoned". The employee is ordered to submit to a drug test that comes out positive. The employee is then fired for his or her culpable misconduct in breaching a significant company rule by attending work while under the influence of an illegal drug. The company has not discriminated against the employee because the employee does not have a handicap (real or perceived). There is no duty to accommodate because there is nothing to accommodate.

So, unless the employee raises the issue of addiction, the employer should presume it is not a factor. One caveat regarding this should be heeded. The employer cannot make this presumption by turning a blind eye to an obvious problem. If the company suspects that the employee has an issue with substance abuse, it has a duty to raise this issue with the employee. Moreover, in a safety sensitive environment, supervisors and management cannot ignore issues in front of them and claim that their "hands are tied". Supervisors need to understand their rights and obligations in ensuring the workplace is safe including ensuring employees are free from impairment. Where there is evidence of drug use, there is a positive duty to intervene.

Role of the Human Resources Practitioner

The first task for the practitioner is to determine whether or not drug testing is required by the organization. Following the threefold test enumerated above, the practitioner must ask, "Is the testing required for a purpose rationally connected to the performance of the work"? Practitioners cannot go on a crusade against drug use. Rather, there has to be evidence that drug use has impaired the performance of work. In other words, there has to be some indication that drugs are being used in the workplace and that such use poses a threat to safety or efficient production.

The practitioner must adopt the workplace rule, policy or standard in an honest and good faith belief that it is necessary to the fulfillment of the work-related purpose. Many workplaces are free of drug use. Even where there is some evidence of drug use, it might not be widespread. In these cases, therefore, the practitioner should deal with instances of drug use as they occur. There is no need for a sweeping policy to eradicate a problem that is not endemic.

The practitioner should also be aware that the workplace rule, policy or standard must be reasonably necessary to the accomplishment of the legitimate work-related purpose. That means there are no reasonable alternatives available to accommodate the employee without undue hardship to the employer. It is the practitioner who should investigate and implement those alternatives. In particular, the practitioner should investigate Employee Assistance Plans and other avenues for making rehabilitation available to the employee.

D - E - F

If no reasonable alternatives are available or if alternative policies have been implemented but proven insufficient in dealing with the problem, the practitioner should write a drug testing policy and establish a plan for communicating it to employees (and their unions where appropriate). Implementing the plan will also involve choosing a physician who can supervise the testing, establish testing protocols and contract with a testing facility.

The written policy must identify the accommodation the organization is willing to offer the employee. Typically, the new employee will be given an opportunity to seek rehabilitation or to be retested at a later date. In cases where existing employees have been tested because of a work-related incident, the practitioner will be called upon to draft a "Last Chance" agreement and may need to negotiate the final terms of that agreement. It is important to remember that a "Last Chance" agreement must clearly stipulate that the parties agree that it constitutes accommodation under the applicable human rights statute. (See page 8 for a Sample Last Chance Agreement.)

Barriers to Success/Common Pitfalls

Drug testing remains controversial and is considered by many to be an unnecessary intrusion into individual privacy. But the *Exxon Valdez* disaster made many aware of the need for organizations to monitor and control substance abuse in the workplace, particularly in safety sensitive work environments.

Many employers believe that drug testing could help them cure a number of issues by removing addicted employees from the workplace. This is a naïve and unfortunate viewpoint. Drug testing can help monitor drug abuse in work environments where use is high. In order to manage the problem effectively, however, the organization must also institute measures that will assist addicted individuals in overcoming their problems.

Employees often resent the intrusion of a drug-testing policy and its initial implementation can lead to resistance. The need for the policy must be carefully and credibly communicated to employees, with emphasis on what the organization is willing to do to help affected individuals.

In its design and implementation, the policy must be carefully constructed to avoid unintended discrimination. When Exxon responded to its oil-spill disaster, it implemented a drug testing policy that went too far: recovering alcoholics and drug addicts were removed from safety sensitive jobs. At some point, these people deserve to be recognized as having reached a level of rehabilitation where they no longer pose a significant risk to the organization. It is important that any policy be designed to preserve the dignity of any employee who may be afflicted with an addiction. Educating supervisors and managers on the sensitive handling of these issues is essential to the success of such programs but is often missed.

The most common pitfall is implementing a drug policy when it is not necessary and when other alternatives are available to the organization. Educating supervisors to identify the signs of a problem, establishing attendance management initiatives, creating an Employee Assistance Program and training supervisors on how to confront these difficult issues are some of the steps that can be taken instead of drug testing. A total program will involve implementing a drug testing policy that complements these other initiatives.

ELECTRONIC COMMUNICATIONS

Definition/Background

In the new millennium, employees have easy access to many new tools, which, if not carefully monitored and controlled, can be easily abused. Access to the Internet or company Intranet, availability of company-provided cell phones, pagers and personal organizers, and use of photocopiers and fax machines are all part of doing business in the "electronic age". These tools can help make employees more productive and greatly enhance communications. However, they are also prone to misuse and can cost organizations substantial financial losses through high service fees and lost productivity.

Organizations should develop and implement guidelines for the authorized use of these business tools so that employees know where the boundaries are between acceptable and unacceptable use of company-provided electronic tools, including computers, personal data assistants, telephones, and video and audio equipment.

The policy should outline the privileges and responsibilities that go along with the use of modern business tools. Policies should offer guidelines and should also forewarn employees of the consequences of violating the rules. As with any policy, it is important that the guidelines for using electronic media remain fluid. The nature of technology means it will continue to evolve and new tools are likely to emerge. Unfortunately, even the nature of abuse will continue to evolve and some employees may find ways to misuse their privileges that have not yet been contemplated.

One particularly controversial aspect of electronic communications policies is the need periodically to monitor employee use. This may be as simple as auditing cell phone bills to determine the nature of the calls being made on company equipment. In other instances, the monitoring may involve reviewing an employee's use of the Internet by tracking the Web sites visited, searching transmission logs or cache files, and reading specific e-mails sent or received.

Call centres usually monitor calls on a random basis to ensure the quality of service is being maintained.

An additional concern for organizations is that some abuses may involve illegal conduct and the organization itself may be liable for these actions if it has not taken the appropriate steps to monitor and control these behaviours. These abuses include the use of electronic communications media to harass others.

Benefits/Expected Outcomes

Implementing a comprehensive policy regarding the use of electronic communications will:

✓ protect the company from potential liability arising from the abuse or misuse of communications tools such as the Internet;

✓ protect company assets from potential harm created by viruses, worms and electronic cavesdropping;

✓ ensure that the use of communications tools is consistent with other company policies and values (e.g., policies on harassment and discrimination);

✓ minimize the costs of electronic media by ensuring the best practices are followed with respect to the efficient use of electronic resources and the purchase of appropriate "packages";

✓ protect against losses associated with the inadvertent release of privileged or confidential information;

✓ minimize losses in productivity and morale associated with abuse;

✓ ensure compliance with software copyrights and licensing agreements; and

✓ increase employee awareness of the potential business applications of electronic communications and the potential harm brought by abuse and misuse.

Programming/Implementation
Monitoring Usage

When issuing electronic communications equipment to employees, an organization should provide the employee with a copy of the policy guidelines that govern the use of such equipment. The policy, in particular, should advise employees of the possibility that equipment use may be audited or otherwise monitored. There are several reasons to monitor the use of electronic communications. Organizations can find that electronic communications are far more expensive than first imagined. However, there are many options available to contain costs. By monitoring use, the organization may be able to optimize the choice of service providers and the packages available from them.

Monitoring may include:

⇨ auditing service provider invoices;

⇨ tracking Web sites visited;

⇨ reviewing transmission logs or "cache files";

⇨ scanning information or messages received via e-mail;

⇨ monitoring usage times or other measures of usage; and

⇨ accessing and reviewing information received.

Personal Usage

The policy on personal use of electronic communications will depend on the philosophy of the organization and may be tailored to different groups of employees. Senior employees, for instance, may be provided with cell phones for both business and personal use. As well, incidental use of electronic equipment may be tolerated provided it is kept to a minimum.

Certainly, an employee using the company photocopier to reproduce correspondence for an outside business enterprise would constitute an abuse. An employee who merely copies a single page (for example, a child's report card) may technically be in breach, but such abuse should be well within an organization's level of tolerance.

Passwords and Personal Identifications

Employees are issued electronic communications devices primarily for business use. This carries with it a responsibility to take the necessary precautions to prevent loss of the device or unauthorized use of the device.

The use of personal identifications and passwords is part of protecting the organization against unauthorized use of electronic devices or access to the organization's networks. Passwords should be regularly changed. Users should be advised not to select passwords that are obvious such as nicknames, children's names, birth dates, etc. Secure passwords are typically seven or eight characters in length and contain both alphabetical and numerical characters.

Users must be advised to keep identifications and passwords secure. No employee should let another person use his or her identification or password(s) to access a system. A common ploy has been for an individual to call employees and claim to be a member of the Information Technology (IT) Department and request the employee's identification and password to correct a system problem. Employees should be instructed never to give their information to anyone over the telephone. In cases where a password has possibly been compromised, users should be instructed to change their password immediately.

Electronic Mail

E-mail has greatly enhanced communications within organizations. There are, however, risks for the organization. Some e-mail systems are contained on dedicated lines and are relatively secure from outside "hackers" and "eavesdroppers". Notwithstanding, systems that can be accessed remotely should be secured with proper firewalls to restrict access. Employees also should not treat the e-mail system as a secure communication channel for transmitting confidential, sensitive or privileged communications.

Some employees may use outside service providers at home and may use their home systems to convey messages to work. Organizations should warn these employees of the possibility that messages sent on Internet e-mail can be intercepted and, therefore, no sensitive or confidential information should be sent via this medium.

Privileged communications may include e-mails sent to the organization's legal counsel. These communications are only privileged and protected when access to them is restricted to legal counsel. If others have access to the messages, the privilege attached to the document may be lost. It is akin to having a third party present when you are speaking to your lawyer. To protect the privilege, employees should be instructed not to copy anyone on correspondence sent to the organization's lawyers if the correspondence concerns a legal matter. If the information is to be shared, the employee should first seek the advice of a lawyer on the matter. Privileged documents should only be sent via secure in-house systems and should contain a disclaimer in case an unauthorized party inadvertently receives the document. In case of doubt, employees may be well advised to send the communication through an alternative channel (such as courier).

Merely labelling correspondence as being confidential or privileged does not protect the documents from disclosure. When in doubt, employees should use other means of conveying sensitive information.

All e-mail created by employees in the course of their employment is the property of the organization. Employees leaving the organization should be required to give copies of any e-mail in their possession to their supervisors and should be strictly forbidden from taking any copies of correspondence without expressed written permission. As with any business record, e-mails may be subject to discovery in the event of litigation. The same care and caution taken to protect company records should be taken in creating and maintaining e-mail correspondence.

Subscribed Services

There are many different services available via the Internet that provide subscribers with valuable information. Some organizations send out regular bulletins regarding promotions or sales. Others include news services that give timely updates on industry-specific events. Still others cater to the specific needs of a business. These services can be powerful business tools. They can be used to identify business opportunities, to keep abreast of important changes in an industry or to identify potential cost savings. It is important, however, to monitor the cost benefits of subscribing to such services.

"Netiquette"

Communicating online should not be treated differently than any other form of written communications. Communications via e-mail should be constructed so that the meaning is understood and no inadvertent meaning is conveyed. Users should be advised to consider carefully what they are writing before they send it. The speed of electronic mail has led to many people being somewhat more careless in how they communicate. Sarcasm, slang, colloquialisms and "tech-speak" have all crept into business communications.

Moreover, e-mail has become an overused medium. Many executives spend over an hour a day reading and responding to e-mails. Some spend several hours and much of this is non-productive. Some simple guidelines for employees may help cut down this overuse (and abuse). The following tips may be helpful:

- Do not copy someone on a correspondence unless it is absolutely essential that he or she receive and read it.

- Do not reply to an "FYI" message just to let the person know that you have received it.

- Use good judgment when forwarding e-mails to others. Do not forward an e-mail if you would not have forwarded a copy of the same message in paper memo form.

- Use the telephone to make contact with individuals as often as possible. Human contact, one-on-one, is still the richest form of communicating. E-mail is not a replacement for conversation. When appropriate to discuss a sensitive or emotionally charged issue, meet the person face-to-face.

- Realize that e-mail is provided by organizations as a business tool. It is not for advertising garage sales or conducting personal business.

- Keep messages short. When replying to an e-mail, portions of the original text can be deleted to reduce the size of the message. Users should be asked to clean up their e-mail files at least once a month to prevent using too much memory and slowing down the system.

- Use normal capitalization and punctuation. The use of capital letters may convey a meaning that is unintended. Remember that electronic mail does not transmit emotions very well and your intended message can be misunderstood.

- Do not engage in e-mail wars with others. If an issue seems to be getting heated, pick up the telephone and discuss it directly with the individual. Often the war begins with a simple misunderstanding of a message and escalates into a childish exchange of messages that the participants will likely live to regret.

D - **E** - F

- Make sure you have checked the intended recipient's address and double-checked to whom you are sending the message before pushing the send button. It can be quite embarrassing to have sent a copy of a personal greeting to everyone in the organization.

- Never send a message that is potentially in violation of a *Human Rights Code* or that might be considered a breach of company policy. Before sending confidential or sensitive messages, employees may want to consult with their supervisors as to the appropriateness of the medium.

Downloads

Downloading programs from the Internet can be risky. Employees may inadvertently put the organization in breach of a software copyright or inadvertently import a virus into the organization's network. Notwithstanding, organizations should not necessarily establish blanket restrictions on downloading. There are certainly some useful programs available from reputable sites that are relatively safe to import. Users should ensure they have the proper authorization from the site owner and copyright holder before downloading anything. Moreover, users should ensure they fully understand any restrictions or licensing agreements attached to the download. Many programs are available for free, but the owners do not allow redistribution. When in doubt, the user community should be advised to consult with their IT Department.

Viruses

Viruses can quickly bring down personal computers and information networks. Organizations should take steps to protect themselves such as ensuring all company-owned computers have anti-virus software installed on them. However, additional steps are also advisable. These include advising users not to open e-mails or attachments from sources they are not familiar. The existence of computer viruses is one reason why limitations have to be put on downloading programs from the Internet.

One precaution users should be advised to take is to detach any attachments onto a disc and then scan the disc for viruses before opening them.

Copyrights

Software piracy is easily accomplished, but organizations can face serious legal actions and liabilities if they are responsible, even vicariously, for copyright infringements. Only licensed software should be permitted on company-owned equipment. Periodically, the IT Department should audit personal computers to ensure they are in compliance with copyright laws. Although some users may believe that the IT Department insists on loading software for political reasons (to enhance dependency on their services), it is important for organizations to insist that users consult with the Department before installing new software. A large software provider like Microsoft may occasionally request that an audit be performed to ensure the use of any of its products is covered by a licensing agreement.

Obscenity and Harassment

Unfortunately, with the freedom of the Internet, everyone has potential access to sites containing pornographic, racist or sexist material. Employees may also exchange e-mails containing offensive photographs or inappropriate jokes. In extreme cases, individuals have used organizations' e-mail systems to maintain campaigns of harassment against co-workers.

Role of the Human Resources Practitioner

While the monitoring of electronic communications is typically a responsibility of the company's IT Department, the Human Resources practitioner needs to be involved in the formation and enforcement of any policies. One of the practitioner's priorities is to ensure that the policy is consistent with the culture and values the organization wants to develop and maintain.

The senior Human Resources practitioner should review and approve any policy statement before it is issued. Electronic communications policies involve emerging and sometimes complex issues. It is advisable for the practitioner to have the policy reviewed by legal counsel before it is finalized. The policy should also be reviewed at least annually. Electronic communications is a rapidly changing aspect of modern business. The policy needs to be reviewed once a year to ensure it remains relevant and complete.

Once the electronic communications policy has been approved, the practitioner needs to ensure it is published and communicated in as effective a manner as possible. Having a comprehensive written policy that gathers dust on managers' bookshelves is not an effective way to gain the benefits of having the policy. Any and every employee who has use of company-owned electronic communications devices should be given a copy of the policy and be required to sign an acknowledgement that he or she has read and understood it.

There are a number of ways to do this. Certainly, every new employee should receive a copy of the policy as part of the orientation program. Moreover, every time an employee receives a new piece of electronic equipment is an opportunity to remind him or her of the policy guidelines. Moreover, if there are changes to the policy, every employee who is affected should receive a copy of the new policy. This might be done as part of an annual update on Human Resources policies.

In particular, the practitioner will want to spend some time with employees whose use may be regularly monitored. For example, call centre employees may be subject to daily checks on their telephone manners and the use of electronic media. This can be a sensitive subject and the practitioner may want periodically to check in with these employees to ensure the right to monitor activities is not being abused by supervisors.

The practitioner should definitely be involved in the investigation into any abuses of the policy. Breaches of the policy can have serious consequences such as the loss of certain privileges or the termination of employment. The practitioner's role is to protect the interests of the organization. However, the practitioner has to balance these interests with the interests of the individual and therefore ensure that the policy is enforced in a fair and equitable way.

Potential abuses may also result in the victimization of some employees at the hands of others. The practitioner should be prepared to help any employee who has been a victim of harassment or discrimination, regardless of how the offence was perpetrated. The manner in which this type of abuse is handled will have an immediate and profound impact on the organization's culture.

One of the most important roles of the Human Resources practitioner is to keep abreast of the issues surrounding electronic communications. Not only is this necessary for purposes of fashioning and implementing an effective policy, but also the practitioner will be able to identify opportunities for improved productivity and effectiveness that can be realized through the use of these business tools.

Barriers to Success/Common Pitfalls

The common pitfalls are similar to those associated with any policy implementation. The policy has to be read and understood by all affected employees, or it is of no value. Unfortunately, many policies are championed for a brief period and then can go neglected for many years. Keeping the policy alive through annual reviews and communication processes is an important responsibility the Human Resources practitioner can and should assume.

A second related issue is the inconsistent application of a policy. Typically, policies are not regularly audited for compliance throughout the organization. The result is that enforcement only comes when breaches are inadvertently discovered. This makes it difficult to prevent little indiscretions from becoming major problems.

Organizations may find that when an abuse is detected, the alleged perpetrators claim ignorance of the policy statements or of the consequences of their behaviour. An alternative defence is to point to other abuses that the company has turned a blind eye to and therefore has tacitly accepted. If the organization claims it will continuously monitor use, then that is precisely what it should do. Otherwise it may find that it is creating differential treatment for different groups of employees. If Division A consistently enforces the policy, but Division B is lax, the organization will have difficulty creating a consistent culture and reinforcing the values it wants emulated.

SAMPLE POLICY

The company has a substantial investment in information technology resources and must protect that investment from practices that interfere with the purpose of the resources. A comprehensive policy provides guidelines to assist in the enforcement of practices that will make justifiable, cost-effective use of business resources. Specifically, this policy seeks to ensure that:

- the company is reasonably shielded from usage that will place it at legal risk through inappropriate or inadvertent activities;

- system resources are not wasted or abused, which can result in poor performance, failure of the system and substantially higher cost to the company, each of which ultimately affects all users; and

- the system is adequately protected from outside sources such as computer viruses or hackers that may harm or disable the system, thus affecting the company's ability to conduct business.

Company's Ownership and Disposition of Electronic Information and Right to Monitor Employees' Use

The system, and all electronic information stored on, received by, or transmitted from the system, is the sole property of the company. By using the system, employees consent to having their use monitored by authorized company personnel at the sole discretion of the company. The company will monitor and review an employee's electronic information to assess, among other things, whether there have been breaches of security or violations of any company policy. The company may disclose, when appropriate and without notice to the employee, the contents of an employee's electronic information to any party (inside or outside the company). Further, the company will discard, preserve or relocate electronic information (wherever located) pursuant to such record management procedures as it may adopt from time to time. Employees are required to cooperate with any company records management procedures by, among other things, deleting, preserving or relocating electronic information in their control when and as they are directed to do so. Employees may not attempt to delete or conceal electronic information that may be discoverable in or relevant to any pending or anticipated litigation or similar legal proceeding.

No Right to Privacy

Employees have no personal privacy right in any electronic information, including, but not limited to, electronic information created, received or transmitted while using the system for personal purposes and any usage permitted by the company's policy. Employees, therefore, should not use the system to create, access, receive or send electronic information that may cause embarrassment to the company, themselves or others.

Employees must provide all system passwords and codes to the company immediately upon request. Employees are prohibited from using any encryption software that has not been provided by the company.

Incidental and Occasional Personal Use Permitted

Incidental and occasional personal use of the system is permitted. Personal use of the system that, in the opinion of the company, interferes with the company's business, interferes with an employee's job duties or is in any way detrimental to the company or any of its employees is strictly prohibited. The company, in its sole discretion, reserves the right to prohibit personal use of the system. The company will monitor employees' use of the system to assure that the company's property is being used in accordance with this policy.

Software Ethics and Use of Unauthorized Material

All electronic or digital hardware, software, data files and applications residing on the system are either owned by or licensed solely for the company's use. All software must be used only in accordance with the guidelines of the licensing agreement. Unless otherwise provided in the company's licence agreement, any duplication of copyrighted software, with the exception of backup and archival activities, is a violation of the law and is contrary to the company's standards of conduct. Any person who illegally reproduces software can be subject to civil and criminal penalties, including fines and imprisonment, and is subject to discipline, up to and including termination of employment.

Under no circumstances should any software be installed on any company computer without the authorization of the company's IT Department. Installing software not specifically authorized by the IT Department may introduce computer viruses that could inflict extensive damage upon the system, adversely affecting performance of the individual system, or resulting in a condition that may adversely impact all users of the system. This includes, but is not limited to, games, screen savers, "shareware", "freeware" and any software that is available over the Internet. In the event you need to use non-company-owned or licensed software on the system, or if you currently use any software on the system not designated as company approved, you must obtain written approval from your department head and an appropriate IT representative.

Improper Use

No electronic information should be created or stored on, accessed or sent from the system which might constitute intimidating, hostile or offensive material on the basis of gender, race, colour, religion, national origin, sexual orientation, age or disability. The company strictly prohibits employees from using the system to transmit obscenities, derogatory language or comments, or sexually suggestive or violent language or images.

Employees are specifically prohibited from using the system to:

1. send or forward chain letters or mass mailings of non-business-related subject matter;

2. send copies of documents in violation of copyright or other laws;

3. distribute, send or forward electronic information, without a legitimate business purpose, under circumstances likely to lead to embarrassment of the sender, the company or recipient(s), or to violate the clearly expressed intention of the sender to restrict dissemination of the electronic information beyond the initial address or recipient list;

4. access the electronic data files of others without a *bona fide* business purpose;

5. send confidential company information, unless such information is clearly identified with a "CONFIDENTIAL" label (including any documents that may be attached to an e-mail message);

6. "spoof" another user by sending electronic information using that user's name without authorization;

7. create, distribute, send or forward mass mailing material in any form or post to any "usenet" or other newsgroup, forum or other similar group any material that is off-topic according to the charter or other description of the group ("spamming");

8. visit Internet sites that contain obscene, pornographic, hateful or other objectionable material;

9. visit Internet sites that allow the user to engage in gambling; or

10. conduct an activity that in any way would bring discredit to the company.

E-Mail and Voice Mail

Company-Confidential Information

Company-confidential information should never be sent or forwarded, via e-mail, voice mail or otherwise, to outside individuals or companies not authorized to receive the information. Additionally, company-confidential information should not be sent or forwarded to other employees inside the company who have no legitimate business reason to know the information.

When addressing e-mail messages or using e-mail distribution lists, employees should ensure that all addressees are appropriate recipients of the information. Lists are not always kept current, and individuals using lists should take measures to ensure that their personal lists are current. Employees should refrain from routinely forwarding electronic information containing company-confidential information to multiple parties unless there is a legitimate business need to do so.

Etiquette

Employees must ensure that all electronic information, whether sent internally or to third parties, is written or spoken courteously and in a professional manner. E-mail communications should follow the same standards expected in written business communications and public meetings. Employees should be aware that electronic information, particularly e-mail and voice mail, may be read or heard by persons other than the person(s) to whom the electronic information is sent. For example, voice mail messages are easily forwarded to unintended recipients and may be re-recorded for replay or transcribed to written form without the sender's knowledge.

Employees should also be aware that e-mail, voice mail and other forms of electronic information are discoverable in litigation. When composing e-mails, therefore, employees should keep in mind that it may be a requirement to produce e-mail messages in the course of litigation, including documents that may have already been deleted.

Retention

Employees must be aware of the near-permanent nature of electronic information stored in the system. Simply "deleting" an e-mail or voice mail message or other electronic information does not necessarily delete it from the system and therefore it may be subject to later disclosure by the company. It is the responsibility of every employee to manage the contents of his or her individual e-mail and voice mail accounts in a manner that will not create unreasonable or costly system resource requirements.

The IT Department recognizes that many users of the e-mail system may have a business need to retain certain messages beyond the above guidelines. Documented procedures have been prepared for users to archive so that they can still retain messages for future reference without burdening the system. Users who wish to save items that exceed these guidelines may contact the IT Department for assistance in setting up their account for automatic archival.

Limitation

The company's e-mail system will restrict the types of documents that can be sent or received as attachments to an e-mail message. This typically becomes an issue only when numerous and/or large documents or files are attached to the message. When an attempt is made to send a message that exceeds this limitation, the user will be reminded of this restriction. Files that have certain extensions (e.g., .bat, .exe, .mp3) are known potentially to carry electronic viruses or are typically used for non-business purposes and thus will not be permitted. The list of these file extensions is subject to amendment without notice.

Internet Use

General Internet access (a practice referred to as "browsing") will be made generally available to selected employees, but may be revoked upon request by a supervisor for any employee who abuses this privilege. In broad terms, employees may access the Internet for personal use on their own time (i.e., lunchtime and non-business hours) as long as such usage does not violate any of the "Improper Use" guidelines previously described in the policy.

All employees are directed to use the system in a manner consistent with the standards detailed in the policy. Failure to comply with the responsibilities outlined in this document may result in disciplinary action, up to and including termination of employment, legal prosecution and other remedies as provided by law.

EMPLOYEE ASSISTANCE PROGRAMS

Definition/Background

Employee Assistance Programs (EAPs) emerged in the 1980s to provide help to employees who were experiencing various problems that could affect their work. Initially, programs largely focused on dealing with substance abuse issues, but have evolved into comprehensive programs offered as part of an employee's benefits package. The rationale for employer-sponsored EAPs is that, by providing assistance to employees experiencing problems off the job, the organization will gain from reduced absenteeism, improved productivity and better employee morale.

EAPs are typically provided by an independent third party who confidentially counsels employees who are suffering with such issues as:

⇨ work–home stressors;

⇨ trauma/crisis (e.g., death of a co-worker);

⇨ bereavement;

⇨ drug addiction;

⇨ alcoholism;

⇨ child care;

⇨ elder care;

⇨ obesity;

⇨ smoking;

⇨ change management;

⇨ financial difficulties (bankruptcy); and

⇨ legal problems.

When an employee contacts the EAP provider, he or she first speaks to an intake worker who ascertains the nature of the problem and determines the best course of action. The employee is then referred to a counsellor who provides the requisite assistance. Counselling is short-term, typically lasting four or five sessions. Employees with complex problems who require ongoing therapy or specialized help are usually referred for treatment outside of the program.

EAP providers usually charge a monthly fee, based on the number of employees covered by the service;

however, some charge on the basis of use (fee-for-service).

Benefits/Expected Outcomes

Research indicates that employers save $5 to $8 for every dollar spent on EAPs through reduced absenteeism and disability costs. When employees are able to cope with stressors outside of work, they tend to be more productive and pay more attention to the quality of their work.

Employees who experience undue stress because of personal problems are more likely to become ill and to make use of the company's benefit plans. While it may be difficult to trace a direct correlation, assisting employees with their problems should ultimately result in reduced health care costs, including short-term disability coverage, prescription drug plans and extended medical coverage.

One important consideration is employee safety. Employees who are distracted because of personal financial pressures or marital problems are more likely to cause accidents or to suffer on-the-job injuries. Unfortunately, statistics are not kept in Canada regarding the number of workplace accidents that are related to the use of drugs or alcohol. However, if American figures are an indication, then a substantial number, up to 40%, may be linked to substance abuse. Providing employees with an outlet to deal with problems can have a direct and positive impact on an organization's safety experience.

Programming/Implementation

There are a number of different ways to set up an EAP. Many organizations prefer remaining silent on the matter but will provide assistance on an *ad hoc* basis when the need is indicated. A common approach is for organizations to counsel employees who are having difficulty at work on ways to deal with outside stressors.

For example, an employee may be experiencing increased levels of absenteeism and tardiness, coupled with a drop off in productivity and the quality of their work. If the employee's supervisor suspects that an external cause, such as substance abuse or marital difficulties is responsible, the supervisor will meet with the employee to attempt to identify the problem. It is important, when doing so, for the supervisor to ask open-ended questions and allow the employee to respond. The supervisor should avoid direct leading questions that might suggest the cause or to make any allegations or speculations as to the cause. Otherwise, the employee may become defensive and withdrawn, or the supervisor may be accused later of treating the employee differentially.

More importantly, treatment and counselling depend on having the individual recognize the nature of the problem on his or her own accord. Forcing an employee to address an issue may result in compliance over the short term, but in order to truly assist the employee, the organization depends on the employee's total commitment to addressing the root cause of the problem.

Typically, the *ad hoc* approaches rely on the establishment of "last chance" agreements to delineate what offers of assistance will be provided and what consequences the employee may face for non-compliance. These approaches are reactive at best and may not address a variety of issues beyond substance abuse.

A second type of program relies on internal referral agents. Again, this approach is primarily focused on substance abuse cases and may have limited application beyond that. Referral agents are usually volunteers who themselves have had experience dealing with similar issues. These programs can be more proactive than the *ad hoc* approach. Employees may be more comfortable dealing with a peer, particularly one who has gone through the same experiences. Moreover, the volunteers tend to be committed to helping others and can often approach employees in trouble without attaching any stigma or passing judgments.

In these two types of approaches, organizations may want to establish an ongoing relationship with a rehabilitation facility. A strong, ongoing relationship may provide certain advantages. For some facilities, there are waiting lists. Organizations with good relations may be able to go to the head of the list and avoid delays on behalf of their employees. Many rehabilitation programs are also offered free to the participants. The agencies running these facilities are charitable institutions that rely on donations and government support to meet their expenses. One way to establish a working relationship is to provide some financial support.

Some organizations employ the services of employee assistance counsellors, or at least designate someone (e.g., occupational health nurse) to fill that role. These individuals provide initial counselling to help the individual identify the problems he or she faces, and then refer the individual to specialized experts who can provide more specific, ongoing counselling or treatment. The individual EAP counsellor may be provided with a "no questions asked" budget to get individual employees started on a course of treatment. These internal counsellors should be familiar with the company's benefit programs to ensure they are not directly funding programs that are covered under the extended medical care plans, or that are provided free of charge elsewhere.

Given that there is a high degree of confidence in EAPs to reduce health care costs, many insurance carriers offer programs without charge as part of their comprehensive employee benefit plans. These programs are similar in scope to those provided by third-party specialists. Practitioners may want to check with their carriers, as these programs are not often publicized to the extent they should.

Many EAPs are provided by independent third parties who confidentially counsel employees. When an employee contacts the EAP provider, he or she first speaks to an intake worker who ascertains the nature of the problem and determines the best course of action. The employee is then referred to a counsellor who provides the requisite assistance. Counselling is short-term, typically lasting four or five sessions. Employees with complex problems who require ongoing therapy or specialized help are usually referred for treatment outside of the program.

Confidentiality is key to the success of these programs. The employee needs to be assured that he or she, or a family member, can contact the EAP provider without any information getting back to the employer. When employees have a high degree of confidence in the program, they will be more likely to use the services, and will be more likely to approach their problems proactively.

An independent auditing organization can be used periodically to check on the efficacy of the program.

For obvious reasons, the organization itself cannot survey employees on the use of the EAP, as it could breach employee confidence in the integrity of the program. However, the organization will want to know the level of usage and types of issues that are being addressed, as well as to have some measure regarding the effectiveness of the treatments being provided.

Role of the Human Resources Practitioner

The practitioner should ordinarily not be directly involved in the EAP. In informal systems, the practitioner may help volunteer referral agents organize meetings or arrange to have in-house seminars conducted by subject matter experts. The practitioner can also be involved in educational efforts such as "lunch and learn" seminars.

Employee assistance counselling is sufficiently specialized that the practitioner should defer to experts. Excluding themselves will help practitioners protect the integrity and confidentiality of the program. Moreover, the practitioner will want to avoid any possibility of liability accruing from the advice that may be provided. This includes being held responsible in the mind of the employee for providing poor advice, even if there is no legal liability.

The practitioner is likely to be the initiator of an EAP and will be responsible for putting together a business case to validate the return on investment. One of the first steps may be to check with the organization's benefits carrier to see if a low or no cost alternative is available as part of the employee benefits plan. If a third party is selected, the practitioner will want to establish what services will be available and at what cost.

It is important to establish what reports will be provided to the practitioner to track program effectiveness. It is also a good idea to establish a protocol for periodic audits. Without a clear line of sight between the EAP investment and the monetary benefit to the organization, the program may be vulnerable to cost cutting.

In *ad hoc* programs, particularly in smaller organizations that do not use the services of an occupational health nurse, the practitioner may be responsible for monitoring an employee's compliance to a last chance agreement.

In extraordinary circumstances where a traumatic event has occurred, the practitioner will likely be the instigator in bringing in trauma counsellors. It certainly falls on the practitioner to establish what is the appropriate approach to EAPs to fit the organization's needs and its level of sophistication.

Barriers to Success/Common Pitfalls

Some EAPs fail because the organization fails to promote its program sufficiently, and employees, who might otherwise avail themselves of the services offered, do not, simply because they are not aware of them. In other instances, employees may associate an EAP with substance abuse issues and are unaware of the other services that may be available to them.

Issues such as coping with stress, mental health and substance abuse are complex. In some cases, employees may not be aware of the issues, or are reluctant to admit that they need assistance. Despite the assurance of confidentiality, many employees will continue to believe that there is a potential stigma attached to admitting that they need assistance. Furthermore, employees will not completely trust that the information will be kept confidential. Many employees fear that, since the employer is assuming the bill, then the organization must have access to information regarding who is using the program and for what reasons.

Programs will also fail if senior management is not sufficiently convinced that there is a viable return on the investment being made in the program. Managers are uncomfortable with spending money on a program that provides them with little concrete information. Managers are equally anxious when employees are absent from work for extended periods of time without explanation. The assurances of the Human Resources practitioner that the absence is legitimate and approved do little to alleviate these concerns.

Finally, the program is seldom completely confidential. When an employee is on a 28-day leave of absence, it is easy for those around him or her to speculate as to the individual's whereabouts. Despite this, the practitioner can help overcome this particular problem by educating supervisors and managers on the need to do everything possible to support the employee, and help the employee maintain his or her dignity and feelings of self-worth.

EMPLOYMENT CYCLE

Definition/Background

Total Quality Management and Continuous Improvement are two management approaches that focus on defining the processes of work. Processes involve taking inputs and transforming them into desired outputs. Inputs can be materials, information or anything else that might be transformed. Outputs are the products the process is designed to create. They can be products, work-in-process, information or services.

Organizations can be seen as a way of organizing several related processes. At a high level, the organization takes a variety of inputs such as capital, labour and raw materials, and uses them in combination to manufacture a product or provide a service. The organization has many sub-processes as well. Some of these are directly related to the central process (assembly, sub-assembly, finishing). Others are separate but integral parts of running the business (shipping, order taking, invoicing).

A process orientation helps the organization map out each step in running the business to help it develop an understanding of how the steps are integrated. The organization can use these process maps to analyze how well different aspects of the business are being managed and controlled. Once a process has been designed, for example, it can be used to identify process points where deviations occur. Root cause analysis can then be applied to the more common or costly deviations to help improve the process.

The process approach can also be used to analyze what steps add value to the production of the product (or the delivery of a service) and any steps that are redundant or superfluous. The concept of "re-engineering" the organization is essentially a process orientation that focuses on identifying parts of the process that add value. Processes or parts thereof that do not add value should, in a re-engineering initiative, be eliminated, outsourced, or automated.

Many of the fashionable methods of reorganizing or reinventing the organization are variations on the process orientation. Socio-technical systems analysis, for example, is a complex approach to understanding "technical" production processes in their social context. There is an underlying assumption that social systems (or processes) exist within the organization. These social systems may either complement or run against the designed technical processes. To achieve the optimum efficiency, both should be designed to work hand-in-hand.

The process orientation can be a powerful tool in analyzing the way work is done. The steps can be kept simple. The basic steps are as follows:

- map the process;
- identify and measure deviations;
- fix the existing process;
- streamline the process (eliminate non-value-added activities);
- streamline/fix the inputs (what is given by others); and
- re-engineer the process, if required.

Human Resources practitioners often are asked to act as facilitators for process-oriented initiatives such as Continuous Improvement or Re-engineering. Although some of these have fallen into disrepute, the basic premises are still quite sound. Unfortunately, few Human Resources practitioners were able to use the methodologies and apply them to the management of Human Resources within the organization. With the possible exception of some of the more mundane administrative tasks, practitioners denied their work could be reduced to a process.

The administrative tasks, however, are important, in as much as they need to be delivered as efficiently as possible. If the tasks do not add value, they should be eliminated, outsourced or automated. More importantly, if the practitioner can take a process view of the purpose of having a Human Resources Management function, he or she may be able to see how different activities fit into a complete process. Ultimately, this can provide a strategic platform to develop specific initiatives to define and drive cultural change aligned with the organization's overall vision and objectives.

Such an approach can be termed the "Employment Cycle". Put quite simply, the Human Resources function exists to develop processes to manage the employment of individuals. All of these various processes are integrated by the cycle of employment that defines the relationship between every employee and the organization.

At a high level, the Employment Cycle is a process of taking individuals (inputs), transforming them into employees, and having them leave the organization.

The process of transformation involves such steps as recruitment, orientation, performance management, training and development, and the termination of employment. Each of these can be broken down into a number of sub-processes or activities.

Employment Cycle

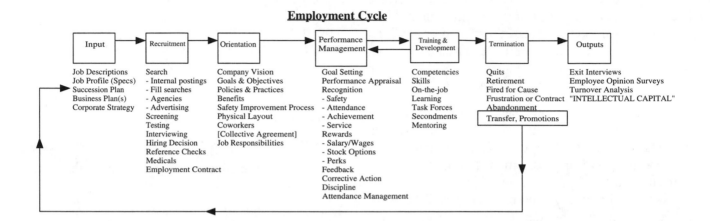

Benefits/Expected Outcomes

The benefits of identifying and mapping the Employment Cycle are, as with any process, to identify points in the process where deviations or errors can occur. The ultimate objective of Human Resources Management is to provide a sustainable strategic advantage to the organization through the development of its people. How it goes about doing this defines its culture. The Employment Cycle is a construct to help the practitioner develop a comprehensive strategic Human Resources plan for achieving this lofty objective.

On the output side of the process, for example, the practitioner can measure deviations by looking at and analyzing turnover statistics. The practitioner will want to know such things as:

— why people are leaving (exit interviews);

— under what circumstances are they leaving (retirement, quit, fired, disabled, etc.); and

— who is leaving (specific locations, functions, departments).

This information is essential for identifying which parts of the Employment Cycle need attention. If people are leaving because of stress experienced on the job, a possible cause might be a poor person-to-job

match. This would mean the recruitment process could have created a deviation. If people, on the other hand, felt that they were unclear of the expectations, the underlying factor may be a problem with their job description or with goal setting. Thus, the problem could exist in the process for developing job descriptions (usually the job evaluation system) or in the performance management process.

Thus, it is essential to be quite specific in identifying why people are leaving the organization. This obviously involves open and candid exit interviews. However, it also involves a careful analysis of the reasons why others, who are not leaving voluntarily, failed to be retained. In many organizations, the culture is such that employees who are terminated for cause or poor fit are blamed for their own demise. In other words, they simply did not work out. Enlightened organizations will take the assumption that the cause for employees not working out ultimately lies in the organization's own processes.

The practitioner also needs to be careful not to jump to conclusions about the root cause within the organization's processes. Once an organization has been able to shift its paradigm from one of blaming the individual to one of self-reflection, it becomes important to carefully understand the root cause. Moving from the proximate cause (the employee could not do the job) to the root cause (we must have recruited poorly) serves no purpose unless the organization identifies the true root cause.

For example, there may have been a mistake made in recruitment because the job specifications were not accurate. Or the error could have occurred because the recruiter was only equipped with the technical specifications and made erroneous assumptions about the behavioural requirements of the job.

Although employees who retire from the organization represent a positive outcome of the process, it remains important to measure this. The practitioner should, of course, not only know who has left but also who the organization anticipates will leave. This is important data in developing a proper succession plan. The person who successfully runs through the Employment Cycle is a vital source of information on what went right. If the person was considered quite successful in his or her job, the practitioner will want to identify those factors that made the individual successful. This will help direct attention on the right process and right factors for developing other successful employees.

Who is leaving is as important as why and how. The organization must concern itself more if employees who occupy positions of strategic importance leave than if others of lesser strategic importance leave. The underlying economic assumption is that organizations have a finite, limited amount of resources. If low-level clerical staff is turning over at a high rate because of poor pay, the organization may tolerate the loss. The alternative may be to limit its budget to pay for technical staff or marketing people who provide a strategic edge. This could ultimately weaken the organization if this group of employees became disenchanted with its compensation.

In other words, the retention of critical staff members may come at the price of experiencing high turnover of non-critical staff. This is acceptable if those people lost are easily replaced and the replacements can be quickly assimilated into the organization. A complex strategy involving compensation policy, job design, recruitment practices, recognition and retention can be developed from this simple premise. The concept of the Employment Cycle helps the practitioner see how the pieces fit together in a comprehensive approach to managing human resources.

On the input side of the process, we will find some of the basic tools of Human Resources Management. Such tools might include the following:

— succession planning;

— job descriptions;

— job specifications (behavioural characteristics/competencies);

— job evaluations;

— organizational objectives/vision/business plan; and

— critical task analysis/physical demands inventories.

Each of these brings value to the organization on its own. They are, however, more powerful when seen in the context of the overall process of Human Resources Management that we refer to as the Employment Cycle. Before an organization recruits, the practitioner should review these elements:

— Does the succession plan identify specific areas of deficiency that can be addressed through recruitment?

— Does the business plan call for replacing this position or are there more viable alternatives?

— Does the job description provide sufficient information to identify the skill set required of the successful candidate? Is that skill set readily available or does it need to be developed by the organization?

— Are the competencies defined that will determine success on the job? Can they be quantified or otherwise measured in the recruitment process?

— Does the organization pay enough to attract candidates of the right calibre?

— Can the candidate physically do the job or is accommodation necessary?

This is not an exhaustive list, but does illustrate the kind of thinking process that can be generated by using the Employment Cycle model. By answering these, and other questions, the practitioner will be able to improve the probability that he or she will get a good person-to-job match in recruitment. This, in turn, will increase the odds that the successful candidate will add value to the organization and will be retained by the organization.

D - **E** - F

The model goes further to tell us that this is only part of the process. The other elements are equally important in raising the performance of employees and achieving competitive advantage through integrated Human Resources Management practices. They are as follows:

— A comprehensive orientation program will help the employee understand what is expected by the organization and what he or she can expect from it.

— A fully integrated performance management process will link a full range of Human Resources practices to improving organizational performance.

— Training and development activities can be designed to address specific organizational deficiencies and result in measurable and desirable change.

— The process will be self-correcting by employing the concepts of Continuous Improvement, and identifying deviations and the corrective action necessary to reduce (and ultimately eliminate) them.

Overall, using the Employment Cycle as a model for the development of a Human Resources Management strategy will help the practitioner and the organization to:

✓ attract and retain employees with critical skills to provide strategic advantage;

✓ align Human Resources activities to the business goals and vision;

✓ integrate processes to reduce redundancy and eliminate activities that do not add value or run counterproductive to the overall strategy;

✓ eliminate "flavour-of-the-month" Human Resources programming initiatives;

✓ identify drivers of organizational culture; and

✓ focus limited resources on activities that bring value to the organization.

Programming/Implementation

The Employment Cycle model is intended first as an abstract construct to help the Human Resources practitioner integrate plans and activities. By using the model, the practitioner can avoid developing processes that do not have immediate impact or that do not add value. For example, the practitioner may be asked to develop a new recruitment process to improve the quality of people hired and reduce turnover. The practitioner might step back from the request and ask the question, "Is the recruitment process the root cause of increased turnover?" The practitioner may conduct an analysis of the Employment Cycle and discover that the organization is very successful in its person-to-job matches, but fails to provide developmental opportunities for key personnel.

The practitioner will be better armed and more credible if he or she addresses organizational issues rather than implementing preferred programs. Many practitioners face the difficulty of asserting their expertise among general managers who have some knowledge of Human Resources practices. It is not sufficient for the practitioner to be an expert at implementing programs that the organization wants developed. The practitioner is a subject expert.

It would be like taking in your car to be fixed and telling the mechanic what to fix rather than explaining what is wrong. He can do exactly what you asked even if it does not address the problem. The practitioner needs to be sure the organization is not simply identifying the things that someone thinks should be fixed. Instead the practitioner should define the problem that needs to be addressed, analyze why it deviates from the expected norm, and then design a fix. Your car may get poor fuel mileage, but that may not be a problem with the car if it was not designed to get good fuel mileage. Addressing high turnover might be a waste of resources, if the turnover does not harm the organization strategically.

The practitioner can use the model to develop an internal audit. The model is not static, so the practitioner can add or subtract elements that are or are not relevant to the given circumstances. The key is first to identify the processes that are, in fact, in place in the organization for managing human resources.

Once this is done, the process can be examined to identify where deviations occur in it. Deviations are exceptions to the expected norm. Again, turnover *per se* is not a deviation. Turnover of staff critical to the attainment and maintenance of the organization's competitive advantage is. The practitioner, therefore, needs to start with a fundamental understanding of the organization's vision and its strategy for achieving its objectives. The practitioner then can audit the existing Human Resources processes to see if they meet the needs of that strategy and to see if they are well integrated.

Human Resources practitioners need to exercise some judgment in using the model to present their strategic plan to their customers (i.e., the management of the organization). For example, by looking at the existing model, the practitioner may find that the organization has implemented a 360-degree feedback system under performance management and, at the same time, finds that its basic performance appraisal system fails to adequately set measurable goals and objectives. Given the limited resources of any organization, the practitioner may plan to abandon the 360-degree feedback process in the short term and focus the organization on improving its goal setting and review activities. This will have a greater impact than trying to fix a more sophisticated system.

Auditing current systems means identifying the following:

— what works;

— what does not work;

— what adds value by being in line with organizational goals;

— what does not add value;

— what fits in the organizational culture; and

— what runs counter to the culture.

The model can be used to show the key players in the organization how each Human Resources Management process fits together. For example, a job description is necessary to do a number of things:

— it is required in order to evaluate the position for compensation purposes;

— it identifies the technical requirements for the position so that recruiters will know what to look for in candidates;

— it identifies the core competencies for the position to drive organizational objectives; and

— it identifies the key results indicators for the formation of position-specific objectives to drive the performance management process.

Seen in isolation, the job description may be viewed by line managers as an unnecessary and tedious task. They may complete it begrudgingly, or are just as likely to ignore the task altogether. In many organizations, rather than gaining line management buy-in, they simply relegate the task to the Human Resources Department.

The practitioner may be able to develop a process model along the lines of the Employment Cycle to demonstrate the importance of job descriptions as keystone inputs into the larger process of managing people. This can go a long way to adding credibility for the function of managing human resources.

Role of the Human Resources Practitioner

In order to use the Employment Cycle model to full advantage, the practitioner needs to be a process thinker. There are a number of resources to consider, including the writings of the "TQM" gurus like Deming or Crosby, Hammer's *Re-engineering the Corporation*, and *The Fifth Discipline*. It is critical for the practitioner to understand this new paradigm and, moreover, to apply it in a practical way.

Applying process thinking starts with mapping critical processes. At a minimum, the practitioner should map the central processes of:

— recruitment;

— orientation;

— performance management;

— developing training plans; and

— termination.

Following this, the practitioner can attempt to define possible deviations that might occur, and measure those that actually occur. This will help point practitioners to the area they should focus their attention on initially. Defining and mapping sub-processes such as the salary administration system or the job evaluation system can be a method of further root cause analysis.

At some point, the practitioner will have a complete picture of the processes that govern how the organization manages its people. These are the essential elements that define the organization's culture. It gives a model that can be used to develop a strategic Human

Resources plan by focusing on those elements that will have the greatest impact on shaping the culture.

Barriers to Success/Common Pitfalls

The Employment Cycle is a model or construct. Practitioners do not commonly use it, although some have built similar models for their own use. The most significant barrier is that practitioners do not use a method to draw their activities into an integrated plan to address the organization's objectives and fulfil its vision.

The lack of a process orientation may prevent some practitioners from seeing the eloquence of the model. Although it might be seen as a mechanistic approach, it is in fact a flexible construct that can fit into a number of paradigms. If the organization takes a more organic approach or even a holographic approach to designing its structure and systems, the model can still assist the practitioner in integrating Human Resources Management activities into the organization's vision.

Ultimately, the model is simplistic. It focuses on identifying the fundamental processes of Human Resources Management. Each of these is well supported by organizational behaviour research and theory. Many practitioners (and general managers) are attracted to new approaches and so-called management theories that prove to be passing fads. Use of this model is premised on the assumption that the practitioner will follow basic proven methods of Human Resources Management, and build on successful application of organizational behaviour and design principles.

Practitioners need to see how they fit into the organization's strategy. Too many have difficulty defining their role and become *de facto* facilitators of the development of the organization's overall strategy. This is a good personal strategy for someone who wants to make a career transition from Human Resources into strategic planning, but does little to demonstrate the power of a sound Human Resources strategy in developing strategic advantage for the organization.

The bottom line is that practitioners should:

✓ keep it simple and stick to basics;

✓ build on successes before adding more sophisticated tools to the mix;

✓ orient the Human Resources strategy to the level of sophistication of the organization;

✓ fix their own processes before becoming facilitators to others in the organization; and

✓ align their goals and activities to the goals of the organization.

EMPLOYMENT TESTING

Definition/Background

"Employment testing" refers to any pre-employment test or assessment that is designed to measure a candidate's knowledge, skills, abilities or behaviours. "Selection" in this chapter refers to both external and internal candidate selection. Employment testing is also used to facilitate employee development but this will not be dealt with in this chapter.

There are literally thousands of employment tests in the market, but for simplicity's sake, we will divide them into two broad categories: aptitude and abilities tests and behavioural assessments.

(See also Recruitment and Selection at page 351 et seq.)

Aptitude and Abilities Tests

Included in this group are tests that measure intelligence, reasoning, written and oral comprehension, physical and psychomotor skills, mechanical aptitude, computer or administrative skills tests. Also included in this group are work samples, where the candidate completes a job task.

Aptitude and abilities tests are usually characterized by the fact that there are right and wrong answers, or, in the case of mechanical aptitude or psychomotor tests, a right way of doing things.

Typically candidates need to score a pre-determined mark on these tests to move forward in the selection process.

Some of the more common tests are:

- Otis-Lennon Mental Ability Test;
- Watson-Glaser Critical Thinking Appraisal;
- Wechsler Adult Intelligence Scale (WAIS);
- Wonderlic Personnel Test;
- Differential Aptitude Tests (DAT);
- General Aptitude Test Battery (GATB);
- O'Connor Tweezer Dexterity Test;
- Purdue Pegboard Test; and
- Stromberg Dexterity Test.

Behavioural Assessments

Included in this group are tests that measure motivations, personality, leadership style, integrity, vocational preference and emotional intelligence.

These tests are usually characterized by the fact that, for the most part, they are not really "tests" at all. There are no right and wrong answers and, in most cases, the candidate does not receive a score as they would with an aptitude or abilities test. Instead, the candidate's results are compared to a desired profile for the job.

Some of the more common tests in this group are:

- California Psychological Inventory;
- Predictive Index;
- McQuaig Word Survey;
- Hogan Personality Inventory;
- BarOn EQ-i;
- Myers-Briggs Type Indicator;
- DISC Personality System;
- Sixteen Personality Factor Questionnaire (16PF);
- Reid Report; and
- Stanton Survey.

Benefits/Expected Outcomes

The goal of any organization when using a selection test or assessment is to improve the ability to predict performance. Organizations want to accurately and objectively assess the candidate's ability and desire to effectively perform critical job functions. By administering a manual dexterity test, for example, a company can gauge an individual's ability to operate a machine safely and productively; or, by administering a temperament assessment, it can gauge an individual's ability to deal with rejection in a telemarketing role. When a company's ability to predict performance is improved, it can then increase productivity by selecting people who are better suited to a job and decrease turnover by not selecting people who are ill-suited to it.

Another potential benefit of employment testing is that it can decrease the costs of hiring. The most costly component of the selection process is the face-to-face interview. A hiring manager's time is extremely valuable and, by using employment testing early in the interviewing process, the company can screen out candidates who are not a good fit. Also, by having objective test data on hand, the hiring manager can utilize the time spent in the interview more effectively. For example, if a test reveals that a candidate has a high need for structure and the company is fairly unstructured and entrepreneurial, this can be identified as a potential "gap" and an area to focus on during an interview.

Increasing Objectivity in Selection

Companies use employment testing because they recognize that the traditional methods of candidate assessment — namely, the résumé, the interview and the reference check — are highly subjective.

Résumés are used by 94% of Canadian companies. Although they appear more rational — probably because they are in writing — résumés are subjective documents prepared by candidates, presenting biographical data which focus on positive elements of candidates' work histories, while downplaying or omitting information that might present their skills and abilities in a negative way. There has been plenty of research on "fudging" of résumés, with some studies indicating that as many as 52% of résumés contain false information.

Interviews are used in candidate evaluation by 98% of Canadian companies and are perhaps the most highly subjective method of candidate assessment. Studies have consistently shown that hiring managers, who mostly have no training in interviewing, are likely to make up their mind on a candidate within minutes of meeting them, based on such non-job-related factors as appearance, likeability and common interests. Furthermore, two interviews for the same job, conducted

by the same interviewer may take drastically different courses based on a number of factors, including the interviewer's mood, time constraints, or the candidate's temperament.

Interviewers can be influenced by a number of psychological factors or effects. The "primacy effect", for example, dictates that hiring managers can be unduly influenced to favour the first candidates they meet. Conversely, the "latency effect" dictates that interviewers will also favour the last candidate they meet because the impression created by the last person interviewed is freshest in their mind. The "halo effect" occurs with the tendency of people to judge the whole person based on their most obvious and strongest attribute. This is a common occurrence in sizing up "super-star" athletes.

While trained recruiters are aware of these effects and can take steps to correct them, hiring managers who ultimately make the decisions are not typically trained to avoid potential pitfalls in interviewing. Objective behavioural assessments can assist the hiring manager to see past these potentially biased perceptions.

Reference checking, used by 67% of Canadian companies, is also subjective in two ways. Few, if any, candidates will seek to provide balance (positive and negative) when submitting the names of references. It is more likely that they will submit positive references only. Additionally, research indicates that reference checkers read a great deal into non-responses. If, for example, a reference does not return a phone call or states that company policy does not permit him or her to provide references, the reference-checker will often treat this in the same way that they would a negative reference.

As indicated in the table on page 157,* employment testing has been shown to be a stronger predictor of performance than any of the three selection methods discussed above.

---

*This table was drawn from two separate presentations: "Employment Testing" by Brenda Tomini, Ph. D., C. Psych., at the Human Resources Professionals Association of Ontario, April 21, 1999; and "Effective Selection and Testing Procedure" by Saville & Holdsworth, February, 1998.

TABLE 1:	Predictive Power of Selection Procedures
The correlations of various selection methods are outlined below, where 1.0 is perfect prediction and 0.0 is random prediction.	
Graphology (handwriting analysis)	0.0
Typical Employment Interview	0.15
Years Experience/Education	0.19
Reference Checks	0.22
Personality Tests	0.39
Structured Behavioural Interview	0.40
Ability Tests	0.52
Work Samples	0.60
Source: Hunter & Hunter, 1984; Schmitt, 1984; Thacker & Cattaneo, 1987; Smith, 1988.	

Employment tests, such as cognitive abilities tests or honesty/integrity tests, can be used on a pass or fail basis to screen candidates for certain minimum requirements. They can also be used to get a better understanding or "second opinion" of personality factors that are deemed relevant to the job, such as extroversion or competitive spirit.

Employment tests are inherently more objective than interviews simply because they ask all candidates the same questions in the same order.

Increasing Productivity/Reducing Turnover

There is certainly evidence to support that effective use of employment testing can increase productivity via improved employee–job fit and turnover reduction. But this does not mean that every company that uses employment testing will realize these benefits. It is the role of the Human Resources Practitioner to ensure that, through the effective selection, design and implementation of the employment testing system, these benefits are realized.

Programming/Implementation

Needs Assessment

Several factors might lead to the use of employment testing in the hiring process. Generally speaking, if the existing hiring process in your organization needs improvement, you might find a combination of any of the indicators listed below:

⇨ high turnover;

⇨ low productivity;

⇨ inadequate succession planning;

⇨ some employees struggling to adapt to organizational culture; and

⇨ inconsistent or inefficient hiring process.

Job Analysis

The first question that the practitioner needs to ask is "what do we need to test for and why?". One mistake companies sometimes make is to test for factors unrelated to success in the role. Therefore, a thorough analysis of the job is a good starting point.

The following example illustrates this point:

> The managing partners at ABC Accounting have decided, due to the growth of their business, that they need to hire two new partners.
>
> In the past, they have not had great success hiring for this role or promoting from within. Although the people selected for the role have been technically very competent they seemed to be missing certain soft skills.
>
> The human resources practitioner meets with the partners and together they analyze what makes the partner role unique. After a long discussion they decide that the following soft skills or behavioural factors are critical to success in the partner role: the desire to influence, a take charge attitude and the ability to cultivate customer relationships.

Based on this information, the practitioner is now ready to evaluate the appropriate employment test.

Selecting an Employment Test

To select a test, the practitioner should evaluate available employment tests according to the following three measures: Job Relatedness, Professional Standards and Interpretation & Administration.

Job Relatedness

To what degree is there an overlap between what the test measures and what is required for the job? ABC Accounting, as we saw in the example above, would like to measure candidates' desire to influence, take-charge attitude and ability to cultivate customer relationships. It is unlikely that an off-the-shelf employment test will measure these things precisely. For most companies, developing an in-house test of their own is not an option because of the high costs of designing and validating such tests.

So, the practitioner will have to review the test to determine the degree to which it measures the qualities sought. Most psychological tests will allow the partners to create a "success profile" in terms of the traits that they feel are job-related. The test may also measure factors that the ABC partners may have overlooked. For example, while The McQuaig Word Survey measures such behavioural traits as competitiveness and sociability, factors directly related to ABC's "success factors", it will also measure a candidate's sense of urgency, possibly another significant factor to success in the role.

To develop a more extensive success profile, a benchmarking process can be employed. Benchmarking will be discussed later.

Professional Standards

The only tests with any value in terms of improving our ability to predict performance are those that meet accepted professional standards for their development and use. Most established test publishers would be able to provide information in three key areas: validity, reliability, and fairness.

Validity refers to the degree to which a test actually measures what it purports to measure. If, for example, a test indicates that an individual has good interpersonal skills, is this really the case? Do other measurements — such as other tests or performance review results — arrive at the same conclusion?

Reliability refers to the degree to which a test measures something consistently. If an individual scores high on the "interpersonal skills" scale when he or she first completes the test, but scores low when completing it a second time a few months later, then the test does not appear to be consistent.

Fairness refers to the degree to which a test does not discriminate, based on any of the prohibited grounds listed by federal or provincial governments, such as race or gender.

It is critical that the practitioner obtain this information prior to developing a relationship with the test provider. If a test does not meet this criterion, it is unlikely that it will improve your ability to predict performance and, if you were ever challenged by a candidate, you would have a difficult time defending your decision.

Interpretation & Administration

The practitioner needs to know in advance what will be required to administer a test, determine scores, and understand the results.

Some tests can only be administered, scored and interpreted by psychologists. Some need to be sent off-site for scoring. Others can be scored in-house, either manually or with software, but require trained interpreters to evaluate the results. Many tests are now on the Internet and can be administered on-line; their publishers often do not require trained interpreters.

The practitioner should select the option that makes the most sense based on the organization's needs and resources. It is always wise to get as much training as possible regarding the psychological theory behind the test, result interpretation and recommended use so that the test will deliver the most value possible to the organization

Benchmarking is the process where a company has existing employees complete a test to establish a basic profile of the job for comparative purposes. For example, a retail company may decide to use a test that measures customer service orientation. This test asks the candidate a number of questions about customer service and gives them a score out of one hundred. Before administering the test to external candidates, the retailer might have their existing customer service people, or at least a sample of them, take the same test. To determine the minimal acceptable score for candidates, they would then correlate the test scores to objective performance data. They might find that their top-performers' average score was 80, while their low performers' average score was 60. Based on these scores, they might assign a cut-off score of 70, which would become the minimum score a candidate would need in order to be considered for the role.

In the long term, if a process like the one above is used, the quality of customer service hires in a company should improve. But be aware that this system is not foolproof. The test will screen out some employees who might have done a good job and give high marks to individuals who, for whatever reason, do a poor job. Testing therefore needs to be used in conjunction with other tools, such as behaviour-based interviewing and reference checking.

Some testing companies will provide norms so that a company can compare the candidate to an industry or educational peer group. For example, the Differential Aptitude Tests (DAT) compare applicants' test scores to a college graduate norm group.

Administering the Test

When administering a test to an internal or external applicant, his or her welfare and rights, as outlined below, need to be protected.

⇨ **Informed Consent:** Applicants have the right to be told why they are being given the test and how it will be used.

⇨ **Access to Test Results:** Applicants are entitled to receive feedback on their test performance. This feedback should be provided by a qualified person who has been trained to interpret the results, such as a Human Resources Specialist.

⇨ **Privacy & Confidentiality:** When collecting information from candidates, the administrator should be certain not to collect any information that is not job-related. Any personal information that is collected should not be shared with any parties who are not directly involved in the selection of the candidate or, if the candidate is hired, his or her ongoing management.

Role of the Human Resources Practitioner

The principal role of the human resources practitioner is to define and implement the recruiting process best suited to the organization's needs and its culture. With respect to employment testing, the practitioner must decide which tests best suit the needs of the organization and where in the process those tests will be administered.

Aptitude and abilities tests typically measure a skill and demand that the potential candidate achieve at least a threshold score in order to be given further consideration. A simple test of a person's mathematical skills, for example, may require a passing grade. However, some care has to be given to ensure the test measures a *bona fide* occupational requirement (BFOR) that does not impinge on an applicant's human rights. It is incumbent upon the human resources practitioner to ensure the administration of

employment tests will pass muster with the appropriate human rights commission in their jurisdiction.

What is considered a *bona fide* occupational requirement? A test for colour blindness may, for example, be essential for positions where the incumbents are required to check colour correctness in a product. In a job where ability to perceive colour is unnecessary, then the test would clearly be unlawful.

Also, because aptitude and abilities tests measure threshold requirements, they should be administered as screening devices early in the recruiting process to fulfil *bona fide* occupational requirements. Most tests in this class are inexpensive and can be administered in-house at little expense. This type of test can be particularly useful in screening a large number of potential candidates at a job fair or in an assessment centre environment.

Similarly, the recruiter should be looking for other requirements early in the process to ensure that only candidates who hold the appropriate qualifications and who have the requisite experience are taken further in the process.

Behavioural assessments can be relatively expensive and time-consuming to interpret. The advent of supporting software can dramatically reduce the cost of administration and speed up interpretation. Nevertheless, human resources practitioners will want to use these assessments judiciously. Alternatives include administering the assessments following the initial screening interview or subsequent to the interview conducted by the hiring manager.

Having assessment results prior to the hiring manager's interview affords the practitioner the opportunity to seed some questions that can be used to validate the interpretation or to identify mitigating factors that may have influenced behaviour. The hiring manager can be given a report before conducting the interview. This can aid him or her in preparing the questions to be asked and in determining the direction to steer the interview. Conversely, the report might unduly bias the manager's opinion before he or she has even met the candidate. The practitioner will want to choose the method they are most comfortable with and that fits the organization's culture.

The practitioner should also be concerned with the tests' vendor. When assessing the vendor, the practitioner will want to check its reputation by asking for references. The practitioner will also want to ensure that the supplier can provide the necessary support, including training, to implement the tests effectively. Finally, in making a selection, the practitioner should analyze the cost versus the benefits of choosing a particular test and a particular supplier.

Many behavioural assessments allow for in-house interpretation. Consulting firms like The McQuaig Institute provide training for users of their assessment tools and software as part of their overall service. This training covers test administration and result interpretation. The human resources practitioner is the logical choice to be an interpreter. Choosing a human resources practitioner provides the additional benefit of enhancing the practitioner's skills as a recruiter by providing insight into behavioural traits as predictors of future performance.

As an interpreter, the practitioner can also gain considerable credibility with internal clients. When presenting potential candidates, the practitioner can give the hiring manager a written report that not only gives the recruiter's observations but also contains language that describes the candidate's behavioural traits. This type of report reflects well on the professionalism of the human resources department and is soundly based on proven assessment tools. In addition, hiring decisions will improve and the credibility of both the process and the practitioner will be further enhanced.

The human resources department is also responsible for maintaining a database of test results and job profiles. This information can then be accessed to determine if the organization has identified the correct behavioural profile for a given position. Sophisticated practitioners can use the data to analyze aspects of the organization's culture. When a particular department contains a large proportion of people who share similar behavioural traits, the department may adopt a particular culture that may or may not be beneficial. Examining this type of trend may assist the practitioner, as well as the hiring manager, in making future selection decisions that can influence the organization's culture.

The database can also be used for internal benchmarking to identify those behavioural traits that seem best suited to a particular role. In benchmarking, the organization identifies employees who are particularly successful in achieving the results demanded of their positions and who exhibit the behaviours that embody or reinforce the organization's culture. Once identified, they are used as models for creating a job profile. While not covered here, the practitioner is also responsible for using the behavioural assessments in other employment contexts, including performance management, succession planning and career development activities.

Finally, it is the practitioner's responsibility to ensure that the tests employed do not infringe on any applicants' human rights. Many tests available from American sources may not pass the scrutiny of Canadian human rights legislation. In particular, the practitioner must be sensitive to whether or not the test measures a *bona fide* occupational requirement.

Barriers to Success/Common Pitfalls

Inappropriate Job Profiles

Comparing a candidate's scores to some sort of job profile or benchmark is a key component in the proper implementation of a testing system. If the job profile is incorrect, then the assessment has a greater chance of not delivering the expected benefits and the test will fail. A job profile is incorrect when it does not reflect the job requirements. Say, for example, a manager builds leadership qualities into the job profiles for entry-level positions.

Often, job profiles are created without doing any sort of internal benchmarking. The benchmarking process greatly enhances the internal validity of an employment test, but it needs to be properly administered. It is possible to get a skewed profile if the performance data is inconsistent.

For example, an insurance company may decide to create a benchmark profile for its sales role by having its national sales force of 300 reps complete a test which measures personality factors. Then, based on the VP Sales recommendations, they divide the reps into three groups, based on sales commissions earned. Group 1, which earned $100,000 or more in commissions in the last year; Group 2, which earned $50,000 to 100,000; and Group 3, which earned less than $50,000.

On the surface this may seem like an objective way to do things. There are, however, several areas where this approach may produce skewed results:

- it may not factor how long the employee has been with the company;

- it may not factor regional differences in sales territories; and

- there may be two few employees who fall into a specific group and the results are not statistically significant.

Assigning a Too High Cut-Off Score

Many companies aim to "raise the bar" for the talent they recruit into the organization, but sometimes they set the bar too high and disqualify suitable candidates. Whenever possible, benchmark your jobs using incumbents. A cut-off point that would rule out a significant portion of your workforce will not only prove to be of little value to your company, but will be difficult to justify from a legal standpoint.

Test Not Appropriate for Job

While some tests have been developed for business use, others are meant to be used in clinical settings. Occasionally, tests that measure personality disorders make their way into the workplace. Use of these tests defies the principle of "job relatedness", is considered invasive and could be challenged by the candidate.

Ensure that the test you select has been validated in a workplace setting and measures job-related factors only.

Test Is Discriminatory

The test must not discriminate based on the prohibited grounds as outlined by the federal government or provinces. Most reputable test publishers will make this information available.

Over-Reliance on Test Results

Remember that the employment test is just one piece of the candidate "puzzle" and should be used in conjunction with other selection methods like the job interview and reference checks. Watch out for managers who may have made bad hiring decisions and are looking for a "magic bullet".

This article was written by Michael Gravelle, Director of Client Services for The McQuaig Institute®, a Toronto-based company with over 30 years' experience providing businesses with tools to improve their candidate evaluation skills. He can be reached at 1-800-387-5455, ext. 361, or mgravelle@mcquaig.com. For more information about The McQuaig Institute, visit their Web site at www.mcquaig.com.

ETHICS

Definition/Background

Corporations today are facing a crisis in ethics. Accounting scandals, executive excesses, bribery, money laundering and the misappropriation of company funds are now common topics in the pages of the business news. One of history's most serious corporate bankruptcies, the collapse of Enron, was perpetuated by accounting fraud and executive misconduct. Ironically, following Enron's collapse, one of the more popular items to appear on eBay was the former energy company's *Code of Ethics*.

Business ethics has been an emerging field for many years. It seems that corporate scandals move in cycles following business trends. In the age of the robber barons, controversy and the suspicion of dubious practices surrounded the rail and oil industries that drove the industrial revolution. In recent years, the energy and technology sectors (in particular, "telecoms") seem to be the breeding grounds of some of the more scandalous behaviours. Perhaps because of the devastating extent and the large number of modern-day examples of unethical (and even criminal) behaviour among company executives, there is a growing need for organizations to establish an ethical and moral grounding for their cultures.

Consumers are demanding more than just good value and high quality from the products they buy. They also want assurance that the organizations which produce and sell the products are conducting themselves in an ethical fashion. Consumers want to know when they buy from a firm that they are not supporting environmentally damaging practices, violations of fundamental human rights, corrupt business dealings or immoral behaviour.

Moreover, employees want to know they are working for responsible firms. An employee's sense of self-worth is partially derived from knowing he or she is part of an enterprise that does worthwhile things. If the organization is mired in scandal or has a reputation for unscrupulous behaviour, employee morale will suffer. In addition, such organizations will inevitably find it difficult to attract employees, especially at a senior level.

While many of the issues facing organizations today involve accounting practices, stock market violations and corporate governance and are therefore beyond the purview of the Human Resources practitioner, they do present a sound argument for corporations to turn their collective minds to the subject of business ethics. In particular, ethics and values should form a core part of any organization's culture and mission.

Some of the unethical practices Human Resources practitioners need to be mindful of include the following:

⇒ improper use of company funds;

⇒ padding of expense accounts;

⇒ employee favouritism;

⇒ accepting or offering bribes;

⇒ conspiring to fix prices;

⇒ collaborating with competitors to fix bids;

⇒ circumventing internal accounting controls;

⇒ improper use of confidential information such as pricing sheets, trade secrets and "insider information" for personal gain;

⇒ stealing trade secrets from other organizations (industrial espionage);

⇒ conflicts of interest;

⇒ accepting or offering inappropriate gifts or entertainment; and

⇒ producing false records.

There is other behaviour that will cast doubt on the integrity of the organization, although it may not be in direct contravention of an organizational rule or of any laws. For example, if two married executives are having a consensual affair, they may not be violating an organizational rule but their adulterous conduct will erode the organization's culture. In the eyes of employees, their behaviour is a direct reflection of the underlying values of the organization.

Benefits/Expected Outcomes

Establishing a written Code of Business Ethics is an important first step in creating an ethical corporate culture. It also can provide the underpinnings of a due diligence defence should the organization face allegations of improper conduct. The Code can distance the organization from the wrongdoing of individuals by clearly and explicitly stating its expectations for ethical conduct by employees and agents acting on behalf of the organization.

Given the current crisis in ethics faced by the business community, organizations can build solid reputations for ethical conduct by publishing a statement with respect to ethical conduct. Those companies that are reputed to be ethical can enjoy certain advantages. For example, many potential employees will be attracted to organizations known for exemplary conduct and, in particular, for their treatment of employees.

In addition, there is a growing interest among the investment community to consider carefully the conduct of organizations when making decisions to invest. In part, this is grounded on moral considerations. Certain investors, particularly high-profile individuals, want to ensure they are not associated with organizations that engage in dubious practices.

There are also the practical considerations of investing in organizations that are less than ethical in the conduct of their businesses. The accounting scandals that dominated business news headlines in 2002 centred around practices that tended to inflate revenues and earnings. These misstatements of financial performance led to artificially high share prices. Once they were uncovered, the shares in those organizations radically fell, resulting in substantial losses for investors. In the telecom industry alone, $2 trillion (U.S.) has been erased and 500,000 employees permanently laid off over the past two years, largely because of corporate greed and unethical practices (*Toronto Star*, November 3, 2002).

Having an established Code of conduct helps employees understand the organization's values and hence will govern the behaviours of those employees. Once the Code is an entrenched part of the organization's culture, it can be somewhat assured that employees will make ethical decisions on its behalf. As well, the Code can help employees who may be exposed to ethical dilemmas by providing guidelines or by giving those employees avenues to seek clarification.

Programming/Implementation

Some organizations believe they are run ethically. However, given the breadth of scandal faced in the business community, these organizations may be asking themselves, "How good are we really?" There are a number of freelance ethicists available who can conduct a benchmarking study and audit of the organization to help establish a baseline. Once this is done, the organization can identify gaps in its current policies and procedures. These gaps will help the organization identify priorities and next steps.

One aspect that certainly needs to be reviewed is the accounting audits. Organizations today need to ensure their auditors are reputable and are briefed on areas of particular interest to the organization. While this is usually beyond the purview of the Human Resources practitioner, the practitioner should ensure that departmental practices are in line with corporate practices. The practitioner should, for instance, ensure that expense accounts and accounts payable are properly documented and authorized.

Many organizations today have established or are contemplating the establishment of ethics oversight committees. The senior Human Resources practitioner should be a key member of such a committee. Even the most comprehensive Code of Business Conduct will not cover every circumstance where ethical questions arise. The Human Resources practitioner is in a central role to ensure other company policies and practices align with the Code.

The role of the committee is to:

✓ investigate allegations brought forth by employees and others regarding breaches of the ethics Code or company policies, potential violations of the law or other improprieties;

✓ provide guidance to employees on ethical dilemmas, including potential conflicts of interest, receiving of gifts, private contracts with company suppliers or customers and whistleblowing;

✓ create a Code of Business Ethics and periodically review it to ensure the Code remains current;

✓ address any issues arising from the application, interpretation or administration of the Code;

✓ initiate any training or education efforts deemed appropriate to support the organization's desired culture;

✓ contract with outside ethicists to conduct benchmarking studies in order to ensure compliance with industry standards; and

✓ ensure compliance with the Code by ensuring every employee has acknowledged receipt of the Code and agrees to abide by its provisions.

Sample Policy

Preamble

The Code of Business Ethics is in effect as of October 31, 2002 and covers all employees of our organization, its subsidiaries and affiliates. Our Organization takes pride in its reputation for integrity, honesty and the ethical conduct of its employees. The purpose of this Code is to protect that reputation and to provide guidelines for the ethical and lawful conduct of all employees.

In many respects, the guidelines go beyond the requirements of law and industry practice. Notwithstanding, nothing contained in the Code should be construed or applied as a binding interpretation or definition of the law or industry practice. Furthermore, any act by a company employee or agent in violation of the law, company policy or the guidelines contained in this Code is considered as being beyond the scope of such person's authority and is not an act by or on behalf of the company.

The company reserves the right to update, amend or modify the guidelines contained in this Code at anytime. In addition, the Business Ethics Committee undertakes to review the Code annually to ensure the highest standards are consistently met and the reputation of the company as a leader in business ethics is maintained.

Employee Responsibilities

Employees are responsible for compliance to this Code and for behaving in an ethical manner as they conduct business on behalf of our organization.

Employees are responsible for reading and understanding the provisions of this Code. Every new employee must acknowledge in writing that he or she has received and read a copy of the Code. By doing so, the employee agrees to act in compliance with the Code at all times. Existing employees may also be required to sign similar acknowledgements on an annual basis and to participate in company-sponsored courses related to business ethics when asked to do so.

Employees may not knowingly help another person act unethically in the conduct of business or to collude with another in breach of this Code or the law. Employees are required to report any suspected breach of this Code or the law to their Manager or to a member of the Business Ethics Committee immediately upon learning of the breach.

It is company policy that no employee may be disciplined, intimidated, coerced or retaliated against for raising a business conduct issue, reporting a perceived violation of the law or otherwise acting in compliance with this Code. Every effort will be made to protect the confidentiality of individuals who report breaches of this Code or company policies, violations of the law, or other unethical conduct to the company.

Additional Responsibilities of Managers

Managers are expected to set an example of exemplary ethical conduct for their subordinates. This includes being open and available to discuss concerns with employees. Managers are expected to be sufficiently familiar with the Code to provide guidance to employees.

When concerns are raised with a manager, he or she will discreetly investigate the matter and make every attempt reasonable under the circumstances to protect the interests of the employee(s) who raised the concern. Managers should, in discharging this responsibility, take the appropriate steps to prohibit retribution against any employee who reports or supplies information about, or assists an investigation into, an allegation of a breach of this Code.

In addition, managers should monitor and ensure compliance with this Code, and with company policies in general, by employees and others conducting business on behalf of the company.

Use of Company Funds

Company funds may only be used for the exclusive benefit of the company. No employee is permitted to use or convert company funds for personal gain or use. Every employee is responsible for the prudent and effective use of all company funds, including those for travel and entertainment.

You must not, on behalf of or in connection with the company, use company funds in any unlawful manner, including the transfer of any funds through market channels prohibited by law.

Use of Company Property and Company Records

Employees may not use company property for personal gain or benefit, unless such property has been properly approved for general or public use. The use of company property under any other circumstances must be expressly approved in writing and in advance of the use. Company property may not be sold, loaned, given away or otherwise disposed of, regardless of condition or value, without written authorization.

Employees must ensure all books, records and accounts accurately and fairly reflect transactions and the dispositions of assets. A system of internal accounting controls consistent with the generally accepted accounting principles must be maintained to provide adequate corporate supervision over the accounting and reporting activities at all levels. No employee will make or authorize any "off-the-book" accounts or otherwise circumvent the system of internal accounting controls.

Company records should not be removed from the premises except for business purposes. You must not remove from the premises any company equipment, credit cards, keys, records, computer systems or other materials if you are terminated or suspended.

Company records must be kept in such a way that an accurate, auditable record of all financial transactions is maintained in accordance with generally accepted accounting principles. No one should make an entry on the company's books or records that intentionally hides or disguises the true nature of any transaction. This requirement applies to all company records including non-financial records (e.g., employee time records, workers' compensation claims, environmental documentation, safety statistics and driver or vehicle records).

Any employee responsible for the creation and maintenance of records and documents must be aware of and adhere to any statutes or regulations pertaining to the proper retention of those documents.

In addition, it is the company's policy to prevent the intentional or inadvertent destruction or concealment of documents except as provided for under law. In the event of an investigation by a regulatory agency, criminal investigation or civil litigation, the company, its employees and agents are required to cooperate to the fullest extent possible. During such investigations, or in the event the company has been subpoenaed to produce documents, any destruction of documents including the destruction of records pursuant to the company's record retention policies must be discontinued immediately.

Electronic Media

All employees are responsible for using sound judgment when accessing or sending information electronically. The proper use of electronic media protects the company from risk. Electronic media is provided by the company to assist in the conduct of company business. All messages composed, sent or received on the system are and remain the property of the company. They are not the private property of any employee, and employees shall not have any personal privacy right in any communications on the company's system. Irresponsible or inappropriate use of e-mail, Internet or access to information through computer networks could result in violation of the law or company policies.

Confidential Information and Trade Secrets

All employees who have or may have access to confidential information must sign a confidentiality agreement in a form approved by the company. By signing this agreement, employees are expressly agreeing not to disclose any private, confidential or proprietary information regarding the company or its customers.

Trade secrets and intellectual capital are the result of the significant investment of company resources. They are important assets that help the company create and maintain our competitive advantage. They must be protected.

All company confidential information will be preserved as a trade secret until the company authorizes its release. If you have access to confidential information including company trade secrets, you must not disclose it or use it in any fashion, either during or after your employment, unless you are expressly authorized to do so by the company.

Insider Information

Insider information is any non-public information relating to the company that could be used improperly for personal advantage. Employees must not disclose material non-public information to anyone outside the company unless they have received expressed permission to do so in advance.

Employees must refrain from using insider information in any business transaction for personal gain or in a manner that disadvantages the company. Employees are also prohibited from trading in the securities of another company if the value of such securities is likely to be affected by an action the company intends to take, of which you are aware, and which has not been publicly disclosed.

Conflicts of Interest

A conflict of interest can arise in any number of situations. It occurs most often when we, or members of our immediate family, obtain a personal benefit at the expense of the company. Any activity, investment, interest or association that interferes or might appear to interfere with our independent judgment or objectivity in performing our jobs is a conflict of interest.

All employees are expected to avoid conflicts of interest. Guidelines for some of the most common conflict of interest situations follow.

Outside Financial Interests: As a general rule, neither you nor your immediate family may have a financial interest or ownership in any company supplier, contractor, customer or competitor with whom you deal in your jobs. "Financial interest" excludes ownership of securities in a publicly traded company that has a fair market value less than your annual income at year end.

Family and Relatives: As a general rule, you must not engage in any business transaction on behalf of the company with a relative by blood or marriage — or with a firm where such a relative is a principal, officer or representative — without prior full disclosure to and written approval from your business unit president.

Using Company Suppliers: Employees who use company suppliers or contractors for personal business are expected to pay fair market value for services rendered and materials provided. In addition, you must disclose in advance this type of personal relationship to your business unit president.

Outside Jobs and Activities: In your employment with the company, you are expected to render your full-time best efforts to the company. You should not engage in outside business interests that divert time or attention away from company duties and responsibilities or that otherwise act to the detriment of the company.

You must not work for any company suppliers, contractors, customers or competitors without prior full disclosure to and written approval from your business unit president.

If an employee thinks he or she may have a direct or indirect conflict of interest, the employee must disclose such potential conflict to the Business Ethics Committee. After an employee has disclosed a potential conflict, a determination will be made as to whether the employee should divest himself or herself of the interest or realign his or her job functions.

Antitrust and Competition Laws

The *Anti-Combines Act* and the competition laws of other countries are designed to preserve and protect competition in goods and services. These laws are a critical part of the business environment in which the company operates. Some violations can result in criminal charges, exposing the company and individuals to fines and imprisonment. Violations can also lead to orders restricting our operations.

Employees may not communicate with competitors in any manner that may be construed as collusion or which is intended to restrict trade or fix prices. Information that cannot be shared with competitors includes:

- prices and pricing plans;
- terms of sale;
- marketing strategies or plans;
- expansion plans;
- territorial or customer allocation;
- reciprocity; and
- refusal to deal.

D - **E** - F

Trade Associations

The company's policy is to belong to trade associations only when such groups contribute significant benefits to justify the time and cost of membership or support. Trade associations, by their nature, involve meetings and discussions with competitors, and care must be taken to avoid antitrust problems.

If you are involved in or observe an activity that could raise an antitrust or competition law issue, you must report it immediately to your manager or the Business Ethics Committee.

Gifts and Entertainment

Whenever exchanges of gifts or hospitality are part of doing business, the company runs the risk of compromising, or appearing to compromise, our business conduct standards.

You must not, nor should any member of your immediate family, accept any gifts or entertainment of an inappropriate nature, money, loans (except on commercial terms from a lending institution) or any other preferential treatment from any company supplier, contractor, customer or competitor without prior full disclosure to and written approval from your business unit president.

Solicitation of gifts from suppliers is prohibited regardless of the value of the gift, the purpose of the solicitation or the use to which the gift will be put.

You must not, nor should any member of your immediate family, give on behalf of the company any gift or entertainment of an inappropriate nature, money, loans or preferential treatment to anyone, including company suppliers, contractors, customers or competitors, without prior full disclosure to and written approval from your business unit president. Gifts must not be made to labour officials.

Inappropriate Gifts and Entertainment

Gifts and entertainment can be said to be inappropriate when they are outside the normal bounds of business or likely to be perceived as influencing the recipient.

Government Affairs

If you represent the company in political and government affairs, or lobby on behalf of the company, you are expected to do so within all appropriate business conduct and comply fully with all laws and regula-tions relating to corporate participation in public affairs.

Filing Government Reports

When you file a report with any governmental department for or on behalf of the company, you must take special care to ensure that the information you provide is true, accurate and complete. Any omission or lack of attention to detail can be construed as a violation of laws or regulations.

Improperly Influencing Government Officials

You are strictly prohibited from offering, promising or giving money, gifts, loans, rewards, favours or anything of value to any government official or employee in order to influence his or her judgment in conducting government duties.

You also are strictly prohibited from making payments of any kind to agents or other intermediaries if you know or have reason to know that they will pay all or part of such payments to accomplish what you are prohibited from doing directly.

No entertainment of a government official, employee, agent or intermediary shall be provided on behalf of the company except routine lunches or dinners occurring during the conduct of regular business, and then only to the extent this is not a violation of policy of the particular government agency involved.

International Business Conduct

Every employee in our international operations will also comply with the laws of the host country. Employees are not permitted to use company funds for any purpose which would be in violation of any law or regulation of any applicable country.

Employees and agents acting on behalf of the company are not authorized to make a payment of money, or anything of value, directly or indirectly, to foreign officials, political parties or candidates for political office to obtain, retain or direct business to any person or influence any act or decision of such official in carrying out his or her official duties.

Agents and Consultants

Agents and consultants who are expected to have dealings with foreign governments or agencies on behalf of the company must comply with the company's policy of strict compliance with the *Foreign Corrupt Practices Act*.

Promotional Activities

Payments only for *bona fide* and reasonable expenses (such as travel and lodging) of foreign government officials who, in the performance of official duties, visit company facilities in connection with the promotion, demonstration or explanation of company products or services is permitted. All such payments must be lawful under the law of the applicable country and be approved in advance by the business unit president.

Suppliers, Contractors and Customers

As agents for the company, employees will base all sales and purchases on the business merits, including product quality, service level and prices, and the consistency and dependability of our customers, contractors or suppliers.

Confidential Information of Others

We will respect the confidentiality of information given to us in confidence by suppliers, contractors or customers. However, certain restrictions about that information may place an unfair burden on the company's future business. For that reason, employees are required to find out what restrictions might exist prior to receiving any confidential information. These restrictions must be disclosed in writing and should be reviewed and approved by the General Counsel before the information can be received.

Payments to Purchasing Agents

Employees, as well as agents retained by the company, must not make payments to purchasing agents or employees of any supplier, contractor or customer to either obtain or retain business, or to realize higher or lower prices for the company.

Employees will not suggest or imply to suppliers, contractors or customers that purchases or sales by the company are dependent upon them buying from or selling to the company.

Environmental Responsibility

Meeting high standards of environmental responsibility is a company value. Failure to do so can damage the company's reputation, lead to fines for both the company and individuals, create liabilities and, in the extreme, imperil the health and safety of employees and others.

We must comply with all environmental laws, regulations and policies and identify and respond to public health concerns. Those who are responsible for or engaged in activities or operations that might affect the environment must be familiar with all laws, regulations and policies that relate to these activities.

Role of the Human Resources Practitioner

While some large firms such as financial institutions are able to afford a full-time ethicist on staff, most organizations need to delegate this responsibility. Quite often, this falls appropriately to the senior Human Resources practitioner. This is consistent with the practitioner's role in establishing company policies and the role of creating and maintaining a corporate culture consistent with the strategic objectives of the organization. In many ways, applied ethics is an integral and fundamental part of what every Human Resources practitioner does on a day-to-day basis.

Certainly, the senior practitioner should be a member of the ethics oversight committee. In some organizations, an ombudsman fields employee concerns and conducts investigations including into issues of unethical practices. In these instances, the practitioner should be the central contact with the ombudsman.

While practitioners should always attempt to avoid the role of organizational policeman, it is vital that they are consulted on allegations of breaches of the Code of Ethics (or Code of Business Conduct), to bring about consistent and fair application of any disciplinary sanctions. Moreover, the practitioner must review such cases, particularly if they may potentially lead to the termination of an employee, to ensure the actions taken are fair, equitable and consistent with the law.

Barriers to Success/Common Pitfalls

Codes of ethics (or codes of business conduct) are seldom seen as central policies and risk, even more so than other policy statements, being given mere lip service. Organizations, and the employees in them, today can easily become overloaded with policies, processes, operating procedures and rules. During times of crisis, as that of 2002, such policies are relevant and timely. Employees may applaud the efforts of organizations that introduce a Code of Business Conduct during such times. However, in many instances, these efforts are long forgotten over time when other matters become more pressing. Keeping a Code of Business Conduct alive and in the forefront of employees' minds is a difficult and often daunting task.

As the Enron example amply demonstrates, having a code is useless when the behaviours of senior management are inconsistent with the intent and content of the policy. In less obvious ways, senior management can render a Code of Business Conduct null and void by the way in which they conduct themselves. The conduct that nullifies the intent of a Code of Business Conduct does not have to be criminal or quasi-criminal acts. The everyday behaviour of the senior management team is the most important guideline for employees to follow when governing their own behaviour.

FLEXIBLE WORK PRACTICES

Definition/Background

Flexibility is defined as the processes required to ensure that an organization, and the individuals and teams within it, can respond and adapt quickly to changing circumstances and the demands arising from them.

Flexibility is an important factor in planning and managing organizational structures, workflows and operations, the deployment and use of people, and the development and extension of the range of skills employees possess (multi-skilling).

The emphasis on increased flexibility has arisen for a number of reasons.

1. The need to be competitive which focuses attention on the more efficient use of human resources.

2. The need to be adaptive. The organization has to be able to respond quickly to change and to the new demands constantly being made upon it in turbulent and highly competitive conditions.

3. The impact of new technology which is changing skill requirements and working arrangements.

4. New organizational structures, leading to the emergence of more fluid forms of organizations to respond quickly to competitive challenges and new consumer demands, in which rapid developments and/or complex innovation takes place. These require a more flexible approach to structure, the definition of work roles and how roles interact.

Although competitive pressures and new technologies may generally indicate that greater structural and operating flexibility is required, the extent to which this applies in any one organization must depend entirely on its environment and its technology. A somewhat bureaucratic and inflexible approach might be unavoidable in some circumstances, whereas a much more flexible approach might be essential in others. There will always be a choice, depending on the situation, of what priorities should be given to the different types of flexibility.

Flexibility affects everyone in the organization, although it will be particularly important for people whose work is subject to constant change or those who have a wide range of skills that can be used on different tasks.

It is no longer possible (if it ever was) to run organizations with an inflexible structure. A bureaucratic approach to managing organizations is only appropriate if they exist in a tranquil and unchanging environment. How many organizations are in that position today?

The fashion for delayering organizations came to the fore when it was at last appreciated that having too many layers in the organizational hierarchy inhibited communication and effective decision-making at the point of action where the need for a flexible response is always greatest. Too many layers also mean, of course, too many managers getting in each other's way and, because they are all busy fighting their own corner, they tend to function inflexibly.

Flatter, delayered organizations can only work well if there is increased emphasis on teamwork and flexibility within teams. Such organizations also encourage the development of project groups or taskforces set up to deal with particular issues and then disbanded. In this way, the organization can respond much more flexibly to new requirements. In fact, project-based and matrix organizations are designed to provide for the flexible deployment and use of people.

The Flexible Organization

An organization is flexible in terms of its adaptability to expansion, contraction or change in the product market. The flexible organization has an inner core of stable, skilled employees with secure employment and career prospects. Outside this core are the peripheral workers who can be placed into the following three categories:

1. The first are a peripheral group of workers who are full-time employees but enjoy a lower degree of job security and have less access to career opportunities. In effect, they are offered a job, not a career.

2. The second peripheral group consists of part-time workers whose deployment is structured to match changing business needs. These employees are used to meet peak manning requirements and to provide relief for vacationing or absent full-time employees. This group can include permanent part-time employees, people on fixed term contracts, job sharers, students, coop placements and call-casual employees.

3. The third peripheral group are the subcontractors who provide specified services for a defined period of time and consist of consultants, self-employed freelancers, people from temporary help agencies and the like.

The main types of flexibility are as follows:

⇨ Functional flexibility in which employees can be redeployed quickly and smoothly between tasks. This can include the employment of multi-skilled craft workers, moving people between different parts of the organization onto different jobs, or moving workers between direct and indirect production jobs.

⇨ Numerical flexibility in which employers can quickly increase or decrease the headcount in line with even short-term changes in the demand for labour to ensure that the number working matches that required.

⇨ Financial flexibility in which pay quickly reflects movements in market rates and/or there is a shift to new pay arrangements that facilitate functional or numerical flexibility.

⇨ Contractual flexibility in which individual contracts and job descriptions provide for the maximum amount of flexibility in terms of the work that employees are expected to perform. These individual contracts and job descriptions may mean abandoning old detailed job descriptions for much broader role definitions that simply indicate, in broad terms, the areas where results are expected, and do not spell out in any detail how individuals are expected to achieve those results.

Job-Based/Functional Flexibility

Job-based or functional flexibility means that workers can be moved from task to task and may be expected to use a wider range of skills within their capability. Organizations may want to introduce this type of flexibility because they need to make the fullest use of their human resources, especially when they are using increasingly sophisticated equipment and systems that must be properly maintained if they are to produce at their optimum levels. Functional flexibility also means that where work loads in different parts of a factory fluctuate widely, people can be moved in quickly to handle the extra demands.

In unionized workplaces, many of the old work rules and jurisdictional issues have restricted the introduction of more flexible practices. Increasingly, the breaking down of these barriers has been a significant issue at negotiation time. Some organizations have overcome these barriers by setting up in "green-field" sites. These may be established in cooperation with the union or may be set up as union-free operations.

Full, functional flexibility is often associated with the harmonization of terms and conditions of employment so that all staff regardless of function are treated equally as far as benefits are concerned.

When implementing job-based flexibility, the process should begin with consultation with employees (and their recognized trade unions if amendments to the collective agreement are required). If such changes are imposed unilaterally, then the employees could claim breach of contract which might lead to constructive dismissal claims should individuals choose to resign over the issue.

Flexible Work

Flexible work can be defined as either being flexible about working hours or flexible about working practices.

The first form of flexible work enables employees to vary their working arrangements according to business circumstances and personal circumstances, enabling them to accommodate essential domestic commitments. Some formulae define the period to be worked and the period when time off can be taken or made up. Other schemes allow for time to be earned which can be saved up over a longer period, and then be used at a mutually convenient time (e.g., during school holidays or to extend annual leave in special circumstances).

The second form allows a range of flexible work practices including any variation on typical patterns, including permanent and temporary contracts. Some of these work arrangements have been in existence for a long time (e.g., part-time work), others are more recent (e.g., telecommuting).

Part-time Work

Part-time work is still the most prevalent form of flexible work. It is used principally for business reasons, including:

— to control costs through flexible staffing;

— to staff for peaks and valleys in product demand (contingency staffing); and

— to provide relief for leaves of absence (vacation relief, coverage for parental leave).

Most part-time jobs are created in low-wage positions. The retail sector uses part-time employees extensively because low margins make it essential for these organizations to control labour costs. As well, these sectors commonly experience significant seasonal shifts in demand that neatly coincide with the availability of students who make up a large proportion of part-time workers.

Some part-time employees are provided with fixed weekly scheduled hours and may be provided with a minimum (as well as a maximum) number of hours. Other part-time employees are used on a call-casual basis. This effectively means they are constantly on call. However, these employees are entitled to turn down hours without reprisal in return for not being scheduled.

In recent years, there was growing speculation that a significant segment of the population preferred part-time work as evident by the growing proportion of part-time workers in relation to the total number of people employed. However, in the very recent times, the number of part-time workers dropped off substantially to the point that many employers who relied on part-time workers were faced with critical shortages. This demonstrated that rather than preferring part-time work, a large number of people preferred part-time work to no work at all.

Part-time work does allow employees more time to spend with their families. Often one parent will work part-time in order to generate some income and to be engaged in a meaningful activity, and still have time to fulfil family responsibilities.

Fixed Term Contracts

Employees may be engaged for a temporary assignment to cover for a specific absence (parental leave) or to work on a defined project. Information Technology employees are often hired on a fixed term contract to implement a new system. This is a cost-effective alternative to engaging consultants to do the work.

Fixed term contracts can also afford workers a lengthy break between assignments to meet family needs or pursue other interests. It also may provide employees with the flexibility to seek out new challenges, manage their own careers and gain variety in their work.

Telecommuting

Telecommuting means working at a distance, away from a normal office environment, and using information technology (telephony) to overcome the distance. The benefits to the organization include:

— flexibility to meet its business needs without the overhead of an in-house workforce;

— ability to cover fluctuations in production and trading; and

— opportunity to draw in key specialist skills.

From the worker's perspective, it means choice and being in control of his or her work. Telecommuting is flexible regarding the location where it is based and the time spent on the job. It can be home-based and/or it can be group-based. It can encompass a freelance worker, pursuing a portfolio career working with several organizations as a lone, mobile worker, or it can use a satellite office/resource centre or any other form of partnership. It can mean carrying out subcontracting work, working on short-term contracts or an annual hours scheme.

The new forms of telecommuting have been summarized as:

— using contractors;

— working on spin-offs;

— using consultants on projects;

— using agency/freelance staff;

— forming strategic alliances with other organizations; and

— using outsourcing services and/or projects.

From the organization's perspective, it implies a change in management strategy (responding to individual demands or business needs) that is new and has not emerged from other, more traditional forms of flexible work practices. It leads to flexible, responsive and networked organizations.

The implications for management styles include a change in roles, from manager to facilitator and from colleague to additional/support worker. For the flexible worker, it means going through multiple roles throughout the working day and being resourceful in finding and creating individual support systems. Communication channels and the quality of the communication are likely to change with infrastructure changes.

Interactions and relationships will change with reference to management and co-workers. Outside the organization, relationships with the community, immediate family and clients will also undergo change.

Freelance/Portfolio Working

This is self-employment for professionals, frequently involving the use of information technology and working from home. A typical example involves a temporary desk with a computer in an office that is used for part of the week. The boundaries between freelance and telecommuting can be a grey area. Freelancers are often called on to bring in specialist skills, to be involved in defined projects, and sometimes as a result of their own request, to work independently. In recent years, executives and professionals who have been displaced through a downsizing initiative have offered their services on a freelance basis. Although for many this was seen as a stopgap measure to pay the bills between jobs, others have set up "rent-an-executive" practices to help organizations on projects or to fill temporary organizational voids.

Job/Work Sharing

Job sharing is a variant of part-time working in which two or possibly three people share one particular job. Whereas it was initially restricted to clerical and administrative jobs, it is increasingly being used at all levels of an organization. In one variation, all employees in an organization may take a reduction in scheduled hours to avoid layoffs. This had fallen into disfavour particularly among unionized workforces who preferred seeing junior employees laid off over

the shared pain of work sharing. Recently, firms in the now volatile dot.com and high-tech sectors have resorted to work sharing as a means of retaining skilled staff. This is a somewhat dubious strategy in that highly skilled employees are likely to leave in search of full-time hours.

The business case for job sharing is well documented. Job sharing may:

— provide flexibility;

— reduce turnover of staff with key skills;

— provide additional cover at peak periods;

— offer employment continuity;

— provide complementary skills; and

— be perceived to be family-friendly.

Critically, it gets over the difficulty, when the right partner or pair can be found, of reducing the hours in a job and restructuring other jobs to meet requests from women returning from maternity leave for part-time working. Experience shows successful job sharers can be men or women.

Flex Hours

Flexible hour arrangements take a variety of forms, including the following:

1. *Flexible daily hours* — these may follow an agreed pattern day-by-day according to typical or expected work loads (e.g., flextime systems).

2. *Flexible weekly hours* — these provide for longer weekly hours to be worked at certain peak periods during the year.

3. *Flexible daily and weekly hours* — these work by varying daily or weekly hours or a combination of both to match the input of hours to achieve the required output. Such working times, unlike daily or weekly arrangements, may fluctuate between a minimum and a maximum of hours.

4. *Compressed working weeks* — employees work fewer than the five standard days.

5. *Annual hours* — these involve scheduling employee hours on the basis of the number of hours to be worked, with provisions for the increase or reduction of hours in any given period, according to the demand for goods or services.

Benefits/Expected Outcomes

The benefits to the organization of flexibility and using flexible work practices are the following:

— flexibility to cover peaks and valleys in product demand;

— ability to bring specialized skills into the organization as and when required;

— takes into account family considerations;

— helps to retain skilled labour;

— capacity to respond quickly and appropriately to new demands and priorities;

— improved utilization of people;

— ability to motivate people by catering more appropriately to their varied and changing needs;

— ability to focus attention on pressing issues without disrupting normal work flows;

— capacity to deploy a wider range of skills; and

— increased scope for deploying people on different work, possibly using different skills, in accordance with operational requirements.

The benefits of increased flexibility can be measured by assessing how quickly the organization and the people in it respond and adapt to new situations. This is likely to be a subjective judgment in many cases, although it will be possible in particular situations to compare employment costs or productivity before and after new flexibility arrangements have been introduced.

Mechanisms and Implementation

Implementation varies according to the needs, structure and culture of each organization and the occupation, industrial sector and hierarchy under consideration. It is comparatively easy to make a case for flexibility but much more complex to see individual initiatives through to implementation.

With ongoing restructuring and organizational transformation, the use of flexibility is expected to increase as organizations operate without slack to absorb the peaks. In addition, they tend to rely more on external specialists for specific projects and a pool of peripheral workers to call on as required.

Flexibility used for structural reasons is different from that introduced for family-friendly purposes; in the latter case, its value is essentially that of skill and experience retention, and motivation and productivity.

Implementation of the new forms of flexible work will place new management style requirements on individual managers, as working relationships will need to be built on openness and trust. The old style values, such as loyalty to the employer, can no longer be taken as givens. There are also likely to be issues around confidentiality of information.

Telecommuting

Processes and practices internal to the organization are likely to be affected in several ways with the introduction of telecommuting (e.g., job content, grading, benefits, technology, methodology, planning systems and output measurements).

Traditional forms of management, such as reward for performance, motivation by control and hierarchical structures (the stick and carrot approach), power based on status and survival by risk aversion, are unlikely to be appropriate to manage the new working relationships. This means a need for new management skills and hence new forms of management development training. Perhaps, for many, there may be a perceived loss of power and status.

Successful management skills will include the following:

— commitment;

— personal responsibility;

— accountability;

— honesty;

— openness and trust; and

— team building and working based on diversity rather than conformity.

Communication style, frequency, participative style, vision, feedback and technology literacy will have an impact on building longer-term working relationships.

The attributes sought after in telecommuters will include:

— balance;

— intrinsic motivation;

— computer literacy; and

D - E - **F**

— trustworthiness with confidential information.

Budgetary considerations need to take account of people within the organization as well as those external to it and contracted by the organization for projects or services of a specific duration.

Job Sharing

Job sharing involves two or more people working part of each day, part of a week or alternate weeks depending on their employer's circumstances. Job sharers can also divide the job by tasks or projects depending on their skills, the requirements of the job and their own needs.

Increasingly, as organizations begin to count hour requirements rather than heads, job sharers can do work that requires a given number of hours. In this way, job sharing is similar to part-time workers jointly being responsible for a particular job. A mix of skills and attributes can combine to give a particularly strong team spirit. For example, for retailers increasingly requiring seven-day cover, job sharing at management level becomes an attractive option.

Each job sharer has a permanent contract with *pro rata* pay and, in some cases, benefits and joint responsibility for the full-time job description.

Communication between the job sharers is particularly important. Thus, to enhance communication, job sharers can have an overlap of one day per week, or one day per month, or a few hours in the middle of each day. The working relationship with the line manager will need to be based on openness and trust, and communication lines will need to be well established. Issues that have arisen revolve around accountability and responsibility, but practice shows that these can be overcome.

Other difficulties have arisen when one sharer is promoted, transfers or resigns, as it can take time to find the complementary match. Organizations have overcome this problem by keeping a register of potential sharers, pooled from permanent employees or those on career breaks.

Formal schemes of job sharing are not necessarily the best way, as each job sharing arrangement can be tailored, for maximum effectiveness, to the needs of a particular organization, department, function, or project requirement.

Role of the Human Resources Practitioner

The areas in which the Human Resources practitioner can advise on the scope for increasing flexibility and help in developing it are the following:

— contracts of employment and job descriptions, by introducing more flexible contracts and less restrictive job descriptions;

— working hours, by designing, negotiating and implementing flexible hours systems;

— job and work design, by enlarging and enriching the range of responsibilities of individuals and teams;

— flexibility agreements, by negotiating agreements with trade unions to abolish demarcation limits and allow management to use labour more flexibly (e.g., machine tool operators carrying out routine maintenance) and monitoring their implementation;

— training, by providing training both to enhance and to broaden skills (multi-skilling);

— resourcing, by seeking ways of using part-time, temporary or contract workers where this is appropriate; and

— pay, by developing flexible reward systems, including performance-related pay and "cafeteria systems" for selecting benefits.

Barriers to Success/Common Pitfalls

The main barriers to success in developing more flexible working arrangements are the following:

— inherent inertia of people and organizations that prefer the *status quo* and are reluctant to deviate from it;

— suspicion about flexible working which may be seen as a threat to security and perceived as an indication that hard-won qualifications and expertise are no longer important;

— problem of maintaining control in situations where there is much more scope for deviating from the norm;

— difficulty of planning ahead when future arrangements are uncertain; and

— reluctance of people to work more flexibly because they are worried about new demands, or because they do not see why they should do new things that are not part of the existing job description or accepted methods of working.

The most common mistake is to assume that because the organization wants to operate more flexibly, everyone will join in enthusiastically. In practice, many people do not see why they should put themselves out and resent being put in a position where they have to change their ways. If asked to do more, they may quite reasonably ask to be paid more. They may not see any reason for putting themselves out for the sake of the organization without reaping some benefits for themselves.

To avoid this problem, it is essential to plan for an increase in flexibility with people in mind. In other words, account must be taken of the likely reactions of individuals to changes in their roles and thought given as to how they will benefit from the new arrangements.

HARASSMENT

Definition/Background

Harassment and bullying are perhaps the most insidious forms of workplace conflict. The victims of harassment and bullying are typically powerless to deal with the stresses imposed upon them, or at least have significantly less perceived power than the harasser or bully. Harassment usually refers to a particular form of discriminating behaviour and is typically gender- or racially-based. Other forms of harassment do exist. *Human Rights Codes* across Canada recognize the rights of every individual to work in an environment free from any type of harassment. In general, the legislation stipulates that no employee shall be discriminated against in any way because of his or her race, ancestry, place of origin, colour, ethnic origin, citizenship, creed, sex, sexual orientation, marital status, family status or handicap.

Sexual harassment is specifically defined as unwanted sexual advances, or visual, verbal, or physical conduct of a sexual nature. This definition encompasses many forms of offensive behaviour including gender-based harassment of a person of the same sex as the harasser. The following is a partial list of examples of sexual harassment:

- unwanted sexual advances;

- offering employment benefits in exchange for sexual favours;

- making or threatening reprisals after a negative response to sexual advances;

- visual conduct that includes leering, making sexual gestures, or displaying sexually suggestive objects or pictures, cartoons or posters;

- verbal conduct that includes making or using derogatory comments, epithets, slurs, or jokes;

- verbal sexual advances or propositions;

- verbal abuse of a sexual nature, graphic verbal commentaries about an individual's body, sexually degrading words used to describe an individual, or suggestive or obscene letters, notes, or invitations;

- physical conduct that includes touching, assaulting, or impeding or blocking movements;

- unwelcome sexual advances (either verbal or physical) and requests for sexual favours; Other verbal or physical conduct of a sexual nature constitutes sexual harassment when: (1) submission to such conduct is made either explicitly or implicitly a term or condition of employment; (2) submission or rejection of the conduct is used as a basis for making employment decisions; or (3) the conduct has the purpose or effect of interfering with work performance or creating an intimidating, hostile, or offensive work environment.

Bullying is a form of harassment where there is no particular prohibited ground for the behaviour. Rather, the bully preys on weaker individuals who have less power than he or she has. Bullying can occur between peers or between a supervisor and his or her subordinates. Unfortunately, bullying can occur right up the organizational ladder. Senior managers can be bullies.

Like any form of harassment, bullying can be either physical or verbal misdeeds. Bullies typically berate and belittle their victims, often in public. The resulting humiliation can cause distress and, if it persists over a period of time, can traumatize the victim. While bullying is just another form of harassment, it has received little attention in Canada. Our schools are now teaching young children how to deal with bullying in the schoolyards, but our business organizations and the agencies that protect employee health and welfare have yet to pay much attention to this serious issue.

The problem with bullying is further exasperated by the fact that the perpetrators are often in more powerful roles and the victims fear reprisal. Moreover, the behaviour often goes unabated and therefore appears to be sanctioned by the organization. Enlightened organizations will include bullying in their harassment policies so that employees have an avenue of redress when they fall victim to it.

Although infrequent, one possible consequence of any workplace conflict is the potential for a physical altercation. When employees are teased or verbally abused and they do not have a ready avenue for redress, they will at times revert to fighting. Supervisors should be alert to signs of an employee or group of employees being singled out and potentially abused, and take proactive steps to protect their rights. Too often physical altercations could have been foreseen by the supervisor. However, it is not uncommon to dismiss the actions of the bully as a mere personality conflict. Organizations should take steps to ensure the issue of bullying is not trivialized at the risk of suffering a poisoned work environment.

Benefits/Expected Outcomes

The obvious benefits of creating an harassment-free work environment include reduced interpersonal conflict, reduced stressors in the workplace and compliance with legislation. Less obviously, promoting such a workplace can lead to substantial benefits for any organization, including:

✓ improved employee morale and a positive employee relations culture;

✓ an environment of open and honest communications;

✓ validation of the organization's core values and code of ethical conduct (whether the code is explicit or implicit);

✓ decreased absenteeism because of interpersonal conflict and stress (see also Stress Management at page 427 *et seq.*); and

✓ increased productivity through the fostering of cooperation.

Organizations that have stood by their anti-harassment policies often also promote diversity, and equal employment and development opportunities. Together, these initiatives create a work environment that is attractive to individuals who fear the potential of a poisoned work environment. Thus, these organizations enjoy the benefit of being perceived as a preferred employer. Their recruitment activities are made that much easier because they have gained a reputation as an employer that lives its espoused values.

Harassment can occur even in the most enlightened organizations. The implementation of investigation processes that are deemed fair and equitable enhances the perception among employees of the efficacy of human resources policies and procedures. When the process works well, the practitioner is viewed as a credible arbiter. One of the greatest challenges faced by the human resources practitioner is the ability to strike a balance between competing interests. In some instances, these may be between an individual and the organization and, in others, between individuals at different levels within the organization. The process of resolving harassment issues gives the practitioner an opportunity to demonstrate his or her ability to strike the appropriate balance.

Programming/Implementation

Organizations must establish policies whereby employees are encouraged to let others know when they find their behaviour to be objectionable or harassing. However, organizations should also recognize that employees might not always find it comfortable to do so. Depending on the size and relative sophistication of the organization, the policy can direct employees to report immediately to a supervisor or any other member of management when they experience or witness sexual or other unlawful harassment in the workplace. Where a supervisor is unavailable or is the perpetrator and the organization has a Human Resources Department, the employees should be directed to report the incident to a human resources practitioner.

For such a practice to work, the employees must believe that they can raise concerns and make reports without fear of reprisal or retaliation. This creates a somewhat delicate dilemma for the practitioner who must investigate all allegations of harassment quickly and discreetly. Maintaining confidentiality of the victim, any witnesses and the alleged harasser should be protected against unnecessary disclosure. However, in order to do a thorough investigation and to have procedural justice, the alleged harasser has a right to know the identity of his or her accuser.

Anyone engaging in sexual or other unlawful harassment should be subject to disciplinary action, up to and including termination of employment. Many organizations have a "zero tolerance" policy when it comes to sexual harassment. However, in some court and arbitration decisions regarding wrongful dismissal, zero tolerance policies have been found to be unfair to the accused. If the behaviour is relatively innocuous and stops as soon as the alleged harasser is advised that the behaviour is unwanted, then a zero tolerance standard may be viewed as too harsh.

Racial harassment, like sexual harassment, can come in many forms, including verbal abuse, verbal conduct such as derogatory comments, epithets, slurs, or jokes, displaying of objects or pictures, cartoons or posters of a racial nature, denying employees promotions or other employment benefits because of their race, and physical abuse. While in some instances of sexual harassment, perpetrators might not reasonably know that their actions are unwanted, in instances of racial harassment, perpetrators ought always to know that their behaviour is wrong.

In addition to a complaint investigation and resolution procedure, organizations should prominently post a policy statement regarding employees' human rights. Such statements give assurances to employees that they are welcome regardless of the colour of their skin, gender or any other natural trait. Such a statement can be as simple as:

> Our organization recognizes the dignity and worth of every individual. Every employee has the right to work in an environment free from any type of harassment. Further, no employee shall be discriminated against in any way because of his or her race, ancestry, place of origin, colour, ethnic origin, citizenship, creed, sex, sexual orientation, marital status, family status or handicap.
>
> Our organization will make every effort to eliminate any barriers that may prevent individuals from reaching their full potential. Hiring and promotional decisions will be based on an individual's merits, his or her contributions to the organization and ability to perform the *bona fide* requirements of the position.
>
> Furthermore, our customers and suppliers, and their employees, also enjoy the same rights. Every employee of our organization is expected to respect the rights of others and to uphold the dignity and worth of every individual they come in contact with during the course of their employment.

Practical Application

Bullying

At a Toronto-based manufacturing firm, a senior Vice President has a reputation for being a hard taskmaster. In fact, he is a bully. He is well known for yelling at employees in his department and employees in other departments. He belittles individual performance in department meetings. His behaviour is degrading to those who work for him. Moreover, his department has the highest turnover rate in the company. One manager had to take considerable time off because of a stress-related illness and was never able to return.

Despite the overwhelming evidence of this bullying, senior management continue to tolerate his behaviour. It is not that they are unaware of it, but rather that they underestimate the organizational consequences of his behaviour. Not only have his actions caused literally hundreds of thousands of dollars in employment-related costs (turnover, absenteeism and increased disability claims experience) but also the failure of senior management to sanction him has validated his behaviour.

This results in it being accepted that others will emulate him to a degree. This creates an atmosphere where employees feel disempowered and are reluctant to voice a differing opinion on any matter. Some senior managers have expressed an awareness of the consequences of his behaviour on his department but still dismiss the concept that the behaviour affects the overall culture of the organization. In truth, it cannot help but have a negative impact on the overall culture.

In one case, the courts recognized the potential harm a manager's bullying could have on the organization's culture and drew the conclusion that it paralleled sabotage. The court held that the actions of the manager did damage to the culture, and were just and sufficient cause to dismiss the manager without notice or compensation.

Sexual Harassment

A female production employee at a Brampton furniture manufacturer was on probation. In fact, her probationary status had been extended by mutual agreement because her productivity continued to fall just short of the established standards. The company concluded that her employment should be terminated because of poor performance. In addition, she had been absent several times during her short tenure.

During the termination interview, she informed the human resources manager that she was nervous at work because her male supervisor leered at her and, on more than one occasion, had touched her breasts and rubbed suggestively against her. She maintained that, because of the environment the supervisor had created, she could not be successful on the job.

The human resources manager at first dismissed her accusations as being retaliation for the decision to discharge her. However, on the advice of outside counsel in response to a grievance filed on her behalf, the human resources manager conducted an investigation.

The investigation not only uncovered supporting witnesses but also other instances of harassing behaviour by the same supervisor against other female employees. The termination was maintained but the company paid a financial settlement to the outgoing employee. The supervisor was subsequently dismissed.

Role of the Human Resources Practitioner

When dealing with harassment issues, the practitioner has a multi-faceted role. The role cannot be solely reactive. In order for an organization to truly rid itself of a poisoned environment, it must embark on proactive programming as well.

In the reactive mode, the practitioner is often positioned as the "complaint department". The practitioner needs to foster an "open door" environment to encourage employees to come forward with any concerns or issues they have regarding workplace harassment. Initially, the practitioner performs a triage function, assessing the severity of the issue and determining the appropriate first response. In some instances, the practitioner may advise the employee personally on how to confront the issue, in others the practitioner may determine that an investigation and formal enquiry is warranted.

In addition, the practitioner may begin the process by advising the alleged victim on where he or she can seek assistance to cope with the stressors created by the situation. Often we refer to the complainant as an alleged victim because the practitioner must reserve judgment until he or she has had an opportunity to review the available evidence that harassment took place. Unfortunately, false accusations and exaggerated claims have become commonplace, and the practitioner needs to remain sensitive not only to the complainant but also to the alleged harassers who may be falsely accused.

If an investigation is warranted, the practitioner will need to decide whether he or she should conduct the investigation or seek other resources. Larger organiza-

tions employ independent ombudsmen to conduct such investigations. Other organizations establish strict policies to have outside counsel conduct investigations. This reduces possible future accusations that the investigation was biased. Using outside counsel also serves to prepare the organization for any potential defence the organization may have to put forward on its own behalf.

Regardless of the knowledge the organization may or may not have of the harassment occurring in its workplace, it is always responsible to some degree. The concept is that, if harassment occurred, the very act itself demonstrates that the organization did not take sufficient steps to prevent it. In defending against this presumption of guilt, the organization will need to put forward a positive defence that proves the organization exercised due diligence in eradicating harassment from its environment. Employing counsel early in the investigation affords the organization the opportunity to gather evidence that it had acted with due diligence.

As well, it is likely that the investigation will conclude with a recommendation to take disciplinary action against someone. If the harassment is proven, the harasser will potentially face termination of employment. If the accusation is proven to be false, the complainant may face sanctions. If the investigation is inconclusive, the organization may still face the prospect of defending itself in a human rights case. Early intervention from legal counsel can lead to a much more effective defence of the actions the organization chooses to take.

Practitioners who conduct investigations should take careful steps to maintain neutrality until the evidence demonstrates clearly what has occurred. Confidentiality is also a key consideration. However, with harassment complaints, it is necessary to reveal to the harasser who the complainant is in order to afford the individual a fair opportunity to answer the charges. It is also often necessary to interview witnesses. Maintaining strict confidentiality is simply not possible. Instead, the practitioner needs to focus on maintaining and promoting sensitivity so that the issue remains contained.

The practitioner makes recommendations on the course of action to be followed based on the findings of the investigation. Here the adage, "justice delayed is justice denied" applies. The investigation should be completed as quickly as possible and, once it is completed, follow-up actions should be swift. A number of organizations have adopted zero tolerance policies. However, practitioners are well advised to consider the question of balance and equity when determining the appropriate level of response. Automatic penalties are seldom perceived as fair. The nature and severity of the misconduct, the performance and service of the individuals, past conduct and any other mitigating factors need to be considered in determining the appropriate courses of action.

These courses of action are not restricted to dealing simply with the immediate situation and fact circumstances; they should also address any environmental issues that could have been an influence. Proactive steps that can be taken include diversity training, harassment awareness seminars and anti-harassment promotional campaigns. Human resources practitioners may also use tools such as employee climate surveys and employee focus groups to investigate if harassment in general is an issue in the workplace. This type of inquiry is not intended to ferret out individual cases of harassment, but rather to determine the need for training interventions or to promote the processes available to individuals who are being harassed.

Barriers to Success/Common Pitfalls

In Canadian culture, one of the most difficult barriers to dealing with harassment is the general belief that it does not occur in our organizations. We believe it happens, but always in some other organization. Every organization faces the potential that harassment is occurring. Moreover, the more general phenomenon of bullying occurs more frequently than organizations care to admit. While harassment, when it is discovered, is recognized as an infringement on an individual's human rights, accusations of bullying are often dismissed as being issues of management style.

Bullying can be just as devastating as harassment. In fact, the only distinction is the grounds behind the behaviour.

Harassment refers to forms of discriminating behaviour against an individual on the basis of a prohibited ground as defined by the relevant human rights code. Bullying is the same behaviour directed at an individual for reasons not covered by the code. For example, in some jurisdictions, sexual orientation is not a recognized ground. This does not mean that discriminating against an individual because of his or her sexual orientation is lawful or less insidious. It simply means those individuals who suffer from such behaviour have to seek redress through other avenues.

Bullying, as the word implies, usually occurs when an individual with perceived power takes advantage of that power to abuse individuals who are relatively powerless. Unfortunately, organizations and individual managers often fail to recognize the damaging effects this type of behaviour has on the organization's culture. Moreover, they also fail to recognize how commonly it occurs.

In some instances, the organization may be prone to pass judgments regarding a situation of harassment based on irrelevant issues. Specifically, senior managers may want to protect a long service manager, even in the face of overwhelming evidence that that manager has engaged in inappropriate behaviour.

Similarly, those involved in the investigation may be prone to biases based on their past experiences with the individuals involved. For example, a junior female employee has had poor performance reviews and attendance issues. Her male supervisor has an exemplary record of superior performance. If the woman raises a complaint of harassment, the investigator may prejudge the situation and conclude that the woman is acting out of vengeance to get back at the supervisor for the poor performance ratings.

HUMAN RESOURCES METRICS

Definition/Background

Searching for the right Human Resources metrics seems to be the Holy Grail of the Human Resources function. A metric is simply a standard of measurement. The objective, from a Human Resources perspective, is to discover those measures that demonstrate the positive impact of Human Resources Management on the overall results of the business.

Human Resources executives want metrics that are clearly aligned with the strategic business goals of the organization. Some metrics are transactional. These typically measure the volume of activities such as the number of offers of employment sent out in a particular period or the number of health claims processed. Others are more tactical and measure the effectiveness of managing an activity. These might include turnover rates or staffing cycle times.

There is a long list of potential Human Resources metrics. The metrics can be divided into different classes or activities. The following is a small sample of the possibilities:

Human Resources Function:

- operating costs;
- cost per employee;
- Human Resources productivity;
- Human Resources/staff ratios;
- return on investment (ROI).

Recruitment:

- applicant conversion rates;
- new hire turnover;
- line management satisfaction;
- time to fill;
- cost per hire;
- strength of employment brand.

Training and Development:

- hours of training per employee per year;
- employees participating in training activities;

- impact on performance;
- ROI;
- development needs of high-potential employees.

Compensation:

- competitiveness;
- compression;
- employee satisfaction/salience with compensation;
- correlations with turnover/performance;
- cost of administration/transaction costs.

Benefits:

- competitiveness;
- employee satisfaction/salience;
- claims processing times and transaction costs;
- total costs.

Organizational Effectiveness:

- turnover by division, department, function or classification;
- costs of turnover;
- absenteeism;
- internal transfer rates;
- performance management analysis;
- succession planning gaps;
- diversity;
- employee satisfaction scores.

Many Human Resources executives do not feel that the Human Resources metrics used by their organizations are effective. A study conducted by the Corporate Executive Board in the fall of 2001 found that the majority of Human Resources executives surveyed indicated that they were not satisfied with the effectiveness or impact of their metrics system, and few believed their system was as effective as those used by other functions.

Measuring grievance activity is an example of a metric that is difficult to assess in terms of its ability to reflect the effectiveness of management activities. A low number of grievances may indicate that the employees are happy with the way in which they are managed. It may also be an indication that supervisors are settling complaints quickly, regardless of their merit, in order to avoid grievances. A high number of grievances may be an indication that there is a general malaise amongst the workforce, or may reflect that employees feel comfortable in using the established process to voice their concerns.

Line managers need to find a use for the metrics published by Human Resources. If the numbers are merely interesting but do not compel managers to deal with the underlying issues, they are of no practical value. Turnover statistics, for example, may be ignored because they are not perceived as being controllable or of having any value. Translating turnover statistics into operating costs may make the process more interesting to line managers and persuade them to manage it through better recruitment and orientation practices.

Benefits/Expected Outcomes

Despite this disappointment with the current state of affairs, measuring the effectiveness of Human Resources Management activities remains on the top of the Human Resources executive's agenda. With better measures, the Human Resources function can achieve better alignment with the corporate strategy of the organization. One of the primary goals of the Human Resources function is to assist line managers in making better decisions regarding people management. Objective and credible measures of effectiveness delivered in real time can only serve to make these decisions better.

In order to become champions of the Human Resources function, Human Resources executives are constantly striving to enhance their credibility with senior management in the organization. Metrics that demonstrate the bottom line impact of Human Resources activities and that show a positive return on the investment in Human Resources programs can go a long way towards building such credibility. There seems to be a movement among CEOs to put pressure on their Human Resources executives to come up with meaningful measures of their activities. In other words, top management wants the function to

justify its existence beyond making employees feel good.

Metrics also serve to identify areas where Human Resources can support the organization's strategic direction and other opportunities, having a positive impact on the business. Surprisingly, many Human Resources departments suffer from not having enough presence among employees. Metrics can create a line of sight with employees. Reporting measures of Human Resources activities serve to keep employees informed about what the department is doing for them. It is a way to demonstrate the value added by the function.

Finally, Human Resources Management has a cost. The Human Resources executive, like all his or her counterparts in other functions, is responsible for managing those costs. This goes beyond simply keeping within budget. It also means examining transactional costs and reducing them through better process management or the introduction of technological solutions. Managing this aspect of the function well is an important way of demonstrating business acumen and bringing credibility to the Human Resources executive.

There are many deficiencies in the way that Human Resources metrics are currently being deployed. Often the link between what is being measured and the strategic direction it is purporting to support is unclear. Human resources executives perceive when line managers do not buy into the usefulness of the metrics. In fact, line managers seldom employ them in making decisions. If the metrics are not being used to help manage the business and impact the overall effectiveness of management, they are of little value.

While measuring Human Resources effectiveness is one of the top priorities for today's Human Resources executive, it is a difficult task. Linking Human Resources performance to business goals is an interesting challenge. Even when a credible measure is found, it has to be sold to line managers in order to become useful. Many things can be measured, but in order to be important, they have to bring meaning to the user. The more a metric can be translated into dollars, the more likely line managers are to understand the importance of tracking such measures.

The advantages of meaningful Human Resources metrics include:

- monitoring performance of the Human Resources function;

- tracking alignment of Human Resources activities with strategic organizational goals and objectives;

- measuring "human capital" as a sustainable source of competitive advantage;

- identifying Human Resources Management priorities; and

- measuring the Human Resources Department's contribution to the bottom line.

Programming/Implementation

Strategic Metrics Cascade Process

One of the most effective ways of identifying, defining and deploying Human Resources metrics is the "Strategic Metrics Cascade Process". This is a means of linking Human Resources objectives to business strategy. The basic process is to break down the overall strategy into specific Human Resources objectives that help drive the desired results, and then to identify the types of measures that might be deployed to track them.

The Strategic Metrics Cascade Process takes its cues from the balanced scorecard approach. It looks from four perspectives at what is important to the business.

1. **Strategic Perspective:** Are the organization's people capabilities aligned with future business needs?

2. **Operational Perspective:** Where must Human Resources excel to enable the business to meet its goals?

3. **Financial Perspective:** Is the Human Resources function adding financial value to the organization?

4. **Customer Perspective:** How do customers see Human Resources?

The approach to ensuring that metrics are properly aligned to the organization's overall goals must be top-down. The Human Resources executive will identify the strategic metrics, because he or she is in the best position to look at the people–capability issues. However, from the other perspectives, line managers must be asked to identify the appropriate metrics because

they will be the determinants of whether or not the function is fulfilling their needs.

The actual cascading process involves a series of steps that break down the strategic goals into smaller sets of specific, measurable Human Resources objectives. The first step is for the Human Resources executive to gather business intelligence. He or she will begin by reviewing the organization's business environment with respect to such things as:

- legislation;

- technology;

- market conditions;

- emerging customer needs;

- demographics;

- competitors; and

- workforce issues (availability, costs, skills, etc.).

Next, the Human Resources executive will review the organization's business strategy in the context of these environmental factors. Beyond just reviewing the strategic plan, the executive should interview line managers, including the CEO, in order to gain insight into how they see the plan unfolding in the context of the Human Resources issues identified in the environmental survey. This also helps to build the executive's credibility and to gain support for the emerging metrics. Finally, the executive can review specific business goals with line managers to understand what measures they see as important in measuring their success.

Once all this intelligence is consolidated, the Human Resources executive can have brainstorming sessions with department staff to begin the process of identifying what people–outcomes are seen as important to the realization of the corporate strategy. This will help the business achieve its goals. Simultaneously, the department should be surveying its internal customers to find out what people and services they require from Human Resources

These two activities will result in lists of potential outcomes and performance requirements for the department. These lists will need to be further consolidated and matched to the strategic plan. This step is a reality check, essential to ensuring the department stays focused on strategic activities. One downfall of many strategic plans is that the organization can easily get preoccupied with other activities that are also deemed important, resulting in a loss of focus. The result is often that the Human Resources Department is overloaded with a list of activities that will be impossible to deliver on. The goal of matching the list of potential activities with the strategic plan is to produce a final list of Human Resources deliverables.

These deliverables are then clustered into the appropriate functional categories (Development, Labour Relations, Compensation/Benefits, Diversity, Staffing, etc.). This ensures the department limits itself to five or six strategic priorities.

For each priority, the department reviews what factors affect the results. Each factor can be broken down into the detailed measures that drive those results. These detailed measures are typically ratios or aggregated data like turnover rates, absenteeism rates, and costs per new hire. The final step is to identify where the raw data comes from that is used in creating the measures.

This is not a scientific process. At every step of the way, Human Resources staff will need to review their choices and use their best judgment. When the first iteration is completed, it is highly probable that the department still will have identified too many measures and will have to cull more. In some instances, there may be duplications in terms of what the metric intended to measure.

Finally, the metrics are matched to the perspective they are attempting to meet (strategic, operational, financial, customer) and presented to senior management for acceptance. The entire procedure is a learning process. It is not perfect, so all participants must accept that there inevitably will be adjustments and refinements, particularly when the organization is just starting out with its Human Resources metrics.

When the metrics have been confirmed, the internal customers are going to expect regular performance reports and accountability for results. A parallel example is the Finance department, which is expected to produce monthly reports and have ready answers regarding any variances that have occurred.

This further helps ensure that the metrics are not only appropriate, but are sufficiently understood, so that root cause analysis can be conducted to determine where deviations have occurred. Ultimately, the Human Resources executive will need to map the strategic processes and understand the constituent parts.

For example, if "time to fill" is identified as an important measure of the efficacy of the recruiting process, it is insufficient to merely track the overall result. If the "time to fill" exceeds the objective, the Human Resources executive is going to need to find out where the deviation occurs in the process. Otherwise, the corrective action may end up focused on the wrong factor.

In the recruiting process, there are several steps or transactions that take place:

- approving a requisition to fill a vacant position;

- sourcing candidates;

- screening candidates;

- interviewing candidates;

- testing;

- reference checks;

- extending offers; and

- receiving acceptance of offers.

If the "time to fill" is in excess of the target, each step should be examined to see if the time taken for the transaction falls within the expected norm. The result may be that only one step is out of sync and the fix is relatively simple. The lesson here is that effective implementation and use of metrics in Human Resources Management dictates a process orientation.

Process Ownership

Process ownership is another key consideration in determining the successful rollout of Human Resources metrics. The perceived lack of value placed on Human Resources metrics is in part related to the fact that few organizations use them in either their day-to-day tactical decision making or in long-term strategy formulation. Line managers do not view Human Resources measures as being true indicators of the business's success. They often do not see the relationship between Human Resources issues and operational results.

Conceptually, line managers may accept the notion that hiring people for the right fit will enhance organizational performance, but they might not see how it will translate into practice. Too often, measures that have a direct impact on the operation's productivity are dismissed as secondary rather than as potential causal links. Absenteeism, for example, is seen as a nuisance but is rarely addressed specifically as a strategic management issue.

To overcome this type of problem, the Human Resources Department should shift ownership of the metric to the true beneficiaries: line management. Managing people is not ultimately a Human Resources responsibility, but is, rather, a line management responsibility. Human resources provides the tools and guidance for the activity, just as finance helps operations identify where key variations occur in their performance and assists them in developing action plans for dealing with those issues.

One of the most powerful ways to get line managers to become interested in strategic Human Resources metrics is to tie those measures to the Performance Management Process and the compensation system. When the size of a manager's bonus is directly linked to the performance of his or her business unit as measured against key Human Resources metrics, the manager will be more likely to pay attention to those metrics.

By tying the metrics to performance management and compensation, the organization ensures that accountability for key Human Resources outcomes is clearly defined. Given Human Resources metrics that are properly aligned, this methodology also ensures that the bonus plan, and therefore management activities, are directed towards common strategic goals. It is obviously important to involve line managers in the process of defining the key metrics to ensure buy-in. Otherwise, the net result may be to alienate managers from the entire process of performance management.

When successfully implemented, Human Resources metrics can go beyond being effective measures of organizational performance to become embedded in the process of strategic decision making. Human resources measures, or at least the key indicators, should be of equal importance to other key process indicators in determining where the organization is going to focus in order to attain or maintain competitive advantage.

Finally, effective Human Resources metrics can be leveraged as a legitimate mechanism for enforcing corrective actions in areas that have been identified as organizational priorities. For example, if the organiza-

tion has identified improved safety performance as a key strategic objective, metrics that define the threshold of acceptable performance can be established. Safety performance may be measured in terms of the frequency of reportable injuries and the severity (in terms of days lost) of those injuries. When a business unit's performance fails to meet the threshold of acceptable losses, the unit manager can be red-flagged and informed that corrective action must take place. Simultaneously, the appropriate staff will be aware of the poor performance and can be dispatched to assist the line manager in taking the remedial steps needed to bring performance in line. Some organizations expect the responsible manager to create a detailed plan outlining the steps that must be taken to improve the performance.

To emphasize the importance of this plan to correct poor performance in a key area, it can be identified as a default category in the bonus plan. If the manager's business unit meets its performance expectations in every other area but fails to achieve the desired results in the key area, the bonus will not be paid. While this may seem harsh, it can be very effective when tied to a strategic objective of obvious importance (as safety should be).

Role of the Human Resources Practitioner

Human resources metrics is a fledgling part of the emerging Human Resources function as a major contributor to high-performance organizations. In order for Human Resources executives to establish measures of Human Resources Management practices as important indicators of the overall reach for competitive advantage, those executives are going to have to pay attention to processes. Achieving buy-in and gaining credibility are absolutely essential to the goal of establishing Human Resources metrics as a fundamental business practice.

Key to achieving this is the development of an overall Human Resources strategy aligned with the organization's corporate goals. The Human Resources practitioner must participate in the development of the corporate strategy. To do this, the practitioner should have a thorough knowledge of the environmental factors that may have an impact on its implementation. In particular, the practitioner must identify the organization's people capabilities and corresponding weaknesses. With this environmental intelligence in hand, the practitioner will be able to identify the strategic priorities from a Human Resources point of view.

Next, the practitioner can begin to develop the metrics. This cannot be done in isolation. The best method is for the senior practitioner to facilitate a series of brainstorming sessions with both Human Resources and line staff. This creates buy-in and ensures all aspects of Human Resources Management are considered. This is a critical stage. One of the outcomes is to have line management accept ownership for managing the numbers. The ultimate role of the Human Resources Department is to gather and analyze data and produce usable reports for line managers. Its second role is to provide consulting support and functional expertise. The practitioner will ultimately be called upon to design and assist with the implementation of the processes that the metrics have been designed to measure.

Some of the metrics will be owned by the Human Resources Department. These include measures of the department's effectiveness in delivering its services, both from a cost and an efficiency point of view. Thus, the practitioner must also implement specific processes to manage the department's activities. The senior practitioner must accept the responsibility for establishing numerical goals and achieving them in these areas.

The successful implementation of Human Resources metrics remains somewhat elusive but intuitively we know it is dependent on tying the measures to compensation and reward systems. This is a bifurcated process. On the one hand, the practitioner must establish a performance management system that aligns the Human Resources objectives with operational goals and hold line staff accountable for the results. Simulta-

neously, the practitioner must establish departmental goals. These goals include both specific operational goals, as well as shared objectives with the larger operational group.

The most powerful Human Resources metrics have a clear correlation with operational results. These measures are more easily accepted by line managers because the relationship is clear. Line managers are willing to commit to the goals when they help them improve operations, grow profits and create competitive advantage.

Barriers to Success/Common Pitfalls

Some of the more common pitfalls encountered include:

- lack of alignment with overall strategic goals;
- metrics created by Human Resources in isolation;
- fuzzy link between people management and organizational goals;
- line management is resistant to accepting ownership for the metrics;
- metrics chosen do not translate into dollars;
- no linkage between the metrics and reward programs; and
- lack of support from top level management.

Final success in implementing useful Human Resources metrics depends on the credibility of the Human Resources function within the organization. Line management must truly believe that Human Resources processes will have an impact on behaviour and performance.

HUMAN RESOURCES PLANNING

Definition/Background

Human Resources planning is the process whereby the organization forecasts its Human Resources needs in order to ensure that the necessary quantity and quality of people are available at a given time to enable the organization to achieve its objectives. Human resources planning is a subset of the Human Resources strategy, focused on identifying the issues surrounding the organization's people resources.

The Human Resources planning exercise is an analytical process that projects how many people the organization will require in different roles in the context of the business strategy. Planning is necessary in order to ascertain the specific needs of the organization so that the Human Resources Department can establish action plans to ensure those needs are met in a timely and appropriate fashion.

Regardless of specific orientation or core values, every organization relies on people to achieve its objectives. Organizations do not merely rely on "warm bodies", but rather require people with specific skills, aptitudes and knowledge. An aeronautical engineer cannot be substituted for an economist. The Human Resources practitioner has a distinct mandate to ensure that the organization's strategies are not frustrated by the failure to have the right people in the right places. In order to fulfil this mandate, the practitioner must be able to forecast issues related to the turnover and attrition of staff, the supply and demand of people with particular skill sets and any other issues related to the ability of the organization to attract and retain the appropriate number of people to achieve its objectives.

By taking a proactive approach, the practitioner will be able to avoid recruiting errors that can be caused by the rush to fill urgent vacancies. Sophisticated practitioners will also take into account changes occurring in the organization's competitive environment so that it has flexible responses to meet emerging demands.

On the flip side, organizations may need to meet emerging issues through restructuring or downsizing initiatives. The practitioner needs to be part of the process leading up to these kinds of changes to ensure they are well planned and therefore have the intended

effect. Lack of planning can lead to a series of counter-productive effects such as unintended turnover.

Moreover, Human Resources practitioners who are aware of emerging trends will be able to respond to the organization's need in innovative and imaginative ways. Flexible work scheduling, work sharing, telecommuting, contracting-out and the use of interim executives are different means that can be used to meet the people requirements of the organization. The practitioner can consider these options and employ them optimally, if there is enough lead time preceding the requirement.

Benefits/Expected Outcomes

Advanced planning of Human Resources requirements can help the organization avoid unnecessary costs by creating more options to address a particular issue. If an organization has enough advance notice that it will be short of people with a particular skill, it may be able to train existing personnel in that skill. This may be preferable to the alternative of having to terminate current staff and replace them with new employees who have the requisite skill.

Those organizations that foresaw the demands created by the need for Y2K systems conversions were able to bring on contract staff to meet the immediate needs of the organization. The advantage of using contracted help included giving the organization the flexibility to reduce staff with minimal impact on operations and morale following a successful conversion. Using this option also allowed those organizations to keep their compensation structures intact.

Organizations that do not forecast their Human Resources needs well may face potential crises when the demands for their products or services cannot be met with the complement of staff the organization has on hand. Such crises take away valuable management time and associated opportunity costs. An organization's opportunities to grow revenue may be foregone if resources are unavailable to take advantage of current market demands.

Planning obviously leads to better decisions by the Human Resources practitioner. These decisions can keep morale in balance by ensuring Human Resources practices, including recruitment, are optimized. Rushing to meet the demands created in a crisis can quickly lead to poor decisions (e.g., poor person to position matches) that will further lead to an erosion of productivity and team satisfaction. The practitioner making decisions in haste can miss opportunities to bring creative solutions to the organization.

Programming/Implementation

There are a number of basic concepts in Human Resources planning including:

⇨ age/length of service profiles;

⇨ manpower planning and budgeting;

⇨ supply and demand forecasting;

⇨ labour market analysis;

⇨ turnover analysis; and

⇨ people utilization (productivity/cost).

Age/Length of Service Profiles

This involves creating profiles of the organization by grouping employees by age or length of service with the organization. Imbalances in age structures may suggest unhealthy gaps in the organization. A department that has a homogeneous age population will be prone to groupthink. Identifying such a profile presents an opportunity to introduce new members from different age profiles.

Keeping an eye on age profiles will also ensure the organization is able to predict attrition through retirements. This can be particularly important in key positions or key functional areas with some employee populations that are more susceptible to the loss of talented individuals.

Too many people in particular age bands may be an indication that there are inherent blocks to promotional opportunities or gaps in the talent pool. In this way, age profiles are an important element to the organization's succession planning exercise. Similarly, lengths of service can be analyzed to determine the impact of turnover. If turnover has been too high, the average length of service will be low and the organization will suffer from a lack of the idiosyncratic knowledge necessary to maintain a strong organizational culture. High average levels of service will indicate that turnover may be too low. The potential effect of this is to foster groupthink or complacency.

The value of analyzing age and service profiles is dependent on ensuring the total population is divided into meaningful groups for analysis. Too many classifications and groupings (high resolution) may cloud trends and issues. Typically, an analysis will look at age and service groupings by division or physical location, job grades, skills groups and/or functional areas.

Large organizations will find that gathering the data can be an expensive proposition if such data are not captured in the payroll or Human Resources information system in a usable format. Therefore, part of the design consideration needs to be to examine the current state of those systems. Setting up and maintaining information systems represent potentially substantial costs. However, these can be set up in conjunction with the payroll system, and developing reports can be a relatively easy and inexpensive exercise provided the data are initially captured in a usable format.

While Human Resources planning is a relatively important process, it alone cannot be used to justify the expense of a human resources information system. Notwithstanding, the data are also critical to the proper analysis of other Human Resources Management issues such as compensation planning, benefit analysis and labour costing. The ability to review age and length of service profiles has to be presented as an added value of such systems.

Implementing the analysis of age and length of service profiles will require:

✓ available information systems for the capture, storage and retrieval of relevant information and the facility to generate statistical reports;

✓ understanding of the organization's current and future Human Resources needs so that the analysis is relevant and solutions address the appropriate issues;

✓ practitioners who are able to interpret statistical data and manipulate that data into meaningful reports to stimulate action;

✓ acceptance of the value of planning for Human Resources needs; and

✓ availability of information systems professionals who understand the needs and objectives of Human Resources planning.

Manpower Planning and Budgeting

A budget is nothing more than a plan that shows how the organization intends to use its financial resources to achieve objectives in the coming year. It is a means of translating strategic thinking into action and a way to control management activities. Budgets rely on forecasts of future activities.

In terms of Human Resources, the budget will have to forecast what each department and functional group predicts it will require in order to fill the anticipated demands placed on it. If a manufacturing company forecasts an increase in production requirements, the operations group will need to determine how much of the incremental demand can be met by improvements in capital equipment and productivity enhancement. Management will also have to budget for a potential increase in staffing levels to meet demand.

Planning in this way can be done by rough estimates (i.e., educated guesses), through specific modelling of manpower needs, or through setting achievable targets. The first is reasonably straightforward. A seasoned line manager can guess that an increase in production of a given amount will require a corresponding increase in manpower. Of course, this methodology is prone to errors. Shortfalls can lead to the obvious inability to fill customer orders. Overstaffing can lead to excessive costs and idle resources. As well, having too many people can erode productivity standards and, if not corrected quickly, can become imbedded in the culture.

As a result of overstaffing, organizations may inadvertently create a culture wherein a productivity ceiling is established through tacit understandings in the workforce. Moreover, behaviours such as increased absenteeism or "coasting" can become an accepted norm. The workforce gains an implicit belief that the behaviour of an individual (e.g., not reporting for work) has little or no effect on the organization's output and therefore the behaviour is unchecked. This, in turn, can create a spiraling effect whereby the behaviours increase and create a need for even more staff. Quietly the organization becomes bloated until its cost structures demonstrate an absolute need to

change in order for the organization to remain competitive.

Clearly, more precise methods help prevent this from occurring. In planning for warehouse staff, a line manager can determine future needs by comparing forecasted demand (number of units to be shipped) with current levels of productivity (units per man hour). The manager will also need to factor in anticipated improvements to productivity that may be brought about by process changes or capital investment. With these inputs, the manager can plan what the anticipated staff requirements will be. Sophisticated planning models will also include data on seasonal fluctuations in demand and correlations between direct labour needs (the staff required to do the central task as, for instance, production) and indirect labour requirements (support staff).

Manpower planning can also be established through the objective setting exercise as part of the performance management process. This can be a stand-alone process or used in conjunction with more sophisticated manpower planning models. The concept is simple. The manager reviews forecasted needs and establishes the benchmark to be achieved. For example, in order to fill an increase of 10% in product demand, the manager may plan for a 5% increase in staff. By doing so, the manager is setting targets for increased productivity. This goal setting exercise then serves as a motivator to the workforce to meet a new higher standard.

Supply and Demand Forecasting

While most people have heard of "Supply and Demand" theory as a concept in the study of economics, here we use the term to refer to the internal needs of an organization. Forecasting an organization's demand on a micro level is not an exact science, given the wide range of variables to be considered. The Human Resources practitioner, trying to predict the organization's needs, should consider the following factors:

- Current staffing levels by job classification and relationship to current levels of output.

- Planned output as forecasted by the strategic/business plan for the next year, three years and five years. Given the high degree of uncertainty regarding future demand for any organization's products and services, sophisticated practitioners may also want to consider sensitivity analysis, whereby the range of possibilities and the probability of outcomes are also explored.

- Planned activities that will have a direct impact on staffing levels (downsizing, capital investments, process changes, acquisitions, "Greenfield" operations, new product offerings, marketing campaigns).

- Ratios of indirect to direct labour. For example, the number of employees serviced by each Human Resources practitioner, or the average number of employees per each front-line supervisor.

- Benchmark data from other organizations that represent industry best practices.

- Organizational objectives that may affect current ratios. Some practitioners may set targets for the Human Resources department to increase its ratios to fill a strategic goal. Developing self-managed work groups should increase supervisor to employee ratios.

- Forecasted retirements and expected employee turnover (both voluntary and forced) should also be factored into the analysis.

- Age and length of service profiles.

The internal supply of people is the number of people who are currently in the organization. This number, however, needs to be adjusted to take into account expected changes such as:

⇨ forecasted turnover and retirements;

⇨ probable promotions and transfers; and

⇨ training and the resulting lateral moves.

The gap between the organization's future needs (demand) and the number of employees it expects to have on hand (supply) dictates the strategies the Human Resources practitioner will need to employ to close the gap. For example, a manufacturing company may introduce a new piece of process equipment that requires a given number of trained operators. If the company has more qualified operators on hand than it will need, the practitioner will have to devise a strategy to retrain, redeploy, or lay off the surplus staff. Given the rapid changes in some technologies, organizations have faced situations where they have sufficient numbers of staff but the people do not have the requisite skills to meet the new demands of the work. In these situations, the practitioner must assess current

skill levels and establish retraining programs for those employees with a demonstrated aptitude to learn the new skills. Employees who cannot learn the new skills may be redeployed elsewhere in the organization or terminated. It is common that, despite needing to lay off employees, the organization will simultaneously need to recruit new employees. This creates a specific need to communicate the impact of the technology on the organization. That impact can be quite devastating to some employees. New equipment technologies such as robotics require fewer operators (often none) and more specialized technicians to service the equipment. This represents a significant shift in demand, from lower skilled operators to highly skilled technicians. The organization's supply of the lower skilled operators therefore becomes redundant. Those operators may well have been with the organization for many years. They also may be less marketable precisely because they had developed idiosyncratic skills unique to the organization. These employees will typically have a strong sense of entitlement. The Canadian Auto Workers Union has described this entitlement as job ownership, and has established a platform to negotiate the number of jobs it expects the automakers to provide in order to develop some degree of job security in the face of rapid technological deployment and outsourcing.

Numerical forecasts of supply and demand are not precisely accurate and therefore the practitioner should include a sensitivity analysis as part of the Human Resources plan. This involves delineating the range of possible (and likely) outcomes and associated plans of action. The success of supply and demand analysis is not determined by the precision of the predictions but rather by the practitioner's ability to use the analysis to develop policies and procedures to forestall crises. Success is also determined by the integration of action plans. An organization will prevent the embarrassment and negative impact created by poor decision-making when the practitioner foresees how changes in demand will affect the total organization.

Specifically, the organization will avoid recruiting new employees for one division when employees from another might be made available at the same time. Even in smaller organizations, the exercise of considering future personnel moves may help managers develop creative solutions to future problems. This could be as simple as moving redundant production operators who have been displaced by more efficient processes or equipment into shipping to handle the increased output enroute to the customer. The organization is better able to respond to shifts in internal demand when issues are contemplated well before they occur. Training or retraining can take many months; to be successful in meeting demand, the training must begin in advance of the anticipated need. The most important advantage to this level of analysis and planning is that it creates operational flexibility and allows the organization to respond rapidly to changes in its environment. Hence, it can be a factor in creating a Learning Organization.

In order to run a supply and demand analysis, the practitioner must possess strong planning skills and a solid understanding of statistical methodologies. A comprehensive Human Resources information system or payroll system will provide most of the necessary data for the analysis. The success of the analysis is correlated to the level of detail available. At a minimum, the practitioner will want to break down the needs and current supply by job classification and to establish age/length of service profiles. More sophisticated forecasting will also incorporate the considerations contained in the organization's succession plan.

One of the most important considerations in employing Human Resources metrics is the buy-in from line managers (refer to Human Resources Metrics at page 185 *et seq.*). Line management ultimately owns the results of the Human Resources plan. They are accountable for the organization's outputs. The success or failure to meet the demands of the customer is theirs. Therefore, the practitioner is well advised to involve this important client group in the planning process.

Involving line managers will improve the quality of the analysis, as they will be able to identify relevant factors that may change during the forecast period. This ensures the underlying assumptions used to develop the forecast are correct and complete. Their involvement also creates a line-of-sight between the line activities and the support provided by the human resources practitioner. As the line managers use the planning tools, they will gain an appreciation for the value brought to them by the practitioner. They will be able to conceptually link Human Resources activities such as recruitment to their end goals.

Labour Market Analysis

Labour market analysis is the study of the external supply of labour available to the organization and trends in the market. Examining trends allows the Human Resources practitioner to consider the factors that may be relevant to turnover. Gaining this kind of understanding is the basis for developing effective retention practices.

Because of the complexity and expense of conducting labour market analysis, organizations mostly rely on external sources such as provincial Labour Ministries, Statistics Canada, banks and consulting firms for published reports on the market. In some instances, specific industry associations may commission a study to investigate the supply, demand and forecast for labour in their sector. For example, during the late 1970s, there was a high demand for engineering projects in the oil, gas and minerals sectors. The construction companies that developed projects like oil refineries and smelters had to ensure there was an adequate supply of skilled tradesmen to complete the projects. Such studies were commissioned through their trade association and revealed to the member organizations where tradesmen could be found across Canada. These studies were conducted with cooperation from unions in the construction industry, and not only examined the number of tradesmen in a particular trade but also provided information regarding the mobility of the available workers.

The supply of labour is affected by a number of factors. The foremost factor is the aging of the population. Demographic analysis provides macro-level data that highlight general trends. In Western countries, and particularly in Canada, the Baby Boomer cohorts have been followed by a relatively small group of Generation Xers who, in turn, have been followed by another large cohort. This trend has been well described in the popular bestseller *Boom, Bust and Echo*.

Looking simply at the age profile of the general population merely tells us broadly what the immigration needs might be in raw numbers to maintain a level of growth. However, in order to be meaningful, we need to understand the characteristics of different segments of the population. In addition to knowing how many young adults are at school-leaving age, we want to know the number who have completed high school, college and university. How many have been trained in particular trades or disciplines? On the other end of the age spectrum, we will want to examine retirement trends. In recent years, there has been evidence of a growing number of people freelancing or acting in interim capacities. Knowing if this trend is continuing or is a short-term aberration will have policy implications for a lot of organizations seeking qualified and experienced people.

A number of years ago, people labelled as Generation X found it difficult to find meaningful full-time employment. They were, in fact, squeezed out of the market by the boomers and the echo. This resulted in a blip in the number of part-time workers. Some analysts interpreted this phenomenon as a growing choice among the employable population. In fact, these part-time workers were merely waiting for an expansion in full-time opportunities.

Supply is irrelevant unless compared to demand. Although the Generation Xers are a smaller cohort, they faced a shortage of available work. This was influenced in some degree by good planning on the part of organizations facing a potential drop in the supply of school-leavers. During the latter part of the 1980s, organizations made long-term structural changes such as flattening the reporting structures that reduced the need for people.

Demand can be somewhat problematic to forecast because firms have been able to anticipate trends and correct for them. To illustrate, the former Ontario Hydro conducted a study during the 1960s that forecast a huge increase in the demand for electricity. To meet this demand Hydro developed a long-term strategy to build nuclear generating plants. During the 1970s, Hydro also made a push for power conservation. Organizations responded so well that the predicted demand was curtailed and there was a reduced need for the generating capacity. As a result, several generating plants fell into disuse shortly after commissioning. The corresponding demand for physicists and atomic engineers also unexpectedly dropped off.

The forces of supply and demand influence the price of labour. Since wages are relatively inelastic (i.e., changes in wage levels are slow in response to market shifts), the price of labour can influence the demand. This creates a cycle of "feast or famine" in certain professions. A shortage of engineers will lead to a premium being paid to engineering graduates. This attracts more students to engineering disciplines. In

short order, there is a glut of engineers and a drop in starting salaries. In turn, fewer students are attracted in subsequent years and supply drops off. The cycle then repeats itself.

M.B.A. graduates commanded a premium during the 1990s. As a result, graduate programs were expanded and the supply dramatically increased. Today the supply is greater than the demand and therefore the premium previously paid is not available to new graduates.

Turnover Analysis

Turnover rates are important in accurately forecasting future demand. They are also strong indicators of potential underlying issues that may demand the attention of the Human Resources practitioner. High turnover may indicate issues connected with recruitment (poor person-to-job matching), management style, lack of training, absence of development opportunities and a host of other related problems.

Simply put, turnover is the number of employees who leave the organization during a specified period of time. Turnover rates are usually expressed as a percentage of the average total number of employees. If an organization had, on average, 1,000 employees during a year and 150 left, its annual turnover rate would be 15%. However, this rate alone does not give a sufficient level of detail to allow the practitioner to determine what courses of action, if any, are necessary.

To be significant, turnover rates should be developed by division, job classification, length of service and age. A sophisticated system allows the user to drill down into the data in order to analyze meaningful trends. For example, the practitioner may want to examine the stability index within a given division. If the turnover rate is 15%, as above, it could represent 150 different individuals who have left the organization, or it may hypothetically represent 999 employees who stayed and one position that turned 150 times. A stability index is calculated as the number of employees with a year or more of service divided by the total number of people employed one year ago.

The practitioner will need to examine where turnover is taking place in order to begin pinpointing the root cause of excessive turnover. It is widely accepted that some level of turnover is inevitable and desirable. The introduction of new people reduces the chances of groupthink developing. New people bring new ideas and help recharge group dynamics. There is no single "right" level of turnover. The rate is partially dependent on industry trends and on specific trends within given professions.

Technology firms tend to experience higher turnover than banks. Within consulting practices and law firms, associates tend to leave more than partners. Human resources practitioners and information technology professionals leave their employ more rapidly than payroll administrators or accountants. There are a number of reasons for these trends. High demand in some industries will drive greater turnover rates within firms in those industries. Thus, low supply of qualified people may also drive turnover. Low demand and high supply therefore may influence greater stability rates. The quick service restaurant market experiences exceptionally high turnover because of low wages and poor working conditions coupled with a high supply of unskilled workers and high demand (i.e., easy to get a job).

Benchmarking an organization's turnover rate against those experienced in the industry is the only way to determine if the rate is high. The practitioner, however, is well advised not to compare the organization's rate to the industry average but rather to compare the rate to the industry's best. This sets the bar high but will be the most accurate indicator of what is possible.

Human resources practitioners tend to be in high demand during upturns in the economy. The practitioner's skill set is applicable across industries, making him or her marketable across industry lines. While this is also true of accountants, there tends to be a greater supply of accountants at any given time and therefore they are less mobile.

In addition to examining where in the organization turnover is occurring, the practitioner will want to examine trends pertaining to the immediate reasons given for leaving. Reasons for leaving include the following:

⇨ death;

⇨ long-term or permanent disability;

⇨ retirement;

⇨ redundancy;

⇨ dismissal for cause;

⇨ transfers;

⇨ temporary leaving (maternity/paternity leaves, leaves of absence, sabbaticals); and

⇨ resignation.

Practitioners are often concerned specifically with voluntary turnover. Involuntary turnover such as retirements and redundancy can be predicted and therefore planned for. Voluntary is more often than not a sign that the organization has failed to meet the needs of the individual. When voluntary turnover rates are high, the practitioner has an opportunity to add value to the organization by discerning the cause and developing an action plan to correct it.

Voluntary leaving may be further broken down by specific reasons such as pay issues, development opportunities, or the transfer of a spouse. Practitioners may differentiate between "push" factors and "pull" factors in this regard. A push factor is internal to the organization, while a pull is an external factor. An employee who has conflicts with his or her boss is pushed out of the organization. An employee who is drawn to the development opportunities of a start-up enterprise is pulled from the organization.

Practitioners need to be careful when analyzing the reasons given by the employee for leaving. The common practice is to solicit reasons from the employee through the exit interview. However, regardless of the assurances given for handling the information with sensitivity and confidence, exiting employees may still be reluctant to report the real reasons for leaving. A departing employee may not want to "burn bridges" by reporting that he or she had problems with the boss. Instead, the employee may merely report that pay is the issue. In fact, pay is a frequently cited reason for leaving, but is usually not the sole or even the primary "real" reason. The practitioner can validate if pay is a salient issue through market surveys and benchmarking.

Another issue with turnover is that it can be a latent phenomenon. The accounting department in a large manufacturing company had been experiencing high turnover (in the order of 40 to 50% annually) for a number of years. However, without any major interventions, the rate slowed to less than 10% for a couple of years. Senior management assumed that the problem had corrected itself. What had happened was a downturn in the manufacturing sector and a corresponding downturn in demand for accountants in the region. In subsequent years, the high turnover resumed.

Most payroll systems and Human Resources information systems provide the necessary data for turnover analysis. The practitioner needs to have an understanding of the concepts of turnover presented here to undertake an informed analysis of the issue within the organization. An understanding of the industry and the labour market is also key in allowing the practitioner to differentiate between push and pull factors. Understanding turnover and ensuring the organization maintains an optimal rate of turnover has obvious implications on recruiting, training and productivity. It also can serve the practitioner well as an argument to support various Human Resources Management initiatives. Reducing turnover through Human Resources programming is a direct and measurable way to demonstrate the added value the practitioner brings to the organization.

People Utilization (Productivity/Cost)

Organizations often cite their people as the most important asset. Practitioners from a humanistic school might shudder at the conceptualization of people as production assets; nevertheless, it is important to realize that every organization must measure the effectiveness of people utilization in the same way equipment or capital utilization is measured. The effective and efficient utilization of people is measured as productivity. Productivity, however, can be measured in a number of different ways. Each organization will need to determine what is relevant to meet the needs of the enterprise in order to define how productivity is to be measured. In high-level terms, productivity is the amount of output divided by the amount of input. A simple productivity measure may look at the total number of units produced in a given period of time divided by the number of hours employed to produce those units.

If it takes 200 employee days to produce 2,000 units, productivity can be stated as 10 units per employee day. If there are 20 days in an average month, the organization knows that it will need 10 employees working at 10 units per day to produce 2,000 units. If demand increases to 3,000 units per month and nothing else changes, the firm will need five more employees.

If productivity improves by 50%, the organization can meet the demand increase to 3,000 units per month with its existing complement of employees. In turn, productivity can be expressed as a cost of labour per unit produced. In our example, the 10 units produced each day have a cost component for labour equal to one-tenth of an employee's daily wages. If wages go up by 3%, the organization will need a corresponding increase of 3% in productivity to maintain its cost structure. An increase of 5% in productivity will yield a financial gain for the organization.

The complexity of calculating productivity is dependent on what the organization wants to measure. Pure productivity does not include indirect labour. Organizations employ people in staff positions such as accounting and Human Resources Management who are not directly involved in production. Their hours of work would not be included in the division. Organizations may also want to exclude hours worked by direct labour in "non-productive" activities such as housekeeping and facilities maintenance.

For those employees not involved in direct production, the organization may want a separate measure of productivity such as a transaction count. An example of this is the number of invoices processed per employee hour in the accounts payable office.

A credible measure of productivity may serve to demonstrate the added value that the Human Resources practitioner contributes. Productivity can be used, for example, as the basis for an incentive scheme. This is at times a difficult proposition because the measure of productivity has to be deemed fair across a variety of different job groupings. In a manufacturing environment, the number of units produced per employee hour may be a fair means to compensate production workers but may bear no relation to the relative efforts of the maintenance department employees. To capture the input of the maintenance department, the organization may establish a standard for production downtime related to planned maintenance activities. These hours would be excluded from the productivity calculation. However, unplanned downtime because of breakdowns would be included. The maintenance department's ability to minimize unplanned downtime therefore has a direct correlation to total productivity.

Organizations that adopt engineered labour standards go beyond merely calculating productivity by past performance. Instead, these organizations examine the nature of each individual task and estimate the time taken to produce each individual component of the total unit of output. This optimizes production methods and allows the organization to set productivity standards for each individual employee. The standard is usually expressed as a range that accounts for different skill levels and physical abilities. The standards then become a basis for training and managing the performance of individual employees.

Engineered labour standards are an excellent and proven means for measuring productivity expectations. However, there are some factors to consider before implementing labour standards. They are expensive to develop and require special expertise and time to study and validate. Employees are very leery of labour standards and tend to be resistant to the implementation of standards as performance measures. Labour standards can be difficult to use to compare relative performance between business units because they are dependent on many variables such as the design and layout of the production process and the relative skill and motivation of the workforce.

Strictly from a people-planning perspective, the calculation of productivity yields a means of forecasting staffing levels required to meet different planned output levels.

Role of the Human Resources Practitioner

Human resources planning is a dynamic management tool used to forecast the demand for people. It serves to define issues related to ensuring the organization has the right people in the right places at all times to meet its customers' demands. These issues can involve virtually every aspect of Human Resources Management.

By forecasting the supply and demand for people, the practitioner is able to establish action plans to meet the most fundamental needs of the client group, that is, to have a sufficient supply of qualified people to meet the organization's strategic objectives. As a dynamic tool, the plan must be sensitive to changes in the organization and its environment.

The plan then acts as a basis for creating a Human Resources strategy. The strategy must be flexible enough to respond to shifts in the underlying assumptions that supported the forecasted needs of the organization.

The senior practitioner oversees the planning activity and must decide on what levels of measurement are suited to the needs and degree of sophistication of the organization. In developing the design of the planning activity, the practitioner should act as a facilitator. In this regard, the practitioner should seek inputs into the design aspects from key stakeholders among the client groups and within the internal staff of the department.

Planning activities that do not involve these key participants are perceived as being developed in isolation by a detached executive. The result is a plan that carries little or no weight in the organization.

Conversely, with line management involvement, the practitioner can show a direct link between planned activities within the Human Resources Department and the needs of the organization. Perhaps surprisingly, some practitioners are reluctant to pay much credence to the power of Human Resources planning partly because the results will dictate where they need to spend the time and resources of the department. This has the potential of detracting those resources away from a pet project and into more mundane activities. Clearly, the danger of such an attitude is that a crisis that could have been prevented through foresight is imposed upon the organization.

The practitioner's greatest gain from forecasting the supply and demand for people within the organization is the ability to meet proactively the needs of internal clients. Some practitioners thrive on the drama of reacting to crisis quickly and effectively. In fact, a few practitioners prefer this drama to the relatively sedate world of working a predictable plan and may even stimulate or accentuate some of the drama. On faith, observers know that the planned approach makes better use of resources and has less negative impact on the culture of the organization.

To counter that need for some excitement in their careers, those practitioners who seek drama should consider the potentially large impact they can have on an organization when the plan becomes an integrated part of the organization's overall strategic thinking.

G - **H** - I

Barriers to Success/Common Pitfalls

Organizations that do not have an established strategy or vision will not foster an environment conducive to planning. The practitioner can overcome such a deficiency by deducing the implied strategy. The danger of such deductions is that the practitioner must rely on assumptions that may not be validated. Moreover, the practitioner in such an environment may face much resistance from his or her client group who will not readily grasp the importance of planning.

Another way the lack of an articulated strategy may be overcome is through the cascading down of specific organizational objectives through the performance management system. Organizations that do not have a sophisticated method for establishing objectives may not provide sufficient information for the practitioner to forecast future demand beyond the immediate needs of the business. Human resources planning will be most successful when the senior practitioner is part of the strategic planning process or, at a minimum, has access to strategic thinking.

Line managers may fail to see the importance of understanding the people implications of the strategy even in organizations that value strategic thinking. Practitioners in these circumstances need to be strong sources of influence and have the requisite credibility to convince senior management that Human Resources planning can add value. In fact, the planning activity is essential to the realization of intended organizational objectives. Ideally, Human Resources planning should be an integrated part of the development of a comprehensive Human Resources strategy. Unfortunately, many practitioners fail to create such a strategy and therefore miss an opportunity to bring heightened value to their organizations.

The skills of the practitioner should always be considered in predicting the potential success of a Human Resources initiative. The practitioner must be able to identify, gather and analyze relevant data. Subsequently, the practitioner must be able to translate the analysis into a convincing business case and an action plan. Preparing statistics cannot be mistaken for developing a proactive approach to meeting the needs of the organization.

Too many practitioners take a mechanical approach to planning. The process needs to be developed in a way that involves the function's key clients. With line management support, the practitioner will avoid creating the perception that the plan was drawn up by a detached specialist locked away in an "ivory tower".

Even if the organization lacks any kind of strategy at all, there is a significant value gained by inviting the participation of line managers and other internal customers. Their experiences can be drawn upon to bring relevance to any data that are gathered so that the practitioner is able to make the right interpretation. In the absence of involving key clients, the practitioner runs the risk of being unable to identify relevant and important issues. The practitioner must be close enough to the business to understand what factors drive key processes. Failure to do so will lead to the possibility of developing the wrong answers to the wrong questions.

Developing a plan is not enough. The practitioner will only be credible if the Human Resources function is able to meet the demands of the plan. If the plan does not yield the expected results and the organization falls into crisis, the function will lose the confidence of its customers. If these people were previously skeptical, such a failure will unfortunately validate their misgivings. Organizations that do not value strategic planning will remain unconvinced of the value of any planning activities and will be unwilling to continue investing resources in the activity.

HUMAN RESOURCES STRATEGIES

Definition/Background

Strategies are generally the means by which organizations seek to meet a set of intended objectives. Comprehensive organizational strategies that are meant to encompass all aspects of the business should contain an integral Human Resources component. Unfortunately, this is an often overlooked part of the strategy. It is therefore left to the senior Human Resources practitioner to design and develop a strategy to support and enhance the overall strategic direction of the organization.

Certainly, the strategy should address the specific issues to be faced by the Human Resources Department in supporting the overall direction of the business. However, the department impacts on all the people within the organization and the strategy developed for the function should address all aspects of people management.

Developing a strategy goes beyond simply designing a plan of action. Strategy development is a process and should be an integral part of the performance management system. Once a Human Resources strategy has been established, the functions, activities and efficacy can be measured, monitored and managed.

Improved performance is a requirement of every organization. Given the proposition that all resources are ultimately finite, the Human Resources function must ensure its activities are aligned with and supportive of the overall strategy of the organization. The Human Resources strategy should:

✓ assist in the development of overall business objectives;

✓ define how those objectives will be met;

✓ address how the Human Resources function's contribution will be measured and assessed;

✓ energize the organization's Human Resources practitioners to work towards the department's and the organization's goals and objectives; and

✓ enable a systematic planning process and allocation of resources.

The Human Resources component of the organization's strategy is a critical determinant of its success. Ideally, that component is fully integrated into the overall strategy. In today's business context, with the rapid changes in competitive environments, legislation and technology, the adage that people are an organization's only sustainable competitive advantage has never been more true. In the absence of a Human Resources component in the corporate strategy, the senior practitioner must develop a supporting strategy for the management of people.

The Human Resources strategy properly designed and implemented will allow employees to optimize their contribution to the overall performance of the organization. It will also address how individual contributions and the contribution of the human resources function will be measured and assessed. The development of the strategy should follow a structured process linked to the strategic direction of the organization.

The strategic plan must ultimately be articulated in clearly measurable terms that enable the performance and contributions to be easily assessed and monitored (see also Human Resources Metrics at page 185 *et seq.*). The department's customers, including the senior management team, key business units and operations, should assess the performance of the Human Resources function.

According to Mintzberg, strategy should be seen to be crafted, modified and developed in the light of experience and circumstances, and not seen as a highly mechanized, rigid program drawn up by a group of detached senior managers. The effective implementation of a Human Resources strategy will ensure the function remains focused on the *important* rather than the *urgent* concerns of the business. This optimizes the utilization of scarce resources such as time, and drives waste out of processes.

Benefits/Expected Outcomes

Focusing on a well-defined strategy will make it easier for the practitioner to resist the "flavour-of-the-month" fads that are commonplace in the Human Resources Management profession. The department's activities

will be designed to address issues that are fundamental to the achievement of overall organizational
objectives. An approach that is properly aligned to the
business goals will help build the credibility of the
department. In turn, this helps the practitioner build a
strong link with the business and get buy-in from line
management.

Early involvement from the department's internal clients in the design of the Human Resources strategy is
critical to the successful implementation of the plan.
Moreover, if the plan addresses the specific needs of
the client group, it will receive buy-in from them. This
helps the practitioner distinguish between what is
important and what is urgent. The practitioner can
then be assured that the department's activities create
a higher value-added return for the organization.

Important Human Resources initiatives like business
process re engineering and organizational restructuring will only be successful if they form a part of a
comprehensive strategy. Unfortunately, this is a
common issue faced by practitioners. Unless there is
an overall strategy, it is difficult to see how an integrated, holistic approach to Human Resources Management can be provided. Piecemeal initiatives introduced in an uncoordinated fashion without
consideration of the effect of other initiatives can be
counterproductive. Planning is a critical part of
ensuring effectiveness.

It is vital to the success of the organization that a
Human Resources plan is developed which creates an
environment that engages employees and empowers
them to optimize their performance towards organizational objectives.

Defining clear outputs from the Human Resources
Department expressed in business or organizational
terms will enable the senior practitioner and the
senior leadership team to monitor the function's
value-added contribution. Human resources outputs
should be as rigorously evaluated as any other key
process indicators. If the outputs do not yield any
significant advantage to the organization, the related
activities should be reduced or stopped. In times of
cost constraint, organizations cannot afford to fund
programs that do not provide them with a discernible
competitive advantage.

Some Human Resources objectives may be difficult to
translate into measurable targets. The practitioner

needs to take a cautious approach to articulating
objectives that "feel good". Nevertheless, it is at times
necessary to establish an organizational objective for
Human Resources Management that cannot be
directly measured in terms of specific results. The
practitioner will need to make a convincing argument
that the objective will yield indirect yet substantial
benefits. Building teams and empowering employees
cannot be directly measured in terms of a benefit to
the organization's bottom line; however, successful
team development, for example, has been closely correlated to improved organizational performance.

The central aspect of "people management" makes it
absolutely imperative for the senior practitioner to
establish a strategic direction that stretches the department's and organization's goals and objectives. By
identifying the key processes that drive people management within the organization, the Human
Resources practitioner can provide leadership
regarding the management of the organization's culture, values and overall mission. In this respect, establishing "breakthrough" objectives that pose a significant but attainable challenge to the Human Resources
Department can motivate the group to attain or
exceed its mandate and add value to the organization
in an unprecedented way.

Programming/Implementation

There is no single, right way to develop a strategic
plan. The best way to develop a plan for any organization is determined by the particular circumstances in
which the organization finds itself. The skilled practitioner will follow a basic model and modify it,
improve upon it and adapt it to those particular circumstances. The fundamentals of strategic planning
include the following:

⇨ understanding the organization's strategic mission;

⇨ defining inputs (data collection) and outputs of the
   underlying business processes;

⇨ assessing the value-added contribution required of
   the Human Resources function;

⇨ planning for the long term and medium term
   (these plans embrace the purpose, values and
   vision of the organization);

⇨ planning for the short term, which addresses the
   immediate needs of the business;

⇨ acting/implementing;

⇨ learning through the assessment of plan effectiveness and analysis of the gaps between implementation and results; and

⇨ reviewing results and modifying the plan.

Strategic planning is a continuous process, but it is not necessarily rigid. Continuous monitoring is a key to the success of the process and, as such, modifications can take place at any time. (See also Human Resources Planning at page 191 *et seq.*)

Another key to the development of the Human Resources strategy is to ensure it is aligned not only with the organization's overall objectives but also to ensure it is internally aligned. For example, the introduction of a competencies-based performance management system may necessitate the modification of job descriptions, job evaluations and the recruitment process, to name just a few. The process will naturally evolve and the practitioner should expect that it would take many iterations over several years before the process is fully imbedded into the culture of the organization.

Step One — Setting the Stage

Given the importance of securing buy-in from several different constituencies, strategic planning experts suggest a team-based approach that involves key players including customers. In the initial stages, the planning process should encourage a dialogue and debate around the concept of the strategic plan. This is done to ensure participants buy in to the importance and potential positive effect of the process. During this inaugural session, the participants will also:

⇨ discuss and agree on the planning process;

⇨ define the key processes, products, services and outputs;

⇨ identify the key customer groups;

⇨ define the key Human Resources metrics and the data collection methodologies to be followed; and

⇨ delineate the proposed time lines to be adhered to.

Step Two — Understanding the Environment

Before a Human Resources plan can be established, essential information regarding the organization's strategic direction must be understood. A basic element of any organization's strategic plan is an analysis of its **S**trengths, **W**eaknesses, **O**pportunities and **T**hreats (SWOT). SWOT analysis can help the Human Resources practitioner identify key people issues. In addition, the practitioner should understand the following:

⇨ strategic imperatives (e.g., top line revenue, return on capital employed, market share or penetration);

⇨ competitive pressures;

⇨ organizational core competencies;

⇨ key business metrics;

⇨ industry environment;

⇨ organizational vision, values and purpose; and

⇨ management "hot buttons".

Wherever possible, the specific measurable goals should be understood. If the organization intends on building market share, it is important to know by how much as this dictates how share will be gained. In some instances, the market share can be grown organically which dictates that the Human Resources function be prepared to recruit and develop people in the sales and marketing areas. In other instances, the objective to build market share may be large enough to necessitate an acquisition. This will present an opportunity for the practitioner to provide expertise on the assessment of the target organization's core competencies and the compatibility of its culture in terms of potential integration.

It is important for the Human Resources function to identify who are its key internal customers. The function essentially provides services and therefore it is vital to its success to understand what services its customers need and want. The two are not necessarily the same. Involving customers at the outset of the process helps build credibility and improves the chances for successful implementation of any Human Resources initiative. Clearly, the Human Resources function cannot operate in isolation. A disconnect between the objectives of the function and the needs of the internal customer will destroy the effectiveness of the Human Resources practitioner.

Identifying the customer is not obvious. Some practitioners are of the view that the primary customers are the organization's employees. Others see themselves as providing an essential service to the management group. Still others select a balanced approach that combines employee advocacy with the delivery of people management processes. The answer therefore is a matter of choice. The practitioner needs to make this choice based on personal philosophy as well as being the right approach to align with the organization's intended culture.

Once the internal customers are identified, the practitioner can then review the products and services it provides, or should be providing in terms of measurable deliverables. This exercise provides the background for the internal customers to use as a term of reference regarding what they should expect from the Human Resources Management function. The practitioner will also be able to use the identified deliverables as measuring points for determining the level of customer satisfaction with the function.

It is obviously important for any service provider to deliver its products to the satisfaction of its key customers. However, the senior practitioner occupies a leadership role. Accordingly, when the services are identified, the practitioner needs to help the function's customers discern what is truly important to the success of the organization. Gathering customer-related information is not the same as requesting a "wish list" from key customers. The practitioner who truly understands the organization's overall objectives will be able to assist his or her customers in identifying services that are strongly linked to those goals. In other words, the practitioner should help the customer differentiate between the urgent and the important.

Through this process of identifying customer needs and expectations, the practitioner must identify those processes that add value to the strategic direction of the organization and differentiate them from services that do not add value and are therefore unnecessary. Ultimately, abandoning non-value-added activities would be a significant part of any business strategy. In turn, some processes may be non-value-added but remain necessary (e.g., payroll services). The practitioner will need to identify how to minimize the cost of providing such services through process refinement, automation or contracting out. On the flip side of abandonment, there may be instances where customers expect or need services that are not currently provided. The practitioner will need to budget for the provision of these services and may need to reallocate resources from other activities.

Information regarding customer expectations can be gained through focus groups, employee climate surveys and the collection of data on leading indicators (e.g., attendance, turnover, grievance activity, injury rate). Regardless of whom the practitioner identifies as the primary internal customer, the Human Resources function must operate within a "line of sight" of the employees. In order for the practitioner to be successful, employees need to understand the goals and objectives of the Human Resources Department. It is also empowering for employees to believe their opinions on the efficacy of service delivery are being sought. Hence, the employee survey is a powerful and essential tool in the strategic deployment of resources.

As subject matter experts, the Human Resources Department must also be familiar with the context in which the organization operates. The successful practitioner will be able to help his or her internal clients anticipate changes in legislation and jurisprudence that will likely have an effect on the way the organization manages its people. The practitioner should be equally familiar with such environmental factors as the economy, labour market conditions, demographic trends, educational issues and any other matters that can impact on the people side of the business.

Step Three — Planning: Long- and Medium-Term

Long-term planning involves identifying the key business issues that the organization will face in the next five years. This is an inexact exercise but is important in areas of continuous development such as succession planning and training activities. Similarly, medium-term planning looks within a two- to three-year period during which the essential issues will mostly revolve around the development of the Human Resources department in terms of its ability to deliver agreed upon programming and processes aligned with the organizational strategy.

In the medium to long term, the function will need to identify how it will embed key values and processes into the cultural fabric of the organization. Even though it is recognized that strategic plans need to be flexible, they also must be resilient so that efforts to shape a desired cultural outcome are not thwarted by a momentary whim. Medium- to long-term plans usually are developed precisely because it will take several years and several iterations of some processes before they become truly integrated into the organization's culture.

Introducing value statements are a good example of such planning. Writing a set of agreed upon value statements is certainly not sufficient for translating those values into actions within the organization. Value statements are intended to drive behaviours by delineating what is important to the organization. This aids employees in determining how they should behave in a variety of different contexts. For value statements to take hold in an organization, the Human Resources practitioner needs to create a communication strategy and to identify supporting activities that will reinforce the right behaviours.

Value statements are an example of what was earlier described as a "feel good" objective. Practitioners know implicitly that value statements can be a powerful influence over organizational performance, but the effect cannot be directly measured. However, to be clear, medium- to long-term objectives involve any part of the strategic plan that will necessarily take a longer period of time to develop.

Step Four — Planning: Short-Term

Some practitioners differentiate between tactical and strategic planning and assume that short-term plans are synonymous with tactical deployment. In fact, the short-term strategic plan is simply an identification of those activities that will take place over the next 12 months in support of the strategic plan. The development of a comprehensive performance management process is a strategic issue that usually takes several years to develop. In the first year, the practitioner may identify activities to get the process started such as defining core competencies and developing a supervisory training program to support the performance management process. This type of activity is different from short-term activities such as negotiating a renewal collective agreement that are important but not necessarily strategic in nature.

The purpose of the short-term plan is to focus attention and resources on the necessary deliverables defined by the strategic plan. Urgent issues will crop up on a day-to-day basis that will require the attention of the Human Resources Department. However, the senior practitioner should not be distracted by these activities. A written plan executed with the proper level of discipline ensures that the important is not sacrificed in favour of the urgent.

The short-term plan is cascaded down through the function to help establish the goals and objectives of all Human Resources practitioners within the organization. It is important, therefore, that the plan be detailed and challenging enough to energize the people responsible for making it happen. It should also establish a significant milestone or "breakthrough" goal that will serve to motivate the department's employees to maintain the necessary discipline to stay focused on strategy. A breakthrough objective is one which, if attained, will take the organization (or department) forward in a significant way.

The short-term plan should be written in precise language and contain:

✓ defining statement describing the vision and context of the Human Resources strategy;

✓ specific statements outlining measurable objectives;

✓ supporting strategies to complement the attainment of those objectives;

✓ measures of success; and

✓ time lines and accountabilities.

Step Five — Implementation

No plan can be said to be a success until it has been translated into action. Involvement leads to commitment. Therefore, in implementing the plan, cascading down specific objectives is an important means to get buy-in from within the department and from the line managers who must support the department's activities. The performance management system is an integral part of setting the strategic plan into action. As such, the process becomes two-way. The setting of specific supporting objectives is a dialogue and negotiation.

The maintenance of proper and relevant metrics in key results areas ensures the effectiveness of plan implementation is continuously monitored and adjustments can be made as necessary. The closer to real time these measures can be taken, the more effective plan implementation can be managed. For each metric, there should be clearly stated objectives.

Every implementation plan should include a communication strategy outlining who needs to know different aspects of the strategy. More communication efforts will be required as the level of involvement increases. There is no danger of being able to over-communicate. The senior practitioner has to act as a transformational leader to keep the organization sold on the critical importance of the Human Resources Department's activities and their link to the strategic vision of the organization.

Step Six — Learning

Throughout implementation of the plan, the senior practitioner must continuously monitor its effectiveness through the review of the key metrics. From time to time, a key metric may dictate that a process be audited to ensure it is creating the desired results or to determine if adjustments are needed. During these audits or assessments, it may be discovered that the process is not right in the given context or new data may emerge that dictates a change in objectives or approach.

The underlying issue is that the strategic process requires the organization, the specific department and the individual practitioner to set out on an ongoing course of learning. Each failure should represent an opportunity to learn something new. The need might be the development of a specific skill or competency, or it may require organizational changes to support the activity. Regardless, the power of a strategic plan comes from its ability to guide and motivate individual behaviours toward the ultimate objectives of the organization.

Step Seven — Plan Review

Strategic plans need to be reasonable, robust and enduring. Therefore, the overall plan should not require constant review. Short-term plans can be updated annually or even every six months. However, the medium- to long-term plans should only be reviewed every two to three years. One reason for this is that the review itself involves substantial resources from both the Human Resources department and its internal customers. Another is the fact that constant review may create the perception that the plan is a flavour-of-the-month and hence should not be taken seriously. Also, the practitioner should expect that the overall direction and vision of the organization would remain constant over a relatively long period of time.

Critical events, however, such as a merger, acquisition or takeover may dictate that the plan be reviewed sooner. Critical events are any occurrence that has a profound impact on the organization's vision, purpose and core values. A change in legislation may have a significant impact on the way an organization operates but it is only considered a critical event if it changes the fundamental nature of the organization or its culture.

A formal plan review differs from the ongoing learning and adjustment process. It is a formal audit of the effectiveness of the plan implementation as measured by the key process metrics. It is a reality check on the continued relevance of the strategic direction. It is also an opportunity to renew the commitment of the department's internal customers to the function's central mandates.

Strategic Human Resources Management Themes

Human Resources vs. Personnel

For some, the only difference between today's Human Resources Department and the personnel department of yesterday is a name change. There are many organizations left that pose a challenge to the seasoned practitioner to effect a change in the perceived value the function brings to the organization. In many ways, there is little difference in the fundamental services previously provided by "Personnel" and those delivered today by "Human Resources". The similarities include:

- Both recognize that line management is responsible for the management of people, and their function is to provide advice and support services to complement the line manager's responsibilities.

- Both value, to some degree, the balancing of individual and organizational needs and the development of people to achieve their own levels of satisfaction and the objectives of the organization.

- Both understand that matching people to the needs of the business is a fundamental competency of the department.

- Both are responsible for a similar set of processes including selection, competence analysis, performance management, training, management development and reward programs.

- Both models consider communications and participation in the management of employee relations important.

Some might argue that the only discernible difference is the emphasis placed on certain activities and the type of approaches employed. While personnel managers argue that they have some level of involvement in strategic planning, Human Resources practitioners argue that this level of involvement has only evolved because of the influence of Human Resources Management. However, the differences are more substantial and include:

• Human resources practitioners see themselves as an integral part of the organization and believe their activities must be fully integrated with the activities of line management. Personnel managers see themselves as separate business partners whose purpose is to influence line managers.

• Human resources practitioners rely on theories of organizational behaviour, organizational development and design and behavioural sciences to create organizational models and management processes. Personnel managers tended not to have much in the way of theoretical grounding.

• Human resources practitioners see themselves as being primarily strategic and transformational, where the focus of personnel management was to oversee day-to-day transactions between the organization and its employees.

The concept behind Human Resources Management is oriented toward a philosophy of business where the management of people is seen as the most significant strategic concern. Managing Human Resources activities is seen as a senior management responsibility and must be owned by management as a whole in order to serve the interests of the organization. Personnel managers tend toward an employee orientation.

Human resources practitioners strive for a holistic approach where the interests of all individuals are considered but remain subordinate to the common good of the organization as a whole. The primary focus of the Human Resources practitioner is the strategic integration of all business objectives and the development and maintenance of a strong organizational culture.

The practitioner faced with the challenge to have the organization accept the unique mandate that Human Resources should be given recognizes the need for a senior leadership team committed to a clear vision of the organization's future. Senior management needs to recognize the value of having a set of articulated values and a mission statement that describes how the organization intends to operate. Such a management team will likely also recognize the value of the human resources function as the critical component to the successful realization of a competitive advantage through the development of people.

Even in this environment, the practitioner must have the credibility and finesse to be considered an equal member of the senior management team. The practitioner not only contributes as a subject matter expert but also to the overall business decision making. As an integral part of the management team, the senior practitioner is able to bring a convincing argument about the significance of Human Resources Management practices.

Once this credibility is achieved, the practitioner should develop a strategy that takes a holistic approach to people management issues. The strategy is comprehensive and suggests a portfolio of specific strategic initiatives and the development of policies and procedures aimed at supporting business initiatives. The primary focus of the Human Resources practitioner is to take only initiatives that add value to the organization in a measurable or observable way. As with other members of the senior management team, the practitioner always considers the impact of the department's efforts on shareholder value and only undertakes those that increase value.

The personnel manager of yesterday believed in winning the "hearts and minds" of employees as a goal unto itself. Even today, many Human Resources departments have merely changed their names and place the same emphasis on employee advocacy. Hence, people who want to work with people continue to be attracted to the function. The high level of sociability found in a typical "personnel manager" probably runs counter to the need of the Human Resources practitioner who must share the objectivity and results orientation of his or her line management peers.

The Human Resources practitioner also sees value in winning the hearts and minds of employees, not as a goal but rather as a means to orient employees to the aims, values and strategic objectives of the organization. The practitioner sees the value in creating a culture of continuous improvement where employees are responsible for their own development, and the organization as an entity is able to learn from its experiences.

The skilled practitioner will readily recognize the differences. Faced with the challenge of transforming the function into an integrated part of strategic management (as opposed to being a strategic partner on the outside looking in), the practitioner will be able to devise a strategy to achieve his or her personal goals of being recognized as an equal at the senior management table. The strategy should begin by examining the current competencies within the department to understand the type of gaps that have been identified above.

Human Resources Management

Human Resources Management (HRM) is a specific approach to managing people. It recognizes that people are the organization's most valuable asset, and that the adage "the only competitive advantage an organization can maintain is through the development of its people" dictates that the management of employees is the most critical business task.

As an approach, HRM emerged in response to new pressures placed on organizations throughout the 1980s and 1990s such as the following:

⇨ changing consumer tastes and increased demand for customized products and services;

⇨ globalization and increased levels of international competition;

⇨ rapid technological advances;

⇨ changing employee needs and demands; and

⇨ reduced levels of real economic growth.

In response to these pressures, organizations sought new strategies to enhance their competitive advantages including:

⇨ becoming more customer-focused (both externally and internally);

⇨ improving products and services on a continuous basis;

⇨ increasing investment in employees as organizational resources;

⇨ increasing organizational flexibility through the development of a highly committed, skilled and adaptable workforce;

⇨ increasing levels of job satisfaction among employees through the creation of positive employee relations environments; and

⇨ amending the basic relationship between employees and employers through the recognition of a "new employee contract".

Employees in today's organizations tend to want more say in matters that affect how they perform their work. They also tend to be more educated and mobile. Organizations cannot measure loyalty and commitment in terms of long service, but instead see it manifest, in effort and performance. In order to retain skilled employees and get value from their efforts, organizations need to develop strategies that not only reward employees monetarily for their efforts but also help them to acquire new skills and increase their marketability.

The starting point is to recognize the value the organization places in its employees in a substantial way through the corporate mission statement, core values and the strategic plan itself. This recognition has to be more than lip service. The senior leadership team must be willing and able to demonstrate its commitment to employees in its everyday actions and words. One of the most significant manifestations of such commitment is the positioning of the senior Human Resources practitioner as an equal member of the senior leadership team. In order to achieve this level of recognition, the practitioner must demonstrate the following characteristics:

⇨ thorough understanding of the business processes, including expertise in reading financial and other corporate performance indicators;

⇨ personal power developed through the fostering of strong relationships, networks and coalitions used to further the interests of the department;

⇨ proactive problem-solving ability whereby the practitioner takes the lead in new initiatives like process re-engineering, Total Quality Management (TQM), performance management and change management;

⇨ results orientation demonstrated through the promotion and maintenance of key Human Resources metrics;

⇨ active promoter of the devolution of Human Resources responsibilities through constant training, coaching and encouragement of line managers; and

⇨ strategic user of outsourcing to offload non-value-added activities such as payroll administration, routine training, recruitment advertising, pension and benefit administration and outplacement.

Under the HRM umbrella, there are five distinct management initiatives:

1. linking people management to corporate planning (essentially the core argument in favour of creating Human Resources strategies);

2. emphasizing culture and leadership;

3. devolving people management to line managers;

4. viewing employees as assets to be invested in and developed; and

5. viewing individuals as members of a team.

An HRM system operates within a conceptual framework that enables a coherent set of policies and practices to be developed. This conceptual framework is abstract and cannot be articulated as a single appropriate model. Notwithstanding, the organization that wants to adopt an HRM approach to its culture of people management should consider the following:

⇨ strategic integration of people management issues and business strategy;

⇨ will and commitment of senior management to develop an internally consistent and comprehensive approach to align Human Resources Management practices with business goals;

⇨ conviction that managing organizational culture is important and worthwhile;

⇨ leadership that values employee commitment over compliance;

⇨ belief in employees as the organization's most important asset, and a belief that as an asset they are worth investing in;

⇨ recognition of the need to create flexibility and to work toward the creation of a Learning Organization as a response to increased globalization and other competitive threats;

⇨ persistent approach to continuous improvement; and

⇨ strong emphasis on communications and the development of shared expectations.

Devolving Human Resources Responsibilities

Many senior Human Resources practitioners today have adopted a different paradigm regarding the role of the line manager in the delivery of Human Resources Management initiatives. As the Human Resources function has evolved over time in large organizations, it has assumed specific responsibilities for the management of people. For example, the Human Resources Department has become solely responsible for recruiting front-line employees. It is seen as supplying people to the operating departments.

The alternative view is that the function is responsible for designing, implementing and managing the efficacy of the recruitment process. In this paradigm, the line managers own the process and are entirely responsible for making the hiring decision. The Human Resources practitioner may provide certain services such as sourcing candidates, training line supervisors on behaviourally based interviewing techniques, conducting reference checks and arranging for appropriate testing. However, the accountability for the results of the recruiting efforts remains with line management.

Devolving Human Resources responsibilities refers to a specific effort to reverse the abdication of this responsibility by line management. This abdication evolved over time as a natural progression of the division of labour and increased task specialization. Reversing it requires a very specific plan of action. The most challenging barrier to making this happen is that today's supervisors and managers tend to be poorly equipped to reassume these long-lost skills.

Devolving Human Resources Management activities emerged as an issue in the last 10 years as organizations identified the need to flatten their structures. An important part of flattening an organization is the need to develop managers, supervisors and employees with more generalized skill sets. This also means empowering employees at all levels to make decisions or to be involved in processes previously reserved for specialists. Notwithstanding these general trends, the senior practitioner must have significant support from the top management of the organization for devolution to take place. Devolving human resources functions will profoundly change the culture of the organization.

As part of a Human Resources strategy, the senior practitioner, with the involvement of the senior leadership team, needs to identify the list of Human Resources activities to be devolved. In support of this list, the practitioner will also need to identify the prerequisite skills required to perform the identified functions. Once a strategy has been agreed upon for devolving the function, then a gaps analysis can be conducted to determine the current competencies and skills inventory among line managers.

From this analysis, the practitioner can develop a long-term strategy that will identify different potential courses of action including:

⇨ designing specific skills training programs;

⇨ identifying individual development needs and opportunities through the performance management process;

⇨ changing incentive and reward systems to align with the new competency requirements;

⇨ amending job descriptions and specifications to reflect new skills needs;

⇨ identifying skilled role models to serve as coaches and mentors; and

⇨ recruiting new people into key positions to support the change and reinforce the strategic direction the organization is taking.

Human Resources Practitioner as Change Agent

Organizational change initiatives invariably involve changes in the way people are managed. The Human Resources function is uniquely positioned to have the most profound impact on an organization in transition. The breadth of influence inherent in the Human Resources function's reach across the organization puts it in a position to leverage its distinct competencies. Human resources practitioners can add great value to any organization through the application of their specialization in introducing breakthrough initiatives that significantly change the attitudes, behaviours and perceptions of employees throughout the organization. Specific initiatives that are identified

with the Human Resources function and underlie change management efforts include:

- **Human Resources Strategy.** The formulation and acceptance of the Human Resources strategy is a means of gaining buy-in throughout the organization on the directions for long-term organizational development. The strategy provides a comprehensive and coherent plan for introducing the organization's intended vision, culture and core values.

- **Organizational Design.** The function is responsible for consulting with the senior leadership team on the appropriate structures that are consistent with the organization's vision. Moreover, on an ongoing basis, the practitioner is responsible for the design and redesign of jobs to fit the requirements dictated by the introduction of new processes, products, technologies, or methods of operation. Organizations facing challenges from competitive threats or from shifts in the economy have looked to the Human Resources practitioner to develop strategies for creating flatter and more flexible organizations that can respond quickly to changes in the business context.

- **Cultural Change and Cultural Management.** Though much has yet to be written and understood about managing organizational culture, the Human Resources practitioner is uniquely the *de facto* steward of the organization's culture. Every Human Resources process in some way affects the culture, whether in a deliberate or inadvertent manner. The practitioner can ensure the organization yields the intended cultural income by having these processes align with the vision and core values the organization seeks. The practitioner, moreover, can influence employee behaviours and, therefore, attitudes, through effective use of processes such as the performance management system, training and development strategies and reward and recognition initiatives.

- **Change Management.** Many practitioners have inherent facilitation skills to oversee change initiatives and are therefore naturally predisposed to take the lead in change management efforts. Knowledge of the fundamentals of organizational behaviour puts the practitioner in an ideal role as influencer, coach and mentor for line managers faced with the challenge of bringing about changes to the organizational culture. The practitioner's specific knowledge regarding motivational theory and employee motivation can be leveraged to influence employee commitment. In addition, this background can be useful in developing communication strategies and devising ways to involve employees in the change process.

- **Flexibility.** In order to face continuous threats and challenges, many organizations have come to realize that they need to be flexible. Organizations that can quickly respond and adapt to shifts in their environments have a decided competitive advantage over others. This flexibility can be achieved through the design and implementation of appropriate structures and policies that allow the organization to move quickly to make the best use of its people. The ultimate flexibility is created in a Learning Organization that continuously seeks to improve its processes, products and services through the empowerment of its employees to self-develop persistently.

- **Teams.** The introduction of teams can take many different forms. It may at one level involve teaching peers from different business units how to "act as one". In the extreme, the organization may want to fully empower front-line employees in self-managing work groups. The Human Resources strategy should identify the specific goals of the organization in this respect and identify the resources that will be invested to create the level of change desired. Introducing autonomous work groups in an organization will have a profound impact on its culture. Such an introduction will predictably be met with pockets of heavy resistance. The practitioner must develop strategies to overcome or eliminate these points of resistance in an effective manner.

- **Total Quality Management.** While not the specific milieu of the Human Resources practitioner, TQM efforts require the practitioner to become involved in the organizational design aspects to support TQM. Moreover, training and development activities are very significant in supporting TQM initiatives. The astute practitioner will note that the introduction of TQM processes presents an opportunity for the practitioner to influence the behaviours and attitudes of employees.

- **Performance Management Systems.** Managing organizational change does not always involve a specific change strategy, but rather can be intro-

duced through the use of the performance management process in support of the overall business strategy. Practitioners should not ignore the fact that the performance management system is perhaps the single most important process the Human Resources Department oversees.

- **Human Resources Development.** The practitioner is responsible for the level of investment an organization makes in the training and development of its workforce. Training and development programs need to be aligned with the objectives of the organization in terms of both measurable results and strategic direction. The ideal situation for the practitioner is to be able to demonstrate a direct return on investment that correlates the expenditure on training and development with improved bottom-line performance.

- **Reward Management.** The reward and recognition systems used by an organization have a direct impact on motivation and thus performance. Reward systems that are not aligned with the organization's strategic objectives will act in a counterproductive manner and constitute the most serious barrier to change efforts.

- **Employee Relations.** Developing a positive employee relations climate is not a given in Human Resources Management; rather, it requires a deliberate and explicit plan to achieve.

Adding Value and Creating Competitive Advantage

If people are to make the difference in an organization, the practitioner must devise strategies that directly correspond to desired business results. Competitive advantage generally flows from having perceived better value (quality of goods or services), reduced cost structures, or through innovation. The practitioner needs to develop strategies that complement the chosen path of the organization in order to add value.

Product and service quality can be enhanced by such policies and practices as:

✓ explicit job description and detailed process analysis that foster repetitive and predictable outputs;

✓ high levels of participation to promote cooperative, interdependent behaviours between work groups;

✓ team or group orientation regarding performance management; and

✓ continuous training and development of employee skills.

Cost reduction is promoted through a different set of policies including:

✓ short-term results oriented focus on performance management;

✓ compensation based on competitive market rates; and

✓ job specialization requiring minimal training.

Finally, a focus on innovation would require policies that include:

✓ promoting interaction between individual and groups through cross-functional task forces;

✓ focusing performance management on long-term goals and group efforts;

✓ allowing employees to develop many different skills through generalized job design;

✓ allowing high degree of variable pay based on increased participation in the organization (e.g., share options); and

✓ creating broad-banded job classifications and open-ended career paths marked by cross-functional training.

The practitioner at a strategic level helps the organization identify its core competencies and its Strengths, Weaknesses, Opportunities and Threats (SWOT). As the business objectives emerge, the practitioner will need to match the type of people the organization has or will need to recruit for the desired outcome. This may involve redeployment or a strategic recruiting campaign. In addition, the practitioner will need to identify and describe the current organizational culture and determine if it is appropriate to the business strategy.

If the strategy is not in alignment, the practitioner will need to identify those processes that are likely to create an organizational breakthrough and create momentum in redeveloping an appropriate culture. The practitioner may need to examine job design, organizational structure, career ladders, compensation schemes and many other processes to determine

which need to be changed in order to bring the culture into alignment with the organization's objectives.

In addition, the practitioner will need to define to what degree employees will need to be involved in the decision-making process and devise the structures to allow for employee participation. This likely would be part of an overall strategy regarding fostering a positive employee relations culture and may also embrace a labour–management relations strategy.

In turn, these strategic concerns will drive the development of a specific strategy on how the Human Resources function will perform. The practitioner will need to ensure the structure and mandate of the department are consistent with the organization's overall direction. The department can also examine whether or not it has the proper resources in the right places to accomplish its mission in alignment with the corporate vision.

Finally, the practitioner will need to examine specific policies and determine if they are being managed in a way that complements the central thrust of the corporate strategy.

Role of the Human Resources Practitioner

Obviously, the development of Human Resources strategy is led by the senior Human Resources practitioner. In fulfilling this role, the practitioner needs to consider who else in the organization will be affected by the creation of the plan. Following the adage that the only sustainable competitive advantage an organization can achieve is through its people, then it is equally obvious that everyone in the organization is in some way affected by the plan. It is hoped that the impact for all employees will be to create a more positive employee relations climate that allows them to be successful in their individual efforts.

As stated above, it is important for the practitioner to define who are the function's internal customers. The answer to this question is not necessarily self-evident. All employees benefit to some degree from the services provided by the Human Resources Department. However, consider how benefit administration is conducted under different paradigms. If the focus is on the employee as the prime customer, the department will invest in the most effective delivery of benefit entitlements. If the focus is on management objectives, the department may choose the most cost-effective delivery at the expense of transaction turnaround times and delivery excellence.

The choice of focus will dictate how the Human Resources function is organized and what are its priorities. In medium- to large-sized organizations, the delivery of certain services such as benefits administration is most effectively accomplished through a centralized function. However, the senior practitioner may also consider contracting out some services if doing so is consistent with the overall strategic direction of the department.

In decentralized environments, local Human Resources practitioners often face a dilemma as to where their loyalties should lie. It may be seen as essential by the senior practitioner to centralize reporting structures to maintain the independence of local practitioners from their line management customer. While this makes imminent sense, the senior practitioner needs to take care in ensuring the objectives established for the local Human Resources practitioner remain aligned with business unit objectives.

Barriers to Success/Common Pitfalls

One of the most significant caveats the senior practitioner must heed is the tendency for Human Resources executives to establish plans that are imprecise and have no obvious link to the organization's overall objectives. The Human Resources strategy must be derived from the overall strategic plan of the organization. It cannot be created in isolation, but rather should be an expression of how the department will contribute to the goals of the organization. This is one reason why the establishment of key metrics is central to the strategic planning process.

Unfortunately, in many organizations, the involvement of the Human Resources function in the strategic planning process is not seen as a critical need. As a result, Human Resources practitioners often do not have the fundamental skills necessary for the establishment of a strategic plan. Specifically, practitioners do not gain experience in developing a Human Resources strategy linked to the organization's objectives. Moreover, because of this lack of experience, the typical practitioner has not developed the disciplined approach to working within a defined plan of action. Practitioners are often more adept at "putting out fires", rather than establishing courses of action to prevent fires from happening in the first place. This is not unique to the function. Most managers are more comfortable in dealing with the urgent issues of today

instead of focusing efforts and resources on the development of more important long-term strategic objectives. However, strategic thinkers emerge in other functions to fill leadership roles. Until recently, few strategists were attracted to the Human Resources function as a career choice.

The inherent lack of strategic planning skills or experience can lead practitioners to develop plans based on "gut feeling" rather than through the gathering of relevant data. Without supporting data, the practitioner may be able to incite activities that have a positive impact on the organization, but will not be able to validate that impact through measurement. Training is a key area where this type of problem is commonplace. The practitioner may be able to convince the organization to invest substantially in the development of a supervisory skills training program. However, if the practitioner has not identified specific measurable results to be achieved, it will not be possible to assess the return on that investment. It is because of this deficiency that useful and important training programs are often the first things to be slashed from a budget during economic downturns, even though such investments are even more valuable when the organization is facing the challenge of declining financial performance.

While it would seem to be obvious that flavour-of-the-month Human Resources Management products should be resisted, many practitioners are trapped by the lure of being on the leading edge of Human Resources practices. These products are not commonly suited to the specific needs of the organization. For example, 360-degree feedback can prove to be a very powerful tool for identifying the development needs of managers, but it can be counterproductive to introduce the process in an organization that has a weak or non-existent performance management system. Regardless, many practitioners ignore such tenets of good practice for fear of being left behind.

Fashionable Human Resources products are strongly marketed to provide the appeal of a quick fix. The target market is usually the organization's senior leadership and, specifically, the CEO. The vendors of these services know that capturing the interest of the top management group is a more effective way of selling their wares than targeting the human resources practitioner. In fact, even the most senior Human Resources practitioners find it difficult to resist the pressure placed on them by a CEO who has been convinced that he or she has found the next great thing in people management.

As a result, Human Resources practitioners often abandon the fundamentals in pursuit of the quick fix. A sound human resources strategy should be formed around establishing and maintaining robust and resilient fundamental practices. (Refer to the Employment Cycle, at page 149.) The best counter-argument the practitioner can give to a CEO to ward off the introduction of a new fad is to demonstrate that the proposed process has no discernible link to the organization's objectives and cannot provide a measurable value-added return. The practitioner will be particularly credible in putting forth such an argument if he or she has developed and articulated a sound Human Resources strategy supported by relevant Human Resources metrics.

Experienced Human Resources practitioners who understand the strategic planning process can nevertheless be prone to wanting to do too much. Trying to accomplish too much with too few resources will result in failure and will affect the credibility of the practitioner. The adage followed by many marketing professionals, "under-promise and over-deliver", is sage advice to the seasoned practitioner. Remember to keep the plan simple and focused on the fundamentals. A few things done well can have a significant impact on any organization's culture and performance.

In many organizations, the overall strategic plan is developed without input from the Human Resources practitioner and therefore lacks an integrated approach to people management. However, in many other organizations, there is no clearly defined and communicated strategy at all. This can be viewed as a serious handicap to the development of a human resources strategy. However, it can also be viewed as a significant opportunity for the practitioner to take a leadership role by demonstrating the value of having a well-defined strategic plan. In these instances, the organization's strategy exists, but is not articulated. The practitioner needs to deduce what the strategy is and should gain credibility and a more in-depth understanding of the business and the organization's objectives through the process of defining and rendering in writing what is the implicit strategic plan.

Moreover, regardless of whether the strategic plan is explicit or implied, it is always subject to change. By definition, strategic plans should be sufficiently robust and resilient to persist through changes in the environment. However, in order to be truly successful, the plans must also be flexible enough to adapt to those shifts. The Human Resources plan should be consistently monitored and reviewed to ensure its ongoing relevance to the strategic direction of the organization.

Plans need to be modified when environmental circumstances dictate that a change in direction is necessary. Moreover, the plan is a living concept that will evolve over time. However, because practitioners tend to lack the discipline to follow a specific plan, abandonment is more likely than following the plan too rigidly. Performance to plan has to be consistently and constantly monitored to ensure ongoing relevance. If a particular aspect of the plan is not yielding the intended results, it may need to be modified or abandoned. Plan reviews should be detailed and comprehensive to ensure continued alignment with the organization's overall objectives.

The development and implementation of a strategic Human Resources plan cannot be a mechanical process. Nevertheless, it is important that the plan aligns with dominant Human Resources Management practices such as the performance management system so that it has relevance and provides a significant impact on the organization's culture and performance.

The relevance of the plan is critical to its success. Too often, when senior practitioners embark on the development of a strategic Human Resources plan, they do so in isolation. Much time must be spent with the internal clients to understand their objectives and challenges in-depth. By spending sufficient time with key internal clients, the practitioner will gain a greater appreciation for the level of need and the degree of sophistication of his or her customers. A common pitfall is to deliver systems or solutions that are more than the customer group needs or is able to implement properly.

Conversely, some practitioners may meet the immediate needs of the client group, but fail to challenge or stretch the organization's ability to improve the people management practices. In fledgling organizations, the senior Human Resources practitioner can provide the necessary leadership to help the organization mature quickly and gain competitive advantage through solid people management.

INTELLECTUAL CAPITAL

Definition/Background

The movement to understand the meaning of the intellectual capital of an organization has grown in momentum since the mid-1990s. Pioneering Scandinavian companies such as Skandia Assurance have demonstrated the inadequacy of a traditional balance sheet to reflect the health of an organization in the knowledge era, and looked for alternatives. Later championed by Thomas Stewart of *Fortune* magazine, today this is a matter of international interest. The historical models of evaluating a business no longer serve as adequate representations of future expectation.

"Capital" is a term generally associated in organizations with the financial balance sheet, and referring to physical and financial assets. Terms such as goodwill reflected the more intangible assets, usually arising from acquisitions where the price paid exceeded the balance sheet value. This goodwill was generally systematically depreciated, as if it were something of an embarrassment amidst the supposedly more accurate tangible assets and liabilities. The term intellectual capital was generally related to intellectual property — patents, special knowledge, and so on. Attempts to value brands were started but never received the blessing of the accountancy profession. Nevertheless, an accountant's answer to the meaning of "intellectual capital" will almost certainly be "an assessment of the value of future earnings opportunities". The problem is that he or she has no idea how to do that assessment, and so fall back on what they do know, i.e., historical results.

The truth is that there has been a progressively ever-widening gap between the value placed on an enterprise by a market and the value calculated according to accepted financial principles in the balance sheet. This gap is attributed to the importance of knowledge and other factors as the drivers of future value for shareholders.

Calculating the absolute measure of intellectual capital (or "intangible assets") is derived from the simple formula:

Market Value = Tangible Assets + Intangible Assets

Of course, objections can easily be raised to this formula. Market value (the number of shares multiplied by their individual value) fluctuates continuously, and depends on all kinds of factors that have nothing to do with the organization itself. The tangible assets come from the formal balance sheet and are measured at a point in time. The formula can be refined to look at moving averages, and corrected for extraneous factors — but we should not miss the main point. In most organizations today, the intangible assets will be greater than the tangible, and they will be increasing at a faster rate. Thus, high-tech companies like Microsoft will show the intangible percentage of market value in the high nineties, but even highly capital-intensive companies will be in the 50% to 70% range. The ratio of intangible to tangible assets gives us a means of comparing similar organizations.

Today, the market value of an organization is usually calculated on the basis of the assets shown on the balance sheet. The value of the firm may be its earnings multiplied by the price earnings ratio, or a formula that takes into account not only its earning but also its tangible assets (buildings, equipment, machinery). Regardless, the difference between the organization's market value or capitalization and its assets is known as the "intangible assets" or the "intellectual capital". This is generally subdivided into three parts: customer capital, structural capital, and human capital.

By customer capital, we mean factors such as customer satisfaction and, more importantly, loyalty, market share, image and reputation, brand value, competence enhancement, and partnerships. Structural capital includes knowledge, patents, intellectual property rights, systems, processes, databases, and culture. Structural capital is often defined as "what is left when the people have gone home".

The human component is not just the people and their expertise, but their motivation, the way they are led and organized, and so on. Some Human Resources practitioners discuss intellectual capital as if it is only concerned with the latter, but this is not so. Nevertheless, people need to be seen as the source of all of the components of intellectual capital — both in maintenance and growth — and therefore a prime concern of any organization has to be the continual transfer of their knowledge and experience into the "hard wiring" of the organization for the benefit of all.

Each of these components adds value to customers and other stakeholders, and ultimately shareholders, through their competitive strength and effectiveness. Each needs to develop and improve in order to provide increasing value. It is often said, somewhat insincerely, "our people are our most important asset". However, none of the various components of intellectual capital can be maintained and grown without them. It is people who create new systems, innovate, develop relationships and make up effective teams. Therefore, a prime concern of any organization has to be the effective utilization and growth of their knowledge, expertise and experience. This requires a culture of empowerment, innovation and learning, and processes that support them.

The components of human capital may vary from organization to organization, but are likely to include the following:

— technical and professional knowledge and expertise;

— personal competencies that support high performance;

— visionary and supportive leadership;

— commitment and enthusiasm for change and learning;

— effective teamwork;

— individual potential for growth; and

— networks of contacts both internally and available externally.

There are aspects of culture — internal communications, systems and processes, norms and expectations — that clearly have a major influence on all of the above.

How Human Capital Contributes to Value

Seeing people as the key drivers of value in an organization, one can categorize individuals and their roles by the value that they add today, or are creating for the future. Some people do very low added-value work — putting right things that have gone wrong, administration and book keeping, compliance with the law; all these may be necessary, but do not actually contribute to value. Others are distinguished by their competence, special knowledge or creativity — and whose loss would be much greater than the loss of a building or machine. People can be static, doing what they did yesterday, with the same level of competence. Or people can be incrementally different each day, as they learn, innovate and contribute more — progressively increasing their ability to add value and to contribute at a higher and/or different level in the future.

Looking at individuals on this basis may raise questions about the alignment of Human Resources policies with a value-based mindset — for example, retention and reward practices. Losing individuals of high added-value, who are also very difficult to replace, has to be seen as a serious asset loss. Whereas accounting standards bodies are struggling to create valuation criteria and techniques for intangible assets generally, they do not see people as part of them because of their transience and variability.

The purpose of studying intellectual capital in an organization is to be able to prioritize attention on the drivers of future value. It is not the physical and financial assets that create future value — important enablers as they are. Since it is self-evident that all intellectual capital is maintained and grown by people, the way in which they connect with the strategic drivers of value is critical to understand. We need to be able to balance the positive and negative aspects that we have, and deliberately shift the balance. This means, in practice, having targeted change in, for example, our levels of capability, in the supporting culture, in the way we are organized, and in leadership ability. In short, understanding and managing intellectual capital is the key to Human Resources activities and initiatives being firmly linked to the business priorities. Organizations need to realize that the only sustainable competitive advantage they can gain is through their people. As such, the organization needs a means to measure the value of its people.

Knowledge Management

Knowledge exists in different places, within individuals and in small groups, and is often not made available to others who could use it. There are three driving forces behind the concept of making the management of knowledge a discipline in itself. The first is the ever-growing importance of the "intangible assets" of an organization. The knowledge and experience that an organization has collectively is a part of that capital. Its productive use and growth is a prime concern.

Secondly, a "learning organization" (or one we might say that is readily adapted to change) is concerned about learning at individual, group and organizational levels. The latter embraces the capability of learning from others in order to adapt successfully, both externally and internally, through a series of mechanisms.

Finally, the growth of communication through technology provides its own stimulus and tools to highlight the benefits of shared knowledge.

Information consists of data and experience. Knowledge could be seen as "what the information tells us" (i.e., the result of some analysis or reflection). Arthur Andersen defines knowledge as "information that adds value". Beyond that is perhaps something we could call "wisdom" — the integration of new knowledge with old, mixed with personal judgment and intuition — which guides future decisions. Another way to look at it is to distinguish between that which is "explicit" — openly available — or "tacit" — embedded within the heads of people. Knowledge management is about making the explicit readily available and providing access to the tacit.

We could define knowledge management as follows: "The management of the information, knowledge and experience available to an organization — its creation, capture, storage, availability and utilization — in order that organizational activities build on what is already known and extend it further." Some say that knowledge management is a meaningless term, because knowledge resides in people and cannot be "managed". The emphasis, however, is on the creation and exchange of knowledge. It happens naturally in many small organizations but rarely so in complex ones, and a systematic approach is the only effective solution.

Studies have shown clearly that effective knowledge management is only 10% to 20% about good tools and systems, and is mainly to do with the attitudes and skills of people. Pressure of time, the need for visibility, the power that comes from knowledge, human impatience, inter-departmental rivalry, restructuring — these and other familiar features of organizational life work against a sharing culture.

In an organization committed to investment in intellectual capital and knowledge management, one might see some of the following:

— open access to shared electronic information files, such as on customers and suppliers;

— physical "maps" of where key knowledge is held;

— "telephone directories" that encapsulate each person's special knowledge or experience — "not more than two calls to find out what you need to know";

— honest project reviews available to all;

— systematic transfer of previous knowledge and experience in job induction;

— time spent on planning the transfer of learning (to whom, how and when) at the end of every training event;

— cross-boundary sharing seminars for "communities of common interest";

— systematic "entry, expert and exit" interviews based around individual's knowledge;

— using "decision diaries" to record why major decisions were taken; and

— celebrations of successful reapplication of old knowledge, and of creation of the new.

Benefits/Expected Outcomes

The possible benefits of attention to managing intellectual capital are enormously significant. The organization itself will:

— understand what creates current and future value;

— have balanced performance measures that put intellectual capital components in their proper perspective;

— be able to better balance short-term pressures and long-term needs;

— be able to invest in line with the true strategic priorities; and

— acquire, retain and grow key intellectual capital components.

The Human Resources practitioner cannot enter this field without having goals related to business benefits of value creation. They must build measures to assess and track the changes in human capital. If they do this successfully, then the benefits will become very clear.

Since everyone can be regarded as part of the human capital of the organization, everyone is involved. However, this puts particular focus on those concerned with the longer term, such as research and development people and strategic/product planners. It affects Human Resources practitioners significantly, since they should be the experts in managing and motivating people, and yet it challenges their business knowledge and skills.

Perhaps most of all, this approach affects the finance and accounting function. It effectively questions the time and effort they take on issues such as budgeting, recording and forecasting. It demands more measures than mere financial ones to indicate success, and it challenges their own competence and breadth of thinking.

That goes for top management also. Driven inevitably by the pressures of the quarter, they need to be able to keep the balanced perspective and make investments and decisions about future value. The messages they give through their words and actions are what give meaning to their beliefs and values.

Sears Roebuck is an example of a company that has proved the "service-profit chain" works directly for their bottom line. Having had major problems in the early 1990s as part of their transformation, they created three sets of objectives and measures to match, under the headings "a compelling place to shop, work and invest". This is referred to as the "Total Performance Indicators", or TPI, and all managers are targeted on them. They have found a direct relationship as follows — that an improvement in employee satisfaction of 4% yields a similar percentage change in customer satisfaction, which translates to $200 million of additional revenues. This leads to investor confidence and consequent share value increase.

Implementation

Thinking of people as assets rather than costs generates a different mindset in resourcing decisions. It implies that, to every cost on the "salaries and related expenses" line, there is a balance sheet factor of asset value. However, the latter is hard to quantify. It requires that there are some measures which relate to the value and contribution of individuals, as well as of the other factors above.

The "Balanced Scorecard", put forward in 1992 by Kaplan and Norton, proposed that a set of measures which reflected more than the financial bottom line was needed. They suggested measures on customers, in internal efficiency and on what they called "learning and innovation". Skandia Assurance applied this by introducing a fifth set of measures related to people themselves, which drove all the others. There are no common standards as yet for such sets of measures; however, what is clear is that they cannot be directly financial. It helps to establish chains of cause and effect that directly link subsidiary measures with profitability or value. A good example of this is the "service-profit chain", which links profits to customer retention, and traces this back to employee satisfaction. Measures at each stage directly feed into one another.

The time will come when investors will demand some kind of "intellectual capital" balance sheet. There are "liabilities" associated with human capital, i.e., negative aspects of all the factors listed. The question for organizations is "Do we know where we are on the balance of asset and liability on each factor, and in which direction are we moving?" Companies are unlikely to want to publish their "liabilities"; however, they should be well aware of them internally. Such a balance sheet may lead to an "intellectual capital budget", and certainly to agendas for change aimed at shifting the balance. Watson Wyatt, the consultants, have developed a "Human Capital Index", which is an assessment of good Human Resources practices. They have shown a direct relationship between a high score on their Index and shareholder value growth.

Some organizations publish an "intellectual assets monitor" along with their standard annual reports. This covers the three areas of Customers, Organization (internal structure), and People (competence). Under each, they have measures relating to growth and renewal, to efficiency, and to stability. For the people side, they have the following measures, and each has a target:

Competencies

- Average professional competence (years)

- Customer focused employees (%)

- Growth in professional competence (%)

- Experts with post-secondary degrees (%)

Efficiency

- Value added per expert ($)
- Value added per employee ($)

Stability

- Expert turnover (%)
- Expert seniority (years)
- Median age of all employees (years)

Implementation of this concept then requires the following:

— identification of the critical components of the organization's human capital;

— creating a set of measures that can track them effectively;

— preparing regular "balance sheets" and "budgets" for growing human capital; and

— integrating these into the organization's performance measurement systems.

Knowledge is an asset, and assets require investments — in commitment, resources and managerial time. The following components are likely to be needed:

- Recognizing from top management that this is essential for survival and that everyone must play a part — and acting as role models themselves in committing resources and in their behaviour.

- Establishing a focus for coordination that can decide the framework of tools, systems and cultural factors that are needed for success. Appointing owners of knowledge assets and internal champions.

- Understanding what types of knowledge are strategically important and deserve special attention, and avoiding the clutter of excess information of little relevance.

- Designing systems (such as shared databases, intranets, electronic libraries, virtual discussion groups, archive libraries, search and link facilities) that will enable people to input and access information, knowledge and experience as easily as possible.

- Building work disciplines to capture new knowledge and experiences that may be of value to others.

- Setting up opportunities for sharing, collaborating, connecting and communicating — regularly, normally, openly, face to face as well as electronically, and across organizational boundaries.

- Focusing on listening to others and transferring what is learned around the organization.

- Rewarding the creation of new learning through experimentation and questioning, and empowering people to do it.

- Publicizing good examples of successful knowledge transfer (and also examples of failure) to utilize what has been learned by others (with costs where possible).

Role of the Human Resources Practitioner

This movement is of fundamental importance to those who work as Human Resources practitioners for many reasons. For practitioners who seek to be "strategic partners" with the business, the logic of this thinking puts people as the foundation of the creation of future value.

It means some significant interventions on the practitioner's part. The following list illustrates some of the potential scope available here:

— helping managers understand the true drivers of future value;

— helping managers understand which of the components (including individuals and teams of people) of intellectual capital are strategic for the organization;

— preparing a balance sheet of current assets and liabilities, and a "budget" for acquisition, retention and growth, for those components that are strategic;

— helping to define and create a culture that maximizes creativity, innovation, learning and knowledge management;

— defining credible measures of human asset value and other aspects of human capital that have an accepted place in the performance management system of the organization;

— designing and managing Human Resources systems that are linked to value (current or future), rather than hierarchy job size or yesterday's performance;

— ensuring that high value resources are rewarded and retained;

— working with the Information Technology department to maximize connectivity between people and systems;

— initiating change programs that will develop the organization, its people and its culture towards higher value contribution; and

— measuring the return on Human Resources Management activities more effectively and relevantly.

The Human Resources practitioner will be at the heart of strategic growth in the organization, provided it is able to devise and use credible measures of human capital. This approach enables the practitioner to talk to other functions on the basis that people are assets rather than mere costs. Human Resources initiatives can be prioritized and aligned with the strategic direction of the organization on a rational basis.

The "intellectual capital" or "knowledge management" approach allows the practitioner a basis to determine what are the prime drivers of the organization's success. These can then be measured in a meaningful way and incorporated into the performance management process. Other Human Resources policies and practices can be engineered so that they reward and grow the human capital of the organization. Overall, the approach provides a systematic way to tie all management practices together in a comprehensive process to create value for the organization and define its culture.

In addition, employees should be conscious of their value to the organization and find it rewarded appropriately. Employees, generally speaking, want to work in an organization that is concerned for the long term rather than the short term only. This approach to managing sends a message to employees that the organization is willing and motivated to invest in their growth and development. This makes employees feel valued as contributors to the success of the organization rather than as "costs on legs".

Barriers to Success/Common Pitfalls

There is one overriding barrier and that is the failure of Human Resources practitioners to understand the nature of intellectual capital and the fundamental role they should play in its growth. This may be due to their own lack of business knowledge or other preoccupations with their own agenda.

A second and more difficult barrier is that the financial community has measurement on their side, ostensibly precise, and Human Resources has very little to offer. It seems a truism that "numbers speak louder than words", and the need for credible, meaningful measures of human capital is vital to having a voice in strategic and tactical decisions. This is not easy. But the fact is that the lack of good non-financial measures has allowed the financial ones to be over-dominating. Many Human Resources practitioners are not naturally numerate and some object in principle to the very concept of "measuring" human beings. One important argument is to convince top management that not every measure has to be in dollars in order to be useful.

Linked to this is the pressure for short-term results that most organizations feel, driven either from outside or inside. Arguments about long-term value creation take second place to the needs of the moment to meet commitments made. Traditional budgeting processes force this mentality, and some pioneering companies have become much more flexible and dynamic in the way they do this.

The Human Resources practitioner should be aware of the following:

— preaching the logic of a focus on intellectual capital without practical ideas of how to measure it and shift "the balance";

— failing to establish credible measurements of human capital;

— not prioritizing those components that they can influence, and creating complex presentations and measurements;

— failing to understand the business dynamics sufficiently to work with colleagues on balanced performance management;

— being unwilling to give up established processes based on previous ideas of fairness and value;

— making knowledge management another "initiative" or "flavour-of-the-month"; and

— believing people will naturally cooperate without answering the "what's in it for me" question.

INTERIM EXECUTIVES

Definition/Background

Interim executives fall into three categories: high profile executives who have taken early retirement, executives who are "between engagements", and free-agents. Whatever their motivations are, all three groups have the experience and expertise to add value to an organization. They thrive on tough challenges, ambiguity and have a strong need for personal growth — precisely the characteristics needed by many organizations in today's environment of rapid change.

Ever since the publication of Peters and Waterman's *In Search of Excellence* in 1982, organizations have been seeking ways to transform themselves into more responsive and flexible enterprises. The authors of that groundbreaking work described organizations that were able to thrive in uncertain times because they had insightful leadership and the ability to learn and adapt as an organization. However, Peters and Waterman were unable to foresee many of the dramatic changes that were on the horizon and, as a result, many of the organizations they cited have since fallen on rough times. The authors failed, in particular, to predict the rise of new enterprises founded on emerging technologies, like communications, software and the Internet. Peters and Waterman did, nevertheless, make an important contribution: they made many organizations recognize the need for critical self-assessment.

"Self-assessment" means examining the organization's leadership, mission and, ultimately, the entire set of assumptions upon which it has built its success, to discover whether or not it could survive and thrive amid rapid change. The continued success — survival, even — of many organizations is dependant on their ability to fundamentally transform their business into a flexible, learning enterprise. "Transformation" means changing an organization's culture so that it possesses a built-in ability to adapt quickly to shifts in the business environment that challenge its short-term success and long-term survival.

Shifts in the business environment come from many different directions, including:

- **Increased Competition** — Competitive threats have always been a concern for business leaders. However, new technologies have reduced economies of scale to the extent that size alone is no longer a defence. Small flexible organizations have been able to gain entry into sectors once thought to be the exclusive domain of industrial giants (e.g., steel manufacturing). Improved communication technologies and more efficient transportation networks have shrunk the world and made global competition a new business reality.

More competition due to technological breakthroughs has also become a new reality. The telephone giants, for example, were once believed to hold a natural monopoly because of the need for extensive investment in infrastructure. But cell phone networks and the Internet have now made significant progress towards eliminating this "natural" advantage.

- **Legislation** — The legal environment is also constantly shifting to adapt to new technologies and changing societal norms. The availability of substitute products has led governments to question the notion of natural monopolies and to apply anti-combines regulations more rigorously.

Governments are also seeking ways to protect individual rights to a greater extent than ever before. Legislation covering human rights, occupational health and safety, employment standards and employment equity have become more comprehensive in content and more extensive in scope. Organizations of every size and description must now comply with a myriad of regulations that once affected larger employers only.

- **Economic Cycles** — While economic ups and downs have been a feature of the business environment since the days of mercantilism, cycles have become shorter and more frequent. The dot.com explosion and subsequent bust of recent years demonstrates the incredible speed at which the economy can turn.

Organizations once considered immune to the fickleness of consumer taste are now experiencing a maturation of their product's life cycle. The boom of the fast food industry has, for example, reached its height and is now seeing its growth eroding because of increasing consumer health consciousness and demographic change.

- **The "Green" Movement** — Rachel Carson's pivotal work *Silent Spring* (1962) created a new paradigm of ecological responsibility. Organizations must be aware of their impact on the physical environment and take steps to minimize any adverse effects. This imperative is only partly driven by new laws designed to protect the environment. It is also driven by new consumer awareness and demands for ecologically friendly products.

The green movement has also expanded its scope by demanding that organizations be ethically and morally responsible. This means organizations should have a positive and proactive impact on the local community. It also means ensuring that the business does not inadvertently support practices that violate the human rights of people in parts of the world where environmental and health and safety laws are less stringent. For example, in contracting out work to third world manufacturers, local businesses must ensure that they are not supporting sweatshops that exploit individuals.

- **Technology** — The speed of technological change in recent years has been overwhelming. Everyone has been affected in some way. The computers that now control the engine system of a modern automobile have more computing power than existed in the entire world in the late 1950s. Surgeons can perform delicate operations remotely, thousands of miles away from the patient. Technology poses a threat and an opportunity for virtually every organization in existence today.

Technology demands paradigm shifts. The mere application of a new tool does not guarantee survival. Organizations must review current processes and re-engineer them to ensure that they are actually adding value.

The demands being made on organizations to transform themselves and become more flexible come at the same time that they are expected to exercise greater fiscal responsibility. Organizations today strive to be "lean and mean". Change initiatives often have to be launched in the context of diminishing resources. The importance of leadership in such times is paramount, as can be seen in the case of the high-tech sector.

The proliferation of high-tech firms, including dot.com enterprises, in recent years created an enormous demand for people with technological skills. Many young people enjoyed short-term success because of this high demand for their talents. Their success was short lived, however, because they did not have the general management skills or experience necessary to create organizational cultures that could thrive in chaotic times. Many fledgling high-tech organizations experienced high turnover and unprecedented growth making it difficult, if not impossible, to establish organizational longevity. This, in turn, created a frenzy of merger and acquisition activity that further heightened the risk of an economic downturn.

All of these changes have created a demand for experienced executives, who possess specialized skills as well as general business acumen. At the same time, organizations are more cost conscious and less willing to add significantly to their overhead. Luckily, there are some corresponding trends that are creating a ready supply of talented and experienced executives who are available to meet the near-term needs of organizations facing the challenges of change.

A growing pool of senior management talent has become available to organizations to meet urgent short-term needs. Downsizing in many large organizations has contributed to this pool. Large numbers of executives with proven, hands-on track records have chosen to take early retirement as a lifestyle choice. However, some of these professionals have also found a continued need to be challenged by work, without the commitment to organizational life that caused them to compromise life choices in the past. They welcome the independence of working on a contractual basis to help an organization with a specific and defined project. They gain the satisfaction of personal achievement without the rigours of organizational life that prevented them from enjoying other aspects of their lives in the past.

In addition to those who actively choose early retirement to pursue alternative work relationships, there is a fairly constant pool of executives who have been forced out of organizations during downturns. These executives want to remain in the workforce and are actively seeking new employment. They can, however, afford to be choosy. They do not simply want a job. They are looking, instead, for an engagement that will meet a variety of lifestyle needs. In the interim period, while seeking the best employment fit, they are happy to provide interim services to organizations with short-term needs.

Finally, there is a third group of executives who have simply chosen to work exclusively through short-term contractual arrangements. They value independence and variety to such an extent that their only choice of employment is to work as "free agents". They do not want full-time permanent employment. They seek control over their work lives to the highest degree possible. Essentially, these people are consultants and they usually prefer to work for consulting firms, as opposed to other types of organizations. They want complete independence to choose when they work, who they work for and what work they do.

The Canadian self-employed sector has doubled in the past 25 years and now represents 16% of the total employed workforce. If this trend continues, in the not so distant future, one in five Canadian workers will be self-employed. In the 1990s, individuals working alone constituted 90% of the growth in self-employment. This indicates that there is a tremendous boom in free agents — as opposed to the retail and craft proprietorships that made up the bulk of the self-employed sector in the past.

According to Statistics Canada, the fastest growing category in the self-employed sector during the last decade has been service to organizations. In addition, a recent Statistics Canada study found that the self-employed tend to be highly qualified, more experienced and better skilled than permanent employees in the workforce.

A corresponding trend is that while there was a 37% absolute decrease in the number of senior management positions between 1987 and 2000, in that same period, overall employment grew by over 20%. Thus, organizations that need experienced leadership are finding it difficult to recruit the right candidates. The use of interim managers and executives is fast becoming a common feature of today's organization in Canada. Statistics suggest that, in some areas, as many as 10% of managers are interim or contract executives.

Benefits/Expected Outcomes

Interim executives can tackle a number of different challenges facing today's organization, including:

- **Special Projects** — Organizations sometimes need to initiate special projects to address organizational deficiencies in areas like costs, productivity, process efficiency, and service or product quality. They may discover that they do not have the in-house resources or expertise needed to complete these critical business initiatives. These projects are, therefore, ideally suited to the interim executive.

An interim executive may be employed for a definite period of time, with specific objectives to accomplish. In addition, the executive-for-hire can pass on his or her expertise to internal personnel. This transfer of skill sets is decidedly one of the most important benefits of using experienced individuals on a short-term but dedicated basis.

- **Short-Term Replacements in Cases of Sudden Departure or Leaves of Absence** — Sudden losses can hit any organization. Executives are as susceptible as anyone else to sudden illnesses and the sudden death of an executive can be a crushing blow to any organization. The availability of a pool of experienced talent to draw from is a godsend for any organization dealing with the leadership void created by such a devastating loss.

The number of women occupying senior management positions continues to increase and the reality is that some of these women will take maternity leave at some point. As well, some men now take paternity leave to assist their spouses in the raising of children. Despite the changes in societal norms that have made these changes possible, organizations still fear the disruption such leaves of absence can cause. In the lower ranks of organizations, these gaps have long been filled by temporary staff. Secretarial and clerical temps have become a fixture of organizational life. To some extent, the emergence of the interim executive simply extends the advantages of temporary staffing arrangements to the higher levels of the organization.

The availability of interim executives also makes it possible for organizations to offer the benefit of sabbaticals to executives. There is a growing awareness that organizational life can place a great deal of stress on individuals. One outlet that can help individuals to cope is to provide periodic leaves of absence that allow people to pursue personal goals — whether those are to travel, engage in a hobby or to further advance their education. Finding a short-term replacement for the executive makes it possible to provide sabbaticals with minimal disruption to the organization.

- **Bridging a Transitional Gap** — The demands of modern life sometimes makes it difficult for organizations to manage transitions. For example, when a senior executive decides to retire, his or her internal replacement may already be identified, but may be unavailable in the short term. The replacement may have commitments to an internal project that must be completed or have family commitments that will delay a relocation. Organizations can afford to be patient and take the time to ensure that they have chosen the right replacement when they are able to bridge the gap between the outgoing executive's departure and the incoming executive's arrival with an interim executive.

Organizations sometimes find themselves facing a dilemma when an executive has ceased to make an effective contribution to the organization and, in the extreme, may have become dysfunctional in the exercise of his or her duties. The executive may have reached this point of incompetence as a result of changes in the business environment, like those discussed above, that they find themselves unable to adapt to or cope with. The dilemma arises when the organization believes it cannot fire the executive because it cannot afford to have that position vacant. The organization may believe that just having someone in the position is better than having no one at all. This logic is flawed — and, moreover, it can sometimes pose a real threat to the organization. Bringing in an interim executive to bridge the gap may be an ideal solution.

Impatience to fill organizational voids has led many companies to make poor recruiting choices that they come to regret in the long run. The practice of hiring interim executives helps the organization make better person-to-job matches. Recruiting for a senior executive who has all the right qualities, skills and experience requires a significant investment of time. Organizations can alleviate some of this pressure by employing interim executives to fill the gaps.

- **Leading an Acquisition, Merger, Divestiture or Resizing Initiative** — These are activities that require a specific skill set over a short time frame. In an acquisition there is a need to integrate opera-

tions. This demands a particular talent that may not be required in the long-term. It is a different talent than is required for the on-going management of the business.

In all these activities, the lead executive will face some tough choices, including the need to let people go and to hire new talent. This invariably creates a stigma around the executive that is difficult to erase. Few executives can make the transition from leading a major change initiative to "freezing" the organization in its new form and culture. There are essential differences between the skills and temperament of a transformational leader and a transactional manager. A successful strategy for some organizations has been to employ a "change agent" to effect the transition and then, once the change has been implemented, to bring in a new permanent leader.

- **Leading the Launch of a New Product or Service** — In recent years, a large number of high-tech firms and dot.com enterprises sprouted up from the seeds of many interesting concepts. These organizations typically had the technological expertise to make these concepts operational. But they also typically lacked the necessary skills and experience to market their products or services. In some cases, they had no insight into the infrastructure required to support the successful launch of such concepts.

The reasons behind these failures are varied. While some organizations simply did not recognize the need, others saw the need but decided they could not afford to increase their headcount. Still others may have had a vested interest in developing the requisite expertise internally. An advantage of using interim executives in these cases is that they not only provide the needed expertise immediately, they also create the opportunity for the skills transfer that can be so essential to the development of the organization's own people.

- **Re-engineering a Process or Practice** — Like any major organizational change, the re-engineering of a process or practice can have negative consequences for some individuals. The leader of any such re-engineering can be stigmatized for his or her role in the redesign of a process — particularly if it leads to job losses.

The facilitator of a re-engineering initiative will inevitably face significant resistance from employees who have a vested interest in the way things are currently done. In addition, the facilitator cannot afford to bring his or her own organizational baggage to the change initiative because it will further cloud things. An outsider can introduce a new perspective free from internal political concerns that might otherwise prejudice the outcome of the exercise.

- **Executive Mentoring** — Many times, organizations find themselves with senior executives who have significant skills and who have been identified as important to the firm's long-term future, but who are still deficient in some general skills that are also needed at the top of the organization. A family-owned enterprise, for example, may have identified the founder's children as his or her successors. These children have many advantages, including a predestined career path — usually on the fast track up the corporate ladder — and the benefit of a higher education. Very often, however, they lack the hands-on experiential knowledge that can only be acquired on the job. In order to give these children a more rounded skill set, the founder(s) might consider hiring a seasoned executive who can provide guidance to their kids.

Similarly, the founders of some high-tech firms have found that, despite early and rapid success (or maybe because of it), they do not have the breadth of experience needed to run a larger, more complex organization. Older knowledge workers can be brought in for the short-term to provide guidance and support. The special benefit of such mentoring is that advice will be given on specific real-life situations in real time and that the efficacy of the advice can be measured by the immediate impact of its application.

Interim consultants usually cost significantly less than consultants working for firms that need to cover overhead, partner fees and downtime, in addition to the base cost of the expertise actually employed. This is not to suggest that interim executives come cheap, but simply that they usually bill at a lower rate than their consulting brethren.

Companies that have been compelled to institute a hiring freeze can use interim executives to avoid the additional costs of benefits and other personnel costs (e.g. payroll taxes). Organizations that hire interim executives also avoid the severance costs that can be one of the most significant downsides to hiring a senior executive.

There are many advantages to using interim executives over using internal candidates. Interim executives can hit the ground running. They have proven track records and come equipped with the requisite skills to complete the task at hand. The interim executive is typically called upon to operate at a level in the organization below his or her highest level of experience. This allows him or her to be instantly effective. Moreover, the nature of interim assignments is only attractive to those who get personal satisfaction from hands-on project work.

Programming/Implementation
A. Project Descriptions

To ensure success of any project or limited term assignment, it is very important to define its scope and nature, including the deliverables. An interim executive will likely face some internal resistance to his or her efforts. By defining the assignment in concise terms, the organization can limit this resistance by informing everyone of the precise nature of the interim executive's mandate.

An essential element of the project description will be to identify a corporate sponsor. The sponsor should be a senior executive who will oversee the project or assignment. Naming a sponsor demonstrates the organization's commitment to the interim executive's success and helps keep all employees on side. The more senior and visible the sponsor is, the more likely the interim executive will meet with a high level of cooperation.

In some instances, it may be advisable to appoint someone internally who will help facilitate the efforts of the interim executive. This person will be responsible for evaluating the performance of the executive and conducting periodic reviews at identified project milestones. This person can be the sponsor or another senior staff member. Often, this person will be someone who has a vested interest in the positive outcome of the project or assignment. In certain circumstances, the senior Human Resources practitioner may be appropriate for the role. For instance, when there is a planned or unplanned departure of a senior manager, the Human Resources executive may want to collaborate with the interim executive in the hiring of a permanent replacement.

The criteria for hiring an interim executive should be no less rigorous than those used when hiring a permanent employee. Specifying what experience and qualifications are needed for the job is merely a minimum. To be successful, expected behaviours should also be defined. The senior Human Resources practitioner and project sponsor should interview potential candidates using behaviourally-based interviewing techniques.

Special care should be taken in identifying the personal traits of the interim candidate. A key to success in an interim assignment is the ability to hit the ground running. Short-term assignments and projects, by their very nature, demand the services of a hands-on specialist. Senior executives from large organizations are sometimes much more accustomed to playing the role of a strategic partner and, as a consequence, have been removed from the task of running specific projects. In deciding which executive-for-hire to engage, the organization should ensure that the candidate comes equipped with more than academic qualifications and advanced degrees. He or she should have a proven track record of successful project implementation. Successful candidates should be able to demonstrate that they have rolled up their sleeves and actively led a change initiative.

A specific start date and finish date should be given in the description of the project or assignment. Even in cases where the interim executive is filling a gap created by an unexpected absence of indeterminate length, the time frame should be stated. If it might end up being shorter or longer, that expectation can be included as a project parameter. Providing a "best guess", however, will help the interim executive determine his or her availability for the duration. It is important to determine from the outset that the executive has the time available to see the project through to its successful completion. If the executive has future commitments that might interfere with completing the assignment, then both parties will be aware of the possibility that the executive might not be available for the duration and they can make their decision accordingly.

Perhaps the most critical element of success is identifying the desired results, measurables and appropriate benchmarks. A clear outline of the project's objectives allows the organization to establish evaluation milestones. This, in turn, helps the project sponsor and/or overseer to identify potential problems early on and to take remedial steps, if necessary. An interim executive will most likely have a high profile in any organization and, as the saying goes, "failure is not an option". By identifying measurable goals and milestones, the organization can track progress and ensure that the right resources are directed to the project.

When a project's objective is a skill transfer to enhance internal competencies, the more clearly the organization can identify these competencies and how they are going to be measured, the more likely it will succeed. Timelines are particularly important, not only for the interim executive, but also for the employees who are expected to learn from the experience of working with him or her.

B. Sourcing Candidates

There are four principal sources of interim executives:

- **Word of Mouth:** Potential candidates may already be known to the organization. These might be former executives who worked for suppliers or customers and who are already familiar with the organization. In some cases, they might be former employees of the organization itself who have chosen to take an early retirement. Some care has to be taken to make sure these candidates do not have political baggage that could affect their performance.

  Interim executives are usually good at networking and, as a result, may already be known to senior executives within the organization or to members of the organization's board of directors. One caveat here is that a potential interim executive should not be identified before the project has been clearly defined or the need manifested.

- **Recruiting Agencies:** Some top-level recruiters, like the Caldwell Partners, have established specific practices to identify interim executives and match them to specific assignments. These practices offer the advantages of speed and confidence that the candidate has the qualifications and skills to meet the needs of the organization.

- **Consulting Firms:** Like their recruiting counterparts, some large consulting firms have created pools of potential interim candidates that can be ready to take on an assignment on short notice.

- **Associations of Soloists:** Some free agents have banded together in order to market their individual services more efficiently. This provides a distinct advantage to interim executives who might not have the right network to attract assignments or who lack the skill set or resources to market themselves on their own. These individuals are also able to share the expenses of some limited overhead, such as secretarial and administrative services.

Role of the Human Resources Practitioner

The traditional notion of "an organization" is increasingly being called into question. Organizations no longer need to develop large staffs in order to fulfil their needs, but can contract out a lot of work that was previously an integrated part of the enterprise. The concept of the "virtual" organization is emerging as a desired state. Virtual organizations are made up of networks of different organizations, each of which performs a specific, defined task.

The idea of the virtual organization poses an interesting challenge for the Human Resources practitioner. The practitioner's role could be completely redefined — how, for example, is an organizational culture created in a virtual organization?

One of the first challenges facing the practitioner is to identify opportunities for employing interim executives. The practitioner should be thinking ahead regarding the organization's structural design and identifying specific opportunities to bring in an interim executive, in lieu of replacing a permanent staff member or creating a new position. A proactive practitioner will develop the business case for using the interim executive. In many instances, the practitioner will begin this process by introducing the notion of interim executives to senior management, so that they can consider the possibilities for themselves.

Once the practitioner has convinced the organization that using interim executives is a sound alternative in general and has further persuaded senior management regarding a specific opportunity, the practitioner should help identify the scope of the project or assignment and define the deliverables. Working with the corporate sponsor, the practitioner will need to identify the skill set and behavioural traits necessary for successful completion of the interim assignment. The written project mandate will then be used to recruit the right individual and also as a tool for communicating the interim executive's role and objectives to the permanent staff.

The practitioner should assist the executive team members and others in understanding what the role of the interim executive will be. It is important to get a buy-in for the interim executive's mandate to prevent resistance, either overt or covert, that could ultimately hinder the success of the project. With the project sponsor, the Human Resources practitioner should play an important role as a champion for the assignment.

The Human Resources practitioner will normally be responsible for sourcing and recruiting the interim executive. Practitioners should assert their role in this regard. The potential exists for senior management to think of interim executives as being the same as outside consultants. They may not see the need for Human Resources involvement and may pursue executives-for-hire without consulting the Human Resources practitioner. This is less likely to happen when the practitioner has taken the initiative to introduce the concept of interim executives in the first place. However, if the organization does pursue interim executives without Human Resources involvement, it is absolutely essential that the practitioner asserts his or her role in the process.

Ensuring that the right person-to-job match is made is paramount. Even in short-term assignments, the proper recruiting protocols must be followed. Interim executives are involved in significant projects that, by their very nature, will have a profound impact on the organization's culture. Their behaviours and the results of their efforts must be in sync with the direction and vision of the organization.

The practitioner should promote his or her role as a project champion in a manifest way. He or she can begin by assuming the responsibility for helping the interim executive to assimilate quickly. He or she should orient the interim executive to the organization's culture in order to facilitate a quick transition. The interim executive should be warned about any potential political pitfalls and advised as to where they are likely to get the most support.

Since interim executives are often employed in "change management" projects, they are likely to face a number of Human Resources issues. The practitioner should become an early ally of the executives so that these issues can be confronted in a manner consistent with the organization's culture. Too often, Human Resources practitioners find themselves "outside the loop" on assignments led by interim executives and may also discover that the organization is taking a new direction without their involvement. Practitioners must not shy away from insisting that this does not happen.

As described elsewhere in this book, a central role of the Human Resources practitioner is to oversee the Performance Management Process (see "Role of the Human Resources Practitioner" in Performance Management Process at page 315). This extends to employing interim executives. The practitioner should participate in monitoring the progress of the assignment and provide tools for evaluating the project at predetermined milestones.

The Interim Contract

The Human Resources practitioner is normally responsible for preparing the contractual arrangements under which the interim executive will be employed. First, the contract should specify the term of engagement. The contract should not leave this open, but should stipulate exactly what the start and finish dates will be. If for any reason the contract might need to be extended, it can be specified in the contract that it is renewable by mutual agreement. Specifying a timeframe is important for the both the organization and the interim executive. For the organization, it is important to ensure that its expectations for the completion of the assignment are clear and that it is not liable at a future date for any severance costs. For the executive, a set completion date allows him or her to plan for future assignments or planned periods of "downtime". The contract should also contain an early-out clause that allows either party to sever the arrangement with an appropriate period of notice or compensation in lieu of.

The contract should also, of course, delineate the expected compensation. The amount of compensation will depend on the nature of the assignment. Some contracts will stipulate an hourly rate to be invoiced, while others will stipulate a *per diem* rate, plus expenses. The contract may also include bonuses

for achieving certain objectives or for completing the assignment on or ahead of schedule. Ordinarily, interim executives are not covered by the hiring organization's benefit plan, but some firms provide this benefit coverage in certain circumstances as an added incentive.

The contract might also outline the project requirements and evaluation milestones, either specifically or by inference. One way or another, it is important to identify the criteria that will be used to assess the executive's performance. In some instances, it may prove necessary to terminate the contract for cause. This will be problematic if the expectations were not clearly defined at the outset.

The contract should also include the appropriate confidentiality clauses. Care has to be taken to ensure that covenants contained in such clauses are not too restrictive. By their very nature, interim executives will be working for a variety of different organizations. Non-compete and non-solicitation clauses need to be carefully constructed so that they do not create a restraint of trade that will render them non-enforceable. Confidentiality clauses do not usually pose a problem. Nevertheless, the organization should be aware that the executive will benefit from acquiring new skills and experience that he or she will want to market to others. Restrictions should be limited to proprietary information or other specific information that could potentially harm the organization if disclosed.

Barriers to Success/Common Pitfalls

Using temporary staff has been a common feature in most organizations for a very long time, but using interim executives is a relatively new practice in North America. It is not yet commonplace and there is a danger that organizations will treat the use of interim executives lightly and not take enough care in selecting the right individuals for the job. Hiring interim executives based on their academic qualifications rather than their specific skills can sometimes create a misalignment between the individual's abilities and the project requirements, resulting in a poor performance.

Some organizations are prone to employing interim executives with whom they are already familiar. These individuals may be former employees, the former employees of suppliers or customers, or friends of a member of senior management. By chance, this could work out well. But the organization should not let familiarity lessen their diligence in seeking the right individual for the job.

In some extreme situations, senior executives have been known to employ friends or former associates on an interim basis to assist those friends in being productive between other engagements. This is a problematic practice. It not only reflects poorly on the executive's ethics but employees may well view it as an abuse of power. There will usually be little that employees can do about it, but the practice will erode their respect for the executive. As well, employing someone just for the sake of employing them — even in the short-term — will call into question the benefits of using interim executives.

A corollary to this is the failure to properly define the project requirements and deliverables. In order to be successful, the interim executive must have clear objectives. Some executives are able to overcome this deficiency quickly because they are naturally able to establish performance guidelines for themselves. This may even be desirable to a degree when the organization is struggling with an ambiguous problem. Regardless, to the greatest extent practicable, the organization should set out what it expects the executive to accomplish. It is never enough for the executive merely to occupy a role and maintain the *status quo*. The opportunity represented by using interim executives lies in their ability to bring improvements to the organization. These improvements might be better processes or enhanced internal competencies. In any event, both the executive and the organization will be the better for the experience if expectations for improvement are established from the beginning.

Another common pitfall is hiring an interim executive who has external commitments that prevent him or her from committing the necessary time and energy to the project. This can do serious damage to the completion of the project. Executives who are between engagements may be particularly prone to leaving interim assignments early if a permanent assignment becomes available elsewhere. Some soloists may be simultaneously involved in other projects.

This does not preclude the possibility of using "tweeners". It can be addressed by ensuring both parties are up front about their expectations and by ensuring the timeframes are clearly defined. Executives between engagements may be suitable if the circumstances of the assignment meet their particular needs. Short-term assignments, for instance, will create only minimal interference with their objective of finding full-time employment. As well, the attraction of healthy compensation and a retention bonus may be enough to prevent them from bolting prematurely. The "tweener" may also be particularly suitable if there is a chance that the assignment might be converted to a permanent position, or if other permanent positions within the organization are possible. While it should not be the norm, the opportunity to assess the performance of an executive on an interim basis, without any permanent obligations, can be a very powerful way for an organization to recruit senior staff.

Finally, another common problem is that employees may have difficulty taking direction from an interim executive because accountabilities or objectives are unclear. The active championing of the project by a senior manager and constant monitoring of project success are two ways of combating this problem. The Human Resources practitioner can minimize this problem by being an active participant and an ally to the interim executive.

INVOLVEMENT, EMPLOYEE

Definition/Background

Employee involvement is commonly defined as a range of processes designed to engage the support, understanding, and optimum contribution of all employees in an organization and their commitment to its objectives.

It is a wide-ranging term covering a number of processes and arrangements developed between employers and employees. Frequently, the term is used interchangeably with employee participation, but a distinction between the two is possible. Participation implies involvement in management decision making, whereas employee involvement practices rarely affect organizational decision making.

In brief, employee involvement encompasses those processes and arrangements whereby employees, individually or collectively (whether in unionized or non-union organizations), can be involved in:

— reviewing their contribution to everyday work activities (e.g., through performance management and quality assessment);

— contributing to team briefings and discussions on the ways in which work is performed and could be improved;

— being informed about the economic factors and labour and product market issues affecting their work;

— influencing management's operational decisions about production or service delivery; and

— influencing conditions of employment (e.g., safety).

Employee Involvement from the Employer's Point of View

Employers' purposes in encouraging greater employee involvement are perhaps best captured by the following:

1. To generate commitment from all employees to the success of the organization.

2. To enable the organization to better meet the needs of its customers and adapt to changing market requirements and hence, to maximize its

future prospects and the prospects of those who work in it.

3. To help the organization to improve performance and productivity and adopt new methods of working to match new technology, drawing on the resources of knowledge and practical skills of all its employees.

4. To improve the satisfaction employees get from their work.

5. To provide all employees with the opportunity to influence and be involved in decisions that are likely to affect their interests.

6. To improve decision making processes and to gain greater buy-in to decisions by giving employees input into those decisions that affect the way their work is performed.

Employee Involvement from a Union's Point of View

Traditionally, trade unions have seen the establishment of the right of recognition for collective bargaining as their primary objective. Mechanisms of employee involvement have invariably been viewed as suspect because any power sharing over decisions was generally absent. Moreover, employee involvement initiatives have been viewed by unions as attempts to co-opt the interests of employees and bypass the union. Some unions still question whether or not such initiatives are merely thinly veiled attempts to negotiate directly with employees. In recent years, however, the trade union acceptance of employee involvement is beginning to change perceptibly.

Employee Involvement from an Employee's Point of View

It is likely that most employees (unionized or not) would share the following key purposes of employee involvement:

1. To have a voice in management decisions that affect employee terms and conditions of employment.

2. To ensure proper and equitable rewards for work performed.

3. To ensure proper and fair conditions of employment based on equal treatment.

4. To ensure a safe working environment.

5. To contribute to operational problem-solving.

6. To establish and maintain job security.

7. To help manage workplace disagreements.

It is clear, given these objectives, that employees can achieve greater involvement through unionization. One clear objective, and perhaps the most important one, for employees to turn to a union is to provide them with a voice into these matters. A union thus can be seen as a vehicle for increasing employee involvement. In non-union settings, employee involvement initiatives may be part of a strategy to remain union free.

Notwithstanding, the focus of this publication is on Human Resources practices and not on labour relations. Therefore, we will restrict the discussion for the most part to non-union workplaces.

Public Policy and Employee Involvement

Employers must consult with employees about specific areas of managerial decision making regarding:

— health and safety;

— collective redundancies/downsizing; and

— pay and employment equity.

Health and Safety

Safety legislation requires employee involvement in a number of different ways. The most important statutory requirement is for the establishment of joint health and safety committees. At least half the representatives on the committee must be selected from among employees who do not exercise managerial functions. Where there is a trade union, the selection of the worker representatives is made by the union.

The statutes empower joint health and safety committees to:

(a) identify workplace hazards;

(b) make recommendations for the improvement of health and safety of employees;

(c) recommend the establishment, maintenance and monitoring of programs, measures and procedures respecting the health and safety of employees;

(d) obtain information from the employer regarding potential dangers inherent in materials, processes or equipment used in the workplace;

(e) obtain any reports or test results conducted on equipment or materials for the purpose of occupational health and safety; and

(f) be consulted on any matters related to the health and safety of employees.

Members of the committee are also required to be involved in specific activities relating to the promotion and maintenance of a healthy and safe workplace. Employee representatives from the committee need to be involved in regular workplace inspections, accident investigations and safety audits. Furthermore, if an employee has refused to perform work that he or she believes poses a potential danger to that individual's health and safety, he or she has the right to have an employee representative participate in any investigation into the matter.

Collective Redundancies

Employment standards legislation in many Canadian jurisdictions requires larger employers that are planning the closure or partial closure of a business or operation to participate in the establishment and work of a committee for the purposes of facilitating the reestablishment of displaced employees in employment. The employer is required to fund the activities of such a committee.

These committees often actively participate in helping individual employees in their job searches. They will arrange for résumé workshops, and will serve as contacts for potential employers that may have openings. They also may recommend employment alternatives such as retraining, or other educational initiatives to help relocate displaced employees.

Pay and Employment Equity

Equity legislation, as it can profoundly impact on the terms and conditions of employment for a significant portion of the workforce, contains provisions for consultation with the affected workers.

Where there is a union, the employer is required by statute to negotiate in good faith and endeavour to agree upon the establishment of a plan. Under pay equity legislation, for example, the parties should endeavour to agree on the comparison method that will be used. Under employment equity schemes, the methods for gathering information, as well as the affirmative action plan should be negotiated.

Where there is no union representation, the employer is often required to post any plans with sufficient time before their implementation to allow employees an opportunity to provide meaningful input.

In general, these legislative schemes are intended to achieve the following objectives with respect to employee involvement:

1. to ensure that due weight is given by employers to employees' interests;

2. to promote a more harmonious way of dealing with potentially conflicting employment issues;

3. to recognize (in redundancies) accrued employee benefits and seniority rights through any organizational changes (and with respect to severance or other relocation provisions);

4. to promote a safe and healthy working environment;

5. to ensure greater sharing of information about the organization; and

6. to promote greater understanding by employees of the economic factors affecting the organization for which they work.

Benefits/Expected Outcomes

Assessing Benefits

An employer can assess the benefits of employee involvement by looking for improvements in certain indicators. These will measure:

A. Economically Related and Operational Factors

Improvements include:

— reduction in customer complaints;

— increased productivity;

— introduction of flexible working practices;

— acceptable level of unit labour costs achieved;

— evidence of employee skill development;

— improved product quality;

— greater customer satisfaction with product or service delivery;

— greater over-all cost-effectiveness;

— use of workforce knowledge and experience;

— effective management of change;

— more effective operational problem-solving; and

— continuous improvement, both operationally and in workforce competence.

B. Employee Relations

Improvements include:

— reduction in grievances;

— reduction in absenteeism;

— improved safety performance;

— relatively harmonious workplace changes;

— workforce prepared to contribute effectively towards organizational objectives;

— greater commitment to the organization and its objectives;

— greater trust in the employer/employee relationship;

— workforce feels that its contribution is valued;

— greater job satisfaction;

— personal development of employees;

— better recruitment and retention of labour;

— better educated and informed workforce regarding business and operational issues; and

— better management of conflicts.

Directors and Senior Managers

This group is central to any effective scheme of employee involvement within an organization. They are responsible for determining the relevance of any particular scheme to the achievement of the organization's objectives. They will define the formal responsibilities in the scheme. Their participation or lack thereof signals the degree of senior management commitment to the process.

When sufficiently committed, the management group will ensure the provision of sufficient resources to make employment involvement credible and effective. This group must devise an appropriate monitoring system to audit effectiveness. They will also determine the specific steps to be taken to correct any deficiencies identified by such audits.

The management group is also the most significant barrier to effective implementation of any employee involvement scheme. Increased employee participation may represent substantial erosion of the manager's power and status. In extreme cases, the scheme may represent a direct threat to the continued employment of the manager.

In order to overcome these barriers, senior management needs to invest time and resources in planning the employee involvement initiatives. They should adopt an inclusive approach (consulting widely on proposed arrangements) and identify potential key constraints and define the necessary steps to overcome them.

Line Managers

Operationally, the role of line managers is critical. Line managers can give credibility or not to any employee involvement arrangements through the quality of their contribution. A number of factors will influence the effectiveness of their role such as:

— the clarity of both their role and their responsibilities;

— the degree of training and development received;

— the availability of sources of advice as required;

— their commitment to the purposes of the scheme;

— the quality of working relationship with other participants;

— the level of trust;

— whether the scheme has any effective outcome (Is a management decision influenced? Is action to be taken?); and

— whether there is proper feedback on employee inputs.

Employees

Employee involvement arrangements can affect employees in two broad ways, that is, directly as employees and indirectly through their representa-

tives. Most survey evidence suggests that the critical issue is clearly credibility. As indicated above, this is conditioned by the contribution of the line manager(s). It is determined also by the perception employees (or their representatives) have of their role in the process.

This perception is affected by a number of factors such as:

— whether or not employees feel able to articulate issues and make a positive contribution;

— whether employees have received any appropriate training;

— whether employees have easy and relevant sources of advice;

— whether employees' contributions are valued;

— whether there are clear outcomes to the process.

Trade Unions

The role of trade unions in such schemes may encompass the following:

1. To provide skill development and other training for employee representatives.

2. To provide a source of advice on:

    (a) any legal issues;

    (b) the effect of employee involvement issues on collective bargaining and on union policy.

Programming/Implementation

Given the wide range of initiatives that can be considered as "employee involvement", the organization needs to decide the level of participation that it wants from its employees and the format in which this involvement will take place. Factors such as whether or not the workforce is organized by a union, the size of the workforce, the level of sophistication of the organization and the skills of facilitators and managers will dictate the appropriate forums for employee involvement. The following provides a general overview of the variety of considerations the organization should take into account when establishing an employee involvement regimen.

Direct Participation

This is concerned with face-to-face contact between managers and their employees. Usually, it concerns day-to-day operational issues and the forums commonly used are town hall meetings and team briefings. The processes are information giving, discussion and consultation.

Indirect Participation

This involves the election of (union or non-union) representatives of the workforce. The responsibility is placed on the representatives to reflect workforce opinion and to report back from discussions. Joint health and safety committees are a prime example of this. In large workplaces where direct participation may be more difficult, some employers establish communications committees. The members of these committees are empowered to disseminate information about the organization to their fellow employees.

Again the processes used may be information giving, discussion and consultation. Recognizing that effective communication must be two-way, some employers have dubbed their communications committees as "rumour committees". The employee representatives are mandated to bring any rumours they hear about the organization to committee meetings so that the management group can address them and ensure employees are well informed and not misled by disinformation.

Financial Participation

This is concerned with economic involvement by employees — linking the individual's remuneration to the organization's economic performance. This may be in the form of immediate rewards such as annual profit-sharing bonuses or may be deferred. Share ownership is a method growing in popularity among organizations in the high-tech sectors. Share options, once a perk reserved for senior management, are becoming a greater part of the average employee's total compensation. Cisco Systems now offers options to all its employees including summer students.

Equity participation gets employees focused on the organization's objectives and provides employees with a longer-term perspective on their organization's performance. They also gain a sense of contribution and will concern themselves more directly with performance issues. An alternative to options is the employee share ownership plan that offers shares at discounted prices through payroll deductions. The employee avoids brokers' fees and often can use proceeds from a deferred profit-sharing scheme towards share purchases.

Profit-sharing plans have been criticized because employees often have trouble linking their individual effort to the profits (or lack thereof) of the organization. In companies whose products are commodity priced, employees have little influence on whether or not the organization will be profitable. They can, however, affect expense and operating efficiencies that will optimize profitability or minimize losses.

An alternative to profit-sharing is a scheme known as gain-sharing. This generally is a plan where the employees share in a portion of gains realized through their direct efforts. The company tracks key result areas such as productivity, unit labour costs, safety and attendance, and monitors any improvements in performance. The dollar savings realized through the improvements are calculated and a proportion of those savings is paid out to the employees (regardless of whether or not the organization is showing a profit).

Gain-sharing is used widely as a complementary reward system to any team based employee involvement initiative. Organizations should plan and develop these schemes carefully and avoid making them too complex or too difficult to achieve.

Organizations will not only have to decide on the degree of employee involvement that will fit into its culture but also the types of decisions with which the organization will feel comfortable having employees involved.

Operational Decisions

Employee participation on operational issues arises primarily in the arena of problem-solving. Quality circles were once in vogue as the principal means of having employees participate in operational decision making. These have now fallen out of fashion and have been replaced by forums derived from Total Quality Management. These include Corrective Action Teams, Quality Work Groups or Continuous Improvement Teams (and other equivalent mechanisms). Through these, employees are engaged in problem-solving discussions to identify improvements to production processes, product quality or service delivery.

Health and Safety

In most jurisdictions in Canada, employers are required to form joint health and safety committees. These committees are empowered to regularly monitor the health and safety initiatives undertaken by the organization and to make specific recommendations to improve on those initiatives. They are also given some specific responsibilities for auditing safety programming, regularly inspecting the workplace, identifying potential hazards and requiring work to stop if it poses an imminent danger to workers.

Terms and Conditions of Employment

In unionized workplaces, the union is recognized as the sole bargaining agent on behalf of the employees it represents. To a significant extent, this is simply a formal means of achieving employee involvement through indirect representation. Conflicts of interest are resolved through negotiation, concessions and agreement by the parties. It is acknowledged by both employers and trade unions as a "power-sharing" process. Unions seek in their negotiating the mandate to extend the scope of collective bargaining to advance the level of employee participation. They often insist that such things as the introduction of technological change, plant closures, determination of working practices and work allocation be subject to provisions in the collective agreement. In this way, these issues are subject to negotiations. However, employers take the view that if these issues are to be subject to any discussion, then it is only through consultative committees.

There are many employers and unions that are trying to evolve their relationships into a more collaborative partnership. This may involve mutual interest bargaining approaches or continuous bargaining concepts. These approaches are beyond the scope of this publication, however, they demonstrate the point that unionization is, in itself, a form of employee involvement.

In non-union settings, a few employers have allowed employees either directly or indirectly through elected or appointed representatives to have a voice in changing the terms and conditions of employment (including wages and benefits). These initiatives demand a significant paradigm shift for management. There has to be a high degree of trust in the level of maturity of the affected employees. Moreover, employers must be careful as to how these consultations take place. They are potentially exposed to charges of having an employer-controlled employee association that contravenes most labour legislation in Canada. Nevertheless, where employers have ventured into such initiatives, they are often surprised at the commitment and sophistication employees bring to the process.

Strategic Policy Making

This level of involvement is virtually unknown in North America. A few examples can be cited but they are often specific to individuals (Owen Bieber's inclusion on the Chrysler Board of Directors) or to isolated examples of employee controlled operations.

One of the most well developed arrangements of involvement at the strategic level is co-determination of employee relations in the German system. An aspect of this is the election of worker directors to supervisory boards (the equivalent of a Board of Directors) to sit alongside shareholder representatives and agree to various strategic decisions.

Consultation

As a process, consultation is theoretically distinct from negotiation in a number of respects:

1. The purpose of negotiation is to reach agreement, through concessions, on claims and other issues in dispute between employers and their employees' representatives (usually union officials). Normally, it is concerned with terms and conditions of employment.

2. The purpose of consultation is to exchange information and views about particular workplace issues. The employer invariably reserves decision making authority — although the decision may be modified in the light of views expressed by the employees or their representatives.

The consultation mechanism can be a substitute for union representation. Some employers deliberately use these mechanisms as part of an overall strategy to remain "union-free". Consultative committees recognize that collective (as well as individual) interests exist in the workplace and may have to be accommodated, particularly if a trade union recognition claim is to be avoided. Largely, such committees will provide information — "hard" (about business issues) and "soft" (about welfare and social issues). They are likely to be management driven and designed to reinforce acceptance of management views on workplace issues.

Employers may also involve employees in a consultative process in order to provide them with the knowledge and skills to understand the economic context in which the organization operates. High-level information is discussed, including financial results, operation costs and competitive comparisons. This provides committee members with an understanding of the problems the organization faces and gives them an understanding of why management has to adopt certain inescapable solutions.

This approach to consultation is clearly intended to co-opt the interests of employees. It is an aggressive approach to gain employee commitment to the organization's vision and objectives. This approach can be used either in unionized or non-union settings. Unions find this approach somewhat suspect and believe it is designed as:

— a more economically knowledgeable workforce that acts as a restraint on militant trade unionism;

— a weakening of the link between trade union members and their shop steward representatives.

Consultation may also be integrated into the representative system of employee relations within the organization as an adjunct to collective bargaining. Sub-committees are formed to discuss specific workplace issues. This is commonly found in negotiations within multiple business units. A master agreement may be negotiated at the main table while local issues are deferred to the sub-committees.

Consultation can assist the negotiating process by:

— exploring the economic and market context of bargaining;

— providing a preliminary to specific bargaining issues; and

— solving specific employee relations problems that are normally not subject to bargaining.

It is essentially a means of introducing a more collaborative problem-solving methodology that explores mutual interests.

Unfortunately, some employers marginalize the consultation process. Very little "hard" information is discussed, and there is unlikely to be any effective decision making at committee meetings. It is argued that such committees may, however, have value in three respects:

— as symbolic evidence of management's commitment to the workforce;

— as a channel for outlining management thinking; and

— as a cynical approach to keep workforce representatives busy on trivial issues.

In considering the process of consultation and its possible introduction into an organization, a number of factors have to be reviewed.

— Which issues are to be subject to consultation? Are these concerned with strategic or day-to-day operational matters? Why is consultation being proposed about these issues?

— Is it proposed to consult on a continuing basis about the issues concerned or is the consultation to deal with a one-off, *ad hoc* situation? If it is a continuing arrangement, how frequent will the meeting be?

— How will the mechanisms affect existing managerial/supervisor authority and structures? How does the deployment of the workforce affect the appropriateness of particular mechanism(s) chosen?

— How might the quality of employee relations condition responses to any new consultation initiative? How does the new arrangement relate to other employee relations arrangements? If unionized, what is likely to be the response of union representatives?

— What are the most appropriate mechanisms for consultation (e.g., departmental consultative committee, company-wide council, *ad hoc* working party, employee opinion survey)?

— Is it appropriate for employees to be consulted directly or indirectly through representatives? Who are the most appropriate representatives for management and the workforce?

At the centre of any consideration of employee participation, as at the heart of the employment relationship, is the issue of power. Most forms of employee participation barely shift the balance of economic power between most employees and their employers. However, some can, in a limited way, have an effect on certain managerial decisions.

How Employee Involvement Affects the Organizational Structure

There are two broad ways in which the development of employee involvement can impact on organizational structures. These are team structure and the devolution of management decision making.

Team Structure

Some organizations with well-developed employee involvement seek ways of integrating the schemes into new organizational forms through a reconstitution of managerial, supervisory and workforce responsibilities. The recent wave of interest in workplace teams is based on the belief that devolving decision making and empowering team members increases skill flexibility, adaptability, quality and problem-solving. It has consequential economic effects in terms of unit labour costs. Furthermore, it can have beneficial effects on motivation and job satisfaction.

The implications of workplace teams are many. In terms of organizational structure, the following may need to be considered:

— the caliber of team leaders;

— the role of team leaders in relation to supervisors and middle managers;

— the team's autonomy and decision making authority;

— the devolution of control over the workforce to the team;

— the effectiveness of the team's contribution to problem-solving and quality assurance; and

— the commitment to individual appraisal and development.

Devolution of Management Decision Making

The devolution of decision making is defined as the transference of decision making power and responsibility from managers to employees. It is a formal process of delegating responsibility over certain given aspects of work to those who are most directly involved in the work. It is often referred to as employee empowerment.

There are several factors promoting the devolution of management decision making within organizations. These are:

— financial devolution and the growth of profit centres;

— the development of Total Quality Management systems at the operational level;

— a redefinition of line management's contribution to the management of human resources; and

— the growth of employee involvement initiatives.

There are clear inter-relationships between these factors. However, the extent to which there is devolution on all fronts is dependent on the coherence of management policy. It is clear, however, that whatever degree of progress is made, a number of structural problems can arise in respect of line management.

This arises from a failure to define sufficiently clearly the responsibilities and authority of middle managers. It can occur where workplace teams are introduced and the role of the supervisor is not clearly defined. In particular, middle managers can find themselves in two structures. While their position in the hierarchy allocates responsibility for overseeing the work teams, they may be denied authority over them in decision making.

In some cases, middle managers and supervisors may not universally welcome the introduction of employee involvement. Some, particularly in manufacturing, perceive it as "soft management".

For line managers, the acquisition of defined responsibilities for managing people has highlighted a number of issues. In particular:

— their competence to participate in the processes (e.g., consultation, appraisal, grievance handling, problem-solving);

— the availability and use of sources of information and advice; and

— the development of monitoring and review systems on policy implementation.

Relationships and authority both need clear definition and continual review by senior management. If middle managers are not provided with the required resources, are not sufficiently trained, or are not evaluated on employee involvement in terms of performance appraisal, then it is difficult for them to see employee involvement as being of major importance.

Role of the Human Resources Practitioner

Employee involvement potentially affects the role of the Human Resources practitioner in two ways. The practitioner needs to provide appropriate support services for line managers and to initiate monitoring reports for directors and senior management.

The appropriate support services comprise of:

— advice on processes (What are the particular procedural arrangements that exist within the organization?);

— advice on legal requirements (e.g., on redundancy consultation);

— skill development (To what extent do line managers need training in, for example, communication skills, chairing meetings?);

— updating information (What do managers need to know?); and

— monitoring reports to directors.

Some organizations may choose to audit employee involvement initiatives through regular or occasional surveys of employee opinion (see also Opinion Surveys at page 277 *et seq.*). These are likely to be expensive unless the practitioner gains the credibility to undertake these surveys internally. Focus groups and Town Hall meetings are other forums that can be initiated internally to receive feedback on the efficacy of employment involvement initiatives. They are also a means of increasing employee participation in themselves. The systematic use of management feedback and reporting, if properly organized and collated, can provide a useful monitoring arrangement.

The Human Resources practitioner may also be the chief cheerleader for all employee involvement initiatives. The nature of the employee involvement scheme adopted by the organization will be dictated by the culture the organization hopes to create and maintain. Employee involvement may well represent a strategic cornerstone for the Human Resources practitioner in shaping how the organization performs and how it uses human resources as strategic assets.

Barriers to Success/Common Pitfalls

Organizations can present a range of barriers to the effective implementation of employee involvement initiatives. These can arise from existing structures or current policies and practices.

Paramount to the success of any employee involvement initiative is the extent to which the culture of the organization will facilitate employee involvement. In a "power" culture where authority is highly centralized and decision making is reserved for a handful of senior employees, employee involvement can only be superficial at best. The culture has to be characterized by open and honest communications, devoid of political overtones, and receptive to new ideas. The failure of many "major" employee involvement efforts has largely been attributable to the incompatibility of the initiatives with the organization's climate. In some instances, the initiators have recognized this and employee involvement has become part of a wider change management effort.

Without the commitment of line management and supervisors, employee involvement initiatives will surely fail. This group, however, is the most likely to resist any attempts to increase employee involvement. They perceive these initiatives as a threat to their job security and status. With employee involvement, the role of the supervisor changes from one of directing the workforce to one of coaching and facilitating. Often the initiative is part of a larger effort to flatten the organizational hierarchy that poses a real and obvious threat to the line manager.

Yet, without the support of these key people, the efforts will fail. They occupy critical roles in training and communicating to employees how the changes affect them. They also have the best vantage point with respect to current operational practices and how effective changes are likely to be.

Good supervisors are, by the nature of their competencies, significant influences on the opinions of their subordinates. If they are not convinced that the changes are worthwhile and welcomed, the workforce will also resist the changes. A significant investment in time and training has to be made in the line managers to ensure they have bought into the initiatives, understand their roles in the new culture, and have the new skills required in those roles.

If the current style of management as it relates to dealing with employees is autocratic and power based, the employee involvement initiative will not succeed. There are some recent views that suggest organizations with strong autocratic, results oriented managers should review their operational results before embarking on a change to increased employee involvement. While employee involvement initiatives, when they are successful, benefit the organizations that embark on them, there seems to be a belief that these organizations had weak cultures beforehand. The employee involvement initiative was a means to instill organizational objectives, values and structure that had not previously been strong.

It seems equally valid that an organization with a strong power culture should have positive economic results. The secret is not in the particular style *per se* but rather in the strength of execution.

There must be a level of trust between employees and their managers for any employee involvement initiative to get off the ground. Employees need to feel that they can openly communicate and, at times, criticize, before they will be willing to commit to a high level of participation. Unfortunately, in a lot of organizational contexts, the initiative itself is viewed with distrust. There is a significant body of folklore around employee involvement initiatives and other change management strategies that they are merely vehicles for selling a radical downsizing of the organization to an unsuspecting workforce. The effort has to be seen as a sincere desire on the part of management to solicit the opinions of all employees and all employees have to feel that they will be protected through the process.

Sophisticated organizations will examine the appropriateness of the policies and mechanisms of employee involvement for the current operational arrangements of the organization. This entails a complex analysis of various social and technical systems within the operation in order to gain an understanding for how they interrelate. This is called socio-technical systems analysis.

Unfortunately, this approach leaves most employees and managers a little bewildered. It is complex, and requires a significant amount of effort and resources to get results. The unfortunate part of socio-technical systems analysis is that it tends to be a tool for consultants who benefit from its complexities. In reality, the approach can be simplified.

Essentially, the organization simply needs to understand how the various jobs people perform fit into the work process. If the process is modified physically or in any other significant way, the jobs performed will also likely have to be modified in order to remain compatible.

Common Mistakes and Pitfalls

1. Failure to ensure senior management commitment.

2. Failure of senior management to deal with any resistance by middle and junior managers and supervisors.

3. Failure to define the purpose of the arrangements.

4. Failure to think about the purpose of the arrangements in the context of existing employee relations and management style.

5. Expectation that arrangements can be introduced on an *ad hoc* basis as a quick fix to an immediate problem.

6. Adopting an arrangement because it is currently in favour generally.

7. Failure to recognize that employee involvement is not just about policies and procedures but it is also about management attitudes and styles.

8. Failure to monitor implementation.

9. Failure to act on monitoring reports.

10. Failure to commit resources to information briefs, and training and development.

11. Assuming that all the benefits of employee involvement can be quantified.

LEARNING ORGANIZATION

Definition/Background

There are many definitions of a "learning organization", but they generally involve variations around two main themes. The first is the importance of learning itself — being continually fostered at all levels in an organization and being acknowledged as a significant component of sustained success. The second is to do with the transfer of learning around an organization.

People and organizations have learning opportunities every day, both formal and informal. Learning organizations are distinguished by deliberately and systematically managing the learning available, rather than benefiting accidentally or haphazardly from it. Thus, it is not so much an absolute state, but a way of thinking and operating that permeates the organization. It requires a learning culture, with appropriate systems and processes, that encourages and supports learning and sees it in direct relation to the organizational goals and measures of success.

The ultimate purpose of pursuing a learning organization culture is to help the organization in:

— being flexible and adaptable to change;

— achieving continuous improvement;

— satisfying all the stakeholders in the enterprise;

— reducing costs and overlap of activity; and

— increasing its "intellectual capital".

It becomes an organization that listens to its stakeholders (customers, employees, shareholders, the public at large) and responds accordingly. It is one that encourages innovation and experimentation. Everyone in the organization is affected by something that is essentially cultural. However, different groups will be impacted in specific ways, and have a special part to play in a learning organization culture.

Top Management

It is the specific role of top management to set the values and direction of an organization. Top management also significantly influences the culture by the emphasis it puts on factors of organizational success. For example, if the main concern is in the sales and profit figures, review processes and financial systems will dominate the culture.

To realize a learning organization culture, members of top management need to:

— incorporate in the stated values of the organization one that relates to continuous learning;

— have a specific strategy of promoting learning at all levels and of sharing it across the organization as a whole;

— devote time, money and resources to learning and knowledge management activities;

— allow mistakes to happen without blame but encourage learning from them;

— indicate clearly that the accumulated knowledge and experience of the organization is a valuable asset to be made available to all, and sanction those who do not use it; and

— be visible learners themselves.

"The Training Department"

The unit(s) whose function is concerned with training and development has a major role to play. It may have a focus on training that is essentially teacher-led, rather than learner-led. The skills of individuals may be more aligned to training.

However, a learning organization culture requires them to be:

— catalysts and champions of a learning culture;

— able to see training as but one means of achieving a learning need;

— consultants to business units in understanding a business problem and its implications for learning;

— experts in the definition of learning needs and in the choice of learning options;

— able to construct programs, events and assignments that meet the learning needs of individuals or teams; and

— able to relate learning to creating value and improved business results.

Line Managers

The traditional, hierarchical approach to management has been to see managers as having a central role in the people development process, regardless of their capability or interest in it. Thus, it has been a key responsibility to monitor and review performance, to summarize it and to suggest development actions. Individuals have usually been passive participants in this process, and from time to time may have felt aggrieved that, for example, no appraisal was carried out or the promised training never materialized. In a learning organization culture, individuals take a greater responsibility for their own learning and have a personal interest in the effectiveness of these processes.

However, although the manager's role changes, it is still vitally important. This role would be:

— helping individuals in his or her team to develop their own learning plans;

— contracting with each individual for the time and money needed to implement the plan;

— coaching and role modelling in order to achieve learning;

— encouraging cross-learning between those who work for him or her; and

— setting up work teams and assignments that will achieve the needed results and provide appropriate learning opportunities.

Employees

The great strength of the learning organization is that it reaches every individual and focuses, *inter alia*, on the realization of his or her full capability. It requires people to value continuous learning, to understand how they personally best learn, to be skilled in defining learning needs and to take ownership for their fulfilment. This does not come naturally to many people.

An "individual learning plan" or "personal development plan" should be based on needs identified from:

— the evaluation of performance in the job through appraisal;

— the development of the business and the particular role held by the individual;

— the person's career development plan; and

— any other personal development needs.

Ideally, every individual should be capable of defining these needs, choosing appropriate solutions and managing their completion. In practice, some assistance will be needed from the person's manager or from another professional source. Individuals also need to take responsibility for giving and sharing learning, as well as being concerned for themselves.

Benefits/Expected Outcomes

The intellectual link between the effective harnessing of learning and improved performance is not difficult to make. However, we can be more precise with the benefits that potentially result from an organization well advanced in the learning organization culture. These are as follows:

1. It will be seen as a listening organization and as a consequence characterized by being nimble, adaptable and flexible. It is responsive to its markets and to changes in its environment, and will attain a reputation as a market leader in thinking.

2. It will be an organization that places a high premium on the skills of its people, which are personally concerned about being up to date and able to meet the business challenges.

3. It will be an organization that has eliminated cost overlaps and waste through effective harnessing of all the learning available.

4. The organization will be a good environment in which to work, where experimentation is valued and blame for mistakes unacceptable.

Programming/Implementation

Creating a Learning Organization Culture

Most proponents of the learning organization would be the first to say that it is not, in itself, an innovative concept. It is essentially about learning and change, and such a link has been self-evident for centuries. What is new, however, is the recognition of the need to manage learning and its flow systematically and deliberately. Professor Chris Argyris postulated his theory of single and double loop learning in 1976, referring to the way organizations learn and the difficulty of questioning deeply held assumptions.

In the same period in the United Kingdom, Reg Revans promoted "action learning" (learning from real experiences), and is credited with a simple formula that encapsulates the essence of the learning organization: $L \geq C$. This says that, in order to survive, the rate of learning (L) must be greater than or equal to the rate of change (C) to which an entity is subject.

The term itself gained public attention in the United Kingdom through a work by Bob Garratt (*The Learning Organization*, Director Books, 1987), and this was followed by *The Learning Company* (McGraw-Hill, Maidenhead, 1988) by Burgoyne, Boydell and Pedler. However, it was Peter Senge in 1990 in the United States who generated worldwide interest with his book *The Fifth Discipline* (Doubleday, New York, 1990). This book is actually about systems thinking, but was subtitled "The Art and Practice of the Learning Organization".

Senge refers to five "disciplines" that should interact together for organizations. These are:

1. personal mastery (continuous learning by the individual);

2. mental models (reviewing the way in which we view the world);

3. building a shared vision (pulling people towards a shared goal);

4. team-learning (the benefits of doing things together); and

5. systems thinking (seeing the relationships between all components of an organization) — the "fifth discipline".

There have been a large number of definitions of the learning organization put forward by various authors, but it is best summarized as a way of organizational operation that:

— maximizes the learning of each of its members, individually and collectively;

— manages the effective flow of learning across its various boundaries; and

— converts the learning into appropriate behavioural change as needed.

The clear message here is the deliberate management of learning with the aim of business improvement, and this requires sets of values, systems and processes that together comprise a learning organization culture. A good deal of practical information has been written about maximizing learning. This is not just about "knowledge" (facts and information). It concerns "skills" (what people can do and to what level of competence); "attitudes" (what guides people as important); "experience" (the lessons that have been learned); and, lastly, the "who's who" of people who assist in specific areas.

In order for organizations to be more productive at the effective flow of learning, a new discipline is emerging, namely that of "knowledge management" or "knowledge architecture" (although it embraces all the areas of learning described above). This is not just an issue for information technology specialists, but is about the interaction between people and information technology. In today's complex environments with abundant information availability, information technology has to be harnessed to enable disciplined and filtered access to data in a friendly and helpful way. Developing a learning culture is a powerful way to do just that.

A number of models have been derived to help put practical meaning to the concept of the learning organization. It, for many, remains somewhat of an abstract concept with no practical application. This, unfortunately, is a narrow view. Certainly, organizations have to reach a high level of sophistication before they can appreciate the benefits of creating a learning culture.

From a practical perspective, the organization can do a number of things to encourage the development of a learning culture without necessitating a deliberate approach. In fact, taking a deliberate approach may prove to be too "esoteric" for most line managers, and be dismissed as "fluffy" Human Resources Management.

In strategy development, the participants, usually senior management, should take the opportunity to learn about the organization's environment. What are the organization's strengths, weaknesses, threats and opportunities? They should also take the opportunity to learn about what management theorists are saying about strategic planning. The process of strategic planning provides an opportunity for senior management to become active learners and serve as role models for others in the organization.

When developing policy, the organization and, in particular, the Human Resources practitioner, should establish a process to allow affected employees to have input into the policies. The forum for soliciting input may also provide an opportunity to teach those employees organizational behaviour theory or other disciplines that may have a bearing on the policy decision. Thus, not only will there be buy-in to the policy but also the employees will gain knowledge that might be applied in other contexts.

Information technology provides powerful tools to encourage learning through shared experiences. Electronic mail and project software applications allow for the ready exchange of information and knowledge across functional boundaries.

Certainly, the performance management process can be designed to help facilitate more learning in the organization. The performance criteria established can reward flexibility, individual self-development, people development and innovation. Similarly, a complementary reward system is necessary to reinforce and support a learning culture. Some reward systems, such as pay-for-skills systems, are designed to reward specific learnings. Organizations need to be careful with the implementation and application of these systems to ensure their effectiveness. To be truly effective, the organization should not simply pay for the learning of a new skill but, rather, should reward the application of that skill.

Organizational structures may pose a barrier to learning. Hierarchies and functional boundaries may be too rigid and, as a result, can create "silo" thinking. Short of a complete overhaul of the organization, alternative structures can be introduced in parallel, such as project teams, steering committees or task forces. In some organizations, renegade teams or so-called "skunk works" are encouraged to work outside of the constraints inadvertently imposed on creativity by the organization's structure, culture, rules and procedures.

Certainly, in identifying the organization's vision and values, senior management can put emphasis on learning as a highly valued competency. Again, the senior managers can serve as role models by displaying the behaviours they want to encourage in others. Senior managers should be highly visible learners.

Each of these elements can be seen as practical indicators of how well the organization learns. Increases in the effective use of project teams or an increase in the number of company-sponsored night school courses

taken may be indicators that the organization is starting to learn. Since one does not transform a culture over short periods, step-by-step change management is needed to develop supporting practices and policies and encourage innovation.

Role of the Human Resources Practitioner

The Human Resources practitioner is inevitably involved with any issue that is of a cultural nature, particularly because he or she will be responsible for many of the systems and processes that constitute the cultural environment. Whether or not the practitioner is responsible for the training function, he or she will need to examine its policies and procedures against the characteristics of a learning-based culture. These will include the following:

1. The appraisal process: what is its main purpose? Is it oriented towards an historical record, towards a pay-based performance summary, or is its main output a set of learning and development needs for the individual? Again, is the assessment and feedback relating to performance from one source only (the manager) or from a variety of people who have an input to make?

2. The training planning process: this should not be an afterthought of the appraisal, or based on a set of training courses. It should be in the form described above, as a personal learning/development plan.

3. Describing roles: in a learning organization, fixed defined job descriptions are not conducive to learning through experimentation. Roles should be described, particularly for knowledge workers, only in terms of accountabilities and not specific tasks.

4. The attention given to induction for new recruits or transferees in a learning organization should be significant, enabling them to exploit all the previous accumulated learning relevant to the role they are to fulfil.

5. The remuneration system may need to be examined to see whether it really does support continuous learning, or whether it is built primarily around levels of status. Likewise, non-monetary reward systems such as excellence or quality awards should be examined — do they give a

message of the importance of learning in the criteria that are used?

6. The career management framework: is it built solely on promotional steps and grades, or does it also provide visible career progression through continuous development?

The practitioner may be the instigator of the learning organization approach, laying out a template of characteristics as a goal. He or she would be involved in influencing top management, followed by other layers of management — ideally seeking champions outside of the Human Resources Department. The practitioner should be the monitor and assessor of progress. The Human Resources Department should be a model of the learning organization itself.

Barriers to Success/Common Pitfalls

Many advocates of the virtues of the learning organization tend to forget that organizational behaviour is a complex play of individual motivations and personal power agendas. The barriers to progress are significant, both in the way people naturally behave and also from the structures created in organizational design. Some of the barriers include the following:

— People are too busy with activity and pressures to concentrate on their learning needs and their personal development. Employees may only concentrate on these issues when forced to do so through a defined process or when they have a personal problem. Likewise, the same unintentional neglect may apply to the time given to the learning needs of colleagues in a team or of subordinates.

— When people are too busy with activity and pressures, this state of affairs often leads to impatience in researching what might already be known about a problem, so that many mistakes are repeated or projects duplicated. Furthermore, it may stop people from effective listening (to customers, employees, consultants, advisers), and therefore from taking due account of the knowledge available.

— Sometimes it is more than "busyness". It may be a personal or unit pride or feeling of self-sufficiency that stops the accessing of available knowledge and experience. It may be competitiveness, or, more often, the "not-invented-here" syndrome of

people wanting to own their own solution to a problem.

— The feeling that "knowledge is power" also prevails with many individuals. They may feel insecure to share what they know with others, fearing it will remove their indispensability or give an advantage in political and power battles which are so frequently prevalent in organizations.

— Another human barrier is the entrenched tradition of teaching/training. Those involved often really enjoy their role, and the learner-centred consultant/facilitator skills are hard to acquire and are demanding to put into practice. Training courses are often apparently neat "end-to-end" solutions that place minimal demand on those involved, at least in terms of thorough exploitation of the learning cycle.

However, in addition to the natural tendencies of people in organizations, the structures, systems and processes that are set up have a major influence. Each element can be subjected to the simple question: "How does this approach encourage learning and the sharing of learning in the organization as a whole?" A structure with minimal layers, for example, provides opportunities for individuals to take responsibility, experiment with new ideas and learn new competencies. However, it also prevents the remaining managerial positions from giving the time needed for personal coaching and feedback to the now larger number of employees in their group. Many financial control systems are built on the principle of minimal discretion, and one could argue that traditional Human Resources systems such as "hierarchical" appraisal and job evaluation do not encourage learning and may often mitigate against it.

Finally, the usefulness and friendliness of supporting information systems are crucial in managing the flow of learning. They need to be designed so that there is no excuse for working with and through them, and in a way that delivers clear and visible benefit for the users.

A number of problems in implementation can cause progress to be sporadic or transient. The first is the very acceptability of the term "learning organization", and seeing a link with business benefit rather than the latest initiative from the Human Resources "flavour-of-the-month" menu. The term itself is not so important as the conviction that a culture based on learning is essential for a healthy organization and for continual business improvement. The task of the Human Resources practitioner is to find the bridges in language and concepts that will intercept the agenda of top management, and help it to champion the importance of learning for every individual and of sharing that learning across the organization.

A second mistake is to hold the belief that a learning organization is an absolute state that can be "finally achieved". It is a way of working and thinking, and it takes time to convert an organization that has treated learning in a casual way to start managing it effec-

tively. Organizations take steps forward and backward in this journey, as they restructure and gain or lose people. The aim is to be making steady progress forward over time.

It is also a pitfall to focus exclusively on the learning process itself. There are many environmental factors involved that need addressing, and particularly important is the link to improved results that is the chief end purpose of this approach. Practitioners should take a complete view of this way of thinking and not allow enthusiasts to champion it in a narrow way.

MANAGEMENT DEVELOPMENT

Definition/Background

Management development refers to the ways in which managers within organizations can change over time to enable them to perform better in their existing and future roles. Development is thus a set of positive changes experienced by a person that should relate directly to the areas for which he or she has a current responsibility, or to expectations of future responsibilities. Change, however, is often difficult to achieve and requires some efforts on the part of both managers and their organizations.

This view of management development implies the notion that it is a deliberate attempt to achieve certain goals in terms of managerial performance. Also implied is the idea that management development is an umbrella concept incorporating a range of activities, such as management education, management training, professional development and work experience. Since management development covers such a number of opportunities, it cannot be restricted to a "one off" event or some amalgamation of isolated courses and/or experiences. A broader and more realistic view of management development demands consideration of a wider range of factors that, together, will enable the development of programs more likely to achieve positive changes and results.

Management development may be a formal program, an informal opportunistic process, or a combination of both. Whether it is achieved through a series of structured events or through *ad hoc* personal learning will depend on the organizational circumstances in which individuals find themselves.

Knowledge incorporates both technical abilities, such as reading a balance sheet or learning how to plan a production process, and an understanding of general management concepts, such as motivation, leadership and the dynamics of team performance. Behaviour refers to managerial activities and the way that a person actually performs in different contexts. Knowing and understanding are important, but being able to apply that knowledge is the key to managerial success.

Management development activities should recognize the need to develop both a manager's technical knowledge and his/her skills (behaviours). Both can be either specific or general. Specific development will usually be associated with the requirements of a particular management discipline. The greater the accumulation of specific knowledge and performance abilities, the closer one comes to being an expert in that field. At the same time, however, managers will also have a need for more general knowledge and abilities. These more general abilities include contingency planning, creative thinking, problem solving, decision-making, time management and delegating.

Underlying all this, however, is the basic assumption that individuals seeking management development will be open to learning, self-examination and change. In turn, this is likely to be a function of a person's emotional intelligence. While developing emotional intelligence may, in itself, be a goal of management development, it is also likely to be the case that certain levels of maturity are required for individuals to appreciate the need and, to make the changes necessary, for development to occur.

The nature and sophistication of the knowledge and behavioural qualities required of an individual will vary between organizations and the scope of that person's responsibility. Generally speaking, the higher one is in an organization, the more sophisticated are the requirements and the greater the degree of emotional intelligence and psychological maturity needed to achieve development.

Business organizations need managers who will meet the objectives that combined achieve the organization's vision. Organizational circumstances will dictate the range of technical and general managerial skills and attributes required. Some of these will remain static over time, while others will change, either as a business grows or restructures, or as its external environment changes. Thus, organizations will have core managerial competencies needed to keep them functioning but also need new competencies to help them survive and prosper under different market and environmental conditions.

Such management competencies can be either imported or developed from within. Management development is therefore a means of obtaining managerial skills internally. Since it is becoming more and more widely recognized that management systems and physical assets are not a sufficient condition for competitive success, management development is an important adjunct to the strategic management of a business. In areas where management skills are in short supply, whether general or specific, management development is a more certain way of creating managerial capacity.

Organizations that rely on recruiting talent often end up with a very expensive resource prone to follow supply and demand pricing mechanisms in the recruitment market. However, organizations must also be aware that good management development on its own is not enough — they must also plan to keep the results of their investment. Without a good retention strategy, businesses are likely to become the "universities" of their industry and end up developing managers for competitors who do recognize their value.

Effective managers require four types of skills: interpersonal, management, business, and functional. Management skills may be defined as those things that enable the manager to achieve results through other people. Examples of management skills are contingency planning, creative thinking, problem solving, decision-making, time management and delegating. Where knowledge, such as an understanding of motivation, is an important foundation for good management, the skills are the ways in which such knowledge is converted to practical application.

The only purpose of management skills is to enable the management role to be undertaken in an effective and efficient way. Because management effectiveness is situational, the skills should be used in a way that adjusts to the situation and takes account of the different motivation, abilities and style preferences of subordinates.

Every person who supervises or manages other people should be competent in the management skills appropriate to his or her situation. The results of this competency are felt throughout the organization, for everyone is affected by the way in which management is exercised. Since management skills apply right across the organization, the need for them is unaffected by the structure. However, the structure will affect how managers at each level apply the skills, because of the different responsibilities and the nature of the subordinates.

Benefits/Expected Outcomes

It is difficult to assess the benefits of management development. This is because any comprehensive program should be delivering the attainment of strategic goals and it will always be difficult to know whether the actual results would have been achieved without the investment in the development of people. Under such circumstances, it is better to evaluate the benefits of development in terms of behavioural performance outcomes.

Where development involves cognitive understanding or basic skills development, it is a fairly straightforward matter to assess improvement. Such issues can be tested, observed and assessed in a number of reasonably objective ways, since the outcomes required are usually quite specific types of behaviour. More difficult to assess are the benefits of development processes designed to generate improved performance, but where the behaviour required is very hard to specify. Examples might include managing change effectively; coping well with situations of conflict; and working well with different group dynamics. Since the outcome of improvements in these areas is only likely to emerge in the longer term and the benefits will be somewhat intangible, evaluation becomes problematic.

The best way to move towards satisfactory evaluation of management development programs is to seek specific ways in which behavioural change will enhance organizational performance. These behaviours can then be judged by means of the subjective evaluation of the people who work with the individuals under consideration. The process involved must be some form of feedback, either direct or indirect, and can be part of an audit or an ongoing evaluation exercise. Feedback situations, however, can be very threatening and must be managed and facilitated well if they are to be effective.

Generally speaking, the more open and honest management teams can be with each other, the greater the potential for the useful appraisal of management development programs.

Management development should, ultimately, lead to the continued survival and improved performance of those organizations that implement an effective management development strategy. Such organizations should expect, therefore, to benefit from improved financial returns, better market share, greater efficiency, fewer quality problems, and so on.

If an ongoing program of effective management development is implemented, businesses might also expect to experience other, more specific benefits such as:

— improved levels of expertise;

— reduced employee turnover;

— less organizational fragmentation (departmental silos);

— greater organizational loyalty and employee retention;

— improved market reputation;

— motivated managers;

— organizational flexibility and innovation;

— becoming an attractive employer for the best and brightest;

— reduced conflict between functions; and

— greater consistency of performance.

There is never any argument inside organizations that managing well is better than managing badly. The justification is rarely of the principle. The two issues are likely to be a belief that the organization is already very good, or that the costs of improvement (e.g., training) are not justified by the expected benefits. Justification is made easier when information has been collected to provide very clear evidence of the areas where improvement is needed.

Ongoing commitment to management development on the part of a business can prove problematic if it creates large numbers of skilled and competent managers who are unable to attain positions consistent with their potential. This is encapsulated in the observation that a business can only have one chief executive, even though there may be a dozen or more people capable of performing the role. Recently, when Jack Welsh left General Electric, a senior manager from within was appointed as his successor. This led to several other senior executives leaving the organization. They left not out of jealousy but rather because the opportunity to put to use the skills that they had developed had disappeared. Organizational structure, therefore, has to be crafted in line with the desires for management development as well as all the other demands that influence structure.

Structural provisions that are likely to support a program of organizational management development rest around the notion of flexibility. Such flexibility should provide substitutes for hierarchical progression and lead to rewards that make jobs intrinsically more satisfying. This may involve cross-functional activity, wider use of project teams, provision for the achievement of personal goals and the devolution of responsibility. Many of the trends towards flatter organizations, matrix-type management systems and structures based on core processes, such as new product development, all provide the potential for creating an environment in which consistent management development can be achieved without disillusionment.

All managers use management skills to a greater or lesser extent, and to different degrees of effectiveness. Benefits arise when there is a general state of proficiency throughout the organization. They include:

— improving motivation at all levels;

— reducing employee turnover when caused by the way people are managed;

— enabling subordinates to perform to their maximum ability;

— allowing for more effective use of available time; and

— reducing stress at all levels.

Programming/Implementation

Strategies for Management Development

In the ideal world, all organizations would have clear, logical and widely published strategic plans for all areas of their operations. In reality, this is rarely the case, and there is often much fuzziness within organizations about what people are supposed to be doing, let alone when, how and why. This is especially true for management development, which is often seen as an adjunct to an organization's activities rather than as being central to the creation of competitive advantage.

To play a larger role in the achievement of competitive advantage, strategies for management development need to consider a number of different strategic dimensions.

For the Human Resources practitioner, the first question to be addressed when considering a management development strategy is whether the organization already has a strategy in place. If it does, it may be either explicit or implicit. If it does not, it will probably mean that there is still an implicit strategy in existence but by default rather than as a deliberate decision. Whichever the case, be the strategy explicit or implicit, both are still prone to problems.

Explicit strategies for management development should be fairly easy to identify since they are likely to be a separate, written document, or part of the succession plan or the corporate strategic plan. The practitioner, however, needs to take care when evaluating (or creating) such a strategic plan, to distinguish between strategic objectives and the strategy itself. All too often, a strategy consists of what the organization wishes to achieve and is very light on how. When examining or developing a management development strategy, it is very important to ensure that sufficient attention has been given to what will need to be done.

As an example, a plan which states that "Our strategy is to get people to work more effectively in teams as a means of achieving more effective management" is, in fact, closer to being an objective than a strategy. A more strategic statement would be "Our objective is to use teams as a basis for better management. The strategy for achieving this will be to: identify areas where teams could initially add most to organizational performance; run workshops on the theory of effective team working; employ facilitators to work with these teams to promote effective working in practice; and publish the results of their work company-wide to encourage more teamwork". While being a much more detailed statement, it does convey in clearer terms, how working in teams will be achieved. Thus, explicit strategies should clearly identify strategic objectives and how the organization has chosen to achieve those objectives.

Implicit strategies are much more difficult to deal with, and one of the key jobs of the practitioner is often to make explicit, for the senior management of a business, the implicit strategy being followed and the consequences for the organization. In general, there are three strategies which are often implicitly followed but which organizations may wish to question once they are made explicit. These are as follows:

1. That the overall goals of the business are best met through focused attention on areas other than management development, such as improved quality, increased productivity, better cost control, new products development, and/or acquisitions. Under these circumstances, any management development that may occur will be incidental self-development. The implied strategy is that management development is the responsibility of individual managers who will engage in personal development in order to keep their jobs or attain their ambitions as they see them.

2. That management development is funded as a reward for individuals who perform well or who show promise. Here, the implied strategy is that the organization will benefit from growing an undefined pool of management talent who may or may not be useful to the organization but who will be motivated by the potential for personal development. At the same time, it is likely that management development will be restricted to training and education and that individuals will bear responsibility for ensuring that such activities lead to improved performance in the longer term.

3. That management development is something needed by operational managers rather than the senior managers within the business. Implicit in this approach are the ideas that senior managers are already sufficiently well-developed or are capable of managing their own development in isolation and that shortfalls in the competencies of operational managers are the key to improved organizational performance. It also implies that visible leadership by example is irrelevant in establishing the importance of management development and in obtaining commitment to it from those lower down in the business. This approach is essentially a bottom-down strategy.

Strategic Objectives for Management Development

Missing from these approaches is likely to be specific attention to the other dimensions of strategies that can serve management development activities. In terms of strategic objectives, there are two important dimensions.

1. Whether the organization wishes to maintain its present level of competence or whether it wishes to obtain some sort of change, be it at a cultural

level or in terms of its range of abilities (organizational capacity).

2. Whether the business wishes to focus attention on specific aspects of its activities or whether management development is part of the underpinning for general organizational development. This decision requires an enterprise to distinguish between priorities that it believes will lead to enhanced performance for the business and to focus resources in these areas.

Dimensions of Management Development Strategy

Other dimensions of strategy that an organization should incorporate in its management development plans revolve around a number of alternatives. These include the following:

1. The choice between organizing management development centrally or devolving responsibility to business units. This will depend on whether there are a set of organization-wide objectives to be met or whether there are significant differences in the competencies required at a local level.

2. The decision to use in-house development resources (such as training courses, work experience, facilitators, etc.), or whether to use external third-party providers. The mix adopted will depend on the resources available within an organization, the scale of a management development program and the range of activities required. Other issues, such as the credibility of either in-house or third-party providers and their relative costs, will also affect this decision.

3. In terms of training as a part of a management development strategy, there is also a choice between using public programs containing a mix of people from different organizations, or dedicated courses comprised only of people from that organization. This choice will depend on the degree of customization required, the nature of the management development objectives, the quality of the external provider of public programs (versus in-house or dedicated facilities) and the organization's ability to release large numbers of people at the same time.

4. The alternatives of engaging in management development to meet existing needs or also catering for expected future needs. The former could be described as a sort of just-in-time strategy that ensures a strong linkage between management development activities and people's current occupations and needs. This can highlight the relevance of any learning and ensures more efficient cash-flow management or its resource equivalent. The latter provides for more opportunities to practise new behaviour and to consolidate and put into context knowledge before it becomes critical to an organization's overall performance.

5. The option of creating a fast-track for selected individuals who will receive a lot of attention in terms of management development resources. The purpose of adopting this as a strategy, or as part of a strategy, would be as a support for business needs such as succession planning or staffing new ventures that might require individuals to take on important but unfamiliar roles. While being potentially divisive or elitist, such an approach can ensure the existence of a pool of managerial talent to provide continuity or to cope with rapid change.

Strategies for management development can, therefore, be developed around a number of alternatives in terms of the priorities of the business, be they explicit or implicit, the management development objective they imply and the alternative approaches that may be adopted. The options chosen will depend on the management culture of the organization, the resources available and the specific situation faced by that business. There are no right or wrong strategies, only ones that are more or less logically consistent, comprehensive and related to the needs of the organization.

Problems in Creating a Strategy

Creating a management development strategy is, of course, more difficult in practice than the theory would suggest. In general, there are three main problem areas that can impede the strategist. The first of these is that the organization may, itself, be unclear about exactly what its business objectives are, or what its strategy is for meeting these objectives. If this is the case, the practitioner will have difficulty constructing a competency profile against which to plan development activities, and in knowing whether one area of the business required higher investment than others.

It will also be difficult to decide on whether a centralized strategy is required or whether responsibility would be better allocated to operating or function-based units. Under such circumstances, the default option is likely to be a generic strategy that relies on the notion that management development is a good thing *per se*. It is also likely to take an opportunistic approach focusing on individuals' personal desires within whatever resource constraints exist.

Secondly, the development of a strategy for management development may not be a realistic possibility as a result of a lack of a company-wide understanding of the nature and value of management development. This will make it hard to establish some of the structures required and to gain support for management development activities beyond attendance at education and training courses (such as debriefing forums, mentors, and opportunities to put learning into practice). It may also make it hard to obtain the active promotion of management development by key individuals within the organization. For the practitioner, this may mean that an initial strategy will have to be a general education of the organization as to the meaning and value of management development.

A third impediment can be the lack of an audit, or one that provides insufficient information on which to base a strategy. This might result from inadequate Human Resources records, an unwillingness by managers in the organization to provide information, particularly if they suspect it might show them or their areas of responsibility in a bad light, or insufficient resources being made available to conduct a good audit. It should also be remembered that the managers responsible for conducting an audit need to have a good understanding of what the scope and dynamics are of an effective strategy for management development. This will be necessary in order for them to know what information is needed for a good audit and to be able to translate the audit into a strategy.

The potential problems facing management development strategists also extend into implementation, the traditional graveyard for strategists from all areas of activity. For management development, there are a number of hurdles that the implementation of strategy typically faces.

The most frequent problem stems from changes in the financial circumstances of a business, or changes at key positions within the organization. Either of these can lead to the reduction or withdrawal of funding, or a lack of support for the strategies in operation. Where general economic conditions are in recession, or where enterprises are in volatile markets, such situations have a high probability of occurrence.

Further problems can derive from the increased use of special project teams and matrix-type management structures. Under these arrangements, managers with general responsibilities, who will be critical to the successful implementation of a management development strategy, are likely to have only short-term commitments to their current role. In addition, they can reasonably expect to experience changes in both personnel and position on a fairly regular basis. At the same time, responsibility for the development of the managerial abilities of individuals is likely to be unclear. Such situations can mitigate against managers taking a developmental perspective for their staff and being effective implementers of a management development strategy.

As well as deliberate, or semi-deliberate, inactivity, line managers may not possess the skills required to implement a management development strategy. Thus, while they may support the principles of a strategy, have attended appropriate training courses and possess sufficient experience, they may not be able to operate well in some of the softer areas of feedback, counselling and coaching, which will be necessary to cope with the wider implications of a management development strategy.

Insufficient time may also prevent the implementation of a strategy by line managers. Although the development of people should be a prime concern for line managers and responsible senior staff, flatter organizations and the trends towards leaner businesses has meant that the range of responsibilities of individuals has been increasing. This will restrict the ability for them to take time off to attend courses and gain experience. At the same time, if management development is to mean more than just course attendance, time is required to ensure that people learn from their experiences, are supported in their development and have sufficient opportunities to build on any advances made.

At a more generic level, the implementation of a management development strategy will require change on the part of individuals. In general, people find change a difficult process. The outcomes of change are, by definition, unfamiliar to the individuals experiencing the change and may involve personal risk. This will make the concept of change uncomfortable and, at the extremes, threatening for the individuals concerned. The result can be a natural resistance to the fundamental objectives of management development strategies.

Conclusion

Management development strategies, then, face a number of difficulties in their implementation. Although such difficulties should, in theory, be highlighted as part of a management development audit and contingency plans made to accommodate them, in practice, it is hard to create a plan which accommodates all of these problem areas. The guiding principle, however, is that perfection is impossible to achieve but practice brings it ever more near. Thus, while problems will always occur, unless attempts are made to devise and implement a strategy, the skills to do so will remain dormant and management development will be a by-product, rather than a central theme, of organizational effectiveness.

As stated before, effective managers require four types of skills: interpersonal, management, business and functional. Management skills may be defined as those things that enable the manager to achieve results through other people. Examples of management skills are contingency planning, creative thinking, problem solving, decision-making, time management and delegating. Where knowledge, such as an understanding of motivation, is an important foundation for good management, the skills are the ways in which such knowledge is converted to practical application.

Management Skills

Contingency Planning

Contingency planning may be operational or strategic, but for both, the basic idea is to have an alternative plan ready to swing into action, should the base plan prove to be inappropriate or some traumatic event occur. It is easy to see the value of contingency planning in a military sense: how, for example, to evacuate the forces and aid agencies from a war-torn country, should their work there become impossible. Similarly, large cities have contingency plans for dealing with major disasters, which require coordination of police, fire services and hospitals.

At the strategic level in management, there is considerable appeal in the idea of having a ready alternative strategy which can be put into effect immediately if the current strategy runs into problems. There is a close relationship between strategic contingency planning and scenario planning. The former prepares alternative plans triggered by a predetermined event, while the latter prepares plans to fit a number of different possible futures that the organization may face. In practice, it is time-consuming (and rarely effective) to prepare strategic contingency plans for all aspects of an organization's strategy. Apart from the cost of this, time may make the contingency plan as out-of-date as the base plan and therefore unworkable. However, the discipline of thinking in advance of what could go wrong and how to adapt because of this cannot be faulted and it is worth making selective strategic contingency plans.

The Human Resources practitioner will be familiar with contingency planning as an integral part of preparing for labour negotiations. In preparing for a potential work stoppage, a contingency plan will be developed to transfer production to other facilities or subcontractors. In this sort of situation, if industrial relations is such that failure in bargaining discussions is likely, it is worth ensuring that the organization has a viable alternative plan that can be implemented quickly.

At the operating level, contingency planning may be about overcoming a possible major setback. This may require some changes in current ways of working, in order to be able to set the contingency plan in operation. For example, to ensure that the organization's server continues to operate, it might be necessary to operate more than one server on more than one site, and develop a plan that enables essential services to be taken over by the second site if, for example, there should be a serious fire in the main facility. Each site might also be equipped with an electric generator in case of a power disruption. The value of pre-planning for this sort of disaster lies in the speed at which the organization can restore normal working in the event of a problem.

Because of the time and cost of contingency planning, it is good sense to use the approach carefully. The two major situations where thought should be given to contingency planning are when either the probability of an adverse event occurring is very high (if there are frequent power cuts as experienced in California in

2001, it makes sense to plan for the next one by installing emergency generators), or when the impact of the possible event would be of major consequence.

The decision is a form of insurance. Some risks are worth ignoring, because they are unlikely to happen and would not hurt very much anyway. Others should be guarded against and contingency plans are one way of reducing risks.

Any department manager can undertake contingency planning for his or her functional area. However, many contingency plans require the cooperation and coordination of several different areas of the organization. The example given above of a contingency plan for a possible breakdown in collective bargaining requires leadership from the Human Resources practitioner but will also necessarily involve operations, sales, purchasing and public relations staff. If the organization has a corporate planning function, this may be the best point through which to secure organization-wide cooperation.

The skills needed to develop a contingency plan are the same as for the preparation of any business plan, and all managers should be proficient in business planning. However, contingency planning requires people with an even higher frustration tolerance than business planning because everyone knows (or at least hopes) that much of the effort will not have to be implemented.

The obstacle to overcome in strategic contingency planning is that, after all the effort of putting together an agreed strategic plan, many managers feel that they have had an overdose of the planning drug and want to get back to managing. To gain their commitment, they have to be convinced of the value of the activity. Similarly, the reason for failure to develop operational contingency plans is usually lack of time, and a belief that by the time they are needed they will be out-of-date.

Part of the training needed is, therefore, about building an understanding of where and when contingency planning will be helpful, and helping those trained to select priority areas so that management is not swamped by planning.

Creative Thinking

Everyone thinks and everyone is creative, although clearly some people think more deeply than others

do, and creative talent is shared unequally within the population. By creative thinking, we really mean the ability to come up with new solutions to problems, whether the problem is about resolving a difficulty, applying a new process, or thinking about the next new product concept.

Edward de Bono is a leading authority on creative thinking, and has written many books on the topic. He uses the phrase "lateral thinking" to describe the creative approach to thinking. Most of us use logical thinking, where the process followed is sequential and where frequently the parameters of the problem are perceived according to certain implicit assumptions. For example, we may think people are not working effectively enough despite the supervision and incentives, so we apply more control and increase the incentives to correct the situation because that is the way the organization has always operated.

Lateral thinking moves away from the sequential logic. It might take the same problem of lack of productivity and look at it in quite a different way. Instead of controlling people, why do we not let the groups control themselves? Or should we change the way in which people are expected to fulfil the tasks? Can we eliminate the process altogether?

Logical thinking very often takes us to a solution that may be viable. Lateral thinking may expose us to more possible solutions, one of which may be better than the answer first thought of. We may also expect that some problems cannot be solved at all by logical thinking.

It is believed that logical thinking employs only part of the brain, the left side, which is concerned with reasoning, numeracy and language. Lateral thinking requires that we also use the right side of the brain, which is concerned with colour, patterns and shapes. There are two basic questions to consider: (1) Can individuals improve their creative thinking?, and (2) Does the organization encourage or inhibit it?

The Individual's Perspective

Can individuals improve their creative thinking ability? The answer is yes, although there will always be differences in ability between people. It is possible to use tools to aid creative thinking. There are a number of these, many developed by de Bono. Most work best when used in groups, as thinking is stimulated when ideas flow between people.

One method is to take a word at random from a dictionary and use it to stimulate ideas in relation to the problem. Assume that the problem is the delay in getting through lunch in the organization's cafeteria. We opened the dictionary and hit the word "mobile". This has many meanings and connotations.

1. Able to move about — could we use a conveyor to bring the food to the people?

2. Characterized by great fluidity — let's only serve liquid foods, such as soup, which can be served from a dispenser and consumed quickly.

3. Artistic structure of dangling forms — now it's your turn to continue the exercise!

At the early stages, do not reject ideas that look silly. Apart from the fact that they may not be, one idea can very often lead to a better one — it may be silly to serve only soup, but there may be mileage in the idea of only serving foods which can be put on the plates by a dispenser and which are quick to eat.

Perhaps the oldest tool is brainstorming, which is believed to have been invented by an advertising executive, Alec Osbourne, in 1938. This is a structured approach to idea generation, which encourages the group to think of as many ideas as they can, to write them down without evaluation or criticism and to say whatever comes to mind. Evaluation and refinement is the second stage, which may be used also to link ideas and to expand them.

The key is to have individuals understand that their thinking is often constrained by their paradigms. Paradigms are artificial constructs or archetypes we create to interpret the world. It is our way of thinking. Exercises like brainstorming are ways to break down our paradigms and open our minds to alternative ways of seeing a problem.

The Organization's Perspective

Does the organization inhibit or encourage creative thinking? Culture can encourage or discourage creative thinking. An organization that believes that people will only work if supervised is less likely to provide opportunities or incentives for creative thinking than one that empowers people and gives them the freedom to decide how they will do their jobs. A fear culture will not encourage experimentation. Management styles are closely allied to culture and are important because how a manager behaves will have a direct effect on the creativity of the subordinates. An autocratic style, for example, may not want other people's thoughts. A *laissez-faire* style may also discourage useful lateral thinking unless it is accompanied by a very clear consensus on vision and goals.

Systems may make creative thinking impossible, either because they enforce particular patterns of behaviour or because they destroy the incentives, and everyone knows that in any clash between the system and a new idea, the system will win. Having employees who think creatively is a good objective for organizations. Achieving it is somewhat harder and requires skilled managers.

There is no doubt that skills in creative thinking can be developed and that most people can improve. In fact, many organizations include training of this sort in their internal training offerings. Unfortunately, this is where many organizations stop and this helps explain why many organizations complain that they have few creative thinkers on the payroll.

Recent research in the United States found that the problem was not that organizations were not generating creative ideas; it was that too few of those ideas were ever implemented. In other words, creative thinking was the smallest part of the problem, and the real issue was inability to innovate. Training should go beyond creativity, to the management of innovation. Every manager who would benefit from creativity training would gain even more from training into how to steer the new idea through the organization, overcome the hurdles and turn it into a reality.

A very simple test that can be applied is to listen to how new ideas are treated in the organization. If the new idea is constantly blocked by stock phrases, you will know that the issue is the management process, not lack of ideas. Typical stock roadblocks to progress are the following:

⇨ "We've not done that before."

⇨ "The boss would never agree."

⇨ "We tried it once before."

⇨ "Head office will go bananas."

⇨ "Needs much more investigation."

⇨ "Not in the budget."

⇨ "You're joking."

Next, examine whether the way the organization operates is an incentive or disincentive for creative thinking. Managers need to have the confidence to give their people enough freedom and responsibility to think creatively. They also need the skills to support employee ideas through to implementation. It is the manager's role to make employees feel safe to try out new ideas and experiment with processes that may improve productivity. They also need to be able to help the employee, and the organization, cope with potential setbacks and failures.

The manager needs to be encouraging and resourceful. Many significant breakthroughs occurred in "skunk works". These are unsanctioned project teams who operate without the official organization's blessing. They do not, however, emerge spontaneously. Managers who have the vision, courage and skills to see a project through champion them.

Organizations need to examine their cultures to see if managers are merely charged with maintaining the *status quo*, or whether they are truly empowered to help move the organization forward and create competitive advantage.

Decision-making and Problem-Solving

Managers at all levels spend a considerable amount of their time in solving problems and making and implementing decisions. The nature of the problems and the scale of the decisions may increase as we move up the hierarchy, but the fundamental role exists at every level. There are four decision-making roles:

1. *entrepreneur*, seeks to improve the business unit and adapt it as conditions change;

2. *mediator*, handles conflict and facilitates communication;

3. *resource allocator*, decides who within the unit gets what (resources, money, management time, etc.); and

4. *negotiator*, which may be external (e.g., customers, suppliers) or internal (e.g., industrial relations).

Different types of decisions call for different approaches. A chapter called decision analysis in an operational research book will contain descriptions of rational, analytical approaches, such as pay-off matrices and decision trees. Strategy books support their approaches to decision-making with chapters on subjects such as portfolio analysis, competitive positioning and gap analysis. However, what these approaches do is no different in concept from any form of problem-solving: the ordering of information and the varying of the elements of that information so that different patterns can be seen, leading to new solutions.

Generic Approach to Problem-Solving

A generic approach to problem-solving follows a series of steps.

Step 1: Choice of Problem

At first sight, this may seem to be a luxury, as many problems choose themselves. A claim of sexual harassment by one person against another becomes a problem that has to be dealt with, and the manager cannot sensibly decide to ignore it. However, many problems present themselves in disguise and it is easy to follow the wrong path. Instances of poor internal communication may lead automatically to a problem of how to improve communication; however, the real problem may lie with the culture of the organization and this is the problem that should be solved. A trainer may grapple with the problem of how to improve the process of a particular training course when the real issue may be how to make the content right for the organization, or that those who need the training are never selected for the course.

Step 2: Obtain Information

To begin to solve a problem, it is necessary to be able to understand it. This requires information. With complex problems, the consideration of possible solutions may lead to a need for further information. However, it is important to ensure that this is not just an excuse to delay dealing with the problem.

Step 3: Review the Elements Mentally

Run over the elements of the problem rapidly and several times in your mind. For a serious problem, this may happen without conscious effort. Care is required to avoid "analysis paralysis", or to avoid jumping to solutions. It is vital that the problem be examined thoroughly to ensure it has been properly defined. It is equally important to define the term in simple terms. Even complex issues can be easily defined in a few short sentences once the problem-solver has grasped the true nature of the issue.

Step 4: Talk to Someone About the Problem

Discussing the problem with someone else can have two purposes. The first is that the process of describing it can often reveal new patterns and put the problem in a new light. The intelligent observations and questions of the confidant may reinforce this. The second purpose is that there may be a need to apply expertise that you do not yourself possess.

Step 5: Allow an Incubation Period

Allow the subconscious to get to work. There are many examples of people who have found solutions without knowing they were thinking about the problem. Archimedes may have been the earliest recorded example. (He's the person who discovered interesting things about the displacement of water while taking a bath.)

Step 6: Vary the Way You Approach the Problem

Do not jump to conclusions too fast. The name of the game is rarely how fast you can solve a problem, but how well you solve it. Try to think laterally and use some of the creative thinking approaches to help. Consider whether it is the sort of problem which would benefit from a team approach. If you get stuck, take a break, or vary the approach you are using.

Step 7: Discover the Root Cause

Every problem is the result of some immediate cause. However treating that cause usually will result in treating the symptom, not the disease. The problem-solver needs to ask the question "Why?" The ultimate source of the problem should lie in the breakdown of a process. The problem-solver needs to gain a full understanding of how the process ought to work and what has changed to lead to the problem.

Step 8: Outline Several Optional Solutions

The best solution is not necessarily the first one found. Try to identify several solutions, so that their merits can be compared. Involve the people who will need to initiate the solution and get their opinions. This ensures buy-in to the one ultimately selected. It also provides for a contingency plan, should the solution adopted fail. Try another solution.

Step 9: Evaluate

This should be done in an objective and constructive way. For complex decisions, the evaluation may itself be complex, and the results may take you back to the beginning of the process, if none of the solutions is appropriate or practical.

Step 10: Decide

At some point, a decision has to be made. The majority of decisions taken by any manager may be important but small, and will not need extensive treatment. For major and complex decisions, there is a need to plan implementation and how to monitor progress.

No one in any organization is likely to argue that problem-solving and decision-making are unimportant. It may be much more difficult to agree whether improvement is needed. Training can be offered in approaches to problem-solving.

Since problem-solving and decision-making are fundamental skills for all managers, it is easy to argue that they should form part of lower level management training programs. It may be somewhat harder to gain agreement that more senior levels could improve, and one answer might be to take an action-oriented approach, incorporating these skills into working meetings designed to deal with real issues. The perception is not then one of training, but of an approach that is being used as a means to solve a particular problem.

Delegating

Managing is about getting things done through people. Effective managers realize that they cannot make every decision and, therefore, delegate part of their overall responsibility to others. However, delegating always brings the fear of loss of control and this is not always easy for a manager to deal with. Consequently, there is always a danger that delegation, in theory, is not delegation, in fact, where the delegating manager imposes so many controls that really he or she is still making the decisions.

Effective delegation can be a major contributor to the success of an organization. Apart from enabling superior managers to spend their time on the higher priority items, delegation can be a source of motivation for subordinates and a development tool. Senior managers can make delegation easier or harder in an organization by their behaviour. It can become impossible if, for example, the Chief Executive Officer expects his senior managers to have detailed, up-to-the-minute information on every matter which, of course, they cannot have unless they handle each issue themselves. Information should be expected quickly but not instantaneously.

Managers may be reluctant to delegate because they perceive that it will result in a loss of personal power. This will be particularly true in highly political environments where managers believe attaining and maintaining personal power is a critical need for success and survival. Unfortunately, this view assumes that power is finite, and that by sharing it with others the manager is giving away a piece of his or her power pie. In truth, by delegating, the manager is increasing the productivity and creativity of the organization and hence is increasing his or her personal power. The power pie gets bigger.

Organizations can encourage delegation by taking proactive steps to dissuade political behaviours and by rewarding managers for their ability to develop people. It should be one of the highest honours a manager can receive from his/her superiors to be recognized as a top people-developer.

All managers should be able to delegate effectively, and ability to delegate is one of the critical performance criteria of managers. It is also possible to obtain insight into how managers delegate through bottom-up feedback approaches, which take findings from the subordinates and measure the practices or behaviours of managers.

Training in delegation and related concepts, such as situational leadership, can be very effective. In delegating responsibilities to others, the following checklist might be useful:

✓ *Delegate to the lowest possible level* — much modern thinking (e.g., about customer-focused organizations) stresses the value of delegating to the lowest possible level in the organization. This involves some risk to the manager that can be reduced by ensuring that subordinates are properly trained for the tasks they are expected to fulfil.

✓ *Fit what can be delegated to the motivation and capabilities of subordinates* — think of each subordinate as an individual. Delegation can be used to stretch people. It is worth taking some risks. Most people rise to a challenge as long as it is not overwhelming. At the same time, the people must be competent (or have the ability to become competent through experience or training). Subordinates must have the willingness to accept responsibility. Managers should be equipped to use situational leadership approaches to decide how to manage each employee under their charge.

✓ *Define responsibilities clearly* — ensure that subordinates know what they are responsible for. There is a real danger that things will slip if you think you have delegated something, but the subordinate does not know this.

✓ *Work out goals and objectives with each subordinate* — make expectations clear, but do this in a way that involves the subordinate in setting the goals and objectives of the job and the time scales by which things will be done. This process is aided if the subordinate is aware of the goals for which you are responsible and the overall organizational context.

✓ *Remove obstacles* — see part of your role as the removal of obstacles that make it difficult for the subordinate to perform. This may be ensuring that the right information goes to the subordinate, that you deal with any of your status-conscious peers who will not cooperate with an underling, and that you coach the subordinate.

✓ *Keep aware without looking over the employee's shoulder* — delegation does not work if the manager is continually checking up on the subordinate, asking for continuous progress reports and second-guessing what the subordinate is doing. Nor will subordinates make decisions if the manager keeps making those decisions for them. Yet, the manager has to remain aware, because final responsibility is not lost by delegation. One way is to "walk the job", noticing what is going on, asking the occasional question but not putting people through the "third degree". Supplement this with a regular meeting with subordinates to review progress against the agreed objectives.

✓ *Support subordinates* — if someone has made a serious mistake, corrective action may be needed. Try to treat this in a positive way with the subordinate so that it becomes a learning experience. Do not criticize things that are not serious just because you might have made a slightly different decision, because if you do, the learning experience will be never to make a decision. Do not throw all the blame publicly on the subordinate if things go wrong (whatever you say, do it privately). Use praise when this is justified.

Time Management

Time is one of the scarcest resources a manager has, so anything that can be done to make the use of time more effective is worth encouraging. Time management is largely a matter of common sense. Various studies of how managers spend their time show that the typical pattern is of many short events, with many interruptions and much variety. Since much of the job is about dealing with people and reacting to circumstances, this will always be an element of the job. It is neither possible nor desirable to make every human contact into something cold and clinical. Warmth, joking and laughter are important ways of getting the best from people, as well as making the job more pleasant for the manager. Time management is not about eliminating essential contacts but trying to gain control of priorities.

There is no single, right solution to time management, as the appropriate way has to fit the individual personality type of the manager. One personality type, for example, will find a solution in planning and scheduling. Another needs the pressure of lots of tasks that have to be urgently completed and will only work well under those circumstances.

Areas where it is possible to look for time management improvement are in the planning of time, to make better use of what is available, and in the efficiency with which time is used.

Planning

For many people, a benefit can be obtained by more careful planning and scheduling of time. This would include thinking forward about the tasks that have to be completed and scheduling time for this. Typically, a manager's diary contains appointments, but rarely blocks out the time needed for routine and non-routine tasks. Careful attention to the priorities of the day ("things to do" lists) and for the week ahead is a useful approach for some people. Scheduling should allow for time to prepare for meetings and time to deal with the outcome of meetings. Most recruiters know that unless this is allowed in putting together an interview schedule, all the candidates tend to blur. If there is no preparation, time is wasted by asking questions where the answers are already in the application, and unless notes are recorded at once there is a danger that what you thought about Mr. X will be a virtue attributed to Mrs. Y. The same need exists with other types of meeting.

Efficiency in Use of Time

The second area for attention is situations where time could be used more effectively. Consultants, lawyers and similar professional services providers have a focus on time that is rarely found in management, in that records are kept of how time is used. For many managers, time is treated as if it is elastic when we all know it is finite. For example, time can be saved if meetings are managed better. This again requires considerable planning, in order to be sure that business is conducted in the way that achieves the objectives in the shortest possible time.

Improved Estimating

There are many reasons why time management may become a problem, not least being the need to cope with the unexpected. An avoidable cause is poor estimating of the time needed for each meeting, which results in delays of subsequent meetings, the waste of other people's time and the loss of the essential buffer time between meetings. Attention to both the earlier points should help managers more exactly estimate time needs, and ensure that time schedules are kept to more often.

There are organizations that specialize in training in time management, often with proprietary approaches. These can be effective when they fit the personality types of the managers. Fitting the approach to the personality types might be one way of ensuring that more people could benefit from training that suits them. To work effectively, time management has to be a priority of the whole organization, but not in a selfish way. There are often situations where the selfishness of a senior manager prevents those more junior from managing their own time, such as repeatedly expecting them to drop their own priorities and come into a meeting. In some organizations, this happens too often to be a desirable reaction to changing events.

Role of the Human Resources Practitioner

The Human Resources practitioner plays a critical role in organizational management development. Primarily, he or she bears a responsibility for initiating discussion on the topic within the organization and the development of a strategic management development plan.

They should also be able to perform a management development needs analysis for the business and have an understanding of the varying methodologies that may be utilized for such an analysis. In addition, they should be able to relate management development issues to the strategic intentions of the enterprise as a whole.

A management development audit is a fundamental requisite for organizations intending to undertake or improve their activities in this area. The information needed will include the current state of managerial performance; critical incident analysis to identify shortfalls in managerial skills; the outcomes of previous management development programs; and the future needs of the business as implied by the business strategy.

Information for this can be obtained from sources such as personnel records, performance appraisal forms, employee opinion surveys, focus groups and the organization's written strategic plans. The exercise can be done either on an in-house basis or it can be performed by outside consultants if resources cannot be released for this purpose or an added element of objectivity is required. Practitioners who aspire to assume a more strategic role in their organization are well advised to find the time and resources to conduct the audit themselves.

Once the data are collected, it is usual to write-up the audit as a report to senior management. The report should clearly identify the managerial requirements the enterprise needs to fulfil its business strategy. In doing so, it should clearly distinguish between knowledge and behaviour, and highlight specific or functional requirements as contrasted with more general organization-wide abilities. The overall effect of the audit is a gap analysis that demonstrates the shortfalls in the organization in terms of the competencies required to achieve the business's strategic goals.

Some organizations now appoint a manager for management development, usually as part of the Human Resources function. This can be a useful position, since it means that a specific person, or group of people, will have responsibility for raising the issue of management development within the organization and keeping it on the agenda as a demand for organizational resources. In addition, since management development is something that needs to take place over a considerable period, it is important to have a strategy for development and to ensure continuity over time, which is best achieved if specific responsibility for this can be identified.

On their own, however, management development managers can have little impact on an organization without the active support of its leaders. Chief executives also have to be committed to the concept of management development to provide the impetus for implementation and to legitimize the actions of such appointees. It is additionally important that any management development strategy is derived from, and is commensurate with, the overall strategy for the business. Chief executives and top management must also, therefore, accept responsibility for management development within their organizations.

Responsibility for management development, however, cannot be left to management development professionals and senior management. Development requires individuals to gain experience and then to learn from that experience and, whether this comes from attending courses or performing tasks, line managers are a critical element in the creation of such development opportunities. This is because it is line managers who release people for courses, give people responsibility for tasks, and who are best able to debrief them.

Line managers will thus need to adopt a developmental perspective towards the managers for whom they are responsible. Such a perspective values their personal growth and leads to the active encouragement of people to experiment and to take the risks required to achieve growth. This is an important additional requirement which, if absent, can stifle management development initiatives. As an example, a manager who feels that up-and-coming subordinates are a threat to his or her position, or that failure is unacceptable for a person's résumé, is unlikely to be able to act in a developmental way for his or her staff.

Line managers will also need to possess feedback and counselling skills to enable managers for whom they have responsibility to learn from their experiences. Such attributes and skills are difficult to develop and may themselves require a program of growth to provide the infrastructure from which organization-wide development can be achieved.

The Human Resources practitioner has to apply the management skills in his or her own operations but has a much wider and more important role, which is to improve the proficiency of the whole organization. This is achieved through the following:

1. Management education, training and development, where the practitioner has to help assess needs, develop policies and provide or coordinate specific initiatives to improve skills.

2. The development of procedures that help to reinforce and emphasize good management practices. This may include the wide use of competencies throughout the organization, appraisal systems that relate to the application of those skills seen to be of prime importance to the organization and incentive systems that reinforce the management behaviours required.

3. Policies, such as those for promotion, equal opportunity and disciplinary procedures that reinforce the effective use of management skills.

An audit of management capability in management skills should be taken regularly, as only by knowing where the gaps are, can sensible training solutions be provided to close them. Possible methods for undertaking such an audit include:

— regular appraisals of the manager by his or her superior;

— assessment/development centres;

— feedback methods that take readings of actual management behaviour from, for instance, subordinates; and

— survey methods by interview or carefully constructed questionnaire.

Barriers to Success/Common Pitfalls

There are a number of barriers that can prevent management development from being effective within an organization. The most common problems are associated with resources, senior management and general attitudes, all of which should show up in any comprehensive audit.

The problem with management development is that true growth in managerial competence cannot be achieved in a piecemeal fashion. Intentions made and skills obtained atrophy if they are not given scope to be put into practice. However, budgets for training and development are often one of the most vulnerable parts of an organization's spending plans. This is particularly true in times of economic recession or in difficult trading conditions. If resources are not available to support management development intentions, such initiatives can all too easily die.

Successful organizations, such as Microsoft, Southwest Airlines and Cisco Systems, all support substantial training and development budgets over time, even when economic circumstances are hard.

The attention of senior managers can often be distracted away from management development activities, which can impact adversely on the success of even the best-conceived programs. Their support is required to give authority to the organizers of programs and to provide encouragement to the participants. Active recognition of such efforts confirms the importance of the activity and adds momentum to initiatives. Senior managers, however, also need to be aware of their status as role models for the rest of the business. If their attention is distracted and, as a result, do not have time to engage in the development of their own managerial competencies, it is hard to expect less senior managers to be inspired to develop themselves.

Management development is also hampered by the general attitudes often found in organizations towards training and development. Examples of such attitudes include the views that:

— a training course is a "boondoggle" rather than something important to the organization;

— management development personnel are of low status within the organization and need not be taken seriously;

— development opportunities are "rewards" for good performance rather than a means of developing strengths; and

— other priorities have to be dealt with before people can indulge in the luxury of development.

At the same time, by definition, management development requires change in individuals. While change in cognitive understanding is relatively easy to accept, behavioural or personal change is more difficult and can feel very threatening. It is not unusual for people to resist change and attitudes towards change can, therefore, also act as a barrier to successful management development.

Common pitfalls include:

⇨ confusing education, training and development, and thinking that one will automatically lead to the other;

⇨ not holding any discussion with a person about how he or she is expected to develop, when creating a development program;

⇨ absence of any briefing or debriefing of development events (courses, special tasks, secondments, or projects);

⇨ expecting senior managers without developmental skills to implement development programs for their staff;

⇨ insufficient follow-through of development activities to ensure changes made or skills learned are practised enough for them to become a natural part of a person's managerial repertoire;

⇨ constructing programs of management development that are not aligned with the business's strategy;

⇨ being unclear about the goals of any development or set of development activities;

⇨ finding it hard to distinguish between the offerings of different outside agencies, all of which claim to provide education, training and development, and which all use the same words but are, in fact, quite different from each other;

⇨ allowing individuals to get away with not writing personal management development plans against which they are monitored and appraised; and

⇨ turning management development into a "them and us" situation: "we assess whether you are good enough without affording you the same privilege towards us", so that development becomes a point-scoring exercise.

MERGERS AND ACQUISITIONS

Definition/Background

Since any change in the ownership structure of an organization will, invariably, have an impact on its culture and management, mergers and acquisitions present a unique challenge to the Human Resources professional. Prior to any change in ownership, an acquiring organization needs to exercise "due diligence" in examining exactly what it is purchasing and in determining how the new organization will be integrated into the whole. This chapter will outline the role of the Human Resources professional in this process. But, first, let's define our terms and look at the various ways mergers and acquisitions can happen.

The term "mergers and acquisitions" is often used as though "mergers" and "acquisitions" denote the same thing. Technically, however, they have distinct meanings. A "merger" occurs when two firms amalgamate and it implies a "friendly" decision to combine forces. The shareholders, who agree to combine their equity, receive shares in the newly formed organization in proportion to what they previously held. An "acquisition", on the other hand, is the takeover of one firm by another. The acquiring firm buys enough shares in the target organization to assume control of it and it may be "friendly" or "hostile" depending on the disposition of the management group of the target organization.

In a "friendly" takeover, the target organization's management group will recommend that its shareholders accept the terms being offered. In a "hostile" takeover, the management group will recommend that its shareholders reject the offer. Sometimes this is simply a tactic used to secure a better offer or to attract an offer from a third party. In some instances, management will take other actions to prevent the organization's sale to "unfriendly" interests. These tactics are commonly called "poison pills".

When a selling organization decides to unload a subsidiary that doesn't fit into its strategic plans or is underperforming, the takeover of that subsidiary is always considered friendly because the parent organization wants to sell. In some recent cases, firms have also split off subsidiaries as separate public entities. This also changes the ownership structure and may have some impact on the way in which the parent organization exerts control.

In theory, mergers and acquisitions are undertaken because the acquiring firm believes it can add value to its operations by creating an operating synergy. "Synergy" means that the whole is greater than the sum of the parts. By combining organizations, the acquiring firm hopes to realize cost savings through operating efficiencies, reduced overheads, elimination pf overcapacity, and other uniquely identified opportunities. The merger or acquisition is usually a significant part of the company's long-term strategy.

Opinions differ widely concerning the efficacy of mergers and acquisitions. Studies have shown that expected synergies are seldom realized — that the combined value is no greater than the sum of the parts. In recent years, some organizations have found that they can better increase their value through a strategy of divestiture. Key to this strategy is a reversal in the usual thinking about holding a diversified portfolio.

While diversification is a good strategy for the individual investor, it often does not work for organizations operating a diverse set of businesses. Few conglomerates (General Electric being a highly notable exception) have been successful at managing businesses in different industrial sectors. Markets have become disenchanted with unfocused organizations and have shown a distinct preference for firms that "stick to the knitting" by remaining focused on core activities. Hence, a new movement is emerging whereby organizations are divesting themselves of peripheral or underperforming businesses in order to release funds that can be used to support the core business. This type of financial re-engineering helps the organization become more focused.

Another trend is for organizations to place more value on the concept of organizational culture. In a diversified conglomerate, it is almost impossible to create a unified and dominant culture. The existence of a set of core values and an overriding mission is essential to achieving synergy in any organization. A focused business helps the organization to create a high-performance culture where values, goals and objectives are shared. Examining organizational culture is becoming an integral part of the "due diligence" process and, moreover, is becoming a significant motive behind divestitures.

Regardless of the technical way in which two organizations come together, mergers and acquisitions always have a significant impact on everyone in the newly combined entity. Work practices will change and redundancies will be identified. The name of the business itself may change. The impact of these changes on the employees will depend on the integration strategy adopted by the new organization. In some instances, the acquiring firm merely imposes its own practices and culture on the target firm. This can be a highly successful strategy if the dominant firm has a well-defined culture. Another strategy, often seen in mergers or cases where the culture of neither organization is particularly strong, is to forge a new organizational culture, borrowing some elements from each organization and introducing others that are entirely new. In yet another scenario, where the targeted firm does not fit well into the parent organization, it may be maintained as an entirely separate entity. This latter strategy has been adopted with some success by conglomerates like Bombardier. In its aircraft business, Bombardier has a single selling organization that is able to access a diverse set of product offerings. Its manufacturing divisions, however, are operated separately, to avoid the heavy cost of trying to integrate vastly different organizational cultures.

Whatever integrating strategy is followed, it is important to remember that any merger or acquisition activity will involve some change and that communication is crucial to ensuring the success of any such activity.

Benefits/Expected Outcomes

The expected benefits of merger and acquisition activities are to realize growth opportunities for the organization and to create additional value for the shareholders. In most cases, the decision makers hope to create synergies that will increase the overall performance and value of the organization. These synergies may be created through eliminating redundant organizational activities and through developing operating efficiencies. Some mergers and acquisitions create advantages for the organization that it could not have developed organically. Combining regionally-based

organizations into one national presence is one significant way of creating a marketing advantage that the two founding organizations could not have developed themselves without considerably more time and expense.

Other benefits might include:

• gaining entry into areas of business where difficult-to-penetrate barriers exist;

• reducing the risk of entering into new businesses, products or geographical areas;

• filling gaps in distribution coverage;

• expanding more rapidly;

• creating a dominant position in a fragmented industry sector;

• removing the competition (subject, of course, to anti-combines legislation);

• reducing capital cost of growth;

• improving access to cash reserves and other significant financial assets (including tax deductions); and

• acquiring management talent and other organizational competencies.

Throughout the 1990s, a significant number of high-tech firms grew their business through acquisitions. Their primary motive was to obtain the talent that had become the most significant asset for most organizations in this sector. Not only had it become difficult to recruit talent away from other organizations, but, once recruited, their ideas might be locked up in patents or protected as proprietary knowledge. Some organizations found that it was simply easier to buy the organization, thereby acquiring not only the talent, but also the intellectual capital that went along with it.

Programming/Implementation

The most significant activity preceding a merger or acquisition is the exercise of "due diligence". Due diligence is the auditing process undertaken to confirm that the details of the targeted organization are, in fact, what the purchasing organization believes them to be. In a friendly takeover or merger, the buyer will have full access to the information needed to make an informed decision (such access, however, is usually subject to a confidentiality agreement to prevent misuse of the information). In a hostile takeover, on the other hand, the buyer will have to rely on information that is publicly available.

Due diligence activities include the following:

- confirming that the profitability of the targeted firm is as stated and that its contracts contain no hidden liabilities or adverse clauses that might reduce future profits. Such a review will involve not only looking at its past profitability, but, more importantly, at its potential to maintain and grow profitability. It is also important to note that acquiring firms may be liable for damages arising from past actions of the targeted organization. For example, if land included in the acquisition turns out to be contaminated, the purchaser will be liable for the cleanup costs as well as any penalties under the applicable statutes.

- understanding accounting differences between the two firms, so that results are compared on an "apples to apples" basis.

- assessing the fit between the two organizations. This means examining the entire organization to gain an appreciation for its culture and other intangibles of its operations. Even when organizations appear to be similar on the surface, there may be vast differences in their cultures, relationships with customers, Human Resources philosophies and policies, and information/communications systems. Knowing what differences exist will help the buyer determine what steps and resources will be needed to ensure successful integration.

- refining the post-acquisition plan to ensure that integration activities are well-developed and that those activities can be undertaken quickly, efficiently and effectively. This includes determining the full cost of integration and making a final decision as to what measures will be used to determine the success or failure of the merger or acquisition.

The due diligence audit ought to be a multi-functional activity. Like any audit, it will limited by strict time constraints and by the pressure it puts on the managers and other employees in the organization being audited. To gain practice in conducting due diligence, some firms will literally look at targets that they ultimately have no significant interest in.

What is achieved by the audit depends on the team assembled to conduct it. The size of the team, its

composition and expertise will all influence its effectiveness, as will the targeted firm's ability to cope with a stringent audit of its activities. The assembly of an audit team can also be taxing on the buying organization. For this reason, some firms use third parties to conduct due diligence for them. Unfortunately, this may not optimize the organization's "feel" for the compatibility of cultures, a benefit that can be gained when its own people are employed to conduct the audit.

Planning the Approach

There are always risks involved in a merger or acquisition. No organization can get all the information it wants, given the inevitable constraints of time and resources. A systematic approach to the undertaking can, however, reduce these risks and increase the chances of successful integration.

First and foremost, an organization must develop a strategy that includes a vision and direction for itself. The merger or acquisition should then be assessed as to whether or not it passes the "smell test"; i.e., does it fit into the organization's overall direction? Once a potential acquisition target has been identified, the decision makers have to determine if it is strategically the best option, or if alternatives that better suit the organization's objectives exist — such as building a greenfield site or entering into a strategic alliance.

Many successful organizations are approached by their banks or brokers to review potential acquisition opportunities. Many of these can be quite worthwhile. However, a more successful approach is to define your organization's strategic direction first and then, in a proactive manner, identify potential acquisition targets. Targets should be realistic in terms of size, compatibility and overall fit. To assist in identifying these targets, a profile of the ideal acquisition could be developed and used to compare against potential acquisitions. Such a profile will help the organization to focus its resources on worthwhile activities and protect it, to some degree, from impulse buying. It may come as a surprise to know that large mergers and acquisitions are sometimes made on the whim of a senior manager. For obvious reasons, it is important to take steps to protect the organization against this possibility.

Once potential targets that pass the "smell test" and fit the profile have been identified, the organization will make its preliminary approach. Early discussions will reveal whether the target organization is willing to be acquired. Establishing "friendly" relations at the onset will make the due diligence process easier to manage, and will have a positive impact, down the road, on the integration of the two organizations. This is not to say that "hostile" takeovers never result in successful integrations, only that friendly ones are easier.

The due diligence audit is a key component of the acquisition plan. Equally important is the current state of the buying organization. Knowing what the buying organization's key competencies, strengths and weaknesses are will help in the assessment of exactly how the new organization will complement or augment its existing capacity and capabilities. It is also a necessary step in planning out the integration activities. The acquiring organization must critically assess whether or not it has the resources on hand to successfully amalgamate the two organizations.

Once final negotiations are completed, the integration plan needs to be implemented. As with any other project, the plan should identify the key measures of success, develop monitoring mechanisms to track progress, identify milestones for reassessments and adjustments, and define the point at which the integration can be declared a success.

Following the implementation of the integration plan, the newly formed organization will need some time simply to establish its performance. However, at a predetermined point, a post-acquisition review should be conducted to determine the degree of success and to identify what corrective actions might be taken to ensure the next merger or acquisition is even more successful.

Role of the Human Resources Practitioner

Every merger or acquisition has an impact on the people in the organizations involved. The degree of the impact will depend on an individual's place in the organization, whether he or she initially belonged to the acquiring or the target organization, and the integration strategy adopted by the organization. The chief responsibility of the Human Resources practitioner is to mitigate the impact on people.

While employee reaction to the major changes brought about by a merger or an acquisition will be a very individual affair, it will also, invariably, be emotional. One common reaction is fear. Employees are naturally apprehensive about what the, as yet unknown, impact of the merger or acquisition will be on them. They will want to know how the acquisition will affect their jobs — or, in some cases, whether they will even have a job. For some, there will be sadness in leaving the old culture behind. Still others may find it difficult to accept that anything will change.

On the other hand, many employees will be quite positive about the changes that will result from an acquisition or merger. They will see opportunities for themselves to learn new things and, possibly, for advancement in the larger organization.

The Human Resources practitioner needs to be prepared to deal with the full range of emotional responses and, above all else, to keep the lines of communication open. Negative consequences resulting from some of the issues that emerge can be minimized through a comprehensive communication plan.

If one of the goals of the merger or acquisition is to achieve efficiencies through economies of scale and shared resources, job losses are inevitable. It is, therefore, important that there be a plan outlining how these job losses will occur prior to the completion of the transaction. Employees will want to know which jobs are affected, who will be selected to leave, and what benefits will be made available to lessen the impact. While no implementation plan will ever be comprehensive enough, nor fast enough to satisfy every employee, the quicker it is implemented, the better it will be for getting a recommitment from the surviving employees.

The expectations of managers and other employees in the buying company are as important as the expectations of those in the target company. The goal should be to establish a stable and productive culture in the combined organization as quickly as possible. The timing of announcements should be planned so that they are made in a sensitive and caring manner.

In mergers and acquisitions, the various activities involved require different levels of involvement from the Human Resources practitioner. The senior practitioner should be a participant in the development of a corporate strategy. As a business leader, the senior practitioner may also have some say with respect to potential targets — usually in the form of a veto over any targets that present manifestly insurmountable integration issues. A targeted company with a history of problematic union–management relations, for example, may be specifically excluded from consideration. The senior practitioner may also be able to identify other key cultural issues that should be considered when searching for appropriate takeover candidates.

A Human Resources practitioner should also be included as part of the due diligence process. The degree of the practitioner's involvement will depend on the size and complexity of the takeover target. The practitioner may want to review the skills and competencies of the targeted organization's top managers. He or she will also want to review Human Resources policies and practices to see the extent to which they match or require integration.

In reviewing the target organization, the practitioner will also have input regarding the potential costs of integration. Integrating costs include the cost of severance for redundant personnel, the cost of harmonizing compensation and benefit practices, the cost of implementing a comprehensive communications strategy, and the cost of potential plant closings. At the same time, the practitioner should assess the impact of the acquisition on the existing organization.

It should not be assumed that all the redundancies identified will be in the targeted company. One of the buyer's chief interests is to capitalize on the unique competencies and skills of the target organization's people. Some individuals in the existing organization may find that they are the ones who are going to be displaced by newcomers from the other organization.

The chief role of practitioners is to plan and implement the integration strategy. So, while their role in determining the strategic advantages of the acquisition is minimal, their role in making it work is key. Bringing the organizations together represents significant cultural change and it should be approached in the same manner as any other change initiative. The Human Resources practitioner should be the chief architect of this aspect of the implementation plan and should be held accountable for its success.

Barriers to Success/Common Pitfalls

The most common mistake made in merger and acquisition activities is the failure to assess whether or not the expected goals and benefits have been realized. Success can only be determined if the objectives and measures of success are decided on *before* the merger or acquisition takes place and are reviewed after the fact. A common phenomenon is for an organization to rationalize a purchase post-transaction by rewriting expectations to match the outcome.

Merger and acquisition activities are high risk and, more often than not, they do not result in the desired outcomes. It is not surprising, therefore, that managers want to create an image of success around these activities. A formal review must therefore be part of any comprehensive merger and acquisition process. This will, of course, help management to avoid the many pitfalls surrounding these activities. Once the organization becomes proficient in such measures, it will be able to develop an early warning system that will help it identify when things are going wrong during future mergers and acquisitions. Mergers and acquisitions can be very beneficial to the growth and financial health of an organization, but the right processes need to be in place to ensure that they succeed.

Other common mistakes include:

- failure to define a corporate strategy that supports the merger and acquisition activity;
- poor integration of the combined organizations due to poor planning;
- choosing the wrong acquisition target;
- failure to follow through — from concept to post-purchase review;
- failure to manage expectations in both organizations immediately following the merger;
- not taking the actions necessary to create synergies;
- presuming that the buyer's processes are always better than the targeted company's; and
- adopting the view that the merger or acquisition is chiefly a financial activity.

From a Human Resources management point of view, the most significant mistake is the failure to gain a comprehensive understanding of the critical differ-

M - N - O

ences and similarities of the two organizations. Too often, the Human Resources practitioner is not involved in the early stages of developing the corporate strategy, identifying potential acquisition targets, or conducting the due diligence audit. Many of the failures that occur in integration or in realizing synergies arise from the incompatibility of corporate cultures. Even when the cultures do not match, this deficiency may be overcome through careful planning and the execution of a target-specific integrating strategy. If the Human Resources practitioner is not involved from the outset, the acquiring organization may underestimate the resources required to bring the organizations together.

To integrate two organizations into a single cohesive operating unit, time, money and people are needed in large quantities. In order to properly assess the potential success of a merger or acquisition, the organization should plan to have these resources available and factor them into the cost of the activity.

MISSION STATEMENTS

Definition/Purpose

A mission statement is a succinct statement of the mission or purpose of an endeavour. It gives clear expression to what is to be achieved, in what manner it will be achieved and why it is worth achieving. The terms "mission statement" and "vision statement" are somewhat synonymous. For some practitioners, the distinction may be that a vision statement is a higher level statement that describes what the organization aspires to be. A mission statement is the way in which the vision is achieved. The debate on what distinguishes the two is of dubious value and therefore we will consider them as being the same.

Usually the term "mission statement" refers to organizational mission, but it could equally be applied to any purposeful project. For example, any team or subset, any family, club or association can have a mission statement. We can usefully establish a mission statement for any process or structure we initiate. Indeed, we will undoubtedly have some sense of purpose whether or not we have a statement about it. Purposeful people are clear about the what, how and why of their actions.

A mission statement should make things clear, explicit and unambiguous. It enables all members of an organization to align themselves — or at least to know where alignment is lacking. Modern organizational theory, learning from physics, suggests that shared mission creates a "field" in which energies can flow (as in electromagnetic fields), releasing potentials that otherwise remain latent. Fields are invisible to us, but we know them by their effect.

It is said "purpose throws an anchor into the future". Developing a mission statement can be a powerful management tool for directing the activities of every individual employee towards a common goal. By giving employees a common purpose, it creates a sense that what they do is worthwhile. Employees gain a sense of satisfaction in knowing that their workplace activities are part of a greater purpose. It is the responsibility of management to create that purpose and communicate in a way that leads to action on the part of employees. It is an essential element in creating the overall culture of the organization.

A mission statement, if it is to be of value, must be the result of a process of exploration — of genuine introspection and thought. All too often mission statements are produced superficially, even delegated, as a kind of window dressing operation. When done without real soul searching and due diligence and then assigned to the office wall or used to adorn the annual report, they may impress but will serve little long-term purpose. Done well, they embody the loftiest, most abstract and value laden intent, which is able to mobilize latent human energies towards realizing challenging long-term goals and to invest all such endeavour with meaning.

Benefits/Expected Outcomes

Having a mission statement is like having a compass — it is invaluable for determining direction and as a constant confirmation that you are on track. Sir Edmund Hillary did not arrive at the top of Mount Everest as a result of having just gone out on a hike and discovering it was there. He embarked on a venture with purpose.

Clarity of mission aligns people in an organization. Purpose connects the activities of individuals into a group direction. It provides employees with a sense that what they are doing is important and worthwhile. It provides meaning to their work. In so doing, it changes our way of organizing from something machine-like to something holistic and intrinsically human. A genuine mission statement is a statement of intent to wholeness. However, the greatest value of a mission statement is the process to be gone through in generating it. Done well, this unites and empowers all those who participate.

Assessing the Benefits

The benefits will relate to clarity (i.e., knowing what you are trying to do). After, say, nine months, a re-run of the interviews carried out before the process began should reveal changes. In fact, these changes should be dramatic and far-reaching. The benefits of clarity of purpose should be visible in the everyday life and work of people in all parts of the organization. If they are not, then you need to question the effectiveness of the implementation or perhaps even to question the degree of honesty and integrity behind the development of the mission statement.

Developing a mission statement is often the first step in creating an organizational change strategy. A transformational leader, by definition, is a leader who creates a vision for the organization and is able to communicate in a way to capture the imaginations of employees and other stakeholders. The mission statement should excite people to take action and rally behind the efforts of the leader. The mission must be clear and well articulated. It must be succinct enough that employees and others find it easy to remember and easy to understand.

Mission statements can be abstract but should convey sufficient meaning to employees so that they can translate it into appropriate behaviours. The mission statement must go beyond being a mere marketing slogan in that its intent and purpose is not simply to attract the interest of customers, but is directed at changing the behaviours of employees to reach a specific objective.

Developing a mission statement is a valid and vital activity of senior management — if they are not defining and communicating a direction for the enterprise, who is? It is the highest level of work within any organization. Unless such work is done at the very top, it is difficult for those elsewhere to be clear about the purpose they are serving. However, such work should not only be done at the top. Everyone should be clear about his or her own mission within the whole, and may need to be helped in the process of clarification. That is the role of leadership.

This may be easier said than done. A management team may have differing and overlapping purposes. They may well not have a common purpose at all and yet be acting in the belief that they do. Clarity of purpose is a wonderful foundation for all levels of planning — indeed, one might doubt the value of planning without a shared understanding of the purpose the plans are intended to serve.

Levels of abstraction are the differing levels at which we perceive and interpret the world. For example, to turn facts into data, we have to make observations. By processing the data, we develop information, and then in turn we transform information into knowledge. Each transformation requires a process and is an abstraction from the basic facts. We are generally una-

ware of these transformations and yet we continuously perform them. Purpose is at the top of the hierarchy and thus shapes and determines everything.

If too little attention is given to the higher levels of policies and strategies (usually because of pressure to engage in operational work), the organization becomes mechanistic and without a soul. It resorts to increased control and disempowers people. Through stratification, the higher levels are often considered to be the preserve of the managers, and people assigned to the lower levels are not expected to think or participate. At a minimum, this leads to complacency and alienation. More dramatically, it can lead to demeaning the contribution of the work of individuals.

"Highest level" refers to the level of abstraction away from whatever concrete activity the organization is engaged in (i.e., what it does). Purpose is to do with why the organization does what it does. Human beings are teleological creatures, which basically means goal-seeking. On a personal level, we all have a need to live meaningful lives. Many of us derive such meaning from our work, so belief in its purposefulness is important to us. Meaningless work demeans us. When we work with a sense of purpose, we can call upon resources that in meaningless activity we deny. "Why?" matters to us.

Implementation and Mechanisms

Usually it will be necessary to take the people, who are going to engage with the process, to an off-site workshop. This should be fully residential. Given the importance of the process, people must be prepared to make a sufficient investment of time and energy. Getting away from the organization's own premises into neutral territory helps free people from cultural conditioning. If the surroundings are themselves liberating and inspiring, so much the better. Beware of introducing irrelevant seductions — a social evening with partners is unlikely to contribute and would be better at some other time. Facilities need to be conducive to thoughtful interaction and productive discussion. They should not overwhelm with luxury or underwhelm with privation — appropriateness and quality should be carefully considered.

The process of developing a mission statement has several distinct elements, which are outlined below.

Whose Mission?

Before beginning, it is important to ensure you have the right people in the right circumstances with the right intentions. Developing the organization's mission is a senior management activity. In some circumstances, it may be appropriate for the transformational leader to draft an initial mission statement as a starting point. The purpose of the statement is to provide direction to the organization.

However, even in circumstances where an organizational change is mandated, to the leader, the mission statement cannot be created in isolation from the stakeholders. Thus, before the statement is finalized, the leader must get input from other senior staff members in order to ensure all perspectives are taken into consideration.

One of the objectives of going through this process is to ensure buy-in from the senior management group. Many mission statements fail to create excitement in their organizations because there is little buy-in from senior staff. In some instances, there can be active resistance to any changes suggested by the mission statement.

The first question to be asked by anyone facilitating the development of a mission statement should be "Who owns the mission?". Ultimately, the statement has to be consistent with the direction in which important stakeholders want the organization to go. These stakeholders include owners, customers, employees and the community at large. While it is impractical to include representatives from all the stakeholder groups in the process, their interests should be represented by the appropriate senior managers.

Not only is it impractical to include representatives from all the relevant stakeholder groups but also unwise. The primary objective of a mission statement is to provide direction and influence a change in the organization. Not all the stakeholders are going to agree with the same direction. For example, as a result of the mission statement, the organization may decide to get out of certain businesses or stop serving certain market niches. Jack Welsh, the charismatic leader who transformed General Electric, initially challenged the organization to question the businesses it was in and to get out of those market segments that did not provide a sufficient return on capital.

Design

Developing a mission statement must be seen as a process. The process should be well structured in order to bring minds together and to facilitate genuine enquiry. Start by creating an atmosphere of attentiveness and openness. Some pattern-breaking activity will be helpful. Early in the process, interactive exercises can be used to surface and overcome hidden assumptions and interpersonal blocks. Later in the process, an introspective excursion in beautiful surroundings can help awaken intuition and inspire higher values. Such elements need to be integrated into the context of the process as a whole.

Stakeholders

Purposeful action begins with identifying the stakeholders (i.e., all of the people, including the process owners, who have a stake in the accomplishment of the purpose). Put the full list of stakeholders up on the wall for all to see. It will be important to reference this list from time to time and to question how the mission statement, and its intent, impact on the stakeholders.

Values

Having listed the stakeholders, it is necessary to explore values. Even in long-standing management groups, the values may again be only implicit. Making the value system explicit will remove the cause of much misunderstanding, frustration and stress. Discussing values can start by looking at a hierarchy of values or having a list of values and identifying those that seem relevant. A values hierarchy should include the following:

1. *Transcendental values:* what an organization wants to mean. (How will history remember us?)

2. *Socio-political values:* the organization's role in wider community. (What do people think of us?)

3. *Communal values:* the kind of community the organization is. (What do our employees feel about us?)

4. *Technical values:* our efficacy. (How do we do what we do?)

5. *Economic values:* how we prioritize expenditure. (What gets spent on what?)

Start by working solo and then comparing notes in pairs. Try to identify the stated values in the organization and any areas of difference between stated values and those reflected in behaviour. Identify also any differences between personal and corporate values. This should enable a useful discussion to be undertaken, from which a list of value statements can be derived.

Identifying values can be a difficult exercise. It is important to have participants who are willing to challenge the organization's adherence to a set of values. Most organizations like to consider themselves to be ethical, but not all are. It is perhaps bold to say organizations should not identify ethical behaviour as an inherent value if in fact it has not been an important driver of the organization. This is not to suggest that they should be unethical, rather they should focus on those values that are more descriptive of the organization.

Many organizations like to consider people as their most important asset and assert this as a value. Yet, the organization may be quick to lay-off its most important asset to meet fluctuations in the demand for its product. Value statements are important in that they translate into action. Otherwise, they become meaningless sentiments. Part of the process must be to question how the organization will be affected by the value propositions. It may mean fundamental changes in the organization's culture and its operating philosophies. For the mission statement to be effective, the organization must be prepared to accept these fundamental changes.

Purpose

Now we can set about externalizing all the thoughts we have about the purpose of the business we are in. This is best done as a kind of brainstorm. If there are more than five people, divide into subgroups to give everybody the maximum chance to contribute. Follow the rules of brainstorming (it is not a discussion). Freely associate, suspend judgment, and record the output publicly and in sufficient detail. Use cards to capture each idea as a separate entity so it can be structured and modeled later. In doing so, be disciplined so that each idea is clear and complete in itself.

In setting about brainstorming, take care to make the questions wide, open and generic. It may be helpful to involve the purpose-owners in formulating the questions. The general gist of the brainstorming should ask the following questions:

1. What is the fundamental nature of our enterprise?

2. What is the business we are in and why are we doing it?

Beware of being too specific by asking, for example, "What is our purpose in running hotels?". It may well transpire that the more generic question opens up a totally new way of understanding and does not limit the way people see what they want to do. A classic example of this is the breakthrough that Union Pacific experienced when it stopped thinking of itself as running trains and began to see it was in the business of facilitating movement. *Readers' Digest* reframed its business from being a magazine publisher to direct mail selling. Avoid trite responses (e.g., "to be the best"), avoid comparisons and avoid single words (i.e., use phrases in which the meaning is explicit and dynamic).

Structuring

Having formulated the question and brainstormed, the next step is to structure the outcome. This is the really challenging part of the process — partly because, at a superficial level, the job is complete. The challenge is to think at a deeper level. The framework for structuring the ideas looks at the what, how and why of them. We need to distinguish between ends and means.

The ideas should be put into the following format:

❏ Our purpose is to:

❏ In a way that:

❏ So that:

"Our purpose is to" simply states what it is you do. "In a way that" is mostly about your values, and "so that" is about the meaningfulness of your activity. A simple illustration of this would be "Our purpose is to provide environments for creative thinking in a way that is comfortable, supportive, stimulating and environmentally sensitive, so that our clients get maximum creative output from their events and all of our stakeholders benefit".

Structuring is a tough assignment but well worth the struggle. For example, many people may insist that the reason why they do what they do is to make profits. On the other hand, whereas being profitable may be an essential prerequisite, for many people, the why of their business is to do with their self-perception, their job satisfaction and their desire to continue to add value. Sorting this and other aspects out will give a rich discussion in which, incidentally, there are no "right" answers.

This is not to suggest that profitability should automatically be excluded from the mission statement. Some organizations are hesitant to admit that their purpose is to make money for the owners of the enterprise. They fear that employees will resent the fact that they are working for others to profit or that they will want a piece of the action. Employees, however, want to know the score and profitability is an excellent way of keeping score. It also is a great way of communicating to employees that they are part of a worthwhile endeavour and that they are succeeding.

Incidentally, in facilitating this discussion, expect most ideas to finish up in the mid-section. "Our purpose is to" should be fairly succinct and action-oriented, and "so that" should mostly relate to, and include, all of the stakeholders (but do not make this an explicit requirement). Within each section, some clustering of ideas will make the whole thing simpler to grasp. Do not permit anything to be thrown out — remember that brainstorming is intended to create a complete and rich picture of what is possible.

Integrating

If you have been working in subgroups, this is the time for the groups to bring their different pictures together. Again, use of a flexible and mobile medium will make life easier and allow people to focus on the process, instead of being bogged down in the difficulty of the task. Some editing will be necessary. Straight duplicates can be rejected — have a "parking lot" for this material so it can be checked out again later before finally being scrapped. Some ideas may need to be rewritten to clarify their meaning, to represent similar concepts or in response to new ideas.

Scribing

When the group has generated and agreed upon a complete model, it is time to translate the ideas into linear format. Although the original associative clusters will be meaningful to those who participated, they will not be to others. Translating clustered concepts into ordinary language will make further demands on thinking. However, this is where parallel processing can be employed to advantage.

Assign each person a number of clusters, with some duplication, and share the burden of work. The duplication will ensure that alternative forms of words are considered. There must be consensus on the final form of the words. There is no room here for majority decision-making. Otherwise, there will not be a complete buy-in and the impact of the mission statement on transforming the organization will be reduced.

Timing

Given the importance of this process, it is important to get it right the first time. The facilitator will want to set time lines as guides but should maintain flexibility in the process to ensure all thoughts receive proper treatment. The introduction and scene setting should not be hurried. Get people to talk about the self that others do not usually meet at work. Run some exercises and play a little. You want people thinking "outside-of-the-box".

Many organizations have implicit missions. The process of arriving at a statement of that mission will bring clarity to it, and perhaps through the process, the participants will gain insight into how they can effect their behaviour in ways that enhance the mission. In these circumstances, the process will be relatively easy.

Other organizations may seek to develop a mission statement precisely because they lack a unified direction and purpose. In these circumstances, the process may be more difficult and may demand several sessions. The facilitator needs to be an astute practitioner in such a situation.

One problem facilitators will face is participants who are unwilling or unable to give up their old paradigms. These people will block effective dialogue and will ultimately make it difficult, if not impossible, to reach a consensus. Moreover, these individuals will likely prove to be major detractors during the implementation process and may effectively block any meaningful change in the organization's direction. The facilitator will need to identify these issues and take them up with the head of the organization. Because we are dealing with organizational change, the leader may have to make a dramatic decision as to whether or not these individuals fit into the organization of the future. These decisions, of course, are very difficult. Often the nay-sayers are the individuals who have contributed a great deal to the present organization in both years and efforts. A decision, however, must be made to direct the course of the enterprise.

Having produced a mission statement, it will be valuable to think about the next steps before concluding the session. How will it be used? What practical consequences are there to any emergent ideas? Who will be responsible for putting things into practice? How will other participants know when the promised actions have been taken? When you have considered these questions, your mission statement event is over.

Follow Through

This is the time to put the mission into action. In following through the mission statement process, the following issues also need to be addressed.

Sub-Missions

Components of the organization, such as divisions and/or departments, may want to articulate how they will organize themselves in a way to serve the organization's superordinate objectives. One or two lines of action statements will encourage and enable others to appreciate better their own place in the whole system. This aids in devolving the process of purposing to produce powerful and beneficial action plans.

Strategies

From mission statements and vision, strategies can be developed. Too much strategic thinking is done without vision. This, in turn, leads to reactive management, as there is no conscious attempt to invent the future. Effective strategies always derive from visions of a desired future, not from extrapolation from the past.

In creating the mission statement, the senior management group will need to look at such things as:

- organizational strengths;
- organizational weaknesses;
- external threats and the environmental context;
- opportunities for growth;
- competitors; and
- customers and product offerings.

These same things are reviewed when considering strategic direction. Hence, the process of developing a mission statement can be seen as the initial step in formulating organizational strategies. From the experience of General Electric, under the guidance of Jack Welsh, we know that formulating mission statements and developing strategy is a never-ending iterative process that is fundamental to managing organizations at the senior level.

Monitoring and Feedback

The person without mission, vision and strategies is weak. He or she can only be a reactive victim of circumstance. Mission, vision and strategy are the tools of those who wish to control their future career path.

Organizations are the same. However, the best-laid plans often go awry. Constant monitoring and receptivity to feedback will enable course corrections to be made. For this reason, it is important to establish what results you expect to see, by when, and who will be responsible for measuring them. These are best contained in specific action plans.

The organization must take steps to ensure that internal processes, such as the performance management system, are aligned with the objectives and purpose articulated in the mission statement. This can be a complex and arduous task but is entirely necessary to ensure the organization's culture is transformed to meet the expectations enunciated by the mission statement.

For example, any value statements that have been made to support the mission should be translated into specific competencies or behaviours, where possible. Then, through the performance management process, employees will get significant feedback on how well they are meeting the organization's expectations. Integrating processes is demanding and detailed work. The trick is to develop systems and language which are easy for employees to understand and which provide them with meaningful feedback on how well they are doing.

Facilitators — Internal or External

Given the importance of the mission statement and the process of purposing, it needs to be in the right hands. Internal facilitators will have the advantage of knowing the organization and the personalities involved. However, consideration should be given to whether the mission statement is best facilitated by an external facilitator, who will have the advantage of being free from cultural conditioning and the possible danger of career limiting "gaffs". Either way, developing a mission statement should be seen as the most important management work to be done — and redone.

Role of the Human Resources Practitioner

Is there clarity at the top about the organization's purpose? Is there clarity in the mind of every person within the organization as to his or her own purpose? If a published organizational mission statement exists, is it real and exhaustive, or is it the product of some past "public relations" exercise?

The role of the Human Resources practitioner may be to ensure this clarity of purpose by collecting and processing information. This information can be established through focus groups or employee "climate" surveys. Input from people typical of all levels and all departments within the organization should be gathered. The structure of the interview need not be complex, as we are dealing with such a fundamental issue. If people lack clarity and direction, it will soon reveal itself. The extent to which it is the case will enable a judgment to be made as to whether action is needed. In extreme cases, interviewing may not be necessary, as the lack of clarity may be all too apparent. However, evidence may be needed to obtain approval for action.

The most important role for the practitioner is to ensure that the organization's internal processes are aligned with the mission statement. These include, but are not limited, to the following:

- organizational structure;

- reward systems;

- job descriptions;

- training and development plans;

- performance management system;

- labour relations strategy; and

- recruitment strategy and process.

The trick for the practitioner is to keep processes simple so that they enhance the clarity brought to the organization by the articulation of the mission. This is an important caveat. Many organizations are hindered in their pursuit of a vision by internal processes that confuse employees or are misaligned. Either way the attention paid to these processes will have a profound impact on the achievement of the organization's mission and its culture.

The practitioner may also act as a facilitator in developing the mission statement. This can be effective if the practitioner has the mandate to facilitate the development of the strategic direction of the company and is clear of any cultural conditioning. The practitioner needs to think this over carefully and give thorough consideration to using the skills of an external facilitator.

Barriers to Success/Common Pitfalls

Developing a corporate mission is the work of the senior management, and they may need to be convinced of this fact. Senior management may have to accept that it is they who have not done this work adequately in the past. They may feel they are themselves clear enough about the purpose of the organization and that others can simply be told what to do. This is not an uncommon state of affairs.

There are, however, many examples of senior managers who fail to see the need to make explicit what they believe is the implicit direction and purpose of the organization. Unfortunately, these examples are found in organizations that have failed to find their central purpose and mission in time to adapt to a changing environment. The senior management of these organizations has not survived to see the task completed.

The senior management may well consider they have much more urgent issues to deal with. Indeed, lack of clarity about purpose causes people to be in reactive mode and to tend to "busyness". They will need to be convinced of the need to change and of the benefits of developing clarity of purpose in the organization. They will need to buy into the idea of taking precious time out in order to invest in the organization's future.

Senior managers may well be somewhat afraid that they will not "come up with the goods", or that they may be personally exposed in some way. These fears could well result in the process being trashed as a defensive reaction. Such fears will need to be forestalled and dispelled. Clearly, the mission building event for the top team is a high stakes scenario — it has got to work!

M - N - o

Developing the mission statement will require a focused and facilitated process. It is not a navel-gazing exercise (although it may result in one), but a process involving reflection and deep thought. Usually it will require an intensive residential workshop.

In the follow-through from the event, watch out for a return to normal. If the team members, having returned from the event to a full in-tray, are tempted to publish and forget, the process will not produce the desired results and forecasts of gloom will be fulfilled. There may be the opposite tendency — to involve everyone in high-flown, purposing activities that take them out of their depth, causing them to feel threatened and convincing them of the imprudence of their managers.

Balance and careful planning of all initiatives are activities for which the Human Resources practitioner can assume responsibility. These are clearly needed to keep the organization focused. In consultation with the external facilitator, the practitioner must work at anticipating the subtleties of implementation and provide the necessary guidance to the management team. The difficulties will have been planned for. Nevertheless, close monitoring of this phase will be necessary to prevent unexpected drift.

OPINION SURVEYS

Definition/Background

Employee opinion surveys are a means of measuring employee attitudes towards their work, management practices, working conditions and Human Resources policies (particularly compensation and benefits practices). The reasons for undertaking an opinion survey are as varied as the ways in which such a survey can be carried out. An employee opinion survey provides an organization with a snapshot of the employee relations climate. More importantly, opinion surveys are part of a management process for identifying which practices work and which practices need to be fixed. An employee opinion survey, or attitude survey as it is sometimes called, enables an organization to assess its employees' perceptions about the effectiveness of management practices and to use this information to address a range of Human Resources issues.

An employee opinion survey can be focused (e.g., on pay and benefits) or it may address a broad range of issues. It may be a one-off survey, undertaken to address a particular issue or to evaluate a specific initiative, or it may be part of an internal benchmarking program, where an initial baseline measurement is taken and change tracked at regular intervals. Many organizations use surveys effectively as an ongoing process to monitor the employee relations climate and manage the organization's culture.

Surveys can be useful tools for measuring the effectiveness of management's communications efforts. This may be of particular significance to organizations that are embarking on, or are in the midst of, a major change initiative. Change has always been part of organizational life. However, many change initiatives fail to realize the stated objectives of the organization. Surveys provide organizations with important data to identify and address the real issues affecting employees during the transition. Prior to any change, an organization needs to have an understanding of the context of the proposed change. During the process, surveys can help with the early detection of issues that need to be addressed.

Surveys can also be used prior to the introduction of major Human Resources initiatives, such as the intro-

duction of a new performance management process. The survey can measure employee readiness to accept the new process. An employee opinion survey is a valuable organizational change tool, but is not intended to be a substitute for managerial decision-making or action. The survey results should not determine whether or not the organization embarks on the change. Rather, it can identify issues that need to be addressed through the implementation of a new process or major organizational change initiative.

Surveys can help organizations confirm that employees understand the organization's vision and objectives. They can tell the organization the degree to which employees "buy-in" to the direction the organization is heading. They may also effectively help the organization diagnose potential turnover problems.

Although usually driven by Human Resources, an opinion survey needs senior management support if it is to succeed. Similarly, it needs to be part of the organization's planning process. Surveys should contribute to the setting of the organization's goals.

Employee opinion surveys are designed to open up communications with employees and provide a channel for employees to communicate upwards to senior management. Such a survey is one means to measure that employees are receiving the message. It is also a means to show that management is willing to listen to them, and helps improve management credibility. It aids in building trust.

In some contexts, surveys can be used to benchmark the organization against other firms. Some consulting firms offer surveys that are used with a number of different organizations. Participating organizations then have a basis of comparison using the consultant's database. One such survey is conducted by Hewitt Associates in a "contest" sponsored by *The Globe and Mail* to name Canada's 35 "best" employers. Employee approval is important. Employees who work for the best employers are more likely to recommend their company to friends, feel informed about the business they are in, are inspired to do their best work, and have a strong desire to stay with the company.

Benefits/Expected Outcomes

The benefits your organization could expect as a result of conducting an employee opinion survey include the following:

— increased morale;

— having the opportunity to do something about your employees' concerns;

— an accurate understanding of your employees' opinions, which can be looked at from an overall perspective or by groups (e.g., by business unit, or location);

— an understanding of your organization's culture, and its strengths and weaknesses;

— having a mandate (i.e., employee buy-in) to implement a proposed change;

— a benchmark of current performance, which could be used in the future to assess the effect of any action plans implemented as a result of the survey;

— a measure of management's effectiveness in communicating the organization's vision and goals; and

— having a set of data that allows change to be measured in the future.

It is difficult to assess immediately the deferred benefits and non-financial results of an employee opinion survey. The relationship between the survey and organizational change may be difficult to measure. However, an important question to ask is: "Do the results of the survey match the aims and objectives you originally established for the project?" For example, have you been able to revise your pay and benefits policy? Has your strategic corporate initiative stood up to the evaluation, or are the results more general? More importantly, has the survey met the objectives that sold it to your senior management?

The overall rating of the organization's managerial effectiveness provided by the survey can be termed as an "Employee Approval" rating. This is a legitimate measure that can be incorporated into a manager's objectives. Organizations need to be cautious when establishing employee morale as a management objective. It must be balanced with other objectives including productivity, quality, safety and profitability.

Everyone in the organization is affected by an opinion survey. Well-designed surveys should have questions that can be addressed by all employees regardless of their position, level in the organization or breadth of responsibility.

The key figures in the organization responsible for the success or failure are as follows:

1. The Human Resources practitioners will usually be responsible for the implementation and successful completion of the survey within an agreed budget and timelines.

2. Senior management must have a visible commitment to the initiative or the project will not succeed. The survey will need their buy-in to:

    (a) assure the buy-in of their direct reports and that of people below them;

    (b) ensure that the results are communicated to all employees; and

    (c) ensure follow-up on the action plans that flow from any recommendations.

3. Line managers must support the initiative in order to obtain employee buy-in to the project. Employees will not trust surveys, if their supervisors are not positive and enthusiastic proponents of them. Supervisors need to be the "champions" of the survey, and thus need to be equipped to answer any questions about the survey process. They will also be responsible for implementing the results.

4. Employees — simply by conducting the survey, you will be raising your employees' expectations by sending them the message that their opinions are important. These expectations must be carefully managed to ensure that morale is not affected and that future surveys are well received.

5. Trade union representatives should be consulted during the early phases of the project.

An employee opinion survey will affect the organizational structure in either a positive or a negative way, depending on how well it is conducted and how well it is communicated. It is important that you only ask the questions you want the answers to or that you could realistically do something about, otherwise senior management may be concerned when the results arrive and nothing is done with them. However, managers need to be reassured that the survey is not a witch-hunt, and must be empowered to communicate the results to staff in a positive way.

One of the most important parts of an effective opinion survey is the communication process. It needs to start during the initial phase of the project. Both managers and employees need to be told why the survey is being done and they need to be given clear instructions throughout the project about their participation. This will include a briefing to managers to help them manage employee expectations, a letter to everyone from the managing director, and/or an article in the company newsletter to make sure everyone feels involved in the process. Finally, when the results are available, they need to be communicated to everyone.

Programming/Implementation

Design Considerations and Applications

When undertaking an employee opinion survey, there are a number of steps to be followed to ensure the success of the project. Central to this is the initial design of the survey.

However, before you get to this stage, you must be sure that the objectives and focus of the survey have been carefully thought through. Be sure that you are clear as to why you want to do the survey, and what issues you want it to address.

The process objectives must be clear so that they can be communicated to the employees. The organization must draw the distinction between a one-off survey designed to address a specific issue and the introduction of the employee survey as an on-going process intended as a complementary tool for managing Human Resources issues.

The opinion survey complements other information-gathering methods typically employed by Human Resources practitioners. These include:

— exit interviews;

— turnover statistics;

— focus groups;

— town hall meetings;

— grievance audits; and

— the grapevine.

Using all of these tools will give the organization a complete picture of the culture and which issues are important to employees.

Is the scope of the project something you can realistically handle with the Human Resources staff, or should you employ an external consultant to help you? Some argue that, in addition to bringing expertise to the survey, the presence of an external consultant will assure your employees that the survey is confidential and unbiased. However, if one of the goals is to open up communications and build trust, then using internal resources is a must. Similarly, if the process of surveying employee attitudes is to become a permanent feature of the organization's Human Resources practices, in-house Human Resources practitioners should conduct it.

Once it has been decided to conduct the survey, the aims and objectives have been clarified, and the support of top management has been won, the project methodology needs to be decided. Is the survey to be quantitative (i.e., a questionnaire) or qualitative (i.e., individual interviews or focus groups), or will it involve a combination of these methods?

Selecting the Methodology

There are a number of types of survey that can be undertaken. They range from the purely quantitative through to the purely qualitative.

A quantitative approach involves using a predetermined set of questions. The employee is asked to indicate how he or she feels about the question on a numerical scale. This allows for statistical analysis and provides the organization with a score.

A quantitative approach allows you to explore the opinions of either all or a representative sample of your employees. It is focused and allows employees to respond anonymously. It is also replicative. Large organizations may conclude that it is necessary to sample the employee population. This may be deemed necessary because of the size of the organization. Notwithstanding, it is recommended that all employees be surveyed. Otherwise employees who are not asked to participate may be skeptical of the results and have a feeling of disenfranchisement. One of the underlying objectives of all surveys is to open up communications. Sampling erodes this objective.

The quantitative methodology allows for anonymity and confidentiality. However, trust is built when employees feel free to express the opinions openly and candidly without fear of reprisal. This is perhaps an idealistic goal but can be achieved with patience and absolute integrity.

The quantitative methodology is cost-effective. Questionnaires are inexpensive to create and analysis, including sophisticated statistical analysis, can be contracted-out at little expense. The forms are, if properly designed, easy to complete and can be quickly gathered. Some organizations mail surveys to the employees' homes and ask them to complete them on their own time. The proportion of employees who actually respond gives a measure of salience. However, even though it is a result of their own act of omission, employees who do not participate may feel disenfranchised when the feedback is given to the group. As mentioned before, the quantitative measure can only deal with a limited set of issues and does not lend itself to exploring complex issues in depth. On the other hand, by utilizing a consistent questionnaire, the organization is able to measure year-to-year changes — it is hoped, improvements.

A qualitative approach allows you to explore an employee's opinions and perceptions in detail. It has the advantage over the quantitative approach of exploring issues that are particularly salient to employees. The predetermined questions contained in the quantitative approach limit employee responses to the areas probed. Open-ended questions, typical of the qualitative approach, allow any and all issues to be raised.

The qualitative approach involves interviews of employees either in groups or one-on-one. These interviews follow a script covering the topics the organization wants explored. The questions are phrased in an open-ended manner, and the facilitator is trained to probe responses further to get a comprehensive response from the employees.

Some organizations, again because of their large size, limit qualitative surveys to population samples. For the same reasons outlined above, this is not recommended, if it can be avoided. It sends a much more powerful message if all employees in the organization are interviewed either in groups or one-on-one. However, because of costs, this may be impractical when using a qualitative approach. The organization needs to be aware of the potential pitfalls, so that by design it is over time able to involve as many individuals as possible in the process.

Qualitative research can be used to explore more complex issues than a questionnaire can. It can also assist you with the interpretation of questionnaire findings. The results do not lend themselves easily to interpretation. In fact, one danger is that the facilitator may over-interpret the information. The secret is to organize employee responses with a minimal amount of analysis or interpretation. Any filtering or paraphrasing may lead to distrust. Employees know what they told the facilitator. If they do not hear it when they are getting feedback from the sessions, they will doubt the results.

Ideally, both approaches can be used to complement each other and give the organization a complete picture.

Individual interviews and focus groups can be costly and may provide an overwhelming amount of information. The cost usually limits the use of these qualitative vehicles to samples of the employee population. Some organizations are able to create forums for input from all employees and have found these to be extremely effective in opening communication channels and creating trust.

The method you choose will be dependent on a number of factors, including:

— the aims of the survey;

— the resources available (budget and people); and

— when the results are due.

Designing the Questionnaire

Generally, the questionnaire will contain:

— demographic questions (e.g., job level, function, location, gender); and

— opinion statements which contain a single concept (e.g., "I like my job").

It may also contain an open question that allows respondents to raise issues of particular concern.

Demographic Questions

Demographic questions pertain to an employee's personal information, such as age, length of service, location and position or grade (sometimes, unfortunately, referred to as "tombstone data"). These questions determine what analysis you will be able to do, and they allow you to make sure the responses you have received are representative of your organization. Most organizations will find differences exist in the organizational culture and value set between distinguishable groups within the organization. It is necessary to be able to identify the groups in order to quantify these differences.

You should only ask those questions relevant to your organization and essential for your analysis. This is particularly important if employees (and the organization) are concerned about the confidentiality of the responses. If there are too many demographic questions, it will become evident that the respondents are identifiable. As stated above, organizations may want to downplay the issue of confidentiality. This is a difficult point, as the organization will already need to have some level of trust between the managers and employees to truly create an open communications forum.

Always give instructions as to how the demographic questions will be analyzed and how they should be completed, as in the example below. Your demographic questions should be pre-coded into sub-groups, as shown below. This ensures conformity of response and will assist with data entry.

> The following information will be used to make group comparisons only. Your questionnaire will not be analyzed on an individual basis. Results will not be released for any group of less than 15 people.
>
> For questions A to E, please circle one number only.
>
> **A.** How old are you?
>
> 1. Less than 25 years
>
> 2. 25–34 years
>
> 3. 35–44 years
>
> 4. 45–54 years
>
> 5. Over 55 years

Opinion Statements

The key areas or themes you address in the questionnaire will depend on the aims and objectives of the survey process (i.e., on what do you require your employees to state their opinion?). For example, a general employee opinion survey might contain questions regarding motivation and commitment, Human Resources practices, communication, integration and teamwork, terms and conditions, and performance management. A one-off survey that aimed to assess employees' opinions about the organization's pay and benefits would be structured to deal specifically with these issues.

A questionnaire of approximately 60 questions would allow you to address eight themes/issues, each containing seven to eight questions. A questionnaire of this length would take approximately 15 to 20 minutes to complete. Opinions differ on what is the right number of questions to be asked. For statistical analysis, 60 questions is a reasonable number. However, many practitioners find that this is too many.

The questionnaire should be long enough to include all of the questions you need to ask. If too long, employees will find it overly time-consuming and may feel somewhat alienated from the process. A short questionnaire will usually stand a better chance of being completed in an honest and spontaneous way. Some practitioners strongly believe that the maximum number of questions should be 20, while others advocate as few as 10.

The primary areas that should be covered include the following:

— nature of the work;

— workgroup cooperation;

— opportunities for advancement;

— working conditions;

— performance feedback;

— confidence in management;

— job security (or future employability);

— supervision;

— vision/company pride;

— compensation;

— benefits;

— recognition;

— job expectations;

— use of abilities; and

— seeking outside job opportunities.

The questions you design for inclusion in the questionnaire should:

— be unambiguous;

— contain only one issue;

— be written in plain language;

— not be leading (i.e., not be written in such a way to give you the sought-after response); and

— be strong enough to elicit a response (e.g., "I like my job", rather than "I like my job most of the time").

Scales

Points of view vary regarding the best type of scale to use in response to opinion statements. The use of an unbalanced scale is recommended for the following reasons:

— a neutral response can be a valid response;

— it is useful to know if people do not have a strong opinion (i.e., a neutral response); and

— without a neutral category, people may decide not to respond to the question.

A five-point scale, in particular, is recommended, where responses are graded; for example, on a "strongly agree" to "strongly disagree" anchored scale (i.e., each value on the scale is anchored to a heading).

Some practitioners argue that balanced scales should be used to avoid "central tendency".

Open Questions

The inclusion of an open question in a survey should be considered carefully, as this may add significantly to analysis time and costs. However, the responses to open questions are very useful and enlightening.

You should place the open question at the end of the questionnaire, thus providing respondents with the opportunity to make any additional comments about the survey itself, and to mention issues they feel particularly strongly about or which they feel were not adequately addressed.

When interpreting open comments, it is important not to overemphasize the significance of a few eloquent individuals and use them to generalize about the whole population. Paraphrasing or interpreting should be kept to a minimum and, where possible, the verbatim remarks should be reported.

The Process

Ongoing opinion surveys that form part of the Human Resources landscape in an organization have to be designed as iterative processes. The following are the typical stages of a successful survey process:

❑ *Step 1:* Secure senior management mandate and sponsorship over the process.

❑ *Step 2:* Define the purpose and goals of the process.

❑ *Step 3:* Determine the methodology to be used.

❑ *Step 4:* Design the questions to be asked.

❑ *Step 5:* Draw up a project plan indicating required resources, budget, timelines and milestones, and measures of success.

❑ *Step 6:* Outline the project scope to all management and secure their feedback and buy-in (adjust the project plan as necessary).

❑ *Step 7:* Announce the survey to all employees, explaining the purpose, methodology and significant steps in the process.

❑ *Step 8:* Conduct the survey.

❑ *Step 9:* Collate, analyze and interpret the results. Prepare a presentation report on all findings. This should be done as quickly as possible. Ideally, this should be done in a week, but in no instance should it take more than a month. Speed is an essential ingredient to credibility.

❑ *Step 10:* Feed back the results to management and develop a "draft" action plan. Managers should be desensitized at this stage so that they are not defensive when giving feedback to employees. The draft action plan is set to help communicate to employees management's willingness to accept their perceptions and to deal with any issues that need to be addressed.

❑ *Step 11:* Provide feedback to employees. Clarify any points that were not understood and introduce the draft action plan. Secure any feedback to the adequacy of the action plan. Adjust the plan, if necessary. Where possible, get employee participation in addressing specific issues.

❑ *Step 12:* Implement the action plan. Provide regular reports to employees on the status of the action plan. If an action has been completed, the organization may want to conduct focus groups to see if it adequately addressed the underlying issue.

❑ *Repeat from Step 1.*

Role of the Human Resources Practitioner

The role of the Human Resources practitioner, of course, will depend on whether the survey is conducted in-house or through an outside consultant.

If the practitioner is working in conjunction with an outside consultant, he or she will be accountable for "championing" the survey internally. Specifically, the practitioner will be responsible for:

— ensuring senior management buy-in;

— leading and coaching line managers;

— selling the concept to employees and to trade unions;

— responding sensitively to internal issues and allaying any fears that the survey will be used as a witch-hunt;

— stressing the confidentiality of the survey; and

— making sure that the project schedule is maintained.

If the survey is run in-house, the Human Resources practitioner will be the individual responsible for the design and implementation of the entire process. The practitioner must have superior communication and facilitation skills to manage effectively the process internally. He or she will also need to command a high level of credibility and respect from the employees.

Barriers to Success/Common Pitfalls

The barriers to the successful completion of an employee opinion survey include:

— implementing the survey without setting clear and realistic objectives;

— trying to cover too many issues with one questionnaire;

— failing to get a commitment to the survey from senior management;

— conducting the survey without adequate resources;

— failing to set and stick to a timetable;

— asking questions to which you cannot address the answers;

— failing to communicate the survey process and objectives to all employees before it begins;

— failing to communicate the results to everyone; and

— failing to follow up on the recommendations.

How To Counteract These Barriers

The practitioner should:

— get senior management buy-in;

— set achievable objectives;

— keep the survey focused;

— conduct interviews/focus groups as part of the questionnaire design process to make sure it is relevant;

— set project deadlines;

— budget sufficient resources;

— communicate what you are doing to everyone; and

— communicate what you have done.

There are a number of mistakes and pitfalls to be avoided throughout an employee opinion survey. At each relevant stage of the project, ask if you have:

— defined clearly why you want to undertake the survey;

— avoided raising issues where change could not be made, or where you would not report the results if they were not positive;

— set realistic and achievable objectives;

— agreed to a realistic timetable;

— appointed a project manager/steering group to be responsible for the survey;

— communicated the aims and objectives to all staff;

— designed the survey, avoiding leading, biased and ambiguous questions;

— selected a representative sample of people (if you are not surveying everyone);

— administered the survey within the agreed time-lines;

— communicated the results to all employees (if you do not, the success of any future employee surveys will be compromised);

— agreed to an action plan;

— implemented the action plan; and

— provided follow-up communications to the employees.

If the answer to each of these is "Yes", you should have avoided the most common problems that can occur.

SAMPLE EMPLOYEE APPROVAL SURVEY

Purpose

The Employee Approval Survey is designed to open up communications with our employees and provide a channel for employees to communicate upwards to senior management. It is one means to measure that employees are receiving our messages. The survey will verify that employees understand and buy into our vision.

The survey will provide us with a measure of employee approval that will be incorporated into our management performance objectives. The survey, however, will not be the only means of monitoring employee approval. We will ultimately complement its findings through the use of exit interviews, turnover statistics, human resources practice audits, and focus groups.

Employee approval is important. Employees who work for a Top-100 Employer are more likely to recommend their company to friends, feel informed about the business they are in, inspired to do their best work, and have a strong desire to stay with the company.

The survey is intended to improve management credibility and build trust with our employees. As managers, we need to raise our level of understanding of how employees feel. What are their perceptions? Do employees know what our mission is? Do they know what is expected of them in order to achieve our objectives? These are important elements in creating the positive employee relations environment needed to realize our goal of being a Top-100 Employer.

Managers should not fear the results of the survey. It is a tool to identify areas for improvement. If, through the survey, we open a "can of worms", then we have created the opportunity to fix it. Otherwise, it would still exist and would not be dealt with.

The survey is an ongoing process, not a "flavour of the month" program.

All employees will be asked to participate in the survey at the same time. All employees will be given 30 minutes at work to complete it.

Survey results will be communicated to employees within one month of conducting the survey. Action plans will be developed and committed to within two weeks of the feedback sessions. Wherever possible, affected employees will have ownership of the action plan.

Follow-up communication sessions and focus groups will be scheduled throughout the year to ensure the process is kept current and "alive".

Questions

Questions 1 to 15 will be answered on a 10-point balance scale. The average scores will be the "Employee Approval Rating". These questions will not be changed from year to year.

1. My work is challenging and worthwhile.

   1   2   3   4   5   6   7   8   9   10

2. The company provides employees with the chance for advancement.

   1   2   3   4   5   6   7   8   9   10

3. My supervisor provides me with useful feedback on my performance.

   1   2   3   4   5   6   7   8   9   10

4. My efforts have been recognized by management.

   1   2   3   4   5   6   7   8   9   10

5. I am proud to work for this organization.

   1   2   3   4   5   6   7   8   9   10

6. The company has a strong vision for the future.

   1   2   3   4   5   6   7   8   9   10

7. The company provides me with an opportunity to build my skills.

   1   2   3   4   5   6   7   8   9   10

8. I have job security with this organization.

   1   2   3   4   5   6   7   8   9   10

9. I am paid fairly.

   1   2   3   4   5   6   7   8   9   10

10. I understand what is expected of me in the performance of my work.

   1   2   3   4   5   6   7   8   9   10

11. My fellow employees are always willing to help me out when I need them.

   1   2   3   4   5   6   7   8   9   10

12. I have considered finding work elsewhere.

   1   2   3   4   5   6   7   8   9   10

13. The company provides a good benefits package.

   1   2   3   4   5   6   7   8   9   10

14. The company considers safety to be important.

   1   2   3   4   5   6   7   8   9   10

15. Managers listen to the ideas put forward by employees.

   1   2   3   4   5   6   7   8   9   10

Questions 16 to 20 will be answered "Yes" or "No" and serve as a reality check on issues. These questions may be changed from year to year.

16. I have received a compliment from a member of management in the past week.

   Yes/No

17. I have had a formal performance review in the past 12 months.

   Yes/No

18. I have been on a company-sponsored training course in the past year.

   Yes/No

19. I have presented ideas to improve processes to my supervisor.

   Yes/No

20. I have seen a copy of the Strategic Plan.

   Yes/No

On a separate sheet of paper, write down anything you would like the company to consider that would help us improve.

ORGANIZATIONAL DESIGN

Definition/Background

All organizations have to make provision for the continual performance of those activities which are needed to achieve their aims. Management systems have to be developed such as task allocation, supervision, co-ordination and control. Such systems form the organization's structure. These activities can be arranged in a variety of ways and be reflected in a variety of possible structures. Senior managers need to give thought to the organizational design and make decisions on the most effective structure to serve their objectives.

The organization's structure is a system of communicating to employees the activities they are required to carry out in order to contribute to the success of the enterprise. As soon as more than one person is involved, there are bound to be differences in what is expected of employees in order to profit from their complementary skills. Once this differentiation is made (the distinction between owner and employee, supervisor and worker, producer and seller, engineer and accountant, etc.), then mechanisms for integration must also be put into place (operating procedures, reporting relationships, control systems, etc.) to ensure that the organization functions effectively.

The nature of the differentiation and its required integration produces the distinctive organizational design of each enterprise. There are a number of possible structures that can be effectively implemented.

The aim of organizational design is to establish an effective structure for the organization to perform well in its present environment and to be prepared to seize opportunities in the future. There is no such thing as an ideal organizational structure. Structures are differentiated according to the context of the organization. An effective management structure is one that is appropriate to the organization's situation. Factors that may influence the effectiveness of the structure include the following:

⇨ size of operation;

⇨ range of products;

⇨ complexity of markets;

⇨ nature of ownership;

⇨ product life cycle;

⇨ maturity of the organization;

⇨ organizational culture;

⇨ market relationships; and

⇨ organizational vision.

The optimal management structure is dependent (i.e., contingent) on these factors. In management literature, this view is referred to as the contingency approach to organizational design. Management needs periodically to review the structure of the enterprise to determine whether it is operating to optimal effect and, if necessary, make changes in the organizational design.

Types of Organization

Organizational structures range along a continuum of complexity. As organizations develop and expand in size of operation, range of product lines and market coverage, they will inevitably need to change their structures to deal with the greater managerial complexity generated. A scale of types of organization, ranging from simpler to more complex, can be identified.

Entrepreneurial Organization

This is the usual primary structure in which the organization is built around the founding entrepreneur/owner. Whatever is included in the organizational chart (if there is one), the actual structure is a star formation. The entrepreneur/owner interacts with everyone as he or she thinks fit, and makes all the important decisions.

Entrepreneurial organizations have maximum flexibility in all aspects of the business. Employees accept and work towards the common goals of the enterprise. They tend to be generalists who participate in a variety of different functions. The organization's strengths are the entrepreneur's strengths (in new product design, knowledge of the market, ability to build relationships, charismatic leadership, etc.).

The entrepreneur's obvious commitment and hard work usually generate similar commitment and hard work in the subordinates. However, the success of the organization often depends in very large measure on the personality and skills of the entrepreneur. This makes the organization vulnerable should anything happen to the owner. As well, situations unfamiliar in the entrepreneur's experience may not be dealt with adequately.

In entrepreneurial organizations, the opportunities for specialists to develop fully professional standards are limited by the entrepreneur's interference (particularly in areas that are not the original specialty of the entrepreneur, such as Human Resources Management). Opportunities for individual growth may be limited by the entrepreneur's need to maintain control, while organizational growth may be limited by his or her capacity to exercise control. As a result, the organization will not easily change structure to adapt to a changing business environment if the change results in a reduction in the entrepreneur's sphere of control and power. Often, only when the organization is literally facing extinction, will the entrepreneur face the need for organizational change.

Functional Organization

Increased scale and scope of operations lead to a type of organization based on a group rather than an individual. This is the functional organization where a board of directors or top management committee acting in concert, rather than the single owner, is the final authority. The board or management committee consists of functional specialists who can each contribute his/her knowledge and skill in his/her specialty and expect to have considerable authority over its activities. The chief executive has moved closer to being a chairman rather than a manager, and is responsible for developing the strategic policy framework within which the professional specialties can function.

Organizations will develop different departments around functional specialties depending on the industries they are in and the emphasis they put on managing different aspects of the business. This allows the specialists to maximize the contribution of their expertise and allows the organization to exploit fully the advantages of functional specialization.

For the individual, the functional organization often encourages the development of professional standards allowing for individual recognition in all specialties of the enterprise (production, research and development, marketing, Human Resources). Each functional area focuses on operating efficiency within its specialty.

This helps optimize the organization's overall effectiveness. It also frees up senior management time to look at developing the organization's vision and strategy, as well as to promote functional integration.

However, since specialists inevitably see the whole operation from their specialist point of view, sub-unit optimization occurs. The specialist may assume that what is good for his or her department must be good for the organization as a whole. This can lead to "silo-thinking", where the functional area works in isolation and little attempt is made to integrate its activities with the activities of other functional areas or with the organization as a whole. This may lead to inter-functional rivalry and empire building, as functions compete for scarce organizational resources (particularly budgets and senior management time). It is not possible for all problems of cross-functional co-ordination and conflict to be dealt with by senior management. They, therefore, tend to be neglected until they get out of hand and cause major problems.

In functional organizations, profit responsibility is perceived to be a senior management concern. All other departments are cost centres. Decisions are made with respect to budgets and available spending resources. Decisions regarding the added value of an activity are difficult in this context and often are seen as arbitrary.

Divisional Product-Based Organization

Organizations often grow by expanding their offerings of products or services. These may be differentiated to the point that each product or service group could be produced more efficiently and effectively independently. When organizations expand their range of outputs to this point, a divisional product-based organization becomes appropriate.

In this type of organization, each division will have a number of functions (production, marketing, accounting, Human Resources, etc.) which are duplicated across all the divisions. There will also be some functions that are retained at corporate headquarters (strategic planning, finance, etc.) which are necessary for senior management control and which the divisions can call on for services as required. This structure allows a greater degree of decentralization of authority from the top than is possible in a functional organization. One method of emphasizing the decentralization into divisions is to make them into legally constituted subsidiary companies. In which case, more headquarters functions will be devolved.

In a divisional product-based organization, large elements of profit and loss responsibility can be decentralized to the divisions, with increased motivation for the divisional managers. This structure also allows for different strategies, adjusted to the different products and their markets. Strategies are more easily developed closer to the business environment of the division. Specialized improvements in production and marketing can more easily be encouraged in each division, without having to be concerned with their appropriateness for other divisions.

Perhaps to an even higher degree than is possible with the functional organization, the senior corporate management can concentrate on the strategic thinking and planning for the organization as a whole without the distractions of operational details. On the other hand, it is more difficult to maintain consistent organization-wide policies and procedures across the various divisions. Each division will seek special treatment to be freed from the possible constraints of the corporate entity.

There will also be a degree of duplication of functions. It may be, for example, that the marketing of one product or service in one division is not so different from that of another product in another division, but any economies of scale or synergies are foregone.

Almost inevitably, a continually contentious issue will be: "What is the most equitable way of allocating to the divisions the overhead charges for the corporate headquarters?" It may also be difficult to limit the interference of the corporate headquarters in the day-to-day running of the division, and its relative responsibilities have to be carefully spelled out. This is particularly true during transition. Former functional leaders may find it difficult to let go of the reins and allow divisional general managers (who, by definition, are probably generalists) enough latitude to manage.

Divisional Geographical Organization

For certain products or services, where essentially the same output is delivered over a wide area and there are economies to be gained by producing nearer to the customer, the divisional geographical organization is appropriate, provided the scale of operation is sufficiently large. Chain store retailers, railways, and commodity products (e.g., cement) are some examples

where producing close to the market gives economic benefits.

The advantages and disadvantages of a divisional geographical organization essentially parallel those of the divisional product-based organization. Advantages include the following:

⇨ Large elements of profit and loss responsibility can be decentralized to the divisions, with increased motivation for the divisional managers.

⇨ Different strategies, adjusted to different regional markets, are more easily developed closer to the business environment of the division without having to be concerned with the appropriateness for other divisions.

⇨ Effective co-ordination of operations within the geographically concentrated division will be more easily achieved than across the larger enterprise as a whole.

⇨ Since the geographical divisions duplicate on a smaller scale much of the activity of the enterprise as a whole, the divisions make good training grounds for future senior managers.

⇨ The top corporate management can concentrate on overall strategic thinking and planning.

Disadvantages include the following:

⇨ It is more difficult to maintain consistent organization-wide policies and procedures across the various divisions that may ask for special treatment.

⇨ Since they will have to be duplicated across the geographical divisions, economies of scale in staff and support functions are not easily available.

⇨ There will be a greater need for general managers lower down the organization.

⇨ Almost inevitably, a continually contentious issue will be: What is the most equitable way of allocating to the divisions the overhead charges for the corporate headquarters?

Divisional "Strategic Business Unit" Organization

It may be that the enterprise grows to such a size that it is inefficient for the heads of all the divisions to report to the chief executive directly. A large conglomerate corporation, for example, may have 20 or more operating product or geographical divisions. Then the chief executive's span of control would become too large to exercise any effective oversight, let alone control. In this case, the amalgamation of groups of divisions into a much smaller number of strategic business units (SBUs), each with a group managing director (vice president), constitutes the divisional strategic business unit organization.

The aim is to group the divisions of those products that go logically together into a strategic business unit. This provides opportunities for synergy in the processes of product development, production methods, marketing channels and strategic analysis. It allows for co-ordination between divisions in the same strategic business unit on product development, production methods, marketing channels and strategic analysis. Thus, efficiency and effectiveness can be improved.

The strategic business unit structure gives a greater opportunity for the supervision and, if necessary, control of the operations of the divisions by the group vice-presidents. It also allows greater oversight of the longer-term strategies of the business units by the chief executive. This does mean adding another layer to the management hierarchy along with an increase in overhead costs. Since the divisions in the divisional strategic business units are themselves of considerable size, it is in fact quite difficult for the group vice-presidents to establish their roles and authority. They are often regarded as supernumerary. Good managers do not stay very long in these positions and there is often, therefore, an air of transience about them.

Matrix Organization Structure

This form of organization has one key characteristic that differentiates it from the previous types. It breaks the normally accepted constraint of "one person, one manager" by allowing certain levels in the organization (usually senior managers and technical professionals) to report to two superiors directly. The matrix structure has been most used when the organization's activities are a continuous series of projects, rather than a standardized product, since it allows greater flexibility in the allocation of people to work.

The matrix organization was developed by NASA. Getting a man on the moon was conceived as a large series of highly technical cross-disciplinary projects that had to be staffed and controlled successfully and cost-effectively. The matrix structure is therefore popular in high-tech, knowledge industries, consulting firms, and educational institutions, where the time of

highly trained and expensive staff must be fully utilized on a range of projects.

It is important to realize that the two managers (e.g., Director of Engineering and Product Development Director) are not doing comparable jobs and, therefore, are not simply competing for the subordinate's time. They represent two different aspects of management, normally combined in the one manager but separated in this structure.

These are:

1. **the resource activity** — the manager is responsible for the recruitment, development and deployment of adequate numbers of staff in one specialty (e.g., engineers, mathematicians, computer experts, accountants); and

2. **the task activity** — the manager is responsible for the task allocation and management of the work of an inter-disciplinary project involving a number of different specialists working together on a particular project (e.g., rocket fuel, communication system, space suits, etc.).

The two activities form the two dimensions of the matrix structure. The basic need for a matrix comes about because the task manager cannot, by definition, be a specialist in all the areas needed by the project team. Therefore, resource managers are needed to supply specialists to various projects as required. They also need to monitor that the pace and quality of work is to professional standards. The resource manager may be thought of as a supplier and the task manager as a customer in this system.

This structure is designed to make flexible use of highly trained professional staff on a range of projects. It allows the technical work of a specialist to be managed with regard to standards by a senior member of the specialty, even though the specialist is working with others in different specialties and is managed with reference to progress and deadlines by a non-specialist. The matrix organization encourages co-operation across disciplines and specialties, and breaks down departmental barriers. It promotes decisions that are best for the organization as a whole, rather than allowing sub-unit optimization to occur.

Managing a matrix structure organization involves a greater degree of complexity than managing a more traditional structure. Interdepartmental cooperation and collaboration are a must. The organization needs a culture that fosters quick and positive conflict resolution. Some organizations managing through a matrix develop facilitating roles to ensure coordination between the project-task groups and the resource departments.

Key decisions are not normally made quickly in a matrix organization. The organization typically can encourage a culture of discussion rather than decision. It is also difficult to maintain a balance between the two sides of the matrix. Often, either the resource side or the task side becomes more powerful and distorts the decision-making process.

Hybrid Organization Structures

The six types described previously may be thought of as "pure types", each with a clear rationale. They each have strengths but also weaknesses. Hybrid organizational structures are often developed to combat these limitations. These use a combination of types in order to obtain some of the benefits of more than one.

A common example is the hybrid consisting of mainly functional structures. In this structure, an organization has introduced some divisions for certain products, while still retaining a strong functional structure for the rest. Certain geographical areas, particularly exporting, may also be made divisions in an otherwise functional structure.

Another variation is the hybrid consisting of mainly divisional structures. The divisions may be organized along either product or geographic lines, but the central corporation retains a considerable number of specialized functions in order to ensure better consistency in company-wide standards and practices.

The matrix structure may be introduced for product development without requiring the reorganization of the organization as a whole. It can co-exist along with one of the more traditional structures as the dominant form for organizing the activities of the larger enterprise.

In all these structures, temporary developments in the structure can be made to deal with particular problems. Project teams can be set up to handle tasks that the current stable structure does not tackle very well. Developing a new product, constructing a new plant, and so on, may not fit very well into the normal, routine nature of the organization's current working. Setting up special temporary project teams may be more effective. These teams have to be disbanded on the completion of the project but, of course, their success might lead to a re-thinking of the overall struc-

ture to move it on to a different type. All these types of organizations do vary within themselves. Thus, they can be run to emphasize more or less decentralization, or taller or flatter hierarchies. Not only the choice of structural type but also the fine-tuning within it must be tackled in relation to the organization's aim of performing successfully in its environment.

Benefits/Expected Outcomes

The organizational design of an effective structure will have a number of benefits. They are as follows:

1. Decision making is easier and faster with consequent increases in motivation at all levels in the organization.

2. Control problems are reduced if authority to make appropriate decisions is placed at the right level.

3. Lead times for innovative activities do not increase unduly.

4. More senior executives are free to concentrate on longer-term strategic issues and development of new opportunities.

5. Managing conflict between different departments, functions and geographical areas is facilitated directly and effectively.

6. Overhead costs from undue processing of formal paperwork, committee meetings and other non-direct work can be reduced. Indirect costs can be reduced through the elimination of co-ordination posts. In particular, it is often the case that inadequate organizational design has been dealt with through the appointment of liaison offices (or even whole liaison departments) given the job of smoothing out the difficulties. With proper design, these overhead costs would be reduced.

Organizational development is a particular approach to introducing and managing change through the redesign of organizational structures. It is a set of deliberate strategies and proven techniques for managing change. The use of an organizational development approach to managing change will have a number of benefits. They are as follows:

1. Change will be achieved with less disruption.

2. Those who participate in the change process develop a positive commitment towards the change and its success.

M - N - O

3. More effective organizational structures, cultures, systems of procedures and ways of working are developed and accepted by the participants.

4. Participation in a successful organizational development project improves morale and motivation at any level in the organization.

5. Co-ordination of conflict between different departments, functions and geographical areas can be tackled directly.

Programming/Implementation

Organizational design, in principle, affects everyone in the organization. Changes may have to be made in task allocation, authority structures, levels in the hierarchy, control procedures and co-ordination mechanisms. Putting an effective organizational design into place is not easy because an organizational structure is a complex interaction of three factors:

1. **The resource allocation system** — The allocation of inevitably scarce resources for which there is competition and disagreement within the organization is the fundamental reason for the management structure. It is concerned with rationally making the difficult decisions in the best interests of the organization. However, the organization's best interests are not always easy to discern and are often disputed.

2. **The occupational and career system** — The structure also gives a framework for the members of an organization to identify themselves with particular skills, functions and interests. It is a focus of their motivation and opportunities for career advancement. It includes preferred ways of working, career prospects and most other aspects of their commitment to the organization.

3. **The political system** — The political system links the resource allocation system and the career system. Members of the organization will be very concerned with how the rationally based proposals to change the structure will affect their political clout. Organizational structure ultimately impacts the power, status and prestige of employees. Any proposals to redesign a department, abolish a layer of management, or open or close a regional office will have an impact on the individual agendas of those directly affected.

All members of an organization operate simultaneously in all three systems. Every reaction to a proposal to change the organizational structure must be interpreted not only in terms of the rational resource allocation system arguments of what is best for the organization but also in relation to the occupational and the political systems. On the other hand, because these systems play such a large part in the arguments about organizational design, it is important not to make the mistake of becoming cynical.

Individuals will make arguments in defence of structures that support their power base, status and prestige. However self-serving these arguments might be, they may also have a rational basis. As well, the organization needs to guard against rejecting resource allocation arguments because on the surface they may appear to be merely rationalizations to defend a particular position. The arguments, for example, by which the Human Resources practitioner resists a reduction in the Human Resources Department's functions will be real ones, even though they will inevitably be underlined with occupational and political considerations.

The prime responsibility for establishing an effective organizational design is that of senior management. But, in doing so, it should:

✓ consider inputs from all levels of the organization;

✓ ensure that everyone understands the need for structural change;

✓ explain the nature and reason for the changes; and

✓ communicate, communicate, communicate.

Structural Dilemmas

Senior management can consciously design organizational structures, or they can evolve as a cumulative result of *ad hoc* decisions taken piecemeal. In either case, the structure attempts to organize the behaviour of the enterprise to achieve its aims in the environment in which it functions. Inevitably, attempting to be successful brings conflicting pressures which pull in different directions, leading to a number of structural dilemmas. They are dilemmas because both sides offer attractive outcomes, but they are incompatible. Indeed, they pull in opposite directions. Since a compromise has to be made somewhere between the two sides, each dilemma generates a basic dimension of organizational structure that constrains organizational design. The five key dilemmas that shape the structure of an organization are:

1. centralization vs. decentralization;

2. standardization vs. flexibility;

3. specialization vs. generalization;

4. mechanistic vs. organic; and

5. tall vs. flat structures.

Centralization vs. Decentralization

All organizations have hierarchies that are necessary for the exercise of authority and responsibility. All organizations want also to have full participation of the members, which leads to commitment and motivated behaviour. However, they pull in opposite directions: more emphasis on hierarchy (centralization) means less on participation (decentralization). Too much emphasis on hierarchy leads to control loss, where decisions taken by senior managers are inevitably too far removed from the actual operations, do not reflect knowledge of what is actually needed and are carried out inadequately. Too much emphasis on participation leads to decision inertia where the process of decision making takes much time and is more important than the actual decision itself. The attempt to balance these conflicting pressures in each organization leads to its degree of centralization.

Controlled Decentralization

When organizations grow, particularly when they become geographically dispersed, the centralized hierarchy inevitably loses control over the day-to-day processes. This can lead to the emergence of sub-cultures or counter-cultures that can damage the overall integrity of the organization's dominant culture.

The growth of an organization is an evolution. Smaller organizations, by nature, tend to be centralized. As the organization grows, the senior management team is distanced from the operations and can no longer respond quickly to emerging issues. However, since it has held power and control closely, the senior management group has not prepared the next level of managers for making decisions. Thus, the organization may face a dilemma wherein it needs to empower people in a decentralized structure to foster further growth, but it has failed to prepare those individuals for the assumption of authority.

One solution used by many organizations is to decentralize in a controlled fashion. While this may seem to be an oxymoron, controlled decentralization merely acknowledges the current limitations of people in an organization to manage in a fully decentralized fashion. By setting up a transitional structure, the organization is better able to take deliberate steps in developing its bench strength in preparation for full decentralization.

One method of doing this is to set up arbitrary divisions. For example, the organization may run six plants in different regions across Canada. If the organization has three capable general managers, it can establish regional business units under each individual and begin the process of downloading responsibilities to them. Functional managers in the "head office" are charged with the responsibility of severing solid line reporting structures and now allowing their subordinates to report to the regional managers.

The general managers are also responsible for developing management expertise below them to set the organization for the possibility of establishing six independent business units in the future. This mandate is intended to begin the process of altering the organizational culture and should therefore be part of a larger change management initiative.

Standardization vs. Flexibility

All organizations require standard routines to reduce costs with regard to repeatable operations. All organizations want also to be able to draw on the full range of the knowledge and skills of members for the benefits in flexibility and innovation that this will bring. But they pull in opposite directions: more emphasis on standard routines (standardization) means less on personal contribution (flexibility). Too much emphasis on standard routines leads to the literal application of those routines, where carrying out the routines is given prime importance, even when they hamper the organization from achieving its objectives. Too much emphasis on personal contribution leads to organizational indulgence where the wishes of the members are allowed to override the organization's effective achievement of its aims. The attempt to balance these conflicting pressures in each organization leads to its degree of standardization.

Specialization vs. Generalization

All organizations require specialists to contribute their particular expertise. All organizations want also that their employees accept and work towards the common goals of the enterprise. However, specialists have specialized goals that may work against the common goals of the enterprise. Too much emphasis on specialization (lack of flexibility between jobs, walls between specialties, etc.) leads to sub-unit optimization where it is assumed that "what is good for marketing, or research and development, or Human Resources Management, is good for the whole organization". Too much emphasis on common goals — all generalists working together for the good of the enterprise — leads to groupthink, where dissent from specialists is neglected at the organization's peril. The attempt to balance these conflicting pressures in each organization leads to its degree of specialization/generalization.

Mechanistic vs. Organic Structures

Organizations that tend to put the balance towards the left side of these dilemmas (i.e., emphasizing hierarchy, standard routines, specialist expertise and small spans of control) are often called mechanistic. They are the more traditional structures that aspire to stability of procedures and reliability of outputs. Those organizations that put the balance towards the right side of the dilemmas (i.e., emphasizing participation, personal contribution, common goals and short lines of authority) have been called organic. They aspire to the empowerment of employees and flexibility in response to change and innovation.

These differences in emphasis towards the mechanistic or organic ends of the dimensions can be found in all organizational types. The general structure of a type has to be adjusted to the environment (industry, market and sector) in which the organization functions and to the degree of change and innovation that is required. These adjustments in structures are necessary, since no form of organization is perfect for all situations at all times.

Tall vs. Flat Structures (Organizational Height)

Spans of control (i.e., the number of subordinates reporting to a superior at any level in the organization) which are too large preclude effective supervision. Therefore, all organizations wish to have smaller spans of control. However, lines of authority that are too long (i.e., the number of steps from the chief executive to a particular organization member) reduce effective operation by magnifying distortions in communica-

tion. Therefore, all organizations wish to have shorter lines of authority. However, they pull in opposite directions: for a given size of organization, smaller spans of control mean longer lines of authority (tall structures) and vice versa (flat structures). The attempt to balance these conflicting pressures in each organization leads to the organizational height of the structure.

Organizations contemplating a flatter structure need to consider the degree to which people in the organization are ready to accept new responsibilities and accountabilities. Hierarchical organizations typically are characterized by centralized controls. Decision making cascades down from the top. As the structure is flattened, employees have to take initiatives and become more involved.

This transition can be extremely difficult. With fewer leaders, there may be less day-to-day guidance. As with any organizational transition, flattening the structure must be done in a deliberate and facilitated manner. Employees will be resistant to the new responsibilities thrust upon them. Managers who rightfully fear potential job losses or redeployment will also resist the changes.

The more successful transitions to flatter organizations have focused on creating self-managed teams. Teams are charged with new responsibilities that involve enlarging job scope and loading responsibilities horizontally. Team development has fallen somewhat out of vogue because few organizations were able to fully develop true self-managing teams. However, lessons can be learned from these experiences to assist the practitioner who is asked to develop a change management plan to reduce the layers of organizational hierarchy.

The Organizational Development Process

Organizational development is a particular approach to introducing and managing change. It is a set of strategies and techniques that have three distinguishing characteristics:

1. **A planned strategy** — Planning is necessary for carrying out important organizational, group and job changes effectively. *Ad hoc* changes are unlikely to be adequate. Change is continuous — both environmental and within-organization change. Both types must be monitored to discover the organization's need for change and,

after proper diagnosis, a planned change strategy carried out.

2. **Grounded in theory** — Behavioural science, organizational theory, psychology, sociology, anthropology and political science provide among them a range of relevant concepts and knowledge with which to understand how organizations function and how they may be effectively changed. Organizational development calls on this range of academic work to develop skills to manage change.

3. **A deliberate approach to change** — The way the change process is conducted has an absolutely crucial bearing on what is achieved and at what cost in human as well as financial terms. A stated set of objectives for change may only be achievable through a deliberate and planned change process. Otherwise, other forces could negate it.

The organizational development process begins with awareness of what changes, problems, or opportunities exist that the organization must address. The aim of organizational development is to address these changes, problems or opportunities in an effective and efficient way with minimal resistance, conflict and loss of morale. It is accepted that the commitment of people at all levels of the organization is necessary for effective change to occur. Organizational development seeks to mobilize employees around the need for a positive change and to build upon their contributions to the organization.

There are four general classes of situations where the need to undertake planned organizational change through an organizational development approach is particularly appropriate. They are as follows:

1. Where an organization is failing to accomplish its objectives (in terms of quality, efficiency, profitability, etc.) and the nature of the current organization (its management structures or cultures) is contributing to this failure by constraining the potential performance of the people who work in it.

2. Where an organization wishes to improve its existing capacity to adapt more readily to environmental changes. External changes in the market, for example, may require changes in the product that, in turn, would require changes in organizational structure or culture.

3. Where an organization intends to adopt new technologies or new ways of working, which require changes in structure or culture for their full benefits to be realized.

4. Where new "operating units" are created (in the widest sense — new factories, new regions, new tiers of management) which give the opportunity to design, from scratch, new management structures and the organization's culture. This may include adopting new operating systems and methodologies to make the maximum use of the people involved and not just, as is often the case, to fully exploit new "hardware".

The organizational development approach maintains that all members of the organization can contribute to an effective enterprise and, at appropriate times, all need to be involved. Most employees are under-utilized and are capable of more responsibility. Since job design, control systems and managerial attitudes frequently demotivate individuals in organizations, involving everyone in organizational development can have a substantial impact on the effectiveness of the organization. Individuals have needs for growth and personal development that can be mobilized to achieve the organization's vision.

Role of the Human Resources Practitioner

The prime responsibility for establishing an effective organizational design is that of senior management. Nevertheless, the Human Resources practitioner has particular responsibilities with regard to it.

⇒ To alert senior management to any symptoms of structural inadequacy. It is often the case that some considerable time before the situation becomes so bad that orders are lost, innovative developments are foregone and productivity and profits are down the symptoms will be making themselves apparent. The appearance of these symptoms could be an early warning. The practitioner needs to monitor the organization's environment and to raise with senior management the need for structural changes to cope with new situations before they become problematic.

⇒ To advise senior management on the opportunities for change and the most effective strategy for implementing the desired change.

⇨ To align changes in management structure with other Human Resources Management systems to achieve compatibility. For example, if the reward system is focused on individual achievement, it will cause significant resistance to any efforts to move to team-based structures. The practitioner needs to ensure that systems and programs reinforce the organizational design, rather than working against it.

Barriers to Success/Common Pitfalls

Even before there is loss of profit and crisis, there are warning signs to suggest that the existing organization has an inadequate organizational design needing to be changed. These include the following:

⇨ **Slow reactions to changes in the environment** — As the structure becomes more inappropriate to the needs of the present situation, it takes longer to achieve tasks, such as developing a product modification, opening a new market and dealing with customer complaints. Although these may only involve small degrees of innovation, they become more difficult to bring about on time.

⇨ **Loss of morale in middle management** — Most people in organizations want to do well. If they are frustrated by the structure, they give up trying and coast along with reduced morale and interest.

⇨ **Regular interdepartmental conflict** — Some friction between departments is inevitable. It underlines the fact that different specialists (e.g., accountants, engineers, marketers) have different views of the organization and their contribution to it. If there are no mechanisms to manage the conflict, it will regularly recur. At some point, intransigence sets in and the conflict can become dysfunctional. The organization can become complacent and the conflict will remain unresolved.

⇨ **Work overload on the chief executive and the senior management** — Senior managers should work hard, but excessive hours do not necessarily mean good management. Indeed, when it gets to the not uncommon 80 hours per week, it could lead to deterioration in the quality of decision making. The overload is often the result of too direct an involvement of the top with detail that

should be delegated. It also leaves little time for strategic thinking and preparation for the future.

⇨ **The red tape syndrome** — Paperwork procedures are necessary, even though there will always be some discrepancy between what is reported and what is actually done. The danger sign is when departmental managers give up trying to use the paperwork information for decisions. They regard the paperwork as red tape to be filled in as ritual (because we have always done it). Information flow (and reports) should provide managers with real-time information to help them make decisions in response to the organization's market.

⇨ **A proliferation of committees** — Committees can be a very useful part of the organization's structure, since their membership represents the power balance between departments. However, by their very nature, they are less likely to challenge this balance and more likely to look for ways of hiding, smoothing over, or compromising rather than facing and resolving real decision issues. A warning sign is when a manager claims to have made a decision — but the decision is to raise the issue at the next committee meeting! They also tend to proliferate. Beware of the situation where a committee is set up to review the workings of the committee system. This is a sure sign that the system is being used to procrastinate on topics rather than resolve them.

If the above symptoms are present to any degree, then the organizational design needs to be reviewed.

Common mistakes in implementing a new structure include:

⇨ Being unwilling to re-think and change considerably an established organizational design, which worked well in the past but is barely adequate now and will be inadequate for the future. This is the most common mistake.

⇨ Attempting to establish an organizational design that is inappropriate for the organization in its attempts to achieve its goals in the environment in which it operates.

⇨ Failing to get an adequate balance between the conflicting pressures of the dilemmas of organizational structure in relation to centralization, standardization, specialization and organizational height.

OUTPLACEMENT

Definition/Background

"Outplacement" is the process of giving support, counselling and advice to individuals leaving an organization, to assist them in the transition to the next stage of their careers. Outplacement services are typically offered to individuals who have been compelled to leave because of downsizing or restructuring (see "Outplacement" in Redundancy/Downsizing at page 398). These services are also offered when employees have been terminated because their skills or competencies no longer fit the organization's needs. While these might be considered "near cause" situations, organizations are well-served by assisting terminated individuals in making their career transitions.

For many employees, their first step after termination is simply to find another job. For others, however, the transition may be more complex. Career choices can include the following:

- early retirement;
- full-time study;
- starting a business;
- self-employment/consulting;
- contract/interim work; and
- other career changes.

Outplacement is designed to assist individuals in coping with the complexities of the available choices.

Outplacement is usually funded by the organization as part of the severance package offered to the outgoing employee. In Europe, individuals may also access "retail" outplacement services that they pay for themselves. Retail outplacement exists in North America, but is still in the fledgling stage. Some outplacement agencies act as agents for individuals, attempting to build long-term relationships with them and help them manage their careers over time. This is still a fairly rare activity in North America, but it may represent an emerging trend.

While many organizations contract out for outplacement services with a third party, others choose to offer in-house outplacement services. It has become a very common practice for organizations faced with large-scale permanent layoffs in the "blue collar" ranks to work with the union representing employees to set up outplacement committees to assist them. These can be formed under the aegis of government agencies and may be required by specific employment standards legislation.

Organizations contemplating the provision of internal outplacement services should consider that this will require a sophisticated Human Resources Department, with substantial specialized knowledge. Employees may resent offers of support coming directly from the organization that has just dismissed them. They may also doubt whether such support will be as impartial, specialized or committed to their needs as they could expect from an independent third party.

Outplacement services usually begin at the moment the employee is informed that his or her employment is being terminated. A representative from the outplacement services provider should be on hand to "talk down" the employee from the emotional experience of losing one's job. This helps to ensure that the counsellor is seen as an employee advocate, making it more likely that the counsellor will succeed in minimizing the devastating impact of job loss.

Outplacement coaching is an excellent way to help a displaced employee cope with the challenges of being forced by fortuitous circumstances to make career and lifestyle changes. Successful outplacement counselling will not only provide individuals with new jobs, it will also provide them with a new set of skills that will help them make better career decisions and sell themselves to employers in the future.

Outplacement programs are typically designed around the individual's needs and should reflect the type of position he or she occupied previously. Typical services include:

- personal and career goals review;
- self-assessment (often using psychometrics);
- preparation of self-marketing materials (broadcast and cover letters, résumés, etc.);
- recognition and development of personal networks;

- practice interviews and feedback;

- access to employment opportunities (Internet access, media libraries, etc.); and

- legal and financial advice.

The above services are designed for future job seekers in particular. For individuals looking to change their career direction by seeking opportunities for self-employment, consulting work or further education, specialized advice will be necessary.

Some programs are designed as a series of "how to" seminars: how to prepare a résumé, develop a job search strategy, make use of personal networks and self-marketing. Depending on the sophistication of the individuals involved and their relative position in the organization, these seminars may be one, two or three days in length and they are almost always augmented by individual counselling and support. Seminars can be conducted on the employer's premises, at a hotel conference room or in the offices of the outplacement service provider. An advantage of conducting these outplacement services on site is that it sends a powerful message to surviving employees that the organization is willing to go the extra mile to treat outgoing employees with respect and dignity.

When a large number of employees are displaced because of downsizing or corporate restructuring, outplacement services can be provided on a group basis. One advantage of this is that the employees may be able to create their own support group and network. Given the potentially large numbers of people that may be impacted by any downsizing decision, the provision of group services is a viable means of limiting the costs of outplacement.

On smaller scale projects or when senior staff are involved, outplacement services are usually provided on a one-on-one basis. These services are provided at the offices of the third party provider and entail specific support for job search activities, such as secretarial and message services, office space, database access, resource libraries and dedicated help on job search techniques.

Outplacement services may also include coaching for the managers who prepare the termination letters and conduct the termination interviews. Tips on what to say and how to prepare are invaluable to managers, many of whom have little experience letting people go. Coaching may also include advice on how to make announcements to the rest of the staff that a restructuring is taking place. Some outplacement counsellors also provide consulting services specific to dealing with survivors of corporate restructuring. This ensures that survivors' needs are identified and addressed, helping them recommit to the new organization.

Benefits/Expected Outcomes

Benefits of developing and implementing an outplacement process include:

- improved morale among "survivors";

- reduced litigation and associated costs;

- some discounting of severance costs;

- quicker transition to a new corporate culture; and

- less adverse publicity.

Employees who survive a downsizing need reassurance that their organization cares about individuals — that it is not only interested in reducing costs. These employees may benefit directly from counselling or indirectly from being informed that displaced individuals have been offered support. Organizations should make all employees aware that outplacement services are being provided to outgoing individuals and, where practical, outplacement services should be made visible by having seminars conducted on site.

A primary reason why ex-employees resort to litigation is that their feelings have been hurt and they feel disenfranchised by the organization. Outplacement counselling can address these issues directly. The immediate presence of an outplacement counsellor after the termination interview can help the healing process begin right away. Also, a significant part of any comprehensive outplacement program should be to provide access to independent legal advice. Rather than avoiding the issue of legal consequences, employers are well-advised to be up front with outgoing employees by recommending that they seek legal counsel before a final settlement is reached. This can go a long way towards demonstrating that the organization is being as fair as possible. In legal terms, any assistance the organization offers its employees in making the transition will be to the organization's advantage. To some extent, it may also serve to reduce the overall cost of severance.

In many instances, organizations offer contingency payments to outgoing employees based on how long they remain unemployed. Payments cease at a predetermined maximum or when the employee finds gainful employment, whichever occurs first. As an additional incentive, the employee sometimes receives half of any outstanding payments as a lump sum once he or she finds work. The sooner the employee is able to find new employment, the less it costs the organization. For both the individual and the organization, then, the advantage lies in the employee finding work as quickly as possible. Employers considering contingency payments should be mindful that there are minimums that must be satisfied under employment standards legislation. In Ontario, employees are entitled to the legislated minimum as a lump sum, unless they specifically agree to an alternative arrangement.

By treating its outgoing employees with respect and dignity, an organization sets the stage for reinvigorating its corporate culture. Surviving employees will be more willing to recommit to an organization if they perceive that it truly cares about people.

When larger organizations downsize their operations, they will often be subject to public scrutiny. The media will focus on the impact restructuring has on individuals. Such scrutiny represents an opportunity for the organization to demonstrate its corporate values and to make a positive statement about how it views its place in the community. Outplacement can put a human face on an organization forced to make difficult decisions affecting the lives of valued employees.

Programming/Implementation

Any major restructuring plan should include details of how outplacement will be handled. Organizations may also want to consider providing outplacement services on a one-off basis. Establishing a long-term relationship with one or more outplacement firms gives the organization ongoing recourse to a firm that understands the corporate culture and that will be available as needed.

The organization will want to ensure that the provider it chooses has the facilities and resources to handle its needs. Some outplacement firms are geographically limited in scope. Displaced employees will want access to a service that is relatively close to where they live. For large national organizations, the best choice is to use an outplacement firm that also has offices in many locations across Canada.

In the case of a large project, it is often a good idea to tender out the outplacement work. This may be done on an informal basis, whereby the project is discussed with a few firms already familiar to the organization, or on a more formal basis, whereby firms are asked to submit proposals. Price will be a major factor but is certainly not the only consideration in arriving at a decision. The decision maker must consider the range of services being offered and how well they fit employees' needs, the outplacement firm's resources, expertise and reputation, and the availability of counsellors.

In requests for proposals, the organization should include the following in a tender document:

- time limits for tenders;

- criteria for assessing bids;

- contract terms and conditions;

- confidentiality clauses;

- pricing requirements;

- details of business and relevant Human Resources Management policies or considerations;

- project scope and specification of required services; and

- references.

Any firm that submits an acceptable proposal should then be asked to make a formal presentation to the decision makers. During this presentation, it is important that the organization has the opportunity to meet the counsellors who will be working with their outgoing employees. These people will be acting as *de facto* representatives of the organization, so it is important that they have the right skill set and presence to properly represent the organization's interests.

When assessing an outplacement provider, the organization should be looking for professionalism, responsiveness, compatibility with the corporate culture, quality of materials, and the adequacy of facilities. Whether the contract involves a large-scale project or a one-off displacement, the organization must get feedback from the consulting firm as to what is happening with its former employees. A proper reporting and monitoring mechanism must be put in place to ensure the effectiveness of the program.

The Human Resources practitioner in particular will want to establish a strong working relationship with the outplacement firm. Periodic review of the effectiveness of the outplacement program can be achieved through regular meetings with the consultants, monthly progress reports, and feedback from individuals using the services. If the program is not meeting established targets or the needs of the organization and its employees, the organization must be prepared to make any necessary adjustments to ensure success.

Role of the Human Resources Practitioner

The Human Resources practitioner is responsible for overseeing the entire outplacement process. This responsibility includes the following:

- preparing the restructuring plan, including the requirements for outplacement services;
- setting goals for restructuring and outplacement;
- developing tendering documents;
- reviewing outplacement proposals and assessing presentations;
- following up with any references provided;
- deciding which outplacement provider will be hired and which programs will be offered;
- continuously reviewing the project through regular meetings with the outplacement firm, evaluating its regular reports, and obtaining feedback from former employees;
- approving any adjustments to the outplacement program;
- establishing corporate policies regarding the provision of outplacement services over time; and
- establishing an ongoing relationship with one or two service providers to ensure compatibility with the corporate culture.

Barriers to Success/Common Pitfalls

Outplacement services can be expensive and some organizations may suffer from "sticker shock". Execu-

tive programs typically include the use of office space and secretarial services and are, therefore, quite expensive. Nonetheless, the positive impact an outplacement program can have on an organization's reputation as an employer makes it a worthwhile investment. Moreover, the service will mitigate in the organization's favour with respect to litigation and, in most cases, will preclude any legal actions whatsoever, thereby offsetting that potential cost.

It is very important to ensure that employees understand the purpose of outplacement and what they should expect from the provider. Some employees may feel that the counsellor should, in effect, find a new job for them. They should be made to understand that the counsellor can only provide them with the skills necessary to assess their own abilities and to market themselves accordingly. Employees need to approach outplacement as the job of finding a job. They need to understand that, in order to be successful, they will need to apply themselves. Looking for a job and changing career paths is a full-time activity. Individuals need to get dressed and go out each day to pursue their goals.

Some employees who receive generous severance packages may see an opportunity to take some time off to enjoy pursuits other than gainful employment. This is certainly commendable and, in some instances, may even be advisable. Caution must be exercised, though. While the stigma of losing one's job through downsizing has been largely eradicated, prospective employers are still somewhat suspicious of individuals who have been out of work for a long period of time. The sooner outplacement starts, the better an employee's prospects will be. If an employee wants to take time off, he or she should be encouraged to set aside a specific amount of time, just as he or she would plan any vacation.

Business for outplacement firms has, unfortunately, been good — and is likely to be even better throughout the early part of this new century. As a result, new firms are attracted to the business. There are few barriers to entry in the field and only a minimal investment is required. Organizations need to be careful, therefore, about who they choose as an outplacement provider. New firms need not be avoided, but they should be examined with sufficient scrutiny to assure the organization that they have the specialized knowledge necessary to provide a satisfactory level of service to outgoing employees, and that they have the resources needed to provide the required level of support. Larger organizations are well advised to seek out national firms with multiple offices and proven track records.

Choosing a good outplacement firm will, of course, be essential to the success of any program. It is just as important, however, to follow up on the program on an ongoing basis, to ensure that the needs of the organization and its former employees are being met. The most important indicator of success is when displaced employees find suitable new work. Tracking how quickly employees find new employment and whether or not they are able to secure positions at the same or higher level is one way of determining the success of the program. Surveying employees who have gone through the process is a good way of discovering what adjustments to the process might be necessary.

The biggest barrier to success can be the perception that the organization does not glean any value from outplacement services. On a cost-benefit basis, it is perhaps impossible to assess a return. Cost notwithstanding, outplacement services will have a very positive impact on the organization's culture. When an organization cares enough to provide such services and to follow up and see what has happened to its former employees, it sends a very powerful message to its surviving employees that it truly cares about the welfare of its people.

PERFORMANCE MANAGEMENT PROCESS

Definition/Background

Performance management is the process of managing organizational effectiveness through the periodic review of employee performance against stated objectives, established standards, and/or defined behaviours required by the position. It is the principal means by which the actions and behaviours of employees can be shaped towards the organization's stated direction and strategy.

Performance management is often seen as a procedure rather than as a process. Most employees and managers identify it with the periodic, typically annual, performance appraisal interview that is only one element of the process. Thus, the process is reduced in many instances to a summary and evaluation of performance over the previous year. As a result, it does not often get the commitment from managers and employees to make it a truly effective tool for enhancing performance. It is more productively viewed as an ongoing and continuous process of setting goals, providing feedback (in various forms), and coaching for improvement. It is inevitably an integral part of the overall process of managing the organization and its resources.

The history of performance management stretches back to early 1800s England, when Robert Owen reportedly rated each employee in his mills on that individual's daily conduct and performance. In addition, these daily ratings were summarized yearly to help keep score on the employee's progress.

Performance management is much more than the paperwork exercise that many managers have come to dread. Employed properly, it is a powerful management tool that can be used to effect significant organizational change. It is an approach to managing people and their individual performance in a structured, objective and deliberate way on an organizational wide basis. Successful performance management systems ensure employees understand the organization's culture and goals as well as what is expected of them personally.

The purpose of a performance management process is foremost to motivate individual employees by reinforcing work well done and providing new challenges to be met. At a base level, the easiest way to motivate individuals is to give them clear goals to strive for achievement.

The process should also be designed to ensure that the efforts of the individual are synchronized with the broader organizational goals. This is accomplished in two ways. First, by measuring and reviewing performance against agreed upon objectives and/or established standards for the position. Second, by reviewing observed conduct and behaviour against the core competencies defined for the position.

By having clear, measurable standards of performance and/or objectives, the organization can analyze how performance can be optimized. In terms of behaviour, by defining competencies, the organization is able to articulate expected behaviours in a manner that provides guidance to the employee on what is expected of him or her. Thus, subjectivity can be driven out of the evaluation of the employee's performance by observable and measurable standards of conduct.

The process provides tools for organizing and planning work optimally. Individual efforts are focused on desired outcomes. This prevents misdirection and inefficiency from creeping into the organization.

The performance management process is inextricably linked to compensation systems. Under merit pay or pay-for-performance systems (including incentive bonuses), there must be a connection between measured performance and rewards. If the performance management process is flawed, the motivating effect of the reward systems will be lost. Obversely, if rewards are not connected to performance in a credible and fair way, the efficacy of the performance management process will be eroded.

Benefits/Expected Outcomes

The benefits to creating a comprehensive and effective performance management process are enormous. This is the central process by which organizations manage their human resources. It has been said that the only sustainable competitive advantage an organization can achieve is through its people. Capital equipment and other assets can be replicated but the organization's people are its unique asset. In order to capture and maintain this competitive advantage, the organization needs to adopt a deliberate and structured means to managing employee performance. In doing so, it will reap some or all of the following benefits:

1. Aids the organization in directing and dealing with change.

2. Provides a mechanism for communicating the core values of the organization, its strategic goals and its vision.

3. Provides a sense of direction to employees by having clearly defined organizational and individual goals and objectives.

4. Establishes progress indicators allowing individuals to monitor their own performance and behaviour and to learn from their own results. Provides employees with the necessary tools to measure their own results and to monitor their own behaviours.

5. Identifies developmental needs and helps identify opportunities for individuals to learn. In turn, this helps bring focus to the organization's training programs and forms the basis for creating a learning organization.

6. Improved individual, and therefore organizational, performance against established standards and measured criteria.

7. Provides the organization with the requisite information for succession planning, assessing organizational capabilities, and to modify organizational structures, processes and systems as required.

8. Provides a link between individual efforts and formal business plans.

9. Can be used to support pay-for-performance compensation schemes and incentive bonuses.

10. Improved customer satisfaction by focusing employee efforts and through clearly defined competencies/behaviours.

11. Can be used to identify employee accountability for process outcomes and to encourage employees to identify with customer needs (both externally and internally).

12. Through peer feedback, when used as an element of the process, teams can review their collective performance and identify areas for improvement that can, ultimately, enhance team cohesiveness.

13. Increased performance flowing from the setting of specific, challenging yet attainable, goals. Directs the employee's attention and action and, thus, increases task persistence and motivation.

14. Provides an opportunity to reinforce positive behaviours and extinguish negative ones.

15. Provides an opportunity to transfer skills and learning through coaching and feedback.

16. Provides both the employee and the organization with information necessary for career planning.

17. Employees clearly understand what is expected of them and can, therefore, operate with more autonomy and discretion.

18. Agreement on objectives through the process aids ownership of goals and increases motivation and commitment.

19. Setting objective is the requisite antecedent to change behaviours and create learning.

20. Organizational results become more predictable, aiding strategic planning exercises and providing a means of assessing the organization's abilities to respond to the competitive environment.

Programming/Implementation

Performance management processes can be designed in a number of ways. Ideal systems will include the following elements:

- organizational direction;
- goal/objective setting;
- defined behaviours/competencies;
- identification of developmental and training needs;
- performance appraisal interviews;
- rating/evaluation scales;
- continuous (or frequent) feedback through established and impersonal mechanisms;
- self-appraisal;
- peer, upward or 360-degree feedback mechanisms;
- linkage to business/strategic plans; and
- linkage to compensation systems.

Having a simple, goal setting and feedback system is a more powerful way of motivating employees and enhancing their performance than is the performance appraisal system of annual reviews and ratings. A comprehensive process includes establishing organizational direction, goal setting, continuous real-time feedback, and performance appraisals that recap the results of the previous review period. Ideally, this process can be integrated with strategic planning, annual budgeting, financial forecasting or business plans and the compensation system.

The key to an effective performance management process is to ensure it is well integrated with any and all related systems and processes. If systems are incompatible, the process will not be able to achieve its objectives. For example, the organizational direction might establish a desire to operate in teams, but if the reward system recognizes individual efforts, it will work against the superordinant goal. Learning will not take place as the desired behaviours are not being reinforced by the compensation scheme.

A. Organizational Direction

Organizational direction is required to provide a context for performance management activities. Words like "vision", "mission" and "charter" are commonly used to describe statements of organizational direction. These, however, sometimes redirect attention away from the real purpose of providing direction, which is to clarify for individuals how to contribute to and prioritize the organization's objectives. In this way, individuals come to understand how they add to the inventory of organizational capabilities. In order for an organization to become customer focused, front-line employees need to know what customer expectations need to be met, and how they, as individuals, need to conduct themselves to meet these expectations.

Employees need to know with clarity what their organization is trying to achieve in terms of:

- financial success;

- relationships with its chosen customers; and

- the way the organization wants to be perceived (its image).

Many organizations have attempted to develop their statement of direction through a consensus-building process down the ranks. This approach is flawed. Senior management carries the mandate for defining the direction of the organization. It is expected of them. That is their role. Ultimately, providing the direction is a key element in establishing the culture of the organization. Thus, it forms the context for managing performance.

Senior management must create this context by forming the words that articulate the direction in which they want to take the organization. These words must also be supported by their actions. The actions of senior management, of course, demonstrate their level of conviction and commitment to the values and direction they want to impose on the organization.

The direction established for the organization not only defines the culture but also helps the employees to clearly identify:

- the type of customers the organization wants to attract;

- the needs of those customers;

- the types of products/services the organization wishes to provide;

- the way in which those products/services will be delivered; and

- the competitive advantage the organization wishes to establish to differentiate it from its competition.

The organizational direction often emerges from strategic planning and analysis. In fact, this is the soundest rationale for supporting the performance management process. Notwithstanding, the direction should be established after also receiving inputs from the following sources:

- customer surveys;

- supplier surveys;

- internal surveys, focus groups;

- benchmarking;

- competitive analysis; and

- market information analysis.

Organizational direction defines what the organization does and how it will differentiate itself from the competition. By having a clear organizational direction, employees are able to focus on the correct objectives and, therefore, are equipped to make better decisions and exercise discretion. This is the result of the organizational direction creating a context for managing performance.

Importantly, by defining the direction of the organization, senior management creates a sense of purpose for employees. By understanding what the organization is trying to achieve on many different levels, the employee gains an appreciation that he or she is involved in a worthwhile endeavour. This, in itself, can be a powerful motivator. It also creates employee loyalty.

B. Goal/Objective Setting

Objectives have the potential to be powerful motivators for employees to improve performance, even in the absence of other supporting mechanisms. In order to be truly effective, the organization must link individual employees to its direction and business plans. The objectives, therefore, need to create the requisite organizational benefits. In other words, they should ensure that the employee's efforts add value to the organization.

The goal/objective setting process should contain the following elements:

- The objectives should cascade from the top level down. The objectives will tend to become more specific and exacting as they cascade down from a strategic to a tactical or operational level. This is the essence of the Management By Objectives (MBO) process.

- Objectives should be discussed with the employee with an open mind to allow for bottom-up feedback. This ensures that the objectives will be challenging and achievable.

- Objectives need to be agreed upon by the individual employee to ensure buy-in, commitment and motivation.

- Measures of the objectives should be developed to reflect organizational priorities (e.g., quality, service levels, productivity, cost effectiveness, and profitability).

- Objectives should be specific so that they can be translated into planned tasks and the organization of work. Timelines for the achievement of the stated objectives should be agreed upon.

- Goals/objectives should be reviewed frequently to ensure they remain consistent with and relevant to the organizational direction (which may change if the organization's environment significantly changes) and to ensure any mitigating factors that arise which prevent achievement are accounted for on a timely basis.

- Managers can use the objective setting process as a communications forum to develop team cohesiveness and to effectively delegate responsibilities and accountabilities.

When done effectively, the goal/objective setting process will ensure employees are clear about their roles. Role clarity is an important means of reducing employee stress. By allowing feedback during the process, the organization can identify the resources the employee may need to achieve the desired results. The employee may be able to identify skill deficiencies that can be corrected on a just-in-time basis through coaching, instruction or training.

More and more, organizations are becoming "customer focused" with respect to both their external and internal clients. This vision of the organization will be more effective where the employees are able to identify how to meet the customers' expectations through the goal/objective setting process.

The process for cascading down the organizational direction and the associated objectives should be well defined. The objectives themselves need to be clearly written in clear and concise language that ensures a common understanding of the intent. Many writers on the subject refer to SMART objectives:

- **S**pecific
- **M**easurable
- **A**chievable
- **R**ealistic
- **T**imely

It is important to keep the objectives simple and focused on organizational priorities (like customer needs). Objectives should be restricted to five or six key success factors. Any more and the efforts required become too complex and the focus is lost. When setting objectives, it is also important to stay away from defining the specific tasks or methods by which they should be achieved. This is a coaching activity that comes after the employee has been allowed the autonomy and discretion to develop his or her own methods and plan of action to realize the agreed upon objectives. This reinforces the buy-in.

Notwithstanding, sophisticated organizations utilize the performance management process to influence the development of organizational direction and culture, and to reinforce their stated values. This is achieved not only by ensuring consistency in the defined objectives at all levels of the organization but also by defining the requisite behaviours and competencies. Thus, to some extent, the manner in which the objectives are achieved may be dictated.

Writing objectives is an identifiable skill that can be taught. The simpler the process, the better. It needs to be consistent and repeatable throughout the organization. One should not underestimate the training efforts required to get it right and ensure objectives are written properly. Managers may find it difficult to translate key results expected into individual goals and objectives. This is where training will bring significant value.

C. Feedback

Receiving feedback from the effects of your actions or behaviour is central to human learning and motivation. It is the central feature of the performance management process. Essentially, by providing employees with feedback regarding the effectiveness of their efforts in achieving their agreed upon objectives, the process is creating a learning organization. It is the central feature of the performance management process. Employees can receive feedback in a variety of ways.

At a basic level, employees get feedback through seeing the results of their efforts firsthand. They see the products they have produced, can count the number of transactions they have processed, hear the responses they get from customers over the phone, or feel the reaction of the audience to which they have just made a presentation. Although this is simple, sensory feedback, the fact that it derives from the work itself makes it extremely powerful.

In some contexts, employees may be alienated from the results of their labour. Through the division of labour, the employee's job may be reduced to a single task that contributes to a complex process. For example, in an assembly line, the jobs are simple, repetitive tasks that contribute to the assembly of complex products like automobiles. Employees thus are removed from the bigger picture and lose the feedback of how their contribution adds to the value of the final product by the simple fact that they do not often see the final product.

Most performance management processes are designed around the performance appraisal interview. This tends to be an annual event. It is one way in which managers give specific, job-related feedback to employees. This is covered in more depth below. The performance appraisal interview, however, should not be relied upon as the only source of feedback as it can often be an ineffective vehicle for performance feedback.

Performance appraisals are infrequent, usually conducted annually. Effective feedback must occur often in order to be timely. Feedback must be connected in time with the behaviour of the employee. In the ideal situation, feedback is continuous and real-time.

Appraisals are typically conducted by the employee's supervisor in a one-on-one interview. Even in well designed processes, where the feedback is based on substantive and objective evidence of the employee's performance, the process remains personal. The employee often perceives the feedback, regardless of whether it is positive, negative, or neutral, as being subjective. This can put an employee on the defensive that then clouds the feedback. The employee gets a feeling that he or she is being judged.

Feedback is a strong motivator when it is received from an objective and non-personal source. For example, a simple production count tells employees how well they are performing against any established standards. Technology is providing more and more sophisticated ways of providing non-personal feedback to employees about their performance. Warehouse management systems use radio frequency scanners to read bar codes to provide workers with continuous readouts on their productivity. This allows workers to monitor their own performance against standards.

The combination of a goal to strive to achieve and feedback on how well you are progressing towards that goal is a very simple, yet effective, way of motivating employees. Simple feedback mechanisms can also be very effective. In a crayon factory, the supervisor posts a cumulative production figure on an hourly basis on a flip chart for the entire crew to see. A goal for the shift is also posted so that the employees know what they are aiming for.

In process technologies, such as chemical refining or papermaking, continuous monitoring of the process is a necessity in ensuring consistency in the process itself and in the quality of the product. Technology, specifically programmable logic controls (PLCs), ensures the equipment is operated within its designed limits. That same technology can provide feedback to employees operating the equipment by displaying critical information on computer screens located at their control panels. The employees thus know how well they are doing in managing the process. This can create an ideal situation for continuous, real-time feedback.

This is perhaps contrasted with accounting systems that provide objective feedback, but are often less than ideal. Accounting reports are impersonal, quantitative and objective. Managers require this information to help them make decisions with respect to a number of key areas of the business. At the same time, the information they receive provides them with a score on how well they are doing in increasing revenues, controlling costs and growing profits.

Accounting systems fall short of being ideal in that they are not often timely. Accountants have been referred to as the corporate historians. They report the results of a company's past performance (albeit the most recent past). Even monthly reports make it impossible to correct problems as they occur. Accounting systems are also often focused on outside audiences. They provide information for the benefit of creditors, investors and auditors. While they do provide information necessary to managers, they often do not look at all the key success factors that might help an organization improve its performance. To be truly effective, managers need real-time information measuring key result factors. Monthly labour costs can be useful, but real-time productivity figures provide a manager with a better opportunity to assess how performance can be improved. Reporting results as they happen gives managers the opportunity to identify mitigating factors and root causes. In this way, they can provide just-in-time coaching to employees. This is much more constructive feedback than providing after-the-fact ratings of performance.

Performance Appraisals

Performance appraisal can be defined as the organization's attempt to review the performance of an employee against behaviours and agreed upon objectives. As one of the principal means by which the behaviours of employees can be shaped towards organizational goals, it is a central part of any performance management process.

The performance appraisal is the periodic interview during which employee behaviours are examined, evaluated and documented. However, it is more productively conceived of as part of the ongoing process of setting goals, giving feedback and coaching where necessary. In short, it is an integral part of the performance management process, and a regular forum for consolidating understanding of performance and planning for the future.

There are two purposes in regularly appraising an employee's performance: the assessment of past and current performance, and the assessment of future potential and development themes. In some organizations, these purposes are formally distinguished by separate periodic performance and development reviews. This can be particularly helpful when pay levels are explicitly linked with performance.

More specific purposes include:

— Motivating the individual by giving credit for work done well and new challenges to be met. (It is important to emphasize that reward here embraces the psychological as well as the financial.)

— Ensuring that the goals being pursued by the individual fit with the key purposes of the role and are in keeping with the broader organizational direction. (This can be done through the review of performance against agreed objectives or the review of behaviours and achievements against core competencies regarded as of universal and general importance in the organization.)

— Providing a more micro-level analysis of how individual goals are best pursued and what would be the measurable and/or observable outcome of them having been fully or partially met.

— Providing a structured method for medium- and long-term planning of work.

— Identifying individual developmental and training needs.

— Determining remuneration. (The wish of employees to secure pay raises tends to give rise to a "less-than-honest" discussion, and the difficulty for appraisers in combining the roles of judge/paymaster and coach, have led some organizations to deal with remuneration outside the performance review system.)

More recent research, grounded in behavioural psychology, has demonstrated the worth of rewarding desirable behaviour and the setting of specific goals. The emphasis is firmly towards appraising behaviour and outcomes of behaviour (results) rather than personality. However, placing a monetary value on performance appraisal, is impossible. One reason is that the formal process of establishing goals and providing feedback is indistinguishable, in fact, from the informal management processes of regular review, discussion and joint problem solving.

Separating the benefits uniquely attributable to formal appraisal is therefore difficult. However, the psychological benefits of a good performance appraisal system in enhancing the motivation and output of employees and ensuring a continuous improvement in performance are undisputed.

More specific benefits include:

— the increased performance that, in general, follows from setting specific, challenging, but attainable, goals, which direct attention and action, and increase task persistence and motivation;

— the increased performance that follows from reinforcing positive behaviours;

— the transfer of skills by means of the communications and coaching that occur during performance appraisal;

— the encouragement of employees to monitor their own behaviour and accomplishments to be discussed during performance appraisal; and

— the benefits to the organization of the data that emerge for the purposes of career planning.

An important, although intangible, benefit arises from the demonstrable fairness of a sound performance appraisal process, by virtue of its focus on objective and observable behaviours and outcomes. This, in itself, can increase morale. It can also prove important to demonstrating the fairness of dismissals for incompetence (as a just cause).

A successful performance appraisal system requires the clear support of senior management. Ideally, everyone in the organization should be, and should be known to be, appraised. Different preparation and interview prompts may be necessary for different levels of staff. Training is normally necessary for those who are going to act as appraisers. Broadly, this needs to cover two components: the informational, dealing with the purpose and administration of the system, and the skills required to use the system effectively.

The information component introduces performance appraisal and places it into the organizational context. This will include: procedures and administrative details (including examples of completed preparation and outcome documentation); information on confidentiality and access to documentation; mechanisms for dealing with a dispute on appraisal outcome (appeals); and links with other organizational activities such as allocating training resources, deciding on remuneration, promotion and job transfer. A manual should be prepared that summarizes this information.

The skills concept should cover the generic skills for effective interviewing and coaching.— putting the employee at ease, listening actively, eliciting information, facilitating supportive exploration of situations, checking mutual understanding, summarizing and jointly setting plans. In addition, specific skills in gathering appropriate performance evidence, identifying and itemizing key activities, goals and outcome measures or standards should be introduced and practised with feedback from the trainer.

An integrated system of performance appraisal is central to the management of the performance and development of employees. It makes explicit the requirements that the organization has of the employee's performance and, by involving the individual in that process, maximizes his or her commitment to fulfilling those requirements.

Appraisal processes differ enormously in levels of structure and formality. On the one hand, regular informal conversations with subordinates provide much valuable, although unstructured, feedback. On the other, a formal appraisal meeting often (although not necessarily) has a formal and scripted quality. Regular coaching sessions fall somewhere between the two. All appraisal meetings involve feedback.

The review meeting, which typically takes place once, twice, or even four times a year, provides the forum in which plans are made for the future and a formal review is undertaken of performance in the period since the last review meeting. The employee should be encouraged to explore his or her work achievements and less successful efforts, and to self-appraise. Indeed, an increasing trend is to encourage employees to make some preliminary assessments prior to the performance meeting. Little of which is said to the employee should come as a surprise since the review meeting should integrate and consolidate the feedback, coaching and supervision given since the last review meeting.

The design of a sound appraisal system includes guidance to employees and managers in preparation for the review meeting and is frequently prompted by standardized forms and formats. These normally deal with the setting of goals, a review of past performance against agreed goals or against key competencies and a consideration of the future development needs of the individual.

A successful appraisal meeting requires that certain conditions be met. These are that:

— the purpose is clear;

— there is enough time, and interruptions do not occur;

— the manager and employee are suitably trained, briefed and prepared in advance;

— the physical surroundings are conducive, suitably private and reasonably quiet; and

— there is openness and trust between the participants.

More specific tasks include the following:

— To agree on the main areas of focus for the employee's job. There should be no more than six key objectives if the individual is to maintain focus. In helping an employee prioritize these, it can be helpful to assess jointly his or her importance to the organization. Where generic skill areas are used, definitions should be clearly given and kept simple for ease of reference and use.

— To agree to goals relating to the key success factors. These should be as specific and as detailed as possible. The greater the input of the employee at this stage, the greater the chance of "buy-in" that will lead to success. Goals should be specific, challenging and achievable if they are to have maximum motivational effect. They should also be specific and measurable, and timelines should be established.

— To review and set in context the achievement or non-achievement of previously established goals. A goal that is not met because of external, mitigating factors outside of the control of the employee needs to be acknowledged and recorded as such.

— To discuss performance more generally. This can be usefully structured around headings or competencies key to the organization's direction, although it should also include general questions regarding workload satisfaction and the need for new challenges, development and training.

— To document development and training needs, timeframes and arrangements for future, regular review meetings.

Any points of disagreement, if not resolved, also need to be recorded and dealt with according to an agreed procedure.

Performance appraisal systems differ widely in how structured they are. To some extent, these differences depend upon the level of the role in question. The more scope for personal autonomy in achieving results and the more unique the role, the more likely it is that the appraisal will be "personalized" and less structured.

In general, standardized forms make the appraisal easier for both parties, as well as more readily controlled by the organization. At its most extreme, different levels of skill can be distinguished within each skill area and performance monitored by charting progress through the skill levels. For this reason, standardized numerical rating scales are often employed.

D. Rating Scales

The word "appraisal" carries with in an implication of rating. This rating is usually linguistic, although numbers may be attached (e.g., outstanding (5), good (4), capable (3), requires some improvement (2), requires significant improvement (1)), or a free form qualitative statement from which the reader draws inferences about ratings. Ratings are only one part of the performance appraisal task. An overemphasis on rating can be at the expense of considering the causes of behaviour and the consideration of developmental needs.

Rating is generally understood as being downwards — the manager rates the subordinate. A recent trend is to adopt more imaginative and inclusive approaches to rating. For example, in so-called 360-degree feedback, data are obtained from peers and subordinates.

A rating scale needs to fulfil at least three objectives.

1. It measures the attribute it is intended to measure. The "halo" effect (i.e., the tendency for a high rating in one attribute or behaviour leading to a high rating on other attributes or behaviours) has often been cited as showing that rating scales are inadequate measures. Recent research suggests, however, that the halo effect arises from differing levels of generosity on the part of the raters, which can be moderated by training and guidance in how to use the scales. Further, a person carrying out the rating may still show some differences between scales, indicating relative strengths and weaknesses.

2. It is reliable in that different people conducting the rating should give the same rating for similar performance. Training, cross-referencing between raters and specific behavioural definitions can increase reliability.

3. It discriminates different levels of performance. Some rating scales do not provide enough of a difference in scores between performers. Research and experience indicate that raters are often reluctant to use scores of average and below. This throws great emphasis on the above-average scale points, of which there may be only two or three, giving little scope to reveal differences and providing poor information on relative performance. To alleviate this problem several above-average options should be given, such as requires improvement, capable, strong, very strong, and outstanding.

Rating scales vary in form and level of the detail provided. The simplest provide a behaviour to be considered and a scale. For example:

Self-improvement Orientation — Works towards continual improvement in own performance. Welcomes training, coaching and guidance and actively seeks new skills and knowledge relevant to the role.
1   2   3   4   5   6   7   8   9   10 Not at all   Considerably

Yet another form of rating scale provides levels of competence. A behaviourally anchored rating (BAR) scale includes specific behavioural descriptions given for each point on the rating scale. For example, in the case of a car sales executive (in the area of customer contact), a BAR scale might appear as follows:

Customer contact
6   Has good ideas arising from an understanding of the business and developments in the wider market place. Actively adds these to the activities itemized in 5.
5   Initiates and maintains own database of customers by networking, "cold-calling" and staying in touch actively with former customers. Shows developed product knowledge.
4   Obtains names and addresses of all callers. Shows developed product knowledge.
3   Promptly addresses all callers and answers questions politely and fully.
2   Addresses some callers but avoids others. Answers some questions, but avoids others.
1   Does not leave desk to approach callers.

For a car sales executive in the skill area of **Contacting Customers**, the following scale might be useful.

Level 1: promptly addresses all callers to the showroom and answers all questions politely and fully.

Level 2: obtains names and addresses from all callers to the showroom and stores them appropriately. Follows up inquiries without prompting using this database.

Level 3: initiates and maintains own database of customers by networking, "cold calling" and productively staying in touch with existing customers.

A less standardized approach might itemize dimensions of interest but not specify skills so precisely. For the car sales executive, a scale might be as follows.

Skill in Customer Contact

Needs significant improvement	Needs some improvement	Capable	Strong	Outstanding

Scores are often treated as "real numbers" in statistical and mathematical calculations. Strictly speaking, however, it cannot be assumed that there is an equal distance between each consecutive number and category on a rating scale. For example, the difference between 9 and 10 might be greater than the difference between 6 and 7; or that between "good" and "excellent" might be greater than between "average" and "good". The implication is that if scores on different dimensions are added, the results should be treated with caution. Furthermore, the addition of scores will reduce the richness of the data. For instance, a global rating may be the same for an average scorer across all dimensions and for markedly high and low scores on different dimensions. A variant is to weight scores to indicate their relative importance. For instance, one dimension may have its score multiplied by 2, or one may have its score halved in calculating a global score.

The advantage of using rating scales in performance appraisal is that they provide a quantitative and standardized measure and specific guidance on the behaviour and outcomes associated with a particular score. However, there are disadvantages and these are as follows:

— Ratings can detract from the use of performance appraisal to identify developmental opportunity.

— Research has shown that average or poor scores can prove demotivating for the individual.

— There are certain difficulties, referred to above, with the use of scores.

— Despite the perception that they are scientifically designed, it remains that the scores are somewhat subjectively determined.

On the other hand, the use of standardized scales in an organization is a powerful signal about what kinds of behaviours are expected and can be a means of reinforcing key strategic themes. A mixed approach, therefore, is sound, combining a limited number of competencies along with a qualitative and goal-oriented approach.

Coaching ability									
Takes little interest in the development of the team. Uses disciplinary measures when mistakes are made. "Shows and tells" rather than exploring reasons for poor performance.	1	2	3	4	5	6	7	8	9
Is aware of the strengths and weaknesses of the team. Actively steers learning development by questioning, encouraging and canvassing ideas.	1	2	3	4	5	6	7	8	9

E. Self-Appraisals

Performance appraisal is about making judgments and evaluations of an individual's performance. Therefore, it can be argued that people self-appraise all the time. When people apply for a job, they have to judge their own capabilities against their perception of the requirements of the job. In other words, they have to self-appraise.

In formal performance appraisal situations, we are clearly dealing with a specific context. The key issue is usually: "Will the manager ask for or listen to the employee's own self-appraisal?" The evidence is that individuals, even without assistance or support, are able to make judgments about themselves that are as good as, if not better than, their managers. Hence, there has been a growing trend for performance appraisals to be more of a dialogue, where each party's judgments are brought together (rather than the manager imposing his or her own perceptions on the process).

Another trend has been to use 360-degree feedback. In this, the views of a wide range of people with whom the employee interacts are brought into the process (e.g., peers, people in other departments, customers, suppliers, those who are managed by the employee, etc.). Strangely, some organizations are doing this while not bringing the employee's views into the process. The main merit of 360-degree feedback is to open up the appraisal process and to recognize that one appraiser does not have a total perspective on the employee's work performance. To exclude employees seems odd, given that they are the experts on themselves.

The point that is being made is that the employee's voice needs to be heard but not that it should be the sole perspective. It is clear that people can delude themselves about their capabilities and potential.

Hence, the most effective process appears to be one of dialogue. Individuals need to bounce their ideas off others so that they can improve their own self-appraisal. A key factor in this is managing feedback.

The most controversial issue is the extent to which allowing a person to bring his or her own self-appraisal into formal appraisal processes undermines the power of the appraiser. Managers who prefer "command and control" methods of managing are usually unsympathetic to the views of their staff. They may be forced to listen to the views of the employee, if the formal requirements of the appraisal scheme demand it, but they may take no notice of the employee. This can undermine employees and hinder their ability to assess their own performances.

Ideally, the use of staff's self-appraisals in the formal processes of the organization is linked to other developments in organizational life. If the organization is heavily in favour of empowerment, is using self-managing teams, is developing as a learning organization and is supporting individual self-development, then there is a climate conducive for self-appraisal as a formally recognized process. Indeed, it could be argued that the reverse also applies. That is, an organization cannot be serious about empowerment, self-managing teams, the learning organization and self-development if it does not encourage self-appraisal.

There are two main approaches to using self-appraisal. One method is to encourage employees to bring their self-appraisals into the annual appraisal process. This is done by providing the individual with paperwork to complete prior to the appraisal interview. If the organization is using a system of "competencies", then the self-appraisal will usually ask employees to rate themselves against a list of competencies. The extent to which the self-appraisal is an important feature of the interview often depends on the interview. Some interviewers allow the individual to drive the process and see their main role as facilitating the individual's own self-assessment. Others will record the individual's self-appraisal but treat their own views as paramount.

A second approach to the use of self-appraisals integrates them much more into the ongoing processes of each person's development. An example is in self-managed learning programs. Here individuals draw up a learning contract that is based around their own self-assessment. They are encouraged to check out their self-assessment with others and to revise their learning

contract accordingly. They then embark on a learning program of their own design that, at the end, requires them to assess their own development. In some cases, there is no end to a program but rather individuals continue to use the learning contract and feed their self-appraisals into the organization's formal performance appraisal process.

F. Peer Review and Upward Feedback

There are a number of different approaches in this area with titles such as "peer feedback", "upward feedback" and "360-degree feedback". The core approach in all of these approaches is systematically to collect judgments about an individual using key contacts within an organization.

There are several convincing arguments for using feedback from peers and subordinates to aid in the assessment and development of managers.

— Such individuals have access to immediate, concrete and rich data that are potentially a powerful source of information about their strengths, weaknesses and performance.

— Peers and subordinates may be in a position to gauge more accurately whether a given level of performance reflects the individual's characteristics or situational factors. This can give rise to a greater degree of objectivity and balance in explaining both poor and good performance.

— Information from a number of peers and subordinates cannot be dismissed as the views of an individual's manager. The number of respondents assures individuals that their own ratings are anonymous and confidential, thereby ensuring openness and honesty. As a result, upward and peer feedback carry high credibility and can be very influential to the individual's attitudes to his or her development.

— As managers become more senior and relationships with superiors more distant, there is less opportunity to get feedback from close quarters.

Typically, the judgments are made in relation to competencies or job-related criteria, or other criteria that have been judged to be critical for performance in a role or within an organization. The judgments can either be collected in quantitative or qualitative form. A consolidated report is usually produced that is fed back to the individual.

Peer review and upward feedback can be used within an organization to help achieve a variety of objectives including the following:

— **Performance management:** Such feedback can be integrated with other appraisal systems to gather data about an individual's performance. More usually, the feedback is used to provide additional sources of data to help an individual and his or her manager reach general conclusions about performance. However, more creative uses are also possible. For example, in one organization, all individuals were rated using such feedback and this was directly linked into the amount of bonus payment that they received.

— **Selection:** Peer review has been used quite effectively to help in the selection of individuals for roles. Typically, this occurs when there is a tightly defined group of individuals with a relatively well defined role in common, and where judgments need to be made in relation to technical and professional skills. Research suggests that, in such circumstances, the judgments reached can be quite reliable and valid.

— **As an aid to team-building:** Frequently, peer feedback is used in quite powerful ways to help a team to review its performance and to identify areas of difficulty.

— **As part of an individual development process:** Frequently, 360-degree feedback is used to help an individual manager identify development issues and to review progress in dealing with such issues. For example, individual coaching programs often use 360-degree feedback.

The usability of these approaches is somewhat dependent upon the specific culture of the organization. They are likely to be less effective in highly political environments and in those where the culture of the organization is not very open and where ratings may reflect covert personal agendas. However, they are particularly useful in organizational contexts where individuals work across a variety of boundaries and where the organization is quite fluid in structure and process. In such circumstances, the process can be invaluable in gathering data about the individual in relation to key performance measures that are not easily observable by a linc manager.

It is important to establish criteria by which the individual will be judged. Typically, these will be competencies that relate either to a specific role or to the future success of the organization or of the team of which the individual is a part. The criteria that are chosen should relate to behaviours and performance that would have been observed by the individuals. The fact that subordinates will only have data available on a particular range of behaviours and skills within a relatively narrow set of circumstances needs to be taken into account in both the design of a system and the interpretation of results.

When used to help with individual development, the criteria can be chosen by the individual manager. In such cases, the criteria will relate to issues that the employee is particularly concerned about in relation to his or her personal development.

Feedback can be collected using a questionnaire or by interview. The advantages of a questionnaire approach are:

✓ It is usually easier to administer, particularly in a dispersed organization where a wide range of individuals need to be sampled.

✓ It reassures the respondent of anonymity and thus can encourage greater levels of openness.

✓ It is easier to summarize the data gathered because there is a greater level of control over the range of issues being reviewed.

The benefits of an interview approach, on the other hand, are:

✓ Questionnaires inevitably require questions to be asked in a succinct manner that can give rise to difficulties and the interpretation of meaning (an interview allows the full meaning to be explained).

✓ Questions and judgments can be explored in greater depth in an interview, allowing feedback to be gathered that is richer than that obtained by using a traditional questionnaire method.

✓ If appropriately skilled, the individual gathering the feedback can collate it and present it personally to the individual manager, thus helping ensure that the feedback is appropriately understood and processed by the manager.

Consequently, this can be a more effective way of using peer and upward feedback to help develop the individual.

The mechanism by which judgments are made needs to be determined. Quantitative measures can include rating the individual on a defined scale, or rank ordering the individual. The latter is usable if there is a well-defined group being considered. It is then relatively straightforward for members of the group to rank order each other. In the case of both rating scales and rank ordering, the statistical processes needed to analyze the data are very straightforward. Finally, feedback can be given in a qualitative manner. Generally, this is a preferred option when feedback has been generated in order to help plan development. Usually, the data given are rich and can be very powerful in helping the individual.

Care needs to be taken when introducing such a system into an organization. Organizational culture needs careful attention. Overall, the introduction of such a system can provide a very powerful signal to the organization of what is expected from people in terms of openness and the basis upon which people will be judged and evaluated. While this exercise can be very powerful and positive and can be used as a means of introducing change, it is critical that people feel that the process is consistent with the overall culture of the organization. In the absence of this, the system is likely to lack credibility. Peer and upward feedback is less likely to be effectively used in a very political organization where individuals feel a strong need to manage their impressions. In such environments, openness and authenticity of feedback is less likely to occur.

In general, such a feedback system is most likely to be successfully introduced into an organization as part of a broader process. This could include the overhaul of existing performance management systems. It could be the introduction of a new management development process or it could be an explicit exercise as part of a shift in the culture and values of the organization. Care needs to be taken to explain the rationale behind the process.

Usually, the feedback is summarized in a report that is given to the individual. Where rating scales have been used, it is possible to give individuals an indication of where they fall within the overall population of which they are a part. This allows the individual to make comparisons with his or her peers.

An important factor to consider in providing feedback is to ensure that there are mechanisms in place which help individuals deal with the emotional and motivational consequences of the feedback they receive.

Feedback to peers and subordinates can be very powerful and, while this can be very positive, it can obviously also give rise to high levels of anxiety. Like all powerful tools, 360-degree feedback requires careful handling.

Role of the Human Resources Practitioner

An integrated system of performance appraisal is central to the management of the performance and development of employees. It makes explicit the requirements that the organization has of the employee's performance and, by involving the individual in that process, maximizes his or her commitment to fulfilling those requirements.

The informed Human Resources practitioner should take responsibility for overseeing the performance management process. More strategically, this includes ensuring that the processes it supports are aligned with the organization's purpose. There is also the administrative need to issue prompts, store completed forms and, where necessary, to help to act on development recommendations. Given that the performance management process is a rich source of data on the talents of employees, policies need to be established to deal with the use of this information for internal promotion and succession purposes.

The Human Resources practitioner can also advise on the use of the performance management process in addressing specific issues — such as employee poor performance, where it can be a means of setting a clear framework for expected improvement and review. Its benefits in this regard are that expectations are mutually arrived at (ideally), clear, and the outcome defined and recorded.

Where differences of opinion arise between manager and employee, the Human Resources practitioner may be involved in mediating between the two parties. A typical review format is to:

— make efforts to reach agreement;

— defer the discussion (to allow emotions to subside);

— involve another line manager or Human Resources colleague to mediate;

P - Q - R

— refer to a more senior manager (level to be itemized); and

— record the dispute on the review meeting outcome form.

Clearly, a serious dispute has implications for the managerial relationship between the two parties and, if at all possible, should be avoided.

Peer and upward feedback systems can be managed and run by Human Resources Management professionals within an organization. However, external consultants help to ensure that the process is seen as being fully objective, that replies are confidentially handled and the process is conducted at arm's length to the organization.

An organization looking to introduce such feedback needs to ensure that certain skills are in place. Where the process is to be run entirely internally, there is a clear need for some basic statistical, quantitative skills to be available. In addition, there is a need for specific coaching and counselling skills to be present in order to help deal with the consequences of the feedback.

Performance management is about delivering results through people. The Human Resources practitioner's role is to support this by helping to create the conditions in which people, and therefore performance management, can be successful. Human Resources staff may well perform their role through the design and co-ordination (preferably in partnership with and through line management) of an audit that will assess effects on performance of several factors. For example, clarity about organization goals and plans, structure, values (culture), skills, people and systems.

The audit and the Human Resources function therefore will contribute:

— a clear benchmark of current influences on performance;

— an insight into what needs to be done first and a critical path;

— an opportunity for people to feel involved in the design and focus of a system; and

— an ability to monitor key progress indicators.

The Human Resources practitioner will also need to recognize the interrelationship between performance management and other activities. Overtime, perform-

ance management, training, pay and conditions, recruitment, career planning, could all be part of a single strategy helping people to be effective. Often this linkage is not apparent.

The Human Resources practitioner often takes the role of "system expert" responsible for coordinating set up and providing training in each area. Many organizations pass this role to the line as soon as possible. Performance management is a business process that the Human Resources practitioner facilitates. Human Resources teams have developed internal consultancy skills to help with this role.

Barriers to Success/Common Pitfalls

Performance management processes are complex and can be negatively affected by several things:

— **Lack of senior management commitment:** Senior management needs to support the process both in words and deeds. If their actions do not reflect their rhetoric, it will show they are merely paying lip service to the process. One important, and simple action, to demonstrate commitment is for senior managers to conduct regular reviews with their subordinates. In other words, to lead by example.

— **Poor design:** Many performance management processes are merely a system of performance appraisals. To be truly effective, the process should be comprehensive and should include all the elements discussed herein. Too often the process is seen as a Human Resources Department initiative or project. As such, there may not be sufficient "buy-in" from line management to sustain the process.

— **Not involving senior and line management in the conception and inception of the process:** Truly effective performance management processes are complex and require a high degree of expertise to design and fit into an organization's culture. This is particularly true with respect to the integration of the process with other systems such as accounting and compensation. The skill of the designer is to structure the process and then to get input on the final design from the end users in a process of facilitation.

— **Subjectivity:** Systems that rely on subjective assessments rather than on measurable goals and objectives are open to a number of abuses. Primary among these is a poor linkage between performance management and compensation/reward systems.

— **Lack of management skills in conducting performance appraisals:** Unless managers are trained and provided the skills to conduct appraisals (and to provide regular feedback and coaching), the organization may face inconsistency in the application of the process. This will also lead to a perception by employees of inequity in any pay-for-performance system. Procedural fairness demands that measurable and observable performance standards form the basis for performance management.

— **Overloading the system:** Despite the fact that they are complex systems, performance management processes should be designed to keep them as simple to use for the line manager as possible. Performance management should focus on measuring key success factors and competencies. The process can be separated into smaller, more manageable activities to keep it from bogging down in overwhelming detail. Discussions regarding past performance, goal setting, training and development, and remuneration can take place in four separate sessions. Rather than increasing the manager's workload this separation makes it easier to have effective and more efficient discussion with the employee and can reduce the manager's time commitment.

POLICY MANUALS

Definition/Background

Policy manuals are collections of the rules, conditions and operating philosophies that govern an organization and its employees. They provide explicit statements of how an organization expects its employees to behave and they delineate how employees can expect that organization to respond in certain circumstances. Often, they also contain statements of philosophy to help define the norms and values that shape the organization's culture.

Many organizations today believe policy statements are unnecessary. They prefer to see employees govern their own behaviour within recognized standards of good judgment. This is an appropriate option when the organization has a strong culture that can provide guidance to employees on what constitutes good judgment. Even in an organization with a well-defined dominant culture, however, employees may stray from what is deemed to be acceptable.

In fact, strong organizational cultures may lead employees to behave in ways they believe are good for the company but which can later prove to be detrimental to the organization's interests. In many cases of collusive behaviour, like price fixing, employees have been motivated by what seemed good for the company and not by self-interest. For this reason, it can be important to define where the boundaries are with respect to acceptable and unacceptable behaviour.

Smaller organizations often find it relatively easy to monitor and govern employee behaviour. Group norms emerge naturally. Employees are often hired directly by the organization's founders precisely because they share the same values and have similar backgrounds. New employees learn what is deemed acceptable from the existing employees. They also find that, in addition to potential employment sanctions, they risk the scorn of fellow employees if they stray too far from the accepted norms. The risk of alienation from the work group is a powerful incentive to conform.

As an organization grows, it will attract a more heterogeneous work group and can expect employees to test the boundaries of acceptable behaviour. Employees may not understand the need to dress in a particular way or understand why they cannot take a break whenever they please. The organization will find that it needs to issue a policy statement to let employees know what is expected of them.

There are many ways to bring employee behaviour into conformity with necessary organizational standards. Many organizations find the issuing of *ad hoc* statements and rules followed up by enforcement activities to be a relatively easy way to achieve conformity. But *ad hoc* policy statements can sometimes confuse employees and may serve to dilute rather than enhance the organization's culture. When a statement is issued in reaction to a specific incident, employees see it precisely as a reaction. Such statements are often inadvertently emotive and are written in strong language that demands an immediate change in behaviour. As the problem subsides or becomes covert, the policy statement is forgotten until it needs to be reissued in response to the next outbreak of problematic behaviour.

For example, an organization might realize that tardiness has become endemic. In response, a senior executive might issue a statement saying that lateness will no longer be tolerated and that anyone who is late in the future will be subject to progressive discipline. The problem may go away for a short period of time. It will likely recur, however, because the organization has not addressed the root cause of tardiness. Nor has it taken an approach that enjoins employees to help solve the problem. The result will be compliance rather than a buy-in to the new norm. Fortunately, there are other ways that can prove to be more powerful and enduring.

A more proactive approach is to consider adopting a policy manual that will contain all policies relevant to governing employee behaviour and that will serve to "sell" employees on the organization's culture. A comprehensive and properly written policy manual will go beyond terse statements of rules to describe the vision of the organization's culture and how it will be achieved. Instead of simply meeting unwanted behaviour with progressive discipline, the organization can consider what other steps it is willing to take to assist employees in adapting to the cultural norms. Progressive discipline will be a necessary element but it should be complemented by other responses, such as employee assistance initiatives and consistent reward systems that support the organization's policies.

For example, many companies today find it difficult to establish an acceptable standard of dress. No longer is there a universal understanding of what normal business attire should be. Hence, organizations that do not find "business casual" to be an acceptable standard find that they need to specify what is appropriate dress and what is not. One problem with making lists of appropriate and inappropriate attire is that it can be difficult to make them all-inclusive. Another is that changing styles make it difficult to keep such a policy up to date. Moreover, some employees will find ways to conform to the letter of the policy while breaching its intent. Thus, many organizations find it more palatable and easier to implement a policy guideline that communicates the intent of the policy while leaving it to the employees to interpret how they should conform. Managers and supervisors can then gently correct those who have difficulty meeting the guideline's expectations.

Policy statements are also increasingly necessary steps in conforming to various statutory requirements. These usually take the form of philosophical statements announcing the organization's willingness to abide by relevant legislation, but they may also inform the employee about what steps can be taken in the instance of a breach. Policies that would fall into this category include health and safety, sexual harassment and discrimination, employment equity and pay equity. These policies should specify the obligations of both employer and employee. While they are not specifically required by statute, including them demonstrates the organization's commitment to comply and can prove useful in proving the organization has used due diligence in ensuring no breach of legislated intent occurs.

Policy statements and manuals should be distinguished from programming initiatives. The policy statement is a statement of purpose or intent. It does not address the details of how the company will implement the policy, though it may generally cover enforcement and implementation activities. Within this book, readers are encouraged to refer to specific subject areas for more explicit guidance on how to implement a new program.

Benefits/Expected Outcomes

Policy manuals assist organizations in defining their culture. Organizations that have not developed a strong dominant culture can benefit from establishing a set of policy statements that define the culture they aspire to. A comprehensive manual will contain important cultural drivers, such as corporate vision and strategy, history and future plans, mission and goals, but its central purpose will be to communicate organizational norms and values to employees. It can also prove to be an important orientation tool, indoctrinating new employees into the organizational culture.

Policy manuals are principally used to govern employee behaviour. By establishing a set of workplace rules, the company lets its employees know what is acceptable behaviour and what isn't. Some may go further by outlining the consequences for breaches of policy. Requiring employees to acknowledge receipt of a written set of rules can establish a basis for proving culpability. It can be difficult to hold employees accountable for adhering to a rule they do not know exists. This would not be a concern in the case of behaviour that any reasonable person would find unacceptable — like theft. In the case of a more organization-specific rule, however, there is an onus on the employer to demonstrate that the employee was aware of the existence of the rule or at least ought to have been.

Organizations often establish policies to deal with issues that they have found problematic or that might pose a risk to the organization. Policies on harassment and employment equity, for example, reduce the risk that legislation will be breached or costly penalties will be incurred. Other policies might address concerns that ultimately affect productivity. A dress code might seem like a simple matter of appearance. But the creation of a specific corporate image can be achieved through a policy such as a dress code, which can also have an impact on individual productivity. It has been argued, for example, that relaxed dress codes in high-tech environments help develop a more creative culture.

In its heyday, IBM recognized that its strict dress code might have had a negative impact on creativity, at least to the extent that they had difficulty recruiting young techies who preferred a more relaxed environment. It responded by creating the Thomas Watson

Center, where techies could dress as they pleased. This allowed IBM to maintain its core culture, manifest in the professional dress and decorum of its representatives at the home office.

Strong corporate cultures become self-sustaining. A policy manual is only a tool to describe and support the culture. In order to be effective, the policy manual must be supported by senior management and consistently followed by line management.

Programming/Implementation

A. Publishing/Distribution Strategies

There are many ways of publishing and distributing policy manuals. Some organizations create binders that contain all the policy statements they believe to be relevant in the context of their organization. These binders are often large and distribution is therefore limited to managers, who become the keepers of the policy manual. Employees are invited to reference the manual by asking their manager any questions they might have.

Other organizations supply individual copies to each employee in the form of an employee handbook. This distribution method sometimes creates a constraint on the number of policies that are created.

In both cases, there are usually far too many policies for the employee to absorb. Policy manuals seem predestined to gather dust on employees' shelves. The result is that line management finds that the manuals do not have a significant impact on employee behaviour and that they are still in the position of having to issue reactive notices reminding employees that there is a policy, the breach of which has consequences.

To overcome these weaknesses, the Human Resources practitioner must devise a comprehensive strategy for the development and implementation of a policy regime, in which the policy manual is but one element.

A recommended strategy is to start with the creation of a "Master Policy Manual". This manual will contain every policy and statement of operating philosophy relevant to the organization. As such, it should be established as a controlled document. That is to say, it will be published in limited numbers and only senior managers will be provided with a copy. Each copy will be an original and reproduction will not be permitted.

Each policy statement will be numbered and dated so that the Human Resources Department can ensure each copy is kept up to date.

The next step will be to produce several shorter documents that are derived from the master document. The organization's vision and central philosophies on safety, human rights and business ethics could, for example, be published in pamphlet form, to be given to employees and recruits. To ensure that these pamphlets don't start collecting dust before they've been read, they should be distributed in employee meetings where the significance of the policy statements is discussed. This helps to develop a common understanding and to develop a definition of behaviours that would support the vision and philosophies.

In addition to these individual policy documents, a condensed employee handbook can be created that will contain only those policies most directly relevant to an employee's position and the terms and conditions of his or her employment. Different handbooks can be created for different groups of employees (exempt versus non-exempt, bargaining-unit versus non-bargaining-unit, salaried versus hourly). This piecemeal approach helps to prevent information overload. Each piece can be supported by a specific communications strategy. Every time the handbook is updated, the Human Resources Department can arrange for group meetings to discuss the changes with affected employees.

Special policies that are relevant only to a small group (relocation policies, for example) can be published in a small handbook available on an as-needed basis. A document that describes the organization, its history, products and services, and identifies its senior staff and operating facilities, might also be created. In booklet form, this type of document could also be used as a marketing tool. To ensure consistency, the Human Resources Department might want to work closely with the sales and marketing group.

An essential element of the "Master Policy Manual" will be a statement outlining how policies will be reviewed and updated. Usually, the Chief Executive Officer (CEO) is the only one granted the authority to approve policy changes. But, in some organizations, the Human Resources executive may be empowered to do so. For maximum effectiveness, as well as to ensure the document does not merely gather dust, a routine review of the "Master Policy Manual" should be established. The best way to do this is to charge the Human Resources Department with the responsibility of reviewing the document once every year. A specific time, e.g., every March, should be established for the Human Resources Department to submit any suggested changes to the CEO for approval.

In addition to these internal considerations, the master document may be subject to change when there are changes in the relevant legislation or other emerging concerns, such as the introduction of new technology or work methods. For example, when organizations first introduced Internet access, they needed to establish guidelines for employees, defining what was acceptable and unacceptable personal use. A review of policies may also be precipitated by outside events. In the wake of the September 11, 2001, terrorist attacks in New York and Washington, D.C., many organizations have reviewed their security policies and emergency procedures. It is the responsibility of the Human Resources Department to monitor such *ad hoc* changes and to make the recommended changes to the "Master Policy Manual".

The "Master Policy Manual" will be a comprehensive document. What follows is a brief description of some of the more common elements of such a document.

B. Welcome Message

The welcome message introduces employees to the organization and the employee handbook as described above. For best effect, employees should be introduced to the Employee Handbook during their orientation.

The welcome message sets the stage for the employee's employment experience so it is important to set the appropriate tone. Some handbooks are written in a harsh legalistic tone that can turn the new recruit off. The welcoming message should be positive and sincere and should reflect the organization's culture.

The message will describe the general intent and purpose of the handbook. While some handbooks attempt to be all-inclusive, others only cover the most basic information. Whichever style is chosen, the welcome message should indicate what is covered by the manual and what is not. It should also tell employees where they can seek clarification of individual policies, as well as further information regarding subject matter not covered by the handbook.

To demonstrate senior management's endorsement, the message should come from the CEO. This will show that the organization's commitment to the culture its policies promote comes from the very highest level. It also *de facto* introduces the employee to the CEO and helps develop a connection to the organization's values. If the CEO leaves the organization and is replaced, a new welcome message will need to be created.

The following is a typical welcoming message:

> Welcome new employee!
>
> On behalf of your colleagues, I welcome you to our organization and wish you every success here.
>
> We believe that each employee contributes directly to our growth and success, and we hope you will take pride in being a member of our team.
>
> This handbook was developed to describe some of the expectations of our employees and to outline the policies, programs, and benefits available to eligible employees. Employees should familiarize themselves with the contents of the employee handbook as soon as possible, for it will answer many questions about employment with our organization.
>
> If you have any questions that are not answered by the handbook you should contact your supervisor or the Human Resources Department.
>
> We hope that your experience here will be challenging, enjoyable, and rewarding. Again, welcome!
>
> Sincerely,
>
> Chief Executive Officer

C. Introductory Statement

The Introductory Statement describes the specific purpose of the policy manual and establishes procedures for making changes to the document. It is important to note that the manual may be considered an implicit part of the employee's employment contract. It is, therefore, important for employees to know that changes can be made and to understand how those changes could come about.

In some organizations, a specific time frame for reviewing policies may be established. The Human Resources Department, for example, might be made explicitly responsible for updating the manual once a year, issuing the revisions to policy manual holders and communicating the changes to all employees. Policies may also be revised on an *ad hoc* basis to comply with changing legislation or to address issues that were not considered when the manual was first published.

Many organizations issue their policy manual as a controlled document given only to managers who must acknowledge its receipt. Each section of the manual is numbered and dated. As revisions are made, the revision date is added, along with a clear indication of which policy is being replaced. Distribution of revisions is limited to those managers who possess a manual and who must inform employees of any material changes.

The following is a sample of a typical Introductory Statement:

> This manual is designed to acquaint you with our organization and provide you with information about working conditions, employee benefits, and some of the policies affecting your employment. You should read, understand, and comply with all provisions of the manual. It describes many of your responsibilities as an employee and outlines the programs developed by our organization to benefit employees. One of our objectives is to provide a work environment that is conducive to both personal and professional growth.
>
> No employee manual can anticipate every circumstance or question about policy. As our organization continues to grow, the need may arise and the organization reserves the right to revise, supplement, or rescind any policies or portion of the manual from time to time as it deems appropriate, in its sole and absolute discretion. Employees will, of course, be notified of such changes to the handbook as they occur.

D. Company Vision/Mission Statement

A mission statement is a succinct declaration of the purpose of an endeavour. It gives clear expression to what is to be achieved, in what manner it will be achieved and why it is worth achieving. The terms "mission statement" and "vision statement" are often synonymous. But, for some practitioners, the distinction is that a vision statement is a higher-level statement that describes an organization's aspirations, while a mission statement describes the way in which that vision will be achieved. The debate about this distinction is of dubious value for our present purposes and we will therefore consider the two to be the same.

A mission statement should clearly and explicitly speak to employees about the organization's goals. It

has been said that "purpose throws an anchor into the future". Developing a mission statement can be a powerful management tool for channelling the activities of every individual employee towards a common goal. By giving employees a common purpose, it creates a sense that what they do is worthwhile. Employees gain a sense of satisfaction in knowing that their workplace activities are part of a greater purpose. It is the responsibility of management to create that purpose and communicate it in a way that leads to action on the part of employees. It is an essential element in creating the overall culture of the organization.

A mission statement enables all employees to align themselves with organizational vision, or at least to know where alignment is lacking. Modern organizational theory, borrowing from physics, suggests that shared mission creates a "field" in which energies can flow (as in electromagnetic fields), releasing potentials that otherwise remain latent. Fields are invisible to us, but we know them by their effect.

If it is to be of value, a mission statement must be the result of genuine introspection and thought. All too often, mission statements are produced superficially, even delegated, as a kind of window dressing operation. When created without real soul searching or due diligence, only to be relegated to the office wall or used to adorn the annual report, the mission statement might initially impress but it will serve little long-term purpose. When done well, it will embody the loftiest, most abstract and value-laden goals and will mobilize latent human energies towards realizing those goals. (See also Mission Statements at page 269 *et seq.*)

E. Customer Relations

Many organizations today are attempting to be more customer-focused. This means taking steps to ensure employees understand the importance of each customer contact. In the early '80s, Jan Carlzon engineered a remarkable turnaround in the fortunes of the Scandinavian Air System (SAS) by focusing the attention of every employee on the need to provide service excellence. Carlzon reasoned as follows:

> SAS has ten million passengers a year. The average passenger comes into contact with five SAS employees. Therefore, SAS is the product of the ten million times the five. SAS is fifty million "moments of truth" per year. Fifty million, unique, never to be repeated opportunities

to distinguish ourselves, in a memorable fashion, from each and every one of our competitors. SAS is the contact of one person in the market and one person at SAS. That is SAS.

[See *A Passion for Excellence*, by Tom Peters and Nancy Austin, Warner Books, 1986.]

An important first step for any organization is to communicate clearly and concisely how it wants its customers to be treated. The following is an example of a brief statement regarding Customer Relations:

> Customers are among our organization's most valuable assets. Every employee represents our organization to our customers and the public. The way we do our jobs presents an image of our entire organization. Customers judge all of us by how they are treated with each employee contact. Therefore, one of our first business priorities is to assist any customer or potential customer. Nothing is more important than being courteous, friendly, helpful, and prompt in the attention you give to customers.

> Customers who wish to lodge specific comments or complaints should be directed to the Customer Services Department for appropriate action. Our personal contact with the public, our manners on the telephone, and the communications we send to customers are a reflection not only of ourselves, but also of the professionalism of the organization. Positive customer relations not only enhance the public's perception or image of the organization, but also pay off in greater customer loyalty and increased sales and profit.

F. Ethics and Conduct

Another growing concern for many organizations is the ethical conduct of the organization and its employees. For some, ethical behaviour is a given. But organizations should consider carefully the potential impact of issuing philosophical statements about business ethics before they issue them. These statements should occupy a central part of the organization's culture and they will lose their effect if they are not followed consistently.

Business ethics do not conform to black and white definitions. For example, organizations in the primary and secondary sectors are under increasing pressure to consider how their operations affect the environment. Companies in industries such as oil exploration, forestry, and refining need to be very careful that the statements they make do not to provoke criticism.

Statements of ethics should never be used to create spin for the company's image.

Ethical statements must be supported by commitment and action or they will have no effect. A number of organizations have created senior-level positions for Ethics Officers who act as ombudsmen to help resolve ethical dilemmas and mediate any disputes which arise from the implementation of a policy on ethics. Employees, for instance, might question whether or not the actions of their supervisors comply with the standards set by the policy. Without some assurances that "whistle-blowers" will be protected from retribution, the policy will be nothing more than a motherhood statement.

Here is a sample of a basic policy on Ethical Conduct:

> The successful business operation and reputation of our organization is built upon the principles of fair dealing and ethical conduct of our employees. Our reputation for integrity and excellence requires careful observance of the spirit and letter of all applicable laws and regulations, as well as a scrupulous regard for the highest standards of conduct and personal integrity.

> The continued success of our organization is dependent upon our customers' trust and we are dedicated to preserving that trust. Employees owe a duty to the organization, its customers, and shareholders to act in a way that will merit the continued trust and confidence of the public.

> Our organization will comply with all applicable laws and regulations and expects its directors, officers, and employees to conduct business in accordance with the letter, spirit, and intent of all relevant laws and to refrain from any illegal, dishonest, or unethical conduct.

> In general, the use of good judgment, based on high ethical principles, will guide you with respect to lines of acceptable conduct. If a situation arises where it is difficult to determine the proper course of action, the matter should be discussed openly with your immediate supervisor and, if necessary, with the Human Resources Department for advice and consultation.

> Compliance with this policy of business ethics and conduct is the responsibility of every employee. Disregarding or failing to comply with this standard of business ethics and conduct could lead to disciplinary action, up to and including possible termination of employment.

G. Health and Safety Policy

Health and safety policy statements should occupy a prominent place in the policy manual and are particularly important in industrial settings. Health and safety policies are a necessary part of any comprehensive safety program and should therefore comply with the requirements of a safety audit. These requirements include:

- defining the responsibilities of the employer, supervisors, employees and contractors;

- a general statement that the employer will exercise due diligence;

- specific requirements regarding the use of personal protective equipment and the following of safety rules; and

- a commitment to comply with all relevant legislation and regulations.

Some organizations include all their safety policies including specific issues like confined spaces, hot work and lock-out procedures in their general policy manuals. Quite frankly, this is a mistake because it leads to information overload and diminishes the importance of safety rules. It is strongly recommended that these items be dealt with in a separate safety manual. We do not deal with health and safety issues *per se* in this book, as this subject is worthy of its own guide (see the *Canadian Employment Safety and Health Guide* published in electronic and print formats by CCH Canadian Limited).

A health and safety policy statement might look like this:

> We are committed to providing an outstanding work environment for all our employees. This includes taking every step reasonable in the circumstances to ensure and protect the health and safety of every employee and complying with all relevant legislation and regulations.
>
> This commitment involves everyone doing his or her part. Management will provide the guidance, tools and resources so that every job can be done safely. Supervisors will make sure employees are trained in proper, safe work methods and that safety policies are implemented and enforced. Employees will work safely at all times, report hazards and injuries immediately to their supervisor, and will follow prescribed work practices including the wearing of required personal protective equipment. Contractors are expected to obey all safety rules and conform to this policy.

> Collectively we will work continuously towards the ultimate goal of eliminating personal injuries, accidental losses and damage to the environment. Our goals will be reached with everyone sharing our vision and placing their efforts into creating an outstanding and safe work environment.

H. Sexual and Other Unlawful Harassment

Another area that should feature prominently as a matter of operating philosophy and that serves as a prime cultural driver is the organization's stand on sexual and other unlawful harassment or discrimination. Under human rights legislation, every individual has the right to work in an environment free from harassment or discrimination. To support this fundamental right, organizations should take a proactive step by publishing their stand on the issue and informing employees of the mechanisms that have been put in place to protect them.

The very nature of harassment and discrimination makes its detection difficult. Victimized employees often feel too threatened by their harasser to come forward with a concern or complaint. The policy statement must, therefore, give employees the confidence that their concerns will be addressed with sensitivity and that they will be protected from any retribution.

Sexual harassment is defined as unwanted sexual advances or visual, verbal, or physical conduct of a sexual nature. This definition covers many forms of offensive behaviour, including gender-based harassment of a person of the same sex as the harasser. Since it is not necessarily understood clearly by all, some specific examples of sexual harassment may help to clarify the definition:

- unwanted sexual advances;

- employment benefits offered in exchange for sexual favours;

- reprisals or threats of reprisals after a negative response to sexual advances;

- visual conduct that includes leering, making sexual gestures, or displaying sexually suggestive objects or pictures, cartoons or posters;

- verbal conduct that includes making derogatory comments, epithets, slurs, or jokes;

- verbal abuse of a sexual nature, including graphic verbal comments about an individual's body, sexually degrading words used to describe an individual, or suggestive or obscene letters, notes, or invitations; or

- physical conduct that includes touching, assaulting, or impeding movements.

At a minimum, the statement should announce the organization's commitment to creating a work environment free from all forms of discrimination and harassment, as well as all other forms of coercive or disruptive conduct. Most statements will go further to define the unwanted conduct as actions, words, jokes, or comments based on an individual's sex, race, colour, national origin, age, religion, disability, sexual orientation, or any other legally protected characteristic.

The statement will make it clearly known that such behaviour will not be tolerated. However, each organization should consider how far it wishes to go in outlining what the consequences might be for any breach of this policy. Some organizations have adopted a zero tolerance policy on discrimination and harassment. Others might want to consider that, as despicable as this behaviour might be, the offending individual may truly not be aware of why their behaviour constitutes a breach of another's rights. For this reason, it is advisable for the organization to consider providing ongoing sexual harassment training to ensure that all employees have the opportunity to work in an environment free of sexual and other unlawful harassment.

Controversy still surrounds the treatment of sexual orientation as a prohibited ground for discrimination. Some Canadian jurisdictions remain silent on the protected status of sexual orientation. As a result, a number of court challenges have been launched to sort out the rights of homosexuals with regards to benefit entitlements and pensions rights. Organizations need to consider how they wish to handle this issue. This goes beyond simply including sexual orientation in the general statements regarding discrimination and harassment.

If sexual orientation is recognized as a prohibited ground for discrimination, the organization needs to review other practices such as benefit entitlements, to ensure that it is taking a consistent approach. Organizations should also review the relevant legislation in their jurisdiction to ensure they are in compliance.

Human Resources practitioners should also recognize that many legitimate personal relationships are formed at work. Therefore, not all sexual advances can be characterized as sexual harassment. The key is that unwelcome sexual advances are prohibited as a matter of law and basic human rights.

Employees should be encouraged to report immediately to their supervisor any sexual or other unlawful harassment they experience or witness in the workplace. If the supervisor is unavailable or it would be inappropriate to contact that person, the employee should be instructed to contact a designated member of management — usually a member of the Human Resources Department. The employee must also be assured that he or she can raise concerns and make reports without fear of reprisal or retaliation.

All allegations of sexual harassment should be quickly and discreetly investigated. To the greatest extent possible, the confidentiality of the employee and any witnesses, as well as that of the alleged harasser, must be protected against unnecessary disclosure. When the investigation is complete, the employee must be informed of the outcome of the investigation.

Some organizations engage the services of legal counsel or an outside ombudsman to investigate claims of harassment and discrimination. This ensures impartiality and provides the organization itself with some level of protection. Organizations should understand that they must take proactive steps to eradicate harassment in the workplace or they will otherwise risk being vicariously libel for the actions of their employees. Establishing a policy to protect employees is just one step towards developing a proactive approach. To be complete, the organization should conduct workshops to ensure that a common understanding is reached. These seminars will underscore the seriousness of the issue and demonstrate the organization's commitment to protecting the human rights of all its employees.

I. Employee Relations

Some organizations choose to make explicit statements about how they wish to treat their employees. This is particularly prevalent among employers who have adopted a "union-free strategy". In these cases, "motherhood" statements — to the effect that the organization will treat its employees with dignity and respect — are insufficient.

In stating its employee relations' philosophy, an organization will want to indicate what voice employees will have in such matters as the setting of new policies. It should also make employees aware of what recourse they have if they believe they have been dealt with in an unfair or arbitrary manner. Some organizations establish an open door policy and, going beyond merely saying that managers will maintain an open door, they define the steps an employee can take to have a complaint or concern heard without fear of retribution.

Policies on employee relations are often treated as no more then "motherhood" statements. But much more serious consideration needs to go into their construction. For example, a common statement is "Our employees are our most important asset". This seems innocuous enough. However, if the organization has a policy of laying off employees during economic downturns, it contradicts its own stated values. After all, the organization doesn't sell off its machinery when work orders slow down. The point is simply that all statements must be carefully considered and their impact assessed before being published. Policy writers should never treat their work as trivial or otherwise unimportant.

J. Employment and Pay Equity

Although Canadian jurisdictions have not adopted the strict reporting regimen of the Equal Opportunities Commission in the United States, there have been some attempts at drafting legislation to address this important issue. Many organizations have adopted policy statements — partially in anticipation of potential legislation and partially to comply with existing requirements under federal contractors' rules or the requirements of vendors to certain municipalities (the City of Toronto, for example).

A more compelling reason to adopt such language is that it can send a powerful message about the organization's values. The obvious argument in favour of such policies is that they can aid in the battle against discrimination in the workplace. Organizations may find that they employ a relatively homogeneous workforce because those who are doing the hiring tend to gravitate towards individuals who share their own background and experience. In order to develop a more heterogeneous work population, organizations must take proactive steps to attract people of different backgrounds. Failing to do so not only flies in the face

of human rights statutes, but also deprives the organization of access to a wider pool of potential candidates.

Employment equity policies will mirror the statements made with respect to sexual and other unlawful harassment and may be combined with these in a single blanket policy. Organizations in jurisdictions that govern pay equity (Ontario, Quebec, Federal) may also want to include a statement, like the following one, regarding the company's philosophy of equal pay for work of equal value.

> In order to provide equal employment and advancement opportunities to all individuals, employment decisions will be based on merit, qualifications, and abilities. Our organization does not discriminate in employment opportunities or practices on the basis of race, colour, religion, sex, national origin, age, or any other characteristic protected by law.
>
> This policy governs all aspects of employment, including selection, job assignment, compensation, discipline, termination, and access to benefits and training.
>
> Any employees with questions or concerns about any type of discrimination in the workplace are encouraged to bring these issues to the attention of their immediate supervisor or the Human Resources Department. Employees can raise concerns and make reports without fear of reprisal. Anyone found to be engaging in any type of unlawful discrimination will be subject to disciplinary action, up to and including termination of employment.

K. Organization Description

The description of the organization tells the employee about the past, present and future of the organization and helps frame the context in which the culture has developed. It can form part of the main body of the policy manual or can be published in a separate pamphlet so that it can be used as a recruiting tool or in other marketing initiatives. Human Resources practitioners in larger organizations might seek the assistance of the marketing department in writing the description to ensure consistency with other marketing materials. The description should include the following:

- goods produced and/or services provided;

- facilities and location(s);

- the history of the organization;

- organizational structure;

- role of the Human Resources Department;
- management philosophy; and
- goals of the organization.

L. Acknowledgement Form

If an organization is going to enforce rules established by the policy manual, its employees must, clearly, be made aware of those rules. It is important, therefore, to document employees' receipt and understanding of the manual. Since the manual may be considered an implicit part of the employment contract, it must be shown that employees were aware of its provisions and had agreed to be bound by them.

The simplest way to accomplish this is to include a tear-out sheet for the employee's signature, representing his or her receipt and understanding of the manual. This sheet can then be placed in the employee's personnel file for future reference. Of course, whenever changes are made to the manual, the employee must be asked to sign a new acknowledgement form. This can, admittedly, prove to be a cumbersome process.

Acknowledgement forms should indicate that:

- the employee has received and read the manual;
- the employee understands its contents and agrees to be bound by the contents and to comply with the provisions of the manual; and
- the employee understands that the organization is free to change any policy contained in the manual at its sole discretion.

The wording of a typical acknowledgement form might read as follows:

> The policy manual describes important information about the organization, and I understand that I should consult the Human Resources Department regarding any questions not answered in the manual.
>
> Since the information, policies, and benefits described here are necessarily subject to change, I acknowledge that revisions to the manual may occur. All such changes will be communicated through official notices, and I understand that revised information may supersede, modify, or eliminate existing policies. Only the chief executive officer of the organization has the ability to effect any revisions to the policies in this manual.
>
> Furthermore, I acknowledge that I am bound by the provisions of this manual as they may affect the terms and conditions of my employment. I have received the handbook, and I understand that it is my responsibility to read and comply with the policies contained in this handbook and any revisions made to it.

M. Employment Terms and Conditions

The following are some other employment policies commonly found in Policy Manuals:

- employee classifications;
- probation;
- conflicts of interest;
- moonlighting;
- confidentiality, non-disclosure and non-solicitation;
- immigration law;
- job postings;
- nepotism; and
- termination and severance.

1. Employee Classifications

Some employers use the U.S. Federal *Labor Standards Act* definitions to distinguish between exempt employees (those ineligible to receive overtime payments) and non-exempt employees (those eligible for overtime payments). These distinctions can be used to define eligibility for other benefits or to delineate participation levels.

Employment standards legislation in Canada defines eligibility for overtime but does not draw the distinction as neatly as its American counterpart. Instead, Canadian employers can make the distinction between the two groups by defining them as "Managerial and Professional" (exempt) versus "Administrative and Clerical" (non-exempt).

In a unionized environment, the provisions of a collective agreement may preempt any policy provisions contained in the organization's policy manual. In these situations, organizations will also need to draw a distinction between bargaining unit employees and non-bargaining unit employees.

Since employees are often paid in different ways, a different set or level of benefits may be provided to those who are paid a salary as opposed to those who are paid by the hour.

A further distinction might be made between full-time employees (e.g., those who are scheduled to work more than 35 hours per week) and part-time employees (e.g., those who are scheduled to work less than 25 hours per week). Employees can be permanent or temporary or, in the case of part-time employees, they can be employed solely on an on-call basis. Each of these should be carefully defined to ensure that there is no confusion as to which policies apply to which set of employees.

2. Probation

Some employers mistakenly believe that probation is a matter of employment standards legislation and thereby run the risk of remaining silent on the issue. Probation is a period of time contractually agreed to by the employee during which the employee's suitability for employment is determined. Probation can only be imposed at the beginning of employment. The conventional way of establishing the probationary period is to define it in the letter of offer or employment contract. It may be included in the employment contract by reference to the policy manual but it is strongly recommended that the exact length of the term be put in writing to the individual so that there will be no confusion.

The policy statement provides a guideline to those responsible for writing letters of offer and drafting employment contracts. Some organizations may establish different lengths of probation for different classes of employees. Senior management staff, for example, might be reluctant to leave a secure position if they face the potential of being released from their new employment without significant compensation. Probation essentially establishes a lesser standard for cause, allowing the employer to terminate the employee because their performance does not meet the requirements of the position or because the individual does not fit into the organization's culture. Since termination during probation may be considered just cause, no compensation for breach of the employment contract is due. Hence, senior staff are not often subject to probationary periods. They may, in fact, go to the other extreme of stipulating a minimum level of compensation due if they are prematurely terminated.

The probationary period is not only a time for assessing the employee, it also usually coincides with the waiting period for eligibility for some benefits. In the case of senior staff, the waiting period may still apply even though they are not considered to be on probation. Some organizations leave it to the discretion of the recruiter to decide whether or not to impose the waiting period. It is often waived when recruiting experienced staff, especially during times when skills shortages make recruiting difficult.

Here is a sample of language for a probationary period policy:

> The probationary period is intended to give new employees the opportunity to demonstrate their ability to achieve a satisfactory level of performance and to determine whether the new position meets their expectations. Our organization uses this period to evaluate employee capabilities, work habits, and overall performance.
>
> All new and rehired non-exempt employees work on a probationary basis for the first 90 calendar days after their date of hire. Any significant absence will automatically extend an introductory period by the length of the absence. If the organization determines that the designated probationary period does not allow sufficient time to thoroughly evaluate the employee's performance, the probationary period may be extended for a specified period.
>
> Upon satisfactory completion of the probationary period, employees enter the "regular" employment classification.
>
> After becoming regular employees, employees become eligible to join the organization's Benefit Plan for Non-Exempt employees, subject to the terms and conditions of each benefits program. Employees should read the information for each specific benefits program for the details on eligibility requirements.

3. Conflicts of Interest

An implied term of any employment contract is that employees will not engage in any activities that conflict with the interests of the employer. Conflicts of interest are not always clear-cut, however, and it can be beneficial to provide employees with some guidelines to help them avoid a breach of their responsibilities. A central part of this policy should be to direct the employee to someone in the organization who can clarify whether or not a particular situation constitutes a conflict of interest. This responsibility usually falls to the Human Resources Department.

Conflicts of interest usually arise when an employee sees the potential for outside personal gain by virtue of being an employee of the organization. Personal gains might take the form of bribes, products or services, special fringe benefits or other windfalls. Some organizations find it acceptable for employees to receive small gifts from established suppliers but never from suppliers who are bidding to receive a new order. Others establish that employees may only accept gifts if they have received explicit approval from a designated executive.

Firms may also want to restrict employees from entering into business relationships that have an appearance of a conflict of interest without explicit authorization. For example, if an employee is in the position of negotiating a contract with a firm owned or controlled by a spouse or close relative, there is an obvious appearance of conflict. Appearances notwithstanding, though, the organization will not want to exclude itself from a favourable deal when no actual conflict exists, and will therefore want to leave some "wiggle room" in the policy.

The most important feature of a conflict of interest policy is that the organization require employees to report all potential conflicts of interest. This helps prevent a presumption of guilt from being created.

4. Moonlighting

Organizations cannot completely restrict employees from engaging in outside employment. However, an organization can insist that employees maintain an acceptable level of performance and be available to work as required. No organization should accept an employee's absence from work because of his or her employment elsewhere. Nor should an organization tolerate an employee who is too tired to perform his job because of the extra workload imposed by outside employment.

An organization can require a moonlighting employee to terminate the outside employment if it interferes with the exercise of his or her duties for the primary employer. It can insist that employees refrain from engaging in any outside work that would constitute a conflict of interest, including working for a competitor. Employees can also be restricted from engaging in any activities from which they receive income or material gain for products or services rendered while performing their work for the organization.

5. Confidentiality, Non-Disclosure, Non-Solicitation

The protection of confidential business information and trade secrets is vital to the interests and the success of every organization. Confidential information includes, but is not limited to, the following examples:

- compensation data;
- computer processes;
- computer programs and codes;
- customer lists;
- customer preferences;
- financial information;
- labour relations strategies;
- marketing strategies;
- new materials research;
- pending projects and proposals;
- proprietary production processes;
- research and development strategies;
- scientific data;
- scientific formulae;
- scientific prototypes;
- technological data; and
- technological prototypes.

The duty to keep such information confidential is an implied part of every employment contract. However, some information gained in the course of employment may fall into a gray area. For example, during the course of employment, an employee may come across a problem. During non-working hours, the employee works on this problem and devises a solution that she offers to sell back to the employer. She also decides to sell the idea on the open market. This may create a dispute over who actually owns the "intellectual property" behind the idea. The employee may have worked on the idea on her own time but, at the same time, must acknowledge that she would never have been exposed to the problem that provided the impetus for the idea had she not been an employee of the organization in the first place.

Organizations can protect themselves from such disputes by including an agreement regarding confidentiality, non-disclosure and non-solicitation in the initial offer of employment. All employees may be required to sign such an agreement as a condition of employment. In some organizations, only employees who occupy certain positions of trust are required to sign such an agreement.

These agreements usually have a life beyond the term of employment and prohibit employees from ever disclosing confidential information. They may also impose covenants that prohibit the employee from soliciting business from the organization's customers or from enticing its employees to join another firm. These covenants, however, need to be limited in time and geographic scope or they may be deemed to be too restrictive.

Employees who improperly use or disclose trade secrets or other confidential business information are ordinarily subject to disciplinary action, up to and including termination of employment and legal action, even if they do not actually benefit from the disclosed information. Former employees who breach these policies may be subject to injunctions to prevent them from harming the organization and may be found liable for damages that occur because of such breaches. (See also "Confidentiality and Non-Competition Agreement" in Contracts, Employment at page 128 *et seq.*)

6. Immigration Law Compliance

Employers are prohibited by human rights legislation from discriminating against employees or potential employees because of citizenship or country of natural origin. Notwithstanding this, employers have a positive duty to employ only those who are legally entitled to work and who have received the appropriate visas. A policy can stipulate that employees must be legally entitled to work in Canada and must be able to show proof when requested to do so.

Employers cannot continue to employ anyone who does not have a valid visa. They can, however, re-employ any individual whose visa has lapsed provided the employee is able to regain his or her visa. Employers may be asked by their employees to provide letters of reference to support a visa application and may want to include their position on this in the policy statement.

7. Nepotism

Employing relatives or individuals involved in a dating relationship in the same area of an organization can cause serious conflicts and problems with favouritism and employee morale. Furthermore, personal conflicts from outside the work environment can be carried over into day-to-day working relationships.

Organizations can lawfully impose certain restrictions on relationships between employees, provided that these restrictions are applied consistently and that the potential harm to the organization's interests can be demonstrated. A common restriction is to prohibit spouses and close relatives from occupying positions in a reporting relationship. Restrictions on dating can be more problematic. Organizations can insist that the employees involved ensure that their relationship does not become an issue for the organization and that they disclose any decision to get married or to enter into a common-law relationship.

Organizations need to be careful how they enforce this policy. Many require employees to disclose their relationships and offer the employees an opportunity to remove the conflict by posting one of them to a position where there is no reporting relationship or by asking one of them to leave the organization. In either case, the organization cannot choose which employee will move but must, rather, allow the couple to make that the choice.

Some organizations, rather than restricting nepotism, actually encourage it. This is found particularly in entrepreneurial organizations that want to attract people with shared values and to reward the loyalty of their employees by granting the favour of hiring relatives.

8. Medical Examinations and Health Surveillance

To help ensure that employees are able to perform their duties safely, organizations may require them to undergo medical examinations. Pre-employment medicals are permissible, provided the employer can establish they are necessary to meet the *bona fide* requirements of the job. If a potential employee is rejected from employment because of the results of a medical examination, the organization will have to demonstrate that the individual was unable to perform the *bona fide* occupational requirements and that accommodation of the individual's disability was not possible.

Employers may also conduct medical examinations after an offer of employment has been made. These are often undertaken to determine eligibility for benefit coverage. In the absence of a *bona fide* occupational requirement, the organization cannot use the results of the medical examination to withdraw its letter of offer. It must, rather, accommodate the employee's disability. Offers of employment and assignment to duties cannot be made contingent upon satisfactory completion of a medical exam, except in instances where the employee cannot meet the *bona fide* occupational requirements.

Some employers offer medical examinations as part of the benefits package for senior executives. The results of such examinations, or of any medical examinations, have to be treated as confidential. Unless the employee signs a specific waiver giving the organization access to the information, only a health professional or a designated person within the organization charged with maintaining confidentiality may have access to it.

In some contexts, the organization may need to monitor employees' exposure to hazardous substances and conditions (noise, dust, etc.). Under these circumstances, it is a good idea to establish a policy statement so that employees understand the requirement to cooperate with such medical surveillance.

9. Job Postings

Internal recruiting and promotions from within are other areas where organizations might want to issue a policy statement. Some organizations create job posting policies that state that all open positions will be posted or they restrict postings to non-exempt positions, non-managerial positions or positions not covered by a succession plan. Others offer to post all open positions, subject to the organizations' reserved right not to post any particular position at its sole discretion.

Any posting policy should stipulate how long positions will be posted, as well as how employees should go about applying for them. It might also advise employees that they have a responsibility to inform their supervisor of their application.

Posting policies may set thresholds for employees to meet in order to be eligible to apply for an internal position. Some state, for example, that employees who have been in their current positions for less than a set period of time cannot move to a new position. Others restrict employees to applying only for positions at a higher or equal level to the position they now occupy. Others require the employee to meet minimal levels of acceptable attendance and/or performance.

Some organizations establish a policy whereby all internal applicants are guaranteed to receive an interview. Unfortunately, this sometimes leads to many employees being granted "courtesy" interviews when they are not serious candidates. This practice tends to diminish the efficacy of an internal recruitment policy. For this reason, it is recommended that the internal recruiting process mirror the external process in that only candidates who meet the threshold requirements for the position will be interviewed.

Another policy consideration is the establishment a reasonable time frame for transfers to occur when an internal candidate is successful in landing another position in the organization. Some supervisors are reluctant to release an employee to another department until a replacement has been found. This practice can demoralize the employee and cause his or her performance to fall off. The reasonable notice that would be expected of the employee if he or she chose to leave the organization is a good guideline to follow in this situation. This is the maximum length of time that it should take for the transfer to occur.

In all instances, internal candidates should be assured that they will be given feedback about their application. This increases the potential of the internal posting process by creating an avenue for providing career guidance to employees. It also allows employees an opportunity to express their career aspirations. It is very important that the organization maintain open communications around the posting process so that it maintains credibility with its employees.

Organizations may also consider creating policies for employees to refer friends and relatives to the company. In some instances, an organization may go so far as to offer a "bounty" to employees for successful referrals.

10. Termination and Severance

In the absence of a collective agreement, employees are generally employed with the implicit understanding that they will not be subject to layoff.

Employees paid by the hour are an exception — they may implicitly understand that they have no guarantee as to the number of hours that they will work in a week. Despite the "implicit understanding" of employees, it is still recommended that organizations make explicit statements in their policy manuals regarding any layoff provisions. These statements should stipulate under what circumstances employees may be laid off, what notice of layoff can reasonably be expected and in what order layoffs will be effected.

Salaried employees, on the other hand, are clearly employed with the implicit understanding that they have been hired permanently and will not be subject to periodic layoff. During downturns, organizations that must cut their salaried work force will have to compensate those employees for severing the employment contract. Some organizations seek to limit the costs of "downsizing" by developing clear policies regarding severance pay. These policies often provide a minimum number of weeks to be paid as severance, with an increasing scale of payments based on years of service, up to a specified maximum. Others develop a more complex grid that takes into consideration not only service, but level of responsibility as well.

Organizations should ensure that their severance policies conform to the minimum standards established by the relevant legislation in their jurisdiction. Policies should be constructed so that they comply both with the statutory requirements for individual terminations and the requirements for group terminations. Some organizations develop policy statements that cover individual terminations only and reserve the right to establish one-off policies regarding group terminations on an as-required basis. (See also "Legal Issues" in Redundancy/Downsizing at page 393.)

N. Miscellaneous

In addition to the generic policies discussed above, some organizations may want to include policy statements more specific to their context. These specific policies might cover such terms and conditions of employment as the following:

- timekeeping and work schedules;
- attendance and punctuality;
- pay advances;
- deductions and set-offs;
- paydays;
- overtime;
- meals and breaks; and
- expenses and travel.

(See also Flexible Work Practices at page 171 *et seq.*)

O. Work Rules

Work rules are established to regulate more specific kinds of employee behaviour. They are often necessary to protect the safety of employees, comply with established regulations, protect the interests of the company or reduce the organization's exposure to litigation as a result of the actions of their employees. The organization must not only establish the work rules, but must also stipulate what the consequences of a breach will be.

1. General Work Rules

Some of the general work rules listed below might seem self-evident to the reader. After all, any reasonable individual will know that it is wrong to steal from an employer. However, borrowing from labour jurisprudence, organizations are well advised to ensure they have a set of rules that fulfill the following criteria:

- the rules are known and understood by all employees;
- the rules are reasonable and necessary for the safe and efficient operation of the business;
- the rules are consistently enforced; and
- due consideration is given to any mitigating factors that might influence the consequences of the employees' actions.

In some cases, the organization will want to establish specific policy statements regarding certain rules so that employees are clear about what is and what is not acceptable.

Some organizations simply list examples of unacceptable behaviour as follows:

> To ensure orderly operations and provide the best possible work environment, we expect our employees to follow rules of conduct that will protect the interests and safety of all employees and the organization.
>
> It is not possible to list all the forms of behaviour that are considered unacceptable in the workplace. The following are examples of infractions of rules of conduct that may occur in the workplace:

- theft or inappropriate removal or possession of company property;

- falsification of timekeeping records;

- working under the influence of alcohol or illegal drugs;

- possession, distribution, sale, transfer, or use of alcohol or illegal drugs in the workplace, while on duty, or while operating employer-owned vehicles or equipment;

- fighting or threatening violence in the workplace;

- boisterous or disruptive activity (horseplay) in the workplace;

- negligence leading to damage of employer-owned or customer-owned property;

- insubordination or other disrespectful conduct;

- violation of safety or health rules;

- smoking in prohibited areas;

- sexual or other unlawful or unwelcome harassment;

- possession of dangerous or unauthorized materials, such as explosives or firearms in the workplace;

- any absence without notice or fraudulent use of sick leave;

- unauthorized absence from workstation during the workday;

- unauthorized use of telephones, mail system, or other employer-owned equipment; and

- unauthorized disclosure of business "secrets" or confidential information.

Any breaches of these rules will result in progressive disciplinary steps being taken up to and including the possible termination of employment.

2. Smoking

Virtually every jurisdiction in Canada has legislation restricting smoking in the workplace. Organizations should check local laws and applicable provincial statutes before drafting their policies to ensure they conform to the regulations.

Generally, employers can choose to establish designated indoor smoking areas, to allow smoking only in outdoor areas or to prohibit smoking altogether. In most cases, employers can create designated indoor smoking areas, provided they are limited in size, are

ventilated to the exterior and are away from eating areas.

Smoking policies should state not only if and where smoking is allowed, but should also stipulate when smoking is allowed. An unfortunate side effect of smoking restrictions in the workplace for many employers is that smokers may be losing productivity by taking an excessive number of breaks. And, because the smoking area may be outdoors and not easily accessible, the length of the breaks may be increasing.

Some employers offer smoking-cessation assistance to employees and may even provide incentives to employees to give up smoking.

3. Use of Phones and Cell Phones

In order to control costs, employers may wish to regulate the personal use of cell phones and the making of long-distance calls on company equipment. Some might want to go further and restrict employees from making any personal calls on company phones, so that productivity is not negatively affected. Many employers will allow a reasonable degree of personal use, provided employees do not abuse the privilege.

Employers are becoming increasingly concerned about employee use of cell phones while driving. In a couple of recent U.S. cases, employers were held liable for damages occurring to third parties involved in car accidents with employees who were on their cell phones at the time of the accident. Organizations may want to review their cell-phone policies to add guidelines prohibiting employee cell phone use while driving, or restricting cell phone use while driving to phones equipped with a "hands-free" feature.

To ensure that employees are made aware of this policy, the organization may want to publish it separately and give it to each employee to whom a cell phone is issued. Users will be required to read the policy and acknowledge acceptance of its conditions in writing.

4. Internet Use

Internet access is increasingly being provided to employees to assist them in obtaining work-related data and technology. Unfortunately, the nature of the Internet makes it subject to all kinds of potential abuses. The improper or careless use of this resource may expose organizations to vicarious liability for the actions of their employees and may also increase the risk of harming their computer systems through the inadvertent importation of viruses.

Organizations should be aware of the possible extent of abuse when employees have access to the Internet. They may want to establish a general set of rules prohibiting the following:

- sending or posting discriminatory, harassing, or threatening messages or images;

- using the organization's time and resources for personal gain;

- stealing, using, or disclosing someone else's code or password without authorization;

- copying, pirating, or downloading software and electronic files without permission;

- sending or posting confidential material, trade secrets, or proprietary information outside of the organization;

- violating copyright law;

- failing to observe licensing agreements;

- engaging in unauthorized transactions that may incur a cost to the organization or initiate unwanted Internet services and transmissions;

- sending or posting messages or material that could damage the organization's image or reputation;

- participating in the viewing or exchange of pornography or obscene materials;

- sending or posting messages that defame or slander other individuals;

- attempting to break into the computer system of another organization or person;

- refusing to cooperate with a security investigation;

- sending or posting chain letters, solicitations, or advertisements not related to business purposes or activities;

- using the Internet for political causes or activities, religious activities, or for gambling;

- jeopardizing the security of the organization's electronic communications systems;

- sending or posting messages that disparage another organization's products or services;

- passing off personal views as representing those of the organization;

- sending anonymous e-mail messages; and

- engaging in any other illegal activities.

Policies regarding Internet use need to be thorough and should be handled in much the same way as cell phone use. That is to say, as employees are granted access to the Internet, they should be required to sign an agreement stipulating the terms and conditions they will abide by. The following serves as an example of such an agreement:

> The undersigned agrees to the following terms and conditions that will govern his/her use of the Internet access provided to him/her by the organization:

> All Internet data that is composed, transmitted, or received via our computer communications systems is considered to be part of the official records of the organization and, as such, is subject to disclosure to law enforcement or other third parties. Consequently, employees should always ensure that the business information contained in Internet e-mail messages and other transmissions is accurate, appropriate, ethical, and lawful.

> The equipment, services, and technology provided to access the Internet remain at all times the property of the organization and, as such, the organization reserves the right to monitor Internet traffic, and retrieve and read any data composed, sent, or received through our online connections and stored in our computer systems.

> Data that is composed, transmitted, accessed, or received via the Internet must not contain content that could be considered discriminatory, offensive, obscene, threatening, harassing, intimidating, or disruptive to any employee or other person. Examples of unacceptable content may include, but are not limited to, sexual comments or images, racial slurs, gender-specific comments, or any other comments or images that could reasonably offend someone on the basis of race, age, sex, religious or political beliefs, national origin, disability, sexual orientation, or any other characteristic protected by law.

> The unauthorized use, installation, copying, or distribution of copyrighted, trademarked, or patented material on the Internet is expressly prohibited. As a general rule, if an employee did not create material, does not own the rights to it, or has not gotten authorization for its use, it should not be put on the Internet. Employees are also responsible for ensuring that the person sending any material over the Internet has the appropriate distribution rights.

To ensure a virus-free environment, no files may be downloaded from the Internet without prior authorization from the Director of Information Technology.

Abuse of the Internet access provided by the organization in violation of law or this policy will result in disciplinary action, up to and including termination of employment. Employees may also be held personally liable for any violations of this policy.

5. Drug and Alcohol Use

Employers have a duty and right to insist that the workplace be drug and alcohol free. It is the organization's obligation to all employees to provide a safe environment. This is compromised by any employee whose performance and judgment is impaired because of the use of drugs or alcohol. At minimum, organizations can require employees to report to work in appropriate mental and physical condition, free from the influence of drugs or alcohol, and able to perform their jobs in a satisfactory and safe manner. They can also require that no employee use, possess, distribute, sell, or be under the influence of alcohol or illegal drugs while on company premises or while conducting business on behalf of the company.

Such rules can be problematic for organizations that condone alcohol use among sales representatives who entertain clients. For these employees, it is still a good idea to create guidelines to ensure that they govern their behaviour with good judgment. With the increased liability associated with drinking and driving, some organizations are reconsidering whether the use of alcohol should be tolerated even in these circumstances.

The legal use of prescription drugs should also be restricted. Employees should be required to disclose the use of prescription medicine when its use could potentially impair their ability to perform the essential functions of the job in an effective and safe manner.

Employers should also consider whether or not to provide alcohol at company-sponsored functions. In recent awards, employers have been held responsible for the actions of employees who consumed alcohol at company functions and then proceeded to drive home under the influence. Common policies include restricting the number of drinks bought for the employee by the company, providing free transportation home or providing overnight accommodation.

Organizations can also opt to take a proactive approach by educating employees about the dangers of substance abuse in the workplace. Resources can be made available to employees, including access to substance abuse counselling through a company-sponsored Employee Assistance Program. Employees can also be encouraged to discuss these matters with their supervisor or with the Human Resources Department, in order to receive assistance or referrals to appropriate resources in the community.

Employees with drug or alcohol problems that have not resulted in, and are not the immediate subject of, disciplinary action may be given the opportunity to take time off to participate in a rehabilitation or treatment program through the organization's health insurance benefit coverage, where applicable. In addition, rehabilitation and abstinence may be stipulated as conditions of "Last Chance" agreements imposed as a result of disciplinary sanctions. (See also a sample "Last Chance" Agreement in Alcohol and Drug Addiction at page 8, and "Accommodation" in Drug and Alcohol Testing at page 133.)

6. Personal Appearance

Standards of dress, grooming, and personal cleanliness contribute to the morale of all employees and affect an organization's image. There are no absolutes with respect to dress codes. Many organizations today have no restrictions, implied or otherwise, on how employees may dress during business hours. Others insist on compliance to strict standards of appropriate business attire.

As for personal grooming, most employers expect employees to present a clean, neat, and tasteful appearance following accepted social standards. These standards differ according to the position the employee holds. Employees engaged in manufacturing or mechanical work will obviously become dirty in the course of their duties. On the other hand, a high standard will be expected of those whose jobs involve dealing with customers or visitors in person.

A common approach is to make a supervisor or department head responsible for establishing a reasonable dress code and for setting standards for personal appearance appropriate to the jobs being performed. If a supervisor feels that an employee's personal appearance is inappropriate, the supervisor might ask the employee to leave the workplace until he or she is properly groomed and dressed. Supervisors are sometimes uncomfortable with the notion of confronting employees about such a sensitive issue and often prefer that the organization establish "black and white" rules governing personal appearance. Such rules, however, cannot anticipate every situation and can, in some instances, lead to ludicrous scenarios.

Consider the length of women's skirts, for example. A policy might state that skirts will not be unduly short or might even stipulate that a skirt should cover the leg to a point no higher than two inches above the knee. In the latter instance, one wonders who would be conducting the measures to ensure compliance.

If supervisors absolutely insist on adopting specific rules, the organization should consider the following:

- shoes must provide safe, secure footing, and offer protection against hazards;

- canvas or athletic type shoes are not appropriate professional attire;

- tank tops, tube or halter tops, or shorts may not be worn under any circumstances;

- mustaches and beards must be clean, well trimmed and neat;

- hairstyles are expected to be in good taste;

- excessive makeup is not permitted;

- offensive body odour and poor personal hygiene is not professionally acceptable;

- perfume, cologne, and aftershave lotion should be used moderately or avoided altogether, as some individuals may be sensitive to strong fragrances;

- jewellery should not be functionally restrictive, dangerous to job performance, or excessive facial jewellery, such as eyebrow rings, nose rings, lip rings, and tongue studs, is not professionally appropriate and must not be worn during business hours.

Some organizations designate certain days as casual days. A common reason for allowing casual days is that some employees have to work on days when there is little or no contact with customers or outside visitors (Saturdays and Sundays). Weekdays, typically Fridays, are sometimes designated as casual days as a means of improving employee morale. On these days, the standard dress code is relaxed. However, the organization may be compelled to define acceptable casual business wear.

Listed below is a general overview of acceptable casual business wear, as well as a list of some of the more common items that are not appropriate for the office. Obviously, neither group is intended to be all-inclusive. Rather, these items should help set the general parameters for proper casual business wear.

Examples of acceptable casual business wear include the following:

- slacks;

- casual dresses and skirts;

- casual shirts and blouses;

- golf shirts;

- turtlenecks; and

- sweaters.

Examples of inappropriate clothing items that should not be worn on casual days include:

- jeans;

- jeans that are excessively worn or faded;

- sweatpants;

- warm-up or jogging suits and pants;

- shorts;

- bib overalls;

- spandex or other form-fitting pants;

- T-shirts;

- sweatshirts;

- tank tops;

- halter tops; and

- visible undergarments.

7. Workplace Etiquette

Etiquette is not a common policy consideration. However, larger organizations may find it necessary to establish some standards of behaviour to help employees govern themselves in situations unique to the workplace. All organizations expect employees to treat each other with respect and courtesy. But issues sometimes arise when employees are unaware that their behaviour in the workplace may be disruptive or annoying to others.

Workplace etiquette guidelines are not necessarily intended to be hard and fast work rules with disciplinary consequences. They are simply suggestions for appropriate workplace behaviour to help everyone be more conscientious and considerate of co-workers and the work environment.

Examples include:

- return copy machine and printer settings to their default settings after changing them;

- replace paper in the copy machine and printer paper trays when they are empty;

- retrieve print jobs in a timely manner and be sure to collect all your pages;

- be prompt when using the manual feed on the printer;

- keep the area around the copy machine and printers neat and orderly;

- be careful not to take or discard others' print jobs or faxes when collecting your own;

- avoid public accusations or criticisms of other employees and address such issues; privately with those involved or your supervisor;

- try to minimize unscheduled interruptions of other employees while they are working;

- communicate by e-mail or phone whenever possible, instead of walking unexpectedly into someone's office or workspace;

- be conscious of how your voice travels, and try to lower the volume of your voice when talking on the phone or to others in open areas;

- keep socializing to a minimum, and try to conduct conversations in areas where the noise will not be distracting to others;

- minimize talking between workspaces or over cubicle walls; instead, conduct conversations with others in their workspace;

- try not to block walkways while carrying on conversations;

- refrain from using inappropriate language (swearing) that others may overhear;

- avoid discussions of your personal life/issues in public conversations that can be easily overheard;

- monitor the volume when listening to music, voice mail, or a speakerphone that others can hear; and

- clean up after yourself and do not leave behind waste or discarded papers.

8. Security Checks

Security checks have become a very important subject since the events of September 11, 2001, in the United States. An organization may have a number of security requirements and, in order not to infringe on anyone's privacy rights, it absolutely must ensure that employees are made aware of any security measures that might be taken.

Security provisions can include a requirement that all employees wear identification badges while at work. When doorways are secured with electronic locks, there may be rules against piggybacking on other employees who are passing through and lending of passkeys to other employees.

If work areas are monitored by closed-circuit television, employees should be made aware of this fact. If they might be subject to personal inspections upon entering or leaving the business premises, they should also be made aware of this. And, when inspections are necessary, all employees should be inspected. Random searches should be avoided.

Some organizations restrict the items an employee can bring into the workplace so that large bags or containers cannot be used to sneak materials in or out of the facilities. Desks, lockers, and other storage devices can be provided for the convenience of employees but remain the sole property of the organization. Accordingly, the organization can reserve the right to inspect these if it has cause to do so.

9. Solicitation

Organizations may want to place restrictions on the distribution of non-work-related literature or the solicitation of business other than its own on its premises. While employees may want to promote a charitable cause they are involved with, or sell items related to a home business (arts and crafts, cosmetics, etc.), the organization should decide what it is willing to permit and what it wishes to prohibit.

If an organization allows some activities but not others, however, it may be seen as conferring favour on some employees and not on others. To avoid controversy, it is sometimes easier for the organization simply to prohibit any solicitation on company premises. Another reason to restrict these activities is that employees sometimes engage in promoting their outside interests during working hours, a practice that cuts into their productive time.

In addition, posting written solicitations on company bulletin boards is usually restricted. Some organizations provide employees with bulletin boards so that they can display personal notices (of weddings, births, deaths), letters of thanks and, occasionally, to sell household items. To control these bulletin boards, organizations sometimes require that any notice must receive approval from the Human Resources Department before it is posted.

10. Progressive Discipline

In the absence of a collective agreement, an organization can only impose progressive discipline if there is a specific policy, read and understood by employees, stating that such discipline will result from misconduct on the employee's part. This policy should ensure the fair treatment of all employees and make certain that disciplinary actions are prompt, uniform, and impartial. The major purpose of any disciplinary action is to correct the problem, prevent recurrence and prepare the employee for satisfactory service in the future.

Progressive disciplinary action means that the severity of disciplinary action increases with repeated misconduct. Often the policy will involve four steps: verbal warning for a first offence; written warning for a second offence; suspension for a further offence; and termination of employment for still another offence. The level of disciplinary action imposed will depend on the severity of the misconduct as well as the employee's past record of behaviour. And there may be circumstances that call for bypassing one or more steps. Employee theft, for example, will in almost all instances result in immediate termination.

Some organizations may establish a "sunset" provision as a reward to employees who have made the necessary corrections to their behaviour. A "sunset" provision states that an employee's disciplinary record will be wiped clean after more than 12 to 24 months have passed since the last disciplinary action. At that point,

any future disciplinary actions will start at the beginning of the process.

P. Employment Records

In addition to Employment Terms and Conditions and Work Rules, organizations may want to establish policies regarding the handling of employee records. These policies might include statements concerning employee access to personnel files and reference checks.

1. Access to Personnel Files

Every organization must maintain personnel files for all its employees. Personnel files contain such information as the employee's job application, résumé, training records, documentation of performance appraisals and salary increases, and other employment records.

Personnel files are the property of the organization and access to them is usually restricted to payroll and Human Resources staff, who require access to the information in the regular course of their duties. The employee's direct supervisor is usually also given access.

Employees who wish to review their own files are legally entitled to do so. As a matter of course, no information should be placed in the file that the employee has not seen, or at least been made aware of, or that the employee has not provided to the company. With reasonable advance notice, employees should be permitted to review their own personnel files in the organization's offices and in the presence of a Human Resources practitioner or another individual appointed by the organization to maintain the files. The organization should never permit an employee to remove anything from the file.

If employees require a copy of any document found in their own files, the individual charged with the custody of the files can provide them with a copy. Copies of payroll records and administrative forms are not usually given to employees unless there is a very compelling reason to do so. However, copies of performance reviews and letters regarding performance, including disciplinary citations, are usually provided because the employee should have previously received copies and may have merely misplaced them.

In some instances, the employee may request that a document be removed from his or her file. Ordinarily there is no reason to comply with such a request, but the organization may want to give consideration to such requests as part of their employee relations philosophy. Such requests should be made in writing to the senior Human Resources practitioner or to the employee's immediate supervisor.

2. Reference Checks

Organizations often establish guidelines with respect to what information they will divulge to outsiders and under what circumstances. Employees sometimes require "employment checks" by their bank or financial institution in order to secure a loan or mortgage. In this case, some companies ask their employees to have the institution submit a written request. Others will only provide an employment letter directly to the employee. Still others will limit their cooperation to simply confirming the information that the employee has given the institution.

Organizations also need to establish guidelines for providing references for former employees. Some are under the mistaken impression that they cannot give out any information that might be harmful to the former employee. Fearing possible libel suits, they establish policies that restrict references to mere confirmations of employment. For Human Resources practitioners, such policies may serve to frustrate efforts to conduct thorough checks as part of the recruiting process. Moreover, many line managers simply ignore such policies and provide private references.

References, good or bad, can be given freely by an organization provided they are made in good faith and are believed to be true. In fact, if an employee was terminated for significant misconduct and the organization fails to reveal a material fact to a potential new employer, it may be liable for any damages incurred by that employer if the misconduct recurs.

One stipulation an organization may wish to include in this policy is that line managers be required to secure the approval of the Human Resources Department before giving a reference. This is particularly important when an employee has been terminated and a dispute remains between that employee and the organization. The organization may want to defer giving any references under these circumstances, at least until the dispute is resolved.

Role of the Human Resources Practitioner

The Human Resources practitioner is usually charged with the responsibility of drafting and implementing the policy manual. The first step is to establish the approach the practitioner wants to take with respect to how the policies are written. The range of approaches varies from a thorough and comprehensive compendium of policies to a brief set of operating philosophies that define the organization's norms and values. The approach adopted will depend on the current culture of the organization but will ultimately be determined by the culture the organization wishes to create or maintain.

The practitioner will need to research which policies are deemed necessary and why. In order to implement the policies effectively, the practitioner will need to gain consensus from the line management on the intent behind the policies. Without the support of this group, the policy manual is doomed to collect dust. So the practitioner will want to be reasonably selective, drafting only policies that are relevant to the line managers' experience — ones that help them address problematic issues.

To ensure that the manual is not simply filed away and forgotten, the means of delivery will be another important consideration. The communication strategy behind the introduction of the initial policy manual and its subsequent revisions is critical to successful implementation.

Since a number of policies cover subject areas that cannot be exhaustively defined, employees may occasionally find themselves in a gray area where they need another resource to help them interpret the guidelines. This responsibility usually falls to the Human Resources practitioner, who will be called upon to assist employees with interpretations in the following areas:

- business ethics;
- sexual or other unlawful harassment;
- conflicts of interest;
- moonlighting;
- personal appearance;
- solicitation;

- providing employee references; and

- workplace etiquette.

Barriers to Success/Common Pitfalls

Policies that are not directly relevant to the workplace will be ignored. Consider the situation where the policy manual contains a statement regarding Internet use, but only a handful of employees actually have access to the Internet. The policy may trigger some to question why they do not have such access and may therefore prove counterproductive. Moreover, employees who do not have such access will soon forget about the policy. If they gain access to the Internet at a later time, they will have long forgotten the policy and may well risk running afoul of it.

Policy overload is one of the most common mistakes made when introducing a policy manual. Human Resources practitioners should resist trying to impress their internal clients with thoroughness and quantity. A few well-thought-out and relevant policies will receive a better reception from line management than a comprehensive tome containing every possible policy that can be contemplated. Large binders full of irrelevant and, therefore, useless information do not get used as the reference guides they are intended to be.

Being too thorough can also lead to the creation of policy statements that are too rigid, potentially creating a stifling culture. Employees might test the boundaries of a dress code that lists specific examples of inappropriate dress. Suppose, for example, blue jeans are prohibited. A creative employee may question whether or not this means that black, red or green jeans are acceptable. An alternative policy that simply states that employees dress in a manner appropriate to their position and function will leave room for supervisors to help employees interpret acceptable dress. In most circumstances, employees will rise to

meet the standards when they feel they have been treated as adults.

Organizations should be careful not to publish policies that they are not prepared to endorse fully. This may seem obvious but it is a very common mistake. Statements on ethical conduct, for example, establish an absolute standard for senior management to comply with. Any breach by senior staff that goes unpunished will make the policy a source of employees' contempt. For example, if a senior managers orders the shipping department to go ahead and send defective goods to a customer in the hope that the customer will not notice, the manager may be making a calculated low-risk decision that could save the company a significant amount of money in the short term. But this action also sends a number of conflicting messages to employees, such as "quality doesn't matter" and "short-term financial gain is more important than ethical behaviour".

These are obvious contradictions, ones that are also, thankfully, becoming increasingly less common. More common are the subtle contradictions that do not amount to breaches of policy *per se* but that do contradict the intent of policy. For example, in industrial settings, management often professes that safety is its primary concern. Yet management incentive plans may focus on productivity and quality, with safety amounting to a secondary concern. The everyday behaviour of supervisors may be geared to meeting production goals. Established management systems, such as the compensation system, may inadvertently dilute the effectiveness of the policy statement.

It is important for the Human Resources practitioner to review with senior management the content, intent and possible impact of every policy statement. This can be a difficult exercise because the discussion will involve dialogue about philosophy and values. Line managers sometimes find these things difficult to talk about and may find it difficult to understand why they are such an important part of the operation.

Sample Policy Statements

The following policy statements are provided for illustrative purposes only. Many organizations prefer going into greater detail with respect to processes to be followed, definitions of terms, and delineation of authorities and responsibilities. Others prefer open-ended statements that are flexible and can be interpreted depending on a wide variety of circumstances. The style and content of any policy manual are dependent on the organization's culture and the intent of the manual.

Organizations that are highly centralized and have a command-and-control structure will tend to be more detailed in their manuals. Organizations that are decentralized and lean towards employee empowerment will tend to write their policies as guidelines rather than as strict rules.

Access to Personnel Files

Our company maintains a personnel file on each employee. The file includes such information as the employee's job application, résumé, records of training, documentation of performance appraisals and salary increases, and other employment records.

Personnel files are the property of the company and access to the information they contain is restricted. Generally, only supervisors and management personnel who have a legitimate reason to review information in a file are allowed to do so.

Employees who wish to review their own file should contact the Human Resources Department. With reasonable advance notice, employees may review their own personnel files in the offices of the Human Resources Department and in the presence of a representative from that department.

Bereavement Leave

Death of Immediate Family Member

An employee may be allowed up to five (5) days' absence from work without any reduction in salary in the cases of the death of his or her spouse or child.

Employees may be allowed up to three (3) days' absence from work without any reduction in salary to attend to matters resulting from the death of an immediate family member. The days absent must be taken in conjunction with attendance at the funeral. An *immediate family member* is defined as:

(a) a parent of an employee or spouse, or a lineal grandparent of an employee;

(b) brother, brother-in-law, sister or sister-in-law of employee; and

(c) a grandchild.

Employees may be allowed an additional two (2) days' absence without reduction in salary where the employee must travel in excess of three hundred (300) kilometres to attend the funeral of an immediate family member.

The company reserves the right to request confirmation of death.

Death of a Relative or Friend

An employee may be allowed up to one (1) day's absence without any reduction in salary to attend matters resulting from the death of a relative (not an immediate family member) or friend with whom there was a close personal relationship.

Emergency Leave

Salaried employees may have time off as needed for family emergencies, including the need to care for a family member in a medical emergency. Such leave must be substantiated if requested. The company reserves the right to impose a limit on the number of days taken by an individual if that number exceeds that allowed by provincial statute or otherwise is deemed excessive.

Equal Employment Opportunity

In order to provide equal employment and advancement opportunities to all individuals, employment decisions will be based on merit, qualifications and abilities. The company does not discriminate in employment opportunities or practices on the basis of race, colour, religion, sex, sexual orientation, national origin, age, or on any other ground protected by law.

This policy governs all aspects of employment, including selection, job assignment, compensation, discipline, termination and access to benefits and training.

Employees with questions or concerns about any type of discrimination in the workplace are encouraged to bring these issues to the attention of their immediate supervisor. Employees can raise concerns and make reports without fear of reprisal. Someone found to be engaging in any type of unlawful discrimination will be subject to disciplinary action, up to and including termination of employment.

Hours of Work/Overtime

For the purposes of this policy, our salaried employees are classified in two groups: management and non-management. Management employees include supervisors, professionals (such as engineers and accountants), managers, directors, vice-presidents and presidents. Anyone receiving a bonus under the incentive compensation plan is considered to be management. Non-management employees include everyone else.

Management employees normally work a 40-hour work week. Starting and finishing hours are determined in accordance with the nature of the work, in consultation with the individual's immediate supervisor. Management employees are exempt from receiving any additional compensation for the extra hours that may be worked as a necessary part of their duties. It is expected that managers will have to work extra hours or hours outside their daily norms from time to time.

Non-management employees normally work a 40-hour work week. Starting times and finishing times are determined by department needs and will be communicated to the employees by their supervisor. Non-management employees are eligible for overtime compensation for any hours worked in excess of 40 in a week or eight in a day.

To be eligible for overtime payment, the employee must have the prior approval of his or her manager. All exempt employees claiming overtime must submit a weekly time sheet that clearly states the hours worked and the purpose of the overtime. These sheets must be submitted to their manager for approval.

Overtime is to be compensated at one and one-half times the employee's calculated hourly rate (calculated as his or her nominal annual salary divided by 2080). Employees may accumulate hours for time off in lieu of overtime payment on a one-for-one basis. However, employees will not be allowed to accumulate more than eight (8) hours of banked time at any given time and must take the time off within three months of reaching eight (8) accumulated hours. Failure to take the time off will result in an automatic payout.

Human Rights Policy

Our company recognizes the dignity and worth of every individual. Every employee has the right to work in an environment free from any type of harassment. Further, no employee shall be discriminated against in any way because of his or her race, ancestry, place of origin, colour, ethnic origin, citizenship, creed, sex, sexual orientation, marital status, family status or handicap.

The company will make every effort to eliminate any barriers that may prevent individuals from reaching their full potential. Hiring and promotional decisions will be based on an individual's merits, contributions to the organization and ability to perform the *bona fide* requirements of the position.

Furthermore, our customers and suppliers, and their employees, also enjoy the same rights. Every employee is expected to respect the rights of others and to uphold the dignity and worth of every individual with whom he or she comes into contact during the course of one's employment.

Practice Steps

Whenever an employee believes he or she is being harassed, the employee should make it clear to the perpetrator that the actions are unwanted and offensive.

It is the responsibility of all employees to report a breach of this policy immediately to their supervisor. If the circumstances of the alleged offence make it impossible to report the incident to your supervisor, then the incident should be reported to a Human Resources Generalist.

Any complaints should be outlined either verbally or in writing to the complainant's immediate supervisor, department/general manager or a Human Resources representative. The person who receives the complaint will reduce it to writing in a form satisfactory to the complainant. The complainant will be required to sign the complaint to insure its accuracy and must be willing to testify with respect to the complaint at any level of internal investigation, grievance meetings, arbitration hearings, or at legal proceedings.

An investigation into the complaint will be conducted by the Human Resources Department or company legal counsel, as appropriate, and will be conducted in as expeditious a manner as possible. Every employee is required to cooperate fully with any such complaint.

All reported breaches of the policy are to be investigated. Confidentiality will be maintained to every extent possible; however, the complainant must realize that a complete investigation and follow-up is usually not possible without disclosing his or her name. No employee will suffer from any reprisal for bringing forth a complaint unless the complaint is blatantly frivolous and vexatious.

The Human Resources Generalist conducting the investigation will issue a written report to the complainant with a copy to the Director, Human Resources who, in turn, will decide on the appropriate remedial actions. The appropriate parties will be informed of the final disposition of the complaint within 24 hours of the decision. Whether discipline is imposed or not, the complainant and the person about whose conduct is complained will be advised of the outcome of the investigation.

Remedial actions can vary in accordance with the nature of the offence and any mitigating factors, but may include immediate dismissal for a first offence.

Anyone receiving a complaint from a customer or supplier should also direct the complaint to a Human Resources Generalist for investigation.

Introductory/Probationary Period

The introductory period is intended to give new employees the opportunity to demonstrate their ability to achieve a satisfactory level of performance and to determine whether the new position meets their expectations. The company uses this period to evaluate employee capabilities, work habits, performance and overall suitability for the position.

All new and rehired employees work on an introductory basis for up to six (6) calendar months after their date of hire. The period will vary depending on the level of responsibility of the position. The specific length of the period will be stated in the letter of offer. During the introductory period, the new employee's performance will be reviewed by the supervisor halfway through the period and prior to the end of the period.

Any significant absence will automatically extend an introductory period by the length of the absence. If the company determines that the designated introductory period does not allow sufficient time to evaluate the employee's performance thoroughly, the introductory period may be extended for a specified period subject to the approval of the department manager and Human Resources.

Job Postings

The company recognizes that its strength resides in the skills and dedication of its current employees. The opportunity for career advancement and personal recognition of its Human Resources will be the predominant factor in sourcing replacements for all management vacancies.

All vacancies for non-management positions will be posted for a period of two weeks. Any qualified employee may apply for the position. It is the responsibility of the employee to notify his or her manager that he or she has applied for the position. Employees will not be considered for an open position (except under exceptional circumstances) if:

- the employee has been in his or her current position for less than one year;
- the position applied for is at a lower classification than the position the employee currently occupies; or
- the employee does not meet the threshold qualifications for the position.

Management below the level of general manager positions will only be posted if:

- there are no employees identified to fill the position under the company's succession plan;
- there are no employees who have been identified in their own development plans as potential candidates for the position and who are deemed ready for promotion;
- there are no employees identified for consideration by the hiring manager;
- the company determines that posting is appropriate under the circumstances.

The company shall only consider candidates who meet, at a minimum, the threshold qualifications for the position. The company will respond to every internal applicant; however, only those applicants deemed qualified will be granted an interview. If the position involves the physical relocation of the employee, the company reserves the right to determine whether or not the successful applicant is eligible for relocation assistance under its policies. Successful applicants not eligible for relocation assistance will be solely responsible for their own relocation expenses.

No supervisor or manager shall interfere with the employee's right to express interest in a position or to apply for a posted position. If the employee is a successful applicant for a new position, his or her manager will release that individual to the new department within three weeks of the appointment unless mutually agreed to otherwise.

Jury Duty

It is the position of the company that, as a matter of good citizenship, an employee should serve when called for duty as a juror or crown witness. However, if in the opinion of the employee's manager, the employee is required on urgent company business, the company should request from the appropriate party, as indicated on the summons, that the employee be excused from jury duty.

Employees will be paid regular wages by the company, in addition to any fees received from the government, when absent because of service as a juror or as a crown witness. Employees will not be granted leave under this policy in instances where the employee is serving as a witness in an action against the company or against the company's interests.

Leave of Absence Without Pay

Eligibility

A leave of absence without pay will not normally be considered until the employee has completed one (1) full year of service with the company. The only exceptions are:

(a) the company has agreed that the employee may have time off as a condition of employment;

(b) special circumstances; or

(c) maternity/paternity leave under provincial statute.

Request for Leave

Employees seeking personal time off without pay must make a written request and submit it to their department manager/general manager. Such leave must also be approved by the Director, Human Resources and the appropriate department head.

Length of Leave

Leaves of absence will vary in length, but under no circumstances will exceed six (6) months. Employees must use all accrued vacation time before requesting a leave of absence.

Nepotism

The employment of relatives in the same area of an organization may cause serious conflicts and problems with favouritism and employee morale. In addition to claims of partiality in treatment at work, personal conflicts from outside the work environment can be carried over into day-to-day working relationships.

For purposes of this policy, a relative is any person who is related by blood or marriage, or whose relationship with the employee is similar to that of persons who are related by blood or marriage. This policy applies to all employees without regard to the gender or sexual orientation of the individuals involved.

Relatives of current employees may not occupy a position that will be working directly for or supervising their relative. The company also reserves the right to take prompt action if an actual or potential conflict of interest arises involving relatives or individuals involved in a dating relationship who occupy positions at any level (higher or lower) in the same line of authority that may affect the review of employment decisions.

If a relative relationship is established after employment between employees who are in a reporting situation described above, it is the responsibility and obligation of the supervisor involved in the relationship to disclose the existence of the relationship to management. The individuals concerned will be given the opportunity to decide who is to be transferred to another available position. If that decision is not made within 30 calendar days, management will decide who is to be transferred or, if necessary, whose employment is to be terminated.

In other cases where a conflict or the potential for conflict arises because of the relationship between employees, even if there is no line of authority or reporting involved, the employees may be separated by reassignment or terminated from employment.

Note: this policy is not effective retroactively.

Personal Appearance/Dress Code

Dress, grooming and personal cleanliness standards contribute to the morale of all employees and affect the business image the company presents to customers and visitors.

During business hours or when representing the company, you are expected to present a clean, neat and tasteful appearance. You should dress and groom yourself according to the requirements of your position and accepted social standards. This is particularly true if your job involves dealing with customers or visitors in person.

Your supervisor or department head is responsible for establishing a reasonable dress code appropriate to the job you perform. If your supervisor feels your personal appearance is inappropriate, you may be asked to leave the workplace until you are properly dressed or groomed. Under such circumstances, you will not be compensated for the time away from work. Consult your supervisor if you have questions as to what constitutes appropriate appearance. Where necessary, reasonable accommodation may be made to a person with a disability.

Reference Checks

It is the company's policy to provide references for former employees when requested to do so by the employee. The employee may make a verbal request of a former manager or colleague, or a written request to the Human Resources Department to have a reference provided.

Managers providing references must be honest and forthcoming in all respects. No reference will be provided to any former employee who has been terminated by the organization for cause without the expressed approval of the Director of Human Resources for the business unit. Under certain conditions, only the Human Resources Department will be authorized to provide references. It is the responsibility of the individual manager to ensure there are no restrictions on providing references before proceeding to provide a reference.

No references are to be provided for existing employees without the expressed approval of the Director of Human Resources for the business unit.

Smoking in the Workplace

In keeping with the company's intent to provide a safe and healthful work environment, smoking in the workplace is prohibited, except in those external locations that have been specifically designated as smoking areas. In situations where the preferences of smokers and non-smokers are in direct conflict, the preferences of non-smokers will prevail.

This policy applies equally to all employees, customers and visitors.

Statutory Holidays

Holidays will be determined by the prevailing statutes of the province in which the employee works. In locations where a collective agreement is in force, the minimum standard will be equivalent to the number of days granted to employees covered by the respective collective agreement. Holidays include:

⇨ New Year's Day;

⇨ Family Day (Alberta only);

⇨ Good Friday;

⇨ Victoria Day;

⇨ St. Jean de Baptiste Day (Quebec only);

⇨ Canada Day;

⇨ Civic Holiday (in accordance with provincial statutes);

⇨ Labour Day;

⇨ Thanksgiving Day; and

⇨ Christmas Day.

Travel Expenses

Employees will be reimbursed for reasonable actual expenses that result from transacting company business. These expenses will ordinarily include transportation, lodging, meals and other items as defined in this policy. Unless otherwise stated in this policy, exceptions to this policy require the authorization of the appropriate corporate officers or his/her delegate. Exceptions are expected to be unusual in nature and non-recurring.

Commercial Air Travel

The standard airline mode is coach/economy class. For international flights of seven hours or more, business class is authorized. Travel between Canada and the United States is considered domestic travel. Use of business class is an exception to policy and the additional cost will not be reimbursed unless authorized by the president of the business unit.

Travellers should try to use the company's preferred airlines when routes and fares are comparable. Air travel should be booked far enough in advance to take advantage of advance booking discounts. Typically, 14 days in advance is the industry threshold, although additional savings are often available when flights are booked 21 days or more in advance. Non-refundable tickets should be used to the fullest extent possible. In conjunction with advance booking, non-refundable tickets are an effective means to secure substantial discounts on airfares.

Memberships in airline, car, hotel and credit card clubs are not reimbursable.

Points accumulated through loyalty programs provided by airlines or credit card companies, with the exception of those provided through corporate credit cards, are the property of the employee and are for his or her personal use.

If an employee wishes to travel a class other than coach/economy, he or she is required to include the difference in the fares as personal expense and report it as a deduction on the expense report. The deduction should represent the actual amount of the ticket less the value of the lowest fare ticket available for that trip, assuming seven-day advance booking as computed by the authorized travel agency. A letter or itinerary from the travel service company must accompany each expense report to document the personal portion; notations of telephone conversations with the travel service company are not acceptable.

Employees cannot use a less expensive class of travel than authorized and use the "savings" for travel of a spouse or other person.

Employee piloting or crewing of employee-owned, borrowed, rented or chartered aircraft for use on company business is prohibited. No exceptions to this section may be granted.

Personal Cars

Personal cars may be used on business trips with the manager's prior approval. An employee who uses a personal car for company business will be paid a mileage allowance plus reasonable parking and toll charges. No additional allowance will be paid for passengers who travel with the employee.

Rental Cars

Generally, rental cars may be used only when less expensive transportation is not available or convenient. Employees should use the company's preferred car rental agency and the approved standard mid-size car. A larger vehicle may be rented when the number of passengers justifies the need.

When renting and using a rental car, the employee must rent under the corporate rate and decline Loss Damage Waiver (LDW), Personal Accident Insurance (PAI) and Personal Effects Coverage (PEC). The rental agency will provide an insurance card in the glove compartment of the rental car. The collision deductible is a risk to be assumed by the company and personal accident (medical) insurance is covered under other insurance policies. Any cost incurred over the provided coverage, under the collision deductible due to an accident, will be paid by and charged to the department involved. Details of all accidents must be reported to corporate risk management.

Since refueling charges are usually high, cars should be refueled before they are returned to the rental agency.

Memberships in rental car clubs are not reimbursable.

Related Transportation Costs

Parking, tolls, taxi/limousine and similar travel costs are reimbursable. Traffic citations and parking tickets received while on company business are not reimbursable. Transportation to and from work, except in connection with a business trip, is a personal expense even if the employee works overtime, weekends, holidays, etc.

Accommodations

Lodging accommodations will be arranged using reasonably priced facilities. Preferred hotels should be used when available and the corporate discount should be requested at the time the reservation is made. Deluxe accommodations may be used only when less expensive accommodations are not available, and require appropriate explanation on the expense report. On extended trips, travellers should explore the economies associated with weekly or monthly accommodations.

Meals and Beverages

Meals and incidental beverages while on travel status will be reimbursed, provided they are kept within reason. Employees may want to discuss a reasonable limit on these expenses with their department manager prior to taking a trip on company business. All meals over $10 require a receipt.

Other Items

Such things as personal items, luggage and cash that are lost or stolen while travelling on company business are not reimbursable.

Child care, pet boarding and other personal expenses are not reimbursable.

Laundry, valet and dry-cleaning services should be considered only in exceptional circumstances such as when extended travel is necessary or trips are prolonged unexpectedly.

In-room movies and fees to use hotel health clubs are not reimbursable.

Vacation

Employees will earn vacation based on continuous service over the course of the *calendar year.*

Vacation Period

The following stipulations apply:

1. One (1) week vacation is the number of workdays in the regularly scheduled work week of the employee at the time of vacation.

2. When a holiday falls on what is normally a workday in an employee's vacation period, the individual shall be allowed an additional day off with pay. Such day must be taken in conjunction with the vacation or before the calendar year end, subject to the approval of the department head.

3. The first two weeks of vacation entitlement must be taken in minimum blocks of one (1) week. Other entitlements must be taken as full days, subject to the approval of the department head, but employees are strongly encouraged to take full-week blocks.

Vacation periods should be arranged to meet the preferences of the employees, if it is practical to do so without interfering with their work. The exceptions are:

1. Vacations may not be carried over from one year to the next. The company reserves the right to schedule any vacation that has not been used or booked by September 1 of each year to ensure there is no carry-over. The only exception to this is in the event that an employee's vacation is cancelled by management because of unforeseen circumstances. In these instances, the employee may be allowed to cash out his or her entitlement.

2. An employee must have been employed by the company at least six (6) months before any vacation time off is taken, unless prior arrangements were made as part of the offer of employment.

However, in view of the number of employees to be considered, the responsible department manager or general manager may designate and fix vacation periods. In fixing vacation periods, preference, where practical, would be given to those employees with the greater length of service.

Vacations may be scheduled at any time throughout the year.

Vacation Entitlement: Non-Management

The following stipulations apply:

(a) When employment began prior to April 1 of the reference year, the employee is entitled to two (2) weeks for that year.

(b) When employment begins after April 1 of the current year, vacation entitlement will be paid at the applicable rate at calendar year end or the equivalent days as approved by the department manager within that year.

(c) For those employees who have completed three (3) or more years of continuous employment but less than ten (10) years of continuous employment on or before December 31 of each year, the length of vacation period for that year will be three (3) weeks.

(d) For those employees who have completed ten (10) or more years of continuous employment but less than twenty (20) years of continuous employment on or before December 31 of each year, the length of vacation period for that year will be four (4) weeks.

(e) For those employees who have completed twenty (20) or more years of continuous employment on or before December 31 of each year, the length of vacation period for that year will be five (5) weeks.

(f) For those employees who have completed twenty-five (25) years of continuous employment, the vacation for that year *only* will be six (6) weeks. For each full year thereafter, vacation entitlement reverts to five (5) weeks.

Vacation Entitlement: Management

The following stipulations apply:

(a) When employment began prior to April 1 of the reference year, the employee is entitled to three (3) weeks for that year.

(b) When employment began after April 1 but prior to September 1, the vacation entitlement will be the equivalent days and be taken within that year.

(c) When employment begins after September 1 of the current year, vacation entitlement will be paid at the applicable rate at calendar year end or the equivalent days as approved by the department manager within that year.

(d) For those employees who have completed one (1) or more years of continuous employment, but less than ten (10) years of continuous employment on or before December 31 of each year, the length of vacation period for that year will be three (3) weeks.

EMPLOYEE ACKNOWLEDGMENT FORM

The policy manual describes important information about the company, and I understand that I should consult the Human Resources Department regarding any questions not answered in the manual.

Since the information and policies described here are necessarily subject to change, I acknowledge that revisions to the manual may occur. All such changes will be communicated through official notices, and I understand that revised information may supercede, modify, or eliminate existing policies. Only the President and the Director of Human Resources are empowered to adopt any revisions to the policies in this manual.

Furthermore, I have received the manual, and I understand that it is my responsibility to read and comply with the policies contained in this manual and any revisions made to it.

_____

Employee's Name (printed)

_____

Employee's Signature

_____

Date

RECRUITMENT AND SELECTION

Definition/Background

Recruitment is the process by which vacancies in an organization are filled. There are six distinct stages in the recruitment process.

Needs Identification

The need to recruit may arise in two ways. A vacancy is created by an internal transfer or promotion or by the termination of an incumbent's employment (either forced or voluntary). Otherwise, the need is identified for an individual to take responsibility for a number of related tasks. However, there may be several ways of meeting that need or filling the created vacancy other than through recruitment.

Identification of Key Skills

These are knowledge and attributes desirable or necessary to perform the role. The drawing up of a job specification that defines the required and desired behaviours necessary for success is an important aspect of the process. It is not enough simply to specify what experience the person has had or what qualifications he or she has attained. The process of recruitment is a complex set of activities designed to find the best person to match all the requirements of the job including the individual's fit with the organization's culture.

Targeting Candidates

This involves a number of means to identify possible candidates, including

— internal advertising (job postings);

— succession plans;

— external advertising;

— targeted (executive) searches;

— recruitment agencies; and

— Internet postings.

Surveys of recruitment methods indicate that internal advertising is the most frequently cited method, reflecting the wish of organizations to promote from within. This provides those with a wish to broaden their skills the opportunity to do so through job change. It also helps to ensure procedural equity by demonstrating the availability of internal opportunities.

Selection

The most suitable candidates are selected by way of a thought-out process, normally involving shortlisting, interviewing and formal assessment (e.g., the use of psychometric tests or job sample exercises). This process should be tied into the key skills, knowledge and attributes identified at the beginning of the process. Where internal candidates are competing against others, a selection process needs to be seen as valid and fair, so as to minimize the risk of the process being perceived as having a bias against internal candidates.

The Hiring Decision

This is key in ensuring that the integrity of the process is maintained and that professionally obtained data are used to best effect, although it is often a neglected part of the process. A structured process in which final candidates are assessed against the range of key areas (skills and attributes) is helpful.

Orientation/Induction and Follow-Up

This involves setting up a means of introducing and integrating the individual to the organization. Introducing individuals to their broader work context will help ensure their motivation as well as provide information about standard practices and the way things are done.

Following up with successful candidates is useful in helping to identify aspects of the recruitment process which may be associated with success or failure, although care must be exercised not to generalize from the unsuccessful cases that inevitably attract attention.

The principal purpose of the recruitment process is to ensure that the best qualified person carry out an appropriately defined set of tasks. The starting point of the process is the identification of a perceived need, normally by a manager wanting a set of related tasks to be done or a defined vacancy to be filled. However, it is important to note that there are a variety of ways in which these perceived needs can be met, including:

— contracting out the activity to a supplier (e.g., payroll administration, software design, logistics and distribution);

— reorganizing the work so that it is done by others (e.g., using overtime, or broadening others' responsibilities which can create opportunities for development);

— using short-term measures in anticipation of a future reduction in demand of the skills implicit in the vacancy, such as contingency workforces, temporary help agencies, or "interim managers" deployed from a management consultant, to bridge the gap.

The perceived need normally arises from the departure of an existing employee. However, expansion and strategic change can result in the creation of new roles. Indeed, external management recruitment is often a key component of change strategies where the infusion of new skills, approaches and values by "outsiders" is seen as important.

However, external recruitment can often be demotivating to others within the organization. For managerial jobs, hiring from outside the organization, reduces the opportunities for management development through internal promotions. Clearly, a balance needs to be struck between these considerations. Some organizations find it helpful to have an explicit policy on management recruitment in which the priority placed on internal recruitment is plainly stated.

Benefits/Expected Outcomes

Recruitment costs range from between a very small percentage of starting wage/salary to as much as 100% in the case of senior managers hired through executive search firms. The financial benefits of getting the process right, however, are seemingly less quantifiable — especially when benefits may be expected in years to come rather than being immediately apparent. Since recruitment has a clear cost, which may directly affect a budget and no measurable longer-term benefit other than getting the job done, there can be a tendency to adopt a less than thorough recruitment process. This is often a false economy, for two reasons.

1. Recruitment costs are trivial in relation to the costs of employment multiplied by the likely period of tenure, particularly when recruitment is followed by a period of initial training.

2. The benefits of successful recruitment, although intangible, extend many years ahead.

Reducing staff turnover through a recruitment process that selects the individuals most likely to succeed and remain in employment, while keeping to a minimum total expense, is therefore often a principal goal.

The more broadly defined business benefits of sound recruitment depend very much on the role and the organization. These benefits range from requiring an operative who simply performs a job to a set of standards, to recruiting a manager to achieve strategic change and make future innovations. Tomorrow's organizational success may therefore depend upon the enlightened recruitment practices of today.

If an organization is to maintain a competitive edge in the future, it must adopt an approach to recruitment that is linked with its strategic goals. For example, a mature business with a need to develop new activities will need to recruit managers with entrepreneurial flair who can help develop and redefine the business. A manufacturing company with an ever-shortening product lifecycle will need employees with the flexibility and aptitude to acquire new skills. In knowledge-intensive organizations, including those where research and development is a key need (e.g., pharmaceuticals, consulting firms or software design), the recruitment process must ensure the balance of skills and characteristics is attained to promote the appropriate level of innovation.

The outputs of most jobs cannot readily be quantified in terms of financial benefits to an employer. The problems are most extreme with senior managers, where decisions may have considerable longer-term impact but little in the way of short-term effects. The exception, perhaps, is in the area of sales where output has a clear and monetary value. What can be achieved is the assessment of the benefits of recruitment against a perceived need. In the case of a particular job, this is clearly whether the need was met or not. However, this notion can be generalized to the organization, when the perceived need then follows from the organization's strategy. Questions that may arise include the following:

1. Is the organization meeting its need to attract the employees of tomorrow?

2. Given the changing business, what skills are likely to be needed in the future?

3. How far are our current recruitment practices meeting these future needs?

4. To what extent does the organization depend upon specific technical skills or skills of general management, now or in the future? What are the implications in terms of recruitment policies?

A consideration of these issues will form an important precursor to an enlightened recruitment strategy.

Programming/Implementation

Needs Analysis and Job Specifications

A job specification is the outline of the knowledge, skills and behavioural attributes of the ideal candidate to undertake a particular role. It is therefore the keystone to the recruitment process, to which each stage of the recruitment process should be tied. More specifically, the purpose of assessment and decision making is to find the candidate who most closely fits the job specification.

The job specification is often arrived at using job analysis, some methods of which are outlined below. At a theoretical level, the most systematic and scientific way to do this would be to study those traits, experiences and skills that best predict success, by comparing the recent job performance and behavioural attributes of a number of different candidates. In practice, however, the step from job analysis and candidate profiling tends to be an intuitive one, based largely on experience. Nonetheless, job specifications are a fair and justifiable way of describing the ideal candidate, insofar as they are based on what is needed to actually fulfil the requirements of the job.

A good job specification is concise and to the point. It is written in plain English and provides a common language among those responsible for assessing a candidate. This helps considerably in the understanding and description of the relative strengths and developmental needs of the candidates under consideration.

Human Resources policies and strategies have a significant bearing on job specifications, in that it is often desirable to incorporate into the specification the future needs which the organization might have. For example, an organization in pursuit of a growth strategy may well have a general need for entrepreneurial individuals or for those with an international orientation. The succession plan and the organization's depth chart need to be considered in order to ascertain future needs the organization anticipates from planned internal movements.

Job Analysis

There is a significant risk in determining a job specification on the basis of current work, as opposed to future requirements. A mechanistic approach to job analysis should therefore be avoided. There are various techniques that can be used singly or together, to analyze a job. These are:

— observation of either the task or the behaviour of an individual undertaking the task;

— interview the incumbent (to identify the behavioural attributes of "good" and "poor" performers);

— interview the manager and or clients (internal and external) of the incumbent;

— diary or log-keeping by the incumbent outlining the tasks undertaken and the method used;

— critical incident evaluation which can be incorporated into an interview (eliciting information about particular incidents characterizing either good or poor performance in a particular job);

— repertory grid (in essence, the technique asks the interviewee to draw contrasts between good and poor performers — both generally and with regard to very specific tasks); and

— standardized instruments to analyze jobs. Examples are the Job Components Inventory and the Position Analysis Questionnaire. These ensure coverage of different potential elements of a job. Their output, however, may lack the richness and strategic overview of more discursive techniques.

Drawing Up the Job Specification

This is a skilled task. It is not a job description, which many job specifications tend to be. It is, rather, a description of the person who could best do the job. It may otherwise be called the "person specification". It needs to take into account how much training and development is available, in order to assess which skills are actually needed by the new entrant and which could be acquired through training. This will clearly affect the specification (e.g., "knowledge of accounting systems relating to car purchase" in contrast to "clear indication of a willingness and aptitude to learn new administrative tasks and aptitude for detailed work requiring numeracy"). This becomes particularly important in trying to identify those with potential rather than simply experience and skill.

Job specifications need to address the following characteristics of the "ideal candidate":

— achievements and professional qualifications;

— intellectual abilities;

— special aptitudes and skills;

— interests and motivations;

— disposition (personality);

— practical considerations (working hours, willingness to travel); and

— relevant experiences.

Examples of elements in a person specification are given below.

Using the Job Specification

The job specification provides an ideal basis for the construction of structured interviews. The interview should cover areas identified in the specification. For instance, in order to identify and qualify an individual's level of initiative, he or she can be asked to "Give an example of a time at work when you took the initiative on a project. What was the outcome? What did you learn from the experience?"

In the use of psychometric tests, every method of assessment should be specifically related to the measurement of one or more parts of the job specification. In this way, the tests are demonstrably relevant and, therefore, defensible. It also increases the efficacy and validity of the tests as predictors of future performance.

Rating scales to assess the relative strengths of different candidates can consist of the elements of the job specification with an accompanying rating scale. This can eliminate biases that might be present by adding a more objective means of assessing candidates against relevant criteria.

Internal Sourcing of Candidates

The first and most important source of potential candidates is internal, within the organization itself. There are a number of ways to identify internal prospects to fill a vacancy.

Succession plans are formal means of planning for predictable vacancies and recruitment needs. Succession plans look at turnover, anticipated retirements, expansion plans, possible mergers or acquisitions and other statistical sources of information and attempt to predict the future recruitment needs of the organization. They also look at the current incumbents in key jobs and plan possible future moves.

When anticipated recruitment needs are identified, the succession plan then evaluates the current pool of likely internal candidates to fill expected and unexpected vacancies. It is basically the drawing up of an organizational depth chart. It should be the first source of information on possible candidates to fill a role, once the need is identified.

Candidates who have been developed to take on ever-increasing opportunities are thus easily placed when a suitable opening occurs that matches their training, experience and behavioural attributes.

Ideally, the performance management process drives the succession plan. However, many organizations fail to link the two activities closely enough. As a result, some good internal candidates do not sufficiently get identified for future promotions in the succession plan. As well, imperfections in the performance management process result in the organization's failure to identify the career aspirations of many of its own talented people.

For this reason, a process of posting available internal job openings should supplement the succession planning process. The succession plan should take precedence over the posting procedure. The organization spends a lot of resources on developing particular employees for future roles. It needs to assess the efficacy of these efforts and to capitalize on opportunities to bring them to fruition in order to justify their considerable investment.

Notwithstanding, the internal job posting, which is essentially advertising internally, internal posting procedures should be undertaken in all but the most senior of positions within the organization. Internal posting procedures bring the following benefits:

— identify individual aspirations and ambitions;

— identify the individual development activities employees may have undertaken on their own accord;

— identify suitable individuals who are missed in the succession plan; and

— provide a system of recruitment that is perceived as being procedurally fair.

Special care must be given to protect the integrity of internal posting procedures. Once candidates have been identified who meet a certain threshold of qualifications and criteria, they must be subject to the same processes and scrutiny as an outside candidate. Courtesy interviews should be avoided as they raise people's expectations unfairly and can make a mockery of the process. Instead, internal applicants who are not being considered should be interviewed and told why they are not receiving further consideration. During the interview, the applicant can be told what areas of weakness have been identified and how he or she can overcome them.

If the succession plan clearly identifies an individual who has been specifically groomed for the vacancy, the position should not be posted. Employees recognize natural progressions and will perceive that the posting is only being put up by rote. Again, this will detract from the efficacy of the process. As well, if there is an identified need to bring in new people to fulfil an organizational requirement, such as to improve the organization's depth, it should be identified to employees. The key is to create an open dialogue about the recruitment process so that employees understand the organization's objectives and so that the culture is enhanced rather than detracted from.

Recruitment Advertising

The objective of recruitment advertising is to ensure that a sufficient pool of suitable candidates is generated from which to make a selection decision. This stage of the recruitment selection process is crucial, since the effectiveness of any selection decision is constrained by the capabilities of the available candidates.

External advertising was once probably the most widely used method of attracting a pool of candidates — especially when there were no suitable internal candidates. Other methods include internal bounties, the use of recruitment agencies, search consultants and informal networks.

Recruitment advertising is best considered as part of a broader process of selection. This ensures that the content and placement of advertising is driven by an accurate job specification, derived from a thorough analysis of the job and the behavioural attributes necessary for success. Effective recruitment advertising is critical in ensuring the organization attracts candidates who are suitable for the job. This narrows the selection process to identifying those candidates with the behavioural attributes to fit the organization's expectations and culture.

Advertising can be expensive. While it is important to ensure that suitable candidates are attracted, this should be done at the minimum of cost. Not only is it expensive to design the advertisement and to buy media space, but also expense will be incurred should the advertisement fail to attract suitable candidates. Furthermore, it is possible that the advertisement attracts a surplus of suitable candidates. In this event, unnecessary costs are incurred in both the placement of the advertising and in the subsequent processing of applications.

The recruiting organization is faced with a number of decisions concerning the use of advertising. These include the choice of media, the level of exposure, the design of the advertisement itself and the subsequent evaluation of the process. The efficacy of job advertisements has been relatively neglected in terms of research into recruitment and selection practices. This is despite the large sums of money involved and the importance of advertising in the overall process of selection.

Advertising is best seen, perhaps, as part of the process of building a relationship between the organization and the candidate. The aim should be to attract the attention of the best candidates who may not even be seeking another role, while not raising false expectations and allowing a healthy amount of self-selection. Notwithstanding, recruitment advertising is also advertising for the organization itself. The form and content will project an image of the organization. Care should be given to ensure the image is consistent with how the organization wants to be regarded. This is an often overlooked aspect of developing an organization's culture.

Content of the Advertisement

The information and the design of the advertisement are crucial. The content of an effective advertisement is likely to include the following:

1. **Information about the organization** — Limited information about the organization may increase the appeal of a role and, to a limited extent, helps to raise company profile. However, the use of a third party, such as a recruitment consultant or a Post Office Box, will be considered where it is important to conceal the identity of the recruiting organization.

2. **Information about the job** — Research has shown that recruitment is more successful where such information gives the applicant a realistic preview of the job. An outline should be given of the approximate remuneration, benefits and location of the job. Significant requirements that may not be readily known, such as the need for extensive travel, should also be included as this assists in self-selection out of the process.

3. **Qualifications and experience required** — Consideration should be given as to whether such requirements are expressed in terms of the ideal as opposed to the minimum requirements.

4. **Instructions for responding** — Applications tend to be increased if box numbers are avoided and if telephone numbers are given. Some organizations specify that only principals should apply to attempt to dissuade recruitment agencies from contacting the firm. Others also note that only candidates to be considered for an interview will be contacted. This is an appropriate touch to forewarn candidates not to expect a "nice no" letter but may also increase the frequency of telephone inquiries.

The content of the advertisement must conform to relevant legislation. Information can be obtained from the relevant Human Rights Commission on what is and is not appropriate content for employment advertising. In a general way, human rights legislation prohibits an employer from soliciting information that might identify an individual based on a prohibited ground for discrimination. Some employers may be exempt from these provisions if the nature of their organizations' activities dictates special requirements. If in doubt, such organizations should seek legal counsel before advertising. In addition to these legal requirements, on a practical level, the barring of certain categories of potential applicants on the basis of criteria, implicit or otherwise, which are not directly related to likely performance, reduces unnecessarily the number of suitable applicants.

Choice of Advertising Media

To be effective, the advertisement must reach the target audience in the most cost-effective manner. This presupposes that the target has been clearly defined. Reference should be made to the job specification produced in relation to the job.

The predominant medium for recruitment advertising has until recently been print. This is because the printed word is effective for conveying detailed information. An additional advantage is that the date of delivery of the advertisement can be quite precisely targeted. Other media have been recently used quite extensively because of a general shortage of labour but continue to be used to a far lesser extent than newspapers. Television and radio advertisement can reach a large audience; however, they tend to be expensive and reduce the amount of self-selection out of the process. Organizations using these media run the risk of being flooded with applicants that will slow the selection of suitable candidates considerably. Air Canada recently (2000) used the broadcast media to reach a large audience because of the extensive recruitment needs created from the fallout of its merger with Canadian Airlines.

The press can be subdivided into three categories: national, local and trade publications. The choice among these three should be driven by a consideration of the target audience, the nature (and number) of the positions to be filled and the importance of filling the positions relatively quickly. It should be noted that the general readership patterns of applicants is not necessarily the same as that when they are looking for jobs.

The national press (principally *The Globe and Mail* and recently the *National Post*) has the advantage of a wide geographic distribution. It is relatively costly and reaches a limited demographic. National papers target high-income earners, executives and professionals.

Thus, their recruitment advertising tends to focus on professional and senior management positions.

The local press tends to be further subdivided into two categories: big city dailies and community papers (usually published two or three times per week). Most of the broadsheet dailies have effectively segmented their recruitment advertising by concentrating advertisements for particular categories in different sections of the paper.

For example, the *Toronto Star* advertises management and career positions in its Business section three times per week, while advertising lower level white-collared positions and skilled labour openings in its Progressive Positions section. Other lower skilled clerical and blue-collar positions are run in the classifieds.

Community papers will run employment advertisements in their classified sections as well. These also tend to cater to lower level clerical and semi-skilled positions. The local press facilitates the targeting of the advertisement to a specific locality. This is necessary where the nature of the job vacancy is such that applicants are unlikely to wish to relocate, or where it is likely that suitable applicants can be found in a particular area. Considerations of fairness also apply to the choice of media. The choice of media should not mean that groups of potentially suitable candidates are unlikely to be exposed to the advertisement. Practitioners often overlook other community papers that cater to specific ethnic communities. These can be an excellent means of reaching parts of the population that do not tend to subscribe to the regular mainstream print media.

In order to facilitate international recruitment needs and fulfil immigration requirements, employers will have to demonstrate that they have advertised for the position nationally. This may mean advertising in a number of local papers when the national print media (as limited as it is) is inappropriate for attracting likely candidates.

The use of trade press offers a cost-effective means of reaching a relatively specific target audience. It tends to be most effective when recruiting people who have specific skills or areas of expertise. Unfortunately, lead times for advertising tend to be inconvenient to the timing of recruitment needs and these publications tend to be published only monthly. They are, however, well suited to general advertising for potential career opportunities. Some employers conduct advertising campaigns that, rather than be directed towards particular openings, are designed to generate interest in the organization as a preferred employer in the particular industry.

Evaluation

Most organizations will want to undertake some form of evaluation of their recruitment advertising. The temptation is to monitor the number of responses obtained for a position as a result of a particular advertisement or campaign. A more appropriate criterion is to analyze the number of shortlisted and appointed candidates.

Use of Advertising Agents

Some organizations are likely to benefit from using outside agencies to design and place their recruitment advertising. Apart from access to levels of expertise, which only the largest of employers is likely to match, they may also be able to obtain media buying discounts on behalf of their clients.

Alternatives

Given the large sums of money involved in recruitment advertising, organizations should be aware of possible alternatives or complementary methods of attracting a pool of candidates. Organizations recruiting large numbers of employees as a result of setting up a new operation or because of rapid expansion may obtain free communication in the form of press coverage. IBM took advantage of this recently when it was attempting to recruit hundreds of programmers in Toronto. It attracted thousands of potential candidates as a result.

Companies recruiting at senior levels, in which the number of potential candidates is likely to be low, may find that resources are more effectively used employing the services of executive search agents (head-hunters) who are able to deliver a personal message to specific individuals.

Executive Search

The work of executive search consultants, or "head-hunters" as they are often called, has a certain mystique. Clandestine meetings and well-developed personal networks both contribute to this, although the more recent use of extensive databases, greater rigour and a transparency of approach is changing the image of search firms. Their primary use is to recruit senior executives, and they are likely to add particular value in the following circumstances:

1. When the likelihood of attracting potential candidates by means of advertising or through recruitment and selection firms is likely to be small either because of the seniority of the role or the specialist nature of the position under consideration.

2. When there is a need for complete confidentiality for both organization and potential candidate.

3. When there is need to identify a specific group of potential candidates (targeted search) and persuade them to leave their current employment (often with a competitor).

4. When there is a need for a careful evaluation of potential candidates before they are introduced to their prospective new organization.

5. When the level of position being recruited makes it improper for the internal Human Resources practitioner to lead the process.

Executive search has grown rapidly over the past generation and it is now common for companies to use search consultants for most senior roles. Having originated in the United States, executive search is now an established part of the Canadian business scene. This dramatic change has been prompted by the following factors:

1. Developments in information technology allow extensive databases to be kept, which has meant that more proactive methods of searching for candidates have become feasible.

2. Severe competition for high quality senior managers has meant that organizations are prepared to pay a high price for effective recruitment.

3. Internationalization of business has meant that organizations require external assistance when recruiting in territories that are unfamiliar to them. Similarly, the shortage of certain required skills makes international recruitment a necessity in some circumstances.

4. Because of a general drive to make recruitment more professional and a desire to outsource activities, organizations prefer to have search agencies handle their more senior or specialized requirements.

5. Increased strategic responsibilities for the internal practitioner means organizations are unable to handle recruitment internally from a practical and economic standpoint.

The character and complexity of executive search have changed considerably over time. Initially, the most prominent search consultants were well connected socially and were able to establish credible relationships at very senior levels within businesses. Such individuals became confidants to chairpersons and chief executives and were able to provide them with external counsel on confidential personnel issues. Such individuals were also able discreetly to sound out potential senior candidates. Some headhunters work today in this way and are to be seen having long lunches and earnestly networking. However, modern day executive search is a hardheaded, business-focused activity backed up by extensive databases and research facilities. Increasingly, the search business is employing different specialists. Some consultants have different people fronting the organization, while others search for appropriate candidates, and still others conduct assessments to shortlist the candidates to be presented to the client.

When To Use Executive Search Consultants

Organizations contemplating the use of such firms should ask themselves, first, the extent to which the above factors are relevant to their particular requirement. Many organizations automatically go to search above a certain level in the hierarchy regardless of the merits of doing so. Use of search consultants, however, should occur on a case-by-case basis.

The alternatives are to use a selection or recruitment firm, which will typically advertise on behalf of the organization. In addition, some search consultants also offer a service whereby they use their databases to generate names of potential candidates that the organization is then responsible for processing. Where feasible, organizations should not neglect to ask their own employees for potential referrals and contacts, as all too frequently the candidates produced by search consultants are known to at least some members of the employing organization. Some firms will identify potential candidates from internal sources of information and then have a search consultant make the first contact. This helps broach the subject of whether or not the candidate would be interested in considering an opportunity without embarrassment to the recruiting organization.

Choosing a Search Agent

Barriers to entry into headhunting are low and, therefore, there is a proliferation of consultants. The choice for potential clients is further widened by the fact that it is relatively easy for individual consultants to break away from larger firms and set up their own practices. It is important to examine a particular reputation that a consultant has built up and, in particular, to assess the sectors in which it is especially strong. While many search firms claim to offer a general service, in reality, the work that they do may well be focused on specific areas.

Apart from differing in terms of sector specialization, some firms have a reputation for strong international search success or for operating at particular levels of management. In addition, there are some specialist firms that focus on identifying chairpersons or non-executive directors. The experience that a firm has in the relevant area is fundamental to its ability to conduct a successful search.

It is also important to assess the background and qualities of the search consultant who is likely to handle the assignment. Clients should examine the background of such consultants carefully and also establish that they have the relevant experience. It is important to meet the consultant personally as some firms can delegate work to less senior staff once the sale has been made. Clients should also endeavour to meet the researcher assigned to the assignment. These people are agents of the organization and represent the organization to others.

Search firms vary in their attitude to research and how systematic an approach they adopt. Clients should identify the particular approach to research that they require from their consultant. Sophisticated firms will present their clients with a list of contacts both successful and not. It is important to get feedback from the field to ensure the search is on the right track. Good intelligence garnered from contacting potential candidates will let the firm know if its compensation package is competitive and will identify any other potential barriers to the recruitment process.

In selecting a firm, it is sometimes helpful to look at past job specifications and person profiles that they have produced. In addition, given the importance of presenting the organization to potential candidates, it is important to identify the extent to which the search firm's values and ethos are congruent with the hiring organization's own culture. The organization needs to decide whether the search consultant identified will be adequately able to establish a rapport with potential candidates.

Negotiating a Contract

Traditionally, search firms charged a fee based on a percentage of the successful candidate's first-year base compensation. Most firms charge a minimum of 15% of first-year earnings and often cap the fees at 35% for higher end positions. However, there is now considerably greater flexibility in terms of the arrangements. The degree of flexibility depends largely on the current economy. In times of a shortage of available candidates, organizations will find that fees are not particularly flexible.

The higher-end consultants operate on the basis of a retainer calculated on a fixed commission. Typically, the retainer is paid in thirds. One-third up front, one-third upon presenting the shortlist, and one-third at the completion of the assignment. The full amount is expected even if, in theory, the position is not filled. However, these firms will continue their search until the organization is satisfied that they have properly addressed its needs.

Other firms are known as contingency agencies. They get paid only when a placement is made. Unfortunately, they tend not to scrutinize candidates as carefully as retainer agencies do, and substitute the quality of search with volume. Some less scrupulous operators will send résumés for potential candidates to an organization even if they have not been given the assignment. They do this in the hope that a candidate may attract the organization's interest sufficiently to overlook this tactic. Contingency agents do not typically take the same approach as retainer firms and should be considered cautiously.

Contingency agents typically source candidates for client organizations across three job categories: temporary, contract, and permanent. They tend to specialize their services within specific fields (e.g., media, legal) and/or job function (e.g., accounting, secretarial), where they can acquire expertise in relevant salary levels and advertising strategies. Their aim, typically, is to obtain a small number of suitably trained and qualified candidates for a role. The principal benefits are therefore that the client avoids the lengthy processes of advertising, inspecting résumés and shortlisting. In addition, by virtue of their expertise, the recruitment consultants should gain access to a well-qualified pool of potential candidates.

All organizations should establish a policy for dealing with recruiting agents. No résumé should be accepted from an agent unless the organization has a signed contract with that agent to work on the specific assignment. Unsolicited résumés should be returned with a note explaining the organization's policy.

In setting a contract, it is important to define the period over which a contract is expected to run. Most search firms should be able to produce a shortlist in 30 working days, although many try to extend this period. It might also be important to identify how many other assignments a consultant is working on. Since few are inclined to turn work away, there is a significant risk that a good consultant may be overloaded and thus may not be able to give research the full attention that it deserves.

Given the high cost of using a consultant, organizations should insist on a written report outlining the agent's activities and providing specifics on the candidates contacted, interviewed and shortlisted. An organization may also want to get a specific guarantee from the agent should the candidate not work out. Guarantees vary in length but invariably involve finding a replacement as opposed to providing a refund.

Positioning a Search Assignment

Effective research requires a considerable investment on the part of the client organization in terms of briefing the headhunter. In doing this, it is important to explain why the search is being made, why the vacancy occurred and to provide a detailed job specification. Given that external recruitment at a very senior level is often part of a change process within an organization, it is important also to give a search firm a clear sense of an organization's strategic priorities as well as its cultural values. The headhunter will invariably meet the line manager who will be responsible for employing the potential candidate. Developing a close relationship over time with a particular firm can

be particularly helpful in terms of developing mutual understanding of the organization's culture.

In considering a potential search assignment, it is important for an organization to define a list of potential target organizations from which candidates may come. Since search companies are precluded from poaching candidates from existing clients, it is important to choose a firm that is not working with companies that are considered fruitful targets.

Most search companies will agree to provide references for their candidates. It is important that these are handled in a sensitive and thoughtful manner, as there can be many potential problems with views obtained from references.

Some search consultants will also undertake psychometric testing and evaluation of candidates. It is advisable, however, for clients to insist that such valuations be conducted by a third party, in order to guard against conflict of interest and ensure the validity of the results.

Caveats

A number of factors can produce a poor fit between an executive selected through the use of an executive search firm and the hiring organization.

1. A talented candidate who is initially ill-inclined to leave his or her existing employer can be oversold a role by the agent and, upon joining an organization, rapidly become disillusioned.

2. There is a tension between seeking a candidate who has a distinct set of skills and who will "add value" to an organization and yet who will, at the same time, adapt satisfactorily to an existing culture. This issue needs to be thoroughly thought-out prior to an executive joining an organization.

3. Search processes build up their own momentum, particularly when the search consultant is keenly motivated to tie up an assignment quickly. There may be a tendency for the hiring organization to shortcut its own processes and rely on the expertise of the agent.

For these reasons, organizations need to satisfy themselves that they understand the style, strengths and limitations of potential hires. The established process should not be compromised simply because an agent has been involved in identifying the candidates. The decision to hire is still with the organization. Use of systematic internal assessment methods are therefore essential, although often overlooked.

International Search

Many search firms claim to offer international search. However, often this is delivered through loose associations. When conducting an international search, it is important to choose genuinely international firms. However, even in these cases, co-operation between offices can be grudging. It is important therefore to contact and interview consultants in the various offices that will be contributing to a search effort.

Interim Management

A relatively recent development is the growth in "interim management", whereby senior managers are seconded to an organization for a defined period, often associated with the implementation of a significant project or change program. There are some consultants who specialize in providing these short-term executives. As well, some of the larger management consulting firms offer this alternative as part of their package of services.

Graduate Recruitment

Organizations typically recruit graduates for the following reasons:

1. to provide a pool of high potential managers who can be developed for future senior positions within the business;

2. to undertake roles that require a high level of intellectual ability (e.g., consulting, engineering, software design, accountancy, etc.);

3. to perform roles that require specific knowledge and skills associated with particular degree courses; and

4. to bring fresh ideas and energy to an organization, challenge its existing management and add to a talent culture.

The impact of new technology, the move to flatter organizational structures and the need to keep pace with a fast-changing external environment are all factors that are promoting a general increase in graduate recruitment by organizations, although the broad trend is subject to severe yearly fluctuations created by the economic climate.

However, the increased demand for graduates has been matched and even exceeded by a corresponding increase in the supply of those who possess higher education qualifications. The important implication is that many organizations face a tough task in identifying the best graduates from what is rapidly becoming a large pool. In addition, simply possessing a degree may not be so distinctive an indication of underlying ability as has been the case in the past.

Organizations utilize a variety of methods for recruiting graduates. These include:

— running in-house block graduate recruitment and training schemes that take a set number of graduates per year;

— farming out the graduate recruitment process to third-party agencies in order to avoid the expense of fully fledged, in-house recruitment schemes;

— recruiting graduates to specific roles on an ongoing basis through co-op programs.

It is likely, because of the supply and demand changes outlined above, that the proportion of graduates recruited into organizations through block schemes will diminish, with more graduates being taken on for specific roles through co-op programs and on an ongoing basis. This is the pattern in many other industrialized countries, especially in Europe. The move towards self-managed development and to learning skills on the job as opposed to through more rigidly defined training programs is likely to diminish further the importance of block selection schemes.

A number of issues need addressing when formulating an organization's graduate recruitment policy, as outlined below.

1. *The benefits of recruiting and subsequently training inexperienced graduates, as opposed to the greater flexibility offered by taking more experienced graduates who have already proven themselves in previous roles, or who have been trained at other people's expense.* The argument in favour of early selection is that it allows a business to pick the best and brightest. Organizations therefore need to weigh up the extent to which the best graduates are only likely to be attracted by a coherent training and development program. Organizations also need to consider whether they have the ability to retain such

people over time and thereby capitalize on their investment.

2. *The extent to which it is possible to identify potential at a sufficiently early stage before graduates have been tested in the workplace.* This problem is confounded by the fact that many organizations have been engaging in something of a game of leapfrog in order to get the best graduates early on. (For some, the closing date for applications occurs within a few weeks of the first term in the graduate's third year.) This means that many are recruited without the benefit of even knowing what their degree results are.

3. *The extent to which organizations should focus on generalist skills or focus instead on recruiting graduates who display clear functional aptitudes and preferences.* The latter course may be safer but risks excluding graduates who may have decided not to specialize at an early stage.

4. *The extent to which salaries can be set at appropriate levels to attract high ability graduates, against the stiff competition of management consultants or south of the border where graduates can be put to productive use relatively early on.* The risks of creating internal inequities in compensation, and the productive worth of graduates to the organization, should both be assessed before setting graduate salaries in order to compete with high prestige recruiters.

Organizations must constantly evaluate their need for graduates and ensure that their recruitment policies are assessing and selecting the best graduates for the organization, as well as the extent to which the graduate program as a whole is meeting its key strategic objectives within the business. Some organizations may be well served by recruiting graduates who do not perform at the top in academics but possess the generalist's skills and behavioural attributes to fit into the organization's culture.

Organizations running successful graduate recruitment schemes build a strong image for themselves with higher education institutions. Regular efforts should be made to check the impression that an organization's promotional and marketing activities have on potential applicants. Useful sources of information in this regard are university career offices.

The levels of satisfaction of graduates who have been developed in the past by an organization can have a critical influence on its image within institutions, because many graduates retain relationships with their universities for a certain period after leaving. It is important, therefore, to assess the extent to which graduates' expectations are being met and to ensure that a realistic image is being projected by the organization. Some organizations use previous graduates to promote their recruitment activities to great effect.

It is equally important for organizations to evaluate the assessment frameworks that they use when selecting graduates. There is a risk in recruiting according to a very defined and established profile that can result in uniformity within the graduate pool and therefore the future management population. In this context, it is important to reflect upon the balance of qualities required by a business and help ensure that these are appropriately represented within the graduate pool recruited.

Technically driven organizations employing graduates for their technical skills can fail to assess adequately for broader managerial competencies and can experience problems later on when they require managers to move out of technical roles into more generalist positions. In addition, some organizations can risk overemphasizing the importance of intellect at the expense of other qualities and risk recruiting graduates who may not be able to bond effectively with their existing organizations, or translate intellectual ability into practical action.

At a strategic level, it is important for organizations to assess the cost of their graduate recruitment policies and evaluate whether the resources deployed in training and developing graduates might produce better results if put to other uses. In addition, it is important for organizations to monitor the time that it takes them to deploy graduates in productive roles in order to evaluate the success of their recruitment programs. In the long term, it is important to look at the extent to which the graduate recruitment scheme is truly providing the senior managers of the future in order to shape appropriately the initial selection criteria.

It is important to develop a clear view of the qualities (knowledge, skills and behavioural attributes) required from graduates and identify the disciplines and backgrounds that are most likely to produce candidates with the relevant characteristics. Targeting particular institutions, or indeed specific courses, is frequently found to be useful. Indeed, successful recruiters work hard to build long-term relationships with such institutions and endeavour to get high potential graduates to undertake work placements with them. The choice of target universities can be tested against the views of line managers within the business and, if possible, validated by looking at graduates who have been successful within the organization in the past.

It is important to time the whole graduate recruitment process rigorously. Typically, such processes include initial presentations, open days for graduates to talk to line managers and, if possible, graduates already on the program, a systematic screening process to identify candidates for interview, first and second interviews, an assessment centre and psychometric testing. Some organizations and industry associations also sponsor specific courses designed to familiarize candidates with key aspects of the business or industry.

Given that a very large part of the selection occurs at the application form stage, it is important to think through the design of such forms and to develop systematic screening processes. Some organizations use psychometric testing and, in particular, ability tests to screen out candidates. These can be useful in assessing potential, especially where no track record exists to confirm an aptitude (e.g., a history graduate considering software design). Care needs to be exercised in that relatively few tests are in widespread use and it is not uncommon to find graduate applicants who have sat the same test on several occasions. There is likely to be an increase in performance on a particular test with practice.

Interviewing

In the 1950s, interviews were regarded as having the scientific status of palmistry. They were wholly unreliable, it was argued, in that different interviewers' judgments of the same candidate would differ. Some psychology departments dispensed altogether with the interview as a selection device, even for so humanistic a discipline as clinical psychology. This same logic also gave rise to a huge increase in the use of psychometric tests, whose objectivity was easier to demonstrate.

It is now known that, when properly formulated and conducted, interviews can be as reliable as many psychometric tests and produce results which are equally valid, in the sense of predicting future success. Given that tests are measuring different attributes to interviewees, the optimal approach is to combine both.

The Interview as a Science

Current thought on the scientific basis of interviewing concerns how data of greatest relevance can be sought and how interviews are best structured. The basic aim is to elicit from the interviewee evidence that relates to his or her abilities, interests and motivation, on the basis that previous behaviour is a powerful predictor of future behaviour. The generation of questions requires considerable judgment and is normally carried out ahead of the interview. This helps to ensure that different interviews are conducted in a more consistent and therefore reliable manner.

This is the basis of so-called "criterion-based" or "behaviourally-based" interviewing, where the interviewer gathers evidence that supports or refutes the interviewee's claim to possess particular skills or characteristics. The generation of questions normally involves drawing out from the candidates evidence about how they have behaved in circumstances relevant to the prospective role.

For example, given an international role, then previous overseas work will be particularly relevant and questions such as, "And how did you adapt to the culture of life in ...", are appropriate. In assessing effective abilities, as distinct from abilities measured by tests, questions that deal with problem solving in a work context will be relevant. Replies may be interpreted in terms of how the interviewee uses data, whether he or she uses a previously derived rule of thumb or looks at each situation on its merits, and whether others are involved or not in the problem solving process. Follow-up questions are needed that probe the replies in more depth.

Questioning normally involves a balance between open, exploratory questions (e.g., "Tell me about the job with ...") and more direct, closed-ended questions (e.g., "You were with our competitors for some time. How much did your team increase its productivity?" "How was this accomplished?"). Common errors include too direct and closed a style and a plethora of leading questions that tell more about the interviewer's view of the world than it does the interviewee's.

The Interview as a Human Exchange

Although the above ideas represent a sound underpinning of the interview, the nature of the social exchange between two people during an interview cannot be overlooked. The etymology of "interview", from the French *entre voir* (to see between), emphasizes the reciprocal nature of this exchange. In the context of a job interview, the possibility that the interviewee assesses the interviewer, both personally and as a representative of his or her potential employer, gives rise to some important implications.

— Employers should see the interview as a means of promoting the image of their organization. A professionally organized approach to recruitment helps promote this image.

— Candidates should be given honest information about the role and its requirements, so that they can judge their own capabilities and, if appropriate, select themselves out of the role (the so called "self-selection model" of recruitment).

— Candidates' expectations should be managed so they are positive but realistic. A candidate who is oversold a role and does not anticipate significant problems will rapidly become demotivated and disillusioned. This is similar to the culture shock experienced by people when they arrive in a foreign land.

— Interviewers should encourage an open, exploratory approach and allow space for two-way dialogue. This needs to be taken into account when using the structured approach outlined above, which if used mechanically, can reduce the interview to something of an interrogation.

Although the interview should be seen by both parties as a two-way process, the onus is on the interviewer to set the tone and establish good rapport, which is a prerequisite of sound interviewing. The skills of warmth, empathy and positive regard should be employed during the interview. Good quality interviewing is more likely to be obtained when interviewees are relaxed and put at their ease, and when the purpose and possible outcomes of the interview are explained and understood.

Introducing professional interviewing is never straightforward since the majority of those who conduct interviews regard themselves as experts. A useful first step is to seek to ensure uniformity of approach through introducing the kind of structured approach noted above as a supplement to existing interviews and in this way convince managers of the benefits that can be derived from a more systematic approach. The benefits are particularly apparent where different interviewers are dealing with candidates for similar roles.

The basis of systematic interviewing can be listed as follows:

— The objectives of the interview are formulated and the requirements of skills, experience and motivation defined.

— A series of questions that measure each area are generated.

— A means of summarizing the questions and possible replies is drawn up (the structured interview schedule) in order that different interviewers can conduct the interview in similar ways.

— A means of rating the skills against each set of requirements or skill areas is established. A four-point scale, such as the following, would often suffice:

    (a) Unacceptable

    (b) Borderline

    (c) Acceptable

    (d) Strong.

Working jointly with managers who may be using a structured interview in formulating its design will help to ensure its relevance and their ownership of the process.

Evaluating the effectiveness of interviewing is less than straightforward. One approach, emphasizing inputs, is to ensure adequacy of interviews through training and specifying procedures. However, there is no guarantee that the approaches will be fully implemented. A more powerful approach keeps a healthy focus on the outputs of interviewing, i.e., its success rates. For example, the introduction of a systematic approach to interviewing could be evaluated by inspecting key manpower statistics, such as retention rates and performance levels, before and after implementation.

Training

Training in interviewing skills can be powerful, although benefits will be greatest in the circumstances outlined below.

— Training is relevant to real job vacancies likely to have been encountered by trainees. A just-in-time approach that provides the training when a manager is about to be involved in hiring a new person is an excellent means to ensure the learned skills are put into practice.

— It is active and involves plenty of feedback (the use of video equipment is invaluable, once initial inhibitions are overcome) and trainees continue to monitor their own skills following training. There is evidence that even professional psychologists get into bad interviewing habits a few years following qualification. Thus, good interviewers will always be prepared to put their skills to the test by inviting feedback from others and assessing their success.

Panel Interviews

Although a one-on-one interview is by far the most common, some organizations use a panel interview as part of the recruitment process. Panel interviews can take place early on as part of the screening process, or can be used later in the process to validate the selection of finalists. Any organization choosing panel interviews as part of the recruiting process should document when and how panels are to be used.

Panels offer an entirely different context for the candidate and are, in themselves, a test of the candidate's ability to present himself or herself in a group setting. Panels are particularly popular in organizations that value team dynamics. The setting allows the interviewers an opportunity to observe how the candidate asserts himself or herself in a group. It also ensures the group buys into the final selection. This sets the stage for the chosen candidate's success on the job.

Panels may consist of three to eight interviewers. Too large a group will be unwieldy and may put undue pressure on the candidate. The panel is usually made up of a cross-section of people from the individual's potential peer group. In some organizations, some of the panelists may also be chosen from the candidate's potential subordinates. In others, the panel may be a standing group selected to serve for a specified period of time. This type of panel may be involved in a wide variety of internal and external searches over the course of a set time frame (often one year). In these cases, participation is seen as part of the panel member's personal development.

Before the Interview

Before the interview takes place, the panel should be assembled and briefed by a trained facilitator. The facilitator will also participate in the interview as an observer. In the briefing, the panel is asked to develop questions for the candidate. The facilitator assists them in framing the questions in a way to elicit responses related to the candidate's past work behaviours. It also ensures the panel does not delve into questions that are irrelevant or prohibited under human rights legislation.

The questions form a script to be followed during the interview. However, the facilitator will also train the panelists on how to form follow-up questions so they are satisfied they have received a full answer. In order to ensure full participation, the facilitator may assign questions to be asked by individual panel members. This ensures not only participation but also buy-in. By assigning questions, the facilitator can judge how long the interview process will take. It is essential that the process is limited to no more than two hours. Any longer and the process may become an ordeal for the candidate and turn off his or her interest in the organization.

During the briefing, the job description and specifications should be reviewed with the panel members to help them in keeping questions relevant and to ensure they have a good understanding of the qualities that will make a good candidate. Typically, the briefing session is significantly longer than the actual interview. This is one of the reasons panel interviews are not commonly used.

However, failure to properly brief and train panel members can result in an unpleasant experience for both the candidate and the panel members. The panel must be made aware that not only are they there to judge the fit of the candidate to the job and the organization but also to represent and sell the organization as ambassadors. Their behaviour and conduct may be a determining factor in ensuring the chosen candidate successfully integrates into the culture of the organization.

To start the process of forming the questions, the facilitator may ask the panel members to make a list of the things about the candidate they will need to know in order to form an opinion about the match between the candidate and the job. Next, the facilitator asks the panel to explain why items on the list are relevant and what on-the-job behaviours would demonstrate the candidate's abilities with respect to those factors. This validates the list. The panel then develops questions designed to gain insight into how the candidate fits the specified requirements.

In framing questions, the facilitator should heed a number of *caveats*. Panel members do not often have experience in interviewing. The facilitator must emphasize that an interview is not an interrogation and the process is not an overt attempt to see how the candidate handles stress. Rather, the panel interview is a means of efficiently gaining a cross-section of opinion and of assessing the candidate in a different context. It also is a way to get peers to buy into the final selection of candidates and to get the candidates' acceptance of the team they may be joining.

Facilitators should also ensure the panel members are briefed on the requirements of the relevant *Human Rights Code* (or Act, as the case may be) to ensure inappropriate questions are not asked during the interview. It is unlikely in today's organizational context that overtly discriminatory questions would be posed. However, at times, panelists may stray into trouble through innocent inquisitiveness. The facilitator's role is to guide the panel away from any potential traps.

Finally, as part of the briefing, the panel should review the résumés of the candidates they are going to meet. Panel members can often be strict scrutineers of candidate's qualifications. The facilitator will need to explain why a particular candidate was chosen for an interview. If, for example, the job calls for a university degree and a candidate has been chosen who does not have a degree, the facilitator will need to explain that the candidate was chosen based on his or her having the requisite experience to overcome this deficiency. Taking the time to review the threshold qualifications and explain any apparent discrepancies is a necessary step so the panel does not perceive that the exercise is merely a matter of superficially involving them.

During the Interview

During the interview itself, the facilitator acts as the gatekeeper. He or she introduces the candidate and the individual panel members. Following this, the facilitator gives a brief overview of the process. This will include describing the organization, the position and what the candidate should expect from the interview. The facilitator proceeds to ask for the first question. Normally, the facilitator then simply observes the process and keeps minutes. However, the facilitator may intervene when:

⇒ panel members are having difficulty framing a follow-up question;

⇒ a panel member delves into a prohibited area or asks an irrelevant question;

⇒ a panel member is taking up too much time or the candidate is giving a response that is too long-winded; and

⇒ the candidate is too nervous and not responding well to the questions being posed.

The intent of any interview is to get information. The nature of the process should not interfere with good intelligence gathering. Many interviewers form opinions about candidates who are nervous and unresponsive and, therefore, fail to probe for more information that may assist in making a better decision. The facilitator must be a skilled interviewer who can help the panel overcome some of the pitfalls of the process.

A portion of the interview should be reserved for the candidate to ask questions of the panel. Practitioners will recall that the recruitment process in its entirety is a two-way process. Not only is the organization assessing the fit of the candidate but also the candidate is assessing whether he or she wants to join the organization. The facilitator will want to brief the panel beforehand on how to field the questions.

For some organizations, this may be problematic. It is essential that the panel be free to answer any questions put to them with candour. Part of a good recruitment process is to ensure the candidate understands all the positives about the organization and some of the potential problems he or she may face. By giving the candidate exposure to a group of peers and subordinates, the organization is affirming its integrity and willingness to be completely open with its employees. The only real *caveat* is to advise panel members to check overly negative responses. If there are too many concerns about how the panel might respond, the organization should re-think the use of panel interviews rather than disallowing this portion of the process.

After the Interview

Following the interview, the facilitator should thank the candidate and explain the next steps. Those steps are to complete all the scheduled interviews, assess the results of interviews and any testing that may have been conducted and arrive at a hiring decision. Although some panel interviews are conducted as part of the screening, it is recommended that they occur towards the end of the recruitment cycle. Conducting panel interviews takes a significant amount of manpower. The mere scheduling of interviews can be quite onerous. It is not a cost-efficient way of screening out candidates.

Rather, panels should be used to affirm the selection of a short list of candidates for final selection. Panels should be afforded a veto on candidates but should not be charged with the mandate for final selection. This remains the responsibility of the hiring manager who cannot abdicate the accountability.

Thus, following the interview, the facilitator must debrief the panel. This consists of reviewing their observations and helping them form a consensus opinion on the suitability of candidates. No individual can cast the veto. The panel collectively decides if they prefer one candidate to another, or if collectively they would choose not to pursue any of the candidates presented. The panel must clearly state the reasons for the collective opinion which the facilitator documents and presents to the hiring manager.

Tips

Panel interviews can be a powerful addition to the recruiting repertoire when used properly. Secrets to a successful panel process include:

✓ having a skilled and experienced facilitator;

✓ taking time to brief the panel on the process;

✓ reviewing candidate profiles with the panel before the interview;

✓ developing behaviourly-based questions relevant to the job specifications;

✓ observing established guidelines for the interview, including time lines;

✓ allowing the candidate to ask questions openly of the panel members;

✓ conducting a full debriefing and documenting the panel's findings;

✓ respecting the collective opinion of the panel when making the final hiring decision;

✓ incorporating the panel interview as a consistent part of the recruitment process; and

✓ focusing on making the panel interview a positive experience for both the candidates and the panel participants.

References

A reference report is an assessment of an individual by a third party. The purpose of taking references as part of a selection process is to obtain, in confidence, factual information about a prospective employee and, if appropriate, opinions about his or her character and suitability for the job. The candidate, of course, should be told if references are to be taken up.

References may be personal, academic or related to prior employment. Personal references are often of little value and probably should not even be required. Academic references are a useful way of checking an individual's qualifications and, if possible, an opinion of his or her capacity to learn. Many employers have found that applicants frequently misrepresent themselves by "faking credentials". Similarly, many universities report that inquiries on graduates and former students often reveal that the individual never graduated or may never have attended the university listed.

The most common references are taken from previous employers and are intended to serve as a way of predicting future job success, based on previous performance. It confirms what the candidate told the hiring organization through the interview process and offers a different perspective on the candidate's achievements and behaviours through the eyes of the referee.

However, due to perceived litigation risks, some organizations have a policy of restricting employee references to factual information, like dates of employment, job title and salary. In any case, an effective reference procedure makes it clear what the selector wants. It should ask for information the referee should reasonably be expected to supply and should make it as easy as possible for him or her to do so. Referees should know that they cannot be held liable for the information they supply, provided it is given in good faith and is based on reasonably held beliefs.

Controversial Issues

While factual references are reasonably straightforward, character references are an entirely different matter. There will always be a problem in assessing what weight to attach to opinions given by someone nominated by a candidate. The bias towards bland, positive statements is well known. Indeed, these considerations beg the question, should references be used at all? If they are, character references should only be used to supplement other information gathered during the selection process.

There are several methods of obtaining references and selecting an appropriate one will often depend on the type of role. Written references can save time, particularly if standardized, pre-printed forms are sent to the referee. These obviously provide a more specific and dependable check than general letters of reference supplied by the candidate. It may be beneficial to supplement written references with a verbal interview over the telephone. For more significant appointments, a face-to-face meeting may also be justified.

Whether verbal or written, the content and format of the reference report are important. More structured reports provide an easier comparison between candidates, although care needs to be taken in order to ensure that all relevant areas are covered. It is therefore useful to include an open-ended section where the referee can comment on any additional points of interest or concern. Rating scales or forced-choice questions designed to measure more specific attributes are also favoured by some organizations.

There are a number of conflicting views about when references should be taken. Experience suggests that informing candidates that references will be taken up encourages them to avoid making claims that will not hold up. If references are to be taken early on in the selection process, it may possibly eliminate some unsuitable candidates without incurring the cost of an interview, although most candidates will not wish to reveal to their employer their intentions until they have been offered the job.

Issues of confidentiality, time and financial resources can sometimes make it difficult for potential employing organizations to take up references on candidates. Printed reference forms sent out or completed via telephone interview are a useful way of addressing some of these issues. Only the people involved in the selection decisions should have access to such material.

Reference-taking agencies offer an anonymous service that can help overcome some of these problems. One variant used by such agencies is "throw off" referees — where referees are asked to give the names of others who know the applicant well or who could provide further information on some matter of interest. Obviously such secondary references provide an opportunity to cross-validate information gained from primary sources, and in doing so, gain a clearer picture of the individual concerned. When taking references, some useful questions to ask are as follows:

Factual

— What was the period of employment?

— What was his or her job title?

— What were his or her job responsibilities?

— What was his or her salary package?

— Are you aware of any convictions (other than spent convictions) recorded against him or her (please specify)?

— What is the reason for leaving?

Opinions

— How would you describe his or her job performance?

— What sort of potential for promotion does he or she have?

— Would you re-employ him or her?

— Do you know of any reason why we should not employ him or her?

Practice Tips

In the United States, many employers are reluctant to provide reference checks for fear that they may be sued for libel or defamation of character. This fear has spread north of the border and many recruiters may find it difficult to get a former employer to provide much more information than a verification that the person worked for it. This may make it more difficult to properly screen a prospective employee.

Recruiters should not be deterred, and there are a number of steps that can be taken to ensure getting a proper validation of the candidate's qualifications and abilities. When checking references, the steps a recruiter can take to ensure he or she gets a complete and accurate picture of the candidate include:

✓ asking the candidate to contact their referees beforehand to let them know they can expect a call from the recruiter;

✓ having the candidate sign a release authorizing the referee to give a reference;

✓ sending the referee, when time permits, a request in writing for the reference;

✓ having a list of questions scripted beforehand;

✓ asking direct questions — begin with questions that verify facts stated in the candidate's résumé;

✓ trying to deal invariably with the employee's direct supervisor;

✓ mining for other references;

✓ arranging for a time when the referee is free to give answers;

✓ arranging to meet with the referee face-to-face, if possible; and

✓ ensuring you have set aside enough time to do the reference check properly.

Canadian employers are not likely to face lawsuits for the references they provide for former employees. The information employers offer is privileged and therefore protected, provided it is given in good faith and is honestly believed to be true. Canadian employers are well served to provide references. More and more often, the courts are awarding additional severance payments in cases where the employer has refused to provide a reference. The rationale being, that by failing to assist the former employee, they are prolonging the employee's search for alternative employment.

In addition, there have been a few cases where a former employer has been held vicariously liable for the actions of a former employee, precisely because it failed to warn a prospective employer about difficulties experienced with the employee. In one instance, a "bouncer" was dismissed from a tavern after he was charged with assaulting a patron. The tavern failed to disclose this to another establishment which was considering hiring him in a similar capacity. The new bar subsequently hired the bouncer. There he got into trouble again and assaulted a customer. When the customer sued for damages, the former employer was held to be partially responsible.

If an accountant were dismissed from his or her former place of employment, a new employer looking to place that individual in a position with fiduciary responsibilities certainly deserves to be told the truth. These are important considerations and are in part why reference checks are so important.

In order to foster a climate in which there is a *quid pro quo* among employers in Canada, organizations should follow a few simple guidelines when giving out references. These include:

❏ provide a written reference to departing employees upon request;

❏ have exiting employees, regardless of the reasons they are leaving, sign an authorization to the organization to give out references;

❏ designate an individual, usually a senior Human Resources practitioner, to be the prime contact for reference checks;

❏ establish a policy that no one in the organization provide references without the authorization of a senior Human Resources practitioner;

❏ ensure anyone who is authorized to provide a reference is briefed on what to say or not to say, and ensure the referee holds no malice towards the former employee;

❏ encourage anyone giving oral references to keep notes on exactly what was conveyed;

❏ do not exaggerate, even when giving a positive reference;

❏ do not speculate on how an individual will perform — stick to what the person did when he or she was an employee;

❏ ensure, if the person has been fired for just cause, that the matter has been properly settled with the necessary written releases before making any statements, whether positive or negative; and

❏ ensure the information given is complete and accurate. (**Note:** If the employee was fired for cause, that should be stated. Otherwise, the organization may be exposed to a suit for negligent disclosure or vicarious liability.)

Sifting and Shortlisting

In many selection decisions, the number of applications received means that it is necessary to perform some form of sifting or shortlisting of candidates before more intensive selection methods can be employed. This is made more difficult if the applicants are relatively homogeneous (e.g., final-year undergraduates), and it can be both time-consuming and expensive. For reasons of time alone, many organizations use agencies or recruitment firms to reduce the workload. Others are employing software that can select out candidates who do not meet threshold qualifications or other identified criteria for the position.

Regardless of who carries out the initial stages of recruitment, the sifting of applications is often performed using a set of criteria that are linked to subsequent job performance. These criteria vary widely and can be informal and *ad hoc*. For example, applicants who take a "year out" between university and work or who have made a handwritten application may be judged to have a low commitment to their careers. Such informality reduces the fairness of the sifting process for the candidate and its efficacy for the recruiting organization.

Application Forms

Sifting and shortlisting can be made more fair, convenient and systematic through the use of standardized application forms. Their principal functions are to assist in the selection of candidates, to provide information for subsequent interviews, and to serve as a basic personnel record. Application forms may represent a marginal improvement over unstructured applications based on résumés. However, in order to comply with human rights legislation, many firms have trimmed down application forms that are usually only used for lower-level positions. Firms prefer résumés for candidates seeking managerial and skilled positions.

Role of the Human Resources Practitioner

This is an area where the Human Resources practitioner is often consulted by line managers to define and implement a process. Recruitment is a significant area where the practitioner's skills can add considerable value. It should not simply be a question of responding immediately to a request and initiating a process without proper thought. The skilled practitioner considers all the stages necessary for a successful process, including whether recruitment is indeed the answer to the line manager's problem.

The Human Resources practitioner is also in a position to consider recruitment from the broader organizational perspective. This is important where a manager's wish to make a rapid appointment may put at risk the need to be seen to be acting fairly towards others in the organization and, for example, post the vacancy internally. A manager may also be responding to an immediate need and not have considered longer-term or more strategic issues. A sensible question about any recruitment is, "What will be the shape of this role in three or five years' time?". In a managerial context, the practitioner may also have the information to identify internal candidates whose development will be furthered by the role.

The primary role is that of internal consultant and implementor, advising managers on how best to organize the process and to carry out specific steps as appropriate. The aim should be to allow a manager or supervisor to make a choice between a small number of suitable candidates. It is important that the ultimate responsibility is in managers' hands since they are then most likely to be committed to the decision.

In general, the contribution to recruitment will be greatest when Human Resources reports through the line management structure rather than through a centralized Human Resources Department. Under these circumstances, there is more opportunity to understand the business requirements and anticipate any future changes that may have a bearing on the recruitment.

A central Human Resources function will be invaluable in the case of internal, middle to senior managerial recruitment in an integrated organization, where it can help to identify candidates for a role. It is also in a position to formulate more general policies about recruitment, including the balance of internal and external recruitment and graduate schemes.

Executive recruitment is beyond the scope of the Human Resources practitioner. Even the most objective and skilled practitioner must avoid participating in the recruitment of peers and superiors. However, most senior Human Resources directors will see it as their role to consider the shape, skills and development of the executive team, and will know a small number of executive search firms should the need arise to fill a vacancy at this level.

Recruitment places a number of demands on the Human Resources Department. The administrative burden created by the volume of potential applications to a vacancy is clear. It is important, too, that the logistics of recruitment are well handled since the process will be the only contact many candidates will have with the organization. Clearly, they should be left with positive feelings about the recruitment process and the organization. Otherwise, all potential candidates may question the integrity of the process and the organization itself.

It need hardly be said that response letters need to be written quickly and the arrangements for interviewing (room availability, payment of expenses) smoothly organized. The candidate should see the process as professional and relatively seamless. The organization must present itself favourably as the candidates are also assessing whether or not they want to join the organization.

Many Human Resources Departments are seen as supplying only these administrative skills. If recruitment is to be seen more strategically, then Human Resources practitioners will need the following skills:

1. They will need a sound understanding of the business, its strategy and future possible developments.

2. They will have to possess a good understanding of the technicalities of recruitment, including how candidates are best targeted, interviewing skills, the role and use of psychometric tests and relevant employment law, particularly where issues of adverse impact may arise. Specific training can help in understanding the technicalities of recruitment.

3. They require knowledge and experience as to when to use outside consultants and how their specific skills may add value.

4. They need the people and influencing skills to deal effectively with line managers.

Human Resources practitioners are the keepers of the process. They must ensure that the integrity of the process is maintained and that it is consistently applied. They may help line managers in making a decision to hire but, apart from hiring Human Resources staff, should not be responsible for the decision making themselves.

Specific responsibilities of the Human Resources Department include:

— establishing and maintaining the succession plan;

— assisting line managers in determining recruitment needs;

— facilitating the defining of job specifications;

— maintaining the internal posting process;

— sifting and sorting incoming résumés and applications;

— screening the initial slate of candidates;

— testing (when qualified to do so);

— facilitating the behaviourally based interviewing process;

— providing training on the recruitment process and interviewing skills to line managers;

— being the principal contact for search firms and contracting with those firms when appropriate;

— defining and auditing the effectiveness of the recruitment process for the organization; and

— maintaining the organization's Internet page for recruitment purposes.

Barriers to Success/Common Pitfalls

When it comes to recruitment, and in particular assessing people through interview, most managers feel themselves to be experts. The most significant barrier is perhaps the limitations that we all have in relation to judgments about people, and the need that follows to organize a systematic process that results in decisions based on sound data.

A further barrier can arise from the organization's culture. Even in today's business climate, it is not usual to find cultures that are truly founded on merit. Recruitment, particularly through internal processes, continues to be influenced by nepotistic attitudes based on managers' wishes to know their new recruit and, therefore, to feel safe. Part of this preference is based upon the perfectly sound argument that data are already available on people who are known. However, nepotism is always unacceptable because of the demotivating effects it has on others in the organization.

Organizations tend to seek to replicate previous success formulae, and in any event, most managers value in others what they see in themselves. The result is a tendency of managers to recruit others in their own image, giving rise to what might be referred to as "corporate cloning". This may well be justified and desirable when a business is operating in a constant and unchanging market. However, business conditions change and the more uniform a set of employees, the more risk there is of groupthink. Some banks, for example, in the mid-to-late-1980s hired large numbers of entrepreneurial risk takers, who arguably took too many risks. A more balanced recruitment strategy, reflecting a wish to assess and balance risk, may have been more successful.

A final barrier to success in this area is the tendency for individuals and organizations not to follow up their decisions to see what might be learned. Too often, the risk of finding unpalatable data prevents our looking for it, even when it might provide valuable learning opportunities. Where recruitment is large-scale, systematic follow-up is essential if the optimal recruitment approach is to be found for a given set of circumstances.

Ten common pitfalls are as follows:

1. There is no real need for the role, which can be met by others, or the role changes rapidly after recruitment. Job analysis and the drawing up of the job specification need to accommodate future change will help reduce this risk.

2. Advertising is poorly targeted, or the job undersold, resulting in a poor pool of candidates. A key aim is to ensure that the best possible people apply. A good selection process can be completely negated if selection is among poor candidates.

3. An external candidate is hired to a vacancy not posted internally, giving rise to resentment and a reduction in development opportunities.

4. A job is oversold to a candidate and false promises made to attract a new recruit. These nearly always backfire. Unrealistic expectations result in culture shock and may give rise to claims of wrongful hire.

5. Shortlisting discards good candidates by too rigid a set of criteria of selection (e.g., the inexperienced with high potential may be inappropriately ruled out).

6. Interviews are too short, hurried and conducted poorly. The evidence suggests that with moderate guidance, managers' interviewing skills can be significantly enhanced.

7. Good selection data are wasted by too hasty a final decision-making process and an over-reliance on the hunches of the most senior manager.

8. Psychometric tests are used inappropriately, without due regard to their limitations or issues of adverse impact and unfair discrimination.

9. So-called "experts" (consultants, psychometricians, graphologists, Human Resources professionals) take over the process so that a line manager feels little ownership of the selection decision. When problems arise, they correctly blame others and try to overturn a decision rather than working with it.

10. A candidate oversells his or her strengths, creating stress and personal discomfort on arrival. Modern recruitment processes encourage individuals to appraise their own skills honestly in relation to a role.

POSITION REQUISITION FORM

Position: _____

Department: _____

☐ Full Time   Part Time, please specify # of hours per week: _____

☐ Permanent   ☐ Temporary/Contract   ☐ Student

Reason for Vacancy: _____

_____

Is this position budgeted for?   ☐ Yes   ☐ No, please attach business case

Proposed salary range: _____

Briefly describe the duties of this position: _____

_____

_____

Is there a written job description?   ☐ Yes (please attach)   ☐ No

This job reports to: _____ # of Subordinates:_____
Please attach departmental organizational chart

Anticipated start date: _____

If temporary/contract/student, anticipated end date: _____

Requested by: _____ Date Submitted to HR: _____

Approval: Departmental Director _____

              Director, Human Resources _____

RECRUITMENT AND SELECTION GUIDE

MANAGEMENT POSITION
(Sample)

CANDIDATE NAME:

INTERVIEWED BY:

DATE:

GENERAL INTERVIEW QUESTIONS

Before the interview begins, choose the questions you wish to ask out of each section. As you ask questions of the candidate, fill in relevant comments and circle relevant keywords mentioned, where possible. Once the interview is over, you can come back to each section and assign a rating based on the rating scale in the assessment section at the end. This will give you time to reflect on how the candidate has answered all of the questions.

Some key things to remember:
- Always begin with rapport-building questions that are casual and put the candidate at ease.
- Look for trends in personal growth and development of leaderships skills over time.
- Be inquisitive. Get examples to turn generalities into specific responses.
- Listen four times more than you talk.

EXPERIENCE

<u>**Related Experience**</u>   **Comments**

☐ Let's begin with your work experiences. Could you give me an overview of your career so far?

☐ I would like to begin by having you outline for me your present/previous position and how you feel it is related to and/or has prepared you for this position.

☐ How do you think your previous job experience has prepared you for this position? Can you give me an example of what is particularly relevant to this position?

☐ What do you feel you can offer our company? (What do you think your main contributions to the position will be?)

Key words: Dedication ~ Lead ~ Problem solving ~ Loyalty ~ Directed ~ Created ~ Developed ~ Implemented ~ Improved ~ Reduced ~ Changed ~ Coaching and motivating employees ~ Integrity ~ Enthusiasm

RATING   1   2   3   4   5   6

1

Education
Comments

☐   Please tell me about any specific training you have had that is related to this job.

Key words: Management/Supervisory skills ~ Business communications ~ Labour relations ~ Microsoft applications ~ Operations management ~ Project management ~ Strategic planning ~ Team facilitation

RATING   1   2   3   4   5   6

Job Stability/Persistence/Goals
Comments

☐   Describe a recent goal or project at work where you experienced tremendous adversity – or where the results were illusive:

     o   What was your goal?
     o   What roadblocks did you encounter?
     o   How did you respond?
     o   What was the outcome?

☐   Tell me about a time at work when morale was low in your department:

     o   What was the situation?
     o   How did it affect you?
     o   What did you do about it?
     o   When did this occur?

Key words: Managed emotions ~ Adopted and maintained a positive mindset ~ Tried to relieve the stress by relaxation, exercise, etc. ~ Prioritized what needs to be done in a logical or optimal order ~ Checklist to keep on track with the tasks (planning) or any tool to help the person keep focused

RATING   1   2   3   4   5   6

2

LEADERSHIP

Provide Leadership

☐ How would you define leadership?

Comments

☐ What is the importance of leadership in an organization? What have you done to develop your leadership skills?

Key words: Empower ~ Lead by example ~ Create and foster change ~ Mentoring and coaching ~ Vision ~ Clear direction ~ Unified

RATING 1 2 3 4 5 6

People Leadership

Comments

☐ Letting people know how they are doing is a key leadership responsibility. Let's go back over the last few times you discussed an employee's performance.

- o What did you discuss?
- o What did you say?
- o How did he/she respond?
- o What was the outcome?

☐ A work stoppage has just concluded. A number of employees participated in it, while others came to work. To insure that your department/organization continues to work effectively, what steps can you take?

Key words: Tact and diplomacy ~ Empowerment ~ Coaching ~ Leading ~ Motivate ~ Communicate effectively ~ Feedback ~ Conflict resolution ~ Positive reinforcement

RATING 1 2 3 4 5 6

3

Planning and Organizing

Comments

☐ Thinking back on your most recent job, describe the project that you feel best demonstrated your skills in planning.
- o Who did it involve?
- o What was the process taken to implement it?
- o How did it measure progress against the plan?
- o What were the biggest challenges?
- o What were the major deliverables?

Key words: Action plan ~ Charter ~ Teamwork ~ Effective allocation and use of resources ~ Delegated responsibilities if appropriate

RATING   1   2   3   4   5   6

Teamwork/Collaboration

Comments

☐ Describe what you believe are your strengths when collaborating with others. Describe a difficult situation where you had to use your strengths to create work plans with other functional areas that had the same objectives. What was the outcome?

☐ Tell me about a situation in which you were required to work with people at various levels within your organization. What was the most important step that you took to work effectively with these people?

☐ Tell me about a time where you had to work closely on a team with others to get the job done.
- o What was the situation?
- o What role did you play?
- o In your experience, what have been the pros and cons of working on a team?
- o What did you do to get people working together?

Key words: Collaboration ~ Use of diverse resources and skills ~ Gathered appropriate information ~ Empowerment ~ Effective communication skills ~ Created and fostered a team environment

RATING   1   2   3   4   5   6

4

Financial and Operational Management

Comments

☐   You have been asked to recommend some criteria for reducing the budget. What criteria will you recommend?

☐   Can you give me an example of a time when you had to deal with employees not reaching productivity goals?
- o   What was the situation?
- o   How did you handle it?
- o   What was the outcome?

☐   Can you give me an example of how you have approached an ongoing reoccurrence of non-compliance to standard operating procedures? What was the outcome?

Key words: Used a planned approach to deal with situation ~ Created and fostered change ~ Communicated importance of standard operating procedures and impact on cost/financial performance

RATING   1   2   3   4   5   6

Customer Orientation

Comments

☐   We all have customers that demand more from us than others. What type of customer demands do you find most challenging? What have you done to minimize the impact of this type of customer on you and your staff?

☐   Tell me about a time when you dealt with an irate/difficult customer. How did you handle the situation? What was the outcome?

Key words: Used problem solving skills ~ Ability to think on one's feet ~ Adaptability ~ Collaboration with customer ~ Clear communicator

RATING   1   2   3   4   5   6

5

Problem Solving

Comments

☐ Tell me about a time when you had to work closely with someone you found very difficult to get along with.
- o What was he/she like?
- o How did you handle him/her?
- o What was the outcome?

☐ In working closely with others day after day, disagreements are bound to arise. Tell me about a serious disagreement you have experienced with a co-worker.
- o What was the situation?
- o How did you handle it?
- o What was the outcome?

Key words: Used conflict resolution techniques such as took him/her aside and probed underlying reasons for disagreement(s), asked for suggestions on how to solve the situation ~ Situation handled with tact, diplomacy and courtesy ~ Ability to recognize own role in conflict

RATING   1   2   3   4   5   6

Communication

Comments

☐ What specific information do/did you share with your staff? How often do you share this information and why?

☐ Give me an example of a time when you were able to communicate successfully with another person even when you felt the individual did not value your perspective.

☐ What do you find to be the most challenging aspect of communication? Can you give me an example of how it has interfered with your interactions? What steps have you taken to improve?

Key words: Effective oral communication skills ~ Ability to change style to suit target audiences ~ Awareness that communication styles can develop respect and mutual understanding along with productive working relationships ~ Ability to recognize room for improvement

RATING   1   2   3   4   5   6

6

VALUES AND BEHAVIOURS

Comments

Work Ethic

☐ Give me an example of a time when you had to go above and beyond the call of duty in order to get a job done.

☐ There are times when conscientiousness can work against us. This happens when we keep doing something the same way after we should have changed our approach. Has this ever happened to you? If so, give me an example.

RATING 1 2 3 4 5 6

7

P - Q - **R**

Motivation

- ☐ Give me an example of a time you felt you were able to build motivation in your coworkers.

- ☐ Have you ever had a job that you felt really passionate about?
    - o What was it?
    - o What did you find exciting about it?

- ☐ Tell me about a time or situation at work where you found it difficult to get motivated.
    - o What was the situation?
    - o When did it happen?
    - o How did it affect you and your work?
    - o What ultimately happened to resolve it?

- ☐ Tell me about a project where you had to work to your limit to get a job done.
    - o What was the situation?
    - o How long did it last?
    - o In what way were you stretched?
    - o When did this happen?

Comments

Key words: Enthusiasm for accomplishing tasks/projects ~ Ability to overcome obstacles and learn from them ~ Motivation to complete tasks and pride in them

RATING   1   2   3   4   5   6

8

Maturity and Judgment

Comments

☐ Tell me about an assignment or project at work where you've been unable to achieve the goal.
- o What was the background?
- o What happened?
- o In your mind, why were you unable to achieve the goal?

☐ Tell me about a time when you were passed over for a promotion or raise or an assignment you felt you deserved.
- o What was the situation?
- o What did you do?
- o Why do you feel you didn't get it?

☐ There are often peak times at work where the load is particularly heavy. Describe an experience you've had working under tremendous pressure.
- o When did this happen?
- o In what way was the pressure heavy?
- o How long did it last?
- o What was your strategy for coping?

Key words: Took a step back and assessed situation ~ Looked for feedback on things that could have been approached differently ~ Delegated responsibilities ~ Sought out additional resources ~ Aware of room for improvement

RATING   1   2   3   4   5   6

9

P - Q - **R**

Self-Control   **Comments**

☐ Describe a time when you were faced with problems or stresses at work that tested your coping skills. How did you handle it? What was the outcome?

☐ Can you give me an example of something at work where, in spite of your efforts, you were unable to achieve good results?
- o   What was the situation?
- o   How did you handle it?

Key words: Prioritizing in a logical or optimal order ~ Taking a step back from situation to reevaluate ~ Sought assistance proactively

RATING   1   2   3   4   5   6

Self-Confidence   **Comments**

☐ You've been appointed as the new manager of your group. The others in the group have more seniority and two of them also interviewed for the position you've been appointed to. How will you approach your new assignment?

Key words: Used tact and diplomacy ~ Showed strong leadership skills ~ Fostered a team environment ~ Empowered others in group

RATING   1   2   3   4   5   6

10

CLOSE THE INTERVIEW

☐   What did you like most about your last job? What did
    you like least? Why did you leave your last job?

☐   What are your long range plans?

☐   What are your earning expectations?

☐   When would you be available?

☐   Do you have any questions?

IF APPROPRIATE, OBTAIN REFERENCES

TELEPHONE REFERENCE CHECKS

11

P - Q - **R**

EVALUATION OF CANDIDATE'S POTENTIAL TO PERFORM

Immediately after the interview is over, read all your notes, and then complete the Evaluation of Candidate's Potential to Perform below. Complete the Evaluation prior to comparing your thoughts about a candidate with other interviewers (if applicable).

RATING OF POTENTIAL
Assign a rating, based on your notes, to each and every one of the elements listed under the key functional, leadership and behavioural competencies using the following rating scale: **Exceptional (6):** Clearly exceeds the requirements for the role (Is this a good thing? Could he/she be overqualified?). This is a key strength for the candidate. **Superior (5):** Candidate fully meets and partially exceeds the requirements for the role in this area. Minimal developmental support is expected. **Competent (4):** Candidate meets the requirements for the role in this area. Expected development in this area is consistent with what would normally be required for new incumbents to the role. **Developing (3):** Partially meets the requirement for the role. Candidate has the ability to develop this area of competency with some support and has demonstrated some level of capability or capacity. **Weakness (2):** Candidate does not meet the requirements in this area. Significant development would be required or this represents a key weakness for the individual. **No Competence (1):** Candidate does not have any of the requirements in this area.

EXPERIENCE	RATING	COMMENTS
Experience		
Education		
Job Stability		
AVERAGE RATING		

LEADERSHIP	RATING	COMMENTS
Provide Leadership		
People Leadership		
Planning and Organizing		
Teamwork and Collaboration		
Financial and Operational Management		
Dock, Storage and Distribution Mgmt.		
Customer Orientation		
Problem Solving		
Communication		
AVERAGE RATING		

12

VALUES AND BEHAVIOURS	**RATING**	**COMMENTS**
Work Ethic		
Motivation		
Maturity and Judgment		
Self-Control		
Self-Confidence		
Conscientiousness		
AVERAGE RATING		

OVERALL RATING			
Use the approach below to determine the overall rating for the candidate. Note the average rating for each area from the tables above in the appropriate section. Multiply the average rating by the weighting indicated and total the score. This total score can then be used to identify the top candidate for the role.			
AREA	**AVERAGE RATING**	**WEIGHT**	**TOTAL** Average Rating x Weight
Experience			
Leadership			
Values and Behaviours			
	TOTAL	**100%**	

CHECKLIST	**(poor) 1**	**2**	**3**	**4**	**5**	**6 (exceptional)**
Appearance	☐	☐	☐	☐	☐	☐
Interpersonal Skills	☐	☐	☐	☐	☐	☐
Verbal Communication	☐	☐	☐	☐	☐	☐
Attitude	☐	☐	☐	☐	☐	☐
Personality	☐	☐	☐	☐	☐	☐
Service Orientation	☐	☐	☐	☐	☐	☐
Leadership Skills	☐	☐	☐	☐	☐	☐
Management Experience	☐	☐	☐	☐	☐	☐
Interest in Position	☐	☐	☐	☐	☐	☐

13

MAKE YOUR SELECTION

Compare the completed evaluations of all the candidates. As you consider your decision, remember that research has demonstrated that focusing on behavioural competencies during the selection process leads to more accurate selection decisions. Furthermore, technical competencies are generally easier to teach, train and learn than behavioural competencies.

RECOMMENDATION/DECISION   ☐   **Offer to be made**   ☐   **Decline**

RATIONALE FOR DECISION

Document your selection decision and the rationale behind it. Provide enough information so that you are able to defend your decision.

_____

_____

_____

_____

_____

_____

_____

_____

14

OFFER LETTER

Date _____

Dear (Name):

We are pleased to offer you the position of Sales Representative for the Ontario region. In this capacity, you will be responsible for developing and executing a sales plan to market our products to prospective clients in the region and to service and manage our existing customer base. You will report to me, the Ontario Sales Manager. We have agreed that you will join us on (date).

You will be responsible for maintaining regular contact with our customers in the region to ensure their ongoing requirements are identified and fulfilled. In addition, you will be required to identify potential new customers and devise strategies for securing new business. Specific performance goals and objectives will be reviewed with you once you commence employment.

Your scheduled regular hours of work will be 8:00 a.m. to 5:00 p.m., Monday to Friday, with a one-hour period for lunch. However, the company reserves the right to change your hours of work, if and when required. It is also understood that you will work the appropriate number of hours for the completion of your work as required. Your compensation includes an annual base salary of ($X) paid semi-monthly by direct deposit. A review of your performance will be scheduled following the successful completion of a three-month probationary period.

In order to give you the time to determine whether our working environment will be satisfactory and for us to determine your suitability, it is agreed that the first 90 days of your employment will be an introductory period. During this period, the company may terminate your employment without cause upon two weeks' notice in writing or corresponding payment in lieu of notice.

You will be entitled to a three-week vacation each calendar year as per our vacation policy. The Ontario Sales Manager must be notified in advance of taking the vacation.

You will be eligible to participate in our benefit plans for salaried employees immediately upon employment. In addition, after you have achieved two years' service, you are eligible for benefits under our group pension plan. The details of these plans will be reviewed with you once you start employment. You will also be eligible for reimbursement of automobile expenses associated with the carrying out of your sales duties.

Following your introductory period, in the event that it becomes necessary to terminate your employment relationship with the company for reasons other than cause, the company will provide you with the following notice based on your completed years of service:

☐ 6 months to 1 year: 1 month's notice;

☐ 1 to 3 years: 2 months' notice; and

☐ more than 3 years: in addition to the 2 months' notice, an additional 2 weeks' notice for each completed year of service to a maximum of 6 months' notice.

In the case of the termination of your employment by the company for reasons other than cause, the company may, at its sole option, provide payment of salary in lieu of such notice. If the company has cause to terminate your employment, this may be done without any notice or payment. The company guarantees that the amounts payable upon termination, without cause, shall not be less than that required under the notice and severance pay provisions of the *Employment Standards Act* (or any other applicable provincial statute), if any, provided that all such payments pursuant to the Act shall be deemed to be payments on account of amounts owing under this heading. In the event your employment is terminated without cause, the company shall continue your group insurance benefits for such period as the *Employment Standards Act* shall require, provided such coverage is available from the insurer.

You will be eligible to participate in the incentive compensation plan, the details of which will be reviewed with you in the first week of your employment. This is our discretionary incentive bonus plan payment under which is subject to your meeting of the established performance standards. For the current year, the bonus will be prorated according to the months of your actual employment.

It is agreed that you will adhere to all company policies, rules, systems and procedures as shall be in force. The company reserves the right to change the provisions of any of these policies at any time. Any representations or agreements contrary to what is set forth in this letter are superseded by this offer. The terms and conditions of your employment are outlined in the preceding paragraphs. Please read the letter carefully, sign it and return it along with the Confidentiality Agreement/Non-Competition Agreement [see Sample Confidentiality and Non-Competition Agreement], to constitute our agreement.

We are excited about the prospect of you joining our company. We believe you have the skills and qualifications to add to our success and we look forward to seeing you on (date).

Yours very truly,

(Name) _____

Ontario Sales Manager

_____

I, (New Employee), have received, read, understood and agree to the above-mentioned policies, together with the information contained within the letter.

Signature _____   Date _____   Witness _____

REDUNDANCY/DOWNSIZING

Definition/Background

Redundancy may also be referred to as downsizing, right-sizing, or, sometimes, reorganization. Its effect is the termination of an employee or employees. Usually the term is applied in the case of more than one termination of employment. In recent years, in Canada, there has been growing public interest in this issue because of rapid technological changes, plant closures and the impact of free trade on branch plants. In broad terms, redundancy arises when:

— the employer ceases to carry on the business that employs people;

— the business is closing down at the site where a particular group of employees work and is relocating to another site;

— the business is closing down a particular site and ceasing operations;

— fewer employees are required to do a particular kind of work.

The acid test of redundancy is whether employers need fewer employees, either across the organization or at a particular location. The amount of work need not have changed but it must be capable of being done by fewer people. Changes to operating processes or the introduction of new technology may reduce the need for people in some jobs.

Redundancy is not considered just cause for dismissal in most instances. Employees whose positions have been determined to be redundant are entitled by statute and under common law to notice and/or severance pay. As well, employees may be entitled to additional assistance in some jurisdictions. In some provinces, legislation requires the employer to form employee–management committees to oversee the outplacement of displaced employees. All employers are advised to develop a clear and fair redundancy policy.

There are a number of different ways for the employer to determine which employees should be declared redundant. These include:

— a voluntary scheme where employees are invited to apply for redundancy;

— application of reverse seniority (i.e., last in, first out);

— an early retirement scheme (voluntary or compulsory);

— a compulsory scheme where the organization identifies and selects employees who are to be made redundant; this method usually considers such factors as performance, qualifications, flexibility, attendance, work ethic and service (seniority); and

— a negotiated scheme with the union that combines voluntary leaving (up to a certain level) and the application of reverse seniority.

Changing business needs are often driven by a requirement to reduce operating costs in order to increase profitability. This may be achieved by changing accepted work practices, relocation, or rationalization of the business from a multi-site to single-site operation. At other times, technological change will mean that fewer employees are required to produce the same output, or that the skills required will change. Both the size and the skills of the workforce may need to change.

Sound Human Resources planning, involving at least annual reviews of likely business and people needs, will often be able to predict the changing needs and take gradual steps to achieve key business objectives. However, there may be occasions where more wholesale change is required within a shorter time scale. A successful merger or a change in market demands may alter the needs of the business in terms of both the numbers and skills of the workforce to such an extent that natural attrition is simply not sufficient. Redundancy, in these situations, can form an important plank in the overall Human Resources planning strategy. The organization needs to ensure that it continues to employ and develop the right staff necessary to achieve its overall business objectives.

Achieving a reduction in workforce numbers is a relatively simple, if somewhat unpleasant, task. The more difficult, but essential, requirement is to achieve that reduction and maintain morale and workforce efficiency. The organization must continue to meet the needs of the business. The remaining workforce will need to feel that those leaving have been treated fairly and with respect. The future needs of the business are for the remaining workforce to feel a new commitment based on open communication and fair working practices. In other words, redundancy affects stayers as well as leavers. The Human Resources practitioner has a key role to play in developing a redundancy procedure with senior management, and ensuring that it is implemented and carefully monitored.

Redundancy affects the whole organization. The structure within that organization must be able to support what is a time-consuming and often stressful event. At first glance, the "hard issues" seem self-evident. A reduction in the workforce will obviously result in lower costs. These, however, have to be balanced against the closing costs (notice and severance) and losses in organizational capabilities. Careful analysis must be conducted so that the organization does not get seduced by the prospect of short-term cost advantages at the price of long-term productivity losses.

Even where technology or process changes provide the organization with the opportunity to produce at the same or higher levels with fewer people, there may be an opportunity cost to letting experienced employees go. These employees have valuable idiosyncratic knowledge that is difficult to replace. Organizations should consider whether or not retraining and retaining these individuals create greater organizational capabilities. In other words, every avenue should be explored before declaring people to be redundant.

Even when the hard issues in terms of determining economic costs, impact of technology and business objectives are well defined, the soft issues of Human Resources concern (morale, motivation, commitment) will have a profound impact on subsequent business performance. These are usually less well recognized and defined.

Throughout the 1990s, many organizations delayered. As part of a strategy to reduce staff, these organizations removed management levels so that there were fewer decision-making layers and more autonomy at the front line. As a result, decision making has been devolved. Managers are now often expected to carry out several different functions, and carry more responsibility. Most managers will now need a wider repertoire of skills that extend beyond technical or commercial competence to include clear responsibility for staff management and communication. These skills are often tested to their limits at a time of major organizational change when downsizing is necessary.

Fewer people in an organization means that those remaining will need to develop a wider range of skills. Instead of being specialists, there is now the need for the workforce to have broader and more general skills as well as retain some specialist knowledge. Some employees respond well to the need for flexibility, others feel confused and demoralized by new demands.

In many organizations, the changes have led to a feeling that there is no longer a "job for life". New organizational structures support the idea of flexible working commitments to a particular organization, less working through a hierarchy to gain promotion to "the top" and more project-based work and task-centred assignments. Simply put, in many organizations, there is no structure left that allows a ladder-rung rise to the top. Managed careers, succession planning and grooming for the top have now given way to a looser commitment, gaining experience in one setting, then moving on to learn more in other organizations.

This has been termed as the new employment contract. Organizations should not view the contract with employees as a simple exchange of money for labour. Rather the organization needs to provide employees with opportunities for personal growth and the acquisition of marketable skills. This is the trade-off for the loss of job security (a job for life).

Organizational structures may well no longer envisage the need for long-term planning, for organization development programs, or indeed for organization investment in anything except project-necessary training. This is perhaps an overly simple viewpoint. Instead, organizations need to ensure they are building organizational flexibility into their development plans so that they can be more responsive to the ever-changing environment.

Consultation is at the heart of any successful downsizing effort, and agreed systems for formal consultation should be in place within any organization, large or small. Formal communication is essential and is required by legislation in some jurisdictions. It is also important to establish the informal networks for ensuring that views are heard and ideas discussed. Creating a climate where there is a free exchange of information is a much wider management task but its application to redundancy is essential.

Visible management is absolutely necessary because the whole exercise cannot be conducted through intermediaries, memos and long-winded letters. Employees like to have contact with management at such a time, and although there is the chance that this will sometimes be confrontational, such concerns are usually exaggerated. In an organization where formal and informal communication have been developed over several years, there is no indication that management feel threatened or at risk.

A policy to promote visible management and informal communication is an effective way to improve decision making and achieve buy-in at all times. At a time of redundancies, consultation with employees may provide alternative ways of tackling the problem, or at least of minimizing hardship. Employees are concerned adults and should be treated as such; their involvement in consultation is often helpful to management rather than a hindrance. Some enlightened organizations have asked their employees for input as to the criteria that should be used in determining who should be declared redundant. By doing so, employees gain a sense of procedural justice and trust in management decisions.

Communication is two-way. Management needs feedback from employees on how the downsizing efforts are being perceived by the employees. One novel idea is to form a rumour committee. Representatives from among the employees are selected to meet with management frequently. During these meetings, they bring any and all questions being raised by employees for management to respond to. Handled properly, these meetings can increase the trust level among employees and reduce the distractions caused by persistent rumours and misplaced perceptions.

Consultation should always take place before any public announcements; employees feel aggrieved when they are the last to know. This may mean working extremely quickly in some situations.

Legal Issues

The effect of "redundancy" has been described as "group termination", "mass layoffs", or "collective dismissals". Special measures have been reduced in most Canadian jurisdictions to deal with these issues and cushion the impact these organizational changes have on employees.

Although the legislation varies from province to province (and for the federal jurisdiction), most consider any displacement of more than 50 employees in a short time period (two to four months) to be a group termination. The usual provision requires companies to provide significantly more notice of the impending termination than they would in the case of an individual employee's termination. This notice varies from four to 16 weeks, depending on the size of the group and the jurisdiction. The notice may or may not be inclusive of the requirements for individual notice. In Ontario and the federal jurisdiction, there is an additional requirement for severance.

Other legislated requirements include providing notice to the appropriate Ministry, providing notice to any trade union representing affected employees, and forming a joint relocation/adjustment committee to provide assistance to displaced employees.

These requirements are set as minimum standards and may not cover the common law obligations of the employer. Practitioners should review the legislation carefully and seek legal counsel as necessary. (For more information, refer to CCH Canadian Limited's *Canadian Master Labour Guide*.)

Benefits/Expected Outcomes

Sometimes redundancy is the only means to ensure other jobs remain. An organization that backs away from acknowledging the need for redundancies may well place in jeopardy the jobs of the entire workforce. It is important to communicate this to employees and provide them with sufficient supporting information to prove the case. This helps build trust and rallies the surviving employees around a common cause — survival.

A well-handled redundancy program secures the future of the business. It enables those staff remaining to be recommitted to the organization. By adopting new working patterns, they can help the organization realize its strategic objectives. It is vitally important to the organization to gain buy-in from the "survivors", so that they can give support and practical help to those who are leaving to enable them to return to the labour market quickly or to make the transition into retirement in a smooth and optimistic way.

A voluntary redundancy or early retirement policy may well enable the business to reduce its workforce with minimum hardship or disruption. Well-managed, such a program may give some employees the opportunity to pursue new careers or to utilize leisure time in a way that gives them great personal satisfaction. The workforce remaining will also feel that the process of losing staff has avoided acrimony or hardship. In turn, they may feel more job security and a sense that they are working for a decent, fair-minded organization.

A compulsory redundancy policy may sometimes be required where a voluntary policy has not secured the necessary reduction in the workforce or in situations where the organization needs to select and retain key staff. For such a program to work, there needs to be a great deal of professional consultation and careful planning to develop a fair selection criteria for a redundancy policy that is not dependent upon the whims of individuals, but based on an objective matching of individual skill and experience profiles to organizational needs.

A properly managed redundancy program will:

— enable the business to retain a sharp commercial focus with lower overhead, increased operating profit and levels of efficiency;

— provide an opportunity for the organization to review all management and operating procedures;

— ensure that target numbers are reached without losing key staff whose skills are essential to the future of the organization;

— ensure that those leaving feel that the process has been fair-minded, supportive, responsible and decent;

— provide those leaving with practical help towards career or life transition, creating as little hardship as possible; and

— ensure that those remaining with the organization continue to meet the required business needs without undue loss of morale or positive commitment.

Redundancy is likely to have an effect on all employees within the organization, including those who do not appear to be directly involved. Even a small-scale downsizing exercise in one part of the business will often create uncertainty throughout the larger organization.

The organization needs to consider who will be affected by the downsizing, including the following:

1. Senior managers will be affected because they are the key communicators. Some feel that redundancy initiatives are an admission of failure. The initiative, however, has to be seen as a positive and necessary step to ensure the survival and/or continued success of the organization. Managers usually cope better with growth than with shrinkage. Downsizing must ultimately put the organization into a growth mode.

   As well as making decisions on paper and in the relative comfort of the boardroom or office, senior management will also need to be visible in the workplace, approachable and capable of providing a clear message concerning the current and future needs of the organization. The whole redundancy exercise must be owned and communicated from the top and carefully managed throughout. It must be part of the vision established for the future of the organization.

2. Operational managers will be left with the task of communicating this message in the workplace. It has been demonstrated in many studies on organizational communication that employees want to receive news from their immediate supervisors. It is a source they trust and can relate to.

   Since the message may well affect them too, operational managers could be in a very difficult position of both giving and receiving messages of redundancy. It is seldom a pleasant or easy task and one that many would wish to avoid. Handling redundancy situations can be very stressful, particularly for operational managers who feel a sense of divided loyalties and a conflict of emotions.

3. Trade unions will be affected because they will want to ensure that everything possible has been done to try to avoid the need for downsizing. Union representatives will want to ensure that the process selection criteria established are fair and consistent. Unions will want the opportunity to negotiate closing agreements to ensure that staff being made redundant will receive the best possible notice and severance payments, usually

above the statutory minimum level. They will also want to know what support is being offered in terms of counselling, outplacement job searching facilities and financial advice.

4. Employees made redundant will obviously be affected. They will need to know what options for redeployment are available, what levels of support and financial compensation are to be offered, what the precise timelines of the downsizing will be, and what rights of appeal or areas of negotiation are open to them.

5. Employees who are not being made redundant will also be affected. They may register concern for their work colleagues and also be unsure of their own long-term position.

6. The local community may be affected. Redundancy could have a widespread impact on the economy of some areas.

7. Supplier organizations may be affected. They may be dependent upon trading with your organization for their own survival.

Skills and training to handle the redundancy exercise will be needed at many different levels, since the impact of the decision will be felt throughout the organization. Handled poorly, a downsizing can result in a much weakened organization that will have difficulty surviving.

The skills and knowledge required will include:

— credibility to provide clear messages at a time of uncertainty;

— interpersonal and cross-disciplinary skills to communicate at all levels;

— leadership and influencing skills;

— analytical tools to make objective decisions;

— knowledge of objective skill-based or competence-based selection criteria;

— flexibility, yet staying power, and ability to keep the end goal in sight; and

— working knowledge of employment law relating to statutory requirements.

It may almost appear tactless to talk of a "successful" redundancy program. However, there are clear criteria by which success may be measured.

The first means of measuring success is to go back to the carefully set objectives of the exercise, in terms of numbers, timelines, and cost, and see to what extent they were met. The clearer the objectives were in the first place, the easier it is to measure success at the end of the venture.

It is fairly simple to measure the financial or business success for the organization in terms of reduced costs, increased operating profit, better margins or any standard measure of efficiency. However, it is also important to measure the effect of the program on the softer issues that also influence business performance. These include issues concerned with morale, motivation, stress levels and absenteeism. Attitude surveys, briefing meetings and good line management reported up and across the system will all provide the ways and means to gain this information.

Perhaps the most compelling of all methods, however, is the in-depth case study that looks at the whole process in detail. The Human Resources practitioner who provides both an objective analysis and an anecdotal account of events will be well placed to prepare such a case study that moves beyond simple surface data to look at the underlying effects of the changes on both the organization and individual. Case studies provide qualitative as well as quantitative data.

Success for the organization concerned may well be in terms of increased business efficiency without reduced morale or increased stress. For those leaving, the measure of success may well be in terms of the length of time it takes to find another job or to settle into retirement. It is also important that they retain respect for the organization. Again, this is relatively easy information to obtain and should be fed back to those remaining in the organization as a sign of a positive and caring policy that enables ex-employees to make a purposeful and successful transition in their life.

Implementation and Mechanisms

An effective redundancy policy will be designed to allay the fears of unfair or underhand practices. Such a procedure will include the following:

— An introductory statement of intent to maintain the organization's competitiveness and maintain job security to every extent possible. The statement may also state the organization's objective to increase the opportunities for individual growth and employability in the future.

— Details of the processes of consultation with employees and (where applicable) their trade union representatives.

— Measures to minimize or avoid redundancies; for example, through natural attrition, restrictions on recruitment, retraining, reducing overtime, early retirement, and/or ending the use of temporary or contract staff.

— Guidelines on selection criteria to be used when redundancy is unavoidable.

— Details of severance terms, relocation expenses, retraining and outplacement counselling.

— An appeals procedure, including, if possible, an alternative dispute resolution process.

— A statement on the specific outplacement assistance available to employees.

Employers should endeavour to incorporate these principles into a formal written policy. Where applicable, they should secure a closing agreement with the recognized trade union representing the employees that incorporates the same principles.

In addition, the policy will need to contemplate the questions that typically arise, including the following:

— the effect on earnings of demotions (or policy of protected earnings) for employees accepting demotion as an alternative to redundancy;

— relocation details and allowances where employees have accepted work for the same organization in a different location;

— the questions of whether and when redundant employees may leave during the notice period without losing entitlement to redundancy payment, or, in the alternative, what incentives are being offered to stay until the closing date;

— the questions of what benefits can be retained as, for example, pension accruals, and for how long; and

— the question of what payments are to be made upon the termination of employment (e.g., vacation pay).

While experiences may vary, the best practices approach to downsizing is founded on the following tenets. Employers should:

— give plenty of warning;

— enter into consultation with recognized trade unions to examine ways of avoiding the redundancies or of reducing the number of staff involved;

— try to achieve the reduction in staff with as little hardship as possible and in a fair manner;

— look at alternatives to dismissal;

— enter into consultation with recognized trade unions about the selection criteria to be used and the way in which they will be applied; and

— make sure that the selection criteria to be used are both fair and objective.

Such a best practice guide should be helpful when formulating a redundancy policy in any organization. It makes sense not to wait until redundancies are required before putting any such planned policy in place.

Best practice suggests consultation at the earliest stage possible and certainly within the statutory minimum time limits. If a redundancy policy has been established in the past, this will make it considerably easier. However, employers are free to depart from an agreed redundancy procedure, providing that they act reasonably in doing so. Consultation should precede any public announcements.

In addition to the statutory requirements to consult during downsizing, organizations are required on the basis of "good faith" to disclose during contract discussions for the renewal of the collective agreement any plans to downsize or reorganize that may affect unionized employees in the future, if such plans are known at the time of bargaining.

Planning

Planning for any redundancy exercise will be critical to its success. In an ideal situation, the organization will have put in place clear policies concerning handling redundancy issues well before they were needed. There will have been discussions with management, employee representatives and a subsequent Human Resources briefing paper and procedural document. Relevant staff will have been trained in the procedures and well briefed. Clear measurement criteria will have been developed to identify the progress of the program, the resettlement rate of displaced employees, the effect on business performance and the morale of the survivors.

Unfortunately, planning for redundancy and agreeing on a policy and procedural route has not generally attracted the positive interest of senior management in all but the largest of organizations. It may appear defeatist in a time of "feast" to develop procedures to handle the times of "famine". Many organizations simply do not envisage that they will ever need to develop a formal redundancy program and would rather respond in an *ad hoc* way to the few isolated cases they expect to encounter.

Either as an agreed procedural policy, prepared in advance or as a response to a specific need, the main features of any redundancy policy may be outlined as follows:

1. Establish with senior management the anticipated Human Resources needs of the business both now and for the foreseeable future. Include consideration of required competencies and skills inventories, training resources, and staffing for contingencies.

2. Conduct an audit with line managers of the current workforce in terms of competencies and skills matched to the business needs and objectives. Look at age ranges, experience and length of service, and anticipate future attrition rates and turnover.

3. Complete a skills gap and head count analysis between requirements/needs and supply. Present this to senior management and begin discussing possible routes to achieve any required reduction or methods of avoiding or minimizing redundancy. This could include:

    (a) reduced recruitment;

    (b) reduction of the use of contract/temporary staff;

    (c) retraining;

    (d) job sharing arrangements; and

    (e) reduced overtime.

If it is clear that a formal redundancy program will be required to make the necessary reductions, then the following procedure may be helpful:

1. Identify with senior management a timeline for the process, target objectives and measurable criteria for assessing success.

2. Nominate a team to drive forward the changes required, which should always include a strong ownership by the senior management group.

3. Establish an overall manager of the project and determine the role of other team members.

4. Begin consultation with trade unions and employees on the need for reducing staff numbers. Consider their views carefully and involve them in an active way in seeking solutions. Set out a clear policy of consultation with them, bearing in mind best practice and the disclosure of information required by law. There may be some occasions when commercial sensitivity of the information makes it difficult to share information at this stage. Wherever possible, though, it is best to consult widely and openly at the earliest possible stage. This will be an important policy to establish with senior management.

5. Consult with senior managers to determine a clear policy on redundancy if one is not already in place.

6. Decide with senior management and unions whether to:

    (a) develop a voluntary redundancy/early retirement policy; and

    (b) instigate a compulsory program (either as a first step or as a back-up to a voluntary program).

7. Develop selection criteria for compulsory redundancy programs and for voluntary redundancy requests. Ensure that they are fair, consistent, objective and non-discriminatory.

8. Put in place an administrative team to process voluntary redundancy requests or necessary information for compulsory redundancy casualties. In the case of large-scale initiatives, a 24-hour help line may be a valued resource to employees. Ensure that the team is able to put together for each individual, in a speedy and accurate way:

(a) details of leaving dates;

(b) notice and severance payments;

(c) pension entitlements;

(d) vacation, sick pay and any other additional payments; and

(e) review and appeals procedures including, where applicable, alternate dispute resolution processes.

9. Check all policy and procedural decisions with employment and company lawyers for compliance and with the finance departments for income tax considerations.

These plans should be well in place before any announcement is made. Once the news is out, there is likely to be a great deal of anxiety, and you will need to react quickly and communicate accurately. The planning stage is most important and often requires the Human Resources practitioner to take a lead role. The plan should take the following format:

1. Source outplacement support providers within agreed delivery and budget boundaries.

2. Arrange training/briefing for senior and line managers in handling the redundancy announcement. Prepare written material for the announcement and supportive letters for all staff affected.

3. Brief line managers and senior managers prior to the announcement. Have in place any internal or external support and all written documentation. Agree on policy and process for the announcement. Ensure strong, positive senior management presence throughout.

4. Ensure, once the announcement is made, that all support and advice is in place. Continue to liaise closely with unions and senior managers, possibly developing a daily briefing session. Establish and manage the appeals procedure and ensure the smooth running of the administration team supplying information to employees who are affected.

5. Establish an employee communications (rumour) committee to monitor and respond to employee perceptions and concerns.

6. Review all operations regularly against the set objectives and timescale established at the beginning of the program.

Outplacement

Outplacement may be defined as the process whereby individuals leaving their employer are given support, counselling and advice to assist them to achieve the next stage of their career.

For some people, the choice will be entirely voluntary; for others, there will have been a compulsion to leave. Some individuals will see the next stage of their career as being to find another job, while others may be seeking to retire, to return to full-time study, to embark on self-employment, or some form of consulting work. The choices open to people leaving an organization are often complex and wide. Outplacement is designed to help people make these choices in a strong and positive way.

Some organizations may wish to run their own outplacement provision. This generally requires a sophisticated Human Resources Department with the appropriate facilities and considerable specialized knowledge. Many employees resent being offered assistance by the very organization that dismissed them, and feel that such help cannot be as impartial, specialized or personally committed as that provided by an outside consultant.

Consultants can offer the specialized assistance to help displaced employees assess their career goals against their strengths and weaknesses. They usually offer confidentiality and discretion. As independent counsellors, they can provide advice with respect to any financial or legal matters the employee needs to consider.

Most outplacement firms offer a variety of services depending on the individual's needs and the organization's budget. These could range from group seminars on résumé writing to individual counselling. For executives and managers, outplacement firms will often provide them with an office for an agreed upon period of time along with secretarial services, a private phone and access to a computer.

Likely Content of Outplacement Programs

Outplacement coaching is often the best way to help people deal with the changes they need to make in their lives. Good outplacement is not a set program but rather an individually tailored response to the needs of the people. Typically, it is likely to include:

— an opportunity to review personal and career goals;

— a period of self-assessment (possibly including psychometrics);

— preparation of self-marketing material, including a résumé and covering letter;

— recognition and development of contact networks;

— practical experience of interviews; and

— opportunity to review potential employment opportunities.

More specialist advice will be available in terms of:

— routes to self-employment;

— training and education opportunities; and

— opportunities for career change.

Location of Outplacement Services

Outplacement can take place on site where an employee works, at nearby hotels, or in the offices and training rooms of outplacement companies. Typically, an outplacement program may consist of a one-, two- or three-day training event, together with individual counselling, specific help with job search techniques and further back-up support.

For one-to-one programs, outplacement may be conducted in designated offices that will also include database facilities, resource libraries and some level of secretarial support.

Styles of Outplacement Support

On large-scale projects, the help is often given on a group basis. On smaller-scale projects, or where senior staff is involved, outplacement provision may be provided by one-to-one counselling and support, sometimes for extended periods.

The options available are often extremely wide, reflecting both cost factors (group outplacement programs are usually less expensive) and needs (one-to-one outplacement may generally provide a longer-term and tailored level of assistance). It is perfectly possible to vary the provision made according to individual needs and reflecting overall financial parameters.

Other Outplacement Services

Major outplacement providers will also develop individually tailored courses to prepare the way for redundancy notices, to handle the announcements that need to be made and to be on hand to help people when they receive the news. Outplacement companies can also provide services for the "survivors" in an organization, to ensure that their needs are met and that they recommit themselves to the "new" organization.

The range of services available shows the extensive development of outplacement during the last decade. It has become a very practical consulting specialty, covering all aspects of the human face of change.

Outplacement provision should be explored well before the need arises. While cost considerations are important, it is much more critical that you feel certain that the outplacement consultant has the resources and ability to handle what is a most sensitive piece of work. Developing a long-term relationship with one or two providers is preferable to issuing an invitation to tender.

Good outplacement companies will be able to advise on handling the announcements and the general management coaching issues that may arise. They can "dock" on to your own services and provide much needed assistance and specialized knowledge.

Role of the Human Resources Practitioner

The Human Resources practitioner should play a leading part in ensuring that all people have received effective training to be able to conduct this highly sensitive exercise with clear business objectives in mind. These objectives must be balanced by a sincere concern for the needs of individuals at a time of major change. Drawing together the right team with the right attitude may be difficult, but the skills and knowledge identified above should assist. Once that team is in position, the additional training required could include the following:

1. Training for senior managers in:

    (a) handling the media;

    (b) making the corporate announcement;

    (c) communicating the organizational message to the workforce; and

(d) encouraging voluntary leaving/early retirement.

2. Training for operational and line managers in:

(a) applying redundancy selection criteria;

(b) interviewing staff;

(c) encouraging voluntary leaving/early retirement;

(d) telling staff their post is redundant; and

(e) handling the announcement for other staff, including "survivors".

3. Training for redundant employees in the form of outplacement support (externally or internally) to assist with career appraisal, self-marketing and job search.

Ironically, one of the management groups most affected by redundancy in the past has been Human Resources. In many organizations, their responsibilities have been devolved to line managers. Often, such managers have inadequate skills to manage the task, which in any case vies with other pressing management concerns for attention.

Many organizations simply do not have the resources in place to manage a redundancy exercise. They may need to call in an interim management team or a consultant to advise and manage the process. This in itself requires careful management.

Any redundancy exercise involves a great deal of information gathering, planning and consultation. The planning involved is extensive, detailed and requires meticulous care, combined with vision for the future and nerves of steel for the present. In brief, the Human Resources practitioner will be involved in the following:

1. Clear information gathering on the skills and numbers of employees currently employed, the number of temporary or contract positions and the projected figures for natural attrition and retirement, if no policy is implemented. This information may be available from existing staff records, including performance reviews and training needs analysis, but will need to be updated by a clear skills audit. Usually, such an audit may be designed by the practitioner in consultation with line managers who are generally responsible for its implementation. This

information may then be set alongside the anticipated needs of the business to indicate the scale of downsizing that will be required.

2. The most important feature of any redundancy program is to be seen to adopt practices that are fair, consistent, non-discriminatory and as objective as possible. It is often the responsibility of the Human Resources practitioner to ensure that these principles are developed and applied.

3. The practitioner will need to work closely both with senior managers and with line managers. Cross-disciplinary teamwork in this way can ensure that all the information is consistently collected and analyzed. Timelines must be maintained by regular monitoring.

4. It is likely that the Human Resources practitioner will play a key role in processing such information and, in particular, for preparing clear reports for use by senior managers and line managers. Reports need to be concise but accurate, since major organizational decisions affecting the lives of individuals will be made on the basis of the information provided to senior management.

Barriers to Success/Common Pitfalls

Handling a redundancy program will never be easy and there will be a number of barriers that impede progress. None is insurmountable. The key throughout is effective communication and strong management.

The first barrier may simply be the perfectly natural reticence experienced by many organizations to the whole idea of making people redundant. Concern for the individuals, or even a pride in their organization, makes cutbacks seem such a defeatist step to take. As a consequence, it is often the case that cutbacks are neither clean-cut nor deep enough. At the time, the organization appears to be saving jobs, but in reality, when more cuts are needed later, the surviving workforce can feel cheated and very insecure.

The problem needs to be addressed at the very outset of the program by ensuring that information is available to tell the organization precisely how many people it needs and how many it must lose. In addition, clear management of the process aimed at holding on to the business objectives will be required, with a definite leadership from a visible and active senior management team.

The second barrier may be the somewhat overly optimistic expectation that the problem can be resolved simply through natural attrition, a few early retirements and some voluntary leaving. Although such methods can be very effective, they need to be very actively managed and marketed. This is a high-profile management task.

Any redundancy program must be given a high profile. Sufficient resources must be allocated in terms of time, people and information, to allow employees to come to terms with the changes. It may well be worth using an outside consultant, who has extensive knowledge of the job market and whose independence can help employees see that they do have the skills and experience to find alternative openings.

The third problem, paradoxically, may be that too many people or the wrong people want to leave the organization. This becomes a particular difficulty when these people possess essential and scarce skills. If a redundancy program is not carefully managed, then all staff will feel insecure and may begin to look for openings outside the organization.

Strong leadership from the senior management team and clear, open communication about the future is essential. Staff remaining must feel that management are in control, are handling the issues sensitively but with resolution, and have a vision for the future which includes them. A key element in promoting such a view is the extent and quality of the open communication, both in group briefing and in the opportunity for individual talks with line managers and senior managers who know what is happening.

Rumour and gossip abound at a time of redundancy, as do stories of unfair treatment, overgenerous "payoffs", or, the contrary, "penny pinching". Such gossip can seriously affect morale, make some people more determined to stay and turn relationships sour between the organization and employees.

Once more, open communication, including regular newsletters and the involvement of trade unions, will do much to alleviate the problem. More than anything, senior managers must be encouraged to be visible and open to discussion without becoming defensive. Establishing an employee communications

(rumour) committee can prove invaluable in reducing employee anxieties.

Loss of momentum is a common problem. Sometimes the timelines for the redundancy program are too long. Employees hear the news of major change but then note that nothing much is happening for over a year or more. It is then possible simply not to think about it any more. Careful timing of announcements and action is needed to keep the pace lively and realistic. In addition, good management will drive the process forward rather than letting it run out of steam. This will often be a task for the Human Resources practitioner.

Checklist of Common Pitfalls

✓ Redundancy programs are often developed without a great deal of forethought and tend to be reactive rather than carefully planned. The need is to consider issues relating to redundancy and agree on organizational policy as part and parcel of good Human Resources Management.

✓ The team responsible for implementing the policy must be carefully chosen, bearing in mind the need for skilled and credible communicators and people with clear objectives.

✓ Failure to consult may well be in breach of employment law. In many cases, there is far too much secrecy and a wish to keep everyone in the dark until the last moment. Employees are overprotected and treated as children, who at best should be shielded from the facts and at worst may become delinquent if not firmly kept in place. While there are some occasions when confidentially is important, the general principle should be to consult widely and early.

✓ Senior managers must own the whole process. They must be visible and be prepared to attend briefing meetings, see individuals and constantly communicate. This is not an exercise that can be conducted by memo, delegation and one-way lectures.

✓ Timelines must be carefully thought out and slippage avoided wherever possible. Momentum must be maintained and largely provided by the energy of the team and planned time limits.

✓ Inadequate information and insufficient opportunity to look at options will inevitably impede any program. Employees need to know exactly what their financial and employment position would be if they leave or if they stay. They also want impartial and realistic advice about future options as well as individual assessment of their abilities and detailed career advice. Information must be confidential, accurate and readily available.

✓ Sensitive information needs to be handled with excellence in terms of communication skills. Many managers faced with telling staff that their posts are redundant resort to platitudes and expressions of sympathy that fail to impart information. Staff will need training in the principles and practice of handling group and individual announcements.

✓ The Human Resources practitioner needs to be absolutely sure of the employment law and individual circumstances that govern every decision. He or she must be clear on the selection criteria for redundancy and prepared to justify this before a tribunal if required.

REWARD MANAGEMENT/ COMPENSATION POLICIES

Definition/Background

Reward management is concerned with designing, implementing, maintaining and communicating reward processes. These processes are devised and managed to provide and maintain appropriate types and levels of pay, benefits and other kinds of reward. Reward processes should be based on reward philosophies and strategies that, as part of the organization's overall Human Resources strategy, help the organization to improve business performance and achieve its objectives. Reward management affects organizational performance because of the impact it has on people's expectations as to how they will be compensated. It has essentially a supporting and enabling role and should not be relied upon as the sole lever for improving performance.

Reward management functions within the context of the organization's environment, culture, business and Human Resources strategies. It consists of a number of processes that are concerned with job evaluation, market rate analysis, job analysis, designing and maintaining pay structures, paying for performance, skills and competence, and performance management, and also the procedures needed in order to manage these processes. Reward management is not only about financial rewards, but also about other rewards that provide motivation. There are four main areas in the reward management process:

1. non-financial rewards that satisfy the individual needs for challenge, responsibility, variety, influence in decision making, recognition and career opportunities;

2. employee benefits (including pension plans) that satisfy the employees' needs for personal security and provide remuneration in forms other than pay which may be tax efficient;

3. pay structures that define fair and competitive levels of remuneration through the combined results of wage and salary surveys and job evaluation; and

4. measurement and management of performance, i.e., measures of performance in relation to outputs (contribution and the achievement of objectives and standards of performance) and inputs (application of skills and competencies and behaviours affecting performance), leading to the design and operation of pay-for-performance schemes, continuous development and training programs.

Reward management can have a far-reaching effect on all aspects of the operation of an organization and the way in which it manages its human resources. The aims should be to achieve the following:

1. **To improve individual and organizational performance** — Reward processes can drive and support desired behaviour at all levels in the organization. Reward processes can:

   (a) align compensation levels to the level of contribution and value to the organization;

   (b) reward people in relation to organizational and/or team performance;

   (c) provide incentives relating compensation directly to output;

   (d) align pay increases or bonuses to performance levels, contribution or increases in competence and skill;

   (e) deliver the message that performance is important by rewarding it through incentive, performance-related pay or bonus schemes; and

   (f) develop a performance-oriented culture.

2. **To encourage value-added performance** — Attention can be focused on areas that add value to the organization and its customers. Maximum added value can be achieved by introducing schemes relating rewards specifically to improved performance in those areas and away from non-value-added activities. The performance management processes can also be used as a way of setting goals, measuring contribution and devel-

oping the capability to perform better in specified areas.

3. **To support the management of the organization's culture** — Performance management and pay-for-performance processes can be used to reward people not only for results but also the extent to which they have developed and demonstrated requisite competencies. These competencies are observable in the actions an employee takes to support such values as innovation, quality and teamwork. The way in which the reward processes are evolved and managed will demonstrate the organization's commitment to those values and other values such as equity, flexibility and risk-taking.

4. **To achieve integration** — Reward management should be a key component in a mutually reinforcing range of Human Resources Management processes. Performance management processes can be used to achieve a number of inter-related purposes, such as, clarifying roles, integrating individual and organizational objectives, identifying training needs, providing the basis for continuous development and measuring performance as a means of deciding on performance-related pay increases.

5. **To support managers** — It will give managers the authority and skills needed to use rewards to help achieve their goals by providing them with a strong framework of guiding principles and procedures.

6. **To empower individuals and teams** — The reward system should raise performance and quality through empowered people who have the scope and skills needed to succeed and are rewarded accordingly. Reward processes should encourage personal development and teamwork.

7. **To compete in the labour market** — A well-devised reward system will help attract and retain high quality people, while at the same time allowing the organization to be cost-competitive.

8. **To motivate** — It will encourage employees to achieve superior levels of quality performance. Pay-for-performance schemes will undoubtedly motivate if managed properly but other non-financial aspects of reward, such as recognition and opportunities to achieve, learn and develop, can also be powerful motivators.

9. **To increase commitment** — Reward processes can increase commitment by linking rewards to organizational performance through gain-sharing, or profit-sharing or profit-related pay schemes. A carefully structured, competitive and flexible benefits package can also help create the right attitude among the employees.

10. **To achieve fairness and equity** — It will reward people fairly and consistently across the organization according to their contribution and merit and not according to irrelevant factors or considerations prohibited by statute (i.e., human rights legislation). In some jurisdictions, legislation requires that specific elements be considered in determining equitable pay scales between male and female dominated job classes.

11. **To support new developments** — The introduction of new and more sophisticated techniques and processes and the use of new technology may require higher levels of performance, the use of new or a wider set of skills, or the acceptance of more responsibility. Increased demands on individuals and teams can be rewarded specifically, or different pay structures can be introduced that reflect the new systems of work.

12. **To enhance quality** — Reward management will help to achieve continuous improvement in levels of quality and customer service.

13. **To promote teamwork** — It will assist in improving co-operation and effective teamwork at all levels by introducing team bonuses and skill-based pay schemes that recognize the additional skills and responsibilities required from team members. Including the ability to manage teamwork as an essential managerial competency that can be appraised and rewarded can reinforce this.

14. **To encourage flexibility** — The requirement to adopt a flexible approach to managing organizations and their human resources arises from the need to be competitive, adaptive and to manage the impact of new technology. Flexibility in reward processes can be achieved by:

(a) increasing the proportion of variable pay in the total package;

(b) using broad-banded pay structures that allow for more scope to reward extra skills, responsibilities or improved performance;

(c) not using an overly mechanistic system of relating rewards to performance;

(d) keeping the job evaluation process up-to-date so that it can be adjusted to meet specific needs;

(e) relating pay increases entirely to performance and to market rate movements, thereby avoiding an explicit link with increases in the Cost-of-Living and allowing scope to give larger awards to good performers and less to poor performers; and

(f) allowing greater choice in the benefits received.

15. **To provide value for money** — You should assess the costs as well as the benefits of reward management practices and ensure that they are operating cost-effectively.

Until recently, there was little strategic direction in reward management and changes came about as reactions to immediate pressures in competitive labour markets. Since the mid-1980s, reward management has moved from a back office administration role to a major management role for change. Organizations have become aware of the importance of "culture" to the success of the enterprise and the compensation system can play a major part in shaping the culture. In particular, there has been a great emphasis on creating a pay-for-performance environment. Senior managers now recognize that compensation policy is an important ingredient of business strategy.

Reward management processes work best if they are part of a coherent set of people management activities, which are carried out within the context of the process of strategic management and Human Resources Management. Human Resources Management is a strategic, management-driven approach to the management of the organization's most important assets — the people working there. The framework for compensation strategies is provided by the process of strategic management and, therefore, must be aligned with it. In this way, the people management processes support the organization's vision and mission, and help define the organization's culture.

Benefits/Expected Outcomes

The reward management strategy will contribute to the achievement of corporate goals by:

- integrating the reward policies and processes with the key strategies for growth and improved performance;

- reinforcing the organization's values, especially those concerned with innovation, teamwork, flexibility and quality;

- reinforcing the culture and management style of the organization;

- driving and supporting desired behaviour by indicating to employees what types of behaviour will be rewarded, how this will take place and how their expectations will be satisfied;

- providing a competitive edge to attract and retain the level of skills needed; and

- enabling the organization to obtain value for money from its employees.

Assessing the Benefits

The benefits of effective reward management policies are that they will improve individual and organization performance, and help to achieve sustainable competitive advantage and increase shareholder value.

Reward management policies that are not clearly thought out, that do not align with the business objectives, and that are not competitive will result in poor organizational performance and a demotivated workforce. It is not easy to measure the direct financial impact, but areas such as employee absenteeism and high turnover are likely outcomes and can and should be measured. It is easier to measure the success of specific reward management policies as and when they are implemented.

Planning and Implementing Reward Strategies and Policies
Compensation Philosophy

It is important for the Human Resources practitioner to develop a compensation philosophy that defines:

- what the organization is prepared to pay for (e.g., skills, qualifications, experience, performance);

- what the organization is not prepared to pay for (e.g., minor changes in market pressure, individualism at the expense of team performance, unwarranted differentials);

- when it will implement change (e.g., when the people are trained and in place to deliver it effectively, when it is right in terms of operational and/or Human Resources strategy);

- where the first change should come (e.g., only after a properly validated pilot study in a represented part of the organization); and

- what external or internal factors will be considered in determining changes to the compensation system (e.g., market fluctuations, ability to pay, competitive pressures, organizational performance).

Once the compensation philosophy has been clarified and agreed upon, the next stage is to set priorities and plan the details of and allocate responsibility for implementation. To do this, the following questions need to be answered:

1. Where do you want to make the most impact? This involves deciding which policy changes will have the greatest symbolic importance and enable further change.

2. How will you get there? This is about the speed and nature of change, that may be:

   (a) **evolution** — gradual change over something like a three-year period;

   (b) **revolution** — a few key symbolic acts to mark a significant change in the culture; or

   (c) **opportunism** — could be used at any time; for example, using a change of location as a chance to change both working practices and pay systems.

Total Remuneration

Total remuneration involves treating as a whole all aspects of the pay and benefits package offered to employees. The cost to the organization and the value to the individual of each element can be assessed with the aim of achieving an appropriate balance between the various components — either cash or benefit-related. Total remuneration can also include some of the less tangible elements of the reward package, such as opportunities for career advancement or the chance to work with recognized professionals. Only the tangible elements will be considered here.

The kinds of elements which are considered as part of the total remuneration package and which, importantly, can be "flexed" to suit employees and business needs would be:

— basic salary;

— bonuses;

— profit-sharing;

— allowances (e.g., shift premium/overtime/isolation pay);

— share options;

— vacation and holiday entitlements;

— private medical insurance;

— pension plans or retirement savings plans;

— life insurance/accidental death and disability insurance;

— meal/leisure facilities;

— relocation assistance and/or loans;

— employee product purchases;

— professional dues;

— child care;

— company cars or allowances;

— disability insurance;

— mortgage subsidy; and

— retirement/redundancy options.

Pay Structures

A pay structure consists of an organization's pay ranges for jobs grouped into grades or for individual jobs, salary lines (or pay curves) for job families, or pay scales for jobs slotted into a pay progression. A system of individual job rates (spot rates) could also be regarded as a pay structure.

In a typical graded structure, jobs will be allocated to job grades according to their relative size; in a formal system, this is determined by a job evaluation system. There will be a pay range for each grade that defines the minimum and maximum rate of pay for all the jobs in the grade. This pay range will usually take account of market rates for the jobs in the grade.

The purpose of the pay structure is to provide a fair and consistent basis for motivating and rewarding employees. The aim is to support the objectives of the organization by having a logically designed framework within which internally equitable and externally competitive compensation policies can be implemented. The structure should also allow the organization to reward and recognize employees according to their role, level of responsibility, performance against objectives, contribution to organizational goals, skill and competence.

Pay structures should:

— be appropriate to the type and needs of the organization: its culture, size and complexity, the degree to which it is subjected to change, and the type and level of people employed;

— be flexible to internal and external pressures, particularly those related to market rates and skills shortages;

— provide flexibility to allow movement of employees around the organization without the need to reflect slight differences in job size by changing rates of pay;

— give scope for rewarding high-level performance and significant contributions, yet still reward and recognize the effective, reliable core employees;

— help to ensure that consistent decisions are made on pay in relation to job size, contribution, skill and competence;

— clarify pay opportunities and career ladders;

— be logical and clear so that they can be communicated to employees easily; and

— enable the organization to control the implementation of pay policies and budgets.

The Basis of Pay Structures

Pay structures are based on decisions about internal equity and external comparisons. They must also take into account the organization's compensation philosophy.

Internal Equity

Internal equity is maintained through the process of job evaluation. The relative size of jobs is measured on the basis of what needs to be done to achieve a standard and acceptable level of job performance. This provides the reference point for the rate within the range that should be paid to an individual who is fully competent. In a graded structure, the same assumption is made for all the jobs grouped into the grade, although their relative job sizes may differ. Other factors that may be evaluated include the physical work environment; requisite qualifications; and the level of responsibility.

External Comparisons

External comparisons are usually made through market rate surveys, and decisions on external comparisons follow the organization's policy on how its pay levels should relate to market rates. This policy will depend on the organization's views as to whether it should pay above, the same, or less than the market, and will be influenced by such factors as:

• the level of people the organization wants to attract and retain;

• the degree to which it is thought that pay is a major factor affecting attraction and retention rates; and

• what it can afford to pay.

There may be different structures according to level or type of responsibilities. For example, an organization may have one structure for salaried staff and one for hourly workers. Other organizations may differentiate between line management and professional staff. This is important in organizations that employ technical specialists whose progression may be limited in traditional managerial hierarchies. These organizations create technical ladders for scientists or research staff that recognize that progression relies more on professional competence than managerial responsibility. The pay structure needs to be aligned with the organizational structure.

Types of Pay Structures

Graded Pay Structures

The following factors are present in a graded pay structure:

1. It consists of a sequence of job grades each of which has attached a pay range.

P - Q - **R**

2. Jobs are allocated to grades on the basis of an assessment of relative value according to a number of identified factors (responsibility, skills, work environment).

3. All jobs within a grade are treated as the same for pay purposes.

4. A pay range is attached to each grade defining the minimum and maximum rate payable to any job in the grade. The span of this range allows for pay flexibility and recognizes that people in jobs placed in the same grade will perform differently and possess different levels of skills and competencies. The centre of the range, i.e., the mid-point, is the job-rate. This is the target pay level for a fully competent individual based on market data and the organization's compensation philosophy.

5. The size of the range can vary between organizations (depending on the width of the grade bands) and within an organization (if it is believed that the higher the grade, the more scope there is for differences in performance). For example, the spread between the minimum and mid-point of the range may be 15% for administrative and clerical job classes and increase to 20% for managerial and professional job classes.

6. In each range, there will be a reference point that defines the pay for fully acceptable performance. It is often the mid-point of the range and is usually related to market rates in accordance with the organization's market stance.

7. Pay increases and progression through ranges will depend on assessments of performance, contribution, skill or competence and, to some degree, on length of service or time in the grade.

8. Progression through the structure (i.e., from grade to grade) will be based on promotion or on upgrading when the job changes in a significant way dictating that it should be placed in a higher grade.

Pay ranges are established through the use of market surveys. Benchmark positions are identified and a survey is conducted to determine the competitive levels of pay. Regression analysis is then used to plot a salary line that matches the levels of pay to the job evaluation system. This salary line will reflect the organization's compensation philosophy (i.e., to pay at the upper quartile, the median or the lower quartile, respectively). Discreet job classifications are then created to group like positions or positions at the same level within the organization's hierarchy.

One issue that arises from this system is that some professions do not fit easily into the salary line. Information Technology professionals typically place lower on the salary line according to the evaluation of their relative worth within the organization than the marketplace dictates. The same is true with respect to other professional groups such as corporate lawyers and occupational health professionals.

Part of the problem is that evaluation systems are limited in their ability to represent market value. While they can accommodate the majority of jobs within an organization, the design of a system to take into account all factors in determining job value would be too complex. For this reason, organizations will separate some jobs from the central pay structure and create parallel structures to accommodate specific job families.

Nevertheless, the advantages of graded structures are:

— they are easy to explain to employees and clearly indicate the relationship between various job levels;

— they can be useful in communicating opportunities to progress through a range;

— they allow a degree of flexibility in that an individual can be assigned to different jobs without the need to change pay;

— they represent a well-defined framework for managing reward and career progression; and

— they provide better control over pay for new hires, individual performance-related pay increases and promotion increases.

The disadvantages of these kinds of structures are:

— the grade boundaries divide jobs into separate entities creating discontinuity that puts pressure on the evaluation process and the selection of the grade boundaries;

— there may be a tendency for "grade drift" as jobs get pushed into the next grade as a result of pressure from employees and their managers;

— it can impose a degree of hierarchical rigidity that may not match the fluidity with which roles develop; and

— some people will inevitably hit the ceiling of their range and, if the size of the job has not changed sufficiently to require regrading, they have nowhere to go unless they are promoted. They are likely to get demotivated if they are not rewarded appropriately.

Broad-Banded Pay Structures

The features of broad-banded pay structures are as follows:

1. They usually cover the whole workforce, although top management may be excluded.

2. They may contain no more than four bands; the span of each may be 200 to 300% above the minimum compared to 40 to 50% ranges in a conventional graded pay structure.

3. There will usually be a number of pay zones that indicate the range of pay for particular jobs or job families. Levels of pay are related to market rates. The size of the pay zones is sufficient to allow for appropriate pay progression related to growth in job knowledge and performance and competency growth.

Broad-banded pay structures are being introduced for the following reasons:

• They provide more flexibility in making and administering pay decisions.

• They recognize that in delayered organizations, careers are more likely to develop within broadly homogeneous areas of responsibility rather than progressing up a number of steps.

• The existence of a few broad-bands reduces the problem of grade drift.

• More authority can be devolved to managers to manage rewards in their departments.

Disadvantages of broad-banded pay structures are:

— controlling pay decisions, so that a fair degree of consistency is achieved, can be difficult and requires a lot of detailed administration;

— they demand a high degree of pay literacy among line managers; and

— the impact and operation need to be evaluated regularly.

Individual Pay Ranges

The features of individual pay ranges are as follows:

1. They define a separate pay range for each job — the relationships between jobs are usually determined by points factor job evaluation that may in effect convert dollars to points by the application of a formula.

2. There is a reference point in each range, aligned to market rates, and the range is usually expressed as plus or minus a percentage of the reference point.

3. It avoids the problem of grouping a number of jobs with widely different job sizes into a grade and therefore may be more suitable for senior levels.

4. They can encourage individuals to put pressure on management to have their jobs re-evaluated on the grounds that more points may mean more pay.

5. They can be more difficult to control than a conventional graded structure.

Pay Structure Checklist

The following checklist is a useful guide for developing and implementing a pay structure:

✓ analyze present arrangements — the type of organization and employees, the organization's reward strategies and policies, the existing pay structure and how effectively it operates, and any specific objectives that the new or revised structure is expected to achieve;

✓ set objectives and timetable for the review;

✓ estimate the likely costs of conducting and implementing a review;

✓ decide on the extent to which employees should be involved in the review;

✓ brief employees on objectives of the review;

✓ make preliminary decisions on what type of structure or structures are required, in light of the analysis of present arrangements;

✓ analyze and evaluate benchmark and related jobs;

✓ obtain market rate information;

✓ make a final decision on the type of structure required and the main design and operational features;

✓ prepare a detailed design for the structure and how it will be managed and maintained;

✓ communicate the details of the structure to all staff;

✓ train managers in how to operate the structure;

✓ monitor the implementation of the structure; and

✓ evaluate the application and impact of the structure.

Market Rate Surveys

In order to develop and maintain competitive pay levels and salary structures, it is necessary to monitor the external market. This can be done in a variety of ways such as salary and benefit surveys, company annual reports, informal contacts and job advertisements. Market data can be used to ensure that the pay and benefits packages are comparable with equivalent jobs in other organizations and to obtain guidance on compensation reviews by monitoring the rate at which salaries are increasing in other organizations.

The data can help to:

— determine starting rates;

— design and modify salary structures;

— determine rates of progression in salary structures;

— review pay, incentives, bonuses and other forms of performance-related pay;

— decide type and level of benefit provision;

— identify special cases where premiums are required because of skill shortages or other factors; and

— decide on appropriate salary increases.

The main sources of data available are:

— general published surveys;

— specialized industrial, professional, occupational or local surveys;

— company surveys (carried out by the company itself);

— published data in professional products (e.g., *Canadian Industrial Relations and Personnel Developments*, published by CCH Canadian Limited), trade journals and newspapers; and

— analysis of job advertisements.

There are many drawbacks to using market data, and different surveys of the same types of jobs may produce different results because of variations in the sample, timing and job matching. The more you are able to track actual salaries paid to people in identical jobs in similar areas, the greater the accuracy of the market rate information. Therefore, company (do-it-yourself) may be the most accurate; however, the effort and cost involved may be prohibitive. Many organizations rely on published surveys, although judgment may be required in the interpretation of the data. That judgment should be based on data that have been collected and analyzed systematically from other sources.

Choosing a Market Data Provider

Participation in surveys is voluntary and therefore the sample of organizations surveyed will vary from one survey to another, and this will inevitably produce different results. When deciding which survey to use, the main considerations should be:

• the size and stability of the database;

• whether the survey includes a good range of companies in terms of location, company size and industry;

• the basis used for comparing jobs;

• flexibility in the timing of data provision;

• ability of the database to be manipulated in order to obtain more specific and relevant market comparisons;

• how up-to-date the data are; and

• how easy the survey is to understand and use.

Defining the Market

There is no such thing as a definitive market rate. There are local markets, national markets, industry markets, markets for specific professions, and so on. The following gives a general guide as to which markets should be considered:

Job Group	Market
Secretarial/clerical	Local market
Professional/technical	Specific job markets
Senior management	National or industry specific market
Top management	Industry specific and/or company size

Job Matching

Market comparisons are most valid when like is compared with like. The various methods of job matching are as follows:

1. **Job Title** — This method can be misleading as job titles give no real indication of the content of the job, and are sometimes used to convey status irrespective of the real level of work involved.

2. **Brief Description of Duties and Level of Responsibility** — Some surveys limit their job matching definitions to a two- or three-line description of duties and an indication of the level of responsibility in rank order. This provides some guidance on job matching and reduces major discrepancies, but can still only provide generalized comparisons.

3. **Capsule Job Description** — Specialist surveys frequently use capsule job descriptions that define the job in approximately 250 words. They considerably increase the accuracy of comparisons but are not always capable of dealing with specialist jobs.

4. **Full Job Descriptions** — These can be more accurate on a one-for-one basis but require a lot of time and labour to prepare. A further limitation is that comparator companies may not have available their own job descriptions for comparison.

5. **Job Evaluation** — This provides a more accurate measure of relative job size but requires a common method of evaluation. The degree of accuracy will depend on the quality of the evaluation process and depends on the quality assurance process both within organizations and across survey participants as well as of the survey producer.

Remuneration Definitions

Definitions of the remuneration elements analyzed may vary from one survey to another, and care should be taken when comparing the results of different surveys. The following are the most common definitions:

1. **Basic (or Base) Pay** — This means gross pay before income tax and statutory deductions. It includes merit increments or incremental payments that are added into salary but excludes performance-related bonuses, overtime pay, fringe benefits and most allowances, unless they are a guaranteed payment such as a location allowance. Which allowances have been included should be made clear.

2. **Total Cash or Total Earnings** — This is the sum of the basic annual pay and any cash bonuses or other cash compensation (e.g., car allowance) received over the previous 12 months.

3. **Total Remuneration** — This is the total value of all cash payments and benefits received (note that valuing the benefits depends on agreed assumptions).

Presentation of Data

Data on pay may be presented in two ways:

Measure of Central Tendency

The measure of central tendency is the point around which values cluster. These consist of:

— the arithmetic mean or average which is the total of the values of the items in the set divided by the number of individual items (the average may be distorted by extreme values); and

— the median which is the middle item in the distribution of individual items (the median is unaffected by extremes).

Measures of Dispersion

Measures of dispersion are the range of values in the set. These consist of:

— the upper and lower quartiles which are the values above and below which 25% of the individual items fall;

— the upper and lower deciles which are the values above and below which 10% of the individual items fall (this is less frequently used but provides more detail on the spread of the market);

— the interquartile range which is the difference between the upper and lower quartile values (this is a good measure of dispersion);

— the total range which is the difference between the highest and lowest values (this can be misleading if there are extreme values at either end).

Tables of values should identify the job, the size of the sample and, where appropriate, may analyze data according to size, type and location of organization. The significance of the information may be revealed more clearly if the data are presented in graphical form.

Market Movements

Market comparisons involve not only assessing current market rates but also trends in pay increases. The percentage increase in average or median pay between surveys can be misleading because of changes in the sample of organizations included and changes in the sample of jobholders provided by organizations.

This can be partially avoided by providing comparisons between only those organizations that subscribed to both surveys. This does not solve the problem of changes in jobholders within these organizations. A more refined matching process will compare only those individuals who have remained in the same job between consecutive surveys. However, this measure may not distinguish between general pay reviews, individual incremental increases, merit or performance-related payments.

Checklist for Using Market Rate Surveys

✓ Who produced the survey?

✓ What is the survey data based on in terms of the salary levels presented — Are these actual salaries, estimated market rates, recruitment salaries, etc.?

✓ Sample composition — Who participated in the survey?

✓ Data collection — How were the data collected?

✓ Job matching — How accurately are benchmark jobs or levels of responsibility matched?

✓ Timing — How up-to-date are the data?

✓ Presentation — How well does the survey illustrate current practice and the reliability of data in analyses?

✓ Salary increases — How valid is the information provided on pay increases?

✓ Other data — What else does the survey contain?

✓ Cost — Is it worth the price in terms of the savings in organizational resources to obtain equivalent data and in terms of the time/effort involved in participation?

✓ Integrity of data — Does the producer maintain consistent and professional standards?

✓ Purpose — Why was the survey produced and is this influencing the results in any way?

Role of the Human Resources Practitioner

Any change in the reward management policy will affect every employee in the organization, and for that reason implementation takes time and must be carefully planned. Communication is the key and the quality of the communication will largely determine the acceptability of the proposed changes.

The impetus for a major change in policy will probably come from the Board of Directors. The Human Resources Director will be required to get approval for new policies from the Board or the Compensation Committee; these must then be communicated to the line managers and through them to the rest of the employees. Line managers are being increasingly encouraged to take ownership of reward practices. The Human Resources Department will need to take the following steps to ensure that freedom is exercised within the framework of generally understood guidelines on corporate pay policies and how they should be implemented:

1. discuss with managers, team leaders and staff the key reward processes which will maintain standards — these will include processes for job evaluation, tracking market rates, performance management, performance rating and pay-for-performance, skill or competence;

2. ensure all concerned thoroughly understand and appreciate the new responsibilities and accountabilities;

3. train managers and team leaders so that they have the level of knowledge required to make informed, business-led decisions about compensation issues;

4. develop information systems and processes that reduce the administrative burden on line managers and minimize non-value-added activities;

5. ensure that the compensation specialists have the skills to provide guidance and support to line managers rather than exercising control over the process;

6. audit reward management processes and compensation practices to ensure their most effective use;

7. ensure that managers understand and accept that they are still interdependent with other operating units and must consider the implications of what they are doing for other parts of the business; and

8. achieve a balance between giving managers space and freedom to act, while ensuring that their actions do not contravene fundamental policies and guidelines.

It is important to assess regularly the effectiveness of the compensation system in order to ensure it is supporting the organization's objectives. A regular review provides a basis for the development of revised reward policies and practice.

The review should cover reward philosophies, strategies, policies, guiding principles, practices and procedures. Any written policies and principles and any documentation of schemes, structures and procedures should be part of the review. More importantly, the auditor should find out how the processes work in practice by interviewing practitioners, managers, line supervisors and employees, to get their feedback on the systems.

It is important to gain an understanding of employee views and attitudes that are likely to affect reward strategy development. Probably the best way to do this is to hold focus group discussions to obtain the views of employees on specific issues and discover which issues are particularly salient. Alternatively, a survey can be conducted if the population is too large to solicit input from everyone in face-to-face meetings.

The review should consist of the following stages:

1. analyze the internal and external circumstances of the organization and the present arrangements for reward management;

2. diagnose the strengths and weaknesses of the present arrangements in light of the analysis;

3. define the reward philosophy of the organization;

4. develop reward strategies and objectives;

5. develop any new or revised policies required to implement the strategies;

6. design and develop processes in the main areas of reward management — pay structures, job evaluation, financial incentives, non-financial incentives, performance management and employee benefits (this will include defining performance criteria);

7. implement the new or revised parts of the reward management process; and

8. evaluate the effectiveness of the processes by references to objectives and performance criteria.

Barriers to Success/Common Pitfalls

The design and development of reward management processes is a matter of selecting the optimal mix of rewards and benefits within the appropriate structure and of ensuring a fit with the culture of the organization. There is no one right mix or structure, and no ideal approach.

The following are some of the internal factors that have to be taken into account:

— financial resources available to introduce new practices;

— human resources available to introduce new practices;

— organizational climate;

— employee attitudes (what they feel about the organization and its reward policies);

— organizational structure (hierarchical, flat, matrix, homogeneous, diversified, decentralized, formal or informal, flexible or rigid);

— how well individual accountabilities and objectives are defined;

— historical practices and precedents;

— organizational processes (teamwork, networking, individualistic, command or consultative);

— technology;

— recruitment and promotion practices;

— differentiation (the spread of pay from the top to the bottom of the organization); and

— whether the organization is unionized or non-union.

External factors that may need to be considered include business performance, competition, economic trends, trends in market rates, critical skill shortages, legislation, employment law and income tax laws.

Effective and successful implementation of reward strategies depends on the following key elements:

— a well-articulated link between business and reward strategies;

— a sensible fit with the culture that the organization has and/or wants to develop;

— a comprehensive and coherent compensation philosophy that underpins all actions taken to further reward strategy achievement;

— both long- and short-term implementation and maintenance plans about what will happen, when, and for what reason, and how the ability to manage new approaches will be developed and maintained;

— a managed pace of change within either an internally agreed, or an externally set, agenda for new ways of working;

— effective and continuing communication to all parties involved which is aligned to the new values being developed, and which is open, honest and credible; and

— having processes in place, from the start, to monitor how changes are working, evaluate results and implement changes in direction, while admitting honestly when initiatives have not delivered to expectations.

Specific Reward Systems
Pay-for-Performance (Merit Pay)

Performance related pay increases link pay progression to a judgment on an individual or a team's performance as determined by a performance review process. It is commonly asserted that performance reviews and salary reviews should be temporally separated. This is to ensure that the performance review does not become tainted by considerations by both the supervisor and the employee on how it will affect the employee's compensation.

Pay-for-performance (also known as merit pay) is associated with graded pay structures, individual job range structures and salary lines. Normally, merit pay provides for an increase in base pay that is governed by the individual's most recent performance rating. This rating may take account of inputs (i.e., skill and competence) as well as outputs (i.e., results against objectives). Some schemes allow for bonuses to be paid which may also be calculated on a rating of an individual's performance.

Pay-for-performance is usually applied to individuals. In some organizations, the focus is on team-based pay, often through some form of group bonus scheme. Even within individual schemes, attention is given to the employee's ability to work as part of a team.

The primary objectives of a merit pay scheme are to:

• focus attention and effort on key performance issues, both for the individual and the organization;

• differentiate rewards to people consistently and equitably, according to their contribution and competence;

• help to change (or maintain) cultures which need to become more performance and results oriented, and where some key values need to be reinforced or changed (e.g., customer service focus); and

• improve the recruitment and retention of high quality employees who will expect to be rewarded in line with their achievements and skills.

Pay-for-performance schemes can have a profound impact on the organization's culture. The emphasis is on managing performance and development. By supporting these goals, the compensation system becomes a key cultural component. Other benefits include:

- provides managers with the authority and accountability to reward individual performance;

- encourages managers and employees alike to participate in setting specific, measurable and relevant performance objectives; and

- aligns well with other Human Resources strategies (e.g., competency-based performance management systems).

Implementation

Size of Increase

Although performance is a key factor in determining an individual's pay progression, other considerations will need to be taken into account as, for example:

- internal comparisons and potential salary compression;

- the individual's position on the pay range (referred to as the compa-ratio);

- market rates for that type of work in that industry;

- total budget available for pay increases; and

- market trends related to pay increases.

Individuals may receive more at earlier stages in a role than they do once they have matured, and may sustain, but add less value to, their own job performance. This is reflected in the individual's position in the salary range. An employee who is new to a position will be paid at the minimum of the salary range. This usually represents about 80% of the job rate or midpoint for the position.

The idea is that the individual is not yet fully competent and only has the threshold qualifications to perform the job. As the individual progresses, compensation should accelerate at a pace slightly above the annual norm to bring him or her closer to the job rate. Depending on the position and the individual, it is usually expected that he or she will become fully competent in a period of three to five years and, therefore, should be at the mid-point of the range.

Pay above the mid-point may represent a senior employee who is being partially rewarded for his or her service, or an employee who is outpacing the normal learning curve and should be considered for promotion.

Increases are determined by first conducting market surveys to ascertain what current competitive compensation levels are, and what the norm for increases is in the marketplace. This is reviewed in relation to the organization's budget (and ability to pay), and a benchmark is established. The salary ranges may be increased by the target amount and a grid or matrix is developed to differentiate between different levels of performance and different positions within the salary range. Merit increases below the current rate of inflation are hardly worth giving and so a minimum level might be established. Thus, poor performers will not be given an increase and employees who meet the expectations of their position are given the minimum increase.

If a lot has to be spent on anomaly pay to keep pace with market rates, there may be less money available to cope with performance pay. Restricting performance pay too much, however, can be risky, and results in cynicism towards a system which can be perceived as reducing everyone to the same common denominator or only rewarding a very select (and sometimes covert) few. This is another reason to establish a threshold of performance below which increases will not be available.

An employee's position in the pay range can be assessed by the "comparison" (or "compa-ratio"), which shows the relationship between the individual's pay and the reference pay point for a fully competent performance in that grade or job (often the mid-point or median). The compa-ratio is stated as a percentage of mid-point. A compa-ratio of .80 is 80% of the job rate.

Those individuals below 1.00 typically have more opportunity to develop within, and contribute more to, the role and may justify faster or greater pay increases as they move towards the reference point. All graded pay systems create the problem of what to do with able employees who have reached the top of the range and have no immediate prospects of promotion. One approach is to make unconsolidated bonuses to those who sustain high performance over a period of two to three years.

Performance Ratings

Merit pay is based on the individual's performance rating and his or her position in the salary range. Many organizations establish a salary increase grid or matrix to provide guidelines to managers and supervisors on the recommendations they can put forth for an individual's merit pay.

Performance Matrix

Performance Assessment	Position in Pay Range				
	.80	.90	1.00	1.10	1.20
Outstanding	6%	5%	4%	3%	0%
Superior	5%	4%	3%	2.5%	0%
Standard	4%	3%	2.5%	0%	0%
Developing	3%	2.5%	2.5%	0%	0%
Unacceptable	0%	0%	0%	0%	0%

Introducing Pay-for-Performance

The process of introducing merit pay and how it is communicated and managed in the context of overall performance management can become more important in employees' minds than the amounts paid out.

It is important, therefore, that you consider the following and satisfy yourself that the organization is ready for pay-for-performance, and that it is appropriate to the type of work done:

1. *Match the culture* — merit pay schemes should be tailored to the core values of the organization and consistent with the daily work of employees.

2. *Link merit pay to the business strategy* — rewards should focus on achievement of goals that directly link to the direction the organization wants to take.

3. *Balance performance measures* — ensure that outputs and inputs have potential to be rewarded, and that there is a balance between "harder" goals such as financial achievement and "softer" goals such as customer service.

4. *Consider teamwork* — design rewards that are team-based for those projects where teamwork (sometimes across divisions) is essential.

5. *Set a balance of objectives* — ensure that goals are set which are both short- and long-term. It is tempting for managers to set only short-term goals which may allow employees to be rewarded more easily at the organization's expense.

6. *Involve those critical for the scheme's success* — consulting managers who will be responsible for the scheme's success and testing potential models

on them is more likely to ensure the longer-term success of the final design.

Addressing the above should avoid unrealistic expectations of a scheme which may fall into disrepute if it is not perceived to be a panacea for any performance difficulties the organization may be facing.

Competency-Based Pay

A competency-based pay system rewards people for demonstrating the competencies that the organization values for its success. Individuals can be rewarded for acquiring new competencies or for demonstrating a specific relevant competency on-the-job. Competency (a slightly different idea from skill) is often defined as a personal trait or quality that may be relatively hard to develop or change (although some are more easily developed than others). It tends to be the way in which a skill is applied rather than the skill itself. In practice, there are significant overlaps between a "competency" and a skill.

Examples of competencies are "organizational leadership" and "customer orientation". Competencies are seen to make the difference between average and outstanding performance. Examples of these might be "achievement drive", "flexibility", and "conceptual thinking", although appropriate competencies for your organization would need to be defined before this approach could be adopted.

Implementation and Mechanisms

Key design issues are as follows:

1. Define the competency clearly and succinctly. Describe what will be observed when the individual demonstrates superior performance, average performance or unacceptable performance in exercising the competency. Clarity of the definition and use is essential before individuals can be rewarded based on competencies.

2. Limit the number of competencies that are identified as relevant for the position. If too many are identified, the individual will not be able to focus on developing them in order to strengthen his or her overall performance. As well, there will be a point at which adding an additional competency will no longer add value, and this should be taken into account at appropriate points in the structure.

3. It is vital to ensure sufficient differentiation in the competencies at different levels in the system to avoid overlaps and role confusion.

4. Any existing systems such as job evaluation need to be fully integrated with a competency-based approach, often by using newer approaches such as job family modeling.

There are three main types of competency-based pay structures, all of which are associated with "job families" (e.g., information technology (IT), research, secretarial, insurance claims).

Narrow Banded Career Ladders

This could be a conventional "time" graded structure where a ladder of competency levels for each specialist employee group is developed and each grade defined accordingly. Alternatively, a competency matrix scheme could be used which defines both the nature and sophistication of the competency required at different levels of the structure. Each level of the competency may relate to a different point on a salary range. Below is an example of a competency matrix.

Competency Matrix

Competency: Flexibility

Definition: The ability to adapt and work effectively within a variety of situations, and link various individuals and groups. Flexibility entails understanding and appreciating different and opposing perspectives on an issue, adapting one's approach as the requirements of the situation change, and changing or easily accepting in one's own organization or job requirement.

Competency Levels:

(1) Accepts need for flexibility: understands that other people's points of view are as good and reasonable as his or her own. Acknowledges that people are entitled to their opinions and accepts that they are different.

(2) Applies rules flexibly: bends the rules or alters normal procedures to fit a specific situation to get the job done and/or meet company goals. Steps in for co-workers in an emergency.

(3) Adapts tactics: decides what to do based on the situation. Acts to fit the situation or the person faced.

(4) Adapts own strategy: changes the overall plan, goal or project to fit the situation.

(5) Makes organizational changes: makes small or temporary changes in own or client company to meet the needs of the specific situation.

(6) Adapts strategies: makes large changes in own or client company to meet the needs of a specific situation.

Broad-Banded Structures

This may involve only four to six grades in the whole organization below senior management levels, each of which has a very broad pay range. There may also still be a job evaluation process that allocates jobs within broad grades or into zones within grades.

Within these grades, there is still the facility to progress individuals on the basis of demonstrated competency usually linked also to performance. "Role size" may be the core factor in differentiating levels of job, but its impact in relation to variations in competency is reduced. Pay progression rules focus on the individual and cost control is through departmental/divisional budgets.

Competency and Performance Pay Curves

This provides different pay progression tracks along which people in a family of jobs can move according to their competency and performance. A job family pay curve contains a number of competency bands, each of which constitutes a definable level of skill, competency and responsibility. Individuals move along these bands at a rate related to their performance and capacity to develop.

This applies particularly to knowledge workers and ensures that:

⇨ competency development is seen as progressive rather than leaping from point to point;

⇨ there is recognition that individuals develop at different rates; and

⇨ the approach acknowledges that roles may expand to the level of competency of the jobholder.

The actual design chosen will depend on the needs of your organization, and the analysis should be undertaken in a similar way to that for a skill-based pay system. However, there is an added dimension here.

The competencies that will be rewarded within a job or job family need to be defined using an analytical framework which ensures you discover the depth and differentiation needed. This can be achieved through structured interviews or a workshop approach, providing those involved know not only what performance in that job looks like but also what exceptional performance looks like. The performance management system must align with the competency-based pay scheme. This will require careful thought and planning.

The competency-based approach helps organizations develop career streams to provide opportunities to employees to develop within their chosen discipline. The approach gives employees an understanding of the differences in competency requirements not only between the different streams but also at different levels within a stream.

Skill-Based Pay

A skill-based pay system recognizes the achievement of increasing levels of skill which the organization values. The increase in reward may recognize the number, the type, and/or the depth of skill developed.

A skill tends to be defined as input, and can be acquired through study, training and experience, rather than a competency that describes the "how" or the process by which the skill(s) are used. As it is often possible to reward individuals who have grown in horizontal as well as vertical skills, this kind of approach suits organizations where it is important to recognize people for their ability to perform certain tasks or roles, either alone or as part of a team. If there is a need to measure performance as well, then a performance-related pay dimension can be added to the reward "mix".

The kinds of organizations that benefit most from this approach tend to have one or more of the following characteristics:

1. They have fast-changing technologies and/or markets; need individuals who can "multi-skill" quickly; and exist where traditional job demarcation ceases to have value (e.g., project-based organizations).

2. They have a strong need for teamwork or "cellular" activities such as in certain manufacturing industries (e.g., automotive, process industries).

3. Organizations operating these structures tend to have a leaner workforce than would be possible in more traditional structures. They tend to be put in place for technical and operator jobs, although some exist in service industries. Skill-based pay systems are commonly found in collective agreements for teachers.

It is important to establish the right conditions before introducing a skill-based scheme. A high level or range of skills should be required. There is also the need to move people quickly from one project to another, and to have an open culture that encourages the participation of all concerned in the design and operation of the system. A conducive industrial relations climate is also vital.

The suggested process steps are as follows:

1. Identify all jobs implicated in the scheme.

2. Group jobs into job families where the "core" skills are similar. Analyze the skills within the job families.

3. Define the skills clusters and levels within the families. A skill cluster can be encompassed by a specific training input and/or development event before extra pay is warranted. A skill level is a pay grade related to the ability to use certain skills. It may be that skill levels are represented by different roles within the family that can be developed through training and experience.

4. Devise skill-training modules and appropriate cross-training patterns for individuals moving through specific job families, including parallel skills where appropriate. Organizations with skill-based pay provide 80 to 120 training hours per person per year using open/distance, interactive and traditional methods. There needs to be facilities and encouragement for continuous on- and off-job development.

5. Determine methods of testing and assessment.

6. Establish base rates for job families (which may also include undertaking market rate benchmarking).

7. Define the range of payments for skills in terms of progressing through skill bands or meeting the requirements of a skill cluster.

8. Establish procedures for making skill-based payments. This includes the timing of the payment — not necessarily immediately after the training/development has taken place but when the skills have been proven operationally. This may have implications for current pay arrangements and, if pay awards are currently made once or twice a year, give thought to making payments dependent on the individual's skill development.

Incentive and Bonus Schemes

An incentive or bonus scheme is primarily intended to motivate employees by offering some kind of material reward in addition to salary for performing up to a certain standard or accomplishing a particular task.

Generally, the scheme will focus on performance over a one-year period and will make payments on an annual basis. At one time, only senior management and sales representatives were included in such schemes, but their use is now spreading to more junior levels where targets are more difficult to measure. Some of the reasons why these schemes are being more widely used are the following:

— bonus can be linked to agreed targets and achievements, thereby linking compensation to performance against an established set of objectives and creating an incentive for the employee;

— bonuses can be structured to reward behaviour and performance when it happens in order to positively reinforce desired behaviours;

— payment is made only if performance targets are met each year and is not perpetuated as part of base salary;

— lump-sum payments are appreciated by many people and, when paid in a timely manner, may provide tax savings to employees through retirement savings opportunities;

— it is possible to reward people at the top of their salary ranges without damaging the pay structure; and

— good work can be rewarded more immediately.

Different schemes may be more applicable to certain groups of staff, but with all schemes it is important to be clear on what the business needs are and what behaviour needs to be reinforced in order to meet these needs.

Shop Floor Incentive and Bonus Schemes

These schemes reward the number of items produced, the time taken to do a certain amount of work and/or some other measure of performance. They may relate to part or all of the pay received by an employee. Some of the schemes are described below.

Individual Piecework

A uniform price is paid per unit of production: operators are rewarded according to how many pieces they produce. The system is easy to operate and simple to understand; as long as there is supervision to ensure quality standards are maintained, it can be left to run itself. This type of scheme has become more inappropriate as new technology has changed work arrangements, and has largely been replaced by work-measured schemes and other forms of incentive or bonus schemes.

These schemes have been criticized in that it encourages employees to work at a high pace and may sacrifice safety.

Work-Measured Schemes

A standard value or time for completing a task is worked out. This may be broken down into smaller components to which standard minute values can be allocated. Incentive payments are made when performance exceeds the standard.

This is commonly used in automotive maintenance shops. If the task is valued at three hours, the employee gets three hours' pay for completing the task, no matter how long it actually takes him or her. Employees who work efficiently and get the work completed in less time are therefore paid more.

Measured Day-Work

The pay of the employees is fixed on the understanding that they will maintain a certain level of performance. The principles of measured day-work are that there is an incentive level of performance and that the incentive payment is guaranteed in advance. The employees are therefore put under an obligation to perform at the level required.

Group or Team Incentive Schemes

The bonus is related to the output achieved by the group in relation to defined targets and is paid either equally or proportionally to individuals within the group. They are most appropriate where teamwork needs to be encouraged and workers have limited scope to control the level of their own output and are expected to support others in the team. They should be based on a system of measured work and the targets and standards should be agreed upon by the team. The team should be provided with the information it needs in order to monitor its own performance and be given sufficient authority over the structure of the work to optimize the outputs.

Productivity-Based Schemes

If properly measured, productivity can be a sensible basis for the payment of a bonus. Usually it will be measured on a department or factory basis. Productivity is generally defined as the ratio of inputs to outputs. Individual productivity bonuses are becoming increasingly popular as technology provides consistent and objective measures of productivity.

An example of this is a warehouse management system that can track productivity on a real-time basis. Employees receive constant feedback through hand-held devices on how well they are performing against an engineered standard. In this way, an employee is able to make adjustments to his or her work immediately and reap the benefits.

Staff Incentive and Bonus Schemes

There are two main types of schemes: individual bonus payments and group bonus schemes.

Individual Bonus Payments

These are related to the achievement of specific targets, the completion of a project or a stage of a project to a specified standard, the receipt of an appropriate rating, or any combination of these. They can be more explicitly linked to performance if they are related to the degree to which targets have been achieved. For example:

— only just achieved target (the threshold bonus);

— completely achieved target (the full bonus); and

— significantly exceeded target (the exceptional bonus).

Group Bonus Schemes

These relate the reward to the satisfactory completion of a project or stage of a project, or the achievement of a group target. They are used by organizations that want to reward collective effort, and are particularly helpful in areas such as research and development and information technology where work is strongly project-based.

Implementation and Mechanisms

Shop Floor Incentive and Bonus Schemes

Analyze the existing situation and decide if an incentive scheme of any sort is suitable. Some of the questions that need to be asked are as follows:

⇨ Does productivity need to be increased and, if so, is that a matter of improving systems of work or the quality of management or supervision, rather than relying on an incentive scheme?

⇨ What is the scope for increasing work rates?

⇨ What is the union's attitude to incentive schemes?

⇨ How likely are employees to respond positively to incentive schemes?

⇨ To what extent is the work carried out on an individual, team or production line basis?

Evaluate the alternatives and decide whether the incentive scheme should be individual or team-based, and which type of scheme is appropriate.

Staff Incentive and Bonus Schemes

The design of the scheme should address the following questions:

⇨ Who are the participants in the scheme?

⇨ Should the scheme be individual or team/group-based?

⇨ What are the measures of performance?

⇨ How is the performance measured and who measures it?

⇨ What is the formula for deciding on the payments and the extent to which a discretionary element is required?

⇨ How much money will be made available for bonuses and how and when should they be paid?

⇨ What is the procedure for monitoring the scheme?

For both shop floor and staff schemes, the three essential prerequisites for introducing a successful scheme are:

1. the senior members of the organization are committed to a program of change;

2. a team of managers is developed, which knows what is required and has the enthusiasm to make it work; and

3. the rest of the workforce is convinced that the project is worthwhile.

It is important to have employees participate in the process, and that they know how to obtain performance improvements and understand how they will benefit from them.

Executive Bonus Schemes

An executive bonus or incentive scheme is generally designed to reward the attainment of predetermined targets of organization growth and profitability. In some cases, schemes may also include an element of individual achievement through the setting of personal objectives. The payments made for reaching these targets are in addition to annual salary and may be very substantial.

Since these schemes only pay out if targets are met, the scheme introduces a certain amount of risk into the remuneration package that is believed to be appropriate for employees at the executive level. If the organization does not perform, the executive may receive no payment at all, but if the organization performance is outstanding, the executive may receive considerable rewards.

Generally, the schemes are based on short-term targets set each year with payments made annually. This has led to criticism that such schemes lead to short-term thinking and may lead to a reluctance to incur expenditure that does not produce immediate results such as capital investment, maintenance and training. Also there is often an expectation on the part of executives that something will be paid and therefore schemes have a tendency to be designed such that company performance would have to be very poor for the scheme not to pay out. This may create a culture of entitlement where risk is avoided.

Over the last few years, there has been an increase in the introduction of long-term incentive schemes that operate in a similar way but with performance measured over a three- to five-year period, with payments made at the end of the period. The bonus payments may be made in cash, in shares, or in a combination of the two. Generally, where they are made in shares, there will be some restriction placed on the sales of the shares.

Where long-term schemes have been introduced, they are usually in addition to the existing short-term scheme and are therefore used to balance the short-term and long-term focus of the executives.

The use of executive bonus and incentive schemes has extended rapidly and the majority of organizations now have schemes in place. In fact, it is becoming increasingly difficult to maintain a competitive overall level of compensation without such a scheme. Before a scheme is introduced, it is essential to know where the organization is planning to go and what constitutes success. Only by knowing this can there be any clear view as to what the executives have to do and achieve in order to make the organization more successful. The scheme should ensure that executives are focused on the right priorities.

The aims of an executive bonus scheme are to:

— motivate executives in order to improve organization performance;

— focus executives on the key measures of organization performance;

— provide executives with a share of the organization's success;

— reward personal commitment; and

— help recruit and retain high-calibre executives by ensuring a competitive remuneration package.

It is important that the incentive scheme is related to other parts of the remuneration package; therefore, before the introduction of such a scheme, it would be wise to review the existing package. Since the incentive bonus will be paid in addition to annual base salary, it must be decided whether base salary levels will be set at a competitive market position with the potential of a large bonus payment in addition, or whether base salary will be set at something below a competitive position with the potential to improve this position substantially if the organization is successful.

The suggested steps for implementation are as follows:

Step One: Define the Participants in the Scheme

Only those executives who can exert personal control over the performance measures should be included. This will include heads of major functions and divisional/subsidiary heads. If there is some form of bonus or incentive scheme already in place for all employees of the organization, then the executive scheme may be an extension of this with additional or different performance criteria and/or higher potential payments, or it may be instead of, or in addition to, the existing scheme.

Step Two: Define the Performance Criteria

These will be either financial or non-financial measures, or a combination of the two.

Financial Measures

The principal measures are as follows:

1. **Profit before tax (pre-tax profit)** — This is the main indicator of corporate success and is often used as the sole criterion. The bonus is based on a percentage of profit. Typically, a payment would be made after the achievement of a threshold figure which would be set to protect the interests of the shareholder.

2. **Profit after tax (post-tax profit)** — This measure is more closely linked to shareholder interest, as it gives an indication of the funds available for reinvestment and payment of dividends. It can, however, be affected by changes in tax laws, and because of this is rarely used as a chief measure. The choice of before- or after-tax profit will depend on whether the executives are expected to take tax considerations into account when making decisions.

3. **Earnings per share** — This relates post-tax profits to the average weighted number of ordinary shares in issue during the year, and is increasingly being used as the chief measure in executive incentive schemes.

4. **Return on capital or assets employed** — This is a key measure of company performance, but can be open to manipulation since the ratio could be improved by the sale of assets. For this reason, it is rarely used as a sole measure.

5. **Cash flow** — It may be useful to emphasize the importance of managing cash by including this as one of the performance measures, but it is not suitable as a sole measure as it only relates to one aspect of management responsibility.

Non-Financial Measures

There may be other aspects of an executive's job which can and should be measured, particularly in service areas such as Human Resources Management. Job-related targets may be set which indicate what needs to be achieved in order to earn a specified level of reward. This could be the completion of a project that meets specific objectives within a specified time scale. The objectives may be cost reduction, improvement in customer service standards, increase in productivity, improvement in quality, and so on. The scheme may be designed so that a payment is made only if the objectives are fully achieved, or they may provide for a partial payment if the results are less than 100%.

Achieving the Right Mix

The mix of financial and non-financial measures will depend on the nature and requirements of the business. It is important that the executives understand the measures and that performance against these measures can be communicated on a frequent basis. Therefore, schemes should not be made too complex; the use of more than three or four factors is not recommended.

There is always a danger that important aspects of a job, such as team building, leadership and development, may be neglected because of the focus on areas where rewards can be achieved. If the discussion on the setting and achievement of targets takes place as part of the normal assessment procedure, this may help to put all aspects of the results achieved by the executive, both those covered by the incentive scheme and those not specifically covered, into perspective.

Step Three: Define the Level of Payments

There are three levels that need to be decided.

Target Level

How much will the scheme pay out if the performance targets are met? Assuming the performance targets are tough but achievable, typical levels would be 20 to 30% of base salary. Payments for reaching target performance should be self-financing, based on the assumption that the organization will benefit as well as the individual.

Starting Point or Threshold Level

Some schemes may make no payment unless the target levels of performance are met; most schemes, however, will have a starting point (i.e., the level of performance required in order to make a payment). This point will depend on how demanding are the target performance levels. If they were reasonably tough, then it would be appropriate to set the starting point for payment of a bonus at 90% achievement of the target level of performance. However, it is important to provide a significant incentive to achieve the target. Therefore, it may be appropriate to gear the incentive payment so that the difference in the amount received at the starting point and that received at target level is greater than the difference in performance levels. The executive may be eligible for a 10% bonus if 90% of the targets are reached, and a 30% bonus if 100% of the targets are reached.

Upper Limit or Maximum

Many schemes cap the payment levels by setting an upper limit that may be earned. This is generally either because it is believed that above a certain level executives cannot influence organization performance by their own efforts, or to avoid the executives being so focused on their own personal targets that they neglect the needs of the business. If there is to be a limit, then this will depend on the level of performance an executive can achieve. In some schemes, the gap between the target and maximum may be the same as that between the starting point and the target, perhaps 10% either side of the target. In other schemes, the gap between the target and maximum may be wider. This will depend largely on the ability of the management to bring about results. Similarly, the difference in payment levels for reaching target and maximum performance may be the same, or larger than the difference between reaching threshold and target performance levels.

Even when there is no maximum limit set, it may be necessary to make provisos in the scheme rules for the handling of windfall profits that may arise from circumstances outside the control of the executives. It would be appropriate for the remuneration sub-committee of the board to discuss and adjudicate this issue. If it is decided to limit the payments in the event of such a windfall profit, then the circumstances in which this could happen should be spelled out clearly in the rules of the scheme. This will avoid the potential demotivation of such a rule being brought into effect unexpectedly.

Step Four: Maintenance of the Scheme

A compensation committee to ensure that the plan is run properly and the interests of the shareholders protected should supervise the operation of the scheme. The rules of the scheme should be set out in a document given to all participants. This should allow them to work out how the incentives are calculated and what they have to do to achieve certain payment levels.

Profit-Sharing

In a profit-sharing plan, a payment is made, in addition to annual salary, which is related to the profits of the business. The payment may be made in cash or shares in the organization. The amount to be distributed may be decided by a pre-set formula that may be published, or it may be at the discretion of the management. Generally, all employees of the organization will participate in the scheme. These types of scheme differ from incentives and bonus schemes in that usually the same percentage is paid to all employees and the sole determinant of the amount paid is the profitability of the organization. It is unusual to find other measures of performance affecting the payment levels.

The philosophy behind these schemes is that the company has a moral obligation to share its prosperity with its employees. The profit-sharing scheme should not then be regarded as a type of incentive scheme, but rather as a way of engendering a "team" culture, whereby all employees will feel that they can make a contribution towards the profitability of the business and will in return receive a share in this prosperity.

The aims of a profit-sharing plan are to:

⇨ create a common interest in the company, thereby encouraging employees to identify themselves with the organization;

⇨ encourage employees to develop a concern for the progress of the business as a whole;

⇨ create more co-operation between employees and management;

⇨ recognize that employees help to produce the profits of the company and therefore have a right to share in them;

⇨ demonstrate, in practical terms, the goodwill of the organization towards the employees; and

⇨ reward success in a business where profitability may be cyclical.

Types of Scheme

The main types of scheme are as follows:

Cash

This is the most common approach whereby a proportion of the profits is paid in cash directly to the employees. In most schemes, all employees with more than one year's service are eligible. Different approaches include the following:

1. A predetermined formula for distributing a fixed percentage of profits which may be published to staff thereby committing the organization to using it. This makes clear the relationship between profits and amount to be paid. However, there is little flexibility, and amounts to be paid out will fluctuate, sometimes widely, according to changes in profitability.

2. The board determines the profit share at its discretion with no predetermined formula. This allows consideration of not only the profitability of the organization but also what proportion it is felt should be distributed, expectations of the employees and the general climate of industrial relations in the organization. This is a more common approach, allowing flexibility in the amount to be distributed rather than being committed to expenditure over which there is little control. It also allows random fluctuations to be smoothed out. However, since one of the main reasons for introducing a profit-sharing scheme is to develop commitment from the employees by giving them a chance to share in the success, this approach clearly has disadvantages. Employees may be suspicious of the decision-making process and the scheme may not be perceived as a real-

istic profit-sharing device if employees feel they are insufficiently rewarded for improved performance or protected from the reverses.

3. The third approach is a combination of the two. A profit threshold exists below which no profits will be distributed, and a maximum limit set on the proportion of profits that will be distributed.

Distribution of Profit Shares

The choice here is primarily between distributing profit shares, either in relation to pay, or in relation to pay and service. Where pay only is used, it is felt that profit shares should relate to individual contribution, which is best measured by pay. Length of service is not taken into account as this is already reflected in the individual's level of pay. Where a combination of pay and service is used, the argument is that loyalty to the organization should be rewarded and encouraged. Occasionally, profits are distributed in relation to pay and some measure of individual performance, but there is a difficulty here in measuring the relationship between performance and profit below the executive level.

Very rarely, a totally egalitarian approach will be adopted, distributing profits as a fixed sum regardless of earnings or service.

Amount Distributed

Ideally, the share should be between 5 and 10% of pay in order to be meaningful.

Timing of Distribution

Most schemes distribute the profits annually, although some may do so twice yearly and a few do so quarterly.

Implementation and Mechanisms

Surveys that have been carried out show that the average performance of those organizations with profit-sharing schemes tends to be better than those without; however, these organizations do not perform better just because they have profit-sharing. It is probably more that, because they are good organizations, they introduce profit-sharing.

What makes these organizations successful is that managers demonstrate the following:

✓ have clear objectives and are able to harness the resources needed to achieve them;

✓ recognize that their chief resource is people;

✓ see their employees as part of a team that works together to make the business successful and shares in its success, and are also able to engender this attitude among their employees; and

✓ are able to generate a commitment to success.

The main question to be asked when considering the introduction of a profit-sharing scheme, or the continuation of an existing scheme, is: "Do you believe that the organization has a moral obligation to share its prosperity with its employees, in addition to the benefits already provided?" If the answer is "Yes", then it should be remembered that for the scheme to be successful it is not sufficient merely to introduce a scheme but for managers to believe that the employees are part of a team, to communicate this philosophy to the employees effectively, and to create a common commitment to success. The introduction of the scheme will then reinforce these values by rewarding the employees with a share in this success.

Gain-Sharing

Gain-sharing is a formula-based company or division-wide bonus plan, which allows employees to share in the financial gains made by a company as a result of improved performance within the employee's control.

The formula determines the payout through a performance indicator such as added value or another measure of productivity (e.g., customer service, delivery or cost reduction). It differs from profit-sharing in that the latter is based on more than improved productivity, and contains factors that are outside the individual employee's control such as taxation, depreciation methods, bad debt expenses, etc.

The specific aims of gain-sharing are to:

⇒ establish clear productivity targets that are objectively measurable;

⇒ encourage full employee participation in the improvement of operating methods; and

⇒ share performance gains with employees who have collectively contributed to those improvements.

Apart from selecting appropriate measures, the way employees are involved in the design and implementation of a gain-sharing program is important to consider. There should be agreement on the areas of performance to be addressed and mutual discussion

of the ways in which they can be improved, to ensure credibility for the bonus system.

There are several methods of designing a gain-sharing program. The most common are:

● the *Scanlon Plan*, which is based on labour costs as a proportion of total sales (if costs fall below this ratio, then savings are shared);

● the *Rucker Plan*, which is also based on labour costs, but as a proportion of sales less the costs of materials and supplies (the value added);

● *Improshare*, where an established standard defines the expected hours required to produce an acceptable output (it tends to be based on work measurement).

Gain-sharing plans based on improvements to value added are becoming more common. Typically, the employees' share is between 40 and 50%, and the remainder funds operating expenses and profit.

Organizations introduce gain-sharing for a number of reasons. Primarily, the reasons are:

— the need to encourage teamwork and encourage employee ownership of improved performance;

— building greater employee awareness of business performance issues;

— increased competition (and/or declining productivity); and

— disillusionment with traditional pay and incentive schemes which appear to have little value as motivational tools.

When considering the introduction of gain-sharing, the following plan should act as a guideline.

1. Be clear about your reasons for introducing such a scheme and what its objectives are. Understand the potential benefits as well as the possible risks.

2. Conduct a cost-benefit review. If the costs of introducing and maintaining the scheme equal or outweigh the likely financial gains, then the scheme design may be faulty or inappropriate.

3. Review the organization's cultural "map" (i.e., the business strategy, technology, management style, work structure and skills) to ensure a good fit with this kind of incentive plan.

4. Sound out managers', employees' and (if appropriate) union representatives' attitudes to gain-sharing (either formally or informally).

5. Draw up preliminary proposals on the type of plan and possible formulae.

In considering the type of formulae to use, the following provides a checklist of questions to address:

✓ How should value added be calculated? Consult the accounting standards and principles upon which the value-added statements in the company's annual report are based.

✓ What threshold should be used to trigger payments? Analyze value-added figures over three to five years. The figure chosen must cover payroll and operating costs and operating profit. If value added rises above the threshold, then a payout is possible. Review this figure annually.

✓ How should bonus relate to improved performance? Most gain-sharing plans use a shared model (i.e., bonus is maintained as a fixed percentage), on the basis that employees should continue to share equally in the organization's success.

✓ What happens if value added falls below the reference point? This effectively means that employees have not "paid their way" and the organization should bear the loss. Some organizations set up a reserve fund (typically 25% of the employees' share) and any surplus is distributed at the end of year as a terminal bonus.

✓ What should be the target for bonus levels? Up to 10% annually? Many schemes in successful organizations average 20%.

✓ Should there be any limit to the amount shared out? You may wish to cap the bonus to, for instance, 25% in a period. Any residual bonus can be paid out at the end of the year. It may be necessary to set up a new "threshold" for the following year.

✓ How should the bonus be distributed? Usually the bonus is distributed in proportion to base pay, but it can be in flat-rate sums for all.

✓ How frequently should it be distributed? Often, every quarter. Some schemes every month, so that there is a more immediate link between performance and reward. The administration of schemes with frequent payments may be costly.

Value-added formulae may be criticized because they do not highlight key performance factors that can be influenced by the employee, and there have been attempts to introduce measures such as quality, customer service and cost, as well as productivity. It may, however, be difficult to establish measures in these areas which make sense to an employee, especially when an added-value formula alone can be relatively complicated.

STRESS MANAGEMENT

Definition/Background

Stress has been called the "repetitive strain injury" of the new millennium. Like RSI, the exact causes of stress are difficult to pinpoint, it is not easy to diagnose and the prognosis is often uncertain. More and more employees seem to be suffering from stress and are requiring time off from work because of it.

Managers cringe at the mere mention that an employee is off work suffering from stress. They know that the problem will be difficult to manage and will likely be a recurring issue with the employee. The truth is that, despite the widespread acceptance of stress as a modern-day feature of work life, managers and supervisors know little about it. They are likely to rely on their intuition in dealing with stress issues. Their common sense approach may demonstrate compassion and sympathy for the employee, but will seldom address the root causes that have led an employee to become disabled by the stresses placed on him or her.

Managers often define stress narrowly as a specific manifestation of an employee's inability to cope with certain situations or elements in the work environment. The employee on stress leave is usually the employee who is suffering from situational anxiety or emotional exhaustion. There are, however, countless other causes of an employee's inability to cope. These could include chronic illness, substance abuse, or declining productivity.

The point is that we often equate the definition of stress with the outcomes of an individual's ability or inability to cope with the stresses in his or her life. Everyone experiences stress in his or her work life. Stress is merely an individual's response to situations that he or she perceives to be challenging or threatening. Some people thrive on challenges and even threats. In other words, they adapt well to circumstances that test their abilities to adjust to new situations. Others do not cope as well.

Managers and supervisors often find it difficult to believe that an individual could be stressed by the pressures and circumstances faced in the workplace. Managers often try to put themselves in the place of the individual and can be quite skeptical of any suggestion that a particular job is stressful. They will think back to a time when they might have done the same job and recall that they were able to handle the demands placed on them without undue stress. In the minds of these managers, the job is not stressful and therefore the person must be very fragile, experiencing stress off the job, or be faking illness. Again, managers jump to conclusions without examining the potential root causes of stress on individuals.

For those who adapt well to the challenges and threats they face in the workplace, stress may in fact lead to very positive outcomes. These individuals get a "rush" from the increased demands placed on them. This feeling of being "more alive" can be very motivating for the individual. This is the "good" stress known as *eustress*. In moderation over a short period of time, the elevated responses to the environment will turn the individual "on" and actually help him or her achieve success in the face of challenges. However, for the most part, what we deal with in the workplace is *distress*. This is when the challenges or threats are beyond the individual's capacity to cope and result in exhaustion, anxiety or inappropriate responses and coping mechanisms.

Stress is very much an individual issue. The ability to cope with the stress of work will depend on a diverse set of factors, including the employee's physical health, family situation, time constraints, emotional capacity to deal with change, and the match between his or her skill set and the demands of the job. Some people literally thrive on chaos, while others require structure and routine in their daily lives in order to cope with the demands placed on them.

Sources of stress — or "stressors" — in the modern work environment include:

- Role-Related Stressors;
- Interpersonal Stressors;
- Organizational Stressors;
- Work–Family Conflicts; and
- Physical Environment.

Role-Related Stressors

There are many different types of role-related stressors. Role conflicts are one type that can be seen when competing demands are placed on the individual. For example, an individual new to an organization may be socialized by his or her peers as to the way things are done. That individual naturally wants to get along with his or her co-workers and will follow their example accordingly. The supervisor, however, may want things done differently and place different demands on the individual, who also wants to make a good impression on the boss. This creates a conflict between the individual's desire to fit in and his or her desire to be a good employee.

Another role-related stressor occurs when employees are asked to do something that they cannot reconcile with their personal values. For example, a manager who has to terminate employees during an economic downturn may find the task very difficult if he or she personally believes that the organization should make every effort to maintain full employment.

In many organizational contexts, employees are being managed in a matrix structure. Employees may find themselves on a cross-functional team wherein they are responsible jointly to a team leader and to a department manager. If these two provide conflicting directions to the individual, an internal conflict will follow. The employee is left to choose whose directions to follow. Similarly, a matrix organization is a loose structure that relies on general directions rather than specific procedures to advance projects. Some individuals find this unnerving and have difficulty adapting.

Role-related stress can also arise when there is a poor fit between an individual's skills and behaviours and the demands of the job. Poor person-to-job matches happen surprisingly often because people have made career choices that are not well-suited to their individual abilities. Take, for example, a Credit Collections Officer who had been appointed from the accounting office because of her strong abilities in identifying credit risks. The Collection position offered more money and a better chance for advancement. However, the individual did not have the skill set required to deal with irate customers who could not, or would not, pay their bills on time. These interpersonal conflicts led to poor job performance, declining health, increased absenteeism and family conflicts. The com-

pany, which was unaware of the poor match, was prepared to dismiss the employee if her performance did not improve. Instead, the Human Resources department intervened and conducted a career assessment for the individual. It was determined that her skill set was poorly aligned with the requirements of the job and that she was better suited to a straight accounting job. She was moved back to her former position with expanded responsibilities and was soon contributing at a high level.

Another role-related stressor is role ambiguity, which can arise in a variety of organizational contexts where individuals may be uncertain what is expected of them and what level of responsibilities they have. Role ambiguity can be the result of not having a performance management process in place to inform individuals as to what their goals and objectives are (see Performance Management Process at page 303). At a more basic level, it can be the result of not providing written job descriptions. Some employees function best when they have a highly structured work environment. They not only require job descriptions, but also prefer working with written procedures and guidelines that tell them exactly what to do in different situations.

Role ambiguity can also be created at times of significant organizational change. In stable environments, employees who require definitive structures may comfortably move up to high levels of authority because the expectations are widely known and understood. If this environment is disrupted by the need to change the organization and meet the challenges of a new business climate, however, the individual may find it difficult to cope with the ensuing ambiguity. In this scenario, a manager — even one at a senior level, who has performed well in the past — may find himself or herself unable to cope with the uncertainty and ambiguity caused by the evolving demands.

One of the most obvious stressors created by the individual's work role is the potential for work overload. Overload means the quantity of work exceeds the individual's capacity. The result is missed deadlines, poor quality output and extended hours. In some organizations, employees (managers, in particular) who put in extra-long days are admired for their devotion to the job. These organizations need to be careful that they are not reinforcing a bad behaviour. The organization may be ignoring the fact that either the scope of the job is too much for the individual or the individual simply does not have the skills to perform the job.

Managers and supervisors also need to be careful not to push employees to work harder to increase productivity. The manager needs to understand the work processes and find ways to improve employee skills, change work methods or processes, and introduce new technology where applicable. The manager also needs to be able to identify if an employee has the ability to perform the work at a suitable level of productivity. If an individual does not have fine motor skills, for example, no amount of pushing is going to make him or her productive at assembling small parts. Selection techniques that identify specific job requirements help ensure that undue workload pressures are not put on individuals who cannot match the requirements of the job (see "Role of the Human Resources Practitioner" in Recruitment and Selection at page 370).

The opposite of work overload is, of course, work underload. It can be equally stressful. Employees who are not sufficiently challenged will feel at risk of potentially losing their jobs. They may also feel trapped in an environment where their skills are not being appreciated or used to their fullest. These employees can be disruptive to others because they have too much time on their hands. Not understanding the root cause may lead managers to take disciplinary action against these employees if they are disruptive. While it may not be obvious at first, managers with employees who are being underutilized should give them more work and perhaps even promote them.

Employees who feel the pressures of stress often refer to how they are feeling as suffering from "burnout", meaning they are emotionally exhausted, lethargic and apathetic. More specifically, "burnout" is seen after prolonged exposure to certain types of stressors associated with working in occupations where the employees deal largely with people issues. These stressors are related to having to help individuals in crisis situations. Doctors, nurses, firefighters and police officers are especially prone to burnout. The symptoms include exhaustion, insomnia, moodiness and depression. It is also marked by depersonalization. As a protection mechanism, the burned-out employee depersonalizes events and begins to view the people being served in an impersonal way. To a nurse, for example, the patient Mrs. Smith might become "the kidney in room 201".

Interpersonal Stressors

Interpersonal stressors stem from the conflicts that arise occasionally between individuals. We often call these "personality conflicts". However, this is an oversimplification that tends to lead people to the conclusion that two individuals simply cannot get along and that this cannot be changed. Personality involves an enduring set of individual traits that cannot always be changed. But interpersonal conflict does not stem from the personalities *per se*, but rather from specific behaviours. Behaviours can be changed.

The most infamous form of interpersonal conflict is workplace harassment. Harassment can take many different forms, including sexual harassment, racial discrimination or bullying. The result of harassment is usually far more serious than hurt feelings. Individuals who are harassed can experience diminished self-worth and suffer from psychological trauma.

Management style is often cited as a cause of interpersonal conflict and stress. Managers need to know that the success of their leadership style is dependent on the specifics of the organizational situation they face. Managers who have a relatively inexperienced workforce will need a different style than those who supervise a group of experienced veterans. The style employed for managing highly motivated individuals is different than the style employed when employees are not motivated.

Managers seldom oversee homogeneous groups and need to be adept at employing different styles with different individuals. Also, when the Human Resources practitioner is selecting candidates to work for a particular manager, the practitioner needs to be aware of the manager's style and how the recruit will fair under his or her tutelage.

Organizational Stressors

There are many organizational events that can cause employees a great deal of stress. The most often cited barrier to managing organizational change is fear among employees. When an organization is undergoing a significant change in its culture — whether due to a merger or acquisition or because a change initiative has been introduced to meet an external threat — employees will experience a significant degree of uncertainty. Downturns in the economy that result in layoffs or plant closings are other obvious organizational stressors. (See also "Role of the Human Resources Practitioner" in Mergers and Acquisitions at page 266 and Outplacement at page 297 *et seq.*)

In a rapidly changing environment, one of the first fears employees have is that they might lose their job. However, employees are also afraid of the ambiguity often associated with change. They fear they may not have the skills to adapt to new technologies or processes. They fear that with downsizing the survivors will have increased workloads and increased pressures to produce.

For many working people, much of their identity and self-worth is associated with their jobs. Even if their position is stable, employees may feel unsettled during a merger because the new organization may have a different set of values.

Work–Family Conflicts

The most obvious potential conflict between a person's work and family life is the competing demands placed on the scarce resource of time. Parents who are unable to work extended hours because they have to tend to the needs of their children may feel guilty that they are not putting in the requisite time. They may fear being overlooked for promotion because they are perceived as not being committed to work. Those who put in the extra hours will feel guilty that they are ignoring the needs of their children. Gaining a proper balance is difficult.

Shift work complicates the demands on an individual's time. Employees who work afternoon shifts often have the feeling that they literally never see their families, who are either asleep or at school when they are at home. Employees who are required to travel a lot also experience this feeling of being separated from their family's lives.

Time conflicts between work and family life continue to increase. In many families, both parents have to work. A significant percentage of families are headed by a single parent, often the mother, who has to balance a full-time job with the full-time responsibilities of running a household. Working people not only have to make time for their children, but are also experiencing demands from aging parents who require elder care.

Stressors experienced at work are sometimes taken home and can lead to conflicts with one's spouse; stressors at home can be carried to work and can lead to conflicts with co-workers. Stress can build on itself and lead to a growing cycle if the individual does not have suitable outlets for relief or the emotional capacity to cope.

Physical Environment

Last but not least, the actual physical working environment can be a significant source of stress on the individual. Conditions that can be distressful to an individual include:

- excessive noise;
- vibrations;
- poor lighting;
- unpleasant odours;
- poor ergonomics;
- safety hazards;
- poor housekeeping; and
- stale air (or "sick building syndrome").

Employees who work outdoors face the added stress of poor weather. Extreme heat or cold can be very stressful to cope with. In cold storage freezers, for example, employers are encouraged to have cold stress relief policies in place to ensure that employees can get a break from the extreme conditions. In glass factories such as AFG's Scarborough, Ontario facility where temperatures can be extremely hot, maintenance workers are encouraged to take as many breaks from the heat as they deem necessary. Just having the freedom to escape helps to relieve the psychological effects of working in an extreme environment.

In most office environments, employees are encouraged to bring a personal touch to their working space. Employees will often have family photos, a house plant or two, and other personal items to help create their own space. This personalization can reduce the alienation some people feel by making them feel more "at home" when they're at work. A sterile environment may be aesthetically pleasing, but can create a psychological distance between the employee and his or her workspace. Allowing a sense of ownership creates a connection between the employees and their work that allows them to take ownership of their work output.

Benefits/Expected Outcomes

While a moderate amount of stress can be motivating and even lead to improved productivity over a short period of time, it is a given that stress costs employees and employers significantly in the long run. Losses incurred by organizations as a result of stress include:

- lost productivity;

- increased absenteeism;

- increased employee turnover;

- workplace accidents and injuries (Workers' Compensation); and

- increased insurance (short-term and long-term disability).

Employees can suffer greatly from a wide variety of stress-induced consequences, including:

- heart disease;

- high blood pressure;

- sleep disorders;

- substance abuse;

- situational anxiety;

- exhaustion (physical/emotional);

- eating disorders;

- ulcers;

- marital strife; and

- burnout.

Dealing with workplace stress in a proactive way will pay tremendous dividends for any organization. There are two ways to help employees manage stress. Organizations can take steps to remove the stress inducers or they can help their employees develop better coping mechanisms to deal with the stressors. The best strategy is to do a bit of both.

The objective is not to remove all stressors. This would be impossible and, in the long run, an organization completely free of stress would likely become very complacent. Such an organization would not be able to compete in an ever-changing economy and would eventually become extinct. In reality, we can

reduce many common stressors and help employees cope with those that cannot or should not be eliminated. Helping employees achieve a balance between their work and family lives, for instance, will provide them with the necessary psychic energy to deal with changes in the competitive market. In this way, the organization is able to create a flexible and adaptable environment that provides it with a distinct competitive advantage.

Programming/Implementation

There are two strategies that can be followed to deal with stress in the workplace. The more obvious strategy is to design specific interventions to help people deal with the threats and challenges they face in the workplace. These interventions include:

- work breaks (afternoon naps);

- sabbaticals;

- stabilization zones;

- relaxation and meditation seminars;

- fitness and lifestyle programs;

- Employee Assistance Programs; and

- social support and social activities.

The second strategy looks to the root causes of stressors to remove or modify them. These interventions include:

- job redesign;

- changing management policies and practices;

- organizational communications strategies;

- modifying the physical work environment; and

- reassignment to get a better person-to-job match.

Work Breaks

All employment standards legislation in Canada provides for daily breaks from work. Employees are entitled to breaks from work to eat their lunches or dinners, as well as breaks to rest. Many companies also encourage specific breaks from the usual work activity to allow employees a change of pace. For example, employees in manufacturing can be taken off the production line to attend a daily Total Quality Management meeting. These meetings give employees a break from the physical aspects of their jobs and allow them to become engaged in the decision-making process. This kind of break allows them to be reinvigorated. Moreover, it provides the company with an opportunity to communicate with its employees and keep them informed as to how their efforts impact the company as a whole.

Another innovation, this one borrowed from Japanese management practices in manufacturing, is the stretch break. The potential for injuries and psychological stresses to employees engaged in physical labour can be dramatically reduced through simple stretching exercises at the beginning of the work shift. Stretch breaks throughout the day can also reduce the possibility of physical fatigue and diminish the potential for repetitive strain injuries.

Employment standards legislation stipulates that all employees should be granted a minimum amount of time off with pay for statutory holidays and vacations. Vacations in particular are important breaks from work that allow employees time to spend with their families and to pursue outside interests. Legislation stipulates not only the minimum time off to be granted, but also requires that the time be given in one-week blocks.

It is important that vacation be used to allow employees to regenerate. Once legislated minimums have been satisfied, some companies allow employees to take their vacation time off in shorter segments, including in one-day blocks. This may be a mistake because it might not allow employees a sufficient amount of time away from the workplace to rest and forget about work.

Sabbaticals

Sabbaticals are a common benefit in academic circles. Universities and colleges allow academic staff time off to write (and publish), to conduct field research or to attend courses elsewhere. Some organizations, such as McDonald's Corporation, allow senior staff who have attained at least 10 years' service to take a sabbatical of up to six months (without pay) every five years. The staff member must make a proposal as to what he or she plans to use the time for, but there are few limitations on what is and is not allowed. The primary stipulation is that the employee must be pursuing an activity that helps in his or her personal development. This could mean finishing a degree requirement at university or it could mean sailing around the world.

The activity does not have to be work-related. Rather, it is intended to help the individual to develop his or her self-worth. This kind of break creates a more rounded individual who is better equipped emotionally to handle the threats and challenges faced at work.

Stabilization Zones

One of the most stressful assignments an employee can face is a placement in a foreign country. In addition to any specific workplace challenges that might exist, the employee and his or her family may have to cope with a different culture and language in their everyday lives. It is natural for expatriates to miss the familiarity of their homes. Stabilization zones give them the opportunity to escape temporarily from the foreign culture.

A stabilization zone may be a club in the living compound that features food and drink from the employee's homeland, it may be a specific event such as a "Canadian night", or it may be a periodic trip to a more familiar culture. Canadian employees in the Middle East, for example, may be given weekend trips to European destinations that are more like home.

Relaxation and Meditation Seminars

Seminars are available to companies to teach employees specific relaxation techniques like isometric exercises, breathing techniques and visualization. Meditation is a specific relaxation technique that teaches individuals to use a repetitive mental device like a chant or mantra to help them relax. The Chinese martial art of Tai Chi is another specific exercise employees engage in to relax. Unlike other martial arts, Tai Chi does not involve strenuous physical exertion or physical contact. Rather, it focuses on flexibility and the fluidity of body movement.

Fitness and Lifestyle Programs

Awareness of the importance of physical fitness has been increasing, seemingly in conjunction with increased awareness of workplace stress. People who are physically fit are better prepared to meet the challenges and threats faced in their work environments. Companies are aware of this and are focusing significant resources to sponsor employee fitness programs. Many organizations even feature exercise facilities at work to allow employees to use their work breaks to develop physical fitness. Others sponsor health club memberships or make arrangement with local clubs to provide discounts to employees.

Lifestyle programs are more inclusive than fitness programs. Lifestyle programs can be aimed at diet and eating habits, smoking, weight loss, or dealing with work–family pressures. There are many programs available at no cost to the company through local health agencies or from service providers, and these can be conducted in a "Lunch and Learn" format.

Other programs such as smoking cessation clinics have a cost. Some companies sponsor these programs for employees who are able to successfully stop smoking for a specific period of time. This creates a minor incentive to encourage those employees who need that little extra push to change an ingrained habit.

Employee Assistance Programs

Employee Assistance Programs (EAPs) are designed to provide interventions for employees who need help overcoming significant personal problems such as substance abuse, financial difficulties, marital problems and family dysfunctions. These programs began as treatment programs for alcoholism, but have become more inclusive.

EAPs can be delivered in a variety of ways. Some employers have trained counsellors on staff to provide guidance to employees. Others train individual employees as referral agents to guide peers as to where they can seek help. Still others engage the services of professional EAP providers.

Employee Assistance may be provided in cases where an employee's problem has spilled over into the workplace, such as when an employee's alcoholism has led to drinking on the job. However, the intent of EAPs is not to be merely reactive, but to also provide a proactive service where employees can turn for help without any stigma or embarrassment.

The proactive aspect of EAPs has evolved even further to include trauma counselling. In one case, a small private construction company suffered the loss of a founding partner, who died suddenly in his early forties. He was a charismatic leader loved by his employees. The firm engaged the services of an EAP professional to provide grief counselling to employees to help them deal with the sense of loss they felt with the passing of one of their leaders. This trauma counselling parallels what we are seeing in schools that assist students in dealing with such traumas as the loss of a popular student to early childhood disease or major catastrophes like the "9-11" terrorist attacks in the United States.

Social Support

Social interaction creates a bond between workers that is very effective in helping them cope with everyday stresses. The perceived threat created by the boss's style of management can be mitigated when an employee gets to know the boss as a person. "Letting your hair down", as the saying goes, allows people to feel more comfortable around each other and can dramatically reduce the stresses found on the job.

Bonding among employees also helps an individual create a support network to help him or her cope with stress at work. Knowing that others share one's experiences and can be relied on as sounding boards provides a safety valve for workers much in the same way a break in the workday helps them recharge their batteries. Supporting each other emotionally is an important aspect of employees' work lives that is often downplayed.

Companies can promote this through company-sponsored events such as picnics and Christmas parties or through the indirect sponsorship of social club activities.

Job Redesign

When designing jobs, an organization needs to ensure that the work is sufficiently challenging and motivating for its employees. At the other end of the spectrum, the organization has to be careful not to create jobs that are overloaded. As the organization grows, the demands placed on individual employees will change. The demands for more production can increase the workload of an entire department or may be focused on a select group of employees.

For example, a growth in sales in one particular region may impact on the credit department responsible for processing credit applications and approving new customers. If the credit department is organized along geographic lines, the impact of the sales spurt may be felt by only a small number of employees in the department. If only one employee is affected, his or her individual performance may suffer. Reorganizing the workload is an obvious way of dealing with this issue. However, the first trick is to identify the issue. Surprisingly, in this type of scenario, some managers are quick to blame the employee for not keeping up with the demands.

Whenever a shift from the norm occurs in employee performance, the question a manager or supervisor should ask is "What has changed?" Unfortunately, this is a difficult discipline to adopt. A corollary of work redistribution is the question of when to increase staffing levels. The first reaction when the workload increases is to have employees work harder to pick up the slack. However, in today's organizations that purport to be running "lean and mean", there isn't much slack to pick up. It is therefore important to monitor workloads and add staff in a timely fashion.

Managers should keep in mind that new staff members will require a period of time to learn the job and achieve an acceptable level of productivity. Bringing a new employee on board before there is a requirement for a "full-time" equivalent will allow him or her enough time to learn the necessary skills and become proficient in them before the demands become too great.

As workloads increase, an alternative to adding staff is to examine work processes to see if there are more efficient ways to handle them. In manufacturing organizations, the layout of the production facilities can have a dramatic effect on work efficiency. In start-ups, layout is not always an important consideration and many workplaces evolve without any particular direction as the organization grows. These facilities can often be organized in more efficient ways to allow employees to do more in the same amount of time.

Specific Change Management efforts, such as "socio-technical design" initiatives, focus on the relationship between employees and their work. These design efforts examine the technical processes involved in production and the social systems underlying them. The idea is that work should be organized in a way that maximizes production while at the same time optimizing employee interaction and communication. In this way, employees can be more engaged in their work and be better able to solve problems quickly and autonomously. This gives employees the ability to respond quickly to production difficulties and disruptions.

Other job design initiatives focus on employees' need to participate in meaningful ways in their work. The thought behind these efforts is that employees become alienated from their work and work product because the division of labour results in work segments that are too distant from the whole. Employees in this situation do not connect the work they are required to perform with the overall goals and objectives of the organization. As a result, they develop feelings of powerlessness and meaninglessness. In extreme cases, they become removed from the organization's social norms and feel isolated from the organization. Ultimately, this increases the stress placed on them to produce more.

To combat this problem, organizations have employed a number of different job redesign strategies. These include:

- **Job Rotation:** Employees are moved from one job to another on a set schedule to give them variety in the tasks they are able to perform. The jobs they rotate through are often associated with each other and together form a distinct segment of the overall work process. Job rotation allows employees to become multi-skilled over time. In conjunction with self-managing work teams that are empowered to establish the rotation schedule, job rotation can benefit employees by allowing them to be more engaged in the processes of work.

- **Job Enlargement:** Job rotation allows employees to learn different skills by performing in distinctly different jobs. Job enlargement takes the tasks found in different jobs and combines them within one job. It also allows employees to become multi-skilled.

- **Job Enrichment:** Employees will be more engaged and empowered if the work they perform is more meaningful and provides them with opportunities for growth and recognition. Where job enlargement adds different tasks, they are usually of a similar nature in terms of the complexity and skill level required to perform them. Job enrichment adds tasks vertically. In addition to the central responsibility to perform a production task, employees are assigned additional responsibilities to plan, schedule, and coordinate their work with the work of others. Employees may also be given the autonomy to work with others to decide on such things as vacation scheduling and work assignments.

These job redesign strategies look at different aspects of work and try to reconnect employees with the meaningfulness of their work lives. They help to reduce stress by giving employees back a sense of control over a significant part of their lives. They are also intended to demonstrate to employees that the work they do and the contributions they make to the organization are worthwhile.

Management Policies and Practices

Proactive Human Resources practices and policies can have a dramatic impact on reducing stress in the workplace. Some policies are obviously designed to help employees deal specifically with competing demands and thereby reduce the stressors found in their lives. These include policies on flexible work schedules, company-sponsored day-care facilities, vacation policies, and sabbaticals.

Management practices that can reduce employee stress include:

- **Performance Management Processes** — Establishes goals, objectives, and job expectations for the employee and therefore reduce ambiguity. (See Performance Management Process at page 303 *et seq.*)

- **Conflict Resolution Processes** — Provides employees with avenues to redress interpersonal conflicts. (See Conflict Management at page 103 *et seq.*)

- **Employee Orientation** — Ensures new employees are socialized into the cultural norms of the organization and reduces the possibility of conflicting demands being placed on them by supervisors and peers.

- **Attendance Management Programs** — Helps identify employees who are suffering from the effects of stress. (See Attendance Management at page 33 *et seq.*)

- **Job Analysis and Redesign** — See page 433.

- **Anti-Harassment Policies** — Provides employees with emotional support and assurance that they can work in an environment free of harassment.

- **Organizing Work Teams** — Allows individuals to identify with their work and gain a sense of empowerment that allows them to cope with stresses. The team provides emotional support to the individual, and having a common set of goals

helps the employee identify with the product of his or her efforts.

- **Leadership Style** — Leaders learn to adapt their style to the characteristics of a particular situation.

- **Change Management** — Proactive change management strategies are deliberately designed to minimize the impact on employees. The precise objective is to reduce fear and help employees deal with the specific stresses associated with change. Severance policies, for example, are created to ensure that employees who are displaced as a result of organizational changes are well taken care of. Moreover, a progressive severance policy gives some assurance to the surviving employees that the organization they work for is humane and will take care of them in similar circumstances in the future. (See "Downsizing and Survivor Management" in Change Management at page 75.)

Organizational Communication Strategies

Many of the stressors at work can be attributed to poor communication. Employees who are confused by ambiguity in their roles or who are uncertain about the expectations being placed on them simply need someone to communicate with them.

In employee surveys, one of the most common complaints is that the organization needs to improve its communication. Improved communication, especially during times of rapid change, helps reduce employee uncertainty. An effective communication strategy can also increase employee engagement. Employees will feel more involved when they are included in the organization's regular communication. One of the more unfortunate but commonplace events is when an organizational announcement is released to the media before employees have been informed of the event.

Communication strategies have to follow deliberate plans. Organizations should schedule regular meetings with employees to share important information with them. While employees are often flattered when the CEO communicates directly with them, they also want to get regular information from their immediate supervisors. Therefore, effective communication strategies usually cascade information down through a series of open forums.

Supervisors should aim to have short daily communication meetings with their charges. As one moves up the organizational hierarchy, the communication sessions can be longer and less frequent. The supervisor may hold five-minute meetings daily to let the employees know what current events are taking place in the organization. The manager at the next level may attend those meetings weekly for ten minutes, while the manager at the next highest level would only attend monthly. The top person in the business unit should attempt to share monthly business results with employees. This helps employees connect their efforts with the goals and objectives of the business.

By having an established communication protocol, employees become accustomed to receiving information and participating in the process. This reduces uncertainty and increases the psychological contract between employees and the organization. It helps employees put meaning into their efforts at work. It also ensures there are no surprises. Employees who are kept informed are able to accept change more readily. They are also less prone to participate in the rumour mill. Rumours, although often based loosely on fact, can be very damaging because they may breed suspicion and distrust among employees. The best way to dispel rumours is through proactive communication.

Communication is a two-way process. A full strategy will include avenues for bottom-up communication. This may include instituting employee opinion surveys and suggestion programs. Employee attitudes should be monitored continuously to determine if organizational changes are leading to increased stress levels or a decline in morale.

Physical Work Environment

As more is being learned about work life, more attention is being paid to the physical work environment. Some work environments cannot be altered because of the nature of the work being performed. Still, other steps can be taken to mitigate the damaging effects of the environment on an employee's psyche. In harsh environments, employers obviously need to equip employees with personal protective equipment to shield them from the hazards of the environment. In extreme conditions, allowing the employees frequent breaks will help to reduce the stressful impact of the environment.

Where the stressful impact of the work environment can be reduced, it should be. While this may seem like a given, many managers have difficulty equating an investment in improved lighting, reduced noise, or ergonomically correct workstations with a return in terms of reduced absenteeism and improved productivity.

Person-to-Job Match

Sometimes an employee may simply be in the wrong job. The ability to cope with stress in the workplace is very much an individual thing. Employees without the right disposition or skill set will find a certain position stressful, while those who are well-matched to the requirements will find the position challenging and rewarding. Using the right assessment tools will help to ensure that candidates are well-matched to the demands of the job. Being well-matched goes beyond having the right training and qualifications. Assessment tools like behavioural profiles will match the behavioural demands of the job to the personality traits of the individual. This type of matching is a better predictor of success then mere interviewing techniques and will help an organization avoid placing individuals in positions they will find inordinately stressful. (See also Recruitment and Selection at page 351 *et seq.*)

When an employee is placed in a job that does not match his or her innate abilities, he or she must expend a lot of energy to fulfil the role demanded of him or her. Using this energy will leave him or her emotionally exhausted and unable to cope with other stressors, such as family demands. This is a particularly problematic situation because the outward manifestations of stress may appear to be rooted in a problem outside of the workplace. As a result, the true root cause at work may go undetected and a cycle of growing distress will be created. Assessment tools are surprisingly reliable in identifying situations where an individual is acting in a role that goes against his or her natural behavioural tendencies.

Role of the Human Resources Practitioner

The Human Resources practitioner will play the central role in dealing with the problems of stress in the workplace. This role has several facets. First, the practitioner is responsible for measuring the impact of stress. This is accomplished through maintaining a database of metrics that will include absenteeism rates, usage of disability plans (and premium costs), Workers' Compensation experience ratings, injury frequencies and employee productivity (see Human Resources Metrics at page 185 *et seq.*). Next, Human Resources practitioners provide an avenue for employees to raise concerns about issues that may be causing undue stress, such as harassment or bullying. The practitioner is expected to act as an impartial ombudsman to investigate such complaints.

Practitioners are also expected to initiate proactive programming to provide employees with assistance in developing coping mechanisms. Practitioners should coordinate the development of an EAP and facilitate "Lunch and Learn" sessions. In short, they should be a resource for employees to gain access to programming.

A primary responsibility of the Human Resources practitioner is always to ensure organizational policies are in place that meet the needs of both the organization and its employees. It is the practitioner's role to introduce policies related to vacations, work breaks, shift scheduling, emergency leave, and a host of other policies. In fulfilling this aspect of the role, the practitioner needs to go beyond simple compliance with the relevant employment standards legislation and ensure that the policies meet the needs of the organization's employees. As the cultural environment shifts, the Human Resources practitioner is in a position to stay ahead of trends and meet emerging employee needs long before legislation catches up.

While all of the above are important, the most dramatic effect the practitioner can have on reducing employee stress is to ensure that the basic tools of Human Resources management are in place and are being used effectively. Principal among these are:

- Performance Management Process;

- Recruitment and Selection Practices;

- Employee Orientation Programs;

- Job Evaluations and Job Descriptions;

- Job Analysis and Design;

- Employee Communication Strategies; and

- Change Management Strategies.

In combination with teaching employees how to cope better with stress and providing them with outlets to deal with conflicts, these basic tools can create a very positive work environment where stress is viewed as a mere challenge to be faced and overcome.

Barriers to Success/Common Pitfalls

The greatest barrier to successfully introducing stress management initiatives into an organization is a general disbelief among managers that the problem is real, or that it has a significant impact on every organization. Stress is very real and no one is immune. Objectively examining the root causes of stress in the workplace will help any organization reap benefits in terms of productivity and morale.

The sources of stress are quite varied and therefore a comprehensive strategy is needed to combat its adverse effects. However, dealing with stress as a stand-alone phenomenon tends to turn senior managers off. By virtue of the status they have attained and the challenges these individuals have faced, they have demonstrated an innate ability to cope with stress. As a result, they are often sceptical about how significant the phenomenon really is.

Notwithstanding this scepticism, they do understand the specific problems associated with stress. It is an easier sell to convince them of the need for more sophisticated management practices, such as performance management tools and job redesign, than to convince them of the need for a stress management initiative. They are also more inclined to attack measurable problems like absenteeism and safety. Finding a metric related to stress alone may prove difficult and is unnecessary. Surrogate issues like days lost will suffice to convince senior management that the issue needs to be addressed.

Since a comprehensive approach is necessary, practitioners need to avoid over-selling any particular initiative. When all the statistics are added up in terms of absenteeism, for example — absenteeism due to smoking, substance abuse, tending to family emergencies, short-term and long-term disabilities, and so on — the results show that organizations "save" several times the number of actual days lost. In other words, there is a fair amount of double counting going on and claims for the success rates of various programs tend to be exaggerated. The practitioner should guard against promising too much of any particular initiative.

While specific programs such as EAPs or health club sponsorships will form a part of a strategy to mitigate the impact of stress, the practitioner will gain more credibility by focusing efforts on specific management processes such as attendance management and performance management. Sound Human Resources practices will have the greatest impact on reducing stress in the workplace and carry many other benefits as well. Staying focused helps Human Resources practitioners maintain credibility and helps them to deliver positive organizational results.

TERMINATIONS

Definition/Background

Whenever the employment relationship between an organization and an employee ceases to exist, it can be said that the contract of employment has been terminated. There are many different ways that a contract can come to an end, however. Many terminations are voluntary on the part of the employee. The employee, for example, may quit to take a position elsewhere or choose to retire. In the case of a fixed term contract of employment, the contract may merely expire.

An unfortunate part of human resource management, however, is that organizations must on occasion bring employment relationships to an end. Decisions to terminate employees are never easy and, in some cases (too many, in fact), the decision is often delayed. Employees may be let go because of incompetence, misconduct, reorganization of the business or because of an economic downturn. Other terminations do not fit neatly into any of these categories, but are motivated by an organizational shift in culture or by the realization that the fit between the employee and the organization is no longer a good one.

Terminations play a big part in the role of the human resources practitioner. When an employee quits, it may be a signal that the human resources management practices that are in place are not working as expected. At a minimum, a resignation triggers the need to conduct an exit interview to determine whether or not changes in practices need to be made.

Even normal retirements should be considered in terms of developing policies and mechanisms to cope with the impact on the organization. Since the retirement is a planned event, the human resources practitioner should, in addition to developing retirement income and benefit plans, be proactive in planning for succession.

The most problematic terminations, however, are the ones driven by the organization. When the organization decides to end an employment contract, the impact on the organization is traumatic. It is never easy to inform an employee that their services will no longer be required. If not handled properly, the impact can dramatically reduce the morale and productivity of other employees. Poorly handled terminations can also result in litigation, in the form of either lawsuits or actions taken through government tribunals.

Terminating an employment relationship is almost always an expensive proposition. Prudent human resources practitioners will take steps to manage the costs by reducing the incidence of unplanned terminations and establishing policies on the handling of terminations to minimize other negative consequences.

It is important for the human resources practitioner to distinguish among the many different reasons for terminating an employee's position. Often, a termination is labelled part of a reorganization, to avoid spelling out the real reasons. Reorganizations do not take place very often at most organizations. When they do, they almost by definition involve more then one position. More common are terminations that happen because the employee is no longer considered a good fit for the organization or because the performance of the employee has not kept pace with the changing expectations of the organization.

Terminations for cause gain more media attention because they often result in a legal dispute between the organization and the employee. In some instances, the organization has alleged cause when none exists. The problem, in part, is that terminating "with cause" has become increasingly hard to defend in the courts. However, another part of the problem is that practitioners have difficulty themselves in distinguishing between a poor organizational fit and cause.

Less frequent are actual cases of "constructive dismissal". This term refers to unilateral actions taken by the company that would be construed by any reasonable person as an attempt to terminate or frustrate the employment relationship. Organizations have become quite aware of this and tend to guard against it. Employees still question certain decisions by organizations as having the potential of being construed as "constructive dismissal" but the actual incidence of the phenomenon has become dramatically reduced over the years through better human resource management practices and a general awareness of the concept.

This chapter will focus on terminations for cause and those motivated by a bad fit between the organization and the employee. Terminations driven by reorganization, redundancy and economic downturns are handled elsewhere in this work.

Just Cause

Terminations for cause include gross misconduct, dereliction of duty and incompetence. The behaviour in question must be extreme to be sufficiently serious to be considered as a breach of the contract. Some examples are more or less obvious. The following types of misconduct almost always justify terminations for cause:

- theft or embezzlement;

- violence in the workplace;

- criminal acts in the workplace;

- criminal acts outside the workplace that damage the employer's reputation;

- repeated acts of harassment against other employees;

- dishonesty;

- gross insubordination;

- significant violations of corporate policies;

- sabotage; and

- conflicts of interest.

Theft is almost always considered sufficient cause for termination. It represents an irreparable breach of the trust necessary between an employee and the employer. Still, the existence of certain factors can sometimes mitigate in the employee's favour. A long serving employee who takes a few office supplies home has stolen from the company. However, the breach is not necessarily beyond repair. The severity of the "crime", the employee's record of service and position, the nature of the employment relationship all need to be factored into a decision to terminate. An employee with a fiduciary duty to the employer, for example, will be held to a much higher standard than is applied to other employees. Employees will also be held to a higher standard in environments susceptible to losses through theft and where trust is therefore of paramount importance.

Organizations need to take care when terminating an employee for something as serious as theft. Although the burden of proof does not necessarily have to meet the standard of "beyond a reasonable doubt" applied in criminal cases, there must be clear and cogent evidence that more than meets the standard of "on the balance of probabilities". Some employers opt to file criminal charges that, if proven, will discharge the onus in a civil action. Others, however, are loath to file criminal charges for fear that any publicity could undermine public confidence in the organization's security measures.

Another consideration when deciding whether to terminate an employee for serious misconduct, particularly criminal misconduct, is the representations the organization might have to make to a third party regarding the employee's dismissal. Organizations are shielded from liability when providing references for former employees, provided the statements are made in good faith. But if the grounds for termination cannot meet the burden of proof required in a potential litigation, the organization may want to avoid making any statements about the dismissal at all.

If, on the other hand, the employer is aware of gross misconduct that brings the employee's character into question and this misconduct has the potential to affect the individual's employability, the employer has a duty to inform any potential future employers of the risk. For example, if a firm's accountant was dismissed for embezzling money and that accountant then applied to a bank for a senior position handling accounts, the former employer would be seriously remiss not to inform the new organization of the past misconduct.

Even where theft has been proven, there are a few cases where mitigating factors have convinced arbitrators and courts that termination was too severe. These cases are rare and usually involve some proven mental illness. However, practitioners should provide ample time and opportunity to employees who stand accused of gross misconduct to bring forth anything that might mitigate in their favour.

Violence in the workplace is becoming all too common. The decision to terminate an employee who has acted violently towards others in the workplace must be weighed against the degree of violence exhibited, the damage done or injury inflicted, and the employee's service and record of conduct. Organizations have both an implicit and explicit duty of care. It is expected that employers will take all reasonable steps to protect the health and safety of all employees. Hence, there is a distinct onus on the organization to reduce violence in the workplace. Similarly the organization must ensure that all employees enjoy a work environment that is free from harassment and other behaviours that infringe on their rights to a work environment free of discrimination. However anti-harassment policies have to be written and implemented with a certain degree of caution. Some acts are of such a nature that a mere warning to the offender is sufficient to prevent a recurrence. Others are so egregious that a single act may warrant termination of the offender. Organizations need to be astute in balancing the rights and interests of all parties in a fair and open manner.

Other types of criminal or quasi-criminal behaviours are usually considered as cause for termination (with the caveats outlined above). There has to be clear and cogent evidence that the employee committed the alleged act and the act caused irreparable harm to the organization. The behaviour does not have to be limited to that engaged in during working hours or acts directly against the organization. Serious misconduct outside of the work environment which harms the organization's reputation or which reflects on the employee's character to such a degree as to undermine the organization's confidence in the employee may also be considered as just cause for terminating the employment relationship.

Sabotage includes deliberate acts that are intended to disrupt operations. Loosening the screws on a machine so that it won't work is a clear example of sabotage. However, sabotage can take more subtle forms. For example, an employee may fix a bid on a project in such a way that the organization will not be awarded the contract. A manager's consistent and overt attempts to resist changes initiated by the organization or to actively disrupt the culture are very subtle forms of sabotage that may, nevertheless, be considered cause for termination.

Dereliction of duty occurs when an employee fails to act with due diligence in the exercise of his or her role and that failure results in a significant loss to the organization. A clear example would be a security guard who sleeps on the job while the place is being robbed.

Incompetence is one of the most difficult things to prove. An employee may be incompetent in the eyes of the employer, but even demonstrated incompetence can fail to pass the test for "just cause" termination. A cut and dried case of incompetence would be where someone cites a specific qualification on his or her résumé that he or she did not actually possess. (This misconduct also involves misrepresentation and dishonesty.) Sometimes, however, incompetence manifests itself because of the employer's actions. These could include promoting the individual beyond the level of his or her ability, or introducing processes or systems that the individual cannot cope with. In these instances, the employer bears the onus of mitigating the impact on the employee.

Without Cause

Most employment terminations are made without cause. In part, this is due to the fact that proving cause has become quite onerous. For the most part, however, the organization simply does not have legal grounds to terminate the employment relationship without compensating the employee for the breach. In legal jargon, these terminations have become known as "wrongful dismissals". Unfortunately, in practice this turns out to be a misnomer.

A dismissal motivated by bad faith or because of a prohibited ground under human rights legislation would be clearly wrongful (and one hopes these instances are becoming more rare). More often than not, the only thing wrongful about a termination is the amount of compensation offered in order to sever the relationship. In other words, how much money will it take to get rid of the employee? An organization's decision to terminate an employee because he or she is deemed to no longer fit into the organization's culture is almost always the right decision. The only question to be answered is what the cost is going to be.

The Ten Per Centers

Recently, there has been some discussion in Human Resources circles regarding the concept of removing the bottom 10% of employees in terms of performance. This is the group that falls on the left tail of the bell curve. Fans of Jack Welch, the former CEO of General Electric ("GE"), will know this group as the "C" players.

Welch insisted every manager be graded rigorously according to what he termed the "vitality curve". On this curve, "A" players consistently make their numbers and embody the values of GE. These are typically the top 20% of the employee population and are the organization's *de facto* leaders. The "B" players make up the bulk of the population and either make the numbers or live the values of the organization. Over time, they can be assisted in achieving both. The bottom 10% are the "C" players who neither meet their numbers nor live the organization's values. Welch believed that these people had to be removed — quickly.

To keep the organization vital, in Welch's view, the bottom 10% have to be continually pruned. This view earned him the nickname "Neutron Jack". Despite this reputation, Welch saw himself as primarily a people manager. He estimated that 60% of his time was spent choosing, developing and firing people. He personally interviewed every single candidate for the top 500 positions at GE.

One thing that particularly bothered Welch was "false kindness". He coined this term to describe failing to fire someone who is incompetent. The fallacy of false kindness is that it prolongs an untenable situation that causes those who work under the incompetent manager to suffer from mismanagement, and the organization as a whole fails to achieve its goals. The manager himself or herself suffers by not being able to achieve self-actualization.

Welch was extremely successful in turning GE around and dramatically improving its market value. He has become a hero among CEOs and those who aspire to run large organizations. His views have been popularized in the media, as well as through his own books about his life at GE. However, there are many who view Welch's opinions as too extreme and believe they should be tempered in practice. Human resources practitioners in particular find that Welch's views run counter to their beliefs regarding good people management practices. Those who favour Welch's opinion have one overriding argument that trumps all others: he was incredibly successful. The market value of GE went from $13 billion when he took the helm in 1981 to $400 billion when he retired in 2000. He must have been doing many things right.

What are the arguments against Welch's people management practices? From a practical point of view, one of the first considerations might be the cost. As any human resources practitioner knows, it is very difficult to prove a case for cause with a long-term employee. The "ten per centers" who need to be culled are typically longer-term employees. (Short-term employees who are "C" players clearly have to be removed quickly. A new employee who can neither embrace the organization's values nor perform to meet their goals and objectives is a bad hire. This represents a problem with the recruiting process that should be addressed as soon as it is identified.)

Longer-term employees may have been continually promoted until they reached a level where they can no longer perform at their optimum level. This has become known as the "Peter Principle". The actual problem is even more complicated. As time passes, the job requirements change, new technologies, systems and processes may be introduced, and the individual may have difficulty keeping up. The speed of change today can be incredible. There is a distinct onus on the organization to provide the training and support to help employees cope with these changes and to keep their skills current. However, there is also an individual responsibility to take steps to manage one's own career and keep pace with the changing environment.

The human resources practitioner's instinct is to have a counselling session with all individuals whose performances are falling short and to clearly define the deficiencies. Then, an action plan to correct the deficiencies is identified, with appropriate milestones put in place to check the individual's progress. The timeline for improvement is dependent on the individual's tenure and the level of responsibility of the position they hold. For a long service employee, a year would not be unreasonable.

Using the "rule of thumb" of one month's severance pay for every year of service, letting these employees go would not be cheap. It may, therefore, seem prudent to spend the time and resources to correct the problem rather than terminating the employee. As well, taking these steps will create a case for termination should the efforts ultimately fail.

Unfortunately such efforts typically do fail, because there are so many intangibles that have led to the individual becoming a poor fit. The right individuals, the "A" and "B" players, do not let their skills and competencies slide. They are flexible and adapt easily to new situations. Even with the proper documentation from counselling for substandard performance, the practitioner will recognize that proving cause for incompetence will still be an uphill climb. Usually, courts are looking for wilful misconduct or dereliction of duty. In the absence of these conditions, even when an organization believes it has cause for termination, most practitioners (including Neutron Jack himself) would advise the organization to provide a generous payout. The real purpose of counselling in these situations is to ease the individual and the organization into the realization that a fit no longer exists.

Clearly, the organization has to assess the "opportunity cost" of not acting sooner. During the improvement period, the organization suffers from continued substandard productivity and has to expend resources to support the underachiever. Moreover, when the individual is a manager, the diminished productivity extends to the department the manager oversees. Morale deteriorates and the organization may risk losing some "A" and "B" players who do not wish to work under an incompetent manager. These people do not always have the patience to wait for a turnaround. The theory is that this opportunity cost invariably far outweighs the cost of terminating the poor performer. To not act is not an option for any organization that wishes to compete at a world-class level.

The time spent trying to rehabilitate the poor performer is not only costly, it is often not effective. The employee who was a good fit 20 years ago, who is not a good fit now, has failed to recognize the shifting environment around them. These employees often do not have the flexibility to adapt under any circumstances. This does not necessarily make them unemployable, but it does indicate that the best thing for them and the organization is that they continue their career development elsewhere. Surprisingly, many individuals who are displaced from an organization go on to other opportunities better suited to their competencies, and where they are able to thrive amid change. In smaller or weaker organizations, their experiences and abilities may be welcome additions.

One of the difficulties in arriving at a decision to terminate these employees is that managers may feel "organizational guilt". Perhaps, had the organization identified the individual's weaknesses earlier, the action plan for performance improvement could have

been more effective. Or, had the organization been able to measure competencies more scientifically, it would have made better decisions regarding promotions and avoided putting the individual in a position to fail. These are legitimate concerns and are very often true root causes for the inadvertent development of "C" players, but they do not justify perpetuating the problem and hurting the organization and other employees. They do justify the generous treatment of the departing employee. In addition to severance costs, decision makers may also want to consider including outplacement counselling as part of the termination package.

Many practitioners also have difficulty with the notion of grading managers on a bell curve. Even those who accept the concept fully have difficulty in convincing their internal clients that the results of performance assessments fall within a normal distribution. They should be assured that, by definition, measurable behaviours like performance will be distributed evenly around an average. When charted, this distribution takes the shape of a bell. This is not a matter of opinion nor is it an arbitrary construct employed to manage a process. It is an empirical observation and a statistical reality.

One of the problems in applying this statistical reality to work performance is the concept of average performance. For many people, "average" connotes a mediocre or even poor performance. People do not like to be considered "average". In fact, with any population being graded, half the people will be above average and half the people will be below. Unless the population of the group being measured is very small, the distribution of grades must resemble a bell curve. Otherwise the grading system would be suspect.

This is the heart of the matter. Many performance management systems suffer from grade inflation because managers are reluctant to grade anyone as being average or below average. This is one of many reasons why good performance management systems are built around objective measures of performance and why human resources practitioners use the term "making your numbers". Using numbers makes the employment of statistical methods easy, as well as difficult to refute.

While many elements of managerial performance are difficult to measure or put into reliable numbers, leading edge practitioners insist on forcing a normal distribution of the performance management results to ensure the integrity of the system. This means putting systems in place that ensure performance evaluations are subject to rigorous review across many levels of the organization. These systems have to be designed to introduce an element of consistency in the grading. Essentially, they involve creating an ongoing dialogue and developing a sense of discipline around the critical evaluation of employee strengths and weaknesses at the managerial level.

One method for forcing this distribution of grades is to have open succession planning discussions and a review of the "C" players at the senior management level. While this may introduce some degree of subjectivity into the system, it helps create a dialogue around expected performance and to develop a buy-in to the culture of high performance. In these sessions senior managers are forced to bring forward a list of their "C" players and to prepare a discussion as to what should be done with them. Their lists will be subject to the scrutiny of others who will be allowed to question any exclusion from the list.

Another one of the biggest concerns regarding culling "ten per centers" is its impact on the organization's culture. Practitioners may fear that institutionalizing such a practice will create a culture of fear that might manifest itself in all kinds of undesirable behaviours. When people are afraid that their positions might be eliminated if their performance falls off, instead of working to improve themselves and their work, they may seek to hide performance deficiencies or "cook" the books.

The problem here is one of perspective. The objective of culling the bottom 10% is not to provide motivation to others. The "A" and "B" players, after all, do not need motivating. Instead, the practitioner should look at the exercise as analogous to managing a sports team. Some players' skills may be sufficient to get by but will not help the team get into the playoffs and win the championship. The team has to trade these players or face elimination. The goal is to create a culture of winning and success. The "C" player is a major barrier to creating this culture.

Getting rid of the "C" players is a downside activity. It is painful and difficult but it must be done. The upside is to replace them with top performers who can bring energy and vitality to the organization and help it grow. This creates a positive and energized environment for everyone. Instead of a culture of fear, then, this type of management style creates a culture of success. Still, one should be aware that at some point the organization will need to put systems in place to ensure that it attracts and retains top performers only. In this way, the need to cull poor performers will be reduced dramatically over time. Unless the culture of success is actively promoted and maintained, complacency will creep back into the organization.

Benefits/Expected Outcomes

There are many benefits to having a written termination policy. These include:

- reduced exposure to litigation;
- improved morale from increased organizational performance and from policies which protect the interests of employees;
- improved productivity; and
- reduced losses from employee misconduct.

Simply put, a written termination policy sends a powerful message regarding the organization's standards of conduct and expectations of performance. When done right, this can create the culture of success discussed above. Employees are reassured when the organization has policies that protect employee interests.

Senior executives often negotiate "golden parachutes" into their employment contracts. These are generous severance arrangements that protect the executive from the downside impact of a change of ownership in the firm or a change in senior management. The rationale behind this is that by protecting the executive, he or she will always act in the interests of the firm, even when doing so may be contrary to his or her own interests.

A similar effect occurs when all employees are aware of the company's policy to protect them if there is an extraordinary event that will affect their employment. It can create a sense of fairness and let all employees know how departing employees are being treated. It is essential that employees who are being let go for reasons other than cause be treated with dignity. Employees who sue their former employers often do so because of hurt feelings.

Having a written policy that forms part of every employee's contract of employment can also save the company money. Without a written policy, the practitioner must formulate a severance package for each departing employee. Often, the employer will err on the generous side in order to reduce the possibility of litigation. A written policy allows the organization to pay a smaller amount, provided it is accepted by employees and exceeds the minimum standards dictated by the relevant legislation.

Having a written policy defining what might constitute termination for cause, sets a tone for what is and what is not acceptable behaviour within the organization. It will also reinforce the ethical standards of the organization. Written policies do act as deterrents, so the incidence of misconduct as a rule should decrease.

Programming/Implementation

The first step in implementing a termination policy is to get a consensus from senior management as to what they want to do and what statements they want to make about the organization's culture. This begins with the senior human resources practitioner who prepares and delivers an educational seminar on what is involved in employee terminations.

Because culling bottom performers remains controversial, the practitioner should anticipate significant dialogue on the subject. However, poor performers must be addressed in some manner. An important element of the Performance Management Process is the ongoing dialogue regarding succession planning, top performers, fast-trackers and poor performers. At a minimum, the organization will want corrective action plans for the poor performers. It stands to reason that these action plans will include the possibility of termination if the corrective steps are not successful.

The outcome of this meeting with senior management will be to establish the ongoing process of discussing performance and dealing with any problems as they occur. As well, the senior management team will dictate what form the termination policies will take. The practitioner should then draft the policy statements and employment contracts, as applicable, and seek final approval for implementing the new policies.

With respect to employment contracts, it is simply not advisable to try to enforce a new employment contract on existing employees. The recommended approach is, rather, to include severance clauses on all future employment contracts. In some instances, these may be extended to employees who are being offered significant promotions, but the practitioner is well advised to tread carefully in this regard. (See also Contracts, Employment at page 125 *et seq.*)

Policies regarding arrangements are usually less controversial but the practitioner might expect senior employees to object. In many instances, senior staff are made exempt from these policies and alternate arrangements are worked out with them.

The human resources department will also want to provide some degree of training for managers in conducting termination interviews. This training is best delivered on a just-in-time basis. On the flip side, human resources practitioners should be well versed in how to handle these situations with dignity and fairness.

Role of the Human Resources Practitioner

The role of the human resources practitioner is first and foremost to oversee all employee terminations, thereby protecting the organization's interests and limiting its exposure to third party actions and liability. Moreover, if an organization is going to accept the notion of culling the bottom performers on a continuous basis, the practitioner has to take responsibility for putting systems in place to monitor performance.

Achieving a balance between employee advocacy and serving the interests of the organization can be difficult because of this. Human resources practitioners do not relish the role they must play in employee terminations. It clearly runs against the grain of acting as an employee advocate and it means that human resources practitioners can be feared and mistrusted by employees. It can be argued that by ensuring that employee misconduct is controlled and performance standards are maintained at a world-class level, the practitioner helps to create an environment in which all employees can thrive. Some employees, those who harass others or infringe on their rights, must be terminated in order to protect other employees.

It is also the human resources practitioner's role to ensure the employee receives fair treatment when a decision is made to terminate his or her position. Protecting the person's job is not in the interest of the organization nor is it ultimately in the employee's interest. The practitioner's role should not be to perpetuate a bad situation through the exercise of "false kindness", even when the employee believes this may be in his or her best interests. While some readers may think it is a stretch to call this behaviour altruistic, the practitioner helps both the organization and the individual out by ending a non-productive relationship.

Included in the practitioner's role are the following activities:

- establishing rules and policies to define employee misconduct and its consequences;

- establishing policies governing severance packages including compensation and outplacement assistance (for terminations due to reorganizations, economic downturns and for any reason other than "cause");

- establishing contractual arrangements that contemplate possible termination of employment;

- reviewing all proposed terminations to ensure legislative and policy compliance and vetoing those that put the organization at risk of successful litigation or human rights violations;

- establishing performance management systems to identify poor performers and action plans to deal with substandard performance where appropriate;

- counselling managers on how to conduct termination interviews and accompanying the manager at the interview;

- reviewing and responding to demand letters from terminated employees or their counsel regarding severance packages; and

- coordinating the organization's defense in allegations of wrongful dismissal.

Establishing rules defining employee misconduct may seem unnecessarily redundant. Everyone knows that stealing from your employer is wrong. Presumably, we also know that taking illegal drugs into the workplace is also wrong. The rules are not intended to tell employees things that they should already know. Rather, by setting out these rules explicitly in writing, the practitioner establishes a standard for employee behaviour within the organization. Rules give the majority of employees a feeling of security by assuring them that the organization is willing to take steps to protect its interests and the interests of its employees. Moreover, by putting rules in writing, the organization can also forewarn employees of the consequences of breaking them. This can help to counter arguments of mitigating factors. If the employees are clearly aware of the consequences of misconduct, then there are very few excuses available to them.

Some organizations establish policies regarding the termination of employees "without cause". These policies outline the amount of notice and severance that the employee might receive, the benefits they can expect to continue, along with any other assistance they might be provided with. In the case of unionized employees, this type of policy will be enshrined in the collective agreement. For others, the policy will usually be contained in an employee handbook that is considered part of the employee's contract of employment. Still others establish their policies by including severance provisions in specific employment contracts. The advantage of this latter approach is that it allows the organization to tailor the severance provision to the individual, thus avoiding the "one size fits all" approach.

Practitioners should insist that the organization give them enough authority to block any termination that is being entered into in bad faith or which is motivated by grounds that are prohibited by legislation. Fortunately, instances like these are rare. Unfortunately, when they do occur, the offending manager usually acts without consulting human resources. Nevertheless, by establishing a policy that all terminations must be reviewed by the human resources practitioner, the organization can hold the manager accountable in instances where they violate the policy.

Once the idea is accepted that every organization has poor performers who it should get rid of, the human resources practitioner should facilitate an ongoing dialogue regarding "C" players. This means ensuring every consideration is given to the factors that may have led to the employee's poor performance so that any decision to terminate is not made in haste. The practitioner also needs to ensure that managers are not overly protective of these poor performers and that the managers understand that the employees will be treated with dignity and care.

Barriers to Success/Common Pitfalls

The first barrier to creating an effective termination policy is that terminating anyone is an emotional and potentially traumatic experience for a manager. It is, therefore, not surprising that managers are resistant to doing it.

Legislation and civil jurisprudence regarding "wrongful" dismissal are not barriers to terminating employees. There is a popular view that it has become more difficult to terminate an employee, but this is not the case. What has happened is that, in the absence of "just and sufficient" cause, it has become more costly to end an employment contract. In other words, the cost of doing business has increased.

The law, therefore, forces businesses to carefully consider the costs versus the benefits of terminating an employee. However, managers do not readily understand this concept and often find it easier not to act at all. This occurs not just with employees whose performance has slipped over time but can also be witnessed in cases of employee misconduct where the organization may have cause to terminate the employee without notice or compensation. Small indiscretions may go unpunished and create an atmosphere where a certain level of misconduct is inadvertently condoned. This is very dangerous for an organization and can have a significant impact on its culture. It also reduces the organization's chances of demonstrating cause.

Employment law is becoming increasingly complex. Many practitioners themselves have a difficult time keeping up with the ever evolving jurisprudence and constantly changing legislation. Educating managers on the complexities of employment law is not necessary. Instead the practitioner should establish simple policies for managers to follow, allowing them to act without contravening the law of the land.

One of the most common barriers to having an effective termination policy and process is the quality of the performance management system. Senior practitioners who have accepted the challenges of turn-around situations are often faced with having to terminate employees who are not only unaware that their performance is considered substandard, but have even been told that they are performing well. When the performance management system works, employees can come to the decision that their employment has to be severed before the organization does. By nature, people want to succeed at what they do for a living. When employees are led through the performance management process to understand why they are not succeeding, they will likely be more willing to accept the organization's ultimate decision to terminate them.

When a termination policy is first introduced, there is a significant risk that some employees will reject the established severance portion of the policy. Senior managers in particular may feel that they would fair better in the absence of a policy. The practitioner should ensure that the policies are introduced at a time when employees can be offered some consideration for accepting the change in policy. Salary increase time is usually a good time. The practitioner may also want to consider reducing any potential controversy by exempting employees in senior posts.

(See also Employment Cycle, at page 149 *et seq.*)

TURNOVER

Definition/Background

Employee turnover rates are important in Human Resources planning partly because of their effect on demand and supply forecasts and partly because they may be indicators of other problems, such as poor motivation.

Turnover is defined as the number of employees who leave employment over a specified period. A turnover index allows comparison between areas of the organization and with other organizations; this is the number of employees leaving in a period divided by the average number employed during that period, expressed as a percentage. Thus, a company with an average employment of 100 and a turnover of 45, would have a turnover rate of 45%.

However, this turnover index can mask serious differences in the stability of different parts of the organization. The example above could have been made up of 45 different departing employees, leaving only 55 with more than a year's service, or 99 who did not change and one who was replaced 45 times, or any combination within the limits of these figures. Stability is clearly higher in the second example than the first. The stability index is calculated as the number of employees with a year or more of service divided by the total employed one year ago, expressed as a percentage.

Employee turnover should be examined by relevant employee categories, not only of the grade or skill level but also by department and locations. The crude figures have some value but should be further analyzed to explain why people have left. First, look at those figures where reasons are available from the act of leaving itself. These include the following:

— death;

— retirement, which may be normal, early at the organization's initiative, through ill health, or early at employee's request;

— redundancy;

— dismissal, which is capable of being broken down into a number of headings (e.g., just cause, frustration of contract, abandonment of position);

— transfer, to other parts of the organization in or outside the country;

— temporary leave, for example, pregnancy; and

— resignation.

Employee turnover should be examined by relevant employee categories, not only of the grade or skill level but also by department and location.

The final category is capable of providing very useful information, if a system is set up to capture the reasons why people resign. This needs care in design; otherwise it will generate the wrong reasons. For example, it is easy for a manager, if asked, to quote pay as the reason for resignation, while the truth is that the employee disliked the manager. Actual reasons can be classified to suit the needs of the organization. Exit interviews can be a useful way to determine the actual reason(s) an employee resigned. A Human Resources practitioner should conduct exit interviews, as employees may be reluctant to be completely candid with their supervisors.

When interpreting ratios, it is important to consider the nature of the industry and national turnover levels. Some industries, because of low pay and limited chances for advancement, expect to have very high rates of turnover. There may be little that the Human Resources practitioner can do to reduce this. The retail sector, in particular, faces this challenge, and designs its Human Resources policies and practices to accommodate this reality. In the high-tech sector, high turnover has become a way of life despite escalating pay. Here innovative practices such as offering stock options at all levels of the organization have been employed.

However, once external contributing factors and internal structural issues are accounted for, the measure of turnover can be a valid and significant indicator of management performance and the effectiveness of Human Resources policies and practices.

Benefits/Expected Outcomes

With the exception of reasons for resignation, all the elements needed for the analysis of employee turnover should be easy to gather and regularly monitored. Data should be separated into meaningful employee groups so that specific problem areas can be isolated. Measuring turnover rates is an inexpensive way to monitor employee morale and to detect any "management" problems early.

Unwanted employee turnover is expensive for the organization in terms of recruitment and training costs and the lower productivity of new employees. The expected benefits of lower turnover rates can be set against the costs of any measures to improve the situation, to allow an economic judgment to be made. The organization needs a means of measuring turnover. "What gets measured gets managed."

Unlike other measures, there is no single right level of turnover. Zero turnover is not only impossible but also undesirable. Organizations need to have some level of turnover to ensure a healthy inflow of new ideas to counter the onset of groupthink. Each organization will have to determine its own optimal level of turnover based on the industry in which it operates and its Human Resources Management philosophies.

Implementation and Mechanisms

The key to meaningful information is having a Human Resources Information System that will allow a breakdown of information into useful categories. Without this, figures can be produced manually. This may make it more difficult to manipulate the statistics to gain further insight into the real problems and issues.

Statistics should be reported regularly. In addition to useful employment categories, the stability and turnover indexes can be presented by length of service.

Ensure that attention is focused on the figures that matter. If only gross figures are discussed with management and there has been an increase due to a downsizing initiative, it may be too easy to rationalize the total turnover as a result of the reorganization. Detailed analysis might show that there are other reasons that should be addressed. Reports should highlight the areas that need attention.

When comparing the indexes with those of the industry, it is of more value to compare the organization with the best, rather than the average, in the industry. Comparisons of indexes in this way show that improvement is possible. A full benchmarking study might be considered which would provide an

understanding of how to improve. Many larger Human Resources consulting firms have developed databases to assist organizations with these comparisons.

Provided the information system exists, there is little additional cost to the employment turnover analysis. Where cost benefit analysis may be important is in the justification of actions to reduce turnover and increase stability. The costs of the turnover should be calculated, as this will enable the benefit from the improvement to be assessed. The final part of the equation is to set realistic targets for improvement.

Role of the Human Resources Practitioner

The Human Resources practitioner is responsible for making sure the turnover statistics are gathered and analyzed. The practitioner needs to interpret the results of the analysis in the context of other information. It is important that the practitioner ensures that turnover statistics are not held up alone to prove managerial effectiveness.

The practitioner should conduct exit interviews with all employees who have resigned. This will provide good information as to the reasons they have chosen to leave the organization. This will ensure better analysis.

The practitioner also needs to ensure that other measures of employee satisfaction are taken. These may include opinion surveys, focus groups, audits of Human Resources practices and grievance analysis.

Barriers to Success/Common Pitfalls

Turnover statistics are good measures of management performance and the effectiveness of Human Resources policies and practices. They are, however, not always sufficient. Organizations with low turnover are not necessarily well managed. Employees may not be leaving because they do not have, or believe they do not have, available suitable alternatives. High pay rates and generous benefit programs can mask a host of sins and create "golden handcuffs" that keep employees from leaving. Instead employees "quit and stay". In other words, they remain with the organization but are so disillusioned that their productivity suffers.

Employees may express their discontent in other ways, including increased absenteeism, unionization and, in extreme cases, sabotage. At the other end of the spectrum, employees may like working for the company but have developed into a pattern of complacency that will not be measured by turnover.

Human Resources practitioners need to interpret turnover statistics in context. They should be examined along with measures of productivity, absenteeism and efficiency. Exit interviews and employee opinion surveys can also provide complementary data that, along with the turnover statistics, can help the Human Resources practitioner develop a complete picture of the organization's culture.

If the analysis is incomplete, the organization may draw erroneous conclusions. An organization may have a 10% turnover rate across the board, but the rate may be broken down to a 40% turnover for employees with less than five years' service, 15% for employees with 10 to 15 years' service, and 3% for senior employees. This tells a very different story. It is absolutely essential that the statistical analysis be thorough.

VIRTUAL ORGANIZATION

Definition/Background

Charles Handy has defined a virtual organization as an "activity without a building as a home" (*Harvard Business Review*, May/June 1995). *Webster's New Collegiate Dictionary* defines "virtual" as "being such in essence or effect though not formally recognized or admitted". The virtual organization appears to the consumer as any other "traditional" organization. Any differences are transparent to the customer.

The virtual organization performs the same functions as the traditional organization, but owns fewer of the factors of production. It works more as a network that pulls together what is needed to offer a product or service to the market. This can be achieved through one or more of the following:

⇨ strategic alliances;

⇨ contracting out of activities to third-part providers;

⇨ creation of a network of independent or dependent contractors;

⇨ establishment of processes where people work at a distance (e.g., telecommuting); and

⇨ changing how a service is delivered through technology (e.g., electronic data interface).

From the viewpoint of the customer, the virtual organization may appear to be identical to a traditional organization. Seen from the inside, it may be very different. Although the term "virtual organization" is fairly new, the concept is not. It began as early as the 18th century when merchants contracted with craftsmen to produce goods for sale. The true virtual organization may be nothing more than a marketing and coordinating office.

The central organization focuses on developing a brand name. It contracts out the product design to specialists who design the product to meet specifications determined by market analysis. The organization then asks manufacturers to bid on the production of the product. Third-party logistics firms arrange for the warehouse and distribution of the products. Freelance sales representatives and brokers sell the product through distribution channels like retail chains.

Even complex products can be built and sold this way. The big five auto makers (GM, Ford, Toyota, Honda and DaimlerChrysler) have all moved towards the virtual organization. Although none has completely strayed from the traditional model, they have adopted many aspects of the virtual organization.

For example, these large manufacturers have all embarked on single-source contracts for major components. The contractor is responsible for research, design, cost control, and scheduling production in synch with the larger organization. Partially to spark creativity, some auto companies have contracted out product design work. General Motors sometimes initiates competitions for new designs between its internal designers and outside firms.

Many organizations have found that distribution and supply chain management have become very complex and can be done more efficiently and effectively by specialized firms. The central organization may be a franchiser whose key function is to develop a brand image. Franchisees manage direct sales to customers, while supply chain specialists ensure the supply of product is always available. Manufacturers and other suppliers are responsible for producing the products according to set specifications. The central organization coordinates the activities of the others.

The network of independent organizations operates with a symbiosis that in some respects looks very much like a single enterprise. Certainly, the end user is unaware of the complex relationships behind getting the product into its hands. Though, in the case of Nike, the famous sport shoe company, consumers have become acutely aware of their offshore contracts with third world manufacturers. Nike has come under severe criticism for the practices in those countries that may infringe on human rights.

The modern stimulus for the development of the virtual company is partly driven by the electronic revolution which makes it possible to do many things on distributed sites that previously could only be done by grouping people together. All parties along the supply chain can access data gathered at the point of purchase. The distributor is alerted to the need to replenish stock as it is sold. As warehouse inventories are reduced, the manufacturer can plan production accordingly.

This type of interdependence requires the forming of strong relationships and allows for the creation of new value-added services. Retailers can carry fewer inventories and thus reduce their costs by shifting the management of their "back rooms" to a supply chain management firm. This type of arrangement requires a significant amount of trust between the organizations.

Some of the elements of the virtual organization have similarities with flexible working practices. However, applying flexible working does not necessarily create a virtual organization. There needs to be an overarching vision of a coherent organization run on non-traditional lines, and what results is something which is fundamentally different from the traditional organization as we know it — yet it can perform all that a traditional organization can.

The virtual organization is an alternative way of organizing the factors of production in order to give continuing customer satisfaction. The concept may be applied to the whole organization, or to significant parts of it where the nature of the work makes the process applicable, and which are in effect a business within a business. They may also be used to construct a completely different product or service that may not have been economic by thinking in the traditional way. The virtual organization can only be appropriate when it can enable the organization to create a sustainable competitive advantage.

Benefits/Expected Outcomes

Saving in Capital Expenditure

If fewer or smaller buildings in prime sites are required, there will be an overall saving in capital expenditure needed to support and maintain the facilities. Third parties can offer cost savings by distributing capital cost among many different customers. Operating a fleet of private trucks can be quite expensive, particularly because the trucks often travel empty. A third-party logistics provider can operate a large single warehouse for several customers and can coordinate the use of their assets for optimal efficiency. This can be a tremendous cost saver for the central organization.

Reduction in Overhead

The big benefit is that the virtual organization can offer a considerable competitive advantage through lower costs, when used in a type of business for which it is appropriate. This may be partly because of a saving in rents, but is also because the infrastructure needed to support these facilities is avoided. Since the central business is relieved of direct responsibility for managing significant functions, there is an opportunity to operate with very little infrastructure. Expensive senior management salaries can be kept to a minimum.

Lower Fixed Cost Base Reduces Risk

The virtual organization can be more flexible than its traditional counterpart. Contracting out, alliances, and working at home mean that the core of the organization is better protected from reductions in sales volumes and has more flexibility to increase output when the market expands.

Lower Operating Costs

The emergence of the virtual organization coincides with the development of technologies that make it possible for the central organization to coordinate the activities of the network. However, increased costs, particularly labour costs, are an additional impetus for the emergence of the virtual organization. Labour costs are inelastic and, in some union environments, the costs have continued to increase despite downward pressures on product prices. Globalization has also resulted in the availability of lower cost competitive products.

Some organizations, such as the "Big Three" auto makers, have contracted out major parts of the production and assembly process to third parties who are able to pay lower wage rates and have more operational flexibility. While this may not be a true virtual organization, it demonstrates clearly one of the advantages.

High Motivation of Employees and Associates

It would be too much to claim that every single employee of any organization will be more highly motivated if that organization moves to the virtual form. For many, the change would be stressful and, for some, it would be inappropriate for the type of work in which they are involved. However, some people relish the greater empowerment and trust that comes to them as a necessity from the way a virtual organization has to be managed.

Small virtual organizations may be established, as much for lifestyle satisfaction as for economic reward, and whether or not this has been delivered will become obvious without any special assessment basis. Large virtual organizations will have been established primarily for economic reasons. Key non-financial aspects that should be monitored include customer satisfaction with the products and services compared with competitors, and employee morale. Both of these aspects are critical for ensuring long-term economic success.

Programming/Implementation

The virtual organization will only be viable when it offers the customer something that is at least as good as, and preferably better than, can be obtained from a traditional organization. Sometimes the virtual organization may be in a better position to meet the needs of a specific segment of the market than a traditional organization, while in other situations the lower cost base may mean that a price advantage can be offered to customers.

Although there may be savings in both capital and operating costs, it would be wrong to overlook the fact that a new service or a new way of doing things may incur different types of costs of their own. Nike is probably one of the best known virtual organizations. Its advantage over its competition is primarily its ability to create brand loyalty. However, in order to create the superior image of quality and desirability, Nike has to incur significant marketing costs. Having the likes of Michael Jordan and Tiger Woods as your spokesmen is very expensive. To balance the equation, the organization needs to keep operating costs low by farming out manufacturing to low-cost producers.

The key to success is a thorough understanding of the market that is to be served, and a careful assessment of the financial and human resources needed. As the virtual organization is no more than a different way of organizing resources to meet a market need, measurement of success is little different from the methods applied in traditional organizations. Customers and shareholders judge based on the benefits and results they gain, and are less interested in the internal workings of the organization that produce these benefits

and results. Although, as mentioned earlier, there is growing awareness of the practices of some firms like Nike.

The management skills needed to make a success of a virtual organization will have different emphases from those needed in a traditional business. This is something of a generalization, because in every business there is a strong situational influence on the critical management skills for success. So it is with the virtual organization; one built on a mix of employees and self-employed associates would require specific skills from particular managers. If you add to this a network of strategic alliances and contracted-out activities, the number of key managers is increased, as are the particular skills needed.

There is also a difference between an organization which changes to a virtual form, where change management skills will be critical, and one which was established in this way from the outset and does not have to ask employees to change their behaviour or expectations.

All managers are critical to the success or failure of the concept, particularly senior managers with an overall corporate responsibility, and other managers who have a direct responsibility for any parts of the organization run in a non-traditional way. Employees and associates also bear a high level of responsibility to work in a way that makes the concept work. Empowerment brings responsibility. It is not just to self-manage, but also to take the personal steps to ensure communication and coordination with other parts of the virtual organization.

Key skills needed include:

⇨ managing and being managed in a dispersed and empowered organization;

⇨ communication skills (including the regular and disciplined use of modern methods such as e-mail, shared databases, and video conferencing);

⇨ continuous attention to the building of trust in relationships;

⇨ visionary leadership skills, which are made more difficult because the opportunity for frequent informal contact is much reduced;

⇨ experience in gaining results from people who may not necessarily be employees, or who may be employed by an alliance partner;

⇨ tolerance of a higher level of ambiguity within the organization than might be necessary in a traditional situation;

⇨ relationship building and management at all links of the value chain;

⇨ understanding that the relationships needed for successful strategic alliances can only be developed in an atmosphere of cooperation and appreciation of the needs of all parties (there should not be a loser for every winner in contractual relationships in a virtual organization); and

⇨ organizing ability, in order to ensure that the organization can deliver on its promises to customers and can deploy reliable resources at every stage of the value chain.

None of these skills is unique to virtual organizations. Training can improve capabilities where they do not exist, but the most critical issue is one of attitude. Those who are not committed to the concept of the virtual organization are unlikely to be able to apply all these skills. A manager who believes that people will only work if they are under observation and that only employees can have a commitment to the organization will fail. So will managers who believe that because of high levels of commitment, no management effort at all is needed to run a virtual organization.

The degree to which the working relationship is exercised through means other than employment clearly affects the structure of the core organization. Many traditional management roles may not exist. Things which are critical for the value chain will continue to exist, but possibly through people who are associates and not employees, alliance partners, or bodies to whom functions have been contracted out. Activities which were required only to enable a critical activity to be performed may not be needed at all; for example, a virtual office, formed from dispersed home-based workers, does not require security personnel, or a cafeteria, or an army of cleaners.

Virtual organizations are likely to have a "leaner and meaner" structure than comparable traditional organizations. The difference goes deeper than this, in that they also have to be goal-centred. They cannot be bureaucratic organizations (although this does not mean that they do not need essential administrative procedures). The organization specifies what it requires; the supplier determines how to deliver to these specifications.

Role of the Human Resources Practitioner

The Human Resources practitioner is unlikely to be the initiator of the virtual organization concept. Human Resources Management, in fact, may be determined to be an overhead that can be saved in the virtual organization.

However, if a traditional organization makes the strategic decision to move towards becoming a virtual organization, the practitioner's expertise should contribute to three main areas to ensure success:

1. ensuring that the organization has, or can obtain, the human skills needed;

2. applying appropriate change management concepts in order to implement the new concept; and

3. developing new Human Resources practices and policies that take account of the different requirements of the new form, in order to help ensure that the organization is successful in the future.

In extreme forms, the virtual organization may not have a Human Resources Department because there are almost no employees. These are the exception. In the majority of situations, normal Human Resources functions will continue to be needed, although the core of employees may be smaller. What changes is the way in which the organization is managed, and this suggests some key questions that will affect the practitioner's role.

⇨ What competencies are different, compared with similar functions in a more traditional organization?

⇨ How do these affect recruitment and selection profiles?

⇨ What training is needed to enable managers and other employees to work effectively in the virtual organization?

⇨ What additional communication policies are required to overcome feelings of isolation in employees and other associates?

⇨ What are the implications for career management?

⇨ How can individual performance be assessed fairly?

⇨ Is the practitioner satisfied that persons not regarded by the organization as employees, in fact, are not considered to be employees in terms of the law?

Questions such as these are more likely to be thought through when an organization is established from the outset in a virtual form. A more specific audit may be required when a traditional organization changes in whole, or part, to a virtual form because patterns of management will have already been established.

Barriers to Success/Common Pitfalls

It can be misleading to generalize because the variety of forms of virtual organizations means that there is no universal truth that can be proclaimed. Barriers that might emerge from an increase in use of dependent contractors (home-based workers) will differ from those that emerge from the introduction of "branchless banking". The points listed therefore should be taken as possible barriers:

⇨ the vision of the new organization is not widely shared, so that there is a lack of faith in its ability to succeed;

⇨ a belief that coordination is someone else's responsibility;

⇨ managers who believe that they cannot manage without having direct control over those whom they manage;

⇨ employees who feel isolated and believe that out-of-sight means out-of-mind;

⇨ a lack of trust is developed;

⇨ loneliness of employees or associates who miss the social contact of a normal office environment;

⇨ a belief that it is impossible for the organization to offer a quality product when many elements of that product are delegated to contractors or alliance partners;

⇨ unwillingness to accept the additional responsibilities that come with higher levels of empowerment; and

⇨ employees of any level who can no longer see career opportunities.

Many of these problems can be overcome through a carefully structured change management process, and the formulation of deliberate strategies to overcome or compensate for each of the barriers. At the same time, it must be acknowledged that because of personality or deep-seated beliefs, there will be many people who are unable to operate in a non-traditional organization. Avoid the following:

⇨ a virtual organization achieved through creeping incremental steps without any clear idea of where the organization is heading;

⇨ a failure to realize that relationships become both more important and harder to build and, therefore, require more attention;

⇨ an inability to trust employees who are outside of the direct line of sight;

⇨ assuming that everyone will adjust to a different way of operating without training, coaching or other specific help;

⇨ considering only the cost-saving arguments, with little thought to the human aspects of organizing the work;

⇨ making unwarranted assumptions about the capabilities of alliance partners based on wishful thinking rather than fact; and

⇨ a failure to achieve genuine alliances of different partners who are working towards a common vision.

TOPICAL INDEX